Dover Memorial Library
Gardner-Webb University
P.O. Box 836
Boiling Springs, N.C. 28017

CLINICAL NEUROPSYCHOLOGY IN THE CRIMINAL FORENSIC SETTING

Clinical Neuropsychology in the Criminal Forensic Setting

edited by
Robert L. Denney
James P. Sullivan

THE GUILFORD PRESS
New York   London

© 2008 The Guilford Press
A Division of Guilford Publications, Inc.
72 Spring Street, New York, NY 10012
www.guilford.com

All rights reserved

No part of this book may be reproduced, translated, stored in a retrieval system, or transmitted, in any form or by any means, electronic, mechanical, photocopying, microfilming, recording, or otherwise, without written permission from the Publisher.

Printed in the United States of America

This book is printed on acid-free paper.

Last digit is print number: 9 8 7 6 5 4 3 2 1

Library of Congress Cataloging-in-Publication Data

Clinical neuropsychology in the criminal forensic setting / edited by Robert L. Denney, James P. Sullivan.
    p. ; cm.
  Includes bibliographical references and index.
  ISBN 978-1-59385-721-9 (hardcover : alk. paper)
  1. Forensic neuropsychology. I. Denney, Robert L. II. Sullivan, James P., Ph.D.
  [DNLM: 1. Forensic Psychiatry—United States. 2. Neuropsychology—United States. W 740 C6415 2008]
  RA1147.5.C55 2008
  614.'1—dc22

                                                                         2007046186

*We dedicate this work to the memory of Theodore H. Blau,
PhD, ABPP, ABPN, the true pioneer in our field.
We also wish to express our appreciation to our families,
and above all, to Him who makes all things possible.*

About the Editors

Robert L. Denney, PsyD, ABPP, ABPN, has been a forensic psychologist and neuropsychologist at the U.S. Medical Center for Federal Prisoners in Springfield, Missouri, for over 15 years. He is also Associate Professor and Director of Neuropsychology at the School of Professional Psychology at Forest Institute in Springfield. Dr. Denney is board certified in forensic psychology by the American Board of Professional Psychology and in clinical neuropsychology by both the American Board of Professional Psychology and the American Board of Professional Neuropsychology. He is a Fellow and past Program Chair of the National Academy of Neuropsychology. Dr. Denney was on the editorial board of the *Journal of Forensic Neuropsychology*, for which he edited special issues on negative response bias and criminal forensic neuropsychology. He is coeditor, with Jim Hom, of *Detection of Response Bias in Forensic Neuropsychology* and coauthor, with Shane S. Bush and Mary A. Connell, of *Ethical Practice in Forensic Psychology: A Systematic Model for Decision Making*.

James P. Sullivan, PhD, ABPP, is in full-time independent practice in the area of criminal forensic neuropsychology, based in Tucson, Arizona. He is board certified in both forensic psychology and clinical neuropsychology by the American Board of Professional Psychology.

Contributors

William B. Barr, PhD, ABPP, Departments of Neurology and Psychiatry, Comprehensive Epilepsy Center, New York University School of Medicine, New York, New York

Robert L. Denney, PsyD, ABPP, ABPN, U.S. Medical Center for Federal Prisoners, Springfield, Missouri; School of Professional Psychology, Forest Institute, Springfield, Missouri

Jerid M. Fisher, PhD, ABPN, private practice, Pittsford, New York

I. Bruce Frumkin, PhD, ABPP, Forensic and Clinical Psychology Associates, Miami, Florida

Robert L. Heilbronner, PhD, ABPP, Chicago Neuropsychology Group, Chicago, Illinois; Department of Psychiatry and Behavioral Sciences, Northwestern University Medical School, Chicago, Illinois

Stephen Honor, PhD, ABPP, private practice, Smithtown, New York

Paul M. Kaufmann, JD, PhD, ABPP-CN, Law/Psychology Program, University of Nebraska, Lincoln, Nebraska

Bernice A. Marcopulos, PhD, ABPP, Neuropsychology Laboratory, Western State Hospital, Staunton, Virginia

Joel E. Morgan, PhD, ABPP, private practice, Madison, New Jersey; Department of Neurosciences and Neurology, New Jersey Medical School, Newark, New Jersey

James P. Sullivan, PhD, ABPP, private practice, Tucson, Arizona

James A. Tyson, PhD, Behavioral Health Unit, Family Health Services, Twin Falls, Idaho

Danielle Waller, MS, LCSW, Mitigation and Sentencing Services, Springfield, Illinois

Timothy F. Wynkoop, PhD, ABPP, private practice, Toledo, Ohio

Kathy F. Yates, PhD, Nathan Kline Institute for Psychiatric Research, Orangeburg, New York; Department of Psychiatry, New York University School of Medicine, New York, New York

Preface

Forensic neuropsychology is a fascinating area of practice. Effective application of neuropsychological principles to forensic issues requires excellent clinical skills, critical thinking, and a willingness to remain solidly anchored to scientific principles. Virtually all neuropsychologists will find themselves in the forensic setting at one time or another. However, neuropsychologists rarely become involved in *criminal matters* unless they specifically choose to do so. Criminal forensic neuropsychology is occasionally exciting, often frustrating, but always challenging.

To remain relevant and effective, the application of clinical neuropsychology within the criminal setting requires specialized knowledge beyond that of even well-trained forensic neuropsychologists. It takes an ability to interact successfully with criminal personalities, law enforcement personnel (such as county sheriffs and deputies, U.S. Marshals, and prison officers), jail and prison settings, and even handcuffs and chains. It also requires an understanding of unique criminal law concepts such as competency to proceed, insanity, criminal intent, volitional control, and dangerousness. These latter issues come directly from state and federal statute and case law. Additionally, the neuropsychologist must become comfortable reviewing and understanding criminal investigation records. Most clinical neuropsychologists do not have this expertise, but they must obtain it to become competent providers of evaluation services in the criminal setting.

In this text, a number of authors who are very accomplished in different areas of criminal forensic work introduce and review topic areas we believe are most relevant and important for competent criminal forensic practice by neuropsychologists. In Chapter 1, Robert L. Denney and James P. Sullivan introduce the foundational practice, U.S. Constitutional, and case law issues that are key and upon which the remaining chapters build. In Chapter 2,

James A. Tyson and Sullivan present the ethical concepts and principles that are unique in the criminal practice setting. Paul M. Kaufmann, in Chapter 3, presents critical issues related to the legal admissibility of neuropsychological evidence in the criminal courts. In Chapter 4, Denney reviews concepts and strategies useful in detecting negative response bias and malingering in this unique setting. I. Bruce Frumkin explains in Chapter 5 the important constructs and procedures related to the assessment of *Miranda* waiver and false confessions. Bernice A. Marcopulos, Joel E. Morgan, and Denney cover one of the most common areas of criminal-related assessment, competence to proceed, in Chapter 6. In Chapter 9, Kathy F. Yates and Denney address the evaluation of mental states related to alleged offenses (including insanity and diminished capacity). Next, William B. Barr focuses on aspects of neuropathology in terms of its relationship to criminal acts and violence. In Chapter 9, Robert L. Heilbronner and Danielle Waller provide direction for the neuropsychologist when asked to participate in mitigation-related assessment during the sentencing phase of death penalty litigation. Timothy F. Wynkoop addresses a relatively new area for criminal forensic neuropsychology in Chapter 10: evaluations within the juvenile justice system. Next, Stephen Honor and Sullivan provide a pragmatic review of issues a neuropsychologist needs to know when interacting with criminal attorneys and attempting to carry out neuropsychological consultations in jail settings. In Chapter 12, Jerid M. Fisher reviews important issues to consider when communicating with attorneys, judges, and juries in the form of written reports and courtroom testimony. Finally, Sullivan and Denney close the book with a discussion of professional guidelines and competence standards as they relate to achieving "authentic professional competence" in the area of criminal forensic neuropsychology.

It is our intent in developing this book to provide a resource that is useful for clinicians not only for a reference and guide book but also as a springboard to seek additional training and supervision in the area of criminal forensic practice. Also, by consistently anchoring clinical suggestions and guidelines to pertinent legal constructs and case law, we intend that neuropsychologists performing criminal evaluations will have a better understanding of critical legal issues and judicial reasoning. Providing neuropsychological expertise within the criminal judicial system is an important area of work and one that we consider to significantly benefit society. We strongly believe that appropriately trained and competent neuropsychologists have much to offer in this regard.

Contents

1. Constitutional, Judicial, and Practice Foundations of Criminal Forensic Neuropsychology ... 1
   ROBERT L. DENNEY and JAMES P. SULLIVAN

2. Ethical Issues in Criminal Forensic Neuropsychology ... 30
   JAMES A. TYSON and JAMES P. SULLIVAN

3. Admissibility of Neuropsychological Evidence in Criminal Cases: Competency, Insanity, Culpability, and Mitigation ... 55
   PAUL M. KAUFMANN

4. Negative Response Bias and Malingering during Neuropsychological Assessment in Criminal Forensic Settings ... 91
   ROBERT L. DENNEY

5. Psychological Evaluation in *Miranda* Waiver and Confession Cases ... 135
   I. BRUCE FRUMKIN

6. Neuropsychological Evaluation of Competency to Proceed ... 176
   BERNICE A. MARCOPULOS, JOEL E. MORGAN, and ROBERT L. DENNEY

7. Neuropsychology in the Assessment of Mental State at the Time of the Offense ... 204
   KATHY F. YATES and ROBERT L. DENNEY

8. Neuropsychological Approaches to Criminality and Violence ... 238
   WILLIAM B. BARR

9. Neuropsychological Consultation in the Sentencing Phase of Capital Cases ... 273
   ROBERT L. HEILBRONNER and DANIELLE WALLER

10. Neuropsychology in the Juvenile Justice System   295
    TIMOTHY F. WYNKOOP

11. Conducting Criminal Forensic Neuropsychological Assessments: 326
    Pragmatic Considerations
    STEPHEN HONOR and JAMES P. SULLIVAN

12. Presenting Neuropsychological Findings, Opinions,   349
    and Testimony to the Criminal Court
    JERID M. FISHER

13. A Final Word on Authentic Professional Competence   391
    in Criminal Forensic Neuropsychology
    JAMES P. SULLIVAN and ROBERT L. DENNEY

Index   401

CLINICAL NEUROPSYCHOLOGY IN THE CRIMINAL FORENSIC SETTING

Chapter 1

Constitutional, Judicial, and Practice Foundations of Criminal Forensic Neuropsychology

ROBERT L. DENNEY
JAMES P. SULLIVAN

Clinical neuropsychologists provide services in a wide variety of settings, and a growing number of them are providing services to participants in criminal forensic proceedings (Denney & Wynkoop, 2000; Giuliano, Barth, Hawk, & Ryan, 1997; Mittenberg, Patton, Canyock, & Condit, 2002). Borum and Grisso (1995) surveyed test use in criminal forensic evaluations and found that 46–50% of forensic psychologists indicated they used some type of neuropsychological assessment in their pretrial evaluations. More recently, Mittenberg and colleagues (2002) presented the results of a national survey of board-certified neuropsychologists. The 131 survey respondents indicated that they completed a total of 33,531 annual evaluations, 4% of which involved criminal defendants, that is, 1,341 criminally related forensic evaluations for just 131 neuropsychologists. These results are understandable given what appears to be the comparatively higher rates of brain injury among criminal populations (Barr, Chapter 8, this volume; Martell, 1992a), and suggest a considerable need for competent neuropsychological involvement in the criminal arena.

Indeed, clinical neuropsychology's involvement in the criminal judicial system is quite understandable. By definition, neuropsychologists are behavioral scientists with specialized training in neuropathological conditions. With their dual focus on clinical psychology and neurology, neuropsychologists can bring to the judicial system not only their understanding of neuroanatomy and neuropathology, but also most importantly, their ability to document objectively how neuropathological conditions affect thinking skills, memory, and decision making (Bigler & Clement, 1997; Lezak, Howieson, & Loring, 2004). Maybe even more important is neuropsychology's ability to identify unusual behaviors that are *not* due to neuropathological conditions. The obvious example is feigning cognitive deficits, but non-neuropathological conditions come into play as well, such as psychopathy, other personality disturbances, and general psychiatric disorders. Ruling out neurocognitive deficits in non-neurological conditions is just as important as identifying the presence of potentially disabling neurocognitive concerns. Neuropsychological evaluations can also delineate neurocognitive functioning when diagnostic issues other than neuropathology exist, such as developmental and psychiatric conditions. Criminal courts need experts who can provide clear understanding when there are concerns that a defendant's cognitive functioning may be compromised.

Our purpose in this chapter is to provide the neuropsychologist seeking to expand his or her practice into the area of criminal forensics the core understanding needed to face this challenge. We explain how the practice of neuropsychology in this setting requires a different model of thought. We highlight this model. We present the criminal judicial system and discuss the points in the process when neuropsychologists typically become involved. Finally, we provide the core criminal case law that one needs to understand to step in to this arena of practice. This chapter is not exhaustive; it is meant to be an introduction to the details that are presented in the following chapters.

Application of Clinical Neuropsychology to Criminal Forensic Issues

The application of clinical neuropsychological expertise to criminal forensic matters is a relatively new subspecialty within forensic neuropsychology (Heilbronner, 2004; Heilbronner & Frumkin, 2003; Sullivan & Denney, 2003). As such, several authorities have decried the lack of adequate preparation for many who practice in the area and cite the need for a specialized knowledge base above and beyond that required for sound clinical neuropsychology practice (Denney, 2005; Denney & Wynkoop, 2000; Martell, 1992b; McCaffrey, Williams, Fisher, & Laing, 1997; Sullivan & Denney, 2003).

As with any young field of scientific inquiry, standards of professional practice advanced by regulatory bodies (American Psychology–Law Society, American Psychological Association Division 41, American Academy of Forensic Psychology) have yet to be widely disseminated to cross-specialty practitioners (namely, neuropsychologists). There is often little policing in the marketplace, and there appears to be a wide range of competence among those who advertise themselves as forensic neuropsychologists. Finally, the proliferation of vanity boards and individuals who feel that only a minimal amount of knowledge is sufficient to practice in the area of criminal forensic neuropsychology is not surprising given the youth of this subspecialty.

Lack of knowledge regarding relevant legal constructs is one of the core factors behind criticisms of mental health professionals practicing in forensic areas. Grisso (2003) has characterized this issue with the "five I's." Briefly, the Five I's are "*ignorance* and *irrelevance* in courtroom testimony, psychiatric or psychological *intrusion* into essentially legal matters; and *insufficiency* and *incredibility* of information provided to the courts" (2003, p. 11). Grisso's call for forensic psychologists to establish familiarity with relevant legal doctrines is echoed in the Melton and colleagues (2007) statement that mental health professionals working in forensic areas require familiarity "with the legal doctrines that give relevance to the mental health evaluation" (p. 81). Furthermore, Melton and colleagues make this assertion:

> We, like others, have been troubled by "expert" mental health professionals who testify on a particular legal issue without any understanding of the nature of the issue they are purporting to address. ... Professionals whose practice takes them into interdisciplinary matters, whether legally or behaviorally trained, have an ethical obligation to learn enough to be able to function competently in such a context. (p. 6)

We believe this sentiment is particularly true for mental health professionals who seek to provide expertise to the criminal judicial system. A working knowledge of relevant portions of the U.S. Constitution, judicial interpretation, and subsequent case law is indispensable in acquiring command of relevant legal constructs and doctrines. After years of training psychology interns in the area of mental heath case law, it has become apparent to us that studying such matters helps practitioners apply their clinical skills effectively. Nevertheless, many practitioners in the area of criminal forensic neuropsychology offer something like the following when encouraged to increase their knowledge of relevant legal constructs: "I'm not a lawyer. Why should I pretend to be? I'll do my job and leave the legal issues to the attorneys and the judge." It is in an attempt to respond further to this widely held misconception that Tyson and Sullivan review the latest draft of the "Specialty Guidelines for Forensic Psychologists" (Committee on Ethical Guidelines for Forensic Psychologists, 1991) in Chapter 2, this volume.

Briefly, the Specialty Guidelines address relevant legal construct issues under the headings of Competence (Section III), Methods and Procedures (Section VI), and Public and Professional Communications (Section VII). Guideline III (C) states, "Forensic psychologists are responsible for a fundamental and reasonable level of knowledge and understanding of the *legal and professional standards* that govern their participation as experts in legal proceedings" (p. 658, emphasis added). Guideline VI (A) states, "Because of their special status as persons qualified as experts to the court, forensic psychologists have an *obligation* to maintain current knowledge of scientific, professional, and *legal developments* within their area of competence" (p. 658). Finally, Guideline VII (F) states, "Forensic psychologists are prepared to explain the relationship between their expert testimony and the *legal issues and facts* of a case" (p. 665, emphasis added). To return to the "I'm not a lawyer" objection offered earlier, it should now be clear that acquiring an adequate working knowledge of relevant legal constructs is not an enterprise for individuals who wish to mimic lawyers. Rather, such knowledge is a requirement for neuropsychologists working in the criminal forensic area who desire to achieve *authentic professional competence* rather than a mere pretense of expertise.

It is our hope that this text will serve as a resource for neuropsychologists seeking to increase their involvement in criminal proceedings. We hope it will improve readers' understanding regarding the criminal judicial system, mental health–related case law, and how best to provide competent expert assistance to those in the criminal justice system.

Criminal Forensic Neuropsychology

In the "Petition for the Recognition of a Specialty in Professional Psychology," the American Board of Forensic Psychology and American Psychology–Law Society jointly define forensic psychology in this manner (Forensic Specialty Council, 2000, cited in Packer & Borum, 2003, p. 22):

> [Forensic psychology is] the professional practice by psychologists within the areas of clinical psychology, counseling psychology, neuropsychology, and school psychology, when they are engaged regularly as experts and represent themselves as such, in an activity primarily intended to provide professional psychological expertise to the judicial system.

When neuropsychologists apply their clinical expertise regularly within the judicial system, they are practicing as forensic neuropsychologists. Forensic neuropsychology has become a genuine specialty area within clinical neuropsychology (Larrabee, 2005; Sweet, 1999). In this regard, the application of neuropsychological expertise to criminal forensic matters appears to be a subspecialty of forensic neuropsychology. Although good clinical neuropsychological skill and expertise form the basis of sound practice, forensic neuropsychology, particularly in criminal forensic matters, requires understanding of a unique knowledge domain beyond that of sound clinical practice (Denney & Wynkoop, 2000; Martell, 1992b; Sullivan & Denney, 2003). One important knowledge domain includes the criminal legal system and the point at which neuropsychologists commonly interface with it.

The Criminal Legal System

There are principles and content that neuropsychologists must learn to be truly facile in the criminal setting. One of these areas is the basic criminal legal system. The United States of America is a federation of states. Each state has its own sovereignty in relation to other states and, in many respects, the federal government. By inclusion in the federation, states have handed over certain powers to federal government. The U.S. Constitution outlines what powers are held by the federal government. Those not held by the federal government are held by the states as long as they do not conflict with provisions outlined in the Constitution. Each state and commonwealth has its own constitution as well. The U.S. Constitution spells out the minimal level of rights provided for U.S. citizens; the state constitutions can grant more rights to the citizenry, but not less.

Federal criminal laws typically include things such as crimes against a federal official, violation of another citizen's civil rights, destruction of federal property, and interstate crimes (e.g., mail fraud; fraud over telephone lines; robbery of federally insured banks; various Internet crimes; crimes affecting interstate commerce; and violations of federal drug, firearms, and explosives laws). Also, federal crimes would include any state crime that occurred on federal property (national park lands, railways, airways, and some instances of crime on Native American lands). When crimes allegedly occur in the federal jurisdiction, federal statutes and case law apply. States define their own laws, except as limited by the U.S. Constitution.

Law is therefore established at various levels and sources: There is U.S. Constitutional law and state constitutional law. There is likewise legislative law at both levels. There are regulations promulgated by various agencies set up by their respective governments. Finally, there is case law (common law) written by the court systems.

Parallel systems of courts exist between the states and the federal government. Both state and federal systems have trial courts and appellate courts. Trial courts determine the facts of the case and apply those facts to specific law. Appellate courts review that law and determine whether appropriate legal principles were used by the trial court. The federal system, as well as most state systems, has two levels of appellate courts: the Circuit Courts of Appeals and the U.S. Supreme Court. There are 12 circuits, each comprising several states (with the exception of the District of Columbia, which has its own Circuit Court of Appeals). Each circuit is titled by its respective number, except the District of Columbia Circuit Court of Appeals (see Table 1.1). Circuit courts review decisions of trial courts from states within that jurisdiction, and rulings apply to that group of states. In other words, they have jurisdictional authority for all states in that circuit when dealing with federal laws. Circuit court decisions can be appealed to the U.S. Supreme Court, where the decision is final. The Court customarily deals with U.S. and state constitutional issues, although it also addresses consistency in state and federal circuit court decisions related to federal law and past U.S. Supreme Court rulings. Most states have two appellate levels as well. The

TABLE 1.1. U.S. Circuit Courts of Appeal and Their Respective Jurisdictions

1st Circuit	2nd Circuit	3rd Circuit	4th Circuit	5th Circuit	6th Circuit
Maine	Connecticut	Delaware	Maryland	Louisiana	Kentucky
Massachusetts	New York	New Jersey	North Carolina	Mississippi	Michigan
New Hampshire	Vermont	Pennsylvania	South Carolina	Texas	Ohio
Puerto Rico		U.S. Virgin Islands	Virginia		Tennessee
Rhode Island			West Virginia		

7th Circuit	8th Circuit	9th Circuit	10th Circuit	11th Circuit	D.C. Circuit
Illinois	Arkansas	Alaska	Colorado	Alabama	Washington, D.C.
Indiana	Iowa	Arizona	Kansas	Florida	
Wisconsin	Minnesota	California	New Mexico	Georgia	
	Missouri	Guam	Oklahoma		
	Nebraska	Hawaii	Utah		
	North Dakota	Idaho	Wyoming		
	South Dakota	Montana			
		Nevada			
		Oregon			
		Washington			
		Northern Mariana Islands			

state Supreme Court is the final authority regarding interpretation of state law and the state's constitution, unless it is considered to conflict with the U.S. Constitution or certain federal enactments (Melton et al., 2007). As complicated as this sounds, it is not as complicated as the many possible routes a criminal defendant can take when traveling through the criminal adjudicative process.

The Criminal Adjudicative Process

The sequence of events in the flow of the criminal justice system is a complicated one in which neuropsychologists may be asked to intersect at many locations. Figure 1.1 is a flowchart presented by the Bureau of Justice Statistics (1997), which indicates two parallel processes, one for adults and one for juveniles (a system Melton et al. [2007] termed *quasi-criminal*). This separation occurs once a suspect is arrested. Mental health professionals, including neuropsychologists, are occasionally involved not only in determining juvenile adjudicative competency but also related issues of potential transfer to adult prosecution (Wynkoop, Chapter 10, this volume). A defendant then travels through the prosecution and pretrial stage. Here the flow is divided by the felony and misdemeanor tracks. Notice that there is a line for *pretrial diversion*. This is a formal process, initially developed for juveniles, to allow defendants to participate in rehabilitation programming on a voluntary basis while prosecution is suspended (Ulrich, 2002). This avenue out of prosecution appears to be a common process for mentally ill offenders and, consequently, a point of involvement for mental health professionals (Rogers & Shuman, 2005; Swaminath, Mendonca, Vidal, & Chapman, 2002). Neuropsychologists can be requested to provide input regarding a defendant's mental state at any point through this system. Issues typically include competence at various points in the process, criminal responsibility (sanity), and sentencing concerns. Each of these evaluations requires a specialized knowledge base and forensic practice method that significantly contrasts with standard clinical practice.

Forensic Neuropsychology as a Unique Practice Setting

There are striking differences between neuropsychological practice in the general clinical setting and that in the forensic setting. The goals of the two specialties differ significantly. The goal of clinical evaluation is most often alleviation of human suffering and improved levels of functioning through evaluation and development of efficient intervention. With the exception of

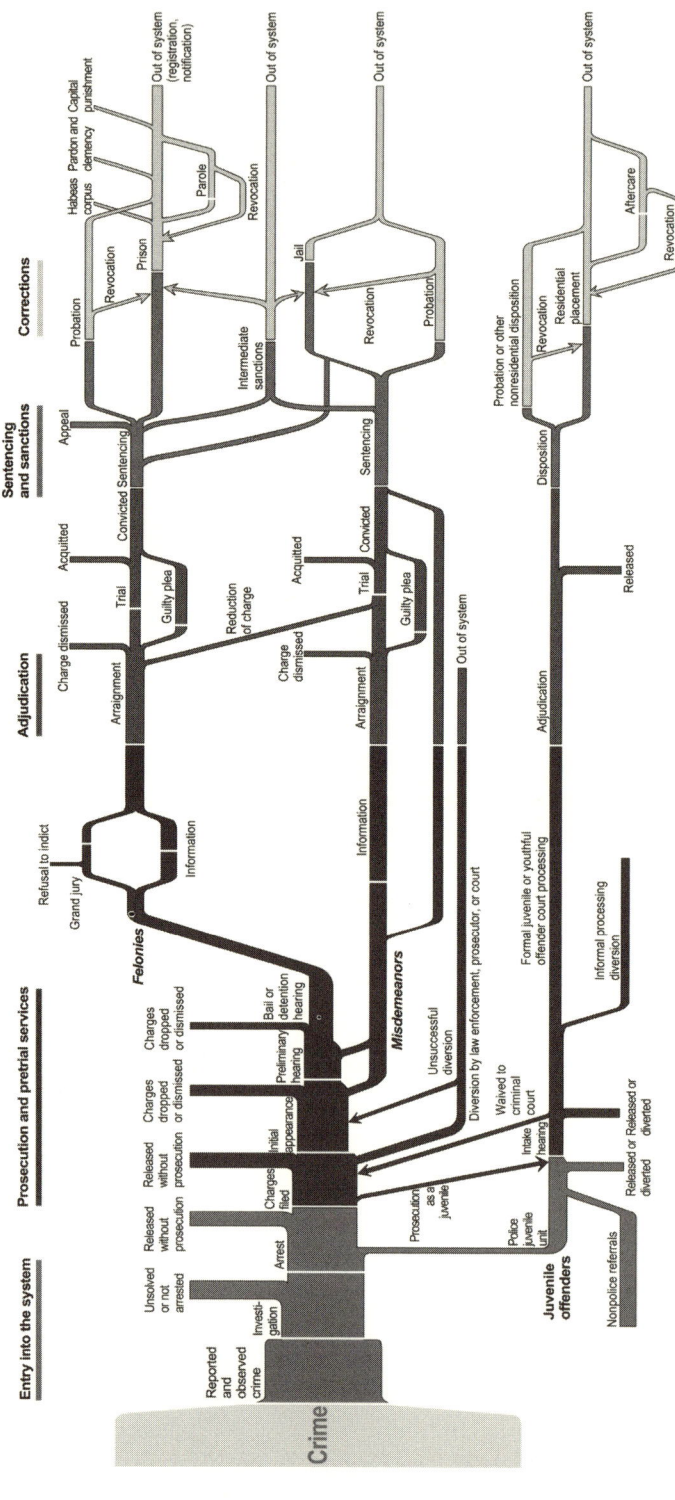

FIGURE 1.1. Sequence of events in the United States criminal justice system. This chart provides a simplified view of case flow through the criminal justice system. Procedures vary among jurisdictions. Width and darkness of the lines are not intended to show actual size of caseloads. From Bureau of Justice Statistics (1997). Available at *www.ojp.usdoj.gov/bjs/flowchart.htm*.

treatment recommendations, the goal of forensic evaluation in the criminal arena is most often to determine whether a defendant's psychological problems meet a specific legal standard. This is a vitally important fact for neuropsychologists to understand. That key difference in goals leads to contrasting *assumptions, roles, alliances,* and *methods* (Denney & Wynkoop, 2000; Goldstein, 2003; Greenberg & Shuman, 1997; Heilbrun, 2001).

Assumptions

In clinical practice, neuropsychologists for the most part assume that patients voluntarily seek help because they are concerned about effects of possible neuropathology and hope to receive guidance and/or treatment to alleviate these effects. There is often a diagnosable condition that occasions the service, whether the service is assessment or intervention. Certainly within the neurorehabilitation setting, an alliance between the patient and provider is required. The overriding theme is one of collaboration, mutual goals, and shared belief. This theme is most often *not* present in the criminal forensic setting. Criminal defendants are typically not self-referred, nor are they necessarily voluntary recipients of services. In many instances they may not have a psychological or neuropsychological complaint. The possibility of harsh punishment can create tremendous motivation for these individuals to manipulate the evaluator in an attempt to ease their way through the judicial system (Boyd, McLearen, Meyer, & Denney, 2007; Rogers, 2008). It is counterproductive to assume that defendants have neurocognitive deficits, want help from the professional, or present themselves in an honest manner within such a harsh and potentially punitive setting. It is no surprise, then, that these differences in assumptions result in different roles for neuropsychologists.

Roles

Heilbrun (2001) outlined differences between the role of treatment clinician and that of forensic examiner appropriate to forensic neuropsychology. As can be seen from Table 1.2 on page 11, these differences reveal themselves through a variety of attitudes and behaviors. The clinical provider maintains a role consistent with helping the patient. Rather than helping the patient, however, the forensic evaluator maintains a more neutral role, consistent with being a "seeker of truth" and a judicial educator (Greenberg & Shuman, 1997; Saks, 1990). Maintaining this forensic role can be difficult. The evaluator should realize that his or her opinion may have the potential to ultimately result in harm, particularly if he or she has the standard psychotherapeutic mindset. Potential consequences of forensic opinions can be substantial. Probably the most serious example includes capital cases, in which the evaluator must provide an opinion on an individual's competence to be executed. No less severe, however, is the forensic neuropsychologist's opinion that a dangerous criminal defendant is not competent to stand trial and will likely never become competent. Such an opinion can ultimately result in a lifelong commitment to a secure mental health facility under federal law (see Title 18, U.S.C., § 4246). Reluctance to be an objective, unbiased seeker of truth, who is willing to make these types of decisions, should lead the ethical neuropsychologist to avoid forensic work.

Alliance

Developing a therapeutic alliance with neurorehabilitation patients is required for successful rehabilitation outcomes. Sohlberg and Mateer (2001) went so far as to include it as a basic principle of cognitive rehabilitation. They noted that "cognitive rehabilitation requires a sound therapeutic alliance among the therapist, client, and family members or caregivers" (p. 21). A therapeutic alliance allows the therapist to foster motivation and hopefulness on behalf of the patient (Parenté & Herrmann, 1996). *Forensic evaluations are not therapeutic endeavors.* As such, the forensic examiner's allegiance is to finding the truth in a thorough, ethical manner. Similarly, one must remember who is truly receiving these services. In general clinical work, the patient is clearly the recipient of services and is typically the client. Forensic examiners must realize that the "patient" is generally not the client in forensic endeavors. More typically, the recipient of services, particularly criminal evaluative services, is the court (and by extension the jury) or attorney. Other distinctions between the two roles are presented in Table 1.2.

Lack of therapeutic alliance in forensic evaluation does not, however, eliminate the need to develop rapport with the defendant, or to treat him or her with dignity and respect. Doing so is always the right thing to do. Additionally, rapport fosters self-disclosure and motivation to perform during neuropsychological testing, and appropriate motivation and effort is critical in forensic neuropsychology (Boone, 2007; Hom & Denney, 2003; Larrabee, 2007). It is possible to maintain a professional and ethical relationship while observing the strict boundaries of the forensic evaluation process.

Methodology

Different assumptions, roles, and alliances necessitate that competent and ethical forensic evaluation requires somewhat different methodology than that of clinical practice. Clinical practice typically incorporates an interview

TABLE 1.2. Differences between Treatment and Forensic Roles for Mental Health Professionals

Dimension	Therapeutic role	Forensic role
Purpose	Diagnose and treat symptoms of illness	Assist decision maker or attorney
Examiner–examinee relationship	Helping role	Objective or quasi-objective stance
Notification of purpose	Implicit assumptions about purpose shared by doctor and patient	Formal and explicit notification
Who is being served	Individual patient	Variable; may be court, attorney, and patient
Nature of standard being considered	Medical, psychiatric, neuropsychological	Medical, psychiatric, neuropsychological, and legal
Data sources	Self-report, behavioral observations, medical diagnostic procedures, and neuropsychological testing; occasional corroborative information	Self-report, behavioral observations, medical diagnostic procedures, and neuropsychological testing; nearly always incorporate corroborative and surreptitious observation by others
Response style of examine	Assumed to be predominantly reliable	Not assumed to be reliable
Clarification of reasoning and limits of knowledge	Optional	Very important
Written report	Brief, conclusory statement common	Lengthy and detailed, documents findings, reasoning, and conclusions
Court testimony	Not expected	Expected

Note. From Heilbrum (2001). Copyright 2001 by Kluwer Academic/Plenum Publishing. Adapted by permission.

with the patient and perhaps an informant familiar with the patient, and neuropsychological testing to characterize the patient's difficulties or to arrive at a diagnosis and make treatment recommendations. The entire process is designed to provide assistance to the patient, his or her caregivers, and medical managers in a timely fashion. Forensic assessment often requires a broader base of information sources than is typical of clinical practice, and the evaluator must place more weight on objective test results than on subjective complaints, self-report checklists, and behavior during clinical interviews. This setting also requires a systematic assessment of negative response bias and malingering. Surreptitious observation can be invaluable, particularly in cases in which signs of poor motivation or symptom exaggeration exist (Denney & Wynkoop, 2000; Wynkoop & Denney, 1999). Consistent with the "truth seeker" role, the evaluator must carry out the evaluation much like a dispassionate detective. It takes time to locate and review past medical and educational records, and to interview others familiar with the defendant. Nonetheless, the forensic neuropsychologist must incorporate information from sources other than the defendant and consider more critically the defendant's self-report. This difference, along with specialized knowledge domains and the contrast in methodology between clinical and forensic practice, is what makes forensic assessment unique.

Denney and Wynkoop (2000) adapted Mrad's (1996) multiple data source model (MDSM) to the practice of criminal forensic neuropsychology. The model represents a synthesis of methods of various authors in forensic psychology (Grisso, 1988; Melton et al., 2007; Shapiro, 1984, 1991, 1999), particularly related to the assessment of sanity (Figure 1.2). However, the model applies to any past mental state evaluation and also demonstrates the core difference between clinical and forensic practice. The model ensures that the evaluator acquires corroborative information beyond that of the defendant's self-report and presentation during interviews and testing. The first two columns represent sources of information (self-report and other, corroborative data) that, when combined, can lead to an understanding of mental state. Each row represents a different point in time (currently, historically, and at a specific time in the past). Arrows reflect areas of expected consistency between information gained from respective sources. For example, self-report clinical history should be consistent with current presentation (when taking into consideration disease process and effects of treatment). Likewise, corroborative information should be consistent both across time frames and with self-report information. In this manner, a reasonable amount of consistency should present across sources and time periods. The middle row directs attention to a particular period of time, and is most relevant for criminal responsibility (sanity) and retrospective competence evaluations. Although originally developed for evaluation of past mental states, it

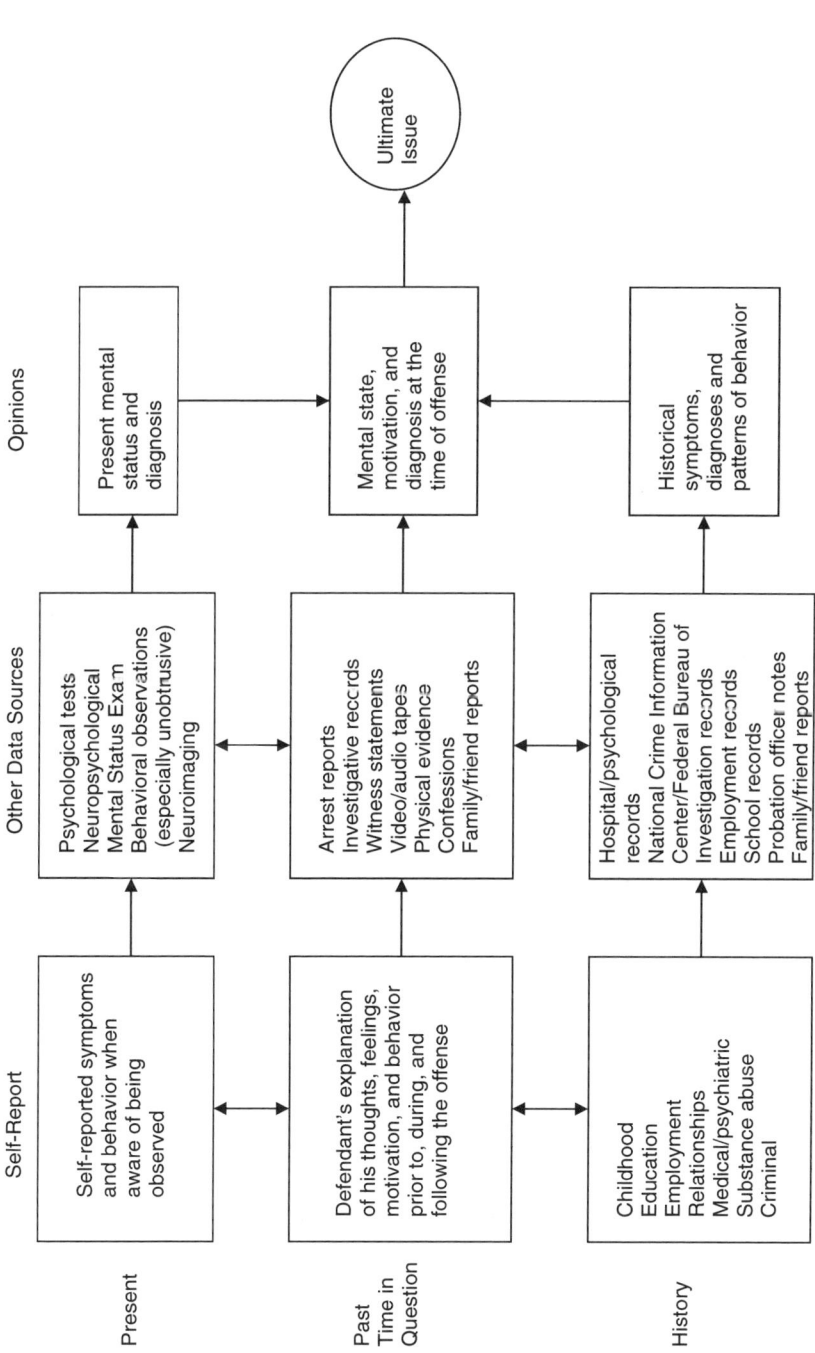

FIGURE 1.2. Multiple data source model reflecting various sources of information that may be needed in a criminal forensic evaluation. From Mrad (1996). Adapted with permission of the author.

can be quite helpful in all forms of forensic evaluation, because it facilitates information acquisition from objective information sources.

An understanding of the differences between clinical and forensic practice is absolutely necessary; however, no less necessary is an understanding of the legal playing field that the neuropsychologist has entered. Consequently, we now turn to the core pillars of criminal mental health law as it relates to potential neuropsychological assessment. Neuropsychologists need to be aware of these issues to practice effectively in this setting.

Key Constitutional Amendments

The United States has a constitutional form of government. As such, the U.S. Constitution is the ultimate legal authority, and all laws must be consistent with the U. S. Constitution based on majority opinion of the U.S. Supreme Court. As noted previously, individual courts can afford a state's citizens more rights than those ensured by the Constitution, but not less. The Fifth, Sixth, Eighth, and Fourteenth Amendments are most pertinent to the practice of criminal forensic neuropsychology and are presented below. Significance sections detail those aspects of the Amendment most relevant to forensic psychological practice.

Fifth Amendment

"No person shall be held to answer for a capital, or otherwise, infamous crime, unless on a presentment or indictment of a Grand Jury, except in cases arriving in the land or naval forces, or in the Militia, when in actual service for time of war or public danger; nor shall any person be subject for the same offence to be twice put in jeopardy of life or limb; nor shall he be compelled in any criminal case to be a witness against himself, nor be deprived of life, liberty, or property, without due process of law; nor shall private property be taken for public use, without just compensation."

Significance

This Amendment establishes every citizen's privilege against self-incrimination and assurance of due process. Privilege against self-incrimination certainly extends to psychological evaluations and is quite relevant during the assessment of competence to stand trial and sanity. It is important that the defendant's words not be used against him or her in any proceeding, unless the defendant places his or her mental state at issue (even then, its protection is open to court opinion). It is not uncommon for a defendant to receive a competency evaluation against his or her will. Certainly, in these situations it is important to limit, in written form, what the defendant reveals about the alleged, or any other, offense, except in cases when his or her report of the offense is substantive evidence of mental illness and incompetence, and there is no other definitive indication of incompetence. At issue here is that, by reporting offenses, the neuropsychologist may inadvertently become an agent of the prosecution. The Federal Rules of Evidence (FRE), Rule 12.2c provides some protection against inappropriate use of such information in the federal jurisdiction; however, the pragmatic extent of this protection is unknown. Moreover, individual states may or may not provide this protection. For example, Virginia Code (19.2–169.1D) specifically dictates that "no statements of the defendant relating to the time period of the alleged offense shall be included in the report." Similarly, a defendant's words during a competence evaluation should not be used against him or her during later, unrelated aspects of the prosecution without his or her permission. For example using the defendant's words from a competence examination as data to provide an opinion on the issue of future dangerousness during a sentencing hearing is prohibited (see later, *Estelle v. Smith*).

Sixth Amendment

"In all criminal prosecutions, the accused shall enjoy the right to a speedy and public trial, by an impartial jury of the State and district wherein the crime shall have been committed, which district shall have been previously ascertained by law, and be informed of the nature and cause of the accusation; to be confronted with the witnesses against him; to have compulsory process for obtaining witnesses in his favor, and to have the assistance of counsel for his defence."

Significance

It is important to understand that criminal defendants have a constitutional right to representation. Inherent in this is the right to effective assistance of counsel, which includes the right to have forensic mental health evaluations, even when indigent (see later, *Ake v. Oklahoma*). It is not unusual for criminal defendants to want to forgo their right to counsel and represent themselves (acting *pro se*). As we see in *Farretta v. California* [422 U.S. 806 (1975)], defendants do not need to be trained in law to represent themselves. Defendants have the right to make that decision even if it is a result of poor judgment, as long as it is not rooted in mental disease or defect. The level of competence to waive this right is discussed further in *Godinez v. Moran*.

Eighth Amendment

"Excessive bail shall not be required, nor excessive fines imposed, nor cruel and unusual punishments inflicted."

Significance

Cruel and unusual punishment involves the nature of a person's criminal sentence. Most commonly, the issue is raised in matters of death penalty. Here psychologists often become involved in identifying relevant aspects of the defendant's current mental health, personality characteristics, or life circumstances, and presenting that information to the jury. With this information, the jury can determine the appropriateness of imposing a death sentence. While presence of mental illness, substance dependence, neuropsychological dysfunction, or traumatic childhood experiences may persuade the jury to withhold the death penalty (mitigating circumstances, see Heilbronner & Waller, Chapter 9, this volume), the absence of these concerns in the face of expected continued violence may be interpreted as calling for imposition of the death penalty (aggravating circumstances). With the exception of dangerousness prediction, most aggravating circumstances are outside the expertise of psychologists. The exact nature of the sentencing process is dictated by state and federal statute. Death penalty appeals are often based on cruel and unusual punishment restriction (see *Furman v. Georgia* [408 U.S. 238 (1972)] and *Atkins v. Virginia* [536 U.S. 304 (2002)]). Cruel and unusual punishment also may relate to general prison sentences and events that occur while the individual is in prison. Psychologists occasionally become involved in malpractice and related treatment issues for sentenced prisoners as well.

Fourteenth Amendment

"All persons born or naturalized in the United States and subject to the jurisdiction thereof, are citizens of the United States and the State wherein they reside. No State shall make or enforce any law which shall abridge the privileges or immunities of citizens of the United States; nor shall any State deprive any person of life, liberty, or property, without due process of law; nor deny to any person within its jurisdiction the equal protection of the laws."

Significance

The Fourteenth Amendment dictates that state (and by extension, federal) laws will not infringe upon Constitutional rights of citizens. It establishes that no citizen's life, liberty, or property shall be taken without due process of law. This "due process clause" is relied upon in court rulings regarding criminal competencies, such as competence to stand trial, to enter a plea, or to face sentencing.

Landmark Cases of the U.S. Supreme Court

The U.S. Supreme Court is the final appellate court of decision for cases involving federal issues. There are nine justices, appointed for life, to the Court. The U.S. Supreme Court's jurisdiction is expansive, because it reviews not only federal court decisions but also state court decisions that involve interpretation and/or potential violation of constitutional issues. All verdicts are final.

Because relevant cases are discussed in detail in subsequent chapters, we limit our current discussion to 12 of the "must know" cases for criminal forensic neuropsychologists. Cases presented here include the U.S. Supreme Court citation, along with a brief description of the case, Court ruling, and particularly significant holdings. Oftentimes, these cases spell out multiple important issues relating to nature of constitutional or procedural law. In addition to the main determination of the Justices are ancillary points (called *dicta*) that may have significance. It is not unusual in the following cases for the appellate courts to rule on several points of law, many of which are not relevant to the practice of criminal forensics. We attempt to bring points out as they relate to mental health issues. Results of the entire appeal process, from the trial court to the U.S. Supreme Court, are not referenced. We chose a bulleted presentation style for issues considered significant for neuropsychologists to facilitate quick reference.

Finally, we need to include a brief word about case citations. The combined numbers and letters in the middle of each citation is the abbreviated title of the reference work (e.g., U.S. refers to *United States Reporter*, a reference specific to U.S. Supreme Court cases; S. Ct. refers to the alternative *Supreme Court Reporter*). Other case reporters exist for federal cases (e.g., F.2d, meaning *Federal Reporter, Second Series*) and other jurisdictions (e.g., Pacific 2d, meaning *Pacific Reporter, Second Series*). The first number of the citation refers to the volume number, and the second number refers to the beginning page of the case. For example, 114 F.2d 240, indicates the case starts on page 240 in volume 114 of the *Federal Reporter, Second Series*. The parenthetical date refers to the year in which the case was published. Case titles are customarily italicized.

Confessions

Brown v. Mississippi, 297 U.S. 278 (1936)

Brown was one of three black men suspected of murdering a white man. Shortly after the murder, he was taken into custody and transported to the murder scene, where he denied committing the murder. Brown was then tied up, hung from a tree, and beaten repeatedly. He was then taken to jail. He was told beatings and whippings would continue until he confessed. He subsequently confessed. He was convicted and sentenced to death in a 2-day trial. Brown filed an appeal on the grounds that his due process rights were violated. The Supreme Court overturned Brown's conviction.

HOLDING

Physically coerced confessions are a violation of Fourteenth Amendment due process rights.

COMMENT

Although *Brown* was not a mental health case, it established the basis from which later mental health–related confession and due process cases derive their import.

Miranda v. Arizona, 384 U.S. 436 (1966)

Miranda was the lead case of four confession cases that were before the Court. Miranda, an indigent Mexican defendant, was arrested on suspicion of kidnapping and rape. He was not advised of any rights. He was interrogated for several hours, while "cut off from the world." He eventually confessed and signed a written statement. He was subsequently convicted. Miranda appealed, contending that his Fifth Amendment right against self-incrimination had been violated because he had not been advised of his rights. The Supreme Court agreed and provided what is known as the *Miranda* warning.

HOLDING

Confessions made by suspects not informed of privilege against self-incrimination and due process rights are not admissible as evidence. All suspects must be advised that they have a

- Right to remain silent, and that anything they say can and will be used against them.
- Right to counsel.
- Right to have counsel provided if they cannot afford one.
- Right to stop interrogation at any time. Once a suspect asks to speak with a lawyer, all interrogation must cease until his or her lawyer is present.

COMMENT

Miranda, likewise, is not a mental health case, but it establishes an important rule of law that impacts all mental health–related confession cases. *Miranda* was challenged in a case that made its way to the U.S. Supreme Court in 2000. The U.S. Court of Appeals had ruled that confessions obtained by federal agents should not be suppressed because suspects were not given a proper *Miranda* warning. The Supreme Court overturned the lower court and affirmed *Miranda* in *Dickerson v. United States* [166 F.3d 667 (2000)], relying on the legal principle of *stare decisis*, which means to leave undisturbed, or to let stand, a settled point of law (Champion, 2001).

Competence to Plead Guilty

Godinez v. Moran, 509 U.S. 389 (1993)

Richard Moran entered a plea of not guilty after being charged with three counts of first-degree murder. Several different mental health professionals evaluated him and suggested he was competent to stand trial. Moran then petitioned the court to dismiss legal counsel, represent himself, and plead guilty to the murders. The trial court found that Moran's decisions to proceed *pro se* (waive his Sixth Amendment right to counsel) and plead guilty (waive his Sixth Amendment right to trial) were knowing, intelligent, and voluntary. Moran was convicted and sentenced to death. Moran appealed, contending that he had been incompetent to represent himself. The Supreme Court upheld Moran's conviction and death sentence.

HOLDING

The competence standard for waiving right to counsel and pleading guilty is the same as that for standing trial (see later, *Dusky v. United States*).

COMMENT

The U.S. Supreme Court decided *Moran* in response to how courts were interpreting the decisions in two previous competence-related cases, *Westbrook v. Arizona* [384 U.S. 150 (1966)] and *Seiling v. Eyman* [478 F.2d 211 (9th Cir. Ariz., 1973)]. These two decisions were interpreted by lower courts to suggest that a higher level of competence was needed to waive these two very important constitutional rights. In *Moran*, the U.S. Supreme Court clarified that no higher level of competence was needed, but the trial court needed to verify on the record that the decisions were knowing, intelligent, and voluntary, and that these focused inquiries did not make the *Dusky* standard more stringent.

Competence to Stand Trial

Dusky v. United States, 362 U.S. 402 (1960)

Milton Dusky, a 33-year-old man diagnosed with chronic undifferentiated schizophrenia, was charged with kidnapping after assisting two teenagers in the kidnapping and rape of a 16-year-old girl. The trial judge found Dusky competent to stand trial after a mental health professional reported Dusky to be oriented to place and time, with some recollection of events (Hooper, 2003). Dusky was convicted, and he appealed, contending he had not been competent to stand trial. The Supreme Court reversed and remanded.

HOLDING

The test for competence to stand trial "must be whether the defendant has sufficient present ability to consult with his lawyer with a reasonable degree of rational understanding, and whether he has a rational, as well as factual, understanding of the proceedings against him."

COMMENT

Dusky is the most significant competence to proceed case. Every forensic examiner should be aware of the High Court's holding in this case and how that decision applies to mental health functioning. Simple orientation to one's surroundings is not enough to make a defendant competent to stand trial. *Dusky* outlines several important factors about competence: It addresses *present* ability, not a person's mental state in the past (e.g., sanity); it requires only *sufficient* ability to consult with counsel with a *reasonable* degree of rational understanding (*sufficient* and *reasonable* do not require perfect ability and understanding); and it requires both *factual* and *rational* understanding of proceedings. In regard to relating to an attorney, many defendants have sufficient ability but simply do not wish to cooperate due to personality factors; such a situation likely does not meet the standard for lack of competence. In regard to rational and factual understanding, it is possible for a defendant to have excellent factual understanding but poor rational understanding due to a delusion about some aspect of the case (e.g., the arrest, nature of the charges, nature of the judge or attorneys involved, or expected outcome). It is important to tease out delusional ideas from the typical pessimism of one who has had many negative interactions with the judicial system. On the other hand, it is also possible to have a delusional defendant who remains competent because his or her delusional thinking does not significantly impact understanding or rational decision making as it pertains to the legal case. In essence, the delusion can be so circumscribed that it does not involve the legal proceedings or courtroom participants. It is up to the forensic examiner to make these fine discriminations.

Drope v. Missouri, 420 U.S. 162 (1975)

Drope was indicted, along with two others, for the rape of his wife. Defense counsel filed a motion requesting a competence assessment given the facts that Drope attempted to kill his wife before the trial, and he shot himself in the abdomen during the trial. The defense motion for a competence determination was denied. During trial Drope's wife reported longstanding history of bizarre behavior on Drope's part, maintaining that he frequently would "roll down the stairs when he doesn't get his way." The defense moved for a mistrial. The trial judge denied. Drope was convicted and sentenced to life. The Supreme Court reversed and remanded.

HOLDING

Once the issue of competence is raised, it must be explored sufficiently before proceeding with trial. Only a "bona fide doubt" need exist to trigger a competence determination.

COMMENT

Drope affirms *Pate v. Robinson* [383 U.S. 375 (1966)] in making clear the threshold for the facts to warrant a formal competence determination is quite low. The presence of irrational behavior, unusual demeanor at trial, and/or prior medical opinions can all be cause enough to consider a defendant's competence. Because of *Drope* and *Pate*, many competent defendants are referred for competency assessment; this explains why research suggests that about 75% of those referred for evaluation are found competent (Steadman, Monahan, Hartstone, Davis, & Robbins, 1982).

Jackson v. Indiana, 406 U.S. 715 (1972) [*competence restoration*]

Theon Jackson was accused of two robberies. By all accounts, he was a mentally retarded, deaf mute, with no means to communicate. The trial judge declared Jackson incompetent to stand trial, committing him to an institution "until such time as he is cured." Jackson appealed, maintaining that since he would never be cured (restored), commitment was a life sentence. The Supreme Court agreed, maintaining that Jackson's due process rights had been violated.

HOLDING

Incompetent defendants can be committed for restoration only for a reasonable period of time either to return them to competence or to determine whether restoration is possible. Incompetent defendants may not be committed indefinitely.

COMMENT

Jackson v. Indiana is a tremendously significant case that crosses boundaries well beyond criminal competence. Having a "rational relationship" between the nature and length of commitment holds true in other criminal matters, as well as civil commitment and juvenile issues.

Capital Punishment

Gregg v. Georgia, 428 U.S. 153 (1976)

Troy Gregg was convicted of the robbery and murder of two men. Gregg was tried, convicted, and sentenced to death under new procedures for capital cases enacted by the Georgia legislature. The new procedures included a bifurcated trial (guilt–innocence phase, penalty phase). Consideration of aggravating and mitigating factors was now required during the penalty phase. The death penalty could be imposed only if aggravating factors outweighed mitigating factors. There was also an automatic appeal of sentence, if imposed. Gregg appealed his death sentence, but the U.S. Supreme Court upheld the sentence.

HOLDING

Georgia's new death penalty procedures were found constitutional, and not in violation of the Eighth or Fourteenth amendments.

COMMENT

In addition to these new procedures making the death penalty constitutional again, the procedures open an avenue for mental health testimony prior to sentencing related to potential increased risk of future dangerousness as well as relevant mitigating factors.

Lockett v. Ohio, 438 U.S. 586 (1978)

Sandra Lockett was convicted of robbery and aggravated murder and sentenced to death. Lockett appealed on several grounds, one of which was that Ohio's death penalty statute did not require consideration of all potentially mitigating factors. On that issue, the U.S. Supreme Court vacated Lockett's death penalty.

HOLDING

The Eighth and Fourteenth Amendments require comprehensive and individualized consideration of all potentially mitigating factors in capital cases.

COMMENT

The Lockett decision opens wide the door for nearly all forms of mental health testimony related to potential mitigating factors. These factors can be any potentially meaningful finding regarding the defendant's biological predisposition, social/psychological history, or current condition.

Atkins v. Virginia, 536 U.S. 304 (2002)

Daryl Atkins and an accomplice abducted Eric Nesbitt, robbed him, shot him eight times, and killed him. The IQ of Atkins was assessed at 59. A rebuttal psychiatrist testified that Atkins was not mentally retarded, but simply a psychopath. Atkins was convicted of kidnapping, armed robbery, and capital murder. He was sentenced to death. Atkins appealed, arguing that it was a violation of the Eighth Amendment to execute the mentally retarded. The Supreme Court reversed and remanded.

HOLDING

In a rare occurrence, the High Court reversed its previous ruling in *Penry v. Lynaugh* [492 U.S. 302 (1989)] stating that execution of the mentally retarded is cruel and unusual punishment and a violation of the Eighth Amendment. The Court cited society's "evolving standards of decency."

COMMENT

This case made a sweeping change. It is a very important case for neuropsychologists who perform death penalty–related evaluations. No neuropsychologist should evaluate a criminal defendant on issues of death penalty sentencing without being thoroughly aware of the details of this case.

Sixth Amendment Right to Counsel

Estelle v. Smith, 451 U.S. 454 (1981) (Fifth Amendment, Sixth Amendment)

Smith was convicted of first-degree murder and sentenced to death in Texas. Smith filed a writ of *habeas corpus* petitioning to have his sentence overturned, because during sentencing, the prosecution used statements obtained from psychiatrist James Grigson during a pretrial competence assessment as a basis for prediction of future dangerousness, without Grigson having warned the defendant that his words could be used against him in sentencing. Furthermore, defense counsel had not been made aware of the competence evaluation. At sentencing, Grigson maintained that Smith, whose accomplice had actually killed the victim, and who had a single prior conviction for possession of marijuana, was a "very severe sociopath" who was "going to commit other similar or same criminal acts." The Supreme Court reversed both conviction and death sentence, remanding back to the trial court.

HOLDING

For statements to be admissible, a defendant must be advised of the purposes of the examination before the examination. To do otherwise is a violation of the defendant's Fifth Amendment right against self-incrimination. To perform a mental health evaluation without defense counsel's knowledge is also a violation of the defendant's Sixth Amendment right to effective counsel.

COMMENT

This case has great significance for forensic psychologists; it was even a basis for creating portions of the "Specialty Guidelines for Forensic Psychologists" (Committee on Ethical Guidelines for Forensic Psychologists, 1991). Psychologists should not perform an evaluation without first making certain that defense counsel has been appointed and is aware of the evaluation. Psychologists must provide adequate warning to the defendant and describe how the information obtained in the evaluation might be used in future proceedings. Finally, psychologists should not testify to issues that were not the focus of the evaluation, particularly when the defendant was not properly warned of the possibility.

Ake v. Oklahoma, 470 U.S. 68 (1985)

Glen Ake, an indigent man, was charged with murdering a couple and wounding their two children. At arraignment Ake's behavior was so bizarre that the trial judge, *sua sponte,* ordered a psychiatric examination. Ake was subsequently found incompetent to stand trial and sent to the state hospital for competency restoration. Six weeks later, Ake was pronounced restored. He informed the court he would present an insanity defense, and he requested psychiatric evaluation at the state's expense. The trial court denied Ake's motion. Ake appealed on Sixth and Fourteenth Amendment grounds. The Supreme Court reversed and remanded.

HOLDING

When the defendant has made a preliminary showing that sanity is likely to be a significant issue at trial, the U.S. Constitution requires that the state provide access to psychiatric assistance on this issue if the defendant is indigent. Additionally, because future dangerousness was a significant factor during sentencing, denial of a mental health expert evaluation served to deny Ake due process.

COMMENT

This decision guarantees indigent defendants access to mental health evaluation if there is reason to believe such expert opinion may be helpful to the defense. In addition to sanity, it is likely this decision would guarantee access to mental health evaluation related to *mens rea* issues, such as ability to form prerequisite intent/diminished capacity.

Dangerousness

Barefoot v. Estelle, 463 U.S. 880 (1983)

Thomas Barefoot was convicted of capital murder following a jury trial. During the penalty phase of this bifurcated trial, psychiatrist James Grigson, who had never spoken with Barefoot, provided testimony about Barefoot's future dangerousness. Grigson, responding to a series of hypothetical questions, described Barefoot as being in the "most severe category of sociopaths, on a scale of one to ten . . . above ten." Psychiatrist Grigson further testified that there was "a one hundred percent and absolute chance" that Barefoot would commit future acts of violence that would constitute a continuing threat to society (Cunningham & Goldstein, 2003). Barefoot was sentenced to death. He appealed, arguing that the use of dangerousness testimony in capital sentencing was unreliable and unconstitutional. The Supreme Court upheld Barefoot's sentence and conviction.

HOLDING

Dangerousness testimony in capital sentencing is not a violation of Fourteenth Amendment due process rights. To disallow prediction of dangerousness by mental health professionals would be tantamount to "disinventing the wheel."

COMMENT

This case provides a glimpse into the U.S. Supreme Court's need to make pragmatic decisions that may not be perfect, but enable the effective resolution of legal disputes. In this regard, the legal system needs the ability for witnesses to respond to hypothetical questions and also to provide testimony related to potential increased dangerousness, even if the science on which those judgments are based is not perfect.

Conclusions

In this chapter we introduced criminal forensic neuropsychology as a subspecialty of forensic neuropsychology, within clinical neuropsychology. In essence, it is the integration of clinical neuropsychology and forensic psychology related to criminal matters. We highlighted the need for a specialized knowledge base to practice effectively in this unique arena. We presented the core differences between clinical and forensic practice. We focused on key principles related to the criminal justice system, specifically pertaining to the United States Constitution and mental health case law. We have become confident over the last few years that this information is vitally important for neuropsychologists entering the criminal setting. We hope this chapter (and text) will serve as a springboard for those neuropsychologists who are seeking authentic professional competence in the area of criminal forensic neuropsychology.

Note

Opinions expressed in this chapter are those of the authors and do not necessarily represent the position of the Federal Bureau of Prisons or the U.S. Department of Justice.

References

American Board of Forensic Psychology. (2003). *Fundamentals of forensic psychology: Description of forensic specialty areas—Revised 2003.* Available at *abfp.com/pdfs/fundamentals_of_forensic_psychology.pdf*

Bigler, E. D., & Clement, P. F. (1997). *Diagnostic clinical neuropsychology* (3rd ed.). Austin: University of Texas Press.

Boone, K. B. (Ed.). (2007). *Assessment of feigned cognitive impairment: A neuropsychological perspective.* New York: Guilford Press.

Borum, R., & Grisso, T. (1995). Psychological test use in criminal forensic evaluations. *Professional Psychology: Research and Practice, 26,* 465–473.

Boyd, A. R., McLearen, A. M., Meyer, R. G., & Denney, R. L. (2007). *Detection of deception.* Sarasota, FL: Professional Resource Press.

Bureau of Justice Statistics. (1997). *The criminal justice system flowchart.* Retrieved September 21, 2007, from *www.ojp.usdoj.gov/bjs/flowchart.htm*

Champion, D. J. (2001). *The American dictionary of criminal justice* (2nd ed.). Los Angeles: Roxbury.

Committee on Ethical Guidelines for Forensic Psychologists. (1991). Specialty guidelines for forensic psychologists. *Law and Human Behavior, 15*(6), 655–665.

Cunningham, M. D., & Goldstein, A. M. (2003). Sentencing determinations in death penalty cases. In I. B. Weiner (Series Ed.) & A. M. Goldstein (Vol. Ed.), *Handbook of psychology: Vol. 11. Forensic psychology* (pp. 407–436). Hoboken, NJ: Wiley.

Denney, R. L. (2005). Introduction to criminal forensic neuropsychology and assessment of competency. In G. J. Larrabee (Ed.), *Forensic neuropsychology: A scientific approach* (pp. 378–424). Oxford, UK: Oxford University Press.

Denney, R. L., & Wynkoop, T. F. (2000). Clinical neuropsychology in the criminal forensic setting. *Journal of Head Trauma Rehabilitation, 15,* 804–828.

Furman v. Georgia, 408 U.S. 238 (1972).

Goldstein, A. M. (2003). Overview of forensic psychology. In I. B. Weiner (Series Ed.) & A. M. Goldstein (Vol. Ed.), *Handbook of psychology: Vol. 11. Forensic psychology* (pp. 3–20). Hoboken, NJ: Wiley.

Greenberg, S. A., & Shuman, D. W. (1997). Irreconcilable conflict between therapeutic and forensic roles. *Professional Psychology: Research and Practice, 28,* 50–57.

Grisso, T. (1988). *Competency to stand trial evaluations: A manual for practice.* Sarasota, FL: Professional Resource Exchange.

Grisso, T. (2003). *Evaluating competencies: Forensic assessments and instruments* (2nd ed.). New York: Plenum Press.

Guiliano, A. J., Barth, J. T., Hawk, G. L., & Ryan, T. V. (1997). The forensic neuropsychologist: Precedents, roles, and problems. In R. J. McCaffrey, A. D. Williams, J. M. Fisher, & L. C. Laing (Eds.), *The practice of forensic neuropsychology: Meeting challenges in the courtroom* (pp. 1–36). New York: Plenum Press.

Heilbronner, R. L. (2004). A status report on the practice of forensic psychology. *Clinical Neuropsychologist, 18,* 312–326.

Heilbronner, R. L., & Frumkin, B. I. (2003). Neuropsychology and forensic psychology: Working collaboratively in a criminal case. *Journal of Forensic Neuropsychology, 3*(4), 5–12.

Heilbrun, K. (2001). *Principles of forensic mental health assessment.* New York: Kluwer Academic/Plenum Press.

Hom, J., & Denney, R. L. (2003). Preface. In J. Hom & R. L. Denney (Eds.), *Detection of negative response bias in forensic neuropsychology.* New York: Haworth Press.

Hooper, J. F. (2003, August 21). *Landmark cases.* Retrieved August 21, 2003, from bama.ua.edu/~jhooper/landmark.html

Larrabee, G. J. (Ed.). (2005). *Forensic neuropsychology: A scientific approach.* New York: Oxford University Press.

Larrabee, G. J. (Ed.). (2007). *Assessment of malingered neuropsychological deficits.* New York: Oxford University Press.

Lezak, M. D., Howieson, D. B., & Loring, D. W. (2004). *Neuropsychological assessment* (4th ed.). New York: Oxford University Press.

Martell, D. A. (1992a). Estimating the prevalence of organic brain dysfunction in maximum-security forensic psychiatric patients. *Journal of Forensic Science, 37,* 878–893.

Martell, D. A. (1992b). Forensic neuropsychology and the criminal law. *Law and Human Behavior, 16,* 313–336.

McCaffrey, R. J., Williams, A. D., Fisher, J. M., & Laing, L. C. (Eds.). (1997). *The practice of forensic neuropsychology: Meeting challenges in the courtroom.* New York: Plenum Press.

Melton, G. B., Petrila, J., Poythress, N. G., & Slobogin, C., with Lyons, P. M., &

Otto, R. K. (1997). *Psychological evaluations for the courts* (3rd ed.). New York: Guilford Press.

Mittenberg, W., Patton, C., Canyock, E. M., & Condit, D. C. (2002). Base rates of malingering and symptom exaggeration. *Journal of Clinical and Experimental Neuropsychology, 24*, 1094–1102.

Mrad, D. (1996, September). *Criminal responsibility evaluations*. Paper presented at Issues in Forensic Assessment Symposium, Federal Bureau of Prisons, Atlanta, GA.

Packer, I. K., & Borum, R. (2003). Forensic training and practice. In I. B. Weiner (Series Ed.) & A. M. Goldstein (Vol. Ed.), *Handbook of psychology: Vol. 11. Forensic psychology* (pp. 21–32). Hoboken, NJ: Wiley.

Parenté, R., & Herrmann, D. (1996). *Retraining cognition: Techniques and applications*. Gaithersburg, MD: Aspen.

Rogers, R. (Ed.). (2008). *Clinical assessment of malingering and deception* (3rd ed.). New York: Guilford Press.

Rogers, R., & Shuman, D. W. (2005). *Fundamentals of forensic practice: Mental health and criminal law*. New York: Springer Science.

Saks, M. J. (1990). Expert witnesses, nonexpert witnesses, and nonwitness experts. *Law and Human Behavior, 14*, 291–313.

Shapiro, D. L. (1984). *Psychological evaluation and expert testimony*. New York: van Nostrand Reinhold.

Shapiro, D. L. (1991). *Forensic psychological assessment*. Boston: Allyn & Bacon.

Shapiro, D. L. (1999). *Criminal responsibility evaluations: A manual for practice*. Sarasota, FL: Professional Resource Press.

Sohlberg, M. M., & Mateer, C. A. (2001). *Cognitive rehabilitation: An integrative neuropsychological approach*. New York: Guilford Press.

Steadman, H., Monahan, J., Hartstone, E., Davis, S., & Robbins, P. (1982). Mentally disordered offenders: A national survey of patients and facilities. *Law and Human Behavior, 6*, 31–38.

Sullivan, J. P., & Denney, R. L. (2003). Constitutional and judicial foundations in criminal forensic neuropsychology. *Journal of Forensic Neuropsychology, 3*, 13–44.

Swaminath, R. S., Mendonca, J. D., Vidal, C., & Chapman, P. (2002). Experiments in change: Pretrial diversion of offenders with mental illness. *Canadian Journal of Psychiatry, 47*, 450–458.

Sweet, J. J. (1999). Introduction. In L. A. Bieliauskas (Series Ed.) & J. J. Sweet (Vol. Ed.), *Series on neuropsychology, development, and cognition: Vol. 2. Forensic neuropsychology: Fundamentals and practice* (pp. xvii–xix). Lisse, The Netherlands: Swets & Zeitlinger.

Ulrich, T. E. (2002). Pretrial diversion in the federal court system. *Federal Probation, 66*(3), 30–37.

Wynkoop, T. F., & Denney, R. L. (1999). Exaggeration of neuropsychological deficit in competency to stand trial. *Journal of Forensic Neuropsychology, 1*(2), 29–53.

Chapter 2

Ethical Issues in Criminal Forensic Neuropsychology

JAMES A. TYSON
JAMES P. SULLIVAN

Forensic psychology is a subspecialty of psychology. Often, answers to problems that forensic psychologists address within a forensic context require not only clinical acumen but also awareness of the unique dynamics in forensic contexts. Ideally, forensic psychologists perform assessments that are relevant, accurate, and credible. Such work requires synthesis of clinical judgment and forensic knowledge that provides the trier of fact with data that informs—rather than intrudes upon—the decision-making process. Such assessments must be guided by ethical awareness.

Because this chapter provides an overview, ethical issues in forensic neuropsychology should be distinguished from moral issues. Although both ethics and morals share the common goal of guiding decision making, moral decision making emanates from internally held values that are often deontological or deity-based. Moral values are typically universal and emphasize values such as truth, honesty, or goodness. In contrast, ethical decision making is directed by professional guidelines that, ideally, are morally neutral.

Forensic neuropsychology is a subspecialty of clinical neuropsychology. In the *Archives of Clinical Neuropsychology*, Hom (2003) described the responsibilities of the forensic neuropsychologist:

The primary responsibility of the forensic neuropsychologist is to provide information based on scientifically validated principles and clinical methodology that is pertinent to the forensic question at hand. . . . To best answer the forensic question, the neuropsychologist must use a methodology that has been scientifically validated on brain-impaired individuals, and can distinguish various brain conditions from each other as well as from normal variation. The methodology must be able to determine whether any dysfunction found is, in fact, the result of a neurological condition as opposed to non-neurological, psychological, or even factitious disorders. (p. 826)

Integrating neuropsychological issues within the forensic context requires careful consideration because of differences inherent to the respective areas. Neuropsychology, and the methodology it employs, requires the conceptualization of human behavior along a continuum. Typically, greater dysfunction is equated with increasing departures from measures of central tendency. Within forensic contexts, a dichotomous classification system predominates. One is either guilty or innocent. One is competent or incompetent to stand trial. The American system of justice's orientation toward dichotomies necessitates an adversarial approach that can be unsettling to the neuropsychologist indoctrinated in academic collegiality and relativism.

In some ways, this potential conflict is related to another fundamental issue. Specifically, psychological and legal systems differ in their conceptualization of the search for "truth" and tolerance for indecision (Faust, 1991). Sweet, Grote, and van Gorp (2002) noted that in adversarial proceedings, "neuropsychologists may be asked to answer questions more succinctly and plainly. . . . This can be difficult, as many neuropsychologists by virtue of temperament and training may prefer to equivocate or to qualify their replies to questions, if simple answers fail to convey the 'truth' of a complex set of variables" (p. 116). The Supreme Court has recognized "within the medical discipline, the traditional standard for 'fact finding' is a 'reasonable degree of medical certainty'" [*Addington v. Texas*, 441 U.S. 418, 430 (1979)]. However, there remains limited consensus regarding how one should translate "reasonable degree" into existing neuropsychological methodology.

Equally problematic differences can contribute to additional problems when a neuropsychologist enters the forensic context. Often the identity of the client is less readily apparent. In contrast to clinical settings, the client in forensic neuropsychological assessment is rarely the examinee. This individual is often properly referred to as the defendant. After identifying the client he or she is to serve, the neuropsychologist must then accurately conceptualize the nature of the relationship with the client to address adequately issues of informed consent and notification of purpose.

Of course, the seasoned neuropsychologist is aware of resources to guide his approach to issues of informed consent (e.g., the American Psychological Association's [2002] *Ethical Principles of Psychologists and Code of Conduct* and relevant specialty guidelines). However, ethical decision making for the forensic neuropsychologist requires awareness of not only enforceable ethics codes and aspirational guidelines but also legal guidelines in general, and relevant case law in particular. For example, awareness of *Estelle v. Smith* [451 U.S. 454 (1981)] and its potential applicability is critical knowledge for addressing issues of informed consent during competency to stand trial proceedings. As Weissman and DeBow (2003) indicated, "It is mistaken to assume that it is acceptable to be ignorant of specialized psycho-legal knowledge bases. The long and rather tortuous history of the psychology–law interface makes it clear that ignorance has never been acceptable" (p. 34).

According to Sullivan and Denney (2003), insufficient legal knowledge when applying neuropsychology within legal settings contributes substantially to criticisms of mental health professionals' work in forensic settings. The authors highlight work by Grisso (1986, 2003) that traces incompetence in forensic settings to what has been called the "five I's," which are briefly, "ignorance, and irrelevance in courtroom testimony, psychiatric or psychological intrusion into essentially legal matters, and insufficiency and incredibility of information provided to courts" (Grisso, 2003, p. 11).

Despite the complexities associated with applications of neuropsychology to the criminal forensic context, it is clear that neuropsychology benefits the legal process. Additionally, there is evidence that forensic evaluations constitute a significant portion of contemporary neuropsychological practice. Mittenberg, Patton, Canyock, and Condit (2002) presented the results of a national survey of board-certified neuropsychologists. The 131 survey respondents indicated they completed a total of 33,351 annual evaluations. Of those, 34% could be considered forensic in nature (personal injury, 19%; disability/workers' compensation, 11%; and criminal litigation, 4%). This 4% constituted 1,341 criminally related evaluations per year. This suggests that a minority of responding practitioners is conducting the majority of the criminal evaluations. Similarly, Borum and Grisso (1995) surveyed test use in criminal forensic evaluations and found that 46–50% of forensic psychologists indicated they used some type of neuropsychological screening in their pretrial evaluations. Such evaluations would have been impossible had neuropsychology not advanced to a position that rests on reasonably sound conceptual and empirical bases, and had law not simultaneously established sophisticated rules for the admissibility of scientific evidence [e.g., *Frye v. United States*, 293 F. 1013 (D.C. Cir., 1923); *Daubert v. Merrell Dow Pharmaceuticals*, 509 U.S. 579 (1993)].

Informed Consent

While psychologists are admonished to "strive to benefit those with whom they work and take care to do no harm" (American Psychological Association, 2002), forensic neuropsychologists are often requested to perform services that may or may not benefit the examinee. The possibility of a negative outcome for an examinee means that forensic evaluations constitute a risk for the examinee, of which he or she should be apprised as part of the informed consent or notification of purpose process. Generally defined, *informed consent* can be seen as having three essential elements: disclosure, comprehension, and voluntariness.

In contrast, *notification of purpose*, which is obtained for court-ordered assessments, typically seeks to provide the examinee with an appropriate explanation of the purpose of the evaluation and to obtain the examinee's assent in conducting the examination. Although assent is desirable before court-ordered assessments, it is not required. The defendant has no legal right to refuse participation. According to the Specialty Guidelines for Forensic Psychologists (SGFP; Committee on Ethical Guidelines for Forensic Psychologists, 1991), "If the client appears unwilling to proceed after receiving a thorough notification of the purposes, methods, and intended uses of the forensic evaluation, the evaluation should be postponed and the psychologist should take steps to place the client in contact with his/her attorney for the purpose of legal advice on the issue of participation" (p. 559).

The following sections highlight the existing guidelines and relevant case law that should direct the informed consent or notification of purpose procedures in criminal forensic neuropsychology. In this and subsequent sections, the introductory section will be followed by enforceable guidelines included in the American Psychological Association's (2002) Ethical Principles of Psychologists and Code of Conduct (EPPCC). The aspirational guidelines included in the SGFP follow. In this chapter, we have analyzed the current SGFP (Committee on Ethical Guidelines for Forensic Psychologists, 1991) and the latest official draft of the revised Specialty Guidelines, published January 11, 2006. The dates clarify which version is being referenced. As appropriate, relevant case law is cited further to inform the discussion, after reviewing the aforementioned ethical guidelines.

American Psychological Association (2002) EPPCC

Section 3.10 of the EPPCC (American Psychological Association, 2002) indicates that the psychologist is "to obtain the informed consent of the individual or individuals using language that is reasonably understandable to that person or persons except when conducting activities without consent is mandated by law or governmental regulation or as otherwise provided in this Ethics Code" (p. 1065). The exceptions highlighted here are expanded in Section 9.03 to include instances where informed consent "is implied because testing is conducted as a routine educational, institutional, or organizational activity" (p. 1071) or when testing is conducted to evaluate decisional capacity.

Additionally, Section 9.03 stipulates that even for "persons with questionable capacity to consent or for whom testing is mandated by law or governmental regulations" (American Psychological Association, 2002, p. 1071), the psychologist should notify such persons as to "the nature and purpose of the proposed assessment services, using language that is reasonably understandable to the person being assessed" (p. 1071).

Committee on Ethical Guidelines for Forensic Psychologists (2006) SGFP

The second official draft of the SGFP was published January 11, 2006. When references are made to the SGFP, the authors are referring to the January 11, 2006, draft, referred to as Guidelines. The goals of the Guidelines as stated in that document are "to improve the quality of forensic psychological services; enhance the practice and facilitate the systematic development of forensic psychology; encourage a high level of quality in professional practice; and encourage forensic practitioners to acknowledge and respect the rights of those whom they serve." Unlike the EPPCC (American Psychological Association, 2002) the Guidelines are aspirational and not explicitly enforceable. In fact, Section 2.05 of the Guidelines explicitly state that the guidelines are "not to serve as the basis for disciplinary action or civil liability." Additionally, the architects of this draft intentionally used modifiers such as *reasonably*, *appropriate*, and *potentially* that emphasize the need for judicious application of professional judgment and discretion in reaching ethical decisions. This draft version of the Guidelines is very explicit concerning the need for clarification of any possible risks in the informed consent or notification of purpose procedure (Table 2.1).

The most recent draft of the Guidelines provides more extensive clarification than is apparent in the original version approved March 9, 1991. The SGFP (Committee on Ethical Guidelines for Forensic Psychologists, 1991) stipulates that "forensic psychologists have an obligation to ensure that prospective clients are informed of their legal rights with respect to the anticipated forensic service, of the purposes of any evaluation, of the nature of pro-

TABLE 2.1. Section 8 of the Specialty Guidelines for Forensic Psychologists

8. NOTIFICATION, ASSENT, CONSENT, AND INFORMED CONSENT

Because substantial rights, liberties, and properties are frequently, immediately, and irrevocably at risk in forensic matters and because the methods and procedures of forensic practitioners are complex and may not be accurately anticipated by the recipients of forensic services, forensic practitioners inform service recipients about the nature and parameters of the services to be provided.

8.01 Timing and Substance

Forensic practitioners notify clients, examinees, and others who are the recipients of forensic services as soon as is feasible regarding the provision of all reasonably anticipated forensic services and all relevant professional conduct. In determining whether the information and subsequent explanation provided as the basis for consent are reasonably adequate, relevant factors include whether the person is experienced or trained in psychological and legal matters of the type involved and whether the person is represented by counsel when providing the consent. Normally, more experienced persons need less information to provide adequate informed consent than would others. When questions or uncertainties remain after the forensic practitioner has made the effort to communicate the necessary information, forensic practitioners recommend the person seek legal advice regarding the possible consequences of the forensic services.

8.02 Communication with Legal Representatives Seeking to Retain a Forensic Practitioner

Forensic practitioners seek to insure that attorneys and others considering to contract with them for services are knowledgeable about factors that might reasonably affect the decision to retain them. As part of the initial process of being retained, or as soon thereafter as previously unknown information becomes available, forensic practitioners disclose to the client all information that would reasonably be anticipated to affect a decision to retain or continue the services of the forensic practitioner. This disclosure includes all information that the reasonably prudent recipient of service would desire to know. The factors to disclose may include a) the fee structure for anticipated services; b) prior and current personal or professional activities, obligations and relationships that would reasonably lead to the fact or the appearance of a conflict of interest; c) the forensic practitioner's knowledge, skill, experience, and education relevant to forensic services in the matter being considered, including any significant limitations; d) the substantial scientific bases and limitations of the methods and procedures which are expected to be employed, including any limitations; and e) any other factor that might reasonably be anticipated to substantially limit the forensic practitioner's ability or qualification to testify or that might substantially limit the weight accorded to the forensic practitioner's opinions.

(continued)

TABLE 2.1. *(continued)*

8.03 Communication with Forensic Examinees

Forensic practitioners disclose to the examinee who is the identified client; the purpose, nature, and anticipated use of the examination; any factor reasonably expected to substantially impair the objectivity, competence, or effectiveness of the forensic practitioner; who will have access to the information; associated limits on privacy, confidentiality, and privilege including who is authorized to release or access the information contained in the forensic practitioner's records; the voluntary or involuntary nature of participation, including potential consequences of nonparticipation, if known; and if the cost of the service is the responsibility of the examinee, the anticipated cost of the service, the means by which the cost will be calculated, and the billing arrangements.

Note. From Committee on Ethical Guidelines for Forensic Psychologists (2006).

---

cedures to be employed, of the intended uses of any product of their services, and of the party who has employed the forensic psychologist" (p. 9).

The SGFP (Committee on Ethical Guidelines for Forensic Psychologists, 1991) additionally clarifies courses of action in the event the examinee appears unwilling to proceed, in situations where the examinee may not have the capacity to provide informed consent.

Importantly, the SGFP (Committee on Ethical Guidelines for Forensic Psychologists, 1991) in Section IV-E-3 specifies the following:

> After a psychologist has advised the subject of a clinical forensic evaluation of the intended uses of the evaluation and its work product, the psychologist may not use the evaluation work product for other purposes without explicit waiver to do so by the client or the client's legal representative.

This is reiterated in Section VI-G-2.

> Unless otherwise stipulated by the parties, forensic psychologists are aware that no statements made by a defendant, in the course of any (forensic) examination, no testimony by the expert based upon such statements, nor any other fruits of the statements can be admitted into evidence against the defendant in any criminal proceeding, except on an issue respecting mental condition on which the defendant has introduced testimony. Forensic psychologists have an affirmative duty to ensure that their written products and oral testimony conform to this Federal Rule of Procedure (12.2[c]), or its state equivalent.

These stipulations, more than others, are representative of the influence that relevant case law, Federal Rules of Procedures, and Federal Rules of Evidence exert on criminal forensic neuropsychology.

Case Law

The language of the Section IV-E-3 is remarkable for its directness and absence of relativism. Here, a particular course of action is not "advised" or "recommended." Instead, a course of action is specifically prohibited to the maximum extent possible within an aspirational framework. It is apparent that these prohibitions highlight the influence that case law has on recommended practices, as highlighted in the SGFP, that is, *Estelle v. Smith*.

In *Estelle v. Smith* (1981), the defendant, Smith, was convicted of first-degree murder and sentenced to death in Texas. Smith filed a writ of *habeas corpus*, petitioning to have his sentence overturned. He argued that during sentencing, the prosecution used statements obtained from psychiatrist James Grigson's pretrial competency assessment as a basis for prediction of future dangerousness. Grigson used the information without having warned the defendant that his words could be used against him in sentencing. Furthermore, defense counsel had not been made aware of the competency evaluation. At sentencing, Grigson maintained that Smith, whose accomplice had actually killed the victim, and who had a single prior conviction for possession of marijuana, was a "very severe sociopath," who was "going to commit other similar and same criminal acts." The Supreme Court reversed both convictions and the death sentence, remanding the case back to trial court.

Holding

For statements to be admissible, a defendant must be advised of the purposes of the examination, including the methods to be employed and the intended uses of such data. To do otherwise is a violation of defendant's Fifth Amendment right against self-incrimination. To perform a mental health evaluation without defense counsel's knowledge is also a violation of defendant's Sixth Amendment right to effective counsel.

Comment

This case has great significance for forensic psychologists; it was even the basis for creating portions of the SGFP (Committee on Ethical Guidelines for Forensic Psychologists, 1991). Psychologists should not perform an evaluation without first making certain that defense counsel has been appointed and is aware of the evaluation. Psychologists must provide adequate warning to the defendant and describe how the information obtained in the evaluation might be used in future proceedings. Finally, psychologists should not testify to issues that are not the focus of the evaluation, particularly when the defendant has not been properly warned of the possibility.

Competency

Golding (1999), one of the authors of the original SGFP (Committee on Ethical Guidelines for Forensic Psychologists, 1991), stated that the foundations of expertise require an understanding of the fiduciary role of the forensic psychologist. As an expert, the forensic psychologist must understand his or her role in ensuring the rights of the examinee are not violated. Additionally, he or she has a responsibility to have the requisite legal, ethical, scientific, and professional expertise. In summary, the forensic psychologist is required to understand his or her fiduciary role. A *fiduciary role* means that the criminal forensic neuropsychologist must safeguard the rights of the examinee and is in a special position of trust and confidence. Golding's statement can be seen as a development of Ethical Principle B (Fidelity and Responsibility). The ethical principle Fidelity and Responsibility highlights the importance of diligent execution of fiduciary responsibilities and directs psychologists to obtain and maintain high levels of competence in the areas in which they specialize. This ethical principle suggests that competence is integral to professional relationships and often is evaluated within the context of one's professional relationships.

There are additional pragmatic reasons to achieve and maintain professional competency. Increased and maintained competency can be viewed as a risk management strategy in which the potential for malpractice lawsuits, tort liability, and criminal sanctions are minimized. Additionally, professional competency improves the quality of professional services and, consequently, increases the public stature of the profession.

The following section is organized hierarchically and begins with a discussion of the most relevant standards from the EPPCC (American Psychological Association, 2002). Aspirational guidelines included in the SGFP (Committee on Ethical Guidelines for Forensic Psychologists, 1991, 2006) follow. Prior to discussion of training of forensic psychologists, we describe the differences between a fact witness and an expert. We also highlight relevant case law and Federal Rule of Evidence 702 (1975) governing the admissibility of expert testimony. The competencies that one should develop when expanding the scope of practice to include forensic psychology follows. Finally, training guidelines for competency development through graduate study and continuing education are discussed.

American Psychological Association (2002) EPPCC

EPPCC Section 2.01 provides ethical guidelines on the competent delivery of psychological services.

> 2.01 Boundaries of Competence
> (a) Psychologists provide services, teach, and conduct research with populations and in areas only within the boundaries of their competence, based on their education, training, supervised experience, consultation, study, or professional experience.

The enforceable guidelines described in this section can be viewed as a concrete extension of the ethical principles of beneficence and nonmalfeasance. Specifically, Section 2.01 provides guidelines that enable a psychologist to be reasonably confident that the services he or she provides will be of maximum utility and cause minimal harm. Section 2.01a is viewed as limiting the scope of practice to those areas in which a psychologist is competent. Section 2.01b, however, clarifies that one can appropriately restrict scope of practice and still fail to practice psychology competently if one ignores the way in which individual differences can affect the outcome of service delivery.

> Section 2.01b. Where scientific or professional knowledge in the discipline of psychology establishes that an understanding of factors associated with age, gender, gender identity, race, ethnicity, culture, national origin, religion, sexual orientation, disability, language, or socioeconomic status is essential for effective implementation of their services or research, psychologists have or obtain the training, experience, consultation, or supervision necessary to ensure the competence of their services, or they make appropriate referrals, except as provided in Standard 2.02, Providing Psychological Services in Emergencies.

Fisher (2003a) writes that psychologists have three obligations under Section 2.01b. These include familiarity with professional and scientific knowledge, appropriate skills, and knowledge of when a referral is necessary.

> Section 2.01c. Psychologists planning to provide services, teach, or conduct research involving populations, areas, techniques, or technologies new to them undertake relevant education, training, supervised experience, consultation, or study.

Section 2.01c of EPPCC directs a psychologist who seeks to expand scope of practice to understand the qualifications established by the field within which he seeks entry. While Section 2.01c establishes the requirements for entry into a different subfield of psychology, it fails to articulate the manner for doing so. Typically, training that facilitates entry into a particular subfield occurs at the graduate level.

Committee on Ethical Guidelines for Forensic Psychologists (1991) SGFP

The SGFP (Committee on Ethical Guidelines for Forensic Psychologists, 1991) provides clarification of the competencies one should possess to provide forensic psychological services. Specifically, the SGFP suggests that forensic psychologists should possess a "fundamental and reasonable level of knowledge and understanding of the legal and professional standards, which govern their participation as experts in the legal proceedings" (p. 558). In addition to the rules and procedures governing the admissibility of expert testimony, Goldstein (2005) underscored the importance of forensic psychologists "understanding the constitutional rights of those they are evaluating, applicable rules of evidence, the nature of expert testimony and the relevant statutes and case law related to the psycho-legal question under consideration by the court" (p. 5).

Committee on Ethical Guidelines for Forensic Psychologists (2006) SGFP

The latest SGFP draft (Committee on Ethical Guidelines for Forensic Psychologists, 2006) expands on the aspirational guidelines provided in the previous version. The current guidelines for competency appear directed ultimately toward protecting the rights of the parties employing forensic psychologists. However, the latest draft of the SGFP is more explicit in its direction to psychologists to be more vigilant regarding the extent individual differences may influence the validity of their conclusions. Additionally, competency as expressed in this draft version mandates that the forensic psychologist be mindful of when the rights of a party necessitate that the party consult with an attorney.

A notable addition to this draft version is guidance for the supervision of subordinates. These guidelines are directed at controlling the quality of work done not only by trainees but also interpreters. Forensic psychologists are especially cautioned to avoid employing persons in their forensic evaluations who have multiple relationships with others involved in a particular case. Table 2.2 includes Section 4 of the draft version of the Guidelines published January 11, 2006.

TABLE 2.2. Section 4 of the Specialty Guidelines
for Forensic Psychologists

4. COMPETENCE

4.01 Scope of Competence

Forensic practitioners provide competent services to clients and other recipients of forensic services in a manner consistent with the standards of their profession. Competent provision of services includes the psychological and legal knowledge, skill, thoroughness, and preparation reasonably necessary for the provision of those services. In determining whether to proceed in a particular matter, forensic practitioners consider factors including the relative complexity and specialized nature of the service required, their general training and experience, their training and experience in the specialty area in question, the preparation and study they are able to devote to the matter, and the opportunities for consultation with a professional of established competence in the subject matter in question. Even with regard to subjects in which they are competent, forensic practitioners are encouraged to consult with other experts in particularly complex or contentious matters.

4.02 Gaining and Maintaining Competence

Forensic practitioners provide services only within the boundaries of their competence. Competence can be acquired through various combinations of education, training, supervised experience, consultation, study, and professional experience. Competent services can also be provided through consultation with, and as appropriate, supervision by, another professional of established competence in the subject matter in question. Forensic practitioners planning to provide services, teach, or conduct research involving populations, areas, techniques, or technologies that are new to them undertake relevant education, training, supervised experience, consultation, or study. Forensic practitioners undertake ongoing efforts to develop and maintain their competencies. To maintain the requisite knowledge and skill, forensic practitioners keep abreast of developments in the fields of psychology and the law, engage in continuing study and education, and comply with any continuing education requirements to which they may be subject.

4.03 Representation of Competencies

Forensic practitioners adequately inform clients, examinees, judges, attorneys, parties, triers of fact, and other recipients of their services about relevant aspects of the nature and extent of their experience, training, credentials, and qualifications. The amount and type of information provided will vary according to the service involved and the context in which it is provided. Forensic practitioners do not, by either commission or omission, participate in misrepresentation of their abilities, training, credentials, or qualifications or the manner in which they were obtained.

4.04 Knowledge of the Legal System and the Legal Rights of Individuals

Forensic practitioners are responsible for a fundamental and reasonable level of knowledge and understanding of the legal and professional standards, laws, rules, and precedents that govern their participation in legal proceedings and that guide the impact of

(continued)

TABLE 2.2. *(continued)*

their services on service recipients. Forensic practitioners manage their professional conduct in a manner that does not threaten or impair the rights of effected individuals. They consult with, and refer others to, qualified legal counsel on matters of law and legal process. In their role as forensic practitioners, forensic practitioners do not provide formal legal advice or formal legal opinion. When forensic practitioners provide legal information to examinees or other parties, they explain to parties that legal information is not the same as legal advice or legal opinion. The legal information provided by forensic practitioners may be based on their knowledge and experience in forensic practice. Forensic practitioners encourage parties to consult with an attorney for guidance regarding relevant legal issues and applicability of any legal information provided regarding the most advisable course of action for the person's particular situation.

4.05 Knowledge of the Scientific Foundation for Testimony and Other Sworn Statements

Through reports, written statements, and testimony, forensic practitioners provide scientific, technical and other specialized knowledge to the court that may assist the trier of fact to understand evidence or to determine a fact in issue. Forensic practitioners only offer opinions to the court in those areas for which they are competent to do so, based on adequate knowledge, skill, experience, and education. When providing opinions and testimony that are based on novel or emerging principles and methods, forensic practitioners make clear the known limitations of these principles and methods. Forensic practitioners typically provide opinions and testimony that are a) sufficiently based upon facts or data and on adequate scientific foundation; b) the product of reliable principles and methods; and c) based on principles and methods that have been applied reliably to the facts of the case.

4.06 Knowledge of the Scientific Foundation for Teaching and Research

Forensic practitioners engage in teaching and research activities in which they have adequate knowledge, experience, and education. They adhere to recognized and accepted principles of research design and scientific method, and acknowledge substantial relevant limitations and caveats inherent in their procedures and conclusions.

4.07 Considering Impact of Personal Beliefs and Experience

Forensic practitioners recognize that their own attitudes, values, beliefs, opinions, or biases may have the effect of diminishing their ability to practice in a competent and impartial manner. Under such circumstances, forensic practitioners take steps to correct or limit such effects; decline participation in the matter; or limit their participation in a manner that is consistent with professional obligations.

4.08 Appreciation of Individual Differences

When scientific or professional knowledge in the discipline of psychology establishes that an understanding of factors associated with age, gender, gender identity, race, ethnicity, culture, national origin, religion, sexual orientation, disability, language, socioeconomic

(continued)

TABLE 2.2. *(continued)*

status, or other relevant individual differences affects implementation or use of their services or research, forensic practitioners gain the training, experience, consultation, or supervision necessary. Forensic practitioners are aware of and respect cultural, individual, and role differences, including those based on age, gender, gender identity, race, ethnicity, culture, national origin, religion, sexual orientation, disability, language, and socioeconomic status and consider these factors when working with members of such groups. They do not engage in unfair discrimination based on such factors or on any basis proscribed by law. They take steps to correct or limit the effects of such factors on their work; decline participation in the matter; or limit their participation in a manner that is consistent with professional obligations. They also avoid participating in or condoning prejudicial activities of others based upon such factors.

4.09 Competence of Supervisees and Trainees

Forensic practitioners are responsible for the conduct of those individuals whom they employ or directly supervise. When delegating work to employees, supervisees, students, or research or teaching assistants, or using the services of others, such as interpreters, forensic practitioners avoid using persons who have multiple relationships with those being served that would be likely to result in diminished or impaired performance, exploitation, or loss of objectivity; authorize only those responsibilities that such persons can be expected to perform competently on the basis of their education, training, or experience, either independently or with the level of supervision that is provided; and take reasonable steps to ensure that such persons perform these services competently and diligently.

4.10 Appropriate Use of Services and Products

Forensic practitioners make a reasonable effort to ensure that their services and the products of their services are used in a competent and responsible manner, balancing this consideration with the need not to threaten or impair the legal rights of parties or to interfere with the ability of their attorneys to adequately represent them. Forensic practitioners are not bound to correct all possible misuses of their services but to exercise professional discretion in determining the extent and means by which misuses may be addressed. When asked to engage in conduct or provide a product that they believe is unethical, unprofessional, or falls below the standard of care, forensic practitioners decline to provide the service or product and, if appropriate, inform the person making the request of the reason for doing so.

Note. From Committee on Ethical Guidelines for Forensic Psychologists (2006).

Types of Witnesses, Case Law, and Federal Rule of Evidence 702

Haas (1993) summarized the qualifications a forensic psychologist should possess, especially as they relate to courtroom testimony. Specifically, Haas emphasized that a forensic psychologist must know the difference between what qualifies as expert opinions and what opinions are properly those of a fact witness. Also, he or she should present limitations of his or her knowledge and knowledge bases.

In contrast to fact witness testimony, experts can testify to matters not within their personal sensory experience, and to opinions not ultimately based on personal knowledge. This latitude allows experts to draw upon scientific knowledge that they may have through education, training, and experience, such as general scientific principles and theories.

Prior to 1973, the *Frye* standard governed the admissibility of expert scientific evidence [*Frye v. United States*, 293 F. 1013 (D.C. Cir., 1923)]. Under the *Frye* standard, expert scientific evidence was admissible only if the theories, procedures, or tests, for example, have gained "general acceptance" in the scientific community. Although the Frye standard was widely utilized by the courts, it had the potential to prohibit expert testimony based on scientifically rigorous but emergent scientific approaches.

In *Daubert*, the U.S. Supreme Court was asked to decide whether the *Frye* test had been superceded by the adoption of the Federal Rules of Evidence, specifically 702, the federal rule governing admissibility of expert testimony. This rule states: "If scientific, technical, or other specialized knowledge will assist the trier of fact to understand the evidence or to determine a fact in issue, a witness qualified as an expert by knowledge, skill, experience, training, or education, may testify thereto in the form of an opinion or otherwise" (retrieved October 9, 2006, from *www.law.cornell.edu/rules/fre/rules.htm*).

The majority opinion in *Daubert* held that Rule 702 did indeed supercede *Frye*. However, testimony admitted in accordance with this holding was required to possess the requisite scientific validity to establish evidentiary reliability. Additionally, the testimony was required to be sufficiently tied to the facts in the case so as to offer assistance to the trier of fact. Although *Daubert* is in effect in Federal and many state courts, some states still follow *Frye*. For more comprehensive discussion of these issues, see Kaufmann, Chapter 3, this volume.

Training and Education

In 1995, Donald Bersoff, JD, PhD, chaired the National Invitational Conference on Education and Training in Law and Psychology at Villanova Law School. The conference produced recommendations for three different levels of training in legal and forensic psychology. Packer and Borum (2003) summarized the competencies associated with each level. The goal of the first level of graduate training in forensic psychology, referred to as the entry level, is to produce a legally informed, entry-level clinician. The second level of training is referred to as the proficiency level.

> The goal of this level of training is to establish forensic competence in one or more circumscribed areas related to some other major clinical specialty with which the psychologist has primary identification and expertise (e.g., a general child psychologist who performs custody evaluations as a secondary part of practice or a psychologist with expertise in trauma who performs personal injury evaluations). (p. 25)

The third level of training, the specialty level,

> is oriented toward the training of psychologists whose professional activities focus primarily on the provision of services to courts, attorneys, law enforcement, or corrections, and whose main specialty identification is in forensic psychology. Training at the specialty level can be distinguished from the proficiency level by a requirement that the forensic psychologist possesses depth and breadth of forensic psychological knowledge. (p. 26)

For the aspiring forensic psychologist, however, graduate programs that specialize in forensic psychology are somewhat limited. According to the American Psychology–Law Society website, graduate training opportunities in forensic psychology include eight doctoral programs in clinical psychology and law, six programs in nonclinical psychology and law, and eight master's programs. Intensive clinical training in the form of internships and postdoctoral fellowships is limited similarly. (Information retrieved October 9, 2006, from *www.unl.edu/ap-ls/student/graduate_programs.html*.)

As such, continuing education offers those interested in expanding their scope of practice opportunities and avenues a chance to develop new competencies. In addition to identifying the goals of graduate training in forensic psychology, the Villanova Conference suggested goals stipulating that continuing education in forensic psychology should contribute to improved standards to guide forensic practice and ethical decision making; provide mechanisms for updating best practices in forensic psychology; identify specific pathways for developing forensic skills; create forums for interdisciplinary interchange; and specify research initiatives and dissemination of knowledge gained from research (Bersoff, 1975).

Specific recommendations were drafted to direct attainment of these goals. Many of the recommendations were incorporated into the formation of the American Board of Forensic Psychology, which was created to credential and to certify specialists in the area of forensic psychology. The American Board of Forensic Psychology became affiliated with the American Board of Professional Psychology in 1985.

The SGFP standard of competence for the practice of forensic neuropsychology has evolved from a rather vague suggestion that forensic psychologists possess a "fundamental and reasonable level of knowledge and understanding of the legal and professional standards" (Committee on Ethical Guidelines for Forensic Psychologists, 1991) to a well-defined set of guidelines that define not only the scope of competence and appropriate knowledge base but also how forensic neuropsychologists should establish and represent their level of competence, protect against personal biases, consider individual differences, ensure the use of only competent subordinates, and protect against the misuse of their work products. Continued work of the original SGFP authors, the American Psychological Association's (2002) updated standards for all psychologists (EPPCC), and case law contributed to the development of the current standard. Golding (1999) suggested that competence in the field required an understanding of one's fiduciary role, which, more than a basic understanding of the clients' rights, includes rules, statutes, and case law related to the question being considered by the court. The EPPCC (American Psychological Association, 2002) helped define the limits of a psychologist's competence, stressed the importance of considering individual differences, suggested a means for expanding one's competence, and provided suggested courses of action when one deems oneself incompetent to provide service. Case law regarding the admissibility of expert scientific evidence and subsequent adoption of the Federal Rules of Evidence (FRE 702) contributed to the development of current standards by defining the differences between expert witnesses and fact witnesses, and the acceptable level of scientific precision on which witnesses should base their opinions. Issues and standards regarding competency to practice forensic neuropsychology are likely to remain in the forefront of the field because training opportunities are limited, but the demand for the work products of these practitioners is expanding.

Release of Test Data

American Psychological Association (2002) EPPCC

Fisher (2003a) wrote the following about Standard 9.04: "This standard reflects perhaps the most significant shift in ethical requirements from the 1992 Ethics Code to the current version. The 1992 code included reference to the release of 'raw test data' within a standard broadly prohibiting the misuse of assessment techniques, results or interpretations by psychologists or others not qualified to use such information" (p. 192). Unfortunately, the broad prohibition failed to address adequately how the individual psychologist should respond to requests for raw data. The current standard attempts to provide guidance by operationalizing "test data" and indicating conditions for its release. It is useful to consider Standard 9.04 in conjunction with Standard 9.11, Maintaining Test Security. This standard indicates that manuals, instruments, protocols, and test questions or stimuli are not test data as defined in Standard 9.04. However, it is interesting to note that test materials, as defined in Standard 9.11, are capable of an evolution of sorts. Protocols, for instance, become test data if the psychologist records an examinee's responses therein (Bush & Lees-Haley, 2006).

The distinction between test data and test materials (e.g., manuals, instruments, and protocols) is useful in understanding how to handle requests for test information under the Health Insurance Portability and Accountability Act (HIPAA). Bush and Lees-Haley (2006) noted that "purchasers of neuropsychological tests often must adhere to copyright laws that prohibit reproduction of test materials." As such, an ethical dilemma ensues when a legitimate request for information included in the "designated record set" contains information that would, upon release, constitute a breach of test security. Although Fisher (2003a) indicates that separation of test data, as defined by Standard 9.04, from test manuals or protocols in a separate "binding unit" made possible by the recording of examinee responses on a separate record form may represent one way to resolve this issue, she simultaneously cautions psychologists in this situation to seek counsel in addressing this scenario.

Test security is viewed by the National Academy of Neuropsychology (2003) as both legal necessity and ethical obligation. Its position statement on test security concludes:

> In summary, the National Academy of Neuropsychology fully endorses the need to maintain test security, views the duty to do so as a basic professional and ethical obligation, strongly discourages the release of materials when requests do not contain appropriate safeguards, and, when indicated, urges the neuropsychologist to take appropriate and reasonable steps to arrange conditions for release that ensure adequate safeguards. (p. 3)

Standard 9.04 also stipulates broadly the conditions under which test data are *not* to be released. Specifically, the standard prohibits the release of test data if doing so would result in substantial harm to a client or patient, or to prevent misuse or misrepresentation of data. Fisher (2003b) defined substantial harm as "reasonably likely to endanger the life or physical safety of the individual or another person or cause equally substantial harm" (p. 12).

In criminal forensic neuropsychological evaluations, release of data is often subject to rules of evidence. Specifically, if the attorney decides to utilize neuropsychological evidence, data often must be released as part of disclosure.

With the exception of death penalty cases, the determination as to whether release of test data will result in substantial harm is an easier decision than whether it is likely to result in misuse or misinterpretation.

Committee on Ethical Guidelines for Forensic Psychologists (1991) SGFP

The SGFP (Committee on Ethical Guidelines for Forensic Psychologists, 1991) provides some direction regarding steps the forensic psychologist is to take when disclosure of test data is required. First, test data are not to be released to persons without a legitimate and professional interest in the data. Second, the forensic psychologist is urged to take "reasonable steps that the receiving party is informed that raw scores must be interpreted by a qualified professional in order to provide reliable and meaningful information" [VII-A (2)]. For instance, based on SGFP (Committee on Ethical Guidelines for Forensic Psychologists, 1991), criminal forensic neuropsychologists must take reasonable steps to guard against misinterpretation and misuse of test data. Rapp and Ferber (2003) indicated that the potential for misuse of neuropsychological data, without competent interpretation, is quite high. "The client's test answers, without the psychologist's analysis, are meaningless to, and likely to be misinterpreted by, anyone other than a specifically trained psychologist or neuropsychologist" (p. 353).

Table 2.3 includes guidelines from the revised SGFP. In addition to requiring the forensic neuropsychologist to take reasonable steps to prevent the misinterpretation and misuse of test data, the latest SGFP version specifies the reasons an individual psychologist may object to a request for data (e.g., contractual obligations; federal or state privacy, confidentiality, or privilege regulations; or notice by another counsel of intent to quash or otherwise petition the court to amend or void the subpoena or order for the records). Furthermore, the revised draft advocates consultation if lack of clarification exists as to the proper course of action.

Release of and access to information are critical issues for the practicing forensic neuropsychologist to consider, because the risk for misuse and misinterpretation is high, and requests for the release of information are possible given the nature of the proceedings. Fersch (1980) stated that the adversarial nature of the proceedings amplifies the potential for misuse or misinterpretation of the forensic psychological work. Haas (1993) made even stronger statements regarding this issue, stating that courtroom proceedings can make prevention of misuse or misinterpretation of test data difficult, if not impossible. "In the courtroom, the ethics of the jurisprudence

TABLE 2.3. Section 10 of the Specialty Guidelines for Forensic Psychologists

10.02 Release of Information

Forensic practitioners comply with properly noticed and served subpoenas or court orders directing release of records, or other legally proper consent from duly authorized persons, unless there is a compelling reason not to do so. Reasons to offer an objection to complying include, but are not limited to, contractual obligations, or federal or state privacy, confidentiality, or privilege regulations, or notice by another counsel of counsel's intent to quash or otherwise petition the court to amend or void the subpoena or order for the records. Absent compelling reason otherwise, forensic practitioners make available all records specified in the consent, subpoena, or order. Their decision-making regarding access to and release of information in the record is informed by the relevant jurisdiction(s) of the matter. When in doubt about an appropriate response or course of action, forensic practitioners seek assistance from the attorney, agency or court that has retained them, retain and seek legal advice from their own attorney, or formally notify the drafter of the subpoena of their uncertainty.

10.03 Access to Information

If requested, forensic practitioners provide their clients access to, and a meaningful explanation of, all information that is in their records for the matter at hand, consistent with existing federal and state statutes, applicable codes of ethics and professional standards, and institutional rules and regulations. Unless the party is the client, the party typically is not provided access to the forensic practitioner's records without the consent of the client. Non-client access to records is governed by legal process, usually subpoena or court order, or by explicit consent of the client. Forensic practitioners may charge a reasonable fee for the costs associated with the storage, reproduction, review, and provision of records.

Note. From Committee on Ethical Guidelines for Forensic Psychologists (2006).

---

system demand an adversarial proceeding, in which the opposing attorneys will attempt to present only aspects of the testimony that support their respective sides and where control over the testimony heavily resides with the attorneys and the questions they pose" (p. 255). These adversarial proceedings present additional ethical considerations related to disclosure for the forensic psychologist. Although competent criminal forensic neuropsychological practice requires that the psychologist disclose limits to his or her knowledge bases, the law itself does not require full disclosure. According to FRE 702 (1975), the presentation of limits to knowledge or knowledge bases is largely dependent upon the ability of opposing counsel to elicit such information. "The expert may testify in terms of opinions or inference and give his or her reasons without prior disclosure of underlying facts or data, unless the court requires otherwise. The expert will, in any event, likely be required to disclose the underlying facts or data on cross-examination" (p. 84).

Therefore, the practicing forensic neuropsychologist should be prepared to respond to requests for disclosure.

Multiple Relationships

Blau (1984) wrote that the forensic psychologist might function as treating doctor, expert witness, or trial consultant. The treating doctor's ultimate goal is to improve the mental or physical health of the patient. When called as a witness, the treating doctor does not enjoy the latitude afforded the expert witness and merely reports the facts associated with a particular patient's course of treatment. The expert witness seeks truth and employs scientifically validated principles to inform the evaluative process. The trial consultant evaluates the conclusions of opposing experts in an attempt to impeach their credibility. In less adversarial contexts, trial consultants may inform processes such as jury selection.

Blau's conceptualization, however, may understate the degree of latitude a treating doctor is afforded. For example, competent treating doctors typically utilize expert knowledge about the diagnosis, treatment, and expected prognosis of a particular disorder as part of treatment. In most jurisdictions, the treating doctor would certainly be qualified to provide expert testimony related to the knowledge required as part of competent treatment.

American Psychological Association (2002) EPPCC

The Ethics Code clearly discourages mixing such roles. Multiple relationships are defined by the Ethics Code as occurring

> when a psychologist is in a professional role with a person and (1) at the same time is in another role with the same person, (2) at the same time is in a relationship with a person closely associated with or related to the person with whom the psychologist has the professional relationship, or (3) promises to enter into another relationship in the future with the person or a person closely associated with or related to the person.

Perhaps the most widely cited example of a multiple relationship in a forensic context is when a psychologist engaged in the treatment of a patient is asked to evaluate that patient and offer an opinion during a legal proceeding. The Committee on Psychiatry and Law of the Group for the Advancement of Psychiatry (GAP) cautioned mental health practitioners as follows: "While in some areas of the country with limited number of mental health providers, the therapist may have the role of forensic expert thrust upon him, ordinarily, it is wise to avoid mixing the therapeutic and forensic roles."

Committee on Ethical Guidelines for Forensic Psychologists (1991) SGFP

The SGFP (Committee on Ethical Guidelines for Forensic Psychologists, 1991) advised forensic psychologists to avoid "providing professional services to parties in a legal proceeding with whom they have personal or professional relationships that are inconsistent with the anticipated relationship," and further suggested that "when it is necessary to provide both evaluation and treatment services to a party in a legal proceeding (as may be the case in small forensic hospital settings or small communities), the forensic psychologist takes reasonable steps to minimize the potential negative effects of these circumstances on the rights of the party, confidentiality, and the process of treatment and evaluation."

The latest draft of SGFP (Committee on Ethical Guidelines for Forensic Psychologists, 2006) is similar in tone to its predecessor. However, it provides greater clarification about the situations that may give rise to multiple relationships (see Table 2.4).

Avoidance of multiple relationships is made more difficult in the forensic context because the person being evaluated is often not the client. It is more likely that the forensic psychologist has been retained by the examinee's attorney to conduct the evaluation. Accurate identification of the client in forensic work has significant ramifications in the areas of confidentiality. Greenburg and Shuman (1997) note that "the legal protection against compelled disclosure of the therapist–patient relationship is governed by the therapist–patient

TABLE 2.4. Section 6 of the Specialty Guidelines for Forensic Psychologists

6.03 Multiple Relationships

A multiple relationship occurs when a forensic practitioner is in a professional role with a person and at the same time or at a subsequent time is in a conflicting role with the same person; is involved in a personal, fiscal, or other relationship with an adverse party; at the same time is in a relationship with a person closely associated with or related to the person with whom the forensic practitioner has the professional relationship; or offers or agrees to enter into another relationship in the future with the person or a person closely associated with or related to the person. Forensic practitioners are vigilant in recognizing the potential conflicts of interest and threats to objectivity inherent in multiple relationships with attorneys, judges, parties, examinees, patients, and other participants to a legal proceeding. Forensic practitioners recognize that some personal and professional relationships may interfere with their ability to practice in a competent and objective manner and they seek to minimize any detrimental effects by avoiding involvement in such matters whenever feasible or limiting their assistance in a manner that is consistent with professional obligations.

Note. From Committee on Ethical Guidelines for Forensic Psychologists (2006).

privilege and can only be waived by the patient or by court order.... Legal protection of the forensic evaluator–litigant relationship is governed by the attorney–client and attorney–work product privileges" (p. 52).

Conclusions and Recommendations

Despite the development and existence of resources available to inform ethical decision making, unethical behavior persists (Bersoff, 2003). Some have speculated that most current ethical guidelines fail to clarify the process for synthesizing information and arriving at an ethical decision (Tymchuk, 1986). Others have speculated that ethical guidelines are not optimally effective, because they mistakenly view ethical decision making as a single, unitary process. For instance, in speaking about moral decision making, Rest (1983) suggested that skill in interpreting a situation as a moral one does not mean that a person is necessarily adept at implementing a moral action. Still others have suggested that ethical decision making is a multistep process. Kitchener (1984) developed a model that "distinguishes between the intuitive and the critical evaluative level of ethical justification. The intuitive level includes a person's immediate feeling responses to situations as well as their ethical beliefs about what they should and should not do based on their current developmental perspective and prior learning" (p. 32). A person evaluates his or her own reactions according to existing ethical guidelines. In the event these guidelines fail to define a course of action, the person moves to the critical–evaluative level. At this point, ethical principles provide a foundation for making more difficult ethical decisions. More recently, Bush, Connell, and Denney (2006) have developed a model that more directly addresses the nuances of ethical decision making within forensic neuropsychology. Interested readers are directed to their comprehensive discussion of this topic for more information.

In this chapter we have reviewed some of the sources that can be used to inform ethical decision making for the criminal forensic neuropsychologist. Specifically, we used a hierarchical organization of the EPPCC (American Psychological Association, 2002), the SGFP (Committee on Ethical Guidelines for Forensic Psychologists, 1991, 2006), and relevant case law to highlight important considerations in reaching ethical decisions, especially in the areas of informed consent, notification of purpose, competency, release of test data, and multiple relationships. It should be apparent, particularly given the utilization of an official draft version of the SGFP (Committee on Ethical Guidelines for Forensic Psychologists, 2006) in creating this chapter, that the development of resources to guide ethical decision making is an ongoing process. The evolution of such resources is perhaps most apparent when one examines the influence of case law within the field of forensic psychology and, therefore, in criminal forensic neuropsychology as well. However, it is important to note that the utilization of relevant resources does not represent an endpoint in the ethical decision-making process, and that ethical decision making may be most effective when appropriate resources are implemented within the context of an appropriate model, developed with an awareness of abundant contextual factors that can exert a powerful, and sometimes negative influence, in the form of bias, upon the ethical decision-making process.

Acknowledgments

We wish to thank Allison Day, a graduate student in psychology at Idaho State University, for her assistance in developing this chapter. Her assistance in obtaining the necessary articles, chapters, and books was indispensable.

References

American Psychological Association. (2002). Ethical principles of psychologists and code of conduct. *American Psychologist, 57*(12), 1060–1073.

Bersoff, D. N. (1975). Professional ethics and legal responsibility: On the horns of a dilemma. *Journal of School Psychology, 13*, 359–376.

Bersoff, D. N. (2003). *Ethical conflicts in psychology* (3rd ed.). Washington, DC: American Psychological Association.

Blau, T. (1984). *The psychologist as expert witness*. New York: Wiley.

Borum, R., & Grisso, T. (1995). Psychological test use in criminal forensic evaluations. *Professional Psychology: Research and Practice, 26*, 465–473.

Bush, S. S., Connell, M. A., & Denney, R. L. (2006). *Ethical practice in forensic psychology*. Washington, DC: American Psychological Association.

Bush, S. S., & Lees-Haley, P. R. (2006). Threats to the validity of forensic neuropsychological data: Ethical considerations. *Journal of Forensic Neuropsychology, 4*(3), 45–66.

Committee on Ethical Guidelines for Forensic Psychologists. (1991). Specialty guidelines for forensic psychologists. *Law and Human Behavior, 15*(6), 655–665.

Committee on Ethical Guidelines for Forensic Psychologists. (2006, January 11). Specialty guidelines for forensic psychologists [2nd official draft]. Retrieved from http://www.ap-ls.org/links/SGFP%20January%202006.pdf

Faust, D. (1991). Forensic neuropsychology: The art of practicing a science that does not yet exist. *Neuropsychology Review, 2*(3), 205–231.

Fersch, E. A. (1980). *Psychology and psychiatry in courts and corrections: Controversy and change*. New York: Wiley.

Fisher, C. B. (2003a). *Decoding the ethics code: A practical guide for psychologists*. Thousand Oaks, CA: Sage.

Fisher, C. B. (2003b, January/February). Test data standard most notable change in new APA ethics code. *National Psychologist*, pp. 12–13.

Golding, S. L. (1999, October). *Problems in conceptualizing and implementing reforms in expert witness testimony.* Paper presented at the meeting of the American Psychological Association and the Criminal Justice Section of the American Bar Association, Washington, DC.

Goldstein, A. (2005). *Ethical issues in forensic psychology.* Paper presented at the American Academy of Forensic Psychology Training, Vancouver, BC.

Greenberg, S. A., & Shuman, D. W. (1997). Irreconcilable conflict between therapeutic and forensic roles. *Professional Psychology: Research and Practice, 28,* 50–57.

Grisso, T. (1986). *Evaluating competencies.* New York: Plenum Press.

Grisso, T. (2003). *Evaluating competencies: Forensic assessments and instruments* (2nd ed.). New York: Plenum Press.

Haas, L. J. (1993). Competence and quality in the performance of forensic psychologists. *Ethics and Behavior, 3*(3&4), 231–249.

Horn, J. (2003). Forensic neuropsychology: Are we there yet? *Archives of Clinical Neuropsychology, 8*(8), 826–845.

Kitchener, K. (1984). Intuition, critical evaluation and ethical principles: The foundation for ethical decision making in counseling psychology. *Counseling Psychologist, 12*(3), 43–55.

Mittenberg, W., Patton, C., Canyock, E. M., & Condit, D. C. (2002). Base rates of malingering and symptom exaggeration. *Journal of Clinical and Experimental Neuropsychology, 24,* 1094–1102.

National Academy of Neuropsychology. (2003). *Test security: An update: Official statement of the National Academy of Neuropsychology, approved by the Board of Directors 10/13/2003.* Denver, CO: Author.

Packer, I. K., & Borum, R. (2003). Forensic training and practice. In I. B. Weiner (Series Ed.) & A. M. Goldstein (Vol. Ed.), *Handbook of psychology: Vol. 11. Forensic psychology* (pp. 21–32). Hoboken, NJ: Wiley.

Rapp, D. L., & Ferber, P. S. (2003). To release, or not to release raw test data, that is the question. In A. M. Horton & L. C. Hartlage (Eds.), *Handbook of forensic neuropsychology* (pp. 337–368). New York: Springer.

Rest, J. R. (1983). Morality. In P. Mussen (General Ed.) and J. Flavell & E. Markman (Vol. Eds.), *Manual of child psychology: Vol. 4. Cognitive development.* New York: Wiley.

Sullivan, J. P., & Denney, R. L. (2003). Constitutional and judicial foundations in criminal forensic neuropsychology. *Journal of Forensic Neuropsychology, 3,* 13–44.

Sweet, J. J., Grote, C., & van Gorp, W. G. (2002). Ethical issues in forensic neuropsychology. In S. Bush & M. Drexler (Eds.), *Ethical issues in clinical neuropsychology* (pp. 103–133). Lisse, The Netherlands: Swets & Zeitlinger.

Tymchuk, A. J. (1986). Guidelines for ethical decision making. *Canadian Psychology, 27,* 36–43.

Weissman, H. N., & DeBow, D. M. (2003). Ethical principles and professional competencies. In A. M. Goldstein (Ed.), *Forensic psychology* (pp. 33–53). New York: Wiley.

Chapter 3

Admissibility of Neuropsychological Evidence in Criminal Cases
COMPETENCY, INSANITY, CULPABILITY, AND MITIGATION

PAUL M. KAUFMANN

Courts use neuropsychological evidence with ever-increasing frequency (Heilbronner, 2004; Sweet, King, Malina, Bergman, & Simmons, 2002). Lawyers are seeking neuropsychological consultation on an expanding set of legal issues, in part, because clinical neuropsychologists apply a scientific approach that meets judicial standards for expert testimony (Larrabee, 2005). A recent LEXIS search using the root "neuropsycholo-" revealed 3,294 cases during the past 70 years, 74% of which were adjudicated in the last decade (Kaufmann, 2007). Of those 3,294 cases, approximately 1,775 were in criminal court, with 77% adjudicated in the last decade. Although neuropsychology has long provided the best methods for evaluating brain–behavior relations when diagnosing higher cortical dysfunction, neuropsychological evaluations are also used increasingly to detect malingered neuropsychological deficits (Larrabee, 2007) or feigned cognitive impairments (Boone, 2007). With rapidly increasing use of neuropsychology in our courts, practitioners of law and psychology would benefit from understanding the nature of neuropsychological evidence and the standards for its admissibility.

Although the scope of neuropsychological consulting has expanded into a variety of civil and administrative proceedings (Greiffenstein & Cohen, 2005), this chapter focuses on admissibility of neuropsychological evidence in criminal cases. Grisso (1988) delineated the general questions underlying specific competencies required for participation in criminal proceedings. The constitutional and judicial foundation for criminal forensic neuropsychology (Sullivan & Denney, 2003) requires a unique understanding of procedural and evidentiary standards that extends well beyond routine clinical practice. Denney (2005a) described a set of issues arising in criminal litigation that are increasingly addressed to clinical neuropsychologists, including competence, insanity, culpability, and mitigation.

This chapter begins with two capital murder case vignettes that involved psychometric tests, illustrating how neuropsychological evidence plays a key role in adjudicating cases that affect the life and liberty of accused defendants. Then, the history of psychologist expertise in our courtrooms is traced from its early emergence in *People v. Hawthorne* (1940) to its current status in U.S. Supreme Court jurisprudence as an accepted source of expert testimony required to assist the trier of fact. Next, this chapter outlines the current legal standards for admissibility of neuropsychological evidence by describing key historical developments and legal precedence, reviewing procedural and evidentiary rules, then applying those rules to a recently resolved federal criminal case. The next section examines research evaluating the impact of *Daubert v. Merrell Dow Pharmaceuticals* (1993) and its progeny on admissibility of expert testimony, with emphasis on neuropsychological evidence. *Daubert* factors are reviewed and a legal analysis of hearing testimony illustrates the manner in which neuropsychological opinions appropriately may be excluded from evidence. Finally, this chapter concludes with a warning that legislative and judicial processes are underway that might undermine the reliability of neuropsychological evaluations and forensic consulting, unless neuropsychologists advocate for reasonable protections and take active steps to intervene legally.

Case Vignettes

On July 20, 1986, Wayne Lee Bates escaped from custody for first-degree burglary, broke into a residence, and stole, among other things, a .410 shotgun (*Bates v. State*, 1997). On July 23, Mr. Bates approached Julia Guida brandishing the newly sawed-off shotgun. After a struggle, Mr. Bates forced the victim into a wooded area, tied her to a tree, and shot her in the back of the head, killing her instantly. The State of Tennessee tried, convicted, and sentenced Mr. Bates to death by electrocution.

During a postconviction hearing, a board-certified clinical neuropsychologist, Pamela M. Auble, PhD, ABPP-CN, testified that records showed that Mr. Bates had possible impairments, including a variety of head injuries and a chaotic home life. A neuropsychological evaluation revealed brain dysfunction in several areas, and Dr. Auble further opined that Mr. Bates had diminished capacity at the time of the murder, caused by his premature birth or his mother's alcohol consumption during pregnancy. Moreover, Dr. Auble testified that neuropsychological testing should have been performed before trial. Mr. Bates sought postconviction relief, claiming ineffective assistance of counsel for (1) failing to obtain and introduce evidence from his medical and psychiatric records, and (2) failing to initiate neuropsychological testing for possible brain damage.

Opposing experts offered opinions as to the possibility of neurological damage. The defendant's expert opined that Mr. Bates "lacked ability to conform his actions" and that his emotional control "ranged from limited to nonexistent" (p. 634). The State's neuropsychologist expert found no indication of an "extreme mental or emotional disturbance" (p. 634) when Bates killed Guida. The Tennessee appellate court upheld the conviction and the trial court finding that the State's expert testimony was "the most credible, reasonable, and realistic" (p. 634).

Although Mr. Bates's guilt is beyond doubt, opposing counsels argued aggravating and mitigating circumstances raised by the neuropsychological evaluation during a protracted set of postconviction evidentiary hearings (*Bates v. Bell*, 2005). In March, 2005, federal *habeus corpus* review affirmed the murder conviction of Mr. Bates, but identified flagrant prosecutorial misconduct so profound that the federal court ordered a new sentencing hearing. To date, the State of Tennessee has not resolved the question of Mr. Bates's death sentence.

More recently, the U.S. Supreme Court heard arguments in another Tennessee death penalty case that turned, in part, on the admissibility of a psychological evaluation (*Bell v. Thompson*, 2005). In a 5 to 4 decision, the High Court held that the court of appeals abused its discretion when it supplemented the appellate record by including a psychological evaluation that it deemed "critical." Writing for the dissent, Justice Breyer took the unprecedented step of including extended excerpts of the psychological evaluation of Gregory Thompson and the deposition of the psychologist, Faye E. Sultan, PhD, who performed the evaluation (pp. 2846–2854). Dr. Sultan testified that she partially relied on the intellectual and neuropsychological evaluation of Barry M. Crown, PhD, ABPN, in formulating her opinions. The district court was required to review the psychological evaluation, but determined that it did not show that Mr. Thompson was incompetent for execution (*Thompson v. Bell*, 2006). Mr. Thompson's death sentence is pending appeal.

Courts commonly recognize psychologist experts, but reliance on the board-certified neuropsychologist expert is a relatively recent development.

In the next section I review the history of forensic psychology consultation in criminal courts, with specific emphasis on the emergence of neuropsychology experts who address neurological factors at issue in litigation.

History

> Experience has shown that opposite opinions of persons professing to be experts may be obtained to any amount; and it often occurs that not only many days, but even weeks, are consumed in cross-examinations, to test the skill or knowledge of such witnesses and the correctness of their opinions, wasting the time and wearying the patience of both court and jury, and perplexing, instead of elucidating, the questions involved in the issue. (*Winnans v. N.Y. & Erie R.R. Co.*, 1859, p. 101)

Courts have been wary of experts and skeptical of expert testimony for some time. Following the U.S. Supreme Court lead in *Winnans*, other courts have expressed similar hesitations; see *Rush v. Megee* (1871, p. 73; "We are not enamored with expert testimony, however procured or presented") and *Whitaker v. Parker* (1876, p. 587; "Evidence of experts is of the lowest order and of the most unsatisfactory character"). Although no cases used expert clinical psychologists in the 19th century, courts would likely have exercised caution with anyone claiming psychological expertise. Although the science of psychology was emerging, the practice of psychology was well underway, with practitioners operating under a variety of labels such as phrenologist, physiognomist, graphologist, mesmerist, spiritualist, seer, psychic, medium, mental healer, and psychologist (Benjamin, 2005).

However, scientific advances softened disbelieving courts into admitting appropriate expert evidence, with *Nelson v. Nelson* (1958) responding to *Whitaker*, writing that the "science of comparing . . . is much further advanced today than it was 80 years ago" (p. 770). As the scientific method became more widely understood and accepted, the methodologies of behavioral and social sciences were applied increasingly to the study of psychology. In the wake of World War II, the U.S. federal government funded an increase in the number of mental health practitioners, providing some support for the Boulder Conference in 1949. The Boulder Conference created the scientist–practitioner model of training in clinical psychology that remains at the core of the profession (Baker & Benjamin, 2000). The scientist–practitioner model bolsters the credibility of expert psychologists in our courts.

In what is often identified as the first case recognizing the expertise of clinical psychologists, *Jenkins v. United States* (1962) addressed the admissibility of expert testimony by a psychologist as to the existence of mental defect or organic brain injury. Three psychologists testified that Mr. Jenkins had a mental disease at the time of the crime. The trial court instructed the jury to disregard the testimony of the psychologists, because "a psychologist is not competent to give a medical opinion as to a mental disease or defect" (p. 643). On appeal, the reviewing court cited the greater weight of legal authority, finding that "some psychologists are qualified to render expert testimony" (p. 644) regarding mental disorders, referring to concurring dicta[1] in an earlier case (*People v. Hawthorne*, 1940).

Jenkins outlined a two-part test to evaluate expert testimony. First, the subject must be related to some science, profession, business, or occupation "as to be beyond the ken of the average layman" (p. 643). Second, the witness must have "such skill, knowledge, or experience in that field" (p. 643) to assist the court in its search for truth. The expert opinion must aid the trier of fact in its search for truth. The jury instruction to disregard the psychologists was an error and the court reversed the conviction, ordering a new trial. *Jenkins* commonly is cited for its central holding that "psychologists may qualify as experts on the question of mental disease or defect under the standards set forth" (p. 647). Other courts have relied on the *Jenkins* precedent to recognize the expert opinions of clinical psychologists.

In *United States v. Riggleman* (1969), the sole question for determination was whether the trial court erred in permitting a clinical psychologist to state an opinion on insanity and criminal culpability. Citing *Jenkins*, the *Riggleman* court rejected the rule that only a psychiatrist may testify as to responsibility for criminal acts. The better rule is that "a psychologist's competence to render an expert opinion based on his findings as to the presence or absence of mental disease or defect must depend upon the nature and extent of his knowledge; it does not depend upon his claim to the title of psychologist or psychiatrist" (p. 1191).

In an early case recognizing neuropsychological expertise in a civil proceeding, *Simmons v. Mullins* (1975) found that a psychologist was competent to testify "as an expert on organic brain injury" (p. 897). The following testimony directly confronts the issue of whether opinions regarding brain damage are exclusively the domain of medical professionals.

> Q: Doctor, when you formed an opinion that this girl did have, in addition to some of the emotional problems which you indicated, that she did have minimal brain damage.
>
> A: Yes.
>
> Q: Can you state with reasonable medical certainty whether you have an opinion as to the cause of this minimal brain damage which you found; and if so, what that cause would be?
>
> A: Yes. I am just stumbling over your term "medical." We have to keep in mind that I am not a medical person.

> Q: I think my question was with reasonable professional certainty.
>
> A: Okay. Yes, I feel that this youngster's minimal brain damage results from the trauma she received in the accident. (p. 897)

Citing *Jenkins* and *Riggleman*, the *Simmons* court noted, "It is not essential that an expert witness be a medical practitioner to testify on organic problems" (p. 898). Moreover, a neurosurgeon provided the court some evidence for such conclusions, as follows:

> Q: Doctor, I wonder if you would explain for the Court and Jury the relationship of a clinical psychologist to a neurosurgeon such as yourself. What does a clinical psychologist do for yourself [sic]?
>
> A: Well, primarily in our business, if we have a patient who has complaints, particularly with those complaints representing the possibility of emotional disfunction [sic], behavioral disturbance, things that we cannot measure on the basis of what we can see, things that we cannot measure on the basis of our detailed examinations—with that particular history, we then refer those patients for psychometric evaluation and request then of our psychologist who is doing the examination whether, by his battery of tests, he can or cannot tell us whether he believes there is evidence of disturbance as far as brain function is concerned, whether this would be on the basis of possible organic disturbance or on the basis of psychological disturbance.
>
> Q: And is the psychologist properly capable of determining by his course of tests and his examination, whether the problem is, the problem that your patient is having, is primarily emotional or primarily organic or having to do with the brain, itself, or a combination of both? Is that a fair statement?
>
> A: Yes. We feel very strongly that Dr. Romano can. He has worked with us many, many years and is one of the two psychologists that, in our practice over this period of time, we have come down to, and the only one that we use from the standpoint of this type of testing, because I think that this man is most excellent in his field and we rely heavily on what he reports to us. (p. 898)

Based in part on the reliance of the medical profession on psychologists to make these judgments, *Simmons* concluded that to adopt the appellant's view that psychologists are not competent witnesses to testify on physical matters "would be to ignore present medical and psychological practice" (p. 899).

Generally, psychologists who conduct assessments testify about tests, test results, and their interpretation of those results (*Buckler v. Sinclair Refining Co.*, 1966; *Ross v. State*, 1980; *Executive Car & Truck Leasing, Inc. v. DeSerio*, 1985; *Minner v. American Mortgage & Guaranty Co.*, 2000). Nevertheless, psychologists who offer opinions regarding the physical causes of injury based on their assessments are frequently challenged, with most courts conducting a fact-specific inquiry before recognizing expertise and admitting psychologist opinions. A majority hold that neuropsychologists are qualified to render opinions about the physical causes of brain injury (*Kinsey v. King*, 1982; *Madrid v. Univ. of Ca.*, 1987; *Valiulis v. Scheffeos*, 1989; *Fabianke v. Weaver ex rel. Weaver*, 1988; *Sanchez v. Derby*, 1989; *Hutchinson v. American Family Mut. Ins.*, 1994; *Cunningham v. Montgomery*, 1995; *Huntoon v. TCI Cablevision*, 1998; *Landers v. Chrysler Corp.*, 1998; *Adamson v. Chiovaro*, 1998; *Bonner v. ISP Technologies, Inc.*, 2001; *Rustenhaven v. American Airlines, Inc.*, 2003), though a minority restrict or bar neuropsychologists from rendering causation testimony (*Krevitz v. Savoy Heating and Air Conditioning Co.*, 1981; *G.I.W. Southern Value v. Smith*, 1985; *Lugo v. Citicorp Mortgage*, 1994; *Bergeson v. Ray*, 1998). A resurgent minority has found that neuropsychologists offering opinions about the physical causes of injury are operating outside the scope of psychology practice (*John v. Im*, 2002; *Grenitz v. Tomlian*, 2003; *McCarthy v. Atwood*, 2005).

Some courts have excluded physicians from rendering expert neuropsychological opinions (*Downs v. Perstorp Components, Inc.*, 1999); however, most follow the general rule that "any person whose profession or vocation deals with the subject at hand may testify as an expert" (*Hagen v. Swenson*, 1975, p. 162). Recently, a New York judge held that selected social workers were qualified to offer expert neuropsychological opinions, finding the practice of psychology and social work "wholly equal and the same" (*People v. R.R. & G.A.*, 2005, p. 544). Ultimately, most courts admit neuropsychologist expert testimony with the value of expert evidence addressed under cross-examination and weighed by the jury.

In criminal litigation involving questions of mental illness, psychologists are recognized as experts in matters of competence, insanity, criminal culpability, and mitigation, with few exceptions.[2] Although recent case law demonstrates the majority rule and continuing modern trend toward broader recognition of neuropsychologist expert opinions, a minority still apply the traditional rule that only physicians can offer expert testimony about the physical causes of injury. Courts remain cautious about brain–behavior science and are skeptical about its application to resolve cases and controversies (Keckler, 2006; Kulynych, 1997; Morse, 2006, Redding, 2006). Although most judges are ignorant of the science, they rightfully are concerned with balancing the probative value of neuropsychological evidence against its prejudicial effect, while being mindful of the risks associated with juror confusion (FED. R. EVID. 403, 2007). Criminal courts cannot resolve longstanding philosophical debates about free will and determinism; such matters are nonjusticiable issues. However, even though the jurisprudence of neuropsychological expertise in criminal litigation is neither as long nor as well developed, judges increasingly admit the brain–behavior science of neuropsychologist experts into their courts. Before considering the current and continuing application of neuropsychology in criminal litigation, it is important to understand a few basic legal concepts, and some rules of evidence and procedure in criminal proceedings.

Competence must be distinguished from the affirmative defense of insanity to understand admissibility standards for neuropsychological evidence in criminal litigation. In 1899, the 6th Circuit determined that the Fourteenth Amendment due process clause prohibited criminal proceedings against a mentally incompetent person (*Youtsey v. United States*, 1899). Although history provides different definitions of insanity that are reviewed elsewhere (Denney, 2005b), after John Hinckley, Jr., shot President Ronald Reagan, his Press Secretary James Brady, and two law enforcement personnel, Congress heightened and shifted the burden of proof to the defendant. The Insanity Defense Reform Act (IDRA; 2007) places the burden on the defendant to prove that he or she was unable to appreciate the "nature and quality or the wrongfulness" of his or her acts as a result of a "severe mental disease or defect" at the time of the crime (18 U.S.C. § 17). To meet this burden, the defendant must present clear and convincing evidence[3] [§ 17(b)]. In contrast, the test for competency is whether the party has "sufficient present ability to consult with his lawyer with a reasonable degree of rational understanding—and whether he has a rational as well as factual understanding of the proceedings against him" (*Dusky v. United States*, 1960, p. 402). Thus, while insanity is relevant only to the time of the crime, competency is relevant throughout the entire legal proceeding, including understanding of *Miranda* warnings, entry of a plea, waiver of counsel, nature of trial proceedings, and punishments. Consequently, the consulting expert must understand the rules governing and distinguishing competence and the insanity defense.

Rules Governing Competency and the Insanity Defense

Generally, prohibitions against subjecting an incompetent person to trial extend from arrest until imposition of the sentence (IDRA, 18 U.S.C. § 4244, 2007; *United States v. Johns*, 1984). Retrospective competency determinations, although disfavored, may be conducted provided that a meaningful hearing of the issue remains possible (p. 957). Moreover, the issue of a criminal defendant's mental capacity to proceed may be raised at any stage of the litigation (*Howard v. State*, 1985), whether by the defense, the government, or the court (*State v. Broom*, 1995).

Once competency is placed at issue, the defendant constitutionally is entitled to a hearing (*Pate v. Robinson*, 1966). Competency hearings do not determine whether the defendant is competent, but whether there are reasonable grounds for the court to believe that the defendant may be incompetent (*Calloway v. State*, 1995). However, the mere fact that a defendant is pleading not guilty by reason of insanity does not require the court to order a competency hearing (*State v. Lee*, 1983). The fact that competency has been put in doubt also does not require the court to order a mental examination (*State v. Clemons*, 1997).

A defendant planning to introduce expert testimony relating to a mental disease or defect, or to any other mental condition bearing on the issue of guilt, must file pretrial motions (FED. R. CRIM P. 12.2(b), 2007). However, the court may, in its discretion, allow a defendant to file notice of intent to rely on the insanity defense at a later time (FED. R. CRIM P. 12.2(a)). There is a split of authority[4] as to whether the Rule 12.2(b) notice is sufficient for the court to order a mental examination (*United States v. Banks*, 1991), or whether the defendant expressly must place competency at issue or file intent to rely on the insanity defense (*United States v. Marenghi*, 1995). These jurisdictional variations yield different defense strategies. For example, a defendant who claims that the presence of a mental condition negates an element of the crime may not necessarily be required to undergo a state mental examination. In some jurisdictions, the defendant may present expert testimony about his or her mental condition without being required to undergo an independent examination by the state, so long as that defendant has not placed competency or insanity in issue.

Recognizing that competency to proceed can be raised by either party or the court at any stage of the proceedings, competency may become an issue at the time of issuance of *Miranda* warnings, entry of a plea, standing trial, sentencing, and punishment.

Miranda Warnings

Waiver of the Fifth Amendment right to remain silent raises the first issue of competency, in that such waiver must be made "knowingly, voluntarily, and intelligently" (*Miranda v. Arizona*, 1966, p. 444). Moreover, waiver of the Sixth Amendment right to consult with an attorney must use the same standard, and the right to counsel can be invoked at any time during the proceeding. Indeed, the government has a high burden to show competent waiver, if it intends to use statements made by a suspect during custodial interrogation conducted in the absence of an attorney (p. 503). However, that governmental burden does not necessarily require an express written or oral statement of waiver (*North Carolina v. Butler*, 1979).

Entry of a Plea

Competency to enter a plea applies the aforementioned *Dusky* "sufficient present ability" standard. No higher standard of competency applies to entry of a plea than that required for standing trial (*Miles v. Stainer*, 1997). However, if evidence presents a substantial question of the defendant's sanity at the time of the offense, then the court must ensure that the defendant (1) is fully availed of alternative pleas, (2) comprehends the consequences of failing to assert an insanity defense, and (3) exercises a free choice (*Frendak v. United States*, 1979). Furthermore, even if counsel indicates that the defendant waives a viable insanity defense, the court must ascertain through independent inquiry that waiver is voluntary and intelligent before such waiver can be accepted (*People v. Gettings*, 1988). Defendants pleading not guilty by reason of insanity must be advised of the likelihood of involuntary commitment for mental illness, if the plea is successful (*Morrison v. United States*, 1990). The competency standard for pleading guilty or waiving the right to counsel is no higher than the competency standard for standing trial (*Godinez v. Moran*, 1993).

Stand Trial

The *Dusky* "sufficient present ability" test of competency involves the defendant's ability to communicate with his or her attorney and to understand the nature of the proceedings. Stated alternatively, it is fundamental to our system of criminal justice to prohibit subjecting to trial a person whose "mental condition is such that he lacks the capacity to understand the nature and object of the proceedings against him, to consult with counsel, and to assist in preparing his defense" (*United States v. Renfroe*, 1987, p. 766). The capacity to assist in preparing a defense includes understanding court procedures and roles (accused person, attorneys, judge, jury), and the ability to recall relevant events, produce evidence, testify, confront hostile witnesses, and project a sense of innocence (*Drope v. Missouri*, 1975, p. 172). Essentially, incompetent persons are not really present in the courtroom, even though they physically appear.

Punishment

Although the basic premise that insane individuals should not be punished while "insane" applies to all punishments [IDRA, 18 U.S.C. § 4245(e), 2007], it is rarely invoked except in cases of execution. In yet another inherently confusing choice of terminology, here the term *insane* actually refers to competency to face execution. The Eight Amendment prohibition against cruel and unusual punishment bars execution of insane individuals (*Ford v. Wainwright*, 1986), and it also is prohibited under state laws. However, the standard for legal insanity applied to execution is not the same as the diagnostic criteria for a mental illness (*Billiot v. State*, 1995). Although intelligence is a relevant factor that courts must weigh, mental impairment and brain damage (*Shaw v. Delo*, 1992) do not preclude execution necessarily, so long as the inmate possesses the mental awareness required for execution. In some jurisdictions, sufficient competence for execution only requires that the defendant understand execution proceedings, know that it is a punishment, and appreciate why he or she is being punished (*Rector v. Clark*, 1991).

Individuals with mental retardation can be found competent to stand trial, yet a death sentence is barred as cruel and unusual punishment under the Eighth Amendment (*Atkins v. Virginia*, 2002). The Court reasoned that individuals with mental retardation have diminished capacity that reduces their personal culpability. Similarly, the Court held that states cannot impose the death penalty on juveniles under the age of 18 years (*Roper v. Simmons*, 2005) due to the diminished culpability of psychological immaturity. Capital punishment is reserved for those offenders who commit the most serious crimes, and the death penalty is only for those whose extreme culpability makes them "the most deserving of execution" (*Atkins*, p. 319).

The Insanity Defense Reform Act

A small minority of jurisdictions abolished the insanity defense by statute (*State v. Beam*, 1985; *State v. Korell*, 1984). There is no fundamental Constitutional right to assert an insanity defense, even in capital murder cases (*State v. Card*, 1991). However, such statutes do not preclude all considerations of a defendant's mental state during criminal proceedings. Courts have acknowledged the "constantly shifting adjustment" of tension between the "evolving aims of the criminal law and changing religious, moral, philosophical, and medical views of the nature of man" (p. 1085). Uncertainty regarding the proper treatment of the criminally insane has resulted in wavering standards and inconsistent application by our courts.

After *Hinckley*, Congress passed the IDRA, defining the circumstances when an "otherwise culpable defendant is excused for his conduct because of mental disease or defect" (18 U.S.C. § 17, 2007), but it does not limit evidence offered to negate specific intent[5] (*United States v. Frisbee*, 1985, p. 1220). Under the IDRA, evidence of mental abnormality proving lack of *mens rea*[6] is admissible, although such evidence cannot be used to prove diminished responsibility or diminished capacity (*United States v. Pohlot*,

1987). Although "persistent confusion" remains in the application of terms such as *diminished responsibility* and *diminished capacity* in determining guilt, the IDRA attempted to delineate carefully the proper use of mental health evidence as it relates to legal excuse and criminal culpability (*United States v. Cameron*, 1990).

Cameron summarized how the IDRA altered the use of mental health evidence in federal criminal trials as follows: (1) eliminated the volitional "diminished capacity" element of the insanity defense (§ 17(a)), (2) eliminated all other affirmative defenses or excuses based on mental disease or defect (§ 17(a)), (3) required the defendant to show clear and convincing evidence of insanity (§ 17(b)), (4) limited the use of expert psychological testimony regarding ultimate issues (FED. R. EVID. 704(b)), and (5) linked a "not guilty by reason of insanity" verdict directly to federal civil commitment proceedings [IDRA, § 4242(b)]. Notwithstanding the statutory language or congressional intent behind IDRA, federal courts have struggled with statutory interpretation and application to criminal cases (*Cameron*, p. 1062).

Cameron suggested that federal court decisions are erratic on evidentiary questions involving mental illness, with no less than three approaches to diminished capacity. Some courts view *diminished responsibility* and *diminished capacity* as interchangeable terms meaning that mental health evidence will be admitted on the issue of specific intent. Other courts agree that the terms are interchangeable but contend that such designations do not narrow the use of psychiatric evidence solely to the question of specific intent. This second group applies both terms "to excuse, mitigate, or lessen the defendant's moral culpability" due to "psychiatric compulsion or inability or failure to engage in normal reflection" (p. 1062). Essentially, this approach views these diminishments as a partial legal excuse. Finally, other courts distinguish between diminished responsibility and diminished capacity. They claim that only diminished capacity aims at negating specific intent, whereas diminished responsibility refers to showing that "the accused suffered from an abnormality of mind that substantially impaired his mental responsibility" (p. 1062). Current jurisprudence on these matters remains unsettled.

Modern neuroscience and neuroimaging technology are adding to the confused jurisprudence of diminished capacity, in the form of the neuropsychological signs and symptoms collectively described as frontal lobe syndrome. Frontal lobe syndrome has given rise to the frontal lobe defense (FLD) in criminal cases (*State v. Rogers*, 2000), which some predict will play an increasing role in representation of defendants with a brain injury (Redding, 2006). A recent *New York Times* article proclaimed (Rosen, 2007), "Neuroscientific evidence will have a large impact not only on questions of guilt and punishment, but also on the detection of lies and hidden bias, and on the prediction of future criminal behavior." A subsequent LEXIS search[7] revealed that functional magnetic resonance imaging (fMRI) findings have yet to be used in a criminal trial, but some speculate the threat of presenting neuroimages has prompted more favorable plea agreements (Rosen, 2007). Although a number of investigators believe that neuroimaging used in conjunction with neuropsychological techniques may be applied increasingly to assist the trier of fact (Bigler, 2001), courts are cautious about admitting expert testimony based on functional neuroimages. For example, legal commentators have examined the hypothetical admissibility of fMRI lie detection science under *Daubert*, concluding that the gap between experimental and practical application currently exceeds what federal courts are likely to allow, and fMRI would fail (Alexander, 2006).

Even the most enthusiastic promoters currently urge caution when using neuroimaging evidence in criminal cases, because the scientific basis for such is very limited, as follows:

> [regarding] the role of FLD in violent behavior, a note of caution must be sounded. These studies, still relatively few in number, often include only a small number of subjects, lack control groups, or find "considerable overlap between the values of patient and control groups in studies of the size, shape, or metabolic activity of different brain regions." Moreover, to date, there are no standard criteria available for differentiating between normal and abnormal scan results or for quantifying the extent of brain damage. (Redding, 2006, p. 63)

Others are less diplomatic in their criticism[8] of neuroimaging evidence, suggesting that "brain overclaim syndrome"[9] often afflicts those enamored by fascinating new theories in the neurosciences (Morse, 2006). Morse (2006) concludes, "Brains do not commit crimes, people commit crimes" (p. 397), seemingly unconvinced that defendants' actions are generated by their brains. Morse refuses to yield personal accountability under the law in what he describes as a "fundamental psycholegal error" (p. 397). Although neuroscientists may view a person and his or her brain as one in the same, the law does not, because explaining causation does not excuse conduct.

Definition by exclusion is another way to grasp diminished capacity—by distinguishing it from competency and insanity. Unlike a finding of incompetency, diminished capacity does not delay criminal proceedings, nor is it an affirmative defense. However, mental condition may still be relevant in mitigating punishment, even when a defendant who is competent to stand trial fails to show clear and convincing evidence of insanity, or cannot prove that diminished capacity negated the *mens rea* component of the crime. Consequently, when the battle of neuropsychologist experts does not yield a favorable verdict for the defendant, testimony used by the defense to argue incompetence, insanity, or diminished capacity may be resurrected to reduce a sentence or avoid the death penalty.

In light of these complex, inconsistent, and confusing legal standards, how can neuropsychologists provide meaningful expert testimony to assist the trier of fact in resolving guilt or innocence? Knowing the differing legal standards for insanity and competence in the relevant jurisdiction is essential for neuropsychological consulting on criminal cases, but such understanding is moot if the clinical neuropsychologist fails to appreciate and fulfill the requirements for recognition as an expert and rendering expert testimony to the court. Therefore, in the next section I summarize the relevant case law and rules governing experts.

Qualification of Experts

Under Federal Rules, courts must evaluate expert qualifications, and the relevance and reliability of their testimony before it is admitted into evidence and heard by a jury. Therefore, neuropsychologists consulting on criminal cases should understand the evolution of court standards for evaluating experts as addressed in *Frye v. United States* (1923), *Daubert v. Merrell Dow Pharm., Inc.* (1993) and its progeny, and FED. R. EVID. 104 (Preliminary Questions), FED. R. EVID. 403 (Relevance), and FED. R. EVID. 702 (Testimony of Experts).

In *Frye v. United States* (1923), a defendant convicted of second degree murder appealed, claiming the trial court erred because it denied the admission of expert testimony on a "systolic blood pressure deception test" (p. 1013). Defense attempts to admit this expert and his opinions or to conduct the test in the courtroom were denied. The appellate court affirmed the trial judge, quoting the government's brief and thereby creating the following rule: " . . . when the question involved does not lie within the range of common experience or common knowledge, but requires special experience or special knowledge, then the opinions of witnesses skilled in that particular science, art, or trade to which the question relates are admissible in evidence" (p. 1014). In a two-page unanimous opinion, the appellate court concluded that the deception test had not gained "standing and scientific recognition among physiological and psychological authorities as would justify the courts in admitting expert testimony" (p. 1014). Stated alternatively, the test was denied admission in court because it was not *generally accepted* in the relevant scientific community.

In *Daubert v. Merrell Dow Pharm., Inc.* (1989), infants and their guardians sued a drug company to recover for limb reduction birth defects caused by the mother's ingestion of the antinausea "morning sickness" drug

Bendectin. Merrell Dow won on summary judgement,[10] with the trial judge citing *Frye*, the "prevailing school of thought" (p. 572) regarding Bendectin, and controlling legal authority that epidemiological studies are the most reliable evidence of causation in this field of study. The plaintiffs failed to present "statistically significant epidemiological proof that Bendectin causes limb reduction defects" because their expert relied, in part, on *in vitro* animal and chemical studies (p. 575). The plaintiffs appealed, arguing that the reanalysis of the epidemiological data and the scientific techniques employed by their experts were permissible. The unanimous three-judge 9th Circuit Appellate Court affirmed the trial court, again citing *Frye* and following the precedent set in sister courts, referencing " . . . a well-founded skepticism of the scientific value of the reanalysis methodology employed by plaintiffs' experts; they recognize that '[t]he best test of certainty we have is good science—the science of publication, replication, and verification, the science of consensus and peer review' " (Huber, 1991, p. 1131). The 9th Circuit suggested that *in vitro* studies were junk science, affirming the trial court decision to ignore this new scientific evidence because it failed *Frye's* general acceptance test. The plaintiffs appealed and the U.S. Supreme Court granted *certiorari*.[11]

In a landmark decision that forever changed the scope of expert testimony, the Supreme Court found that the general acceptance test in *Frye* had been superseded by FED. R. EVID. 702, thereby requiring all federal courts to admit any "scientific, technical, or other specialized knowledge" that assists the trier of fact to understand the evidence.[12] "General acceptance" is not a necessary precondition for the admissibility of scientific evidence under the Federal Rules of Evidence. A 7 to 2 majority also held that district court judges (gatekeepers) had the duty to evaluate the admissibility of expert testimony. However, the Honorable Chief Justice William Rehnquist parted company on the issue of the judge's role: "I do not doubt that Rule 702 confides to the judge some gatekeeping responsibility in deciding questions of the admissibility of proffered expert testimony. But I do not think it imposes on them either the obligation or the authority to become amateur scientists in order to perform that role" (pp. 600–601). In candor, Chief Justice Rehnquist acknowledged being "at a loss" to understand what is meant when it is said that the scientific status of a theory depends on its "falsifiability," and he predicted other federal judges would be too. Nevertheless, the 9th Circuit decision was reversed, and the case was remanded for further proceedings.

In the interests of justice and judicial economy, the 9th Circuit decided to conduct the newly required *Daubert* analysis of FED. R. EVID. 702, framing the question in this "brave new world" as follows: "How do we figure out whether scientists have derived their findings through the scientific method or whether their testimony is based on scientifically valid principles?" (p. 1316). In the end, a unanimous 9th Circuit found that the plaintiff expert failed Rule 702 requirements and *Daubert's* holding, because the plaintiff presented only experts' qualifications, their conclusions, and their assurances of reliability. The original summary judgment rendered 6 years earlier was affirmed, and the *Daubert* plaintiffs received due process, equal protection, and justice, but no compensation, because the scientific testimony offered by their expert failed to show with a preponderance of the evidence that Bendectin caused the birth defects.

The Court clarified *Daubert* and broadened its impact in two subsequent cases, *General Electric Co. v. Joiner* (1997) and *Kumho Tire Co. v. Carmichael* (1999). In *Joiner*, a city electrician, who was diagnosed with lung cancer, brought suit against the manufacturer of polychlorinated biphenyls (PCBs) and manufacturers of electrical transformers and dielectric fluid, alleging based on expert testimony that exposure caused his cancer. The district court judge excluded the plaintiff's expert testimony, finding it "subjective belief or unsupported speculation" (p. 140) and Joiner appealed. The 11th Circuit Appellate Court applied a stringent standard of review, reversing the trial court and finding that the judge erred in excluding the expert testimony. The U.S. Supreme Court intervened to reverse the 11th Circuit, thereby affirming and strengthening the gatekeeping function of the trial court, directing appellate courts not to review a trial judge's decision regarding expert admission, unless the judge committed a clear abuse of discretion. Basically, appellate courts were ordered to show great deference to the gatekeeping judges in district courts and to not disturb the decisions of the trial judge regarding the admissibility of expert testimony in the absence of gross error.

In *Kumho Tire*, a vehicle overturned when a right rear tire blew out, killing one passenger and injuring others. The plaintiffs sought to admit the testimony of a tire failure analyst regarding his visual and tactile inspection of the tire, based on the theory that in the absence of at least two of four specific physical indicators, tire failure must have been caused by a defect. The defendant moved to exclude the tire analyst testimony, claiming the methodology failed to satisfy FED. R. EVID. 702 requirements. The trial court applied *Daubert*, and the judge excluded the tire analyst after finding that the methodology employed was insufficiently reliable; Carmichael appealed. The 11th Circuit held that the trial court erred in applying *Daubert*, believing that it only applied to scientific testimony. The U.S. Supreme Court reversed the 11th Circuit and clarified that *Daubert* factors apply to the testimony of engineers and other experts who are not scientists. Experts may also be evaluated and admitted to testify based on skill, experience, and other specialized knowledge, not based only on scientific knowledge.

In 2002, holdings from the *Daubert* "trilogy" were used to amend Rule 702 and codify these U.S. Supreme Court decisions into the current rules governing expert testimony. Rule 702 now reads as follows:

> If scientific, technical, or other specialized knowledge will assist the trier of fact to understand the evidence or to determine a fact in issue, a witness qualified as an expert by knowledge, skill, experience, training, or education, may testify thereto in the form of an opinion or otherwise, if (1) the testimony is based upon sufficient facts or data, (2) the testimony is the product of reliable principles and methods, and (3) the witness has applied the principles and methods reliably to the facts of the case.

The next section shows how these rules applied to a neuropsychologist expert in a recent case. Careful analysis shows the pivotal role of the neuropsychologist expert in assisting the trier of fact to understand the mental condition of a defendant as it may relate to considerations of competence, insanity, culpability, and mitigation.

Admissibility Standards Applied to Neuropsychological Evidence in a Criminal Case

A recently resolved federal criminal case illustrates the current standards of admissibility for neuropsychological evidence. In *United States v. José Santos-Bueno* (2006), the government filed a motion *in limine*,[13] to exclude the expert testimony of a neuropsychologist regarding the impact of a brain injury on the defendant's cognitive abilities.

Mr. Santos-Bueno was charged with transporting illegal aliens in violation of the Immigration and Nationality Act (8 U.S.C. § 1324(a)(1)(A)(ii)). The defense introduced expert neuropsychologist testimony to rebut the government's evidence that Mr. Santos-Bueno formed the requisite mental state to commit the crime. The neuropsychologist's testimony challenged "the accuracy and reliability of inculpatory statements" made by the defendant to law enforcement following his arrest (p. 2). Essentially, the defense asserted that Mr. Santos-Bueno did not have the requisite state of mind to infer that passengers were aliens, and that he was excessively vulnerable to suggestions during questioning due to his cognitive disabilities. The government sought to exclude the expert testimony on three grounds: (1) preclusion under IDRA, (2) insufficient reliability and relevance under FED. R. EVID. 702 and *Daubert*, and (3) the potential to mislead and confuse the jury substantially outweighed the probative value of the expert testimony under FED. R. EVID. 403. Pleading in the alternative, the government also sought to have their own expert examine the defendant under FED. R. CRIM. P. 12.2(c)(1)(B)[14] should the court decide to admit the defense expert.

Federal court authority to review this motion derives, in part, from FED. R. EVID. 104 (a) Preliminary Questions of Admissibility, and (b) Relevancy Conditioned on Fact, as follows:

> (a) Preliminary questions concerning the qualification of a person to be a witness, the existence of a privilege, or the admissibility of evidence shall be determined by the court, subject to the provisions of subdivision (b). In making its determination it is not bound by the rules of evidence except those with respect to privileges.
>
> (b) When the relevancy of evidence depends upon the fulfillment of a condition of fact, the court shall admit it upon, or subject to, the introduction of evidence sufficient to support a finding of the fulfillment of the condition. (p. 11)

As the gatekeeper of admissibility as outlined under *Daubert*, the Honorable Judge F. Dennis Saylor conducted a pretrial evidentiary hearing and rendered an opinion on January 5, 2006.

In analyzing the statutes and evidence, Judge Saylor concluded that only two of four elements of 8 U.S.C. § 1324(a)(1)(A)(ii) were at issue: (1) Did Mr. Santos-Bueno act "knowing or in reckless disregard of the fact that an alien has come to . . . the United States in violation of law," and (2) did Mr. Santos-Bueno act "willfully in furtherance of the alien illegal presence" in the United States? (p. 11). The government attempted to prove these two elements, and the defense relied on the testimony of an expert neuropsychologist to rebut their proof. David Gansler, PhD, ABPP-CN, offered testimony that Mr. Santos-Bueno had suffered a brain injury 6 months before the crime, causing persistent and significant cognitive deficits. Dr. Gansler prepared to testify that people with the defendant's condition "are known to be vulnerable to suggestion" (p. 10). The defense argued that statements allegedly made by Mr. Santos-Bueno during a police interview were unreliable and untrue. In evaluating the admissibility of this testimony, Judge Saylor asked whether such evidence was (1) precluded under IDRA, (2) admissible under Rule 702 and *Daubert*, and (3) excluded under Rule 403.

Neuropsychologist Testimony Not Precluded by the IDRA

The IDRA provides an affirmative defense when showing clear and convincing evidence of insanity (IDRA, §17, 2007), but precludes "the use of noninsanity" psychiatric evidence pointing toward exoneration or mitigation of an offense (*United States v. Cameron*, 1990, p. 1066). Congress intended to preclude "diminished capacity" testimony by restricting the use of the defendant's supposed "psychiatric compulsion or inability or failure to engage in normal reflection" (p. 1061). However, IDRA does not preclude the use of such evidence "to negate a requisite state of mind" that is an element of the alleged criminal offense (*United States v. Schneider*, 1997, p. 201). Some appellate courts admit diminished capacity testimony only for "specific intent" crimes, because it is difficult or rare that a mental condition could negate a "general intent" requirement (*United States v. José Santos-Bueno*, 2006, p. 14). However, there is no agreement as to whether transportation of illegal aliens is a specific or general intent crime, nor did the defense attempt to use this distinction. Rather, the defense asserted that Mr. Santos-Bueno did not have the required mental state, because he did not draw the necessary inferences that the van passengers were illegal aliens. Consequently, the court held that the IDRA simply did not apply to the neuropsychologist's expert opinions in this case.

Neuropsychologist Testimony Meets *Daubert* and Rule 702 Standards for Admissibility

Next, the court turned to *Daubert* and FED. R. EVID. 702, which codifies the requirements for admissibility of expert testimony in federal courts. District courts have broad gatekeeping discretion in this inquiry—a process of evaluating the reliability and relevance of expert testimony (*Kumho Tire Co. v. Carmichael*, 1999, p. 141). Courts may use a flexible approach and enjoy "substantial discretion" in determining whether to admit or exclude expert testimony (*General Electric Co. v. Joiner*, 1997). Although the government challenged neither the scientific reliability of the evidence nor Dr. Gansler's qualifications to conduct an appropriate evaluation or render an expert opinion, the court must conduct a preliminary assessment.

Reliability of Neuropsychologist Testimony

In *Daubert*, the Supreme Court determined that FED. R. EVID. 702 superseded the holding in *Frye v. United States* (1923) and set out a new standard for admissibility of novel scientific evidence. Federal Rules of Evidence allow expert testimony "if scientific, technical, or other specialized knowledge" will assist the trier of fact (p. 589). Rule 702 provides that a witness may qualify as an expert based on "knowledge, skill, experience, training, or education." However, courts must evaluate expert testimony and an expert may testify only if (1) the testimony is based on sufficient facts or data, (2) the testimony is the product of reliable principles or methods, and (3) the witness applied the principles and methods reliably to facts in the case (FED. R. EVID. 702).

Although declining to establish a definitive checklist, the *Daubert* Court examined whether the theory and methods used (1) were generally adopted by the scientific community (*Frye* "general acceptance" test), (2) were subject to peer review and publication, (3) can be or have been tested, and (4) have a known and acceptable error rate (p. 597).

Although the government evidence did not challenge the scientific reliability of the neuropsychological evaluation, Judge Saylor concluded that "the reasoning and methodology applied by Dr. Gansler in drawing conclusions" appeared reliable (*United States v. José Santos-Bueno*, p. 24). Dr. Gansler's reliance on standardized psychological tests (e.g., the Wechsler Adult Intelligence Scale–III), although not infallible, as a tool for assessing cognitive function "is not seriously disputed in this case" (p. 24). Accordingly, the court held that Dr. Gansler's testimony regarding cognitive abilities were reliable sufficiently under *Daubert* and Rule 702, and were not excluded.

Relevance of Neuropsychologist Testimony

In addition to FED. R. EVID. 702 governing expert testimony, the criminal court also addressed FED. R. EVID. 704, as follows: "No expert witness testifying with respect to the mental state or condition of a defendant in a criminal case may state an opinion or inference as to whether the defendant did or did not have the mental state or condition constituting an element of the crime charged or of a defense thereto. Such ultimate issues are matters for the trier of fact alone." Here, all parties stipulated that Dr. Gansler may not offer any opinions on whether Mr. Santos-Bueno "actually knew (or recklessly disregard[ed])" that the van passengers were illegal aliens (p. 23). However, because the defense offered Dr. Gansler's opinion only in rebuttal to the government's proof of actual knowledge, Rule 704 does not apply.

While conceding the reliability of neuropsychological methodology, the government challenged the relevance of the neuropsychological evaluation and expert testimony about cognitive abilities. In addition to arguing that the cognitive abilities of the defendant were irrelevant, the balancing of relevance was the more essential analysis under *Daubert* and the Federal Rules. As such, the *Santos-Bueno* Court asked whether the probative value of the expert testimony "to the extent that any exists—is substantially outweighed by its potential to mislead or . . . confuse the jury" (p. 23). However, this legal analysis also relies, in part, on FED. R. EVID. 403.

Neuropsychologist Testimony Does Not Mislead or Confuse the Jury

Although a court may find neuropsychological evidence reliable and relevant under *Daubert* and Rule 702, such evidence may be excluded if its value to the court does not outweigh its potential to mislead or confuse the jury. In addressing this question, the court applied FED. R. EVID. 403, as follows: "Although relevant, evidence may be excluded if its probative value is substantially outweighed by the danger of unfair prejudice, confusion of the issues, or misleading the jury, or by considerations of undue delay, waste of time, or needless presentation of cumulative evidence" (p. 31). In balancing these factors, the court must decide whether the proposed expert testimony "could improperly suggest . . . the abolished diminished capacity defense is available" or that Mr. Santos-Bueno is "entitled to sympathy and possible nullification" (p. 26). Psychiatric evidence "presents an inherent danger" of distracting the jury from its task of evaluating the government's proof of each element of the alleged offense. In this case, there was concern as to whether Dr. Gansler's testimony might improperly open up the jury to theories of defense that do not exist under current law[15] or provide an erroneous justification for the alleged crime (p. 26).

Consequently, Judge Saylor limited the scope of Dr. Gansler's testimony to those expert opinions addressing how Mr. Santos-Beuno's cognitive disabilities impacted his factual inferences, or lack of such inferences, regarding whether the van passengers were illegal aliens. Furthermore, the Judge excluded any opinions about "alleged difficulty in exercising judgment, his impaired ability to appreciate the consequences of his actions, and . . . to 'execute appropriate plans of action' " as being outweighed by the potential to mislead or confuse the jury (p. 27).

Then, the court applied a similar, albeit briefer, analysis to evaluate the admissibility of neuropsychological evidence and Dr. Gansler's opinion on the defense claim the Mr. Santos-Bueno was more vulnerable to suggestion due to his head injury. Judge Saylor expressed "grave concern about both the scientific reliability and the relevance of Dr. Gansler's statement" about enhanced vulnerability to suggestion (p. 29). The court granted the defense an additional week to supplement the record on this question.[16]

Santos-Bueno illustrates current application of standards for admissibility to neuropsychological evidence in a recent federal criminal case. Although the court applied *Daubert* in its analysis of Dr. Gansler's proposed testimony, the court does not, nor should it, provide a thorough understanding of the significant impact of *Daubert* on the use of expert testimony in criminal cases. The next section focuses on the broader trends and far-reaching implications of *Daubert* and its progeny on the standards for admissibility of expert testimony.

The Impact of *Daubert* on Admissibility of Expert Testimony in Criminal Litigation

Research demonstrates that greater judicial scrutiny after *Daubert* was increasingly fatal to civil cases, with 90% of summary judgments going against the plaintiff (Dixon & Gill, 2002); that is, testimony from plaintiff experts was more readily excluded. In contrast, there has been little change in admission rates for expert evidence in criminal litigation at the trial and appellate levels (Groscup, Penrod, Studebaker, Huss, & O'Neil, 2002). Furthermore, the setting of a standard for appellate review in *Joiner* had little impact on the admissibility of expert testimony in criminal litigation. Nonetheless, *Daubert* and its progeny prompted greater scrutiny of experts by criminal court judges and brought about many changes to the manner in which expert testimony is evaluated. Groscup and colleagues (2002) noted a few general trends in criminal appellate cases, as briefly summarized below.

Since *Daubert*, relevance of expert testimony has been discussed at greater lengths in criminal appellate decisions, suggesting that courts spend more time analyzing the Federal Rules of Evidence or applying the *Daubert* factors. Specifically, judges spent more time scrutinizing expert evidence under FED. R. EVID. 702. However, judges also devoted more time to analyzing FED. R. EVID. 104 (permitting pretrial determinations), apparently because *Daubert* served as a reminder that judges have an obligation to do pretrial assessments of the reasoning and methodology of experts. Although there were increased references to *Daubert*, Groscup and colleagues (2002) noted no concomitant increase in analysis of its four suggested factors. Increasingly, courts are trying to dispose of admissibility issues in Rule 104 hearings as a result of *Daubert*.

Not surprisingly, *Daubert* also caused greater discussion of *Frye*, if for no other reason than to distinguish the holding. Even though *Daubert* and its progeny were superseded by the 2002 amendment to Rule 702, the discussion of *Frye* remains relevant because a minority of states (16) still use its general acceptance standard, including California, New York, Florida, Illinois, and Arizona (Lustre, 2004). Groscup and colleagues (2002) reported a decreased use of the general acceptance standard in jurisdictions adopting *Daubert*, and an increase in reliance on its falsifiability, peer review, and error rate criteria. As courts have adjusted to the gatekeeping function, they have spent less time analyzing *Daubert* when disposing of expert admissibility issues.

In a result with greater implications for clinical neuropsychology, scientific expert evidence is treated differently than medical–mental health, technical, or business evidence. In addition to lengthier discussions of *Daubert*, court consideration of Rules 104 and 403 and the *Frye* general acceptance test were much longer and more influential in terms of admissibility of scientific expert opinions. Obviously, these rules existed before *Daubert*, but results show greater scrutiny of scientific expert opinions on key evidentiary rules, in addition to the *Daubert* factors of falsifiability, peer review, and error rate. This elevated scrutiny has led to greater exclusion of scientific expert testimony when compared with medical–mental health testimony. Clinical neuropsychologists are trained in a scientist–practitioner model and may be retained to offer expert opinions as scientists or board-certified providers of medical–mental health services. Results show that when the expert's opinion is viewed as scientific, *Daubert* factors must be met for the court to admit the expert evidence. For most other experts, presentation of information addressing *Daubert* may be less common. Courts tend to rely more heavily on whether the expert testimony will assist the trier of fact (Rule 702), and that its probative value outweighs its prejudicial effect (Rule 403). Medical–mental health practitioners seeking expert qualification should be more prepared to discuss their indicia of expertise (e.g., education, experience, specialty, board certification, etc.) rather than their own research or an existing body of research.

Courts increasingly rely on neuropsychologist experts to assist the jury in resolving certain legal claims (Kaufmann, 2005). Historically, legal scholars have avoided the legal implications of neuroscience in our courts (Greely, 2006), with only six published articles using the terms *neuroscience* or *neuroimaging* in their titles (p. 607). However, a more recent LEXIS search[17] revealed twenty law review and bar journal articles, with ten published in 2007. Many of the recent publications have focused on neuroimaging techniques for evaluating truthfulness—a task that traditionally is the exclusive province of the jury. Currently, neuroimaging techniques for detecting deceit are no better than lie detectors, with neither technique being sufficiently reliable to be admitted as evidence (Keckler, 2006). Nine years ago, few neuroimaging findings were considered specific enough to address legal questions of cognitive or volitional impairment (Kulynych, 1997). Although neuroimaging has advanced rapidly, a carefully conducted neuropsychological evaluation remains a more reliable and legally relevant source of information about an individual's level of functioning, because neuropsychological tests have much better normative data. Indeed, it is on the basis of reliable and valid normative data that neuropsychological tests meet the requirements of admission under *Daubert* and the Federal Rules (Kaufmann, 2005). Furthermore, although lawyers believe that a neuroimage picture may be worth a thousand words, the general public does not seem to carry an inherent bias toward greater reliance on neuroimages than on neuropsychological test results (Guilmette, Kennedy, Weiler, & Temple, 2006). Finally, neuropsychological evaluations commonly incorporate neuroimaging studies, not to mention other neurological and neurodiagnostic findings, when formulating clinical impressions. As such, it is routine practice for clinical neuropsychologists to use neuroimaging results and other medical information when drawing inferences about brain–behavior relations and when rendering expert opinions.

In summary, *Daubert* assigned, and *Joiner* reinforced, the gatekeeping role of the trial court judge in determining the admissibility of expert testimony, thereby raising the level of scrutiny of experts and the basis for their testimony. *Daubert* also partially defined a road map, in the form of flexible factors, for experts to follow to have their testimony admitted and ultimately heard by the trier of fact. *Santos-Bueno* showed how careful attention to evidentiary and procedural rules in a criminal proceeding, including *Daubert* factors, allows expert neuropsychologists to be recognized by the court in a preliminary evidentiary hearing. Ultimately, Dr. Gansler's expert neuropsychological opinions were admitted as sufficiently reliable and relevant to assist the jury. However, the outcome is quite different when expert neuropsychologists ignore evidentiary and procedural rules, and fail to follow the *Daubert* road map, as illustrated in the following civil case.

Expert Neuropsychologist Excluded for Failing to Follow *Daubert*

Prior preparation prevents poor performance.
—JAMES A. BAKER III (2006)

Baxter v. Temple (2005) illustrates that Mr. Baker's maxim is especially true for experts preparing to render testimony at a preliminary evidentiary hearing. In *Baxter*, the defense filed a motion *in limine* to exclude the testimony of a Barbara Bruno-Goldman, PhD, as insufficiently reliable, under *Daubert*. During the evidentiary hearing, Dr. Bruno-Goldman described the Boston Process Approach to hypothesis testing in the neuropsychological evaluation of a child exposed allegedly to lead poisoning. The defendants argued successfully that Dr. Bruno-Goldman's testimony should be excluded, because the Boston Process Approach has not been subject to peer review and publication, has no known or potential error rate, and is not generally accepted in the appropriate scientific literature. A review of hearing testimony shows how a trial judge used *Daubert* factors to exclude expert neuropsychological evidence and provides instruction for how to avoid such outcomes (Desmond, 2007).

All three neuropsychologists, Drs. Bruno-Goldman, Sandra Shaheen, and David Faust, testified that the Boston Process methodology employed was untested (*Baxter* order, p. 8). Dr. Bruno-Goldman added that the Boston

Process Approach that she employs in forensic examinations "has never been . . . and *cannot be* tested, because it varies from practitioner to practitioner" (p. 9, emphasis added). In fact, Dr. Bruno-Goldman testified that she "could not recall if she had ever administered the same test battery" (p. 9) on the thousands of other patients she evaluated during her career. The *Baxter* court ruled that the Boston Process Approach as employed by Dr. Bruno-Goldman cannot be and has not been tested in this case.

All three neuropsychologists testified that the Boston Process methodology employed was neither subjected to peer review nor described in published articles. Dr. Bruno-Goldman referenced a professional position paper supporting the application of the Boston Process Approach that Dr. Faust noted was not in a peer-reviewed publication. Dr. Shaheen referred to many learned treatises on the general acceptance of the Boston Process Approach in clinical neuropsychology practice, yet admitted that Dr. Bruno-Goldman's specific methodology had not been subject to peer review or described in published articles. Finally, Dr. Bruno-Goldman admitted that she had not previously used the methodology, and it was likely that no other clinician had either. Therefore, the *Baxter* Court found the Boston Process Approach, as employed in this case, had not been subject to peer review and publication.

No evidence was offered on a known or potential error rate for the Boston Process Approach. At one point, Dr. Bruno-Goldman testified that she did not follow the instruction manual regarding time constraints on some tests to "test the limits" of the child's performance. Neither Dr. Bruno-Goldman nor Dr. Shaheen offered any evidence on the reliability of "testing the limits." Dr. Faust pointed out that any variation in the standardized instructions destroys the normative comparisons of the child's performance to like-age peers, making it impossible to determine an error rate or interpret the results. Moreover, although selected individual tests have known error rates, when Dr. Bruno-Goldman modified the Boston Process Approach, she created what Dr. Faust described as an "idiosyncratic combination, if not hodgepodge of multiple influences" (p. 11). The court detailed some departures from standardized techniques. Dr. Faust concluded that the methodology employed was "not scientifically validated . . . founded on guesswork, speculation, and conjecture, which sometimes flies directly in the face of scientific literature" (p. 11). Hence, the *Baxter* court ruled that the methodology employed by Dr. Bruno-Goldman did not have a known or potential error rate.

In concluding its analysis, the *Baxter* Court drew a distinction between appropriate scientific literature for clinical assessment and "a 'forensic' approach to assessing children with lead poisoning" (p. 13). Dr. Faust described how the role of the expert neuropsychologist changes depending on whether a case is a clinical or forensic referral. This important distinction between the roles of clinical provider and forensic examiner has been frequently described (Denney, 2005a; Denney & Wynkoop, 2000; Goldstein, 2003; Greenberg & Shuman, 1997; Heilbrun, 2001). Neuropsychologists in forensic practice must employ objective methods that allow them to be unbiased truth seekers.

The *Baxter* court held that the evidence overwhelmingly showed that Dr. Bruno-Goldman's methodology was not sufficiently reliable for forensic analysis (Desmond, 2007). The evidence failed to meet any of *Daubert*'s flexible factors. Therefore, the defendant motion *in limine* was granted, Dr. Bruno-Goldman's testimony was excluded, and the jury never heard her opinions in the case. On January 31, 2008, arguments were heard before the New Hampshire Supreme Court and the case is pending.

Some commentators have speculated, quite prematurely, that *Daubert* challenges of idiosyncratic test combinations will end the use of flexible neuropsychological batteries in forensic consulting (Reed, 1996). Survey results from 1989 and 2005 show that fewer neuropsychologists use fixed batteries, a decline from 18% to 7% (Sweet, Nelson, & Moberg, 2006). At the same time, a steadily growing majority of neuropsychologists (54–76%), use carefully constructed batteries specifically tailored to distinct clinical populations. An estimated 93% of neuropsychologists do not use the fixed Halstead–Reitan or Luria–Nebraska test batteries, perhaps signaling a newly emerging standard of care. Moreover, judicial decisions heralded the end of fixed battery dominance in forensic consulting (*Chapple v. Gangar*, 1994).

In *Chapple*, a 10-year-old boy, Christopher, sustained a brain injury in a car accident. Three psychologists conducted neuropsychological evaluations, Paul J. Domitor, PhD, Catherine Mateer, PhD, ABPP-CN, and Ralph M. Reitan, PhD, ABPN. Acting in a clinical role, Dr. Domitor employed some Halstead–Reitan tests but augmented his battery with a variety of additional measures (e.g., intelligence, academic achievement, and nonverbal memory). Dr. Domitor concluded that Christopher had a mild cognitive impairment and might be at risk for continuing problems due to frontal lobe injury, but he was unwilling to make a prognosis.

Acting as plaintiff's retained expert, Dr. Mateer reviewed a variety of records, including educational reports showing a decline in the boy's functioning following the injury. Dr. Mateer administered a flexible battery that included only one Halstead–Reitan test (Trail Making), but a much broader range of other measures (e.g., attention, verbal memory, and executive functions). Dr. Mateer, who disagreed with Dr. Domitor, found moderate deficits and concluded that, more likely than not, Christopher would experience permanent residual problems with attention, memory, and executive functions. Moreover, Dr. Mateer opined, with a reasonable degree of neuropsychological certainty, that remediation programs would not make Christopher's problems go away (p. 1495). Dr. Mateer added that the boy was at "much higher risk for difficulties with employment and that there may be various employment he would have been capable of performing that he will clearly not be now" (Mateer Dep. at 87) due to "continuing problems secondary to frontal damage" (Mateer Dep. at 98).

Retained as a defense expert, Dr. Reitan rejected Dr. Domitor's conclusions and took exception to Dr. Mateer's assessment, at one point claiming that it was not a neuropsychological evaluation, but rather "the kind of ability and cognitive testing that might be used to assess a normal child" (Reitan report at 9). Espousing blind interpretation, Dr. Reitan also suggested that Dr. Mateer was biased by her preassessment review of records, including the history of head injury (Reitan report at 16). Dr. Reitan reviewed Christopher's declining academic functioning but could not correlate it with recovery patterns noted by children with significant brain injury (Reitan report at 19). Dr. Reitan speculated that Christopher "may not have been trying hard enough on the tests" (p. 1497) and concluded that it was extremely difficult to make predictions regarding the long-term outcome of children with brain damage (Reitan report at 22).

The plaintiff requested $2 million for lost earning capacity and employment opportunities but received nothing, although the court awarded Christopher $793,013 for other claims. Although the court expressed some reservations regarding the reliability of the flexible battery approach, none of the neuropsychologist expert opinions was excluded. Indeed, the only *Daubert* challenges were raised by the plaintiff against the defense's neurosurgeon and vocational specialist, not the neuropsychologists. While some may debate the meaning of *Chapple* (McKinzey & Ziegler, 1999), none of its holdings address battery selection. Reed (1996) misstated the *Chapple* result, as though it were precedent setting for the admissibility of fixed batteries and exclusion of flexible batteries, when clearly it is not. All neuropsychological evaluations and opinions were admitted and weighed by the court. A more accurate reading of the outcome is that *Daubert* standards will be liberal for professional communities practicing rigorous scientific methodology and conservative for those employing less stringent scientific methodology. Courts clearly make these decisions in each case when the controversy arises (Desmond, 2007).

Wrongful Disclosure of Psychological Tests Threatens the Admissibility of Neuropsychological Opinions

At the same time that clinical neuropsychology has experienced unprecedented growth in forensic consultation, discovery rules and isolated court decisions threaten the validity of neuropsychological methods (Kaufmann,

2005). Specifically, the strong public policy underlying test security (*Detroit Edison Co. v. NLRB*, 1979) is being threatened by the overly zealous discovery demands of litigation. Standardized psychometric tests used during forensic evaluations provide the best technology available to assist the jury in resolving certain legal claims (Kaufmann, 2005). Wrongful disclosure of psychological test materials allows opportunistic litigants and their attorneys to "review test protocols, obtain test items, discover answers, and 'cheat' on future tests" (p. 100), thereby turning valuable neuropsychological methods into junk science in our courts. In keeping with the theme of this chapter, such wrongful disclosure would likely cause judges to exclude neuropsychological evidence in pretrial hearings, because opinions based on tainted data would not be sufficiently reliable under *Daubert*. In *Detroit Edison*, the U.S. Supreme Court ordered that such materials should be released only to psychologists to "insure [sic] the future integrity of the tests" (p. 308).

Although about 20 states have acted to protect psychological test materials from wrongful disclosure, potentially harmful court decisions caused concerned professionals to create the Group Protecting the Integrity of Psychological Examinations (G-PIPE; *Berman v. Kuckarski*, 2006). G-PIPE consists of individual practitioners, neuropsychology credentialing boards, and state psychological associations that are concerned about negative consequences of test disclosure on the objectivity, fairness, and integrity of neuropsychological evaluations and practice. G-PIPE also includes test developers, publishers, marketers, and distributors who are concerned about copyright infringement, trade secret protection, and other intellectual property rights associated with their tests. G-PIPE has addressed challenges to the integrity of neuropsychological evaluations posed by a third-party observer/recording device (TPO) and compliance with court orders protecting the integrity of test materials.[18]

Currently, Florida places the burden of proof on the party seeking to avoid a TPO during a psychological evaluation (*Broyles v. Reilly*, 1997). In *Broyles*, the court set forth a two-part test requiring (1) case-specific reasons why a TPO is disruptive to the evaluation, and (2) no other qualified provider in the area is willing to conduct the evaluation in the presence of a TPO. This legal test was developed originally for medical–legal examinations, and G-PIPE argued that psychological evaluations are distinguishable because they employ psychometric tests. G-PIPE advocates that the party seeking the TPO have the burden to show case-specific reasons why a TPO should be allowed. In a related Florida case, G-PIPE sought to amend a protective order requiring the return of a videotape made during a psychological evaluation (*Florida Department of Transportation v. Piccolo*, 2006).

Although *Berman* is still pending, the *Piccolo* court found that plaintiff counsel did not depart from any established principle of law by retaining a videotape of the neuropsychological evaluation. However, in a concurring opinion, Judge Wallace affirmed,

> ... It appears from our record that the denial of DOT's request will make it impossible for the agency to obtain the services of a clinical neuropsychologist to examine Piccolo. I disagree with the majority's suggestion that this is unimportant because DOT can arrange for Piccolo to be examined by a professional from a different discipline.
>
> Many years ago, the United States Supreme Court recognized the psychological profession's legitimate interest in preserving the security of test materials. See *Detroit Edison Co. v. NLRB*, 440 U.S. 301, 313-15 (1979). The trial court's order fails to strike a proper balance between this legitimate interest and Piccolo's interest in effective legal representation. (pp. 776–777)

In a unanimous decision, a California appellate court held that copyright protection does not preclude a test recipient from obtaining his or her answers and the test questions after completing a mental examination using psychometric tests (*Carpenter v. Yamaha Motor Corp.*, 2006). The court also found that a test recipient could obtain the names of the tests before the examination and—with the assistance of counsel, psychologist, or other expert—could object to certain tests deemed inappropriate for the purposes of the mental examination. Although the *Carpenter* Court acknowledged that disclosure of test materials before the examination "could affect the integrity of the tests" (p. 267), it failed to appreciate that test identification before examination posed a risk. While remanding the case for further proceedings due to deficiencies in the record, *Carpenter* saw no threat in providing test names, because "actual test questions are a carefully guarded secret among the publishers and examiners" (p. 268). Yet in *Detroit Edison*, all of the justices recognized the risk of test disclosure, with the majority commenting that protections afforded by restrictive orders were not persuasive (p. 314), and the minority commenting on the harm associated with inadvertent disclosure (p. 324). In the end, the U.S. Supreme Court has found a better balance in clarifying the strong public policy underlying test security, ordering that psychometric tests should be released only to psychologists.

These Florida and California cases show how easily a court might disclose psychological test materials into the public domain, thereby compromising the integrity of neuropsychological practice and forensic consultation. This chapter has demonstrated the importance of protecting psychological test materials, standardized instructions, and normative comparisons in developing neuropsychological evidence and rendering reliable opinions in court. Precedent-setting court decisions may sway the public policy debate away from test security, in favor of evidentiary discovery rules, such that courts will increasingly find neuropsychological opinions unreliable. Wrongful disclosure of psychological test materials is a looming threat to the admissibility of neuropsychological evidence in our courts, prompting G-PIPE into legal advocacy.

Conclusions

Although neuropsychological consulting has expanded into various civil and administrative proceedings, this chapter has focused on admissibility of neuropsychological evidence in criminal cases. Three out of every four reported criminal cases referencing neuropsychology have been adjudicated in the past decade. This rapid increase in the use of neuropsychology to assist criminal juries demonstrates that neuropsychologist expert opinions meet the criteria for admissibility under *Daubert* and the Federal Rules. This chapter has provided an overview of neuropsychological evidence, the rules for its admissibility, and the most common legal challenges confronting neuropsychologists in recent legal cases.

Criminal courts are admitting neuropsychologist expert opinions on questions of competence, insanity, diminished capacity, culpability, and mitigation. Standardized, norm-referenced, psychometric tests provide the most reliable and valid procedures for addressing questions involving the mental condition of the criminal defendant. Unlike other mental health professionals, psychologists use objective psychological tests as part of a scientific methodology to refine their impressions when formulating expert opinions (Kaufmann, 2005). Applying their unique brain–behavior knowledge base, neuropsychologists use results from psychological tests in conjunction with neuroimaging, neurodiagnostic, and neurological findings, in a scientific enterprise that assists the trier of fact to resolve certain legal claims. Courts routinely find that neuropsychological expertise is based on reliable and relevant methods, and that expert neuropsychologist opinions help the jury. Board-certified neuropsychologists who are versed in the constitutional and judicial foundations of criminal forensic consultation will continue to provide an important expert service.

Although the law seeks every rational means for ascertaining the truth, public policy must promote the truth-seeking function of the judiciary by protecting psychological test materials from wrongful disclosure in a manner that serves all parties and the profession, while preserving justice in our courts. The forensic neuropsychologist expert offers admissible neuropsychological evidence that is more probative than prejudicial on the ultimate issues of guilt or innocence that criminal courts and juries must decide.

Notes

1. Statements of opinion or belief considered authoritative because they are made by the court. Compare to *holding*, which is "a court's determination of a matter of law pivotal to its decision; a principle drawn from such a decision" (*Black's Law Dictionary*, 8th edition). Dicta may be persuasive but do not set precedent. Holdings create binding precedent within the applicable jurisdiction of the court.

2. See also Foster (2004), citing *Russell v. State*, 775 So.2d 866 (Ala. CIM. App. 1997); *People v. Noble*, 42 Ill. 2d 425, 248 N.E.2d 96 (1969); *State v. Alexander*, 252 La. 564, 211 So.2d 650 (1968); *Saul v. State*, 6 Md. App. 540, 252, A.2d 282 (1969); *Span v. Bees*, 23 Md. App. 313, 327 A.2d 801 (1974); *People v. Diaz*, 51 N.Y.2d 841, 433 N.Y.S.2d 751, 413 N.E.2d 1166 (1980); *Com v. Williams*, 270 Pa. Super. 27, 410 A.2d 880 (1979); *State v. Williams*, 278 Md. 180, 361 A.2d 122 (1976); *Saul v. State*, 6 Md. App. 520, 252 A.2d 282 (1969).

3. An evidentiary standard that exceeds the preponderance of the evidence standard used in civil litigation, but is less than the beyond a reasonable doubt standard used in criminal litigation. Therefore, although the defendant has the burden to show that insanity is highly probable, the defense is not required to prove insanity beyond the shadow of a doubt.

4. Courts in different jurisdictions operate under different legal precedents and rules.

5. *Specific intent* refers to the state of mind required to accomplish a precise criminal act that can be negated by intoxication or insanity.

6. *Mens rea* means guilty mind, or the state of mind that the prosecution must prove beyond a reasonable doubt to secure a conviction.

7. Conducted on December 12, 2007.

8. Noting 2007 American Academy of Clinical Neuropsychology (AACN) listserve discussions titled "Functional Neuroimaging: Not Ready for Prime Time" and "fMRI Admissibility Revisited."

9. Morse describes the speculative claims of some practitioners about the implications of neuroscience for criminal responsibility that cannot be conceptually, empirically, or legally sustained, recommending "cognitive jurotherapy" as the treatment of choice for brain overclaim syndrome.

10. There is no genuine issue of material fact upon which the plaintiff could prevail as a matter of law. The trial judge rendered a verdict for Merrell Dow Pharmaceuticals based on briefs without a trial.

11. The most common mechanism used by the U.S. Supreme Court to hear a case by order directing a lower court to deliver the case record.

12. However, about 16 states still use a *Frye* type of standard, including California, New York, Florida, Illinois, and Arizona.

13. A motion to limit or exclude allegedly prejudicial evidence presented to a judge before or during a trial.

14. Rule allowing the court to order the defendant to be examined by a government expert after the defendant provides notice of intent to introduce expert evidence relating to a mental disease or defect.

15. Also called *jury nullification* that occurs when a jury renders a not guilty verdict, contrary to instructions by the judge concerning what is the law, or whether such law is applicable to the case.

16. Defense counsel reported that the admission of neuropsychological evidence was pivotal in the government's offer to let her client plead guilty to a lesser offense (i.e., conspiracy to transport illegal aliens, be sentenced to time already served, and avoid immediate deportation (P. Kelley, personal communication, April 25, 2007).

17. Conducted December 12, 2007.

18. For more information on G-PIPE, contact Laura Lee Shaw Howe, JD, PhD.

References

Adamson v. Chiovaro, 705 A.2d 402 (N.J. Super. App. Div. 1998).

Alexander, A. (2006). Functional magnetic resonance imaging lie detection: Is a "brainstorm" heading toward a "gatekeeper." *Houston Journal of Health Law and Policy, 7*, 1–56.

21 AM. JUR. 2D *Crim. Law* §§ 48, 62, 63, 67, 68, 87, 94, 95, 102, 103, 119, 120 (2007).

Atkins v. Virginia, 536 U.S. 304, 318 (U.S. 2002).

Baker, D. B., & Benjamin, L. T. (2000). The affirmation of the scientist–practitioner: A look back at Boulder. *American Psychologist, 55*, 241–247.

Bates v. Bell, 400 F.3d 635 (6th Cir. 2005).

Bates v. State, 937 S.W.2d 615 (Tenn. Crim. App. 1997).

Baxter v. Temple, No. 01-c-0567 (N.H. Sup. Ct. Aug. 8, 2005) (order granting motion *in limine*).

Bell v. Thompson, 545 U.S. 794 (U.S. 2005).

Benjamin, L. T. (2005). A history of clinical psychology as a profession in America (and a glimpse at its future). *Annual Review of Clinical Psychology, 1*, 1–30.

Bergeson v. Ray, Middlesex Superior Court, Docket No.: 1998-569.

Berman v. Kuckarski (Dist. Ct. App. Fla. 2006) [Brief for Amicus Curiae Group Protecting the Integrity of Psychological Examinations (No. 5D06-2053)].

Bigler, E. D. (2001). Neuropsychological testing defines the neurobehavioral significance of neuroimaging-identified abnormalities. *Archives of Clinical Neuropsychology, 16*, 227–228.

Billiot v. State, 655 So.2d 1, 17–18 (Miss. 1995).

Black's Law Dictionary (8th ed.). (2004). St. Paul, MN: Thomson West.

Bonner v. ISP Technologies, Inc., 259 F.3d 924 (8th Cir. 2001).

Boone, K. B. (2007). *Assessment of feigned cognitive impairment: A neuropsychological perspective*. New York: Guilford Press.

Broyles v. Reilly, 695 So.2d 832 (Dist. Ct. App. Fla. 1997).

Buckler v. Sinclair Refining Co., 216 N.E.2d 14, 19 (Ill. App. Ct. 1966).

Carpenter v. Yamaha Motor Corp., 141 Cal. App. 4th 249 (Cal. Ct. App. 2006).

Calloway v. State, 651 So.2d 752, 754 (Dist. Ct. App. Fla. 1995).

Chapple v. Gangar, 851 F. Supp. 1481 (E.D. Wash. 1994).
Cunningham v. Montgomery, 921 P.2d 1355 (Or. Ct. App. 1995).
Daubert v. Merrell Dow Pharmaceuticals, 727 F. Supp. 570, 575 (S.D. Cal. 1989).
Daubert v. Merrell Dow Pharmaceuticals, 951 F.2d 1128 (9th Cir. 1992).
Daubert v. Merrell Dow Pharmaceuticals, 509 U.S. 579 (U.S. 1993).
Daubert v. Merrell Dow Pharmaceuticals, 43 F.3d 1311 (9th Cir. 1995).
Denney, R. L. (2005a). Criminal forensic neuropsychology and assessment of competency. In G. J. Larrabee (Ed.), *Forensic neuropsychology: A scientific approach* (pp. 378–424). New York: Oxford University Press.
Denney, R. L. (2005b). Criminal responsibility and other criminal forensic issues. In G. J. Larrabee (Ed.), *Forensic neuropsychology: A scientific approach* (pp. 325–465). New York: Oxford University Press.
Denney, R. L., & Wynkoop, T. F. (2000). Clinical neuropsychology in the criminal forensic setting. *Journal of Head Trauma Rehabilitation, 15,* 804–828.
Desmond, J. M. (2007, Winter). Admissibility of neuropsychological evidence in New Hampshire. *New Hampshire Bar Journal, 47*(4), 12–17. Retrieved July 5, 2007, from *www.nhbar.org/publications/display-journal-issue.asp?id=347*
Detroit Edison Co. v. NLRB, 440 U.S. 301 (U.S. 1979).
Dixon, L., & Gill, B. (2002). Changes in the standards for admitting expert evidence in federal civil cases standards since the *Daubert* decision. *Psychology, Public Policy, and Law, 8,* 251–308.
Downs v. Perstorp Components, Inc., 126 F. Supp.2d 1090 (E.D. Tenn. 1999).
Drope v. Missouri, 420 U.S. 162, 171–172 (U.S. 1975).
Dusky v. United States, 362 U.S. 402, 402 (U.S. 1960).
Executive Car & Truck Leasing, Inc. v. DeSerio, 468 So.2d 1027 (Dist. Ct. App. Fla. 1985).
Fabianke v. Weaver ex rel. Weaver, 527 So.2d 1253 (Ala. 1988).
Federal Rules of Criminal Procedure 12.2(a), (b), (c)(1)(B) (2007).
Federal Rules of Evidence 104, 403, 702, 704 (2007).
Florida Dept. of Trans. v. Piccolo, 964 So.2d 773 (Dist. Ct. App. Fl. 2007).
Florida Dept. of Trans. v. Piccolo (Dist. Ct. App. Fla. 2006) [Brief for Amicus Curiae Group Protecting the Integrity of Psychological Examinations (No. 04-11035)].
Ford v. Wainwright, 477 U.S. 399, 409–410 (U.S. 1986).
Frendak v. United States, 408 A.2d 364, 380 (D.C. Ct. App. 1979).
Foster, S. K. (1999). Qualification of nonmedical psychologist to testify as to mental condition or competency. *American Law Reports 5th, 72,* 529–605.
Frye v. United States, 293 F. 1013 (D.C. Cir. 1923).
General Electric Co. v. Joiner, 522 U.S. 136 (U.S. 1997).
G.I.W. Southern Value v. Smith, 471 So.2d 81 (Dist. Ct. App. Fla. 1985).
Godinez v. Moran, 509 U.S. 389 (1993).
Goldstein, A. M. (2003). Overview of forensic psychology. In I. B. Weiner (Series Ed.) & A. M. Goldstein (Vol. Ed.), *Handbook of psychology: Vol. 11. Forensic psychology* (pp. 3–20). Hoboken, NJ: Wiley.
Greely, H. T. (2006). Neuroethics and ELSI: Similarities and differences. *Minnesota Journal of Law, Science, and Technology, 7,* 599–637.

Greenberg, S. A., & Shuman, D. W. (1997). Irreconcilable conflict between therapeutic and forensic roles. *Professional Psychology: Research and Practice, 28*, 50–57.

Greiffenstein, M. F., & Cohen, L. (2005). Neuropsychology and the law: Principles of productive attorney-neuropsychologist relations. In G. J. Larrabee (Ed.), *Forensic neuropsychology: A scientific approach* (pp. 29–91). New York: Oxford University Press.

Grenitz v. Tomlian, 858 So.2d 999 (Fla. 2003).

Grisso, T. (1988). *Competency to stand trial evaluations: A manual for practice.* Sarasota, FL: Professional Resource Exchange.

Groscup, J. L., Penrod, S. D., Studebaker, C. A., Huss, M. T., & O'Neil, K. M. (2002). Effects of *Daubert* on the admissibility of expert testimony on state and federal criminal cases. *Psychology, Public Policy, and Law, 8*, 339–372.

Guilmette, T. J., Kennedy, M. L., Weiler, M. D., & Temple, R. O. (2006). Investigation of biases in the general public in evaluating mild head injury using neuropsychological and CT scan results: Forensic implications. *Clinical Neuropsychologist, 20*, 305–314.

Hagen v. Swenson, 236 N.W.2d 161 (Minn. 1975).

Heilbronner, R. L. (2004). A status report on the practice of forensic neuropsychology. *Clinical Neuropsychologist, 18*, 312–326.

Heilbrun, K. (2001). *Principles of forensic mental health assessment.* New York: Kluwer Academic/Plenum Press.

Howard v. State, 698 S.W.2d 23, 25 (Mo. Ct. App. 1985).

Huber, P.W. (1991). *Galileo's revenge: Junk science in the courtroom.* New York: Basic Books.

Huntoon v. TCI Cablevision of Colorado, 969 P.2d 681 (Colo. 1998).

Hutchinson v. American Family Ins. Co., 514 N.W.2d 882 (Iowa 1994).

Immigration and Nationality Act, 8 U.S.C. § 1324(a)(1)(A)(ii) (2007).

Insanity Defense Reform Act of 1984, 18 U.S.C. §§ 17, 4244, 4245 (2007).

Jenkins v. United States, 307 F.2d 637 (D.C. Cir. 1962).

John v. Im, 559 S.E.2d 697 (Va. 2002).

Kaufmann, P. M. (2005). Protecting the objectivity, fairness, and integrity of neuropsychological evaluations in litigation: A privilege second to none? *Journal of Legal Medicine, 26*, 95–131.

Kaufmann, P. M. (2007). Scientific evidence in the court room: Legal requirements and ethical dilemmas for the expert neuropsychologist. (CE Workshop presented at the 35th Annual Meeting of the International Neuropsychological Society, Portland, OR). *Journal of the International Neuropsychology Society, 13*(Suppl. S1).

Keckler, C. N. W. (2006). Cross-examining the brain: A legal analysis of neural imaging for credibility impeachment. *Hastings Law Journal, 57*, 509–556.

Krevitz v. Savoy Heating and Air Conditioning Co., 396 So.2d 49 (Ala. 1981).

Kinsey v. King, 431 N.E.2d 1316 (Ill. App. Ct. 1982).

Kulynych, J. (1997). Psychiatric evidence: High-tech crystal ball? *Stanford Law Review, 49*, 1249–1270.

Kumho Tire v. Carmichael, 526 U.S. 137 (U.S. 1999).
Landers v. Chrysler Corp., 963 S.W.2d 275 (Mo. Ct. App. 1998).
Larrabee, G. J. (Ed.). (2005). *Forensic neuropsychology: A scientific approach.* New York: Oxford University Press.
Larrabee, G. J. (Ed.). (2007). *Assessment of malingered neuropsychological deficits.* New York: Oxford University Press.
Lugo v. Citicorp Mortgage, No. 925051, 1994 WL 879715 (Mass. Super. Ct. 1994).
Lustre, A. B. (2004). Post-*Daubert* standards for admissibility of scientific and other expert evidence in state courts. *American Law Reviews 5th*, 90, 453–545.
Madrid v. University of California, 737 P.2d 74 (N.M. 1987).
McCarthy v. Atwood, 67 Va. Cir. 237 (Va. Cir. Ct. 2005).
McKinzey, R. K., & Ziegler, T. G. (1999). Challenging a flexible neuropsychological battery under *Kelly/Frye*: A case study. *Behavioral Sciences and the Law, 17,* 543–551.
Miles v. Stainer, 108 F.3d 1109, 1112 (9th Cir. 1997).
Minner v. American Mortgage & Guaranty Co., 791 A.2d 826 (Del. Super. Ct. 2000).
Miranda v. Arizona, 384 U.S. 436, 444 (U.S. 1966).
Morrison v. United States, 579 A.2d 686, 691 (D.C. 1990).
Morse, S. J. (2006). Symposium: The mind of a child: The relationship between brain development, cognitive functioning and accountability under the law: Brain overclaim syndrome and criminal responsibility: A diagnostic note. *Ohio State Journal of Criminal Law, 3,* 397–412.
Nelson v. Nelson, 87 N.W.2d 767 (Iowa 1958).
North Carolina v. Butler, 441 U.S. 369, 373 (U.S. 1979).
Pate v. Robinson, 383 U.S. 375, 377 (U.S. 1966).
People v. Gettings, 530 N.E.2d 647 (Ill. App. Ct. 1988).
People v. Hawthorne, 291 N.W. 205, 208 (Mich. 1940).
People v. R.R. & G.A., 807 N.Y. S.2d 516, 544 (N.Y. Sup. Ct. 2005).
Rector v. Clark, 923 F.2d 570, 572 (8th Cir. 1991).
Redding, R. E. (2006). The brain-disordered defendant: Neuroscience and legal insanity in the twenty-first century. *American University Law Review, 56,* 51–123.
Reed, J. E. (1996). Fixed vs. flexible neuropsychological test batteries under the *Daubert* standard for admissibility of scientific evidence. *Behavioral Sciences and the Law, 14,* 315–322.
Rosen, J. (2007, March 11). The brain on the stand. *New York Times*. Retrieved July 5, 2007, from *www.nytimes.com/2007/03/11/magazine/11Neurolaw.t.html?ex= 1331269200&en=bbdc98f5f3800cd7&ei=5088*
Roper v. Simmons, 543 U.S. 551, 568 (U.S. 2005).
Ross v. State, 386 So.2d 1191, 1195 (Fla. 1980).
Rush v. Megee, 36 Ind. 69 (Ind. 1871).
Rustenhaven v. American Airlines, Inc., 320 F.3d 802 (8th Cir. 2003).
Sanchez v. Derby, 433 N.W.2d 523 (Neb. 1989).
Shaw v. Delo, 971 F.2d 181, 187 (8th Cir. 1992).

Simmons v. Mullins, 331 A.2d 892, 897 (Pa. Super. Ct. 1975).
State v. Beam, 710 P.2d 526 (Idaho 1985).
State v. Broom, 655 So.2d 705, 708 (La. Ct. App. 1995).
State v. Card, 825 P.2d 1082 (Idaho 1991).
State v. Clemons, 946 S.W.2d 206, 222 (Mo. 1997).
State v. Korell, 690 P.2d 992 (Mont. 1984).
State v. Lee, 660 S.W.2d 394, 397 (Mo. Ct. App. 1983)
State v. Rogers, 4 P.3d 1261, 1276 (Ore. 2000)
Sullivan, J. P., & Denney, R. L. (2003). Constitutional and judicial foundations in criminal forensic neuropsychology. *Journal of Forensic Neuropsychology, 3,* 13–44.
Sweet, J. J., King, J. H., Malina, A. C., Bergman, M. A., & Simmons, A. (2002). Documenting the prominence of forensic neuropsychology at national meetings and relevant professional journals from 1990 to 2000. *Clinical Neuropsychologist, 16,* 481–494.
Sweet, J. J., Nelson, N. W., & Moberg, P. J. (2006). The TCN/AACN 2005 "Salary Survey": Professional practices, beliefs, and incomes of U.S. Neuropsychologists. *Clinical Neuropsychologist, 20,* 325–364.
Thompson v. Bell, No. 1:04-CV-177, 2006 U.S. Dist. LEXIS 27283 (E.D. Tenn. May 4, 2006).
United States v. Banks, 137 F.R.D. 20, 21 (C.D. Il. 1991).
United States v. Cameron, 907 F.2d 1051, 1066 (11th Cir. 1990).
United States v. Frisbee, 623 F. Supp. 1217, 1220 (N.D. Cal. 1985).
United States v. Hinckley, 525 F. Supp. 1342 (D.D.C. 1981).
United States v. Johns, 728 F.2d 953, 956 (7th Cir. 1984).
United States v. José Santos-Bueno, No. 04-40023-FDS, 2006 U.S. LEXIS 6275 (Dist. Ct. Mass. 2006).
United States v. Marenghi, 893 F. Supp. 85, 99 (D. Me. 1995).
United States v. Pohlot, 827 F.2d 889 (Dist. Ct. Cal. 1987).
United States v. Renfroe, 825 F.2d 763, 766 (3rd. Cir. 1987).
United States v. Riggleman, 411 F.2d 1190 (4th Cir. 1969).
United States v. Schneider, 111 F.3d 197, 201 (1st Cir. 1997).
Valiulis v. Scheffeos, 547 N.E.2d 1289 (Ill. App. Ct. 1989).
Whitaker v. Parker, 42 Iowa 585 (Iowa 1876).
Winnans v. N.Y. & Erie R.R. Co., 62 U.S. 88 (U.S. 1859).
Youtsey v. United States, 97 F. 937, 940 (6th Cir. 1899).

Chapter 4

Negative Response Bias and Malingering during Neuropsychological Assessment in Criminal Forensic Settings

ROBERT L. DENNEY

Interest in malingering within clinical psychology has exploded in the last 10 years. This trend is demonstrated with the results of PsychLit searches for "malingering" among peer reviewed journal articles (Figure 4.1). This trend is likely in response to the recognition that incentive to demonstrate mental impairment in forensic settings can be tremendous. Whereas much of the research has dealt with civil forensic issues, the motivation is no less significant in criminal settings. Rather than large monetary awards, criminal defendants have the understandable motivation to avoid long prison sentences or even execution. Indeed, research exists to suggest criminal defendants facing more serious charges are more likely than those facing lesser charges to exaggerate deficits (Weinborn, Orr, Woods, Conover, & Feix, 2003). Even sentenced inmates oftentimes have incentive to spend their prison sentence in hospitals. Female staff are more prevalent, and greater opportunity for acquiring drugs of abuse exists. Inmates may also find themselves facing dangers that force them to seek a move to another facility. Feigning psychiatric or physical disease and transferring to a hospital for specialized assessment is a possible solution.

There has also been increased recognition that for cognitive test results to be valid, effort on behalf of the examinee is required. Although this recog-

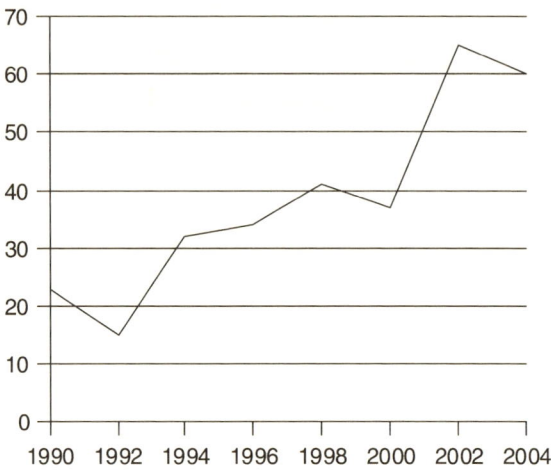

FIGURE 4.1. Number of peer-reviewed malingering-related papers published by year.

nition is not new (e.g., Anastasi, 1961), widespread appreciation of the effect of effort on cognitive test results is more recent. Green, Rohling, Lees-Haley, and Allen (2001) evaluated the performance of a series of 904 patients with head injury and neurological impairment on neuropsychological tests. They found a correlation ($r = .73$) between a well-validated symptom validity test (Word Memory Test [WMT]; Green, 2003) and the overall neuropsychological test battery mean. More strikingly, they found that poor effort suppressed the test battery mean 4.5 times more than did moderate to severe brain injury. In effect, effort has a much greater effect on test scores than does brain injury or a neurological condition. Neuropsychological tests are achievement oriented and require examinee effort to obtain valid results. Consequently, they are extremely susceptible to the influence of poor effort, exaggeration, and feigning.

Researchers also demonstrated that it is virtually impossible to detect malingering reliably without using indices designed to identify it (Faust, Hart, Guilmette, & Arkes, 1988; Heaton, Smith, Lehman, & Vogt, 1978). A new appreciation for the effects of effort on assessment resulted in admonishments to change the manner in which neuropsychological testing is performed in forensic settings. In the Foreword to the WMT (Green, 2003, p. iv), Paul Lees-Haley noted, "Neuropsychological assessments are no longer complete without evaluation of effort." This sentiment has risen to official levels, as evidenced by the position paper on symptom validity testing from the National Academy of Neuropsychology (Bush et al., 2005), which asserts the importance of objectively evaluating evaluee effort in all forensic-related neuropsychological assessments.

The purpose of this chapter is to review important issues regarding assessment of effort and malingering in the context of criminal forensic neuropsychological evaluations. There is great wealth of research dealing with psychiatric symptom exaggeration. Although relevant to neuropsychologists evaluating criminal defendants, the general psychiatric exaggeration literature is too broad to cover in this single chapter. For a broad review regarding detection of deception and malingering, the reader is referred to Boyd, McLearen, Meyer, and Denney (2007) and the classic work by Rogers (2008). For a more comprehensive review and analysis of poor effort and malingering in neuropsychology, I recommend both Boone (2007) and Larrabee (2007). Here I discuss the nature of exaggeration and malingering as it relates to neuropsychology in general, but with specific emphasis on these issues in the criminal forensic setting. I present what is known about the prevalence of malingering; review the accepted classification system and specific measures and strategies for detecting poor effort; address issues of remote memory loss; and conclude with areas of concern and recommendations for future research.

The Nature of Malingering

Malingering, as it relates to neuropsychology, is a clinical determination based on test results and behaviors within a contextual framework. Malingering can be viewed as requiring two components: response bias and conscious intention. *Response bias* is a systematic pattern of performance, such that obtained results do not accurately reflect what the tests are purported to measure. Response bias discloses nothing about the reason for the atypical performance. An example of negative response bias could be something as simple as fatigue. In neuropsychology, we are typically concerned about the possibility of negative response bias rather than positive response bias, because people cannot "fake good" on achievement-oriented testing (it is called "cheating"). Once negative response bias is documented, the conclusion of malingering requires the determination that significant secondary gain is influencing evaluee performance. Because it is a two-part process, I address aspects of negative response bias, then turn to malingering.

Negative Response Bias

Negative response bias (NRB) is a systematically poor performance that is not consistent with genuine neurocognitive compromise. NRB makes no reference to conscious or unconscious motivations. It may arise due to fatigue, anxiety, or the presence of significant psychiatric disturbance. NRB may also arise because of intentional attempts to misrepresent abilities. NRB specifically impacts achievement-oriented test results. Intelligence, academic abilities, and neurocognitive functions, such as attention, concentration, language, visual–spatial learning, memory, abstract reasoning, and problem solving, could all be impacted.

NRB can also take the form of exaggerated self-reports of cognitive impairments or the influence of claimed cognitive impairments of daily functioning. This form of NRB can be identified through inconsistencies between self-report and real-world functioning, and through inconsistencies between real-world functioning and normative-based results on self-report measures.

NRB can also be applied to functioning outside the area of cognitive abilities. Exaggeration of psychosis, anxiety, depression, and dissociation can be presented through self-report measures and overt behavior as well. Studies of the Minnesota Multiphasic Personality Inventory–2 (MMPI-2; Butcher, Dahlstrom, Graham, Tellegen, & Kaemmer, 1989) among forensic populations reveals that this type of exaggeration is less common for neuropsychological evaluations in civil forensic settings (e.g., personal injury), where individuals oftentimes minimize mental health difficulties while highlighting somatic and neurocognitive disability (Lees-Haley, Iverson, Lange, Fox, & Allen, 2002). Nonetheless, NRB can occur with any combination of intellectual or cognitive dullness, specific neurocognitive deficits (e.g., learning or memory), psychiatric manifestations, and general somatic concerns (e.g., neurological and pain). Larrabee (2003b) demonstrated correlations between somatic concerns and cognitive complaints among individuals seeking personal injury claims.

Within neuropsychology, test procedures that have proven reliability and validity may yield scores that are not reliable or valid for a particular individual. Questions can arise because of significant inconsistencies in the test data. These inconsistencies may occur among the following areas:

- ❖ Neuropsychological domains (e.g., impaired attention with normal memory).
- ❖ Test scores and suspected etiology (e.g., impaired IQ with normal memory in hypoxia).
- ❖ Test scores and documented severity of injury (e.g., performance levels characteristic of prolonged coma in traumatic brain injury [TBI] with no actual loss of consciousness).
- ❖ Test scores and behavioral presentation (e.g., failure on measures of recent and remote memory, but ability to report accurate clinical history).

A valuable conceptual model developed by Frederick and presented by Frederick, Crosby, and Wynkoop (2000) is displayed in Figure 4.2. It reveals the fourfold nature of an individual's potential performance across two continua, effort and motivation. Individuals motivated to perform well, and who give their maximum effort, are considered to have provided a compliant and valid performance (upper right quadrant). The remaining three quadrants each represent some form of NRB and are not considered valid reflections of true ability. Individuals who may be motivated to perform well but do not put forth their best effort are classified as *careless*. Their carelessness represents NRB, but in most instances does not represent intentional misrepresentation of ability. Rather, this quadrant likely reflects NRB caused by excessive fatigue or distraction, such as that caused by psychosis or severe headache. However, it may reflect poor effort. The remaining two NRB quadrants indicate individuals who are motivated to perform poorly. Many such individuals do not assert much effort, and their results are best classified as *irrelevant*. These individuals present a picture of cooperation by completing the test, but they are responding in a manner independent of item content (e.g., a random response pattern on the MMPI-2 [Butcher et al., 1989]; irrelevant response pattern on the Validity Indicator Profile [VIP; Frederick, 2003]). Such individuals may later be classified as malingering. At the very

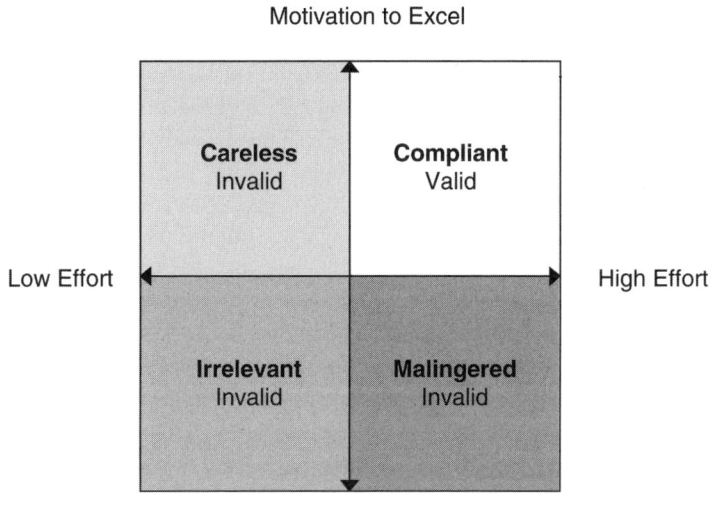

FIGURE 4.2. Fourfold nature of examinee performance. From Frederick (2003). Copyright 2003 by Pearson Assessments. Reprinted by permission.

least, they are noncooperative with the evaluation. The final quadrant represents malingering in its truest form. These individuals are not only motivated to perform poorly but they also put forth effort to perform poorly. This pattern of performance is most clearly demonstrated with below-random responding on forced-choice tests.

Variable effort and motivation can sometimes be secondary to factors outside the examinee's conscious intent or control, such as those found in severe depression and anxiety, as well as somatoform disorder. They can also be under conscious intent and control, such as factors found in factitious disorder and malingering. Factitious disorder and malingering share intentional, volitional distortion or misrepresentation of symptoms, but factitious disorder requires the determination that the subject has a psychological need to assume the sick role (primary gain). Malingering requires the contextual determination that the subject's motivation is for secondary gain, such as obtaining financial compensation or avoiding criminal prosecution.

Malingering

In contrast to the other forms of NRB, *malingering* is the "intentional production of false or grossly exaggerated physical or psychological symptoms, motivated by external incentives such as avoiding military duty, avoiding work, obtaining financial compensation, evading criminal prosecution, or obtaining drugs" (American Psychiatric Association, 2000, p. 739). Rogers (2008) provided a discussion of the possible explanatory models, noting a history of believing that individuals who malinger are mentally disordered. This *pathological* model arose from the explanations of behavior espoused by psychoanalytic thinkers. Rogers also described a second explanatory model that focused on individual character. In contrast to the pathological model, in which malingerers deceive because of some intrapsychic pathology, the *criminological* model emphasizes the propensity for antisocial and psychopathic personalities to lie, cheat, and steal.

The pathological model arose because of the clinical observation that many people considered to be malingering were also noted to have antisocial or sociopathic personality disorders. This view espouses that people with antisocial personality disorder are more prone to malinger because of their propensity to lie. The model, which appears to lack substantial empirical support, appears to be the current view of contributors to the *Diagnostic and Statistical Manual of Mental Disorders*, fourth edition, text revision (DSM-IV-TR; American Psychiatric Association, 2000), where it is suggested that malingering should be "strongly suspected" when any combination of the following are noted: (1) a medicolegal context; (2) marked discrepancy between subjective claims and objective findings; (3) lack of cooperation; and (4) presence of antisocial personality disorder (p. 739). In contrast to these pathological and "bad" models of malingering, Rogers (2008) also proposed an *adaptational* model, whereby malingering individuals are considered to be basically normal people attempting to meet their needs in adversarial circumstances. These individuals perform a cost–benefit analysis when confronted with an assessment perceived as indifferent to or in opposition to their needs. Research seems to support this finding, because the base rates for NRB and malingering appear to be high in adversarial contexts such as personal injury litigation (Larrabee, 2003a), Social Security Disability litigation (Chavez, Abrahams, & Kohlmaier, 2007), and criminal litigation (Ardolf, Denney, & Houston, 2007; Denney, 2007). Furthermore, research suggests that as the potential for greater gains increases, the rates of NRB increase (Bianchini, Curtis, & Greve, 2006). Personal stakes can be high in the adversarial context, and for many people there are no other perceived viable alternatives than to feign or exaggerate illness.

Prevalence Rates

Diagnostic accuracy is dependent, in large part, on one's awareness of prevalence rates for the suspected condition in the relevant population (Baldessarini, Finkelstein, & Arana, 1983; Elwood, 1993). It is no less a concern in the area of malingering detection (Gouvier, Hayes, & Smiroldo, 1998; Rosenfeld, Sands, & Van Gorp, 2000). Indeed, ignorance of such information appears to contribute to the difficulty of malingering detection and misclassification in general (Labarge, McCaffrey, & Brown, 2003; Rosenfeld et al., 2000). There should be no expectation that malingering styles or base rates will remain stable across evaluation settings. Furthermore, there should be no expectation that rates are the same in civil and criminal areas. Rates may even vary within the criminal setting depending on the context (sentenced inmates seeking hospitalization vs. criminal pretrial defendants) and severity of crime and sentence (potential 5-year vs. life sentence). This type of "dose–response relationship" has been found in the civil litigation (workers compensation) arena (Bianchini et al., 2006). Before addressing what little is known about malingering prevalence rates in the criminal setting, I briefly review what is known about those rates in the civil setting.

NRB in Civil Forensic Settings

Mittenberg, Patton, Canyock, and Condit (2002) surveyed members of the American Board of Clinical Neuropsychology regarding the number of times they diagnosed malingering over the course of the previous year. Mean estimated rates of "probable malingering or symptom exaggeration" were between 28 and 33% for personal injury, disability, and workers' compensation cases. This survey appears to have relied on clinicians' recollection of the number of times they identified NRB. This finding may be weakened by fading memory, as well as possibly less than thorough NRB evaluation efforts by a portion of the membership in the first place. Larrabee (2003a) combined results of 11 different malingering studies of over 1,350 civil litigants (for more information about these studies, see Ardolf et al., 2007). He found an overall 40% base rate of NRB among civil forensic cases, with a range from 15 to 64.3%. Consistent with those findings, Chavez and colleagues (2007) evaluated 232 consecutive Social Security Disability referrals and found an NRB rate of 55.8% using the Test of Memory Malingering (TOMM; Tombaugh, 1996), and 61.4% using the Medical Symptom Validity Test (MSVT; Green, 2004). These studies suggest substantial rates of NRB in the civil forensic arena, but much less literature exists regarding NRB in the criminal forensic setting, particularly related to neurocognitive concerns.

NRB in Criminal Forensic Settings

Little is known about the prevalence of NRB in the criminal forensic arena, and much of that information deals with exaggeration of general psychiatric issues. Rogers (1986) identified rates of 20% for suspected malingering and 4.5% for "definite malingering" among criminal defendants. Cornell and Hawk (1989) considered 8% of their pretrial criminal defendants to be feigning psychosis. Lewis, Simcox, and Berry (2002) identified a rate of 31.4% for feigned psychiatric presentation among pretrial criminal defendants.

These studies dealt with general psychiatric presentation. Even fewer studies exist for exaggerated neurocognitive deficit in the criminal population. The Mittenberg and colleagues (2002) survey included estimates of neuropsychological exaggeration for criminal referrals as well, with the mean falling between 19 and 23%, depending on whether cases were referred by the defense or the prosecution. Rates of malingering conclusions were lower when cases were referred by the defense. Frederick and Denney (1998) estimated a 25% prevalence of below-random responding assessed by forced-choice recognition tests for individuals claiming amnesia in a criminal forensic setting. Ardolf and colleagues (2007) reviewed data from 105 presentence criminal defendants who had been referred by the U.S. District Courts for mental health evaluation of their competency to undergo criminal proceedings. These cases were unique in that all had some question regarding their cognitive status and underwent neuropsychological evaluation. These cases varied greatly in their referral diagnoses, as one would expect in a consecutive series of cases. Each defendant was evaluated with multiple measures of NRB (free-standing and imbedded validity indices). Although all cases did not receive all of the same measures, use of multiple measures allowed for use of various NRB and malingering classification schemes, including Slick, Sherman, and Iverson's (1999) multimodal, multidimensional classification of malingered neurocognitive dysfunction (MND).

Ardolf and colleagues (2007) found that 89.5% of their criminal defendants scored positively on at least one measure of NRB, 70.5% of the defendants scored positively on two or more indicators, and 53% of cases scored positively on three or more indicators. Use of the Slick and colleagues (1999) criteria resulted in a 54% rate of MND classification (combined 32% probable and 22% definite; i.e., below-random performance). The Slick and colleagues classification takes into account possible false-positive findings, as well as indications of invalidity of test results apart from the validity indices (e.g., discrepancy between test data and observed behavior, and indications of invalidity due to self-report). As a result, the classification system attempts to avoid both false positives and false negatives, and provides what appears to be a robust estimate of neurocognitive malingering in the criminal forensic venue.

I (Denney, 2007) returned to the previous neuropsychological data, which had increased from 105 to 118 pretrial criminal defendants during the intervening time. I then extracted only those cases with complaints of mild to moderate TBI and obtained data on 67 of them (22.4% moderate and 77.6% mild). As with the larger database, defendants were administered a variety of NRB detection strategies: 73.1% of the defendants were positive on two or more NRB indices (previously 70.5%). Use of the Slick and colleagues (1999) classification system resulted in a combined rate of probable and definite MND of 62.7% rather than the 54.3% rate of the previous heterogeneous pathology data. These rates are similar to the NRB rates found in Social Security Disability evaluations by Chavez and colleagues (2007). Although one can argue that the Slick and colleagues classification system has yet to be validated as an accurate predictor of MND, the results clearly indicate a greater than 50% rate of NRB occurrence in presentence criminal defendants referred for neuropsychological evaluation.

Why Is the Base Rate of Malingering Important?

Diagnostic accuracy is clearly an important endeavor. Psychological tests help in this pursuit of accuracy; however, even the most reliable and valid test has error. That error interacts with the base rates of the condition in any given population. Diagnostic accuracy, then, requires an understanding of the predictive characteristics of the tests we use within a specific population (Baldessarini et al., 1983; Gouvier et al., 1998; Rosenfeld et al., 2000). Neglecting base rate information appears to contribute to the difficulty of malingering detection and misclassification in general (Labarge et al., 2003; Rosenfeld et al., 2000). Identifying the base rate for malingering among criminal defendants referred for neuropsychological evaluations is important, because it sheds light on the predictive value of the malingering detection method used. Establishing a base rate in one's setting may be difficult initially, because it requires (1) the use of NRB indicators on a regular basis over an extended period of time, and (2) a systematic review of that data. Results from my NRB test data (Ardolf et al., 2007; Denney, 2007) suggest that the base rate in the population of male criminal defendants referred for neuropsychological assessment is over 50%.

The importance of a rise in prevalence rates beyond 50% cannot be overstated, because it has relevance for classification confidence. The difference in diagnostic certainty, as it relates to classification accuracy between a low base rate phenomenon and a high base rate phenomenon, is easily demonstrated. First, we must remember test sensitivity (i.e., cases with the diagnosis that have a positive test finding[1]) and specificity (nonimpaired cases that have a negative test finding[2]) are unique to the instrument and do not vary based on prevalence of disorder. The hit rate index refers to the overall correct classification ability of the instrument and is identified as (true positives + true negatives)/N. Predictive value statistics, such as positive predictive value (PPV) and negative predictive value (NPV), incorporate the prevalence of disorder (Baldesserini et al., 1983). PPV is determined by true positives/(true positives + false positives). NPV is determined by true negatives/(true negatives + false negatives). Baldesserini and colleagues (1983) provide these formulas for computing PPV and NPV, incorporating test sensitivity (x), specificity (y), and base rate (prevalence, p):

$$PPV = (px)/[(px) + (1 - p)(1 - y)]$$
$$NPV = [(1 - p)y]/[(1 - p)y + p(1 - x)]$$

Although seemingly complicated, it is really not difficult. Let us assume a reasonably accurate malingering instrument, or combination of instruments, that have a sensitivity of .80 and specificity of .90. In a base rate setting of 20% positive findings, PPV is .667 and NPV is .947. Here, one has more diagnostic confidence in the negative findings. This confidence significantly changes as the base rate changes, however. In a base rate setting of 70% positive findings, PPV is .949 and NPV is .659. Here we have much more confidence in our positive findings, and strikingly less confidence in negative findings. This change in our confidence occurred because the prevalence of the condition (here, NRB) changed from well below 50% to above 50%. As prevalence nears 50%, our confidence in positive and negative findings more closely approximates the sensitivity and specificity of the measure without the influence of prevalence. Knowledge of prevalence rates does not change the accuracy of the test, but it does change *confidence* in the test findings. My data suggest that the base rate of MND among criminal defendants with neurocognitive concerns is well over 50% (possibly over 70%). In this setting, positive findings on NRB indices are quite convincing. Negative results, however, are not as definitive.

Malingered Neuropsychological Dysfunction Classification

Slick and colleagues (1999; hereafter called Slick criteria) proposed diagnostic criteria for MND that includes possible, probable, and definite classifications. This multidimensional approach incorporates several criteria: presence of substantial external incentive; evidence from neuropsychological testing, including negative response bias; and evidence from self-report. Finally, it incorporates a rule-out criterion for the evaluator to consider possible psychological, neurological, or psychiatric reasons for the unusual behavior. Evidence coming from neuropsychological testing is considered for NRB. The finding of NRB does not equate to malingering, it is one of the requirements for malingering. MND requires the presence of a substantial external incentive. *Probable MND* is defined as positive findings on one or more well-validated psychometric tests or indices designed to measure exaggeration or fabrication of cognitive deficits, such that it is consistent with feigning along with inconsistencies from other sources. *Definite MND* is defined as below-chance performance ($p < .05$) on one or more forced-choice measures of cognitive function. Millis (2004) reviewed the Slick criteria and developed a decision tree to assist evaluators in applying the multidimensional model in the assessment setting (Figure 4.3). Larrabee, Greiffenstein, Greve, and Bianchini (2007) discuss recommendations for improvement and validation of this classification system.

Below-Random Performance and Definite Malingering

The Slick criteria differentiate between NRB and malingering. This distinction is important, because the conclusion of malingering must always be clinical; that is, it takes into consideration contextual aspects of the evalua-

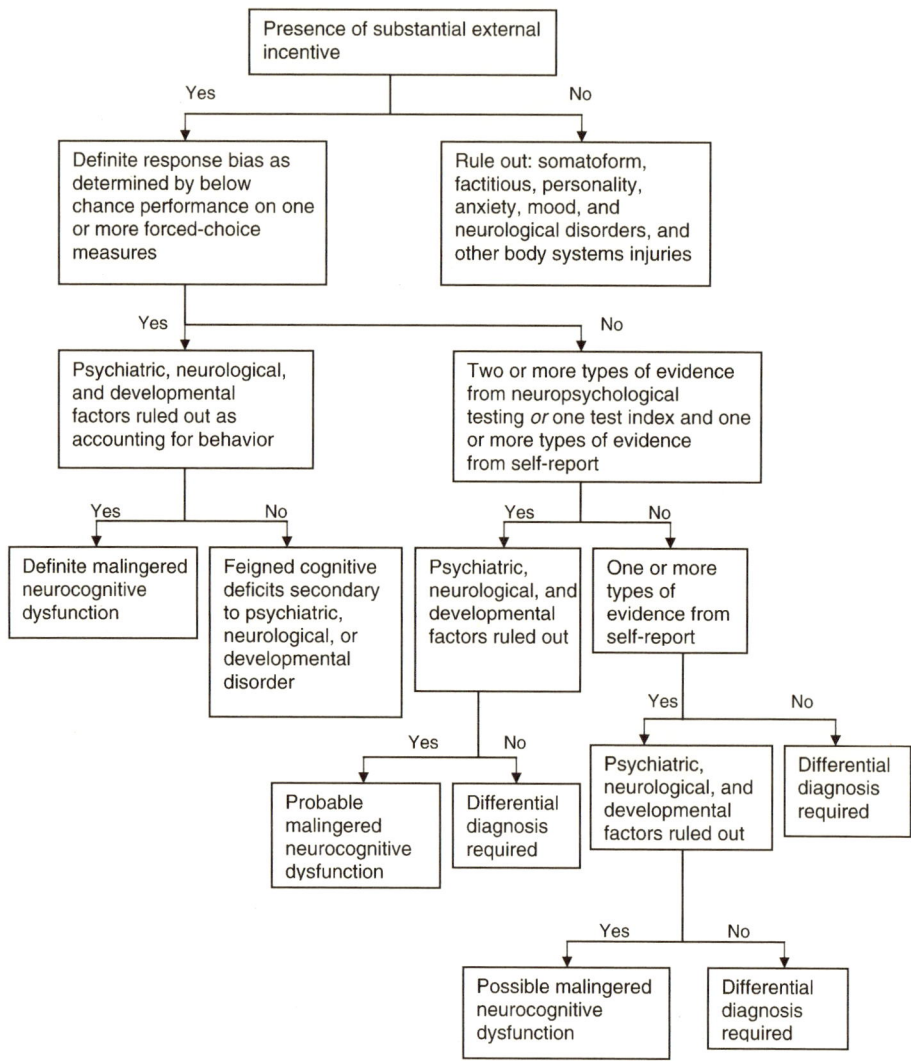

FIGURE 4.3. Diagnostic decision tree for malingered neurocognitive dysfunction. From Millis (2004). Copyright 2004 by W. B. Saunders. Adapted by permission.

tion and clinical judgment. Definite NRB is demonstrated from test results (i.e., below-random performance on a forced-choice measure), whereas definite MND requires a clinical conclusion, even in the presence of below random performance. See Frederick and Speed (2007) for a cogent discussion about the meaning of below random findings on forced-choice tests. The field is currently debating whether below random performance *definitively* indicates willful misrepresentation. Boone (2007) notes the history of the paradigm and points out that it was initially developed to identify conversion disorders. She also notes that published clinical cases demonstrated severe cognitive impairment and no incentive to feign deficits, but significantly below random performance on two-alternative, forced-choice testing. Her argument raises two issues: (1) It is theoretically possible for individuals to perform below random because of purportedly unconscious processes; (2) severely compromised individuals can perform below random occasionally. The second issue might be straightforward and has a statistical explanation. Using $p < .05$ as the cutoff for below-random performance indicates there will be five false-positive findings for every 100 performances from individuals who have *truly no cognitive capability* on the test. We must keep in mind, however, that we never administer these tests to individuals who truly have no ability. The issue of unconscious motivation is understandably much more murky. Results still reveal misrepresentation, but the question remains whether or not it was willful.

I (Denney, 1999) noted that below-random performance demonstrates ability and suggested that it was the most definitive indication of malingering in the context of litigation. I also raised the concern that because "symptom validity testing was originally designed to detect conversion syndromes, one cannot automatically cry malingering when suppressed scores occur" (p. 16). There is some indication, however, that the "conversion disordered" individuals used in the development of the paradigm (Brady & Lind, 1961; Grosz & Zimmerman, 1965; Theodor & Mandelcorn, 1973; Zimmerman & Grosz, 1966) may have been feigning, but the behavior was considered unconsciously motivated given the *zeitgeist* of the time. Pankratz (1979; Pankratz, Fausti, & Peed, 1975) was one of the first to adapt the strategy to neurocognitive functioning and described below-random results as a possible "smoking gun of intent" (Pankratz & Erickson, 1990, p. 385). Bianchini, Mathias, and Greve (2001) suggested that such suppression was clearly indicative of feigning. Larrabee and colleagues (2007) reviewed the issue again and concluded "the interpretation of a significantly below-chance result as definitive evidence of *intentional* exaggeration of cognitive deficits even in the context of objective pathology has become well established in the neuropsychological literature" (p. 346, original emphasis). Given the age-old difficulty with defining and measuring unconscious processes, the contribution of unconscious motivation to below-random performance will undoubtedly remain unclear. Nonetheless, current literature indicates that the field is largely in agreement regarding the significance of below-random performance from individuals in litigation.

Thankfully, both Boone (2007; Boone & Lu, 2003) and Larrabee (2003a, 2005) have demonstrated that below-random performance on two-alternative, forced-choice testing may not be the only definitive test finding regarding NRB classification. Effort tests are developed to have very low false-positive rates (i.e., their specificity rates are kept high, generally greater than 90%). Because the false-positive rate is at or less than 10%, tests can be used in concert to increase diagnostic certainty substantially. Presuming a minimal amount of correlation between tests, positive findings on multiple tests significantly decrease the possibility of false-positive findings (e.g., $.10 \times .10 \times .10 = .001$). In other words, positive results on three NRB indices suggest a less than 1 in 1,000 chance of a false-positive finding. Although it is clear that some level of correlation occurs between NRB tests (Nelson, Boone, Dueck, Wagener, Lu, & Grills, 2003), these correlations are likely kept to a minimum by incorporation of multiple measures from different cognitive domains or testing paradigms (e.g., verbal vs. visual memory, free-standing measures vs. imbedded indices). Accuracy of specificity rates is limited when tests have not been validated using individuals with severe, and specific, cognitive pathology. In this regard it is important for the clinician to understand how well the proposed pathology of the criminal defendant corresponds to validation samples of the particular NRB index. I believe this is the greatest area of weakness regarding the assessment of malingering at this time.

Assessment of Malingering

The detection of deception is a difficult endeavor under any circumstance (Boyd et al., 2007). However, it is made extremely difficult when neuropsychologists rely solely on behavioral clues (Ekman, 1992). Similarly, limitations of subjective clinical judgment necessitate use of objective measures of invalidity and effort during the assessment of neurocognitive function (Bigler, 1990; Faust & Guilmette, 1990; Faust et al., 1988; Heaton et al., 1978). Consequently, neuropsychologists must incorporate objective measures when assessing malingering of neurocognitive and psychiatric impairment. I first review free-standing measures of NRB, then address NRB indices within common neuropsychological tests and batteries.

Free-Standing Measures of NRB

Each of the following measures of NRB has different characteristics. An important consideration is the apparent face validity of each. For example, some measures are based on general intellectual ability, whereas others are based on visual or verbal memory. Although some of these procedures may be termed "floor effect" tests in that they actually measure only a modest level of ability, they, nonetheless, have face validity to the evaluee. In this regard, subjects who wish to exaggerate deficits in certain neurocognitive functions (consistent with their understanding of what true pathology looks like) will likely not exaggerate in every functional domain. This distinction becomes important when psychologists evaluate the meaningfulness of NRB test results. Furthermore, this distinction may explain why certain types of procedures appear to be more sensitive than others. Individuals attempting to deceive an evaluator will likely not suppress every task they perform, because it may too easily appear disingenuous. They suppress the function they see as most likely to appear legitimate based on their understanding of their proposed pathology, as well as specific forensic demands (e.g., competency to stand trial related abilities). Finally, NRB measures differ in their level of transparency as a malingering detection device, which likely affects their sensitivity as well.

General Intellectual Ability

VALIDITY INDICATOR PROFILE

The Validity Indicator Profile (VIP; Frederick, 2003) is unique for several reasons. It is a measure based on verbal and nonverbal intelligence; it combines two-alternative, forced-choice structure with performance curve analysis due to progressive item difficulty; and it establishes a fourfold classification system of performance (compliant, inconsistent, irrelevant, and suppressed). Developed with items adapted from intelligence tests, it assesses general, intellect-related functions and not memory. The nonverbal test can be administered separately from the verbal test for those who cannot read. It uses six different classification strategies developed with a sample of more than 1,000 clinical and nonclinical subjects. It was cross-validated with an independent sample of 312 individuals in five criterion groups: TBI patients; suspected malingerers; normal subjects; simulators; and random responders. In his own review of the test, Frederick (2002) reported sensitivity/specificity rates of 73.5/85.7 for the nonverbal subtest and 67.3/83.1 for the verbal subtest during cross-validation. Frederick suggested that these rates were underestimates of test performance because of criterion group contamination. The VIP is a breakthrough in attempting to understand the nature of malingering as more than simply a dichotomous occurrence, because it takes into consideration motivation and effort. In addition, there are no other free-standing NRB indices specific to general intellectual function.

As a result of this last consideration, the measure can actually provide an estimate of a person's intellectual range of ability. This estimate can be provided when the subject is motivated to perform well and provides adequate effort; it is also available when subjects are motivated to perform poorly and suppress their scores below random performance. By the nature of the binomial theorem, below-random scores indicate just as much ability as above-random scores (Denney, 1999), which can then estimate intellectual ability in the case of the VIP. This characteristic of the VIP was validated in the development samples by correlating it with the Shipley Institute of Living Scale (Zachary, 1986). I have found this test helpful when criminal defendants are claiming mental retardation and are suppressing their scores below random. In these instances, defendants occasionally suppress their score so low that they actually demonstrate intellectual abilities well above that of mental retardation.

A word of caution is needed regarding the use of the VIP with individuals presenting with possible mental retardation. The VIP was validated on 40 nonlitigating subjects with mental retardation (MR) (Frederick, 2003). Subjects were determined to have IQs between 54 and 75, based on Shipley estimates (Zachary, 1986). Twenty subjects' IQs were below 65. There was a clear relationship between IQ and VIP classification, because those with Compliant classifications had higher IQs than those classified as Inconsistent. Those classified as Inconsistent had higher IQs than those classified as Irrelevant. Thirty-two of the 40 subjects with MR produced results considered invalid on the Nonverbal subtest, and 30 subjects produced invalid results on the Verbal subtest. Most obtained results were classified as Inconsistent and Irrelevant. Only one subject produced a suppressed result, and this occurred on the Verbal subtest. These findings have resulted in the recommendation not to use the VIP with individuals who have a bona fide history of MR. However, the manual indicates that it is appropriate to use the VIP with individuals who present themselves as having MR but have no historical documentation to support that conclusion.

DOT COUNTING TEST

The Dot Counting Test (DCT) was originally developed by André Rey (1941) as a method to identify individuals attempting to feign TBI. Frederick (2002) reviewed the history of the DCT and presented Rey's original ideas regarding the procedure. The procedure incorporates 12 cards with dots arranged in various patterns. The first set comprises six cards with dots arranged in random patterns, whereas the latter set has six cards with dots arranged in clear groupings. Individuals are asked to count the dots as quickly as they can as each card is presented. Classically, performance times were compared between grouped and ungrouped cards, on the assumption that disingenuous subjects inadvertently perform too slowly when counting grouped dots compared to ungrouped dots (Frederick, 2002; Frederick, Sarfaty, Johnston, & Powel, 1994). There have also been other variations in scoring methods, typically dealing with the number of errors in counting (Binks, Gouvier, & Waters, 1997; Lee et al., 2000; Paul, Franzen, Cohen, & Fremouw, 1992).

There have been numerous studies of the DCT with simulators, clinical, and forensic samples. Vickery, Berry, Inman, Harris, and Orey (2001) performed a meta-analysis of six studies and concluded the DCT was not particularly effective at differentiating between simulators and honest responders. Boone, Lu, and Herzberg (2002) developed a formula (mean ungrouped time + mean grouped time + number of errors) and found it to be a sensitive index for detecting individuals with noncredible symptoms from different settings. This formula was then formalized as the Effort Index, or "E-score," in the later standardized test publication (Boone et al., 2002). The studies on which this published version is based include a number of normal-effort clinical groups including persons with depression, schizophrenia, head injury, stroke, learning disability, and mild dementia. With the various groups come differing cutoff scores to maintain specificity rates near .90. With these groups, the DCT has an average sensitivity of 78.8%. It is currently not recommended for differentiating feigning persons from those with moderate dementia (Boone et al., 2002) or MR (Marshall & Happe, 2001; Victor & Boone, 2007).

Short-Term Memory

REY 15-ITEM MEMORY TEST

The Rey 15-Item Memory Test (FIT; Rey, 1958) is the most widely known of Rey's malingering tests. It is a simple memory procedure that takes little time to complete and has received a great deal of research attention. Frederick (2002) reviewed the procedure and found sensitivity rates to vary from 40 to 89% depending on the cutoff, with specificity generally placing in the middle to upper .90's. There appeared to be a difference in test performance between civil litigants and criminal defendants. Boone, Salazar, Lu, Warner-Chacon, and Razani (2002) reviewed the test and found sensitivities ranging from 7 to 72% for volunteer simulators, and from 5 to 72% for clinical samples of patients in litigation and those suspected of malingering. Reznek (2005) performed a meta-analysis and found the FIT to have an overall sensitivity of only 36% using the standard cutoff. Nitch and Glassmire (2007) reviewed studies pertaining to the FIT and found sensitivities between 5 and 86% (M = 41.13) using the same standard cutoff. The mean sensitivity for suspected malingerers in clinical settings was 44.2%. Only three of those studies dealt with criminal suspected malingerers (Frederick et al., 1994; King, 1992; Simon, 1994). Sensitivities among these criminals ranged from 43 to 86%, with a mean of 66.33%. It appears the test may be more sensitive among criminal defendants.

Boone and her colleagues (2002) developed a recognition test to add to the FIT, which raised the sensitivity to 71% over the rather modest sensitivity of 47% in a known groups, civil litigation design. This change in the procedure adds little additional time to a test that is already quite time-efficient. There have been no studies of the procedure's effectiveness in the criminal setting using this additional modification. Vallabhajosula and van Gorp (2001) suggested that the procedure, as originally developed, would not meet *Daubert* (*Daubert v. Merrell Dow Pharmaceuticals, Inc.*, 1993) court admissibility standards because of low sensitivity, but Frederick (2002) suggested that it is a reasonable procedure to use so long as it is not used in isolation. Although sensitivity has been somewhat low, the procedure has been generally considered quite good.

Reznek (2005) performed a meta-analysis and found the FIT to have an overall specificity of 85% using the standard cutoff. A 90% specificity rate was obtained if cases with MR were removed. From a conceptual perspective, however, pooling various neuropathologies with psychiatric referrals and normal controls to obtain a global specificity rate is less than fully meaningful, because the procedure clearly has higher specificity rates with mild head injuries compared to severe injuries and dementing illnesses. Nitch and Glassmire (2007) reviewed the procedure's specificity using the standard cutoff over a wide variety of studies and patient groups. As expected, there was such striking variability between groups that the authors recommended caution when using the test to evaluate cases of strongly suspected genuine memory disorder, dementia, stroke, low intelligence, poor education, and psychosis.

FORCED-CHOICE DIGIT RECOGNITION TESTS

The Portland Digit Recognition Test (PDRT; Binder, 1990; Binder & Willis, 1991), the Computerized Assessment of Response Bias (CARB; Allen, Conder, Green, & Cox, 1997), and the Victoria Symptom Validity Test (VSVT; Slick, Hopp, Strauss, & Thompson, 1997) are all forced-choice, digit recognition tests patterned after the Hiscock Digit Memory Test (Hiscock & Hiscock, 1989). In each of these procedures individuals view a five-digit number and are required to recognize the correct number after a delay. There are three distinct series of presentations, each with longer delay times. The increased delays included in each series make the items appear more difficult. The PDRT incorporates a counting backward distraction task during the delays. The PDRT requires about 40 minutes to administer, although an abbreviated form has been developed for individuals who appear to be performing well (Binder, 1993). Binder (2002) reviewed the procedure and noted that sensitivity rates varied from 39 to 77% depending on the type of subject, whereas specificity rates held constant at 100%. In a meta-analytic review of six studies using the PDRT, Vickery and colleagues (2001) found the measure to have intermediate sensitivity (44%) but excellent specificity (97.3%). Greve and Bianchini (2006a) evaluated the effectiveness of the PDRT with a known-groups design that comprised 262 TBI referrals classified on Slick and colleagues (1999) criteria for MND. They concluded that the original cutoff scores for the PDRT were too conservative, because the sensitivity was only .20–.50. Using a lower total score cutoff, they were able to demonstrate a sensitivity rate of 70% while holding to a 95% specificity rate.

The CARB is similar to the PDRT, but it is computer administered. It has three forms, the 111-item original (Conder, Allen, & Cox, 1992), the 72-item CARB-97 (Allen et al., 1997), and a shorter length variation (Green & Iverson, 2001). It can also be set to provide correct–incorrect feedback via color and tone for each trial and even to discontinue after a perfect performance on the first trial. Subjects are asked to count backward from 20 during the delay periods. The CARB uses DOS-based software and has a poorly written manual (Wynkoop & Denney, 2001). The test publisher has a website that purports to provide a Windows version of the test and ongoing software updates; however, this site repeatedly did not function. Allen, Iverson, and Green (2002) reviewed the development and characteristics of the CARB but gave no specific sensitivity or specificity rates. The great benefit of the CARB, however, is that it includes norm references that allow the examiner to compare the subject's performance to known groups of patients with neurological, amnestic, and severe brain injury. Oftentimes, this comparison by itself provides substantial indication of poor subject effort due to presence of clear inconsistency between test results and activities of daily living. Studies supporting the validity of the CARB are not clearly understood beyond the striking finding that larger percentages of litigating persons with disability fail the procedure compared to subjects with more severe brain injuries. Given the research with individuals with moderate and severe TBI, the test appears rather insensitive to brain damage (Conder,

Allen, & Cox, 1992). The mean total CARB score was 96.8% correct with moderate and severe brain injury. When Allen and Green (1999) administered the CARB to 56 patients with severe TBI, the total CARB score correct mean was 98.3%. Green and Allen (1999) also reported results for 40 patients with mixed neurological disease, with a mean total CARB score of 97.2%. Overall, these studies indicate that the CARB is not sensitive to brain damage when subjects are otherwise testable.

There are no specific reports of research directed at the sensitivity of the CARB. Gervais, Rohling, Green, and Ford (2004) compared the CARB with the WMT and TOMM using 519 non-head-injured personal injury and disability claimants. They found that twice as many individuals failed the WMT compared to the TOMM, with CARB results falling in between. They concluded that the CARB was less sensitive than the WMT, but more sensitive than the TOMM. Nitch and Glassmire (2007), in their review, conclude that the CARB appears to be "limited by its negative predictive power; consequently, false negatives may be common" (p. 64).

The VSVT (Slick et al., 1997) is also computer administered, but unlike the CARB it is published by a well-known test publisher and runs well in Windows. The VSVT program presents a total of 48 items over three trials of 16 items. The three trials have increasing delay times before the subject is required to recognize the presented five-digit number from a foil. Also unlike the PDRT or CARB, subjects do not have distraction activities during the delay periods. Uniquely, the VSVT incorporates what appears to be easy items and difficult items by having foils completely different from the stimuli for the easy items and foils only minimally different from the stimuli. While giving the appearance of increased difficulty to the examinee, research demonstrates no actual increase in difficulty between easy and difficult items with non-compensation-seeking neurological patients (Slick et al., 1997). Classification of test results is based solely on the binomial theorem by labeling performance above random (valid), random (questionable), or below random (invalid) for easy, difficult, and total scores. Finally, the program allows for printing of graphs with comparison groups.

There are few findings regarding test sensitivity with the VSVT, because most studies have used a differential prevalence design. Tan, Slick, Strauss, and Hultsch (2002) performed a simulation study with undergraduates. VSVT difficult item scores accurately classified 96% of malingerers. They found that combining easy and difficult items resulted in 100% classification of malingerers and controls.

The original development studies did not include individuals with severe brain injury, because the neurological group comprised non-compensation-seeking patients with seizure disorders. Slick and colleagues (2003) presented VSVT data on six non-compensation-seeking individuals with severe memory disorder (anterior cerebral artery aneurysm, Korsakoff syndrome, anoxia, and epilepsy). None of these subjects' performance was below 22 out of 24 correct for the difficult items, and all obtained 100% correct for the easy items. These results are clearly limited by small sample size. Macciocchi, Seel, Alderson, and Godsall (2006) administered the VSVT to 71 individuals with acute, severe brain injury and found that nearly all subjects (96%) scored better than 44 out of 48 correct on the combined easy and difficult items. They noted that only those individuals with severe visual–perceptual and verbal fluency deficits performed poorly. They suggested that the computer classification system was too conservative and provided alternative cutoffs. These studies suggest that the VSVT is quite resistant to the effects of brain damage in general.

In contrast to these results, Loring, Larrabee, Lee, and Meador (2007) presented VSVT data for various neurological cases evaluated in a medical setting (50 dementia, 38 cerebrovascular, 19 multiple sclerosis, and 27 mixed pathology). There were unacceptably high rates of test failure (i.e., less than .90 specificity) using the criteria of less than 18 out of 24 correct for difficult items among all their clinical groups (22% dementia, 18% clinical TBI, 15% memory complaints, 16% cerebrovascular, 11% multiple sclerosis, and 11% mixed neurological). However, they did find significantly poorer performances in the compensation-seeking cases. Grote and colleagues (2000) obtained a 93.3% specificity rate using 90% correct on difficult items with 30 non-compensation-seeking patients with epilepsy. Loring, Lee, and Meador (2005) found a 71.6% specificity rate among 120 patients with epilepsy using the same cutoff and a 75% specificity rate using the binomial theorem–based cutoff of "questionable validity." It was unclear how many of the Loring and colleagues cases may have been seeking compensation, because theirs was a retrospective study. The VSVT has been studied in Spain (Vilar-López et al., 2007) and appears to have similar effectiveness in a non-English-speaking population. Clearly, there is variability in VSVT findings with clinical groups. Additional known-group studies are needed to establish optimal cutoffs that maintain specificity rates of .90 or greater.

TEST OF MEMORY MALINGERING

The Test of Memory Malingering (TOMM; Tombaugh, 1996) is also a two-alternative, forced-choice test of memory, but it uses line drawings rather than digits. There are three trials of the TOMM. Trial 1 is a learning trial in which all pictures are presented and the subject immediately completes a recognition task. The pictures are then presented again in Trial 2, with the subject again performing an immediate recognition task. There is then a 15-minute delay recognition task (Retention). The TOMM manual suggests that evaluators may wish to forgo the Retention trial if subjects have performed well on Trial 2; however, Greve and Bianchini (2006b) found that doing so resulted in a 3% decrease in test sensitivity.

Initial development simulation studies with undergraduates revealed 84 and 88% detection rates for simulators, with a 100% specificity rate using the recommended cutoffs (Tombaugh, 1996, 2002). A follow-up study using patients with TBI in litigation resulted in 77% correct classification rate, and specificity dropped to still a respectable 90% when including severely impaired neurological patients (Tombaugh, 1996, 2002). Teichner and Wagner (2004) evaluated the performance of the TOMM in elderly patients with cognitive impairment and dementia. Patients with cognitive impairments did not differ significantly from cognitively intact patients (92.7 vs. 100% normal performance, respectively). The false-positive rate for patients with dementia, however, was considered unacceptably high, with false-positive rates of 76% using the standard cutoff for Trial 2. There appears to be little effect from depression and anxiety for community-dwelling older adults (Ashendorf, Constantinou, & McCaffrey, 2004; Yanez, Fremouw, Tennant, Strunk, & Coker, 2006) nor from moderate to severe pain (Etherton, Bianchini, Greve, & Ciota, 2005).

Delain, Stafford, and Ben-Porath (2003) reviewed the performance of the TOMM in a sample of pretrial criminal defendants, and results appeared to support the test's validity in that setting. In a differential prevalence design, Weinborn and colleagues (2003) found that criminal defendants referred for pretrial mental health evaluations were more likely to demonstrate below-cutoff performances on the TOMM than were criminal defendants adjudicated not guilty by reason of insanity (and presumably wanting to perform their best for possible release). Although a number of studies demonstrate the utility of the TOMM in the civil forensic arena, these results also suggest that it is a valid indicator of poor effort among criminal defendants. The TOMM appears to perform as well in at least some Spanish-speaking populations as it does in English-speaking North American populations (Vilar-López et al., 2007).

WORD MEMORY TEST

The WMT (Green, 2003; Green, Allen, & Astner, 1996) is unique in the area of malingering tests, in that it is a forced-choice, two-alternative procedure that also includes legitimate memory assessment for words and word pairs. This computer-administered test automatically calculates z-score comparisons to over 2,800 individuals of various ages and diagnoses that most closely correspond to characteristics of the subject's performance. Comparison groups can also be selected by the administrator. It can be computer-administered in nine languages. Green and colleagues (2002) noted the WMT demonstrates overall sensitivity rates of about 97% and specificity rates of 100% for simulation studies. Tan and colleagues (2002), in an undergraduate simulation study, found the WMT to have 92.6% sensitivity and 100% specificity at recommended cutoffs.

There have been numerous studies of the WMT with subjects with significant neuropathology; however, the findings are difficult to interpret (Green, Iverson, & Allen, 1999; Green et al., 2002; Green, Rohling, Lees-Haley, & Allen, 2001). Results of these studies seem to suggest that more individuals with mild brain injuries fail the WMT than do those with severe brain injuries. Furthermore, those with putatively mild injuries who failed WMT demonstrated significantly worse neuropsychological test scores overall than did those who had severe injuries but passed the WMT. These results strongly suggest that the WMT is not nearly as sensitive to brain injury as it is some other construct, presumably poor effort. Bowden, Shores, and Mathias (2006) sought to replicate the Green and colleagues (2001) finding that WMT failure rates appear higher in mild compared to more severe brain injuries among litigating subjects. They reported data from 100 consecutive subjects, ranging from age 6 to 74 years, who were involved in litigation related to TBI. The researchers found no indication of improvement in WMT (Immediate Recognition only) performance as injury severity increased. They found a significant, but likely inconsequential, effect of WMT Immediate Recognition performance on the outcome measure of delayed memory using 86 subjects ($p < .001$, $\eta^2 = 0.18$). It is difficult to determine the significance of Bowden and colleagues' results, because their research incorporated a much smaller N than did the Green and colleagues data; they did not identify how many cases were pediatric; and they only administered the Immediate Recognition portion of the WMT.

Many of the WMT studies have also included other malingering tests, such as the CARB and TOMM. Gervais and colleagues (2004) reviewed 519 compensation-seeking cases who were given the TOMM, the CARB, and the WMT. They found failure rates of 11% on the TOMM, 17% on the CARB, and 32% on the WMT Primary Effort subtests. These findings suggest that the WMT is a more sensitive measure of poor effort and malingering than the CARB or the TOMM.

Gorissen, Sanz, and Schmand (2005), using the Dutch and Spanish oral versions of the WMT with patients with schizophrenia, nonpsychotic psychiatric patients, neurological controls, and healthy controls as part of a larger neuropsychological assessment, confirmed that the WMT does not correlate with more customary measures of memory, such as delayed verbal and figural memory, regardless of which subject group was considered. Nonetheless, they found that 72% of the schizophrenia group, 25% of the psychiatric controls, 10% of the neurological controls, and none of the healthy controls failed the WMT. When they divided groups based on WMT performance, they found that those in the poor effort schizophrenia group performed more poorly on other neuropsychological tests than did the neurological patients. Additionally, poor WMT scores within the schizophrenia group correlated significantly with the negative symptoms scale of the Positive and Negative Syndrome Scale (PANSS; Spearman's ρ = –0.42; Kay, Opler, & Fiszbein, 1986), yet did not correlate with tests of executive function, such as the Trail Making Test–Part B, the Stroop Color–Word test, or Verbal Fluency test. The authors considered results to possibly reflect an amotivation syndrome. Other studies have demonstrated that incentives may increase cognitive performance among those with schizophrenia (Schmand et al., 1994). Results are difficult to interpret, because there was no apparent motivation for patients in this study to perform well. We are left not knowing how much the poorer performances simply reflected subjects' lack of desire to perform well.

Although the WMT initially received a cool review due to difficult computer software and lack of peer-reviewed and published research (Wynkoop & Denney, 2001), it has now become a widely researched tool with a strong empirical basis (Hartman, 2002; Wynkoop & Denney, 2005). With the new Windows version, the test is easy to use, includes numerous clinical and nonclinical comparison groups, and can be performed in multiple languages. Research with the instrument in different languages is starting to come out, and results suggest it performs just as well in German, Turkish, and Russian (Brockhaus & Merten, 2004; Brockhaus, Peker, & Fritze, 2003; Tydecks, Merten, & Gubay, 2006).

MEDICAL SYMPTOM VALIDITY TEST

The MSVT (Green, 2004) is, in essence, a simpler version of the WMT. Despite the term *medical* in the title, the test uses a verbal memory paradigm like the WMT, rather than any particular assessment of medical symptoms. The MSVT uses 10 word pairs rather the WMT's 20 word pairs, and the word pairs have a much stronger semantic relationship. Consequently, it appears to be a much easier test. As with the WMT, words are presented via the computer in word pairs. Subjects then complete an initial recognition test for each word. There is a 10-minute delay and the recognition test is presented again. There are then paired associate and free recall tasks. The entire test takes about 20 minutes to administer, including the 10-minute delay. The ease of the task is demonstrated by the fact that English-speaking adults and children who could not speak French scored nearly perfectly on the validity scales portion of the test, even when tested with French words (Richman et al., 2006). The computer program includes a feature that easily compares the subject's performance to a large number of comparison groups, including five simulator groups, healthy children and adults, child clinical groups (fetal alcohol syndrome, learning disability, conduct disorder, MR, and attention deficit disorder), and adult clinical groups (mild through severe TBI, neurological with impaired memory, Social Security Disability claimants, chronic pain, major depression, anxiety, soft-tissue insurance disability claimants, schizophrenia and bipolar disorder, and early and advanced dementia). In addition to a strict cutoff for the three validity scales in the measure, a dementia profile is designed to identify those who fail the MSVT, but do so in a manner consistent with genuine dementia (Green, 2004).

Merten, Green, Henry, Blaskewitz, and Brockhaus (2005) performed an analog study of the oral form of the MSVT in Germany. They compared performances between 18 simulators and 18 healthy adult controls. The simulators were warned that validity measures would be included in the test battery. The MSVT results were nearly perfect. Delayed Recognition and Consistency scores demonstrated 100% classification of both simulators and health adults. The Immediate Recognition classified all of the simulators, but one healthy subject's score fell on the cutoff (94.4% specificity). These specificity rates have little meaning, because the study did not include cases with known clinical conditions.

Teichner, Waid, and Buddin (2005) presented results of the computer-administered English-language MSVT with 294 clinical and forensic adult and pediatric subjects. They used the TOMM and WMT as indices within the Slick and colleagues (1999) classification for MND. They did not explain this classification further. All 102 children were considered to have provided good effort. Seventeen of the 192 adults were considered to have provided poor effort (8.85%). All of those poor effort cases were identified by the MSVT (100% sensitivity). The strength of this study lies in the fact that it included subjects with bona fide neuropathological conditions (e.g., TBI, stroke, carbon monoxide exposure, MR, mild dementia). Of the children, 7.8% were misclassified as giving poor effort (92.2 specificity). Of the adults, including those with dementia, 12% were misclassified as having poor effort (88% specificity). Extracting the dementia cases ($N = 15$) from the data reduced the misclassification to 9.4% (90.6% specificity). It is difficult to interpret this data without knowing the details of how the TOMM and WMT were used in classifying the subjects.

Howe, Anderson, Kaufman, Sachs, and Loring (2007) evaluated the performance characteristics of the MSVT among clinical referred memory disorders patients. They included data for 63 subjects, 11 of whom were considered to have a disability-related incentive to possibly perform poorly. Forty-five precent of the disability group failed one or more of the MSVT Validity scales. Two of them had clear indication of invalid responding, and three met the MSVT's valid dementia profile algorithm. Twenty-two percent of the subjects without disability failed one or more of the MSVT Validity scales. After considering the dementia profile algorithm, however, they found a false-positive rate of only 4.76% for their entire sample. Two of these three subjects were considered to have advanced dementia. The third was considered to have early dementia. These data indicate the MSVT is a powerful tool when differentiating valid from invalid performances among memory disorder referrals, including dementia, with a 95.24% specificity rate.

NONVERBAL MEDICAL SYMPTOM VALIDITY TEST

Green (2006) has introduced the preliminary research edition of the Nonverbal Medical Symptom Validity Test (NV-MSVT), a computer-administered test that is very similar in design to the MSVT; however, it uses visual stimuli rather than word pairs. It also takes about 20 minutes to complete and includes a 10-minute delay. In contrast to the MSVT, it incorporates variations during the delayed recognition task that, when compared to the paired associate task, appear to make it particularly capable in differentiating genuine from feigned dementia. At the time of this writing one can compare a subject's performance to a number of normative and clinical comparison groups (including children with fetal alcohol disorder, adults passing and failing WMT and MSVT, good-effort adult volunteers, four groups of adults with dementia, adult dementia simulators, adult male prisoners with end-stage renal disease, and four groups of children stratified by age from 7 to 18 years). A number of clinical researchers are currently collecting data on the NV-MSVT, so comparison groups will likely increase in number and variety.

Green reported results from 107 consecutive compensation-seeking subjects who were also administered other validity measures (Reliable Digit Span [RDS], TOMM, WMT, & MSVT). Failure rates were 32% for the WMT, 25% on MSVT, 20% on RDS, 20% on NV-MSVT, and 8% on TOMM. Preliminary results suggest a strikingly different pattern between simulators and those with genuine dementing conditions. Use of singular cutoffs does not appear to work nearly as well as the overall test result profile. Using an algorithm that compared recognition, paired associate, and free recall, Green reports a 96% correct classification for 128 subjects (40 good-effort adults, 40 adult dementia simulators, 19 good-effort children, and 29 individuals with dementia). When parsing out the 40 simulators and 29 dementia cases from the data provided in the handout and creating a hybrid simulator, known-group design, the NV-MSVT obtained a 95% sensitivity, a 90.6% specificity, and correct classification of 93%. These preliminary results are quite promising, particularly when dealing with the often difficult diagnosis of dementia. The manual should be published by the time this volume goes to press.

Embedded Indices of Neurocognitive NRB

Aside from tests and techniques designed specifically to assess neurocognitive malingering, many NRB indices are incorporated within widely used psychological and neuropsychological measures. These strategies are beneficial because they take little additional time to administer and the connection between poor performance on the validity scale and poor performance on the genuine test is clear. In addition, they can be calculated on testing protocols from evaluations done in the past. The negative aspect of these strategies is that their specificity will likely not be as strong as that of freestanding NRB measures, because they comprise tasks designed to measure actual effects of brain pathology. Vallabhajosula and van Gorp (2001) suggested that the best malingering detection strategies will be measures sensitive to feigning but not to genuine impairment. Nevertheless, the trend of embedding NRB detection methods within already established neuropsychological measures appears to be a reasonable pursuit. Examples of such malingering detection strategies based on established clinical measures include the Warrington Recognition Memory Test (for a review, see Millis, 2002), atypical pattern analysis on the Wechsler Scales, Wechsler Memory Scale—Revised, and Halstead–Reitan Battery (for a review of each, see Mittenberg et al., 2002), RDS (Greiffenstein, Baker, & Gola, 1994; Larrabee, 2003a; Meyers & Volbrecht, 1998; for a review, see Suhr & Barrash, 2007), Rarely Missed Index of the Wechsler Memory Scale–III (Killgore & DellaPietra, 2000; Suhr & Barrash, 2007), California Verbal Learning Test (Millis, Putnam, Adams, & Ricker, 1995; Slick, Iverson, & Green, 2000), Wisconsin Card Sorting Test (for a review of various methods, see Greve & Bianchini, 2007; Greve, Bianchini, Mathias, Houston, & Crouch, 2002), Finger Tapping (Heaton et al., 1978; Larrabee, 2003a), Benton Judgment of Line Orientation (Iverson, 2001; Meyers, Galinsky, & Volbrecht, 1999), Category Test (for reviews, see Greve & Bianchini, 2007; Sweet & King, 2002), test–retest changes on the Halstead–Reitan Battery (for review, see Reitan & Wolfson, 2002), and Benton Visual Form Discrimination (Larrabee, 2003a). Readers are referred to each article to learn specifics of computing these indices, because reprinting them here could compromise test security.

Using Multiple NRB Indices

Larrabee (2003a) pointed out that "assessment of effort in medicolegal settings must be multi-variate" (p. 422). Meyers and Volbrecht (2003) demonstrated that use of multiple *imbedded* NRB indicators within a standard neuropsychology battery can identify invalid performance. Meyers and Volbrecht found 83% sensitivity and 100% specificity in identifying NRB using a positive cutoff rule of 2 or more among a mixed group of clinical cases and analog simulators. There were no false positives using this method. Larrabee (2003a) found that using multiple NRB indicators and a positive cutoff of 2 or more resulted in an overall sensitivity of 87.8% and specificity of 94.4% for the combined samples of litigating and nonlitigating closed head injury evaluees classified based on Slick and colleagues (1999) criteria. He also demonstrates that use of multiple indicators decreases the chance of false-positive identification errors. These sensitivity rates rival, and even surpass, those of many free-standing measures of NRB. Using the aforementioned imbedded indices facilitates the identification of NRB in this regard, with no additional test administration time. Incorporating one or more freestanding indices of NRB would likely increase the sensitivity of this multivariate method without compromising specificity.

Self-Report Measures of Psychiatric Disturbance

Although this chapter is focused on exaggeration of neurocognitive dysfunction as it relates to criminal forensic evaluations, the neuropsychologist performing work in this setting will often face cases in which feigning of psychiatric impairment is also an issue. There is a large amount of literature regarding the detection of feigned psychosis; however, the subject is beyond the scope of this chapter. For a recent review of self-report measures related to assessment of feigned psychiatric impairment, see Berry and Schipper (2007).

Complaints of Remote Memory Loss

Significant retrograde amnesia is rare in the absence of substantial brain damage and typically raises concerns about psychogenic etiology (Parkin, 1996; Ross, 2000). Claims of remote memory loss, when they relate to alleged criminal activity, however, are not unusual (Schacter, 1986). It appears to occur more commonly with acts of violence. Reported amnesia in relation to homicide charges are estimated to range from 23 to 65%

(Bradford & Smith, 1979; Guttmacher, 1955; Evans, 2006; Leitch, 1948; Parwatikar, Holcomb, & Menninger, 1985). Hopwood and Snell (1933) reviewed 100 criminal cases and found that 90% of the amnestic claims pertained to murder or attempted murder charges. In a more recent review, only 8% of 120 cases of nonhomicide violent crimes included claimed amnesia, and there were no claims of amnesia among 47 individuals charged with nonviolent crimes (Taylor & Kopelman, 1984).

Most researchers suggest that a substantial portion of such claims are feigned (Adatto, 1949; Bradford & Smith, 1979; Hopwood & Snell, 1933; Lynch & Bradford, 1980; O'Connell, 1960; Parwatikar et al., 1985; Power, 1977; Price & Terhune, 1919). Schacter (1986) provided this viewpoint:

> In the large majority of criminal cases that involve amnesia, the loss of memory either has a functional origin or concerns only a single critical event. I have found no cases in the literature in which a patient afflicted with chronic organic amnesia has come before the courts on a serious criminal matter that is related to his or her memory disorder. Organic factors may play a role when concussion, alcohol intoxication, or epileptic seizure occurs during a crime, with subsequent limited amnesia for the crime itself, but in these cases memory problems typically do not exist prior to the crime. (p. 287)

Occasionally, criminal defendants experience a neurological condition either severe enough or close enough in time to the crime to hinder recall of events around the time of the alleged offense (Miller, 2003; *Wilson v. United States*, 1968; Wynkoop & Denney, 1999). It is also possible that individuals carrying out criminal activity while intoxicated may subsequently not recall these important events. Other instances could include individuals who experience a TBI during the crime or arrest, or experience a neurological insult, such as cerebrovascular stroke or hemorrhage, after the arrest but before legal proceedings are concluded (Denney & Wynkoop, 2000). Under such circumstances, it is not unreasonable to find loss of memory for events preceding the arrest, including the offense behavior. A criminal defendant's ability to recall events sufficiently to reconstruct his or her activities for the period of time around the offense may be an important aspect of his or her competency to proceed.

Symptom Validity Testing for Remote Memory

Identifying feigned memory loss for a specific period of time or for a specific event is not easy. Most methods used to evaluate amnesia (see Rubinsky & Brandt, 1986; Schacter, 1986; Wiggins & Brandt, 1988) do not avail themselves of the detection of specific past criminal events. One exception is symptom validity testing (SVT), which appears to work well in assessing claims of remote memory loss.

Originally designed to assess psychogenic sensory complaints as mentioned above, SVT was modified for learning and retention complaints (Grosz & Zimmerman, 1965; Haughton, Lewsley, Wilson, & Williams, 1979; Pankratz, 1979; Pankratz et al., 1975; Theodor & Mandelcorn, 1973). Frederick and Carter (1993; Frederick, Carter, & Powel, 1995) adapted this technique to assess memory for events surrounding an alleged offense for which a criminal defendant claimed amnesia. They developed two-alternative, forced-choice questions for events presented in the criminal investigative records for which the defendant claimed no recollection. Upon administration, the defendant performed statistically below expectations for an individual who had no memory for those events. They concluded the man was feigning his amnesia.

The procedure is based on the binomial theorem, which purports that when two possibilities of equal probability exist, results will fall around the mean in an expected bell-shaped curve (Siegel, 1956). Similarly, when an individual with no ability/knowledge is asked a number of questions with only two possible answers of approximately equal probability, results should fall in a random range. Knowledge is demonstrated to a particular level of statistical certainty when results fall outside the random range. Customarily, individuals with knowledge of events in question score well above the random range, therefore demonstrating their knowledge (see Marcopulos, Morgan, & Denney, Chapter 6, this volume, for an example of this occurrence). Likewise, results falling below the random range also demonstrate knowledge, albeit in the opposite direction.

When applied in a criminal context, questions are derived from investigative materials, medical records, or from interviews of witnesses, family members, or law enforcement personnel. Oftentimes, the facts of the case are well described in the indictment and supportive information. This information is combed to create questions about events and facts that the defendant should have known or experienced during the period of claimed amnesia. Enough detail is required to generate an ample number of questions (preferably more than 24); an increased number of items increases sensitivity and overall accuracy. In addition, the information on which the questions are based must be salient enough and be created in such a manner that an individual without significant memory loss would likely have remembered the information. Questions should be developed to include the correct answer and an equally plausible alternative. Questions should also be worded in such a manner that responses avoid direct admissions of guilt (e.g., "investigative records allege ... " or "the prosecution claims ... "). The procedure is designed to identify false claims of memory loss rather than to identify guilt.

Frederick and colleagues (1995) noted the difficulty in creating reasonably plausible alternative answers. Occasionally, the difficulty is in creating equally *implausible* alternative answers. For example, I (Denney, 1996) presented a case in which a male defendant dressed as a woman to rob a bank. Although developing questions can be difficult, research has demonstrated that unequal probability answers actually increase the conservative nature of the procedure (Frederick & Denney, 1998). As in the case of the bank robber, it was important that alternative answers not systematically present more likely possibilities. Biasing the test in this manner would inappropriately increase the possibility that a truly amnestic individual could select wrong answers more often than would occur by chance. It is helpful, therefore, to have a colleague review the questions before administration.

Defendants are instructed that, because of their memory concerns, they will be tested regarding their memory for those specific events in order to understand their memory problem more clearly. Each item is presented after the question of whether they remember this information or not. Items for which they claim recall of the information or "reason out" the solution are discarded, because the test is designed to measure their lack of recollection (Denney, 1996). Items not recalled or invalidated through deductive reason are administered to defendants with the instruction to choose the correct answer or simply guess to the best of their ability if they cannot remember. Subjects are told whether they are correct or incorrect, and the correct answer is noted. Often, the task is constructed so that succeeding queries are more specific variants of the preceding question (e.g., "Investigative records allege you did what, rob a bank or perform a drug deal? No, it alleges you robbed a bank. Was it First Interstate Bank or Seattle First Bank? Was it on 2nd Avenue or 4th Avenue?" etc.). Correct answers are totaled and applied to the following formula from Siegel (1956):

$$z = [(x \pm 0.5) - NP] / \sqrt{NPQ}$$

where z is the test statistic, x is the number of correct responses, N is the number of questions administered, P is the probability of a correct discrimination given no true ability (0.5); and Q represents $1 - P$ (probability of an incorrect discrimination). The correction (adding 0.5 when $x < NP$; subtracting 0.5 when $x > NP$) is made to correct for continuity as the binomial distribution involves discrete variables. A one-tail test is used to identify the exact probability using the Unit Normal Table (z table). The one-tail test is considered appropriate given the intent to identify suppressed performance

(Larrabee, 1992; Siegel, 1956). A z-score of -1.65 is significant at $p = .05$ and -2.33 is significant at $p = .01$.

Denney (1996) and Frederick and Denney (1998) demonstrated that individuals with no knowledge of events in question perform predominantly within the random range, with scores clustering around the mean (50%). Results demonstrated that the procedure was actually slightly more conservative than that spelled out by the binomial distribution. Furthermore, Frederick and Denney performed computer simulations in which P and Q were progressively not equal to 0.5, and demonstrated that the test statistic performed even more conservatively as response options moved away from 0.5 probability. The increased variability led to a decrease in sensitivity, thereby lessening the likelihood of labeling a true amnestic as a malingerer. While the SVT procedure can be time-intensive in terms of acquiring investigative material and developing questions, it has proven itself as an effective tool in identifying feigned claims of remote memory loss.

Malingering and the Criminal Courts

By definition, the term *malingering* indicates intentional misrepresentation for secondary gain. In the correctional environment, this may include feigning mental or physical illness to gain access to drugs, female staff, a safer environment, or a situation in which escape may be possible. In the truly forensic setting (that pertaining to the judicial system) this means feigning or exaggerating disability to delay or avoid prosecution, obviate criminal responsibility, or obtain a lesser sentence. Most commonly, attempts to feign cognitive disability arise in relation to competency to proceed. Although courts have been reticent to allow expert testimony regarding an individual's veracity in personal injury and civil tort actions (*Commonwealth v. Zamarripa*, 1988; *Nicholson v. American National Insurance*, 1998), these instances typically involve the expert providing testimony before a jury. Judges appear to have less concern regarding this issue when it is addressed in a bench proceeding. In fact, it is clear that courts take attempts to circumvent the criminal judicial process quite seriously.

In *United States v. Greer* (1998), the 5th Circuit Court of Appeals affirmed a decision that underscored the seriousness of criminal defendants feigning mental illness. Charles Greer was indicted for kidnapping and various firearms violations. He had a long criminal history and had been committed several times to inpatient psychiatric facilities. He had been found incompetent to proceed on previous occasions and was initially found incompetent to proceed in relation to the state aspect of these charges. He then underwent an inpatient competency evaluation performed by Richard

Frederick, PhD. Dr. Frederick later testified that Greer was not only competent to stand trial but that he was also feigning psychotic illness. After hearing testimony from a defense expert, the court found defendant Greer competent to stand trial.

Greer's bizarre behavior during trial preparation prompted his attorney to file another motion to determine competency. He was examined by a psychiatrist from the Texas Department of Criminal Justice, who opined that he was incompetent. The government did not contest the opinion, and Greer was found incompetent. He was then referred for inpatient mental health treatment to restore his competency. After 2 months of observation, mental health staff were unable to find any active psychotic process or serious mental disease. Mary Alice Conroy, PhD, later testified that in her view he had been malingering. The court found that Greer was feigning mental illness and that he was competent to stand trial. However, on the first day of trial, he took his clothes off and attempted to flush them down the holding cell toilet. He also spit up between 10 and 16 half-dollar-size splotches of blood and was taken to a local hospital. The jail's director of infirmary services testified that an abrasion found in Greer's mouth had caused the bleeding and that such abrasions were commonly caused by self-inflicted scratches. She also testified that it appeared Greer was gagging himself rather than vomiting blood. Without the jury present, the U.S. District Judge told Greer that he believed Greer was a malingerer. He also told Greer that if he acted up or tried to disrupt the trial while in the courtroom, he would be removed from the courtroom and the trial would proceed in his absence. Greer exhibited additional disruptive behaviors during the trial and was subsequently removed. The jury convicted Greer in his absence. At sentencing, the court granted the government's argument that Greer's sentence be enhanced for obstructing justice, since he had feigned mental illness prior to and during trial. He received a 210-month sentence with the enhancement, whereas he would have received a 185-month sentence without it. The court's decision to enhance the man's sentence due to malingering was affirmed on appeal.

Future Directions

Research regarding free-standing and embedded neurocognitive malingering measures has increased in recent years. Although there is a tremendous interest in the subject, most of the work is being done in civil populations. That work needs to continue, particularly in verifying specificity rates among differing neuropathological conditions. However, more work also needs to occur in the criminal setting. There is no guarantee that these measures perform in this setting as they do in the civil (typically personal injury) setting, and the base rates of malingering appear to be higher in the presentence criminal setting than in most civil settings. Additionally, there is increased reason to identify feigned versus genuine mental retardation among criminal defendants in light of the U.S. Supreme Court decision banning execution of mentally retarded criminals (*Atkins v. Virginia*, 2002). Along with that need, there exists a need to validate existing detection methods for use with the MR population. Finally, additional research needs to occur related to sensitivity rates of SVT for remote memory. It is very possible that criterion cutoffs could be established. Denney (1996) and Frederick and Denney (1998) found that most individuals with no memory for events in question fell near the mean, suggesting that simulation designs could be developed to establish criterion-based cutoff scores. Little is known about how standard competency to stand trial measures perform in regard to malingering and exaggeration of neurocognitive dysfunction. Clearly, there is a need for a great deal more research regarding exaggeration of neurocognitive deficits in the criminal forensic setting.

Notes

Opinions expressed in this chapter are those of the authors and do not necessarily represent the position of the Federal Bureau of Prisons or the U.S. Department of Justice.

1. Identified as true positives/(true positives + false negatives).
2. Identified as true negatives/(true negatives + false positives).

References

Adatto, C. P. (1949). Observations on criminal patients during narcoanalysis. *Archives of Neurology and Psychiatry, 62*, 82–92.

Allen, L. M., Conder, R. L., Green, P., & Cox, D. R. (1997). *CARB '97 manual for the Computerized Assessment of Response Bias*. Durham, NC: CogniSyst, Inc.

Allen, L. M., & Green, P. (1999). *Severe TBI sample performance on CARB and the WMT: Supplement to the CARB '97 and Word Memory test manuals*. Durham, NC: CogniSyst, Inc.

Allen, L. M., Iverson, G. L., & Green, P. (2002). Computerized Assessment of Response Bias in forensic neuropsychology. In J. Hom & R. L. Denney (Eds.), *Detection of response bias in forensic neuropsychology* (pp. 205–225). New York: Haworth Medical Press.

American Psychiatric Association. (2000). *Diagnostic and statistical manual of mental disorders* (4th ed., text rev.). Washington, DC: Author.

Anastasi, A. (1961). *Psychological testing* (2nd ed.). New York: Macmillan.

Ardolf, B. R., Denney, R. L., & Houston, C. M. (2007). Base rates of negative response bias and malingered neurocognitive dysfunction among criminal defendants referred for neuropsychological evaluation. *Clinical Neuropsychologist, 21,* 899–916.

Atkins v. Virginia, 536 U. S. 304 (2002).

Baldessarini, R. J., Finkelstein, S., & Arana, G. W. (1983). The predictive power of diagnostic tests and the effects of prevalence of illness. *Archives of General Psychiatry, 40,* 569–573.

Berry, D. T. R., & Schipper, L. J. (2007). Detection of feigned psychiatric symptoms during forensic neuropsychological examinations. In G. J. Larrabee (Ed.), *Assessment of malingered neuropsychological deficits* (pp. 226–263). New York: Oxford University Press.

Bianchini, K. J., Curtis, K. L., & Greve, K. W. (2006). Compensation and malingering in traumatic brain injury: A dose–response relationship? *Clinical Neuropsychologist, 20,* 831–847.

Bianchini, K. J., Mathias, C. W., & Greve, K. W. (2001). Symptom validity testing: A critical review. *Clinical Neuropsychologist, 15,* 19–45.

Bigler, E. D. (1990). Neuropsychology and malingering: Comment on Faust, Hart, and Guilmette (1988). *Journal of Consulting and Clinical Psychology, 58,* 244–247.

Binder, L. M. (1990). Malingering following minor head trauma. *Clinical Neuropsychologist, 4,* 25–36.

Binder, L. M. (1993). An abbreviated form of the Portland Digit Recognition Test. *Clinical Neuropsychologist, 7,* 104–107.

Binder, L. M. (2002). The Portland Digit Recognition Test: A review of validation data and clinical use. In J. Hom & R. L. Denney (Eds.), *Detection of response bias in forensic neuropsychology* (pp. 27–41). New York: Haworth Medical Press.

Binder, L. M., & Willis, S. C. (1991). Assessment of motivation after financially compensable minor head trauma. *Psychological Assessment, 3,* 175–181.

Binks, P. G., Gouvier, W. D., & Waters, W. F. (1997). Malingering detection with the Dot Counting Test. *Archives of Clinical Neuropsychology, 12,* 41–46.

Boone, K. B. (2007). A reconsideration of the Slick et al. (1999) criteria for malingered neurocognitive dysfunction. In K. B. Boone (Ed.), *Assessment of feigned cognitive impairment: A neuropsychological perspective* (pp. 29–49). New York: Guilford Press.

Boone, K. B., & Lu, P. H. (2003). Noncredible cognitive performance in the context of severe brain injury. *Clinical Neuropsychologist, 17,* 244–254.

Boone, K. B., Lu, P. H., & Herzberg, D. S. (2002). *The Dot Counting Test manual.* Los Angeles: Western Psychological Services.

Boone, K. B., Salazar, X., Lu, P., Warner-Chacon, K., & Razani, J. (2002). The Rey 15-Item Recognition Trial: A technique to enhance sensitivity of the Rey 15-Item Memorization Test. *Journal of Clinical and Experimental Neuropsychology, 24,* 561–573.

Bowden, S. C., Shores, A., & Mathias, J. L. (2006). Does effort suppress cognition after traumatic brain injury?: A re-examination of the evidence for the Word Memory Test. *Clinical Neuropsychologist, 20*, 858–872.

Boyd, A. R., McLearen, A. M., Meyer, R. G., & Denney, R. L. (2007). *Detection of deception*. Sarasota, FL: Professional Resource Press.

Bradford, J. W., & Smith, S. M. (1979). Amnesia and homicide: The Padola case and a study of thirty cases. *Bulletin of the American Academy of Psychiatry and Law, 7*, 219–231.

Brady, J. P., & Lind, D. L. (1961). Experimental analysis of hysterical blindness. *Archives of General Psychiatry, 4*, 331–339.

Brockhaus, R., & Merten, T. (2005). Neuropsychologische diagnostik suboptimalen leistungsverhaltens mit dem Word Memory Test [Neuropsychological assessment of suboptimal performance: The Word Memory Test]. *Nervenarzt, 75*, 882–887.

Brockhaus, R., Peker, Ö., & Fritze, E. (2003, July). *Testing effort in Turkish-speaking subjects: Validation of a translation of the Word Memory Test (WMT)*. Paper presented at the joint meeting of the International Neuropsychology Society and Gesellschaft fur Neuropsychologie, Berlin, Germany.

Bush, S. S., Ruff, R. H. Tröster, A. I., Barth, J. T., Koffler, S. P., Pliskin, N. H., et al. (2005). Symptom validity assessment: Practice issues and medical necessity. *Archives of Clinical Neuropsychology, 20*, 419–426.

Butcher, J. N., Dahlstrom, W. G., Graham, J. R., Tellegen, A., & Kaemmer, B. (1989). *Manual for administration and scoring the Minnesota Multiphasic Personality Inventory–2*. Minneapolis: University of Minnesota Press.

Chavez, M. D., Abrahams, J. P., & Kohlmaier, J. (2007). Malingering on the Social Security Disability Consultative Exam: A new rating scale. *Archives of Clinical Neuropsychology, 22*, 1–14.

Commonwealth v. Zamarripa, 379 Pa. Super. 208, 549 A.2d 980 (1988).

Conder, R., Allen, L., & Cox, D. (1992). *Manual for the Computerized Assessment of Response Bias*. Durham, NC: CogniSyst, Inc.

Cornell, D. G., & Hawk, G. L. (1989). Clinical presentation of malingerers diagnosed by experienced forensic psychologists. *Law and Human Behavior, 13*, 357–383.

Daubert v. Merrell Dow Pharmaceuticals, 509 U.S. 579 (1993).

Delain, S. L., Stafford, K. P., & Ben-Porath, Y. S. (2003). Use of the TOMM in a criminal court forensic assessment setting. *Assessment, 10*, 370–381.

Denney, R. L. (1996). Symptom Validity Testing of remote memory in a criminal forensic setting. *Archives of Clinical Neuropsychology, 11*, 589–603.

Denney, R. L. (1999). A brief Symptom Validity Testing procedure for Logical Memory of the Wechsler Memory Scale—Revised which can demonstrate verbal memory in the face of claimed disability. *Journal of Forensic Neuropsychology, 1*(1), 5–26.

Denney, R. L. (2007). Assessment of malingering in criminal forensic neuropsychological settings. In K. B. Boone (Ed.), *Assessment of feigned cognitive impairment: A Neuropsychological perspective* (pp. 428–452). New York: Guilford Press.

Denney, R. L., & Wynkoop, T. F. (2000). Clinical neuropsychology in the criminal forensic setting. *Journal of Head Trauma Rehabilitation, 15*, 804–828.

Ekman, P. (1992). *Telling lies: Clues to deceit in the marketplace, politics, and marriage.* New York: Norton.

Elwood, R. W. (1993). Psychological tests and clinical discriminations: Beginning to address the base rate problem. *Clinical Psychology Review, 13*, 409–419.

Etherton, J. L., Bianchini, K. J., Greve, K. W., & Ciota, M. A. (2005). Test of memory malingering performance is unaffected by laboratory-induced pain: Implications for clinical use. *Archives of Clinical Neuropsychology, 20*, 375–384.

Evans, C. (2006). What violent offenders remember of their crime: Empirical explorations. *Australian and New Zealand Journal of Psychiatry, 40*(6/7), 508–518.

Faust, D., & Guilmette, T. J. (1990). To say it's not so doesn't prove that it isn't: Research on the detection of malingering (reply to Bigler). *Journal of Consulting and Clinical Psychology, 58*, 248–250.

Faust, D., Hart, K., Guilmette, T. J., & Arkes, H. R. (1988). Neuropsychologists capacity to detect adolescent malingerers. *Professional Psychology: Research and Practice, 19*, 508–515.

Frederick, R. I. (2002). A review of Rey's strategies for detecting malingered neuropsychological impairment. In J. Hom & R. L. Denney (Eds.), *Detection of response bias in forensic neuropsychology* (pp. 1–25). New York: Haworth Medical Press.

Frederick, R. I. (2003). *Validity Indicator Profile Manual, revised.* Minneapolis: Pearson Assessments.

Frederick, R. I., & Carter, M. (1993, August). *Detection of malingered amnesia in a competency evaluee.* Paper presented at the Annual Convention of the American Psychological Association, Toronto, Canada.

Frederick, R. I., Carter, M., & Powel, J. (1995). Adapting symptom validity testing to evaluate suspicious complaints of amnesia in medicolegal evaluations. *Bulletin of the American Academy of Psychiatry and the Law, 23*, 231–237.

Frederick, R. I., Crosby, R. D., & Wynkoop, T. F. (2000). Performance curve classification of invalid responding on the Validity Indicator Profile. *Archives of Clinical Neuropsychology, 15*, 281–300.

Frederick, R. I., & Denney, R. L. (1998). Minding your "p's and q's" when using forced-choice recognition tests. *Clinical Neuropsychologist, 12*, 193–205.

Frederick, R. I., Sarfaty, S., Johnston, J. D., & Powel, J. (1994). Validation of a detector of response bias on a forced-choice test of nonverbal ability. *Neuropsychology, 8*, 118–125.

Frederick, R. I., & Speed, F. M. (2007). On the interpretation of below-chance responding in forced-choice tests. *Assessment, 14*, 3–11.

Gervais, R. O., Rohling, M. L., Green, P., & Ford, W. (2004). A comparison of the WMT, CARB, and TOMM failure rates in non-head-injury disability claimants. *Archives of Clinical Neuropsychology, 19*, 475–487.

Gorissen, M., Sanz, J. C., & Schmand, B. (2005). Effort and cognition in schizophrenia patients. *Schizophrenia Research, 78*, 199–208.

Gouvier, D., Hayes, J. S., & Smiroldo, B. B. (1998). The significance of base rates, test sensitivity, test specificity, and subject's knowledge of symptoms in assessing

TBI sequelae and malingering. In C. R. Reynolds (Ed.), *Detection of malingering during head injury litigation* (pp. 55–79). New York: Plenum Press.

Green, P. (2003). *Word Memory Test for Windows: Test manual.* Edmonton, Alberta, Canada: Green's Publishing.

Green, P. (2004). *Green's Medical Symptom Validity Test (MSVT) user manual.* Edmonton, Alberta, Canada: Green's Publishing.

Green, P. (2006). *The Nonverbal Medical Symptom Validity Test: MS Windows computer program.* Edmonton, Alberta, Canada: Green's Publishing.

Green, P., & Allen, L. M. (1999). *Performance of neurological patients on the Word Memory Test (WMT) and Computerized Assessment of Response Bias (CARB): Supplement to the Word Memory Test and CARB '97 manuals.* Durham, NC: CogniSyst, Inc.

Green, P., & Iverson, G. L. (2001). Validation of the Computerized Assessment of Response Bias in litigating patients with head injuries. *Clinical Neuropsychologist, 15,* 492–497.

Green, P., Iverson, G. L., & Allen, L. (1999). Detecting malingering in head injury litigation with the Word Memory Test. *Brain Injury, 13,* 813–819.

Green, P., Lees-Haley, P. R., & Allen, L. M. (2002). The Word Memory Test and the validity of neuropsychological test scores. In J. Hom & R. L. Denney (Eds.), *Detection of response bias in forensic neuropsychology* (pp. 97–124). New York: Haworth Medical Press.

Green, P., Rohling, M. L., Lees-Haley, P. R., & Allen, L. M. (2001). Effort has a greater effect on test scores than severe brain injury in compensation claimants. *Brain Injury, 15,* 1045–1060.

Greiffenstein, M. F., Baker, W. J., & Gola, T. (1994). Validation of malingered amnesia measures with a large clinical sample. *Psychological Assessment, 6,* 218–224.

Greve, K., & Bianchini, K. (2006a). Classification accuracy of the Portland Digit Recognition Test in traumatic brain injury: Results of a known-groups analysis. *Clinical Neuropsychologist, 20,* 816–830.

Greve, K., & Bianchini, K. (2006b). Should the retention trial of the Test of Memory Malingering be optional? *Archives of Clinical Neuropsychology, 21,* 117–119.

Greve, K., & Bianchini, K. (2007). Detection of cognitive malingering with tests of executive function. In G. J. Larrabee (Ed.), *Assessment of malingered neuropsychological deficits* (pp. 171–225). New York: Oxford University Press.

Greve, K., Bianchini, K., Mathias, C., Houston, R., & Crouch, J. (2002). Detecting malingered performance with the Wisconsin Card Sorting Test: A preliminary investigation in traumatic brain injury. *Clinical Neuropsychologist, 16,* 179–191.

Grosz, H. J., & Zimmerman, J. A. (1965). Experimental analysis of hysterical blindness: A follow-up report and new experimental data. *Archives of General Psychiatry, 13,* 255–260.

Grote, C. L., Kooker, E. K., Garron, D. C., Nyenhuis, D. L., Smith, C. A., & Mattingly, M. L. (2000). Performance of compensation seeking and non-compensation seeking samples on the Victoria Symptom Validity Test: Cross-validation and extension of a standardization study. *Journal of Clinical and Experimental Neuropsychology, 22,* 709–719.

Guttmacher, M. S. (1955). *Psychiatry and the law*. New York: Grune & Stratton.

Hartman, D. E. (2002). The unexamined lie is a lie worth fibbing: Neuropsychological malingering and the Word Memory Test. *Archives of Clinical Neuropsychology, 17*, 709–714.

Haughton, P. M., Lewsley, A., Wilson, M., & Williams, R. G. (1979). A forced-choice procedure to detect feigned or exaggerated hearing loss. *British Journal of Audiology, 13*, 135–138.

Heaton, R. K., Smith, H. H., Lehman, R. A. W., & Vogt, A. T. (1978). Prospects for faking believable deficits on neuropsychological testing. *Journal of Consulting and Clinical Psychology, 46*, 892–900.

Hiscock, M., & Hiscock, C. K. (1989). Refining the forced-choice method for the detection of malingering. *Journal of Clinical and Experimental Neuropsychology, 11*, 967–974.

Hopwood, J. S., & Snell, H. K. (1933). Amnesia in relation to crime. *Journal of Mental Science, 79*, 27–41.

Howe, L. L., Anderson, A. M., Kaufman, D. A., Sachs, B. C., & Loring, D. W. (2007). Characterization of the Medical Symptom Validity Test in evaluation of clinically referred memory disorders clinic patients. *Archives of Clinical Neuropsychology, 22*, 753–761.

Iverson, G. L. (2001). Can malingering be detected with the Judgment of Line Orientation Test? *Applied Neuropsychology, 8*, 167–173.

Kay, S. R., Opler, L. A., Fiszbein, A. (1986). *Positive and Negative Syndrome Scale (PANSS) rating manual*. New York: Albert Einstein College of Medicine.

Killgore, W. D., & DellaPietra, L. (2000). Using the WMS-III to detect malingering: Empirical validation of the Rarely Missed Index (RMI). *Journal of Clinical and Experimental Neuropsychology, 22*, 761–771.

Labarge, A. S., McCaffrey, R. J., & Brown, T. A. (2003). Neuropsychologists' abilities to determine the predictive value of diagnostic tests. *Archives of Clinical Neuropsychology, 18*, 165–175.

Larrabee, G. J. (1992). On modifying recognition memory tests for detection of malingering. *Neuropsychology, 6*, 23–27.

Larrabee, G. J. (2003a). Detection of malingering using atypical performance patterns on standard neuropsychological tests. *Clinical Neuropsychologist, 17*, 410–425.

Larrabee, G. J. (2003b). Detection of symptom exaggeration with the MMPI-2 in litigants with malingered neurocognitive dysfunction. *Clinical Neuropsychologist, 17*, 54–68.

Larrabee, G. J. (2005). Assessment of malingering. In G. J. Larrabee (Ed.), *Forensic neuropsychology: A scientific approach* (pp. 115–158). New York: Oxford University Press.

Larrabee, G. J., Greiffenstein, M. F., Greve, K. W., & Bianchini, K. J. (2007). Refining diagnostic criteria for malingering. In G. J. Larrabee (Ed.), *Assessment of malingered neuropsychological deficits* (pp. 334–371). New York: Oxford University Press.

Lee, A., Boone, K. B., Lesser, I., Wohl, M., Wilkins, S., & Parks, C. (2000). Performance of older depressed patients on two cognitive malingering tests: False positive rates for the Rey 15-Item Memorization and Dot Counting Tests. *Clinical Neuropsychologist, 14*, 303–308.

Lees-Haley, P. R., Iverson, G. L., Lange, R. T., Fox, D. D., & Allen, L. M., III. (2002). Malingering in forensic neuropsychology: *Daubert* and the MMPI-2. *Journal of Forensic Neuropsychology, 3*(1/2), 167–203.

Leitch, A. (1948). Notes on amnesia in crime for the general practitioner. *Medical Press, 219*, 459–463.

Lewis, J. L., Simcox, A. M., & Berry, D. T. R. (2002). Screening for feigned psychiatric symptoms in a forensic sample by using the MMPI-2 and Structured Inventory of Malingered Symptomatology. *Psychological Assessment, 14*, 170–176.

Loring, D., Larrabee, G. J., Lee, G. P., & Meador, J. (2007). Victoria Symptom Validity Test performance in a heterogeneous clinical sample. *Clinical Neuropsychologist, 21*, 522–531.

Loring, D. W., Lee, G. P., & Meador, K. J. (2005). Victoria Symptom Validity Test performance in non-litigating epilepsy surgery candidates. *Journal of Clinical and Experimental Neuropsychology, 27*, 610–617.

Lynch, B. E., & Bradford, J. M. W. (1980). Amnesia: Its detection by psychophysiological measures. *Bulletin of the American Academy of Psychiatry and the Law, 8*, 288–297.

Macciocchi, S. N., Seel, R. T., Alderson, A., & Godsall, R. (2006). Victoria Symptom Validity Test performance in acute severe traumatic brain injury: Implications for test interpretation. *Archives of Clinical Neuropsychology, 21*, 395–404.

Marshall, P. S., & Happe, M. (2007). The performance of individuals with mental retardation on cognitive tests assessing effort and motivation. *Clinical Neuropsychologist, 21*, 826–840.

Merten, T., Green, P., Henry, M., Blaskewitz, N., & Brockhaus, R. (2005). Analog validation of German-language symptom validity tests and the influence of coaching. *Archives of Clinical Neuropsychology, 20*, 719–726.

Meyers, J. E., Galinsky, A. M., & Volbrecht, M. (1999). Malingering and mild brain injury: How low is too low? *Applied Neuropsychology, 6*, 208–216.

Meyers, J. E., & Volbrecht, M. E. (1998). Validation of Reliable Digits for detection of malingering. *Assessment, 5*, 301–305.

Meyers, J. E., & Volbrecht, M. E. (2003). A validation of multiple malingering detection methods in a large clinical sample. *Archives of Clinical Neuropsychology, 18*, 261–276.

Miller, R. D. (2003). *People v. Palmer*: Amnesia and competency to proceed revisited. *Journal of Psychiatry and Law, 31*, 165–185.

Millis, S. R. (2002). Warrington's Recognition Memory Test in the detection of response bias. In J. Hom & R. L. Denney (Eds.), *Detection of response bias in forensic neuropsychology* (pp. 147–166). New York: Haworth Medical Press. [Copublished simultaneously in *Journal of Forensic Neuropsychology, 2*(3/4), 147–166]

Millis, S. R. (2004). Evaluation of malingered neurocognitive disorders. In M. Rizzo

& P. J. Eslinger (Eds.), *Principles and practice of behavioral neurology and neuropsychology* (pp. 1077–1089). Philadelphia: Saunders.

Millis, S. R., Putnam, S. H., Adams, K. M., & Ricker, J. H. (1995). The California Verbal Learning Test in the detection of incomplete effort in neuropsychological evaluation. *Psychological Assessment, 7*, 463–471.

Mittenberg, W., Aquila-Puentes, G., Patton, C., Canyock, E. M., & Heilbronner, R. L. (2002). Neuropsychological profiling of symptom exaggeration and malingering. In J. Hom & R. L. Denney (Eds.), *Detection of response bias in forensic neuropsychology* (pp. 227–240). New York: Haworth Medical Press. [Copublished simultaneously in *Journal of Forensic Neuropsychology, 3*(1/2), 227–240]

Mittenberg, W., Patton, C., Canyock, E. M., & Condit, D. C. (2002). Base rates of malingering and symptom exaggeration. *Journal of Clinical and Experimental Neuropsychology, 24*, 1094–1102.

Nelson, N. W., Boone, K. B., Dueck, A., Wagener, L., Lu, P., & Grills, C. (2003). Relationship between eight measures of suspect effort. *Clinical Neuropsychologist, 17*, 263–272.

Nicholson v. American National Insurance, 154 F.3d 875 (8th Cir. 1998).

Nitch, S. R., & Glassmire, D. M. (2007). Non-forced-choice measures to detect noncredible cognitive performance. In K. B. Boone (Ed.), *Assessment of feigned cognitive impairment: A neuropsychological perspective* (pp. 78–102). New York: Guilford Press.

O'Connell, B. A. (1960). Amnesia and homicide. *British Journal of Delinquency, 10*, 262–276.

Pankratz, L. (1979). Symptom validity testing and symptom retraining: Procedures for the assessment and treatment of functional sensory deficits. *Journal of Consulting and Clinical Psychology, 47*, 409–410.

Pankratz, L., & Erickson, R. C. (1990). Two views of malingering. *Clinical Neuropsychologist, 4*, 379–389.

Pankratz, L., Fausti, S. A., & Peed, S. (1975). A forced-choice technique to evaluate deafness in the hysterical or malingering patient. *Journal of Consulting and Clinical Psychology, 43*, 421–422.

Parkin, A. J. (1996). Focal retrograde amnesia: A multi-faceted disorder? *Acta Neurologica Belgica, 96*(1), 43–50.

Parwatikar, S. D., Holcomb, W. R., & Menninger, K. A., II. (1985). The detection of malingered amnesia in accused murderers. *Bulletin of the American Academy of Psychiatry and the Law, 13*, 97–103.

Paul, D. S., Franzen, M. D., Cohen, S. H., & Fremouw, W. (1992). An investigation into the reliability and validity of two tests used in the detection of dissimulation. *International Journal of Clinical Neuropsychology, 14*, 1–9.

Power, D. J. (1977). Memory, identification and crime. *Medicine, Science, and the Law, 17*, 132–139.

Price, G. E., & Terhune, W. B. (1919). Feigned amnesia as a defense reaction. *Journal of the American Medical Association, 72*, 565–567.

Reitan, R. M., & Wolfson, D. (2002). Detection of malingered and invalid test results using the Halstead–Reitan Battery. In J. Hom & R. L. Denney (Eds.),

Detection of negative response bias in forensic neuropsychology (pp. 275–314). New York: Haworth Medical Press. [Copublished simultaneously in *Journal of Forensic Neuropsychology, 3*(1/2), 275–314]

Rey, A. (1941). L'Examen psychologie dans las cas d'encephalopathie traumatique [The psychological examination in cases of traumatic encephalopathy]. *Archives de Psychologie, 28,* 286–340.

Rey, A. (1958). *L'examen clinique en psychologie* [The psychological examination]. Paris: Presses Universitaires de France.

Reznek, L. (2005). The Rey 15-Item Memory Test for malingering: A meta-analysis. *Brain Injury, 19,* 539–543.

Richman, J., Green, P., Gervais, R., Flaro, L., Merten, T., Brockhaus, R., et al. (2006). Objective tests of symptom exaggeration in independent medical examinations. *Journal of Occupational and Environmental Medicine, 48,* 303–311.

Rogers, R. (1986). *Conducting insanity evaluations.* New York: Van Nostrand Reinhold.

Rogers, R. (Ed.). (2008). *Clinical assessment of malingering and deception* (3rd ed.). New York: Guilford Press.

Rosenfeld, B., Sands, S. A., & Van Gorp, W. G. (2000). Have we forgotten the base rate problem?: Methodological issues in the detection of distortion. *Archives of Clinical Neuropsychology, 15*(4), 349–359.

Ross, S. M. (2000). Profound retrograde amnesia following mild head injury: Organic or functional? *Cortex, 36*(4), 521–537.

Rubinsky, E. W., & Brandt, J. (1986). Amnesia and criminal law: A clinical overview. *Behavioral Sciences and the Law, 4,* 27–46.

Schacter, D. L. (1986). Amnesia and crime: How much do we really know? *American Psychologist, 41,* 286–295.

Schmand, B., Kuipers, T., Van der Gaag, M., Boxveld, J., Bulthuis, F., & Jellema, M. (1994). Cognitive disorders and negative symptoms as correlates of motivation deficit in psychotic patients. *Psychological Medicine, 24,* 869–884.

Siegel, S. (1956). *Nonparametric statistics for the behavioral sciences.* New York: McGraw-Hill.

Simon, M. J. (1994). The use of the Rey Memory Test to assess malingering in criminal defendants. *Journal of Clinical Psychology, 50,* 913–917.

Slick, D. J., Hopp, G., Strauss, E., & Thompson, G. B. (1997). *Victoria Symptom Validity Test version 1.0 professional manual.* Odessa, FL: Psychological Assessment Resources.

Slick, D. J., Iverson, G. I., & Green, P. (2000). California Verbal Learning Test indicators of suboptimal performance in a sample of head-injury litigants. *Journal of Clinical and Experimental Neuropsychology, 22,* 569–579.

Slick, D. J., Sherman, E. M. S., & Iverson, G. L. (1999). Diagnostic criteria for malingered neurocognitive dysfunction: Proposed standards for clinical practice and research. *Clinical Neuropsychologist, 13,* 552–553.

Slick, D. J., Tan, J. E., Strauss, E., Mateer, C. A., Harnadek, M., & Sherman, M. S. (2003). Victoria Symptom Validity Test scores of patients with profound memory impairment: Nonlitigant case studies. *Clinical Neuropsychologist, 16,* 495–505.

Suhr, J. A., & Barrash, J. (2007). Performance on standard attention, memory, and psychomotor speed tasks as indicators of malingering. In G. J. Larrabee (Ed.), *Assessment of malingered neuropsychological deficits* (pp. 131–170). New York: Oxford University Press.

Sweet, J. J., & King, J. H. (2002). Category Test validity indicators: Overview and practice recommendations. In J. Hom & R. L. Denney (Eds.), *Detection of negative response bias in forensic neuropsychology* (pp. 241–274). New York: Haworth Medical Press. [Copublished simultaneously in *Journal of Forensic Neuropsychology*, 3(1/2), 241–274]

Tan, J. E., Slick, D. J., Strauss, E., & Hultsch, D. F. (2002). How'd they do it?: Malingering strategies on symptom validity tests. *Clinical Neuropsychologist*, 16, 495–505.

Taylor, P. J., & Kopelman, M. D. (1984). Amnesia for criminal offences. *Psychological Medicine*, 14, 581–588.

Teichner, G., & Wagner, M. T. (2004). The Test of Memory Malingering (TOMM): normative data from cognitively intact, cognitively impaired, and elderly patients with dementia. *Archives of Clinical Neuropsychology*, 19, 455–464.

Teichner, G., Waid, L. R., & Buddin, W. H. (2005, October). *The Medical Symptom Validity Test (MSVT): Data from a sample demonstrating a range of neurological and psychiatric disorders.* Poster presented at the National Academy of Neuropsychology Annual Conference, Tampa, FL.

Theodor, L. H., & Mandelcorn, M. S. (1973). Hysterical blindness: A case report and study using a modern psychophysical technique. *Journal of Abnormal Psychology*, 82, 552–553.

Tombaugh, T. N. (1996). *TOMM: Test of Memory Malingering.* North Tonawanda, NY: Multi-Health Systems.

Tombaugh, T. N. (2002). The Test of Memory Malingering (TOMM) in forensic psychology. In J. Hom & R. L. Denney (Eds.), *Detection of response bias in forensic neuropsychology* (pp. 69–96). New York: Haworth Medical Press.

Tydecks, S., Merten, T., & Gubay, J. (2006). The Word Memory Test and the One-in-Five-Test in an analog study with Russian speaking participants. *International Journal of Forensic Psychology*, 1, 29–37.

United States v. Greer, 158 F.3d 228 (5th Cir. 1998).

Vallabhajosula, B., & van Gorp, W. G. (2001). Post-*Daubert* admissibility of scientific evidence on malingering of cognitive deficits. *Journal of the American Academy of Psychiatry and the Law*, 29, 207–215.

Vickery, C. D., Berry, D. T. R., Inman, T. H., Harris, M. J., & Orey, S. A. (2001). Detection of inadequate effort on neuropsychological testing: A meta-analytic review of selected procedures. *Archives of Clinical Neuropsychology*, 16, 45–73.

Victor, T. L., & Boone, K. B. (2007). Identification of feigned mental retardation. In K. B. Boone (Ed.), *Assessment of feigned cognitive impairment: A neuropsychological perspective* (pp. 310–345). New York: Guilford Press.

Vilar-López, R., Santiago-Ramajo, S., Gómez-Río, M., Verdejo-García, A., Llamas, J. M., & Pérez-García, M. (2007). Detection of malingering in a Spanish population using three specific malingering tests. *Archives of Clinical Neuropsychology*, 22, 379–388.

Weinborn, M., Orr, T., Woods, S. P., Conover, E., & Feix, J. (2003). A validation of the Test of Memory Malingering in a forensic psychiatric setting. *Journal of Clinical and Experimental Neuropsychology, 25*, 979–990.

Wiggins, E. C., & Brandt, J. (1988). The detection of simulated amnesia. *Law and Human Behavior, 12*, 57–78.

Wilson v. United States, 391 F.2d 460 (D.C. Cir. 1968).

Wynkoop, T. F., & Denney, R. L. (1999). Exaggeration of neuropsychological deficit in competency to stand trial. *Journal of Forensic Neuropsychology, 1*, 29–53.

Wynkoop, T. F., & Denney, R. L. (2001). Test reviews: Computerized Assessment of Response Bias (CARB), Word Memory Test (WMT), and Memory Complaints Inventory (MCI). *Journal of Forensic Neuropsychology, 2*, 71–77.

Wynkoop, T. F., & Denney, R. L. (2005). Test review: Green's Word Memory Test for Windows. *Journal of Forensic Neuropsychology, 4*, 101–105.

Yanez, Y., Fremouw, W., Tennant, J., Strunk, J., & Coker, C. (2006). Effects of severe depression on TOMM performance among disability-seeking outpatients. *Archives of Clinical Neuropsychology, 21*, 161–165.

Zachary, R. A. (1986). *Shipley Institute of Living Scale—Revised manual*. Los Angeles: Western Psychological Services.

Zimmerman, J., & Grosz, H. J. (1966). "Visual" performance of a functionally blind person. *Behaviour Research and Therapy, 4*, 119–134.

Chapter 5

Psychological Evaluation in *Miranda* Waiver and Confession Cases

I. BRUCE FRUMKIN

Confessions and self-incriminating statements to law enforcement carry great weight with the trier of fact. They become important components of proving guilt beyond a reasonable doubt. Kassin and Neumann (1997) helped to demonstrate what is commonly believed to be true, that a confession is "devastating" to a defendant. Leo (1996) reports that 80% of suspects waive their rights, whereas Wrightsman and Kassin (1993) report that confessions are produced in 50% of criminal cases and are challenged in court in 20% of these cases. Cassell (1996), in a literature review, found that confessions are needed in 24% of cases to produce conviction. Leo studied 182 criminal cases and found that the strength of the evidence without the use of confession was weak in 33% of these cases. He also found that suspects who incriminated themselves during interrogation were 20% more likely to be charged by prosecutors, and 26% more likely to be found guilty and convicted.

Both anecdotal and empirical data support what is amazing but in fact true: Innocent people sometimes do confess to crimes they did not commit. For example, in the "Central Park Jogger" case, five teens ages 14–16 were arrested. Each confessed and implicated the others on videotape in the crime of attacking and raping a jogger in New York City's Central Park on April 19, 1989. In 2002, Matias Reyes, a convicted murderer and rapist, admitted that he was responsible for the rape and attack of the woman. Reyes's DNA matched that obtained from the crime scene, and the convictions of the five youths were vacated on December 19, 2002.

According to Ofshe and Leo (1997a), not only do suspects sometimes falsely confess to crimes they did not commit, but in fact they also seem to do so regularly. Ofshe and Leo base their conclusions on case studies, laboratory research, and their own work on a large number of probable or confirmed cases of false confessions. It is impossible to assess accurately the number or the percentage of false confessions, because estimates of false confessions vary depending on the design of the study and how the false confessions were operationalized. Some researchers (Kassin & McNall, 1991) estimate that there are fewer than 30–60 false confessions per year, whereas another researcher (Cassell, 1996) reports that number to be as high as 600. In the United States, there is no tally kept of the number of suspects interrogated annually and how many of those result in a true confession, no confession, or false confession. In many states and jurisdictions, police are not required to record the confessions that suspects have allegedly made. A suspect, despite law enforcement claims to the contrary, may deny ever having confessed in the first place. A confession, unrecorded, may later become a challenged retracted confession. A confession is considered so crucial in prosecution that weight is still given to that confession even when a defendant is seemingly exonerated by DNA evidence. Notably, just because a suspect provides a false confession for one element of the offense, not all elements of the alleged offense are false. Thus, a confession is not necessarily completely true or false. There may be varying degrees of truth regarding certain aspects of a confession. Finally, numerous instances of laboratory errors and/or fraud have been documented. Therefore, someone who confesses and later retracts the confession, but is not cleared by laboratory results, may in fact still be innocent.

Mental health professionals have been used to assist the court in cases in which the admissibility of a confession is disputed. Although the frequency of expert testimony varies between jurisdictions, psychologists are often used to assess a defendant's *competency* to have waived *Miranda* rights at the time of the police questioning. Competency to waive testimony is generally offered pretrial at a suppression hearing. In certain circumstances, depending on the legal strategy of a defense attorney, such testimony can be offered at the time of the trial as well. Psychologists are also used to evaluate psychological factors that might be relevant in cases of alleged false and/or coerced confessions. Such expert testimony is usually offered at the time of trial, but it may occasionally be offered pretrial, again, depending on the defense's legal strategy.

Compared to evaluation in other areas of criminal forensic psychology (e.g., competency to stand trial, insanity, risk assessments), evaluating a defendant's competency to waive *Miranda* rights and assessing psychological factors relevant to false and/or coerced confessions are relatively new activities of a forensic psychologist. Psychologists have only been doing these evaluations routinely for the past 25 years and have faced increasing scrutiny in the courtroom for the work they do in this area.

This chapter focuses on the clinical, legal, and theoretical underpinnings relevant to confessions, specifically, a defendant's competency to waive *Miranda* rights at the time of the interrogation, and psychological variables related to false and involuntary confessions. Following each section, a clinical protocol is provided to guide the psychologist in conducting an effective forensic assessment for that particular psycholegal topic. Next, issues pertaining to the admissibility of some of the relevant forensic measures are covered. Finally, the chapter closes with a brief summary outlining special considerations for the forensic neuropsychologist. The goal of this chapter is to provide key information to assist the forensic psychology expert in providing testimony to the court. Issues of *Miranda* rights and false confession are certainly areas of potential concern for defendants with suspected neurological dysfunction. In that regard, neuropsychologists seeking to expand their practice in the area of criminal forensics may find themselves dealing with these very issues and as a result will find this chapter particularly helpful.

Competency to Waive *Miranda* Rights

Heilbrun (2001) defines a *forensic mental health assessment* as an "evaluation that is performed by mental health professionals as part of the legal decision-making process, for the purpose of assisting the decision-maker or helping one of the litigants in using relevant clinical and scientific data" (p. 3). Forensic evaluations need to be functional assessments that relate legally relevant behavior and obtained assessment data to specified legal criteria. In determining whether a *Miranda* waiver is valid, the fact finder is concerned with the "totality of circumstances" surrounding the interrogation, specifically, the nature of the interrogation process and those individual characteristics that may increase or reduce a defendant's understanding (e.g., *Fare v. Michael C.*, 1979). In *Miranda v. Arizona* (1966), the U.S. Supreme Court ruled that any statement arising from the custodial interrogation of a suspect would be presumed involuntary and thus inadmissible, unless the police provide the suspect with four warnings: (1) the right to remain silent, (2) that any statements can be used in court against the suspect, (3) the right to the presence of an attorney before and at all times during the interrogation process, and (4) that an attorney will be appointed if the suspect cannot afford one. As mentioned earlier, a suspect may waive his or her rights if the waiver is made *knowingly, intelligently*, and *voluntarily*. Many jurisdictions have added a fifth prong to the four "rights": that the rights may be invoked at any time during the interrogation and the interrogation must cease. The case of *In re Gault* (1967) applied these protections to juveniles. More recently, the U.S. Court of Appeals for the 4th Circuit attempted to narrow the relevance of the *Miranda* warning for federal law enforcement officials. They cited 18 U.S.C. 3501, which was passed by Congress to reinstate a rule that had been in effect for 180 years prior to *Miranda*, that statements by suspects could be used against them as long as they were not involuntarily coerced, thus negating the need for a recitation of *Miranda* (see *United States v. Crocker*, 1975). *Dickerson v. United States* (2000) overturned the 4th Circuit's decision. Additionally the U.S. Supreme Court held that an act of Congress cannot overrule the Constitutional decision of the Court.

Frumkin (2000) and Frumkin and Garcia (2003) proposed a model for conducting *Miranda* waiver evaluations. Others have proposed similar models (e.g., DeClue, 2005; Grisso, 2003; Heilbrun, 2002; Oberlander, Goldstein, & Goldstein, 2003). There are more similarities than differences across the models. Each model calls for a functional assessment approach. A clinician needs to assess psychological factors relevant to the legal construct of a *knowing, intelligent,* and *voluntary* waiver. Psychologists and attorneys alike mistakenly use these terms interchangeably. However, their meanings are different, and all three prongs must be established for a waiver to be valid and a subsequent statement to be admissible (e.g., *State v. Bittick*, 1986).

Grisso (2003), in his review of case law, defined a *knowing* waiver of rights as dependent upon the individual's understanding or comprehension of each of the four rights, as well as the manner in which the rights were administered to the individual. Obviously, an individual's reading comprehension is highly relevant if he or she is asked by law enforcement to read the rights. Conversely, if the police read the rights to the individual, then reading skills are relatively unimportant to assessment of an understanding of the rights, and the focus moves to verbal comprehension. Was the suspect merely handed the waiver form and asked to sign his or her name, without being asked to read the form first? In that situation, even if the subject reads, the manner in which the rights were administered becomes relevant. The complexity of the wording of *Miranda* waiver forms vary greatly within and among jurisdictions. Therefore, it is the "interaction" of the individual's cognitive abilities with police procedure that is relevant.

An *intelligent* waiver of rights is distinguished from a *knowing* waiver of rights. Grisso (2003) speaks of a decision-making capacity, whereby the subject weighs options and his or her consequences. Although the exact definition of *intelligent* waiver varies based on case law, it is generally thought to signify being able to "fully comprehend the meaning and effect of his decision to waive the rights and make incriminating statements to police officers" (*In re Patrick W.*, 1978). In *Moran v. Burbine* (1986), the U.S. Supreme Court held that "the waiver must have been made with a full awareness of both the nature of the right being abandoned and the consequences of the decision to abandon it" (also see *Cooper v. Griffin*, 1972).

In court, the expert is frequently questioned as to whether anyone who waives his or her *Miranda* rights can be said to have *not* made an intelligent waiver. The answer is "absolutely not!" An unintelligent waiver does not have to do with making a poor choice. An unintelligent waiver results from making a decision to waive the rights based on a misunderstanding of the legal process and how it applies both personally and in the abstract. For example, one may understand (*knowing* component) about the right to have an attorney present during questioning. However, if the suspect erroneously believes a defense attorney would only defend innocent defendants, then an intelligent use of the right to counsel is not realized. One may know about the right to silence, such that one does not have to speak to the police. Yet if that individual mistakenly believes that a judge or jury will think a person is guilty of the crime for not "cooperating" with the police, or that one must state in court what one did that was wrong, then the individual cannot make an intelligent use of the right to silence.

The discrimination between a knowing and an intelligent waiver with *Miranda* is similar to that made for a "factual" and a "rational" understanding of legal proceedings relevant to fitness for trial (*Dusky v. United States*, 1960) and those made in a variety of civil competencies, such as consent to treatment, capacity to enter into a contract, and testamentary capacity (Slovenko, 1999). The "rational" or "intelligent" prong of these various legal competencies involves the ability to manipulate information and appreciate the significance and consequences of one's actions.

In *Colorado v. Connelly* (1986), the U.S. Supreme Court reversed the trial court's suppression of the defendant's confession. The lower court had based its ruling on a psychiatrist's testimony that Frances Connelly was psychotic (hearing the voice of God demand that he confess to a murder), which interfered with his ability to make a free and rational choice and motivated his confession. The Supreme Court found no requirement that for a *Miranda* waiver to be *voluntary*, a waiver must be the product of free will. There does, however, have to be a demonstration that the police overstepped their bounds or were unduly coercive in extracting a confession, for a confession to be involuntary.

I have argued (Frumkin, 2000; Frumkin & Garcia, 2003) that it is beyond the expertise for psychologists to offer testimony as to whether a defendant has voluntarily waived *Miranda* rights. It becomes purely a legal (or moral) issue of where one draws the line as to the limits of coerciveness of police conduct in extracting a *Miranda* waiver or confession. It is not for the psychologist to make that fine-line determination, because the decision to be made is not a clinical one. This is not to suggest that the psychologist does not have useful data to present to the court. Psychological characteristics that may make a person more susceptible to giving in to influences compared to the average person, or psychological factors that heightened the risk for giving a false confession are highly relevant. Such factors may include neurocognitive compromise.

There has been frequent controversy in forensic psychology regarding psychologists offering testimony on the ultimate legal issue, that is, the specific question before the trier of fact. Although many psychologists do frequently testify to the ultimate legal issue, I concur with the opinions expressed by Melton and colleagues (2007) that psychologists should resist such temptations to offer ultimate opinion testimony. Psychologists have no special training in legal decision making, in essence, where to "draw the line" in making legal judgments. This issue is particularly relevant for *Miranda*-related issues. In the case of a *Miranda* waiver evaluation, it is one thing to state the likelihood of a defendant being able to make a knowing and intelligent waiver at the time of the interrogation. It is another matter entirely to state whether such a waiver was indeed valid. The validity of a waiver is based on the totality of circumstances, some of which include nonpsychological variables, such as police conduct.

A Protocol for Evaluating Competency to Waive *Miranda* Rights

A psychologist must conduct a comprehensive evaluation of a defendant's psychological functioning. This assessment should integrate background or third-party data, results from a clinical interview, and data from a host of psychological tests, with legally relevant criteria defining the *knowing, intelligent,* and *voluntary* aspects of the *Miranda* waiver. Psychological tests designed to assess malingering of cognitive and psychological impairment are an integral component of any forensic assessment.

One should inform the defense attorney that the defendant should not be told about the specific purpose of the evaluation (i.e., whether *Miranda* rights were understood or whether the police coerced a statement). Not only would such advance notice increase the likelihood that a defendant might try to exaggerate impairment to come across as incompetent to waive the rights, but also even if the defendant did not try to malinger, the opposing attorney would argue that the defendant did just that. That is not to imply that informed consent should not be given to the defendant. If the evaluation is defense-requested, the defendant should be informed by both the psychologist and the defense attorney that the purpose of the evaluation is to assist the attorney in "better planning for the case." Additionally, it is best if the defense attorney keeps at a minimum any discussion pertaining to the Miranda rights themselves. If an attorney educates the client by speaking about the rights that should have been invoked when with the police, it is more difficult for the psychologist to extrapolate from the defendant's current knowledge what he or she knew when interacting with the police.

Record Review

The next step in the evaluation process is to seek relevant third-party data. The most important piece of this data is a copy of the signed Miranda waiver form or a verbatim copy of the wording used in an oral administration of the rights. Since the complexity of the wording of the warnings can vary greatly within and between jurisdictions, it is important that the psychologist evaluate the defendant, in part, based on the rights actually given. If the warnings were read, then a number of readability formulas enable one to calculate reading ease and grade level for a particular written passage. Both WordPerfect and Microscoft Word allow one to calculate a Flesch Reading Ease and Flesch–Kincaid Grade Level score for any passage based on Flesch's (1994) calculations. Obviously, the relative readability of the Miranda passage is important data if a defendant's reading comprehension or ability to decode written material is measured at a level far below that of the particular Miranda rights read by the subject.

The psychologist should attempt to obtain from the referring source copies of transcripts or records of the interrogation, as well as the defendant's statements, to compare that with the defendant's version of what transpired. Unfortunately, relatively few jurisdictions record an individual's first contact with law enforcement. If there is a recording or transcription, it may have been done after a preinterview, or after the first administration of the rights.

In any event, audio- or videotaped recordings of the interrogation, if they exist, are clearly the primary source for review, because transcripts may vary in accuracy and level to which they capture a suspect's emotional and cognitive state. It is important to obtain transcripts of depositions, again, if they exist, of witnesses (police officers, family members, etc.) who observed the defendant as close to the time as possible when rights were administered. School records, work records, psychological and medical records, and any and all third-party records that enable a clinician to better interpret the findings of the current evaluation are important to obtain. While it is important for the psychologist to obtain an arrest history of the defendant, research has shown (see Grisso, 1981) that there is "no straightforward relation between Miranda comprehension and number of prior felony arrests (our way of defining amount of prior court experience)" (T. Grisso, personal communication, April 16, 2001).

Clinical Interview

Once the psychologist obtains and reviews as much third-party data as possible, the assessment is conducted. It is important first to obtain informed consent from the defendant and to explain the limits of confidentiality. Competency to consent to evaluation does not automatically equate with competency to have waived *Miranda* rights at the time of the police questioning.

Although one would not want to go beyond the scope of the evaluation to assess a defendant's version of what transpired that led to an arrest, it is important that a thorough clinical interview be conducted during the assessment to obtain the defendant's version of occupational, educational, medical, marital, family, arrest, and mental health treatment histories. A history of alcohol and substance abuse is also relevant, particularly if the defendant was under the influence of such substances when interrogated. Such psychosocial assessment is relevant in terms of how one interprets the test data. A Full Scale IQ score in the Borderline range may mean malingering or acquired brain dysfunction for someone who completed a college education, but it may mean something entirely different for an individual whose formal education did not extend past the eighth grade and consisted of placement in special education classes. The traditional mental status examination is also required.

During the clinical interview, the psychologist must obtain the defendant's detailed version of the interaction with law enforcement. The goal of this part of the interview is to have the defendant describe, step-by-step, what happened during the police questioning. Ideally, at some point, the defendant will spontaneously state that the police then read or asked the defendant to read his or her rights. The psychologist wants to determine if the rights can be spontaneously verbalized by the defendant. If the defendant does not indicate that the police read any rights, the psychologist can ask whether the police gave him or her any papers to sign. The psychologist may ask whether the defendant watches police shows on television and if so, "What do the police say to suspects when first arrested?" Once the psychologist ascertains as well as possible how the rights were administered by the police, it is advisable to administer the actual rights to the defendant in the same fashion the rights were given by the officers. If the defendant was asked to read the rights, then the psychologist should give the rights to the defendant to read. If the rights were read to the defendant, then the psychologist should read the rights to the defendant during the interview. Sometimes both methods need to be employed. Immediately after the rights are given during the interview, the psychologist should ask the defendant what rights were just given. It is important to note that just because a defendant can repeat back each of the four or five rights, or can spontaneously utter them without prompting, it does not mean that he or she understands the rights. An individual might verbalize, for example, that whatever one says may be used against the person in court. Further inquiry may indicate that the defendant believes that if one curses at the police, it will be used against the defendant in the courtroom. There may be no indication that the defendant understands that statements pertaining to the alleged offense can be used against him or her in court. It is oftentimes useful to ask a defendant why he or she decided to waive the rights when told that he or she had a right to remain silent; or why one did not ask for a lawyer when told he or she could have one. The answers to these questions could provide valuable information as to the subject's thought processes at the time of the police questioning.

What if an individual understands and appreciates each of the four rights but cannot remember them for any length of time? An argument can be made that if one is allowed to invoke the rights at any time during the interrogation, then the validity of the *Miranda* waiver may have been compromised if the subject cannot remember the rights well enough to invoke them. This issue may be particularly relevant for a defendant who has significant neurocognitive deficits or below-average intellectual functioning.

Psychological Testing

Psychological test results are a major source of data in formulating an opinion on a defendant's competency to waive *Miranda* rights. It must be emphasized that there is no single IQ cutoff or diagnostic category that automatically renders one unable to waive the *Miranda* rights competently at the time of the police questioning. However, research is clear (e.g., Cloud, Shepherd, Barkoff, & Shur, 2002; Everington & Fulero, 1999; Fulero & Everington, 1995; Grisso, 1981) in showing a correlation between *Miranda* comprehension and intelligence. Yet, in a particular case, whereas an individual with mental retardation may be able to understand and appreciate his or her rights, a person of greater than average intellectual abilities may have a misconception of the meaning and effect of one of the rights. Certainly, psychotic thinking may adversely impact the processing of information during the recitation of the rights. However, compromised reality testing, even at the time of police questioning, would not automatically negate a knowing and intelligent waiver. A clinical evaluation has to be functional, and an assessment constructed so as to identify what specifically this defendant understands and appreciates about the *Miranda* rights. Then the psychologist, much the same way one would do for a mental state at the time of the offense evaluation, attempts to make a retrospective assessment regarding the defendant's knowledge, and ability to make an intelligent waiver, *at the time of the police questioning*.

Intelligence tests, such as the Wechsler scales, are useful not only in obtaining various IQ and scale scores but also as behavioral samples that illustrate how an individual responds to various types of tasks. Vocabulary knowledge, verbal abstract reasoning skills, general fund of knowledge about the world, attention and short-term memory, and judgment and common sense are all relevant factors to examine when evaluating one's ability to waive *Miranda* competently. Although the Performance IQ is likely less relevant to *Miranda* issues than Verbal IQ, one should give the complete IQ test to interpret scaled score differences and identify possible issues of organic brain dysfunction. Axelrod (2002) and others caution against using short forms of intelligence tests, such as the Wechsler Abbreviated Scale of Intelligence (WASI). There is poor correlation between Wechsler Adult Intelligence Scale–III (WAIS-III) and WASI scores, and the WASI has poor accuracy in predicting true scores. For example, 16% of WASI scores vary greater than 10 points in either direction. When, on the basis of record review, observation, or psychological testing, brain dysfunction is suspected, traditional neuropsychological measures may be utilized. A psychologist qualified to administer and interpret neuropsychological measures should perform this part of the assessment. Neuropsychological assessment should be limited to measures that serve to inform expert opinion about the psycholegal construct in question. A comprehensive neuropsychological assessment may or may not be indicated.

Depending on how the rights were administered to the suspect, the clinician may well decide to measure reading comprehension by use of standardized achievement tests, such as the Wide Range Achievement Test–4 (WRAT-4), the Wide Range Achievement Test—Expanded (WRAT-E), or the Wechsler Individual Achievement Test–II (WIAT-II).

Personality tests are also important in evaluating competency to waive *Miranda* rights. These tests may provide information regarding an individual's psychological functioning as it relates to reality testing, accommodation, impulse control, coping skills, and other states and traits that could undermine an individual's ability to make a knowing, intelligent, and voluntary waiver of rights. Although the Minnesota Multiphasic Personality Inventory–2 (MMPI-2; Butcher, Dahlstrom, Graham, Telegen, & Kaemmer, 1989), the Minnesota Multiphasic Personality Inventory—Adolescent (MMPI-A), or the Personality Assessment Inventory (PAI) are often used, tests such as the California Psychological Inventory—Revised (CPI-R) or the 16 Personality Factor (16 PF; Cattell, Cattell, & Cattell, 1993) provide better assessment of the more normal or healthier aspects of personality that could be relevant to *Miranda* competency. These tests often include different normative groups and may provide information that the MMPI-2 cannot provide.

If there is reason to believe a defendant is malingering, it is important to administer psychological tests to measure this issue objectively. Malingering is not a dichotomous construct; rather, it falls along a continuum. Individuals exaggerate and/or minimize diverse symptoms to varying degrees. It is important to distinguish malingering of cognitive deficits from malingering of psychopathology. Psychological tests such as the Test of Malingered Memory (TOMM) or the Validity Indicator Profile (VIP) are useful in assessing whether a defendant is attempting to exaggerate or feign memory or intellectual shortcomings. The validity scales of the MMPI tests and the Structured Interview of Reported Symptoms (SIRS) are useful in assessing whether a defendant is attempting exaggerate or feign psychopathology.

Specialized Tests

Grisso (1981), as part of a National Institute of Mental Health–funded research project, studied comprehension and appreciation of *Miranda* rights among juveniles and adults. Four separate tests were developed from this research: the Comprehension of *Miranda* Rights (CMR), the Comprehension of *Miranda* Rights—Recognition (CMR-R), the Comprehension of *Miranda* Vocabulary (CMV), and the Function of Rights in Interrogation (FRI). These tests, if properly used, can provide the clinician and the courts with valuable information in *helping* to assess a defendant's ability to have made a knowing and intelligent waiver of *Miranda* rights at the time of the police questioning.

The first test, the CMR, helps to assess one's *current* understanding of *Miranda*, as opposed to one's understanding at the time of the police questioning. An individual may well understand the rights currently but may not have been able to do so at the time of the police interrogation. The defendant may have been subsequently educated on *Miranda* by defense counsel or by other inmates. Additionally, the defendant may have been in an impaired mental state due to sleep deprivation, alcohol or drugs, or a psychotic thought process at the time of the interrogation. In the same way that *current* psychological or cognitive status may not pertain to a defendant's criminal responsibility at the time an offense was committed, a defendant's current functioning may not be the same as his level of functioning during police questioning.

On the CMR, the subject is shown four cards, each containing one of the four *Miranda* rights. The subject is read each right and asked to state in his or her own words what each right means. In Grisso's research, a national panel of judges, lawyers, and legal scholars decided what type of response would indicate a full understanding of the right, a 2 point response; a partial understanding of the right, a 1 point response; or no understanding of the right, a 0 point response. A scoring manual was developed to allow the psychologist to score the items objectively. Thus, a person can obtain a score of 0 to 8. The obtained score can be compared to various normative groups in the standardization sample.

The CMR-R was developed as a less verbally demanding means to assess one's current understanding of *Miranda* rights. Grisso believed it was possible that a person understood the rights, but because of poor verbal skills, could not communicate the understanding. Thus, the CMR-R was developed to provide an additional, less verbally expressive measure to look at *Miranda* understanding. Again, the defendant is shown one of four *Miranda* warnings. Also shown are three comparison statements. The defendant has to state whether each of the comparison statements' meaning is the "same" or "different" than the *Miranda* right. For each right, there are three comparison statements. The scoring range is 0 to 12.

The CMV was developed to examine a defendant's understanding of the meaning of six words often contained in the *Miranda* warnings. Again, one can obtain a 0–2 score on each of the six words. The test manual is used to score the responses the subject provides.

Whereas the CMR, CMR-R, and CMV were developed to help assess a defendant's current understanding of the *Miranda* rights and to help assess psychological factors relevant to making a knowing waiver at the time of the police questioning, the FRI was developed to help assess ability to make an intelligent waiver of *Miranda* rights. As discussed earlier, an intelligent waiver of rights involves a decision-making capacity, entailing an appreciation of the meaning and effect of waiving the rights. To this end, on the FRI, a subject is presented with illustrations and four brief vignettes depicting (1) an individual being interrogated by police, (2) an individual meeting with an attorney, (3) an individual being questioned by the police, and (4) the same individual later appearing in court. After each vignette, the psychologist asks questions about the stories. These questions are designed to determine the defendant's grasp of the nature and significance of the interrogation process, the right to counsel, and the right to silence. Again, one refers to a manual for scoring based on the national panel's determination of what type of response indicated full appreciation, partial appreciation, or no appreciation or ability to intelligently invoke the *Miranda* rights.

These four tests provide the psychologist with a standardized assessment tool to help in the *Miranda* competency assessment. Unfortunately, some psychologists make inappropriate use of resultant test data. One common error is for the psychologist categorically to equate how well the defendant performs on the tests with his or her ability to have made a knowing and intelligent waiver at the time of the interrogation. These tests aid the psychologist in assessing what the defendant currently understands and appreciates, but they may not reflect a defendant's actual knowledge and/or appreciation in the past, during the police questioning.

Second, the *Miranda* wording on the Grisso tests is likely to vary to a greater or lesser extent from the wording actually given by law enforcement. The psychologist needs to take this into consideration in interpreting the meaning of the results. Particularly if the police version differs significantly from the Grisso tests wording, the psychologist should ask the defendant to state the meaning of the warning he or she was actually given by the police.

Third, the psychologist often puts undue emphasis on the scores or percentiles. Although it is sometimes important to calculate how that defendant's score compares to others' scores, it is more important to examine qualitatively the types of errors made, as well as how a defendant came to obtain a particular score through item-by-item analysis. For example, did the defendant get a particular score of 6 because he or she demonstrated full understanding of two of the rights and partial understanding of the other two rights, or did the subject have full understanding of three of the rights and no understanding of one of the rights?

Another error is made when psychologists compare total FRI scores with the normative group. They use the total FRI score to support conclusions, as if the total score measured a single construct. The three functions measured on the FRI—nature of the interrogation process, intelligent use of right to counsel, and intelligent use of right to silence—measure different aspects of appreciation of rights. According to Grisso (1981, p. 127), "they do not measure a unitary substance or knowledge or beliefs. That is, the accuracy or inaccuracy of a person's perceptions in any one of the three areas is not predictive of the quality of perceptions in any other area." Thus, someone may obtain an average or above average total score on the FRI, yet miss one or more of the items pertaining to intelligent invocation of right to silence. For example, if the defendant verbalized that a judge or jury would think one guilty because he or she invoked his right to silence, that defendant may not have been able to make intelligent use of the right to silence, regardless of the actual total score obtained on the FRI.

Because there are so few test items for each of the Grisso tests, providing percentiles to the court regarding a defendant's performance compared to that of a normative group may inaccurately describe a defendant's true knowledge. The tests' strength appears to be in providing a standardized means of obtaining data for which a panel of experts have indicated a certain level of understanding or appreciation. Providing the court with verbatim responses of the subject is potentially more useful than merely demonstrating how this person compares to others, because a one-point score difference in either direction on a test such as the CMR can drastically change percentile scores.

The CMV appears to be the least useful of the four Grisso tests, because unless most of the six words appeared on the actual waiver form the defendant was given, one is measuring words that in that specific case do not apply. The six words on the CMV are *consult, attorney, interrogation, appoint, entitled,* and *right*. If four or more of the words are contained on the actual *Miranda* waiver form, it may be useful to give the test. Nevertheless, unlike scoring for the other three Grisso tests, the scoring manual for the CMV does not provide thorough discriminations among various types of scores. If one wants to measure vocabulary knowledge, extrapolating from results of the Vocabulary subtest on the WAIS-III is likely a more psychometrically sound approach.

A final consideration is that the Grisso tests should only be used as part of an overall comprehensive assessment. In fact, in the test manual, Grisso (1998) describes the measures as a "helpful adjunct in *Miranda* waiver evaluations when combined with other assessment data" (p. 4). Additionally, it is important to inform the court what research has shown regarding individuals' understanding of *Miranda* rights. Existing research (e.g., Grisso, 1981) has demonstrated that juveniles age 14 and younger are substantially less likely than adults and older juveniles to understand *Miranda* and to make competent and intelligent decisions about their waiver of rights. Adolescents ages 15 and 16, with IQ scores lower than 80, do not understand *Miranda* rights compared to adult groups and to juveniles with higher intelligence. One may want to inform the court of the correlation between intelligence and *Miranda* understanding and appreciation. Grisso's research has also shown that 23% of adults across the board do not understand at least one of the rights. Significantly, 43% of adults offenders and 70% of nonoffender adults believe erroneously that one must incriminate oneself in court. Likewise, 21% of adult offenders and 35% of adult nonoffenders erroneously believe there are penalties for invoking one's right to silence during interrogation.

An often heard argument is that because such a large percentage of adults (and juveniles) have a misconception about how the legal process works in relation to the right to silence, little weight should be given that this particular defendant has the same fallacy in thinking. This is a purely legal question based on whether the courts wish to use an absolute standard in determining *Miranda* competency or use the relative standard of how the defendant compares to others. The original *Miranda* decision clearly speaks about the validity of the waiver in absolute terms. A waiver of rights cannot be valid if it is not made knowingly, intelligently, and voluntarily. It does not make relative comparisons of that defendant's ability to that of others.

As stated previously, it is inappropriate for mental health professionals to offer opinions regarding the *voluntariness* of a *Miranda* waiver. The distinction between a coerced, involuntary waiver and a waiver resulting from legally sanctioned means of extracting a waiver and subsequent confession is for the trier of fact to make. Nevertheless, psychologists and other mental health professionals have special expertise in assessing a subject's psychological functioning. They can describe factors that may contribute to a person being less able to resist police demands to waive his or her rights, or such psychological factors that make an individual more susceptible to police influence.

Some competency to waive *Miranda* rights evaluations involve defendants who are psychotic. Research has shown (Viljoen, Roesch, & Zapf, 2002) that although defendants with primary psychotic disorders demonstrated more impairments than other defendants in their understanding of Canadian rights (similar to *Miranda*), psychosis by itself was not a good predictor of their lack of ability to comprehend the meaning of the rights. However, those psychotic defendants with low IQ were less able to understand the rights than those with higher IQ.

The assessment procedures for providing data relevant to the voluntariness of a *Miranda* waiver are the same as those used to assess the voluntariness of a confession. They are discussed in the subsequent sections of this chapter.

False and Involuntary Confessions

Law enforcement personnel use a variety of tactics and techniques to pressure suspects into confessing their involvement with a crime. Although police are no longer allowed physically to coerce confessions (*Brown v. Mississippi*, 1936), legally sanctioned, sophisticated procedures are taught in police manuals and training programs on how to influence a person believed to have committed a criminal act to confess to that act. The most widely used procedure, commonly referred to as the "Reid Technique" (Inbau, Reid, Buckley, & Jayne, 2001), is sometimes misapplied. It involves nine steps for effective interrogation of allegedly guilty suspects. Although the specifics of the nine steps can be obtained through Inbau and colleagues (2001) and other sources, including their website, *www.reid.com*, the procedures are summarized here. This is important information for the psychologist. Often, what actually transpired when the suspect was with the police is undocumented or unreliable. One may get two versions: the defendant's version and the law enforcement version. Unfortunately, a suspect's encounter with police is rarely taped from start to finish. Sometimes, significant events occur prior to *Miranda* rights being given and interactions being recorded. One has to evaluate how a defendant's psychological functioning may have interacted with techniques and procedures that law enforcement personnel commonly employ.

The key elements of the Reid Technique are the following.

❖ *Step 1: Direct, positive confrontation.* Law enforcement personnel confront the suspect with a statement that he or she is considered to be the person who committed the offense.

❖ *Step 2: Interrogation theme development.* Law enforcement personnel express a hypothesis about the reason for the commission of the crime. This theme development helps the suspect justify or excuse the crime, perhaps by affixing moral blame on an accomplice or victim, or emphasizing the suspect's impaired mental state.

❖ *Step 3: Handling denials.* This step involves dealing effectively with the suspect's initial denials of guilt.

❖ *Step 4: Overcoming objections.* Law enforcement personnel do not allow a suspect's excuses or explanations of why he or she would not have committed the crime (often based around economic, religious, or moral grounds) to be effective.

❖ *Step 5: Keeping the suspect's attention.* Law enforcement personnel reduce the physical distance from the suspect and increase eye contact. This prevents the suspect from mentally withdrawing or "tuning out" from the presentation of the theme.

❖ *Step 6: Handling the suspect's passive mood.* When the suspect weighs the possible benefits of telling the truth, law enforcement personnel express sympathy and understanding.

❖ *Step 7: Presenting the alternative question.* The suspect is presented with two options concerning aspects of the crime. One option is presented as more acceptable or morally blameless than the other. For example, the interrogator may state, "Were you some evil monster who intended to rape and kill the child or were you someone who cared about the child's well-being but events just got out of hand?" Choosing either option is the functional equivalent to giving an incriminating confession.

❖ *Step 8: Bringing the suspect into the conversation.* This involves having the suspect give a detailed account of the crime to the degree that it would establish legal guilt.

❖ *Step 9: The written confession.* This last step converts an oral confession to a taped or electronically recorded confession.

Inbau and colleagues (2001) discriminate between a police interview and a police interrogation. They are different procedures, sometimes only separated by several minutes. An interview is conducted when the guilt of the suspect is in doubt. Police are trained to look at the suspect's body language and quality of statements to determine whether the suspect is innocent or guilty. For example, although they state that nervousness is present in both guilty and innocent suspects, those who are guilty are more nervous, and their anxiety increases during interrogation. Those who are innocent have a decrease in anxiety. A distinction is also made between the emotional offender, who has a troubled conscience and should be dealt with sympathetically and compassionately during the interrogation, and the nonemotional offender, who is not troubled by his or her crime, and is not as emotionally involved with interrogation. A "factual analysis approach" is said to work best with this type of individual. Police are taught that anger, either their own or that of the suspect, is an undesirable emotion, because it inhibits constructive communication. What is needed is trust, rapport, and cooperation. Proponents of the Reid Technique believe that innocent individuals' anger persists over time, whereas truly guilty individuals have difficulty maintaining their anger, because they know they committed the crime. Inbau and colleagues indicate that the interrogation should be done in a controlled environment, isolating the allegedly guilty party from outside influences. There should be no objects in the interrogation room to distract attention from the matter at hand: obtaining a confession. There should be only one person interacting with the suspect, sitting close to him or her, and asking questions. A one-way mirror is preferable in such situations, so others can more closely monitor signs of vulnerability in the supposedly guilty party.

Although Inbau and colleagues (2001) firmly state that at no time is the suspect told that if he or she confesses, there may be leniency (it would not be legally permissive), defendants often state during the psychological evaluation that this is precisely what they are told. Law enforcement personnel rarely confirm this inappropriate practice in their testimony in court. It is not for the psychologist to form an opinion as to which side is telling the truth. Rather, the psychologist can offer both descriptions in court and describe the potential effect each would have had on the defendant as it relates to the voluntariness of a *Miranda* waiver or to psychological factors related to a false or coerced confession.

Gisli Gudjonsson is one of the most prolific researchers in the area of false confessions. His book, *The Psychology of Interrogations and Confessions: A Handbook* (Gudjonsson, 2003), is essential reading for anyone interested in working in this field. A number of researchers (Gudjonsson, 2003; Kassin & Wrightsman, 1985; McCann, 1998; Ofshe & Leo, 1997b) have proposed theoretical formulations, delineating various conceptual categories of false confessions or confessors. However, many times a defendant who gives a false confession cannot be neatly assigned to a category. The confession may seem to meet the description of a combination of different types of false confessions. Kassin and Wrightsman's (1985) three categories, with a fourth added by McCann (1998), describe parsimoniously the various reasons someone may confess to a crime he or she did not commit.

The *voluntary false confession* is the type of false confession a suspect willingly gives to the police because of a desire for notoriety, the need to protect a friend or relative, or some pathological need to be punished. Few referrals of the voluntary false confession type come to the clinician, because law enforcement generally eliminates the individual from serious consideration. Examples of voluntary false confessions can be seen with the plethora of "confessions" to the Lindbergh baby murder (Federal Bureau of Investigation, 2006).

The *coerced–compliant false confession* is that of a suspect who confesses to escape or avoid the stressful interrogation process, or to achieve some immediate goal, such as less punishment or reward for cooperation (e.g., phone call to family member, soda and/or cigarette break, or the promise of placement in a nicer correctional facility). In both the voluntary and the coerced–compliant false confession, the subject knows he or she did not commit the crime. Interrogations, which can last for less than an hour to days, produce tremendous anxiety in both guilty and innocent suspects. Innocent suspects may falsely confess to a crime to end the stress of interrogation, often erroneously believing that since they are innocent, the truth will come out in court. Coerced–compliant false confessors often (as do guilty suspects) retract their confessions soon after they are made. Because police often minimize the legal wrongfulness of the offense, while emphasizing and insinuating that the alleged perpetrator was morally blameless, suspects may confess to end the interrogation, believing that even though they are admitting to the offense, the punishment will not be all that great. For example, someone accused of a sexual offense may be led to believe that if he or she confesses to the crime, the only punishment would be probation and mandated outpatient treatment. Because the criminality of the alleged conduct is minimized, the defendant is minimizing the potential to spend many years in prison.

The *coerced–internalized false confession* is the one confession whereby a suspect, who has been subjected to intense police interrogation, begins to internalize or believe that he or she in fact committed the crime. These individuals tend not to trust their own memories, or they have little memory of their actions around the time of the offense. They become anxious, confused, and are quite susceptible to suggestive techniques. Someone who was intoxicated around the time of the commission of the crime, or perhaps in a psychotic state, may have fuzzy memory for the time period in question. When police lie to suspects about the incriminating evidence against them (police are allowed to give oral misrepresentations about evidence, such as eyewitnesses, DNA, fingerprints, etc., that do not exist; e.g., *State v. Cayward*, 1989), the suggestible individual may begin to believe that he or she in fact committed the crime. Otherwise, why would there be this evidence against them? They begin to doubt their memory and incorporate the version of the crime that the police state transpired into their thought processes. For example, a defendant with substance-induced delirium during the time period of the commission of a crime may begin to incorporate suggestions from the police that he or she must have committed the offense. Law enforcement personnel misrepresent the quantity and quality of physical evidence present at the crime scene. The defendant believes that if police personnel say that his actions were recorded on a security camera and they also have matching DNA, he must in fact be the guilty party.

There is also the *coerced–reactive false confession*, which is a voluntary confession, in that police personnel are not using psychological procedures to induce a confession. In fact, oftentimes the individual has come to the police station on his or her own. The individual confesses because of coercion by some other person, apart from the police. A psychologist may evaluate a battered spouse, who is told by her abusing husband that unless she confesses falsely to injuring their child, the husband will kidnap or injure the other child. Another example might be a gang member threatened with violence from other gang members unless he "takes the rap" for a crime he did not commit.

Not all false confessions fit neatly into one of the four categories. One might add additional categories of false confessions or combine some of the categories. As stated earlier, it is important to stress is that false confessions do sometimes occur, although the incidence of false confessions is difficult to assess. Nonprofit organizations such as the Innocence Project at the Benjamin N. Cardoza School of Law at Yeshiva University, founded by attorneys Barry C. Scheck and Peter J. Neufield in 1992, work in part to exonerate wrongfully convicted persons through postconviction DNA testing.

Expert testimony may cast doubt on the reliability of a confession, even if the confession is found to be admissible. In *Crane v. Kentucky* (1986), the U.S. Supreme Court held that a confession's reliability may be challenged at trial, even if the confession had been deemed to be voluntary. A suspect's psychological vulnerability to interrogation can also be introduced to the trier of fact. In *United States v. Major* (1996), the defendant had witnessed the shooting of a family guide by Russian soldiers during his youth. He said that his past caused him to become "emotionally frozen" when police raided his business with their guns drawn, and psychologically vulnerable and less able to resist the directions or requests of law enforcement personnel. Despite weighing this testimony, based on the totality of circumstances, the court rejected the defense's motion to suppress the defendant's statements after his arrest.

Expert testimony is important in assisting the jury to understand those psychological characteristics that place a defendant at risk for giving a less than accurate and/or false statements to the police. Expert testimony can also assist the jury in understanding why a particular defendant is at greater psychological risk for succumbing to police influence than the average defendant. Testimony can apply to both the voluntariness component of a *Miranda* waiver and the resultant confession.

A Protocol for Conducting Evaluations Pertinent to the Voluntariness of a *Miranda* Waiver and False/Involuntary Confessions

I must emphasize that no scientifically valid process exists for a psychologist or any mental health professional to determine whether a confession is true or false. The determination is properly made by the trier of fact. A confession may not support the facts known about the case (i.e., a defendant confesses that he broke a window, entered the dwelling, shot the occupant, dropped the gun, and ran out the door; yet physical evidence shows no broken window, and no gun was found on the scene). This is information the psychologist may want to point out to the court as one factor, as well as many others, that place the subject at risk for being a less than reliable historian when confessing. Ultimately, the psychologist becomes most useful when discussing *psychological* characteristics that heighten a defendant's risk for giving a false confession or succumbing to police influence. This testimony is rarely disallowed in court.

Often, although not always, evaluations pertaining to the voluntariness or the validity of a confession are requested in conjunction with an evaluation of *Miranda* competency. Although there is no incompatibility in doing an evaluation of *Miranda* (which includes the factors related to the voluntariness of the *Miranda* waiver) and that of the voluntariness of a confession, doing both a *Miranda* competency assessment and false confession assessment during the same session is often problematic. To discuss psychological factors relevant to the validity of a confession, one must ask the defendant why he or she provided a particular statement. It requires the defendant to describe the statement he or she gave to the police as true or false. If false, then the defendant's true actions at the time of the offense have to be assessed to determine why a different version of the event was given to the police. A defense attorney interested in pursuing a motion to suppress statements based on Miranda incompetency may not want the psychologist to have incriminating information provided by the defendant, if in fact the defendant did do the crime. Thus, it is suggested that the evaluation be done in two parts. In the first part, the psychologist evaluates for a knowing, intelligent, and voluntary waiver of rights. The defendant is not asked, and is encouraged not to talk about, what actually transpired during the offense and how it differs, if at all, from statements given to the police. If there is no Miranda waiver issue, then the psychologist can proceed to the investigation of psychological factors related to false confessions. If there is a Miranda waiver issue to be litigated, then it is suggested that the evaluation of confessions take place after the pretrial motion to suppress is litigated. As mentioned earlier, the reliability of a confession is almost always an issue to be determined by the trier of fact. Ultimately, this is the attorney's decision, but the psychologist should discuss with the attorney the danger of doing both types of evaluations together.

Psychological evaluations pertaining to confessions require the same type of third-party data collection review and comprehensive interview that is required in the Miranda waiver competency assessment. Again, special attention is devoted to getting the defendant to detail, step-by-step, what happened in his or her interactions with the police, and to attempt to ascertain the defendant's thought processes and rationale for making various decisions throughout the interrogation. Person-centered variables such as intoxication, sleep deprivation, pain from injury, and so on, are important factors in understanding the defendant's thinking at the time of the confession.

Gudjonsson (2003) describes three general processes related to false confessions: *suggestibility, compliance,* and *acquiescence.* The clinician needs to examine these processes and how they relate to the voluntariness of a confession or rights waiver, and how they relate to a defendant's statements to the police.

Gudjonsson uses the term *suggestibility* to refer to interrogative suggestibility (distinguishing it from the types of suggestibility in hypnosis), which is the extent to which an individual comes to accept messages or information communicated during formal questioning, essentially coming to believe that the information given is true. This interrogative suggestibility operationally comprises two indices on a test designed to help assess interrogative suggestibility, the Gudjonsson Suggestibility Scales (GSS). *Yield* is defined as the subject's tendency to give in to leading questions. *Shift* is defined as the tendency for a subject to change answers after being subtly pressured or given negative feedback. A number of studies have shown that highly suggestible individuals, as measured by the GSS, are particularly susceptible to giving erroneous testimony during questioning (e.g., Gudjonsson, 1984, 1991).

Although there is some interrelatedness between the various types of false confessions, interrogative suggestibility is best demonstrated by the coerced–internalized false confession.

According to Gudjonsson (1997), three components are essential prerequisites to the process and mechanism of interrogative suggestibility. There must be an *uncertainty component*, in which the subject is not certain of the correct answer to a question. There must be *interpersonal trust*, in that the interviewer's intentions are experienced as both constructive and genuine, without any trickery involved. Finally, there is an *expectation* component, in which the subject is reluctant to declare uncertainty and lack of knowledge, because of his or her belief that he or she is expected to know the answer.

A second general process related to false confessions is *compliance*. Compliance differs from suggestibility, in that the former does not require a private acceptance of the proposition or request. A defendant may confess or give statements about a crime, even if he or she does not agree with or believe what was said. Gudjonsson (2003) states that compliance can be viewed in two different ways. It can be conceptualized as a personality trait, such as an eagerness to please, or as a behavioral response to a given situation, such as avoidance of conflict or confrontation with others, particularly those in authority. Compliance is best demonstrated by the coerced–compliant type of false confession.

Acquiescence, the third process described by Gudjonsson, is the tendency to act in accordance with wishes of others to affirm information, regardless of the content (Cronbach, 1946).

Although interrogative suggestibility and compliance are presented as different constructs, there is some overlap. Gudjonsson (2003) describes how they are mediated by similar factors, such as avoidance coping, eagerness to please, and states of anxiety when the individual attempts to cope with pressured situations. Studies have shown a modest correlation between suggestibility and compliance (Gudjonsson, 1989, 1990). Further research (Gudjonsson, 1986; Gudjonsson & Clare, 1995; Winkler, Kanouse, & Ware, 1982) show only a weak relationship between suggestibility and acquiescence. The relationships that exist, according to Gudjonsson, are probably due to a state of uncertainty and low self-esteem that arises when a subject does not know how to answer a question. The subject may give in to leading questions or shift responses under pressure (interrogative suggestibility), or just answer affirmatively, regardless of the content of the question (acquiescence). These behaviors have the effect of reducing tension and restoring self-esteem. Gudjonsson (1990) showed empirically that there is little correlation between compliance and acquiescence. This is not surprising, because the intervening variable, intelligence, has little theoretical relevancy to compliance, which is conceptualized as both situation and personality bound.

The task of the psychologist when conducting evaluations focusing on confessions and the voluntariness of *Miranda* waivers is to assess for those factors that are most relevant to understanding how susceptible a defendant was to police influence and psychological factors at the time of the interrogation. DeClue (2005, p. 155) suggests that, in the assessment, one must "gather and analyze information regarding the physical and psychological environment in which the confession was obtained." That is a good point. The psychologist must integrate the defendant's likely psychological functioning at the time of the interrogation with the interrogation environment itself. Many times, law enforcement's description of the interrogation is at odds with the defendant's version. Psychologists make a mistake if they automatically assign more credibility to one of the versions. Rather, descriptions of the interrogation that differ significantly should be reviewed for internal inconsistencies. For example, a detective writes in his report that the suspect carefully read out loud each of the four *Miranda* rights (written at an eighth-grade level) and indicates that the suspect understood them. Yet documented evidence exists that the defendant reads words at less than a third-grade level. The detective's report, at least in that one aspect, does not appear credible. Likewise, if a defendant states that *Miranda* rights were never given, yet he or she signed *Miranda* waiver form, then the defendant's account is suspect. While it is ill advised, and unlikely to be allowed, to offer opinion testimony that one party or the other's version is wrong, there is nothing to prevent experts from stating why they have questions regarding the accuracy of the report of one party or the other. To be conservative in one's opinion, unless there is factual information proving otherwise, an expert opinion is best offered with the assumption that the police did not engage in improper procedures in their interrogation. An expert can always opine though that if law enforcement in fact used coercive procedures, they would probably have had these effects on the defendant. Experts are well advised to leave it to the trier of fact to decide for themselves whose version of interrogation processes is more believable.

Gudjonsson Suggestibility Scales

Gudjonsson (1997) developed the GSS to *help* assess interrogative suggestibility. There are two parallel versions of the test. This test is commonly used by forensic psychologists to evaluate factors related to the voluntariness of a *Miranda* waiver, as well as factors related to false or coerced confessions.

Although the GSS was initially developed to examine a subject's tendency to give in or yield to leading questions, as well as the tendency to shift or change responses after being subtly pressured or receiving negative feedback, scores on the GSS are directly relevant to issues of compliance as well. Although some individuals may argue that the GSS should only be used in situations of suspected coerced-internalized false confessions, Gudjonsson (1997) states,

> It could be argued that the Scales are relevant to any interview situation, including a clinical interview. It is a common misconception that the Scales were developed exclusively to assess the validity of the individual's self-incriminating admissions to the police. . . . The psychological vulnerability of witnesses can greatly influence the validity of their accounts to the police, and the Scales can be fruitfully used to assess their relevant strengths and vulnerabilities. (p. 29)

Administration of the GSS, which is presented as a memory test, involves reading a complex narrative story that comprises 40 bits of factual information. After reading the story, the subject is told, "Tell me everything you remember about the story." The test's purpose is not to evaluate short-term memory. The subject, after a 50-minute delay for those who demonstrated adequate memory, is again asked to recall everything he or she remembered about the story. If he or she initially does not remember the story well, there is no 50-minute delay. The subject is then asked 20 standardized questions about the story, 15 of which have been specifically designed to be subtly misleading, in that they lead the subject toward inaccurate reporting of what he or she "remembers" of the story. These leading questions comprise the Yield 1 score on the GSS. Regardless of the subject's performance on Yield 1, he or she is then firmly told, "You have made a number of errors. It is therefore necessary to go through each of the questions once more, and this time try to be more accurate." One is then able to assess how much the individual yields to the leading questions after being pressured. This comprises the Yield 2 score. The extent to which the subject "shifts" from the original response, right or wrong, to a different response after pressure comprises the Shift score. The Yield 1 and Shift scores are combined for a Total Suggestibility Score. Each of these indices can be compared to normative groups of various ages, legal status, and intelligence. The GSS was developed using normative data from Great Britain and Iceland. Gudjonsson (2003) reviewed a research study that, in part, looked at differences in suggestibility among people of different ethnic backgrounds. The findings showed that Afro-Caribbean detainees obtained greater suggestibility scores than their Caucasian counterparts, even after controlling for verbal recall of the materials. Nevertheless, according to Gudjonsson (personal communication, 2000), the amount of variance in performance between the true groups was minor compared to other factors, such as intelligence, memory, anxiety, and so forth. There is no reason to believe that Americans as a group would perform differently than a group from the United Kingdom. Although Pollard, Trowbridge, and Slade (2004) found some differences, their study was quite preliminary and they did not use such diverse groups in their normative samples. Brett Trowbridge, one of the coauthors of this study, states that he still uses the norms from Britain and Iceland when using the GSS (B. Trowbridge, personal communication, 2006). There were no substantial differences in performance between groups from Great Britain and those from Iceland.

Even if one argues that normative data should not be used on this test, because it was not normed on an American population, this test provides good behavioral data on ways an individual responds when confronted with leading questions, both with and without pressure, and how easily an individual shifts responses under pressure.

The GSS allows comparisons of a particular defendant's interrogative suggestibility to that of other normative groups. It also provides good samples of behavioral data. The information gleaned from the GSS, combined with other data, can provide courts with useful information regarding a defendant's interrogative suggestibility.

Psychological Variables Related to Suggestibility

A number of research studies, summarized in Gudjonsson (2003) have shown a negative relationship between interrogative suggestibility and intelligence. The lower one's intelligence, the higher the GSS score. Therefore, it is incumbent on the psychologist to administer intelligence tests as part of the overall assessment. Although intelligence is only slightly related to compliance, there are strong relationships with acquiescence and suggestibility (e.g., Gudjonsson, 1990). This finding is not surprising in light of what we observe clinically. Those individuals with low intelligence often attempt to mask their intellectual deficiencies by responding affirmatively to questions for which they do not know the answer.

Other cognitive variables, such as memory, are correlated with suggestibility. In particular, the faster one's memory deteriorates over time, the more suggestible the individual. Individuals with memory impairment often tend to mistrust their own judgments and rely more on cues by others. The Yield score is related more to cognitive variables, such as intelligence and memory, whereas Shift is more related to interpersonal and social factors. Gudjonsson (2003) summarizes the literature in this area well.

Research has also shown that poor assertiveness, evaluative anxiety, state anxiety, avoidance coping strategies, and perhaps trait anxiety are correlated with suggestibility, as measured by Yield and Shift on the GSS (e.g., Gudjonsson, Rutter, & Clare, 1995). Sleep deprivation is also correlated with suggestibility (Blagrove, 1996; Blagrove & Akehurst, 2000; Blagrove, Cole-Morgan, & Lambe, 1994). Gudjonsson (2003) also describes the research demonstrating that suggestibility is negatively correlated with prior convictions.

Gudjonsson (2003) summarized the research about suggestibility, suspiciousness, and anger as well. We know that suggestibility is often influenced by situational factors and experience. Mood variables, such as anger and suspiciousness, have been shown to reduce people's susceptibility to suggestion and their willingness to comply with requests. Finally, there is no simple relationship between mental illness and suggestibility (Sigurdsson, Gudjonsson, Kolbeinsson, & Petursson, 1994; Smith & Gudjonsson, 1995; Young, Bentall, Slade, & Dewey, 1987).

Gudjonsson (2003) has also summarized the research regarding suggestibility and juveniles. Young children yielded and shifted more than did adolescents. Adolescents (age 12 and older) do not have higher Yield scores than adults. They are no more likely to give in to leading questions. Not surprisingly, they are significantly more responsive to negative feedback or Shift scores up until the age of 17, when they appear to respond more like adults.

Personality Testing

A number of personality tests can help the psychologist to quantify the defendant's personality functions, such as various states and traits. These can be integrated with other data to provide the court with information relevant to confessions. Although a measure such as the MMPI-2 (Butcher et al., 1989) may have less utility except to help rule out malingering of psychopathology, tests designed to assess more normal aspects of personality are invaluable in these types of cases. A test such as the 16 PF (Cattell et al., 1993), for instance, contains a Global Factor of Independence, which measures accommodation versus independence traits. Likewise, there are Primary Scales, which are directly relevant to confession issues, such as Factor E, measuring deferential versus dominant personality, or Factor H, measuring shyness versus social boldness.

Interestingly, Gudjonsson (1990) found that the Picture Arrangement subtest on the WAIS-III, which provides a measure of social awareness and participation (Schill, Kahn, & Meuhleman, 1968), has the highest correlation with interrogative suggestibility of the various WAIS-III subtests. Unfortunately, there is not a developed body of research investigating the relationship between neuropsychological functioning and suggestibility.

Gudjonsson Compliance Scale

Frumkin (2000) cautions against the use of another of Gudjonsson's tests, the Gudjonsson Compliance Scales (GCS), developed to measure compliance. The GCS comprises a 20-item, self-report questionnaire. The subject circles or responds verbally (if the items are read) to true or false questions, such as "I give in easily when I am pressured," or "I find it very difficult to tell people when I disagree with them." A slightly modified version of the test is available to be given to knowledgeable informants of the defendant, such as friends or relatives. Since the GCS is a self-report measure, it is susceptible to inaccurate response sets. An individual may consciously or unconsciously want to present as less or more compliant.

Malingering and Deception on the GSS and GCS

The problem with the GCS is that the content of the items and the construct of what the test measures is very obvious to the test taker. It would be easy for a subject to manipulate the results to make him- or herself seem more compliant. Although the test has been shown to discriminate between false confessors and other criminal defendants (Gudjonsson, 1997), more work needs to done in evaluating the test when the defendant attempts to distort the results. Of course, face validity of measures is one of the main reasons that formal measures of malingering and deception are included as part of any evaluation of *Miranda* waiver competency or psychological factors related to false or coerced confessions. See Denney, Chapter 4, this volume, on malingering detection.

Unlike the GCS, the GSS appears to be relatively resistant to feigning. As mentioned earlier, defendants are not informed that it is a test to measure suggestibility. They believe it is a test to measure their memory. In a study by Baxter and Bain (2002), subjects were told prior to administering the GSS that their suggestibility was to be measured. They were instructed to feign suggestibility on the test. Results of the study suggest that only Yield 1 was susceptible to faking.

Admissibility Issues

The GSS and the Grisso measures (CMR, CMR-R, CMV, and FRI) are specialized forensic assessment instruments that are unknown to many psychologists and attorneys. On rare occasions, their use may be challenged on *Frye v. United States* (1923) or *Daubert v. Merrell Dow Pharmaceuticals* (1993) grounds. The *Frye* standard, commonly referred to as the "general acceptance principle," requires that "the thing from which the deduction is made must be sufficiently established to have gained general acceptance in the particular field which it belongs." The D.C. Circuit Court decision, over 80 years ago, had to do with the admissibility of a blood pressure–based lie detection device. Many states still use the *Frye* standard in determining the admissibility of expert testimony. *Frye* was superceded in federal court by

Daubert. Many states have followed suit and adopted the *Daubert* standard for the admissibility of expert testimony in their courts. In *Daubert*, the U.S. Supreme Court held that judges should be given wide latitude in determining the admissibility of scientific testimony based on the scientific reliability and validity of the principles and methods governing the expert's opinion. The U.S. Supreme Court provided guidance to the lower courts in enumerating four factors that judges could consider when evaluating the admissibility of the basis of expert testimony: (1) whether the methodology was being tested or had been tested, (2) whether the methodology had been published in peer-reviewed literature, (3) the known degree of error when using the particular methodology, and (4) whether the principle or methodology in question had gained general acceptance in the scientific community. The *Kumho Tire Company v. Carmichael* (1999) holding expanded the *Daubert* decision to apply to social science and other nonscientific testimony. The nonexistence of error rates was not considered problematic. The trial courts could have broad latitude in applying the standards. Hence, *Daubert* is often characterized as appointing the trial judge as gatekeeper of those standards. See Kaufmann, Chapter 3, this volume, for an advanced discussion of general admissibility issues.

Grisso Tests

The Grisso measures would appear to have little difficulty meeting *Frye* or *Daubert* challenges when both the attorney and the expert are prepared to answer questions pertaining to "general acceptance" and issues of scientific reliability and validity. First, Grisso was recognized with a number of awards, based on the research from which his tests were derived. His research was funded by the National Institute of Mental Health (NIMH). Studies funded by NIMH must meet a model of scientific rigor, relying upon standardized and controlled methodology. His research proposal was arguably subjected to the most stringent scientific peer-review process that science has to offer for behavioral and social sciences. His use of a national panel of judges, lawyers, and legal scholars in defining the various constructs made his tests extremely applicable to the forensic context. According to Grisso (personal communication, 2006), this national panel included representatives from both the defense and the prosecution. The method of development was a functional assessment, specifically integrating test behavior with psycholegal criteria. The reliability and validity of these tests are described in the test manual and in the original publication of this research (Grisso, 1981). The Grisso tests have generally been reviewed positively in a number of authoritative publications (e.g., DeClue, 2005; Frumkin, 2000; Frumkin & Garcia, 2003; Melton et al., 2007; Oberlander et al., 2003; Shapiro, 1991). The results of the entire research project were published as part of a book series by the forensic psychology division of the American Psychological Association (Grisso, 1981). The research and resulting tests were accepted in a number of law reviews, for example, the *California Law Review* (Grisso, 1980). Cloud and colleagues (2002), in the *University of Chicago Law Review*, described a replication of the Grisso study. The Grisso tests have also been taught as part of a number of statewide and national training programs in psychology and the law. Many appellate courts have made reference to his *Miranda* research and/or the resultant instruments in their decisions, for example, *California v. Burnett* (1987), *State v. Whitaker* (1990), *State v. Phillips* (1992), and *In re T.S.D. v. Florida* (1999).

Conversely, several appellate cases have deemed that the Grisso tests did not meet *Frye* or *Daubert* standards for admissibility (*Carter v. State*, 1997; *State v. Griffin*, 2003). However, this should not present a problem for the expert. In the Florida case of *Carter v. State*, a *Frye* state, the defense did not lay adequate foundation for the admission of the results from the Grisso tests. In fact, the psychologist expert testified that the Grisso "test" is not commonly used or nationally recognized. The expert further testified that the defense's attempt to use the results to challenge the defendant's ability to comprehend his rights was "very unusual." Apart from the psychology expert misconstruing the four instruments as one test, as opposed to four different measures, it was apparent in the testimony that the psychologist was unaware of the frequency of the tests use by psychologists who evaluate *Miranda* competency. Moreover, both the psychologist and attorney appeared unaware how well received the test was in the general forensic psychological community and literature. In the Connecticut case of *State v. Griffin* (2003), a *Daubert* state, the psychologist performed the assessment in much the manner recommended in this chapter. She conducted a comprehensive interview and administered measures of intelligence, personality, and the Grisso tests. Unfortunately, she was unaware of the numerous psychology and legal publications that reference the Grisso tests. She testified that she recalled a law review article in which the tests were discussed, that the tests were discussed in seminars, and that peer review had been done when Grisso published certain of his own writings when discussing the test. She testified under cross-examination that she knew of only a "couple of organizations" that used the test. It appears that in *State v. Griffin*, as well as in *Carter v. State*, the defense did not lay the groundwork in showing that the Grisso tests have been peer reviewed and have been accepted as scientifically valid in the community.

Richard Rogers and his coauthors have leveled a harsh critique on the Grisso tests (Rogers, Jordan, & Harrison, 2004; Rogers & Shuman, 2005). Although Grisso (2004) has responded to Rogers's critical appraisal of the tests, a review of Rogers's criticisms and a response to them are summarized.

Rogers, Jordan, and Harrison's (2004) main criticism of the tests is that they do not meet appropriate professional standards in test validation, reliability, and documentation, as set forth in the official *Standards for Educational and Psychological Testing* (American Educational Research Association, American Psychological Association, & National Council on Measurement in Education, 1999). He states that the reliability data are virtually nonexistent, that normative data used the wrong reference group, and that criterion-related validity is nonexistent.

In reference to his criticism regarding criterion-related validity, Rogers, Jordan, and Harrison (2004) erroneously stated that the test was designed to "assess" the legal construct of *Miranda* competency. As is stated explicitly in the test manual, the Grisso tests were never specifically designed for that purpose. The validity of a *Miranda* waiver is based on the totality of circumstances present during the police interrogation. The *Miranda* tests help to assess only two components of a *Miranda* waiver, the knowing and intelligent prongs. Moreover, it does not measure knowledge and appreciation of the rights at the time the rights were given by law enforcement. As DeClue (2005) states, the Grisso tests "are psychological tests that are *directly relevant to* the legal question but *are not tests of* the legal question" (p. 149). Thus, attempting to correlate or relate Grisso test results with legal decision making in motions to suppress hearings would be ill informed. As Grisso (2004) points out, "If the instruments had ever been intended to do what the review demands of them, the criticisms would be on target. An *instrument must be judged according to criteria for its stated purpose*" (p. 720).

Rogers, Jordan, and Harrison (2004) wrote about the tests not meeting professional standards for test development and were critical because there are no published indices of long-term stability of scores, such as the time period between *Miranda* first being administered by the police and examiner evaluation of a defendant's *Miranda* comprehension and appreciation. As Grisso (2004) accurately stated, test–retest reliability is designed to measure error rates in tests, not change in people over time. Grisso used short intervals in examining test–retest effect to avoid issues such as learning that may take place subsequent to the test's first administration. Although *stability* of a test's scores over time may be important information depending on the purpose of the test (e.g., IQ scores), the purpose of the Grisso tests was never to postdict *Miranda* competency, but to aid the clinician in a retroactive assessment of a defendant's competency at the time of the interrogation. A measure Rogers designed to help assess competence to stand trial, the Evaluation of Competency to Stand Trial—Revised (ECST-R; Rogers, Tillbrook, & Sewell, 2004), could suffer from the same criticism that Rogers levels at the Grisso tests, as would most psychological measures.

Rogers, Jordan, and Harrison (2004) speak about problematic interrater reliability in inexperienced test raters, those without training on scoring the

Grisso tests (like the average forensic psychologist not trained as part of the Grisso research project). Rogers believes that it is unknown whether there would be consistency in scoring among testing practitioners. In fact, in the test manual, Grisso (1998) writes that the interrater reliability is quite good when comparing the scoring of trained scorers of the tests and those who had no training in scoring the tests (p. 10).

Rogers, Jordan, and Harrison (2004) are also critical of what they consider to be problems with the tests' internal consistency, lack of standard error of measurement statistics, and validity data. Their critique of the internal consistency of the test (the correlation between items on each of the tests and that between various tests) is unwarranted. What should be critiqued is psychologists' misuse of the test by not taking into consideration poor interitem and interscale correlations. There were fairly low correlations of understanding from one Miranda right to the next, as well as low correlations between the various tests and among the various scales of the FRI. Yet this is the nature of the Miranda issue itself. Research has shown that an individual may have good comprehension and/or appreciation on three of the rights, but faulty comprehension and/or appreciation on the other. The Miranda waiver construct is multidimensional. It only makes sense that the Grisso measures would be as well. This is not a fault of the test but of the heterogeneous nature of the rights themselves. Personality tests are not criticized because of low correlations between someone scoring high on a Depression scale and low on a scale tapping into Schizophrenia. Miranda understanding and appreciation are not unitary constructs, but are multidimensional, comprised of a number of components. Rogers states that the tests do not report any standard error of measurement. However, Grisso (2003) supplied consistency and reliability data on page 10 of the manual.

Rogers further expresses concern that the Grisso tests do not measure understanding and appreciation of the numerous variants of the Miranda rights given throughout the United States. Rogers and Shuman (2005, p. 133) even include my own personal communication that the wording of the Miranda rights on the Grisso tests no longer correspond to the versions of the rights used in St. Louis County, where the test was developed. Because there are numerous wordings of the Miranda rights within and across jurisdictions, it is impossible to develop measures incorporating all possible variants of Miranda. This does not make the test unusable. A test does not have to be universal and measure all things a person needs to know to be useful. For example, few intelligence tests measure constructs such as creativity or ability to work well in groups, yet there is no reason to believe that those constructs are unimportant components of intelligence.

I agree with Rogers that there could have been more psychometric information provided in the test manual. The manual was developed some 17 years after the original development of the test (which originally had not been designed for individual clinical assessments). Yet the test is very good in its intent, as an *aid* for psychologists to use in a retrospective analysis of *Miranda* competency.

The Grisso tests could have been improved by increasing the number of items on the CMR-R and the three scales of the FRI. There are only three comparison items for each *Miranda* right on the CMR-R, and only five questions for each scale on the FRI. Adding items to these scales would have greatly improved the utility of the tests. Yet many well-recognized tests contain scales with few items comprising some of its scales. For example, Rogers, Bagby, and Dickens's (1992) Structured Interview of Reported Symptoms (SIRS), arguably the best stand-alone test to help assess malingering of psychotic symptoms, has a number of scales that comprise less than 10 items each. One supplementary scale contains only two items. No test is perfect, particularly when used in a forensic context. Every psychological test could be critiqued legitimately in a number of ways. It is important for the clinician to be aware of a test's limitations and to use data from multiple sources. In summary, although Rogers's negative appraisal of the Grisso measures are useful in forcing the psychologist to think more critically about how the tests are used, the criticisms are easily addressed and do little legitimately to affect their utility in *Miranda* evaluations.

A yet to be published revision of the Grisso tests by Naomi Goldstein and Lois Oberlander Condie (see Oberlander et al., 2003) unfortunately does not add items to the rights under the CMR-R or FRI tests. It does provide much needed text revision on the *Miranda* warnings that better corresponds to rights actually given to suspects. It also provides updated normative data, adds the fifth *Miranda* rights prong, and includes another test, the Perceptions of Coercion in Holding and Interrogation Procedures (P-CHIP), which asks the defendant to specify the likelihood that he or she may offer a true or false confession under various circumstances. One is hopeful that these revised tests will incorporate some of Rogers's concerns.

Gudjonsson Suggestibility Scales

Frumkin and Garcia (2003) summarize issues pertaining to the admissibility of the GSS. Gudjonsson's work is well known in the field of suggestibility research, but his tests have not been widely used in the United States, mainly because few psychologists do this type of assessment. The GSS should meet *Frye* and *Daubert* criteria when used in conjunction with a comprehensive psychological assessment, and when the psychologist does not go beyond the GSS data to offer ultimate issue opinions regarding the validity of a confession.

In terms of the *Frye* standard for admissibility, psychologists who evaluate for psychological risk factors relevant to false confessions, as well as involuntary or coerced confessions, routinely use the GSS as part of an overall assessment. The test has been aptly described in the professional literature (i.e., DeClue, 2005; Frumkin, 2003; Grisso, 1986; Oberlander et al., 2003). Significantly, a special supplement to *Psychological Science in the Public Interest*, a journal of the American Psychological Society, the largest academically oriented psychological organization in the United States, is devoted entirely to the psychology of confessions and a review of the literature and issues from which the GSS originally derived (Kassin & Gudjonsson, 2004). The increasing widespread acceptance of the GSS is further demonstrated in the *Forensic Neuropsychology Casebook*, which a chapter is devoted to a case example of competency to confess, whereby the GSS was used as part of the neuropsychological assessment (Sullivan, 2005). The American Academy of Forensic Psychology, which is the educational arm of the American Board of Forensic Psychology, conducts workshops throughout the country. Some of its workshops pertaining to *Miranda* waiver and confessions review the use of the GSS.

In terms of *Daubert* criteria, Grisso (1986) points out that "construct validation research with the GSS has placed the forensic examiner in a good position to use GSS scores when considering questions of an examinee's decreased resistance to suggestion or subtle pressure in interrogation by law enforcement officers" (p. 147). Since Grisso's review, the GSS has been validated in a number of other studies (see Gudjonsson, 2003) and an alternate version, the GSS 2, was also developed. The test has shown good test–retest and interscorer reliability (Gudjonsson, 1997, 2003). Attempting an error rate analysis on the GSS is an unproductive exercise. The GSS was not developed nor should it be used to predict or postdict behavior, such as determining whether a defendant gave a false confession. Rather, it is to be used to describe psychological characteristics of the individual and the defendant's susceptibility to certain types of influence by law enforcement. The GSS successfully met a *Daubert* challenge in a New York Federal Court case (*United States v. Raposo*, 1998).

Several state cases (*Commonwealth v. Soares*, 2001; *Misskelley v. State*, 1996; *State v. Romero*, 2003) have addressed whether GSS testimony should be allowed. In *Misskelley*, a trial court's decision not to allow a psychologist to testify on the GSS was upheld by the Arkansas Supreme Court. A psychologist had offered his opinion that the appellant was "quite suggestible" and that the confession was the product of coercion. Apart from this psychologist acknowledging that he had not administered the GSS previously, there are concerns about any psychologist addressing the ultimate legal issue of coerced confession. Whether a confession was the product of coercion is properly for the trier of fact to decide. In *Misskelley*, an opinion should have been offered relative to the defendant's interrogative suggestibility. How susceptible, compared to others, was the defendant to police influence? Testimony framed in this fashion, supported by behavioral and test data, would have provided the court with information that could be incorporated into legal decision making, and may have well been allowed.

In *Romero*, a psychologist was initially excluded from testifying at the time of trial regarding a defendant's susceptibility to interrogation techniques. The GSS was administered as a part of the evaluation. The trial court excluded the psychological testimony at the pretrial hearing "not based upon a lack of competence or not based upon the fact that the tests are not good ... (but) simply based upon it's a comment on the evidence, it's a comment on the voluntariness, it's a comment on the truth or falsity of the testimony" (p. 4). In other words, the court predicted the expert would offer ultimate issue testimony. Rather, the psychologist had described psychological factors that related to the voluntariness of statements. Ultimately, the Court of Appeals of Oregon allowed such testimony, stating, "We conclude that Kolbells's testimony meets the threshold for admissibility. It would have been probative, relevant, and helpful to the trier of fact. Based on the record before it, the trial court would have erred if it had excluded the evidence on the basis of a lack of scientific reliability" (p. 9).

In *Commonwealth v. Soares*, the psychologist expert testified that although the defendant was suggestible as measured by the GSS, "application of results from that test to a custody situation might not be valid" (p. 6). The psychologist also said his opinion would change if, in that custodial situation, it was shown that the interrogation was devoid of physical force or yelling. In *Soares*, the Appeals Court of Massachusetts ruled that the trial court properly discounted such testimony, and that the application of the results of the GSS were not valid. The psychologist in *Soares* appeared unaware that the GSS is highly relevant to police custody situations. There is no physical force or yelling in administering the GSS. Police routinely ask suspects leading questions to get them to give in to such questioning. They also apply subtle pressure to get an individual to shift to a different response. Perhaps, had the expert testified differently, the results of the GSS would have been admitted.

Sometimes it is argued that the GSS should only be used when there is a suspected coerced–internalized false confession. The coerced–internalized false confessor has faulty memory for events surrounding the time period of the offense, and is misled and pressured into believing he or she committed the crime. The argument is that the GSS is not applicable with alleged coerced–reactive false confessions. In those cases defendants do not have episodic or autobiographical memory impairments. They know whether or not they did the crime.

In fact, Beail (2002) cautions against the use of the GSS among people with learning disabilities, because the GSS is more likely to elicit acquiescent responses from those whose semantic memory is poor, while their autobiographical memory may be unaffected. White and Willner (2005) also studied suggestibility in individuals with learning disabilities. They created two Alternative Suggestibility Scales (ASS and ASS 2) based on real events occurring at the residents' day treatment program. The experimental group had witnessed the events described in the ASS, which took place 18 months earlier. The control group attended a different day treatment program, making the information presented in the GSS and the ASS tasks equally unfamiliar. In a second study, both groups of participants were administered the ASS 2, which described events taking place 1 month earlier. The researchers found that suggestibility is decreased by familiarity with the information to be remembered, and that the decrease in suggestibility is greater for the more recent events. They found that decreases in suggestibility cannot be explained simply in terms of increased recall. Thus, they concluded that a person scoring high on the GSS would appear moderately suggestible when tested with familiar material, and only slightly suggestible when tested with both familiar and recent material.

It is a simplification to limit the use of the GSS because it has a memory component. It measures something entirely different from memory. The two studies should not present a difficulty for a psychologist who uses the GSS. According to Henry and Gudjonsson (2003), the Shift type of suggestibility (changing responses based on subtle pressure) is less influenced by memory processes than Yield 1 (giving in to leading questions). Shift is more influenced by social and anxiety processes. Suggestibility, as measured by the GSS, highlights a potential *vulnerability*, which should be interpreted in the totality of circumstances in any given case. It should not be interpreted in isolation from other factors. Moreover the White and Willner (2005) study is methodologically flawed. First, White and Willner changed the post recall instruction on the GSS 2 to make it less harsh. Thus, they not only administered the test in an unstandardized fashion but they also actually changed the nature of the test. The subsequent results from their adulterated GSS cannot be legitimately compared to the original. Second, the authors use a relatively small sample size (only 20 per group) with a mean IQ of 57, as measured by the WASI. Based on research by Axlerod (2002), the WASI was found to be quite poor in predicting Full Scale WAIS-III scores and cannot be considered a reliable measures of intelligence. Even if the IQ scores are valid, it is rare in the criminal justice system to evaluate defendants with such significant mental retardation. The ones that are evaluated have such profoundly impaired memory and vocabulary skills that they are unlikely even to have the GSS administered to them. In the study the authors use a population of such profoundly intellectually impaired individuals that, practically speaking, the results are not relevant to use in most clinical–forensic contexts. They also ignore data from Britain that show the majority of defendants whose convictions have been overturned on the basis of unreliable confessions have been of borderline or low-average intelligence (Gudjonsson, Clare, Rutter, & Pearse, 1993). Finally, the study focused on witnesses, not defendants. The generalizability of their study to defendants is questionable.

Neuropsychological Assessment

Heilbronner and Frumkin (2003) discuss the collaborative relationship between the clinical neuropsychologist and forensic psychologist when involved together in a criminal forensic case. In one model, the clinical neuropsychologist works as a consultant, providing neuropsychological data to the forensic psychologist, who then incorporates the data to the legally relevant criteria based on the forensic psychologist's knowledge of case law and professional standards. The neuropsychologist's "client" is the forensic psychologist. In the second model, both the neuropsychologist and the forensic psychologist are hired by the retaining attorney. This may be done at the outset of the case or after one expert has been hired and evaluation results suggest the need for the services of the other professional. In this second model, the retaining attorney is the "client." Of course, individuals with adequate training can perform both roles simultaneously. These collaborative models are discussed more in Sullivan and Denney, Chapter 13, this volume.

The neuropsychological assessment can be helpful in some *Miranda* waiver and confession cases. As stated earlier, the *Miranda* assessment is functional, based on totality of circumstances; there is no level of cognitive impairment that automatically results in a suspect having given an invalid *Miranda* waiver or having tendered a false or a coerced confession. Yet sometimes the trier of fact will find it useful to understand what is causing the impairment that compromises the waiver or results in a possible false confession. Brain–behavior relationships may in some cases provide insight into the difficulties a defendant has in remembering *Miranda* rights and using executive functions in problem solving, the neuropsychological factors resulting in impaired judgment or impulse control, and/or auditory processing of verbal stimuli. The neuropsychological evaluation should generally be conducted after the initial forensic evaluation, so that the neuropsychologist knows where to focus the neuropsychological assessment. The neuropsychologist can then have more specificity in assessing impairments that impact *Miranda* understanding or appreciation, or affect a defendant's ability to resist or not be misled by interrogation tactics.

References

American Educational Research Association, American Psychological Association, and National Council on Measurement in Education (AERA/APA/NCME). (1999). *Standards for educational and psychological testing*. Washington, DC: American Educational Research Association.

Axelrod, B. (2002). Validity of the Wechsler Abbreviated Scale of Intelligence and other very short forms of estimating intellectual functioning. *Assessment, 9*, 17–23.

Baxter, J., & Bain, S. (2002). Faking interrogative suggestibility: The truth machine. *Legal and Criminological Psychology, 7*, 219–225.

Beail, N. (2002). Interrogative suggestibility, memory and intellectual disability. *Journal of Applied Research in Intellectual Disabilities, 15*, 129–137.

Blagrove, M. (1996). Effects of length of sleep deprivation on interrogative suggestibility. *Journal of Experimental Psychology: Applied, 2*(1), 48–59.

Blagrove, M., & Akehurst, L. (2000). Effects of sleep loss on confidence–accuracy relationships for reasoning and eyewitness memory. *Journal of Experimental Psychology: Applied, 6*, 59–73.

Blagrove, M., Cole-Morgan, D., & Lambe, H. (1994). Interrogative suggestibility: The effects of sleep deprivation and relationship with field dependence. *Applied Cognitive Psychology, 8*, 169–179.

Brown v. Mississippi, 297 U.S. 278 (1936).

Butcher, J., Dahlstrom, W., Graham, J., Tellegen, A., & Kaemmer, B. (1989). *MMPI-2: Manual for administration and scoring*. Minneapolis: University of Minnesota Press.

California v. Burnett, 234 Cal. Rptr. 67, 76 (Cal. Ct. App. 1987).

Carter v. State, 697 So.2d. 529 (Fla. App. 1st Dist. 1997).

Cassell, P. G. (1996). Miranda's social costs: An empirical reassessment. *Northwestern University Law Review, 90*, 387–499.

Cattell, R. B., Cattell, A. K., & Cattell, H. E. P. (1993). *Sixteeen Personality Factor Questionnaire* (5th ed.). Champaign, IL: Institute for Personality and Ability Testing.

Cloud, M., Shepherd, G., Barkoff, A., & Shur, J. (2002). Words without meaning: The Constitution, confessions, and mentally retarded suspects. *University of Chicago Law Review, 69*, 495–624.

Colorado v. Connelly, 479 U.S. 157 (1986).

Commonwealth v. Soares, 51 Mass. App. Ct. 273, 745 N.E.2d 362 (2001).

Cooper v. Griffin, 445 F.2d 1142 (1972).

Crane v. Kentucky, 476 U.S. 683, 106 S. Ct. 2142 (1986).

Cronbach, L. (1946). Response sets and test validity. *Educational and Psychological Measurement, 6*, 475–494.

Daubert v. Merrell Dow Pharmaceuticals, 509 U.S. 579 (1993).

DeClue, G. (2005). *Interrogations and disputed confessions: A manual for forensic psychological practice*. Sarasota, FL: Professional Resource Press.

Dickerson v. United States, 166 F.3d 667 (2000).

Dusky v. United States, 362 U.S. 402 (1960).
Everington, C., & Fulero, S. (1999). Competence to confess: Measuring understanding and suggestibility of defendants with mental retardation. *Mental Retardation, 37*, 212–220.
Fare v. Michael C., 442 U.S. 707 (1979).
Federal Bureau of Investigation. (2006). *Homepage—Famous Cases: The Lindbergh Kidnapping.* Available at http://www.fbi.gov/libref/historic/famcases/lindber/lindbernew.htm
Flesch, R. (1994). *The art of readable writing, reissue edition.* New York: Macmillan General Reference.
Frumkin, I. B. (2000). Competency to waive Miranda rights: Clinical and legal issues. *Mental and Physical Disability Law Reporter, 24*, 326–331.
Frumkin, I. B., & Garcia, A. (2003). Psychological evaluations and competency to waive Miranda rights. *The Champion, 27*, 12–23.
Frye v. United States, 54 App. D.C. 47 (1923).
Fulero, S., & Everington, C. (1995). Assessing competency to waive Miranda rights in defendants with mental retardation. *Law and Human Behavior, 19*, 533–543.
Grisso, T. (1980). Juveniles' capacities to waive Miranda rights: An empirical analysis. *California Law Review, 68*, 1134–1166.
Grisso, T. (1981). *Juveniles' waiver of rights: Legal and psychological competence.* New York: Plenum Press.
Grisso, T. (1986). *Evaluating competencies: Forensic assessments and instruments.* New York: Plenum Press.
Grisso, T. (1998). *Instruments for assessing understanding and appreciation of Miranda rights.* Sarasota, FL: Professional Resource Press.
Grisso, T. (2003). *Evaluating competencies: Forensic assessments and instruments* (2nd ed.). New York: Kluwer Academic.
Grisso, T. (2004). Reply to "A critical review of published competency to confess measures." *Law and Human Behavior, 28*, 719–724.
Gudjonsson, G. (1984). Interrogative suggestibility: Comparison between "false confessors" and "deniers" in criminal trials. *Medicine, Science, and the Law, 24*, 56–60.
Gudjonsson, G. (1986). The relationship between interrogative suggestibility and acquiescence: Empirical findings and theoretical implications. *Personality and Individual Differences, 7*, 195–199.
Gudjonsson, G. (1989). Compliance in an interrogation situation: A new scale. *Personality and Individual Differences, 10*, 535–540.
Gudjonsson, G. (1990). The relationship of intellectual skills to suggestibility, compliance and acquiescence. *Personality and Individual Differences, 11*, 227–231.
Gudjonsson, G. (1991). Suggestibility and compliance among false confessors and resisters in criminal trials. *Medicine, Science, and the Law, 31*, 147–151.
Gudjonsson, G. (1997). *The Gudjonsson Suggestibility Scales manual.* Hove, UK: Psychology Press.
Gudjonsson, G. (2003). *The psychology of interrogations and confessions: A handbook.* West Sussex, UK: Wiley.

Gudjonsson, G., & Clare, I. (1995). The relationship between confabulation and intellectual ability, memory, interrogative suggestibility and acquiescence. *Personality and Individual Differences, 19*, 333–338.

Gudjonsson, G., Clare, I., Rutter, S., & Pearse, J. (1993). *Persons at risk during interviews in police custody: The identification of vulnerabilities.* London: Royal Commission on Criminal Justice, HMSO.

Gudjonsson, G., Rutter, S., & Clare, I. (1995). The relationship between suggestibility and anxiety among suspects detained at police stations. *Psychological Medicine, 25*, 875–878.

Heilbronner, R., & Frumkin, I. B. (2003). Neuropsychology and forensic psychology: Working collaboratively in criminal cases. *Journal of Forensic Neuropsychology, 3*, 5–12.

Heilbrun, K. (2001). *Principles of forensic mental health assessment.* New York: Kluwer Academic.

Heilbrun, K. (2002). *Forensic mental health assessment: A casebook.* New York: Oxford University Press.

Henry, L., & Gudjonsson, G. (2003). Eyewitness memory, suggestibility, and repeated recall session with children with mild and moderate intellectual deficiencies. *Law and Human Behavior, 27*, 481–505.

Inbau, F., Reid, J., Buckley, J., & Jayne, B. (2001). *Criminal interrogation and confessions* (4th ed.). Gaithersburg, MD: Aspen.

In re Gault, 387 U.S. 1 (1967).

In re Patrick W., 148 Cal. Rptr. 735 (1978).

In re T.S.D. v. Florida, 741 So. 2d 1142 (Fla. Dist. Ct. App. 1999).

Kassin, S., & Gudjonsson, G. (2004). The psychology of confessions: A review of the literature and issues. *Psychological Science in the Public Interest, 5*, 31–67.

Kassin, S., & McNall, K. (1991). Police interrogations and confessions: Communicating promises and threats by pragmatic implication. *Law and Human Behavior, 15*, 233–251.

Kassin, S., & Neumann, K. (1997). On the power of confession evidence: An experimental test of the fundamental difference hypothesis. *Law and Human Behavior, 21*, 469–484.

Kassin, S., & Wrightsman, L. (1985). Confession evidence. In S. Kassin & L. Wrightsman (Eds.), *The psychology of evidence and trial procedures* (pp. 67–94). London: Sage.

Kumho Tire Company v. Carmichael, 526 U.S. 137 (1999).

Leo, R. A. (1996). Inside the interrogation room. *Journal of Criminal Law and Criminology, 86*, 266–303.

McCann, J. (1998). A conceptual framework for identifying various types of false confessions. *Behavioral Sciences and the Law, 16*, 441–453.

Melton, G. B., Petrila, J., Poythress, N. G., & Slobogin, C., with Lyons, P. M., Jr., & Otto, R. K. (2007). *Psychological evaluations for the courts: A handbook for mental health professionals and lawyers* (3rd ed.). New York: Guilford Press.

Miranda v. Arizona, 384 U.S. 436 (1966).

Misskelley v. State, 323 Ark. 449, 915 S.W.2d 702 (1996).

Moran v. Burbine, 475 U.S. 412 (1986).

Oberlander, L., Goldstein, N., & Goldstein, A. (2003). Competence to confess. In A. Goldstein (Ed.), *Handbook of psychology: Vol. 11. Forensic psychology* (pp. 335–357). New York: Wiley.

Ofshe, R., & Leo, R. (1997a). The decision to falsely confess: Rational choice and irrational action. *Denver University Law Review, 74*, 979–1122.

Ofshe, R., & Leo, R. (1997b). The social psychology of police interrogations: The theory and classification of true and false confessions. *Studies in Law, Politics and Society, 16*, 189–251.

Pollard, D., Trowbridge, B., Slade, P. D., Streissguth, A. P., Laktonen, A., & Townes, B. D. (2004). Interrogative suggestibility in a U.S. context: Some preliminary data on normal subjects. *Personality and Individual Differences, 37*, 1101–1108.

Rogers, R., Bagby, R., & Dickens, S. (1992). *SIRS, Structured Interview of Reported Symptoms: Professional manual.* Sarasota, FL: Professional Resource Press.

Rogers, R., Jordan, M., & Harrison, K. (2004). A critical review of published competency-to-confess measures. *Law and Human Behavior, 28*, 707–718.

Rogers, R., & Shuman, D. (2005). *Fundamentals of forensic practice: Mental health and criminal law.* New York: Springer.

Rogers, R., Tillbrook, C., & Sewell, K. (2004). *ECST-R: Evaluation of Competency to Stand Trial—Revised: Professional manual.* Lutz, FL: Psychological Assessment Resources.

Schill, T., Kahn, M., & Meuhleman, T. (1968). WAIS PA performance participation in extracurricular activities. *Journal of Clinical Psychology, 24*, 95–96.

Shapiro, D. (1991). *Forensic psychological assessment: An integrative approach.* Boston: Allyn & Bacon.

Sigurdsson, E., Gudjonsson, G., Kolbeinsson, H., & Petursson, H. (1994). The effects of ECT and depression on confabulation, memory processing, and suggestibility. *Nordic Journal of Psychiatry, 48*, 443–451.

Slovenko, R. (1999). Civil competency. In A. Hess & I. Weiner (Eds.), *The handbook of forensic psychology* (2nd ed., pp. 151–167). New York: Wiley.

Smith, P., & Gudjonsson, G. (1995). The relationship of mental disorder to suggestibility and confabulation among forensic inpatients. *Journal of Forensic Psychiatry, 6*, 499–515.

State v. Bittick, 806 S.W.2d 652, 658 (Mo., en banc 1986).

State v. Cayward, 552 So.2d 971 (1989).

State v. Griffin, 78 Conn. App. 646, 656-57, 828 A.2d 65 (2003).

State v. Romero, 191 Or. App. 164, 81 P.3d 714 (2003).

State v. Phillips, 226 Ill. App.3d 878, 589 N.E. 2d 1107 (1992).

State v. Whitaker, 578 A.2d 1031, 1037 (Conn. Sup. Ct. 1990).

Sullivan, J. P. (2005). Competency to confess: A case of false confession and a false friend. In R. L. Heilbronner (Ed.), *Forensic neuropsychology casebook* (pp. 285–304). New York: Guilford Press.

United States v. Crocker, 510 F.2d. 1129 (1975).

United States v. Major, 912 F. Supp. 90, 96 (S.D. N.Y. 1996).

United States v. Raposo, 1998 WL 879723 (S.D. N.Y. Dec. 16, 1998).

Viljoen, J., Roesch, R., & Zapf, P. (2002). An examination of the relationship between competency to stand trial, competency to waive interrogation rights, and psycho pathology. *Law and Human Behavior, 26,* 481–506.

White, R., & Willner, P. (2005). Suggestibility and salience in people with intellectual disabilities: An experimental critique of the Gudjonsson Suggestibility Scale. *Forensic Psychology and Psychiatry, 16,* 638–650.

Winkler, J., Kanouse, D., & Ware, J. (1982). Controlling for acquiescence response set in score development. *Journal of Applied Psychology, 67,* 555–561.

Wrightsman, L. S., & Kassin, S. M. (1993). *Confessions in the courtroom.* Newbury Park, CA: Sage.

Young, H., Bentall, R., Slade, P., & Dewey, M. (1987). The role of brief instructions and suggestibility in the elicitation of auditory and visual hallucinations in normal and psychiatric subjects. *Journal of Nervous and Mental Disease, 175,* 41–48.

Chapter 6

Neuropsychological Evaluation of Competency to Proceed

BERNICE A. MARCOPULOS
JOEL E. MORGAN
ROBERT L. DENNEY

Competency to proceed refers to a criminal defendant's capacity to participate effectively and make decisions on his or her own behalf while being prosecuted. Competency must be distinguished from legal sanity, because it has a very different legal standard, and competency most commonly deals with current mental states (Denney & Wynkoop, 2000; Melton et al., 2007). Competency to proceed is relevant to any portion of the process, from talking to police (i.e., *Miranda* rights to remain silent) to receiving a sentence or even being executed. Because the capacity to understand and waive *Miranda* rights is a unique type of competency with its own issues, it is addressed here (see Frumkin, Chapter 5, this volume). In this chapter, we discuss the role of neuropsychology in determining a defendant's *competency to proceed*, that is, such areas of competency as participating in a trial, pleading guilty (and thereby waiving a Constitutional right to receive a trial), waiving one's right to counsel, being sentenced, and being executed. In addition to describing the basic concepts in competency evaluations, this chapter reviews the contribution a clinical neuropsychologist can make in examining these issues and assisting the trier of fact in criminal legal proceedings. Several cases are presented involving defendants whose competency was questioned due to possible cognitive issues. Inherent in this discussion is an explanation of the unique skills that neuropsychologists may bring to criminal legal matters involving defendants with cognitive impairment due to suspected brain damage or dysfunction, and the specialized instruments used for evaluation purposes.

The Legal Standard

The rationale for questioning/examining a defendant's competency can be historically traced to English common law and the 17th century (Melton et al., 2007). Courts in colonial America relied on English common law as well, and ultimately the U.S. Supreme Court upheld the right of a criminal defendant to be competent through criminal proceedings (*Dusky v. United States*, 1960). *Dusky* protects the Fourteenth Amendment rights of the individual to receive *due process* (called the Due Process Clause). Therefore, it is a denial of due process when an incompetent person is tried for a crime, because, by definition, an incompetent person is one who cannot assist counsel and cannot adequately participate in the legal process (*Youtsey v. United States*, 1899).

In *Dusky*, a definition of competency established by the U.S. Supreme Court has become the standard in all jurisdictions within the United States. It reads, "The test must be whether the defendant has sufficient present ability to consult with his attorney with a reasonable degree of rational understanding and a rational as well as a factual understanding of proceedings against him" (p. 402). Thus, *Dusky* sets the standard for competency in criminal matters in a two-pronged fashion: (1) The defendant must have the capacity to understand the criminal process he or she is facing (which would include an understanding of the roles of the various participants in that process, such as judge, jury, prosecutor), and (2) the defendant must be capable to participate in that process through consulting with counsel in the preparation of his or her defense. Both of these prongs require a *rational*, as well as *factual*, level of understanding. *Present ability* refers to the ongoing legal process at the present time (and presumably the near future), not to the defendant's previous mental state at the time the alleged crime took place (that is relevant to the issue of criminal responsibility or *insanity*; see Yates & Denney, Chapter 7, this volume). By definition, a *competent defendant* is one who is an active participant in the legal process, not a passive observer. Defendants are assumed to be competent unless the issue is brought before the court and the defendant is declared incompetent to proceed. The various nexus points regarding competency to proceed are presented in Table 6.1.

TABLE 6.1. Specific Competencies in the Criminal Justice Process

Competency to:	General issue in question
Confess (or to waive rights at pretrial investigations)	Understanding and appreciation of rights to silenced and legal counsel when the rights may be waived at the request of law enforcement investigators seeking a self-incriminating statement
Plead guilty	Understanding and appreciation of above, and of the right to a jury trial, the right to confront one's accusers, and the consequences of a conviction
Waive right to counsel	Understanding and appreciation of the dangers of self-representation at trial
Stand trial	Ability to assist an attorney in developing and presenting a defense, and to understand the nature of the trial and its potential consequences
Be sentenced	Understanding and appreciation of nature of the sentence to be imposed (after trial has resulted in conviction)
Waive further appeal (when facing an execution)	Understanding and appreciation of right for additional appeal and potential consequences of waiving it
Be executed	Understanding and appreciation of nature and purpose of the punishment, and ability to assist counsel in any available appeal

Note. The wording of these definitions does not conform to prevailing legal terminology. They are intended only to convey the general issues raised in each specific competency. From Grisso (1988). Copyright 1988 by Professional Resource Exchange, Inc. Reprinted by permission.

Most states have attempted to elaborate and refine the *Dusky* standard by adopting some variation of it (Favole, 1983; Grisso, 2003). In so doing, legislatures attempted to specify the standard and make it more explicit and operational by adding additional clarification. In New Jersey for example, fitness to proceed to trial is based on the following:

> N.J.S.A. 2C:4-4(b). A person is mentally competent if (1) the defendant has the mental capacity to appreciate his presence in relation to time, place and things; and (2) his elementary mental processes are such that he comprehends (a) he is in a court of law charged with a crime, (b) there is a judge on the bench, (c) there is a prosecutor who will try to convict him, (d) that he has a lawyer who will defend him, (e) that he will be expected to testify as to facts re: charge or be silent, (f) the role of the jury and the consequences of a plea bargain, (g) that he has the ability to participate in an adequate presentation of his defense.

These minimum requirements for competency were initially outlined in *Wieter v. Settle* (1961; see Table 6.2). Although not jurisdictionally authoritative, *Wieter* demonstrates the basic nature of competency abilities and how such cases can have impact on other jurisdictions. In New Jersey, when issues of competency are raised, most often by the defense,[1] the burden rests upon the State to prove competency by a preponderance of evidence (*State v. Lambert*, 1994). Other States may differ with regard to this requirement, where the burden of proof may rest with the defense to prove incompetence. *Medina v. California* (1992) ruled that it is constitutional to place the burden of proof on whoever raises the issue of incompetence, because all defendants are considered competent unless proven otherwise. However, the Supreme Court ruled in *Cooper v. Oklahoma* (1996) that the standard of proof in establishing incompetency can be no greater than a preponderance of evidence, if the burden rests on the defense. To expect clear and convincing standard of evidence from the defendant violates due process under the Fourteenth Amendment.[2] Incompetent defendants may not be prosecuted under the law until they are judged to be competent as a result of time or treatment (Poythress & Feld, 2002).

Questions of competency should not be confused with questions of knowledge or willingness to participate. Thus, the defendant who willingly chooses not to talk to his or her attorney, or the defendant who is uncooper-

TABLE 6.2. Minimal Ability Requirements for Criminal Competency as Outlined by the U.S. District Court in *Wieter v. Settle* (1961)

1. Mental capacity to appreciate his or her presence in relation to time, place, and things.
2. Elementary mental processes such that he or she apprehends (i.e., seizes and grasps with what mind he or she has) that he or she is in a Court of Justice, charged with a criminal offense.
3. Apprehends that there is a judge on the bench.
4. Apprehends that there is a prosecutor present who will try to convict him or her of a criminal charge.
5. Apprehends that he or she has a lawyer (self-employed or court-appointed) who will undertake to defend him or her against that charge.
6. Apprehends that he or she will be expected to tell his or her lawyer the circumstances, to the best of his or her mental ability, (whether colored or not by mental aberration) the facts surrounding him or her at the time and place where the law violation allegedly occurred.
7. Apprehends that there is, or will be, a jury present to pass upon evidence adduced as to his or her guilt or innocence of such charge.
8. He or she has memory sufficient to relate those things in his or her own personal manner.

Note. Adapted for clarity.

ative or selectively mute would not be considered incompetent to stand trial. If there is nothing in the defendant's history that would suggest some type of mental impairment, the defendant may be merely uncooperative or defiant and choosing not to speak to his attorney or cooperate with the proceedings. Jail officers may observe the defendant frequently talking to other inmates without difficulty. Again, in this instance, the defendant demonstrates uncooperativeness, not incompetence. By all appearances, the defendant has the capacity to participate but chooses not to do so. In a similar vein, defendants often claim no knowledge of the issues and events surrounding the instant offense/accusations. A putative lack of knowledge of the events surrounding the allegations/crime is not necessarily equated with incompetence, unless the defendant is unable to learn as a result of a mental abnormality. Uncooperative or unknowledgeable defendants may be found competent; thus, the legal process would proceed.

Mental health experts performing competency evaluations often offer ultimate issue opinions (i.e., the answer to the specific legal question at hand). Nicholson and Kugler (1991) found that judges agree with expert's opinions regarding competency most of the time, which is why many mental health experts attempt to avoid giving ultimate issue opinions. Regardless of whether the expert provides an ultimate issue opinion, it is important to remember that the concept of competency is a legal one. Competency is not a psychological or psychiatric concept. Whereas, by definition, an incompetent individual necessarily has some mental impairment, not all individuals with mental disorders are considered to be incompetent. In fact, that was one of the interesting points clearly defined in *Wieter*. The psychiatrist was opining that the defendant remained not-competent and was requesting additional time for treatment. The court, however, considered the defendant competent to stand trial even though he was mentally ill. In highlighting the difference between presence of mental illness and lack of competency, the *Weiter* court also made this distinction between expert opinion and findings of the court:

> At that time, in criminal procedure, such a person is not in the position of being evaluated as capable, or incapable, of knowing right from wrong; or as being "mentally ill" or afflicted with "mental disease" from psychiatric standards so that he may, psychiatrically, be concluded as mentally unable to rationally understand the proceedings against him and cooperate with counsel in his own defense. Any such psychiatric conclusion, if arrived at, is not and cannot be legally binding. At most, it is merely opinion testimony, to be resolved by the legal *finder of fact*, in the same manner as is the testimony of all expert expressed conclusions. (p. 322, original emphasis)

From this legal perspective (particularly that outlined in Table 6.2), it is probable that most mentally ill defendants would be considered competent; the status of mental illness is not equated with incompetence. It is very important for the neuropsychologist to understand that mental illness in the form of psychiatric disturbance and/or neurological dysfunction does not automatically equal incompetence to proceed.

Triggering a Competency Inquiry

The threshold to question a defendant's competency to proceed is rather low. It is better to delay the proceedings to guarantee a defendant's competency than inadvertently to roll over the Constitutional right to due process by trying an incompetent defendant. *Pate v. Robinson* (1966) and *Drope v. Missouri* (1975) reveal that competency must be evaluated, if there is evidence to suggest a *bona fide doubt* regarding the defendant's competency. Evidence can be raised by anyone involved in the proceedings, and trial courts should consider any evidence coming from irrational behavior, demeanor at trial, or any prior medical opinions. Disturbing information from even one of these sources may trigger an inquiry into the defendant's competency to proceed. This reasoning is the basis for considering most defendants referred for competency evaluation to be competent (Denney, 2005a; Melton et al., 2007; Steadman, Monahan, Hartstone, Davis, & Robbins, 1982).

Competency to Waive Rights to a Trial and Rights to Counsel

Another landmark case regarding competency is *Godinez v. Moran* (1993), which deals specifically with the level of competence required for a defendant to waive his or her right to trial by pleading guilty or to waive right to counsel by representing oneself (acting *pro se*, that is, as one's own lawyer).

Richard Moran shot and killed a bartender and bar patron in August 1984. A few days later, he shot and killed his wife and attempted suicide by shooting himself in the abdomen. He survived and was prosecuted. He was found competent to stand trial and initially pleaded not guilty. About 2 months later, he requested that his defense attorney be discharged and that he be allowed to plead guilty. The trial court granted his requests once assured that he was not pleading guilty in response to threats or promises, and that he understood the potential consequences facing him. He pleaded guilty and was sentenced to death. In 1987, he filed a petition for postconviction relief, claiming he had not been mentally competent to represent himself. The U.S. Court of Appeals for the 9th Circuit concluded that the Due Process Clause of the Fourteenth Amendment required the trial court to hold a special competency inquiry as to whether he was making a "reasoned choice among alternatives" before accepting his decision to discharge counsel and enter a guilty plea. In other words, the Appeals Court suggested that the *Dusky* standard by itself was not enough. The U.S. Supreme Court took up the question and rejected the 9th Circuit's use of "reasoned choice" and concluded, "We can conceive of no basis for demanding a higher level of competence for those defendants who choose to plead guilty . . . nor do we think that a defendant who waives his right to the assistance of counsel must be more competent than a defendant who does not" (*Godinez v Moran*, p. 332). Although the Court specifically indicated that the *Dusky* standard was not increased, it made this slight enhancement:

> A finding that a defendant is competent to stand trial, however, is not all that is necessary before he may be permitted to plead guilty or waive his right to counsel. In addition to determining that a defendant who seeks to plead guilty or waive counsel is competent, a trial court must satisfy itself that the waiver of his constitutional rights is knowing and voluntary. (p. 333)

Godinez established that competency to plead guilty or waive counsel does not require a higher standard than competency to stand trial. However, the trial court must now specifically place in the record an inquiry into the defendant's thought process to verify that it is a "knowing" and "voluntary" decision. *Godinez* reaffirms *Dusky* and spells out the minimum required standard for defendants to waive U.S. Constitutional rights.

Competency to Be Sentenced

Thus far we have discussed the legal standard of competency to proceed in general terms as it relates to standing trial, waiving one's right to trial and pleading guilty, and waiving one's right to counsel. Each of these competencies dealt with issues before a conviction. Although the *Dusky* standard is still in place for sentencing-related competency, competency to be sentenced is a slightly different issue in regard to the demands placed on the defendant. Up to this point in the process, the defendant has needed to take a more active role. The demands on the defendant are less in the area of assistance and decision-making capacity. This difference is exemplified in a recent case from the U.S. Court of Appeals for the 6th Circuit (*United States v. Liberatore*, 1994).

Anthony Liberatore was charged and convicted of racketeering and money laundering. Three hours before sentencing, however, the defense filed a motion seeking a hearing to determine his competency to be sentenced. After neuropsychological evaluation as part of an inpatient mental health evaluation, Mr. Liberatore was considered by the mental health expert to have primary degenerative dementia of the Alzheimer type and to be not competent for sentencing. It was opined that he would not have the ability to provide proper assistance necessary for sentencing, such as having difficulty following lines of reasoning when discussing his defense with counsel, difficulty remembering what occurred during previous discussions, and difficulty speaking on his own behalf due to memory deficits. The U.S. District Court determined that such difficulties would not necessarily eliminate Liberatore's competency to be sentenced. The court highlighted this analytical inquiry that an expert must perform:

> This intellectual process involves three distinct analytical steps: first, determination of the defendant's mental capabilities; second, determination of the legal standard of competency; and third, comparison of defendant's capabilities to the standard. (p. 578)

The sentencing court had concerns about the last two issues related to the testimony of two experts. Although all the experts agreed that Liberatore had deficits, they differed in their opinions about competency. The court concluded that whereas *Dusky* remained the standard for competency to be sentenced, the demands required of the defendant are less than that of participating in a trial. In this regard the court found that two of the experts placed too much weight on the demands required of the defendant. Finally, a defendant has the right of allocution, that is, the right to speak at his sentencing (*Green v. United States*, 1961). The court clarified that such allocution was not eliminated by lapses in memory or mild difficulty speaking. It appeared the court concluded that speaking on one's own behalf at sentencing did not require the same level of mental acuity that testimony during a trial would require. The court found Liberatore competent for sentencing. On appeal, the U.S. Court of Appeals for the 6th Circuit affirmed the decision and made this observation:

> And although the district court's opinion might be read as proposing a somewhat less stringent standard for determining competency for sentencing than would be required for determining competency for the pre-trial and trial phases of a criminal proceeding, it is clear that the standard that the district court applied in coming to its conclusion is essentially that required by *Dusky v. United States*. (*United States v. Liberatore*, 1995, electronic reference)

Competency to Be Executed

A man or woman who is about to be executed must be competent to undergo the procedure. In 1986, the U.S. Supreme Court determined that executing a person who did not understand the reason for the severe punishment was "cruel and unusual punishment." The decision is spelled out in the complicated due process case, *Ford v. Wainwright* (1986). Defendant Ford was convicted of a capital offense and residing on death row when he became acutely psychotic. The procedure in Florida at the time did not allow for a judicial determination of competency, as it was done by the governor, assisted by a panel of mental health experts. The High Court determined the Florida procedure to be unconstitutional and also provided the finding that it is a Constitutional right to be competent when executed. The court did not spell out what it takes to be competent for execution, but it referenced Florida's standard that a person must have the mental capacity to understand the nature of the death penalty and why it was imposed. Reisner and Slobogin (1990) suggested that the condemned must have "a sufficient understanding to know any fact which might make his punishment unjust or unlawful, and the intelligence requisite to convey such information to his attorneys or the court" (p. 946). This focus suggests the individual must be able to assist, at least minimally, counsel in generating ideas for possible appeals. Such requisite abilities make sense given the U.S. Supreme Court's position against executing mentally retarded persons (*Atkins v. Virginia*, 2002).

Limits to Competency Restoration

The U.S. Supreme Court has determined that there are limits to how long a person can be hospitalized for competency restoration and also to the types of treatments forced on the defendant during that time. The first issue is addressed in the landmark competency case, *Jackson v. Indiana* (1972). Theon Jackson was arrested for two different robberies (a purse with $4 and also $5 worth of cash), misdemeanor crimes. Difficulty arose regarding his competency when it was determined that he was deaf, mute, and mentally retarded. He was considered not competent and committed to a state facility for treatment. After spending well over a year in the facility, his counsel filed a motion for a new hearing, as his continued commitment amounted to a "life sentence" without hope of release after never having been convicted of a crime. The U.S. Supreme Court concluded that a criminal defendant cannot be held for more than a reasonable amount of time without pursuing additional civil commitment proceedings. The court did not spell out what constitutes a reasonable period of time. Once a defendant is considered not restorable, he or she must either be released or committed under civil commitment procedures (typically related to dangerousness to others).

There are also limits regarding the nature of involuntary medication to restore an individual to competency. The U.S. Supreme Court concluded in *Sell v. U.S.* (2003) that the forcible administration of antipsychotic medication solely to restore competency could be done under certain circumstances. First the Court recommended trial courts consider such cases based on *Washington v. Harper* (1990) grounds (i.e., whether or not the person is dangerous to self or others). There was no concern regarding involuntary medication to restore the defendant's competency if the defendant was dangerous to self or others. However, if the defendant was not dangerous to self or others, then the U.S. Supreme Court established that each of these four issues must be resolved affirmatively by the trial court to justify forced medication: (1) there are *important* government interests; (2) those important government interests will be *significantly furthered* by medication; (3) the medication is *necessary* (i.e., there are no less intrusive alternatives); and (4) such medicine is *medically appropriate*. Under these circumstances, criminal defendants can be medicated involuntarily with antipsychotic medications to restore their competency.

A Model for Evaluating Competency

According to Grisso (2003), the procedure for determining competency to stand trial involves several stages. First the question of competency is raised, most often by the defense attorney. However it can also be raised by the judge or prosecution, and can be raised at any point in the proceedings. The second step is performing a competency evaluation.[3] This is discussed shortly. After the competency evaluation, the judge makes a determination of competency or incompetency to proceed based on the information presented from the mental health expert. That information should also include a disposition and plan for restoration of competency if the defendant is found incompetent. The incompetent defendant receives treatment, typically in a state or federal mental health facility. After the treatment, the judge rehears the facts on the defendant's competency and makes another determination of competency. If the defendant is found competent, then the trial proceeds; if not, the defendant receives more treatment for restoration. As noted previously, under *Jackson v. Indiana* (1972), a defendant cannot be institutionalized indefinitely while waiting to be restored to competency. At some point a decision must be made as to whether the defendant is *unrestorably incompetent*. If so, the government must eventually institute a civil commitment related to dangerousness or release the defendant.

Grisso (1988) established a method and conceptual basis for conducting competency evaluations. Grisso (2003) described five components of legal competency that should be used to guide the forensic evaluator: (1) functional, (2) causal, (3) interactive, (4) judgmental, and (5) dispositional. The *functional* component refers to the defendant's specific abilities, behaviors, beliefs, and capacities as they directly relate to the competency issue and legal situation in question. This is not determined by evaluating symptoms or signs of a mental or neurological disorder and making a diagnosis, but by directly observing and testing whether the defendant understands the charges, personnel, and procedures in the courtroom, and whether he or she can work productively with his or her attorney to establish a defense strategy. The *causal* component of the competency evaluation involves ascribing an underlying cause and providing an explanation for a finding of incompetence (e.g., severe memory loss in dementia preventing the defendant from retaining any information regarding his charges and his defense team).

The *interactive* component recognizes the importance of the person–context interaction and that not all legal situations demand the same level of capability. It is the congruence between the situational demands and the defendant's ability rather than absolute ability that is important (Grisso, 2003). Thus, the forensic evaluator must examine what is being demanded of the defendant in making a recommendation to the court. This is a difficult issue, however. One might argue, as Bonnie (1992, 1993) did, that different competencies could require different standards. For example an individual with cognitive deficits might have the capacity to understand his or her options and plead guilty but not have the cognitive capacity to follow a complicated trial process. Or an individual might have the cognitive capability to stand trial with the assistance of counsel, but not to stand trial *pro se* (on one's own, without representation). Conceptualizing competency in this manner fits with Grisso's model (1988, 2003) of assessing competency, which considers context and the congruence between a person's capabilities and the demands of the specific legal situation. However, as we mentioned regarding *Godinez v. Moran* (1993), the U.S. Supreme Court concluded that competency to plead guilty or waive counsel is the same as competency to proceed to trial. They require no special or additional standards beyond making it clear in the record that the defendant was making a "knowing" and "voluntary" decision. *Godinez* certainly did not address whether or not specific case complexity could affect competency for an individual with cognitive deficits. Nevertheless, such an interaction could be argued in the case of a defendant with undisputed cognitive deficits.

The final two components of Grisso's model are judgment and disposition. *Judgment* involves deciding whether the functional deficits eliminate the defendant's capability to understand the charges and proceedings he or she is facing or the capability to assist in his or her defense. In a competency assessment, this is the "ultimate issue." Grisso (2003) advises against deciding the ultimate legal question of competence or incompetence, preferring that the forensic evaluator defer to the court to make this legal decision. However, the court may still want to know the expert's ultimate issue opinion. *Disposition* relates to an incompetent defendant and involves prescribing a plan to address the functional deficits to render the defendant eventually competent to stand trial. Courts need direction when it comes to dealing with mental illness and defect, and this information comes into the record through the mental health expert. Although typically bound by statue to refer for mental health treatment,[4] courts appreciate clinical recommendations and information about the natural course, treatments available, and prognosis of the specific condition. Providing this opinion entails predicting whether the defendant is restorable. Hubbard, Zapf, and Ronan (2003) found that just over half (58%) of the competency evaluations they reviewed included a prediction of whether the incompetent defendant could ultimately be restored. Those found unrestorable were more likely to have a psychiatric history and less likely to have a previous criminal history. Older defendants were more likely to be found unrestorable, presumably due to cognitive impairment (e.g., suspected dementia) limiting their ability to understand and learn about the criminal justice system. Heck and Herrick (2007) recently presented two cases of geriatric defendants undergoing competency to stand trial (CST) evaluations and highlighted the need to determine whether the defendants have reversible cognitive impairment and can be restored, or a progressive dementia.

Neuropsychological Testing in Competency to Stand Trial Evaluations

How does psychological or neuropsychological testing fit with Grisso's conceptual approach to competency evaluation? Although some suggest that formal psychological testing is not always necessary (Melton et al., 2007), it can be argued that testing in many cases is quite useful, if not critical. There certainly appears to be a role for formal competency assessment instruments, such as the MacArthur Competence Assessment Tool—Criminal Adjudication (MacCAT-CA; Poythress et al., 1999) and Evaluation of Competency to Stand Trial—Revised (ECST-R; Rogers, Tillbrook, & Sewell, 2004). We would argue that in cases involving neurocognitive concerns, neurocognitive testing is extremely beneficial. For instance, memory impairment in a defendant is a problem that could possibly impair competency, and that neuropsychological testing can reveal as genuine, malingered, mild, or severe. Neuropsychological assessment can contribute to Grisso's causal and dispositional component of legal competencies. For instance, if the defendant is incompetent because of the cognitive sequelae of a brain injury or other neurological condition, the neuropsychologist can offer a prognosis and an opinion on the likelihood of the defendant becoming competent in the foreseeable future, based on the nature and severity of the disorder or injury and concomitant cognitive deficits, and their relation to the legal definition of competence.

Cochrane, Grisso, and Frederick (2001) analyzed data from 1,710 criminal defendants referred by U.S. federal courts and found that 18% were incompetent to stand trial. Of those defendants, those with psychotic disorders were most likely to be found incompetent (43%). Defendants with mental retardation were found incompetent 30% of the time and those with "organic mental disorder," 38% of the time. Warren, Fitch, Dietz, and Rosenfeld (1991) found that the diagnoses most commonly associated with incompetency were schizophrenia, mental retardation, and mood and organic brain disorders. Thus, because a significant proportion of incompetent defendants have a brain disorder, and neuropsychologists have expertise in diagnosing brain and other mental disorders, the science of neuropsychology could be relevant to competency evaluations.

By virtue of their expertise in brain–behavior relationships, neuropsychologists can contribute to the evaluation of competency when cognitive factors are believed to impact competency to proceed (Denney, 2005a). Neuropsychologists' contribution can be critical, especially in terms of their knowledge of cognitive functions—both normal and abnormal; brain-based functions, as manifested in psychometric data; knowledge of the human nervous system and the behavioral expressions of disease; psychopathology; and exaggeration, dissimulation, and issues of symptom (performance) validity and poor effort. Indeed, one of the more unique and valuable aspects that neuropsychologists bring to CST and other forensic evaluations concerns their knowledge of symptom validity testing (Larrabee, 2005). Defendants have a powerful incentive to malinger psychological and neurocognitive impairment to avoid or indefinitely delay trial and prosecution. Rates of malingering in CST evaluations have been reported to be from 8% (Cornell & Hawk, 1989) up to 15% (Rogers, Sewell, & Goldstein, 1994) or 17% (Rogers, Salekin, Sewell, Goldstein, & Leonard, 1998). A very recent study of 100 males undergoing CST evaluation in a forensic hospital found an even higher rate of malingering (Vitacco, Rogers, Gabel, & Munizza, 2007). Of the sample, 21% were deemed likely to be malingering psychiatric disturbance. Rates of exaggeration appear to be significantly higher when criminal defendants are specifically referred for evaluation related to neurocognitive and memory concerns. Ardolf, Denney, and Houston (2006) found negative response bias rates higher than 50% and possibly as high as 70% for a consecutive series of 105 presentence male defendants referred due to neurocognitive concerns. They found that 21% of the cases performed below random chance on two-alternative, forced-choice testing. Denney (2007) returned to these data, supplemented it with additional consecutive cases, and looked solely at defendants with presenting claims or records suggesting mild and/or moderate closed head injury. He found that 73.1% of this series obtained positive results on two or more indices of negative response bias. Clearly, the detection of feigned or exaggerated cognitive deficits in presentence criminal defendants is a concern. Defendants can malinger cognitive deficits, psychiatric impairment, or both. There are many empirically validated, specific instruments that detect malingered cognitive or psychiatric symptoms, as well as procedures that detect exaggeration and feigned symptoms in commonly used, standardized, clinical tests (Larrabee, 2007). Neuropsychologists have developed a host of test-based strategies designed to measure scientifically an examinee's (a defendant, in this case) cooperativeness and honesty in taking cognitive and emotional/personality tests (see Denney, Chapter 4, this volume), and many have become experts in such matters (Boone, 2007).

Denney (2005a) advocates the use of a multiple-data-source model for forensic assessment. Observing the defendant surreptitiously can be helpful when poor motivation or symptom exaggeration is suspected (Denney & Wynkoop, 2000; Wynkoop & Denney, 1999). The forensic evaluator cannot rely on the defendant's self-report and testing behavior, and must get corroboration from outside sources. Consistency across sources of information is vital.

Case Examples

The following case presentations illustrate situations where neuropsychological evaluations can be quite useful in discerning the extent of a suspected cognitive disorder and presence of malingering.

Amnesia: Real and Feigned

Defendants who present with presumed memory impairment for the alleged crime are not uncommon (Denney, 2005a). Feigned amnesia is much more common in the forensic context, and distinguishing between genuine and simulated amnesia was thought to be a difficult task 20 years ago (Schacter, 1986). But with the advent of symptom validity theory and test development, in large part as a result of neuropsychological research, it is possible to distinguish between feigned and actual amnesia. Because of their training in memory testing, knowledge of memory functions, and advances made in detecting feigned versus genuine neurocognitive deficits, clinical neuropsychologists are in a good position to evaluate claims of amnesia in the forensic context. A number of authors have noted that approximately 30% of criminals claim they cannot remember their crimes (e.g., Cima, Nijman, Merckelbach, Kremer, & Hollnack, 2004; Gudjonsson, Petursson, Skulason, & Sigurdardottir, 1989; Taylor & Kopelman, 1984). Historically, the courts have been reluctant to equate amnesia with incompetence, because claiming amnesia is so common and is most likely an attempt to avoid criminal responsibility (Melton et al., 2007). Even a defendant with genuine amnesia may be considered competent. The trial may proceed even if the defendant has no recollection of the crime, unless the only way the defense counsel can obtain important evidence is by the defendant's own account of the crime (see *Wilson v. United States*, 1968). Amnesia may take several forms: (1) organically based amnesia secondary to cerebral dysfunction, as in the case of severe traumatic brain injury (TBI), stroke, cerebral tumor, or other neurological abnormality occurring after the offense, or alcohol or drug-induced intoxication at the time of the offense (the so-called "state-dependent amnestic syndrome"); (2) psychogenic-based amnesia secondary to psychic trauma or other psychiatric conditions; and (3) malingered amnesia (Cima et al., 2004).

Competency to Stand Trial: Penetrating Brain Injury

A CST evaluation was ordered for a defendant who had been charged with armed robbery in the first degree. After his arrest on those charges, the 27-year-old defendant awaited trial at the local jail. During an altercation with another inmate at the jail, the defendant was stabbed in the head with a homemade knife. The defendant sustained a deep, serious, penetrating brain injury that entered his skull at his left eye and deeply penetrated his left frontal and temporal lobes. He bled profusely and lost consciousness. At the emergency room he had to be intubated, and he required cardiopulmonary resuscitation. Neuroimaging was consistent with traumatic lesions in the left frontal and temporal lobes. There was hemorrhage in the area of the hippocampus, amygdala, and left mammillary body. Severe edema was present, and the defendant survived more than one episode of left unilateral herniation. He underwent craniotomy and neurosurgery to evacuate a large intraparenchymal hemorrhage, and remained in a coma for 6 weeks. Upon awakening, he was densely amnestic, mildly aphasic, mildly disinhibited, had a right unilateral hemiparesis, and was grossly disoriented. He was blind in his left eye. Slowly, over the next 4 months, his cognitive condition marginally improved and he was evaluated for competency at that time. He was seen in the county jail over three sessions.

On neuropsychological evaluation the inmate was cooperative and pleasant. Expressively he was mildly aphasic and had a right upper extremity hemiparesis. He was a high school graduate, and examination of his school records indicated he achieved average grades. Examination of his reading ability placed it in the average, expected range at the 63rd percentile (Wide Range Achievement Test–3 [WRAT-3] Reading). Wechsler Adult Intelligence Scale–III (WAIS-III) IQ scores revealed a Verbal IQ (VIQ) of 77, a Performance IQ (PIQ) of 90, and a Full Scale IQ (FSIQ) of 85. He exhibited executive deficits on the Stroop and verbal fluency fell into the impaired range with T-scores below 30. He achieved normal scores on the Test of Memory Malingering (TOMM), with 43 correct on Trial 1 and 49 correct on Trial 2. Similarly he had a valid profile on the Victoria Symptom Validity Test (VSVT).

Assessment of learning and memory with the California Verbal Learning Test, second edition (CVLT-II) resulted in impaired learning with an overall T-Score of 29 (Trials 1–5). He showed a pronounced interference effect on Trial B ($z = -2.5$). He manifested rapid forgetting of long term retrieval with free and cued delayed recall with z scores of -2.0 and -2.5, respectively. California Verbal Learning Test recognition memory was average ($z = -.5$). He performed similarly poorly on the Wechsler Memory Scale, third edition (WMS-III) Logical Memory, Paired Associate and Family Pictures subtests.

Minnesota Multiphasic Personality Inventory–2 (MMPI-2) performance resulted in a valid profile with a 1–2 elevation. On interview/mental status he was mildly anxious and depressed. He was taking antiseizure (carbamazepine) and antidepressant (bupropion) medication.

Systematic investigation into more specific issues of competency regarding his knowledge of the legal system, awareness of charges against him, roles of the various participants in the legal process, and so on, were all within normal limits. But the defendant had serious defects of episodic memory surrounding the events of the alleged armed robbery. Consistent with the presence of both anterograde and retrograde memory impairment, the defendant had little difficulty remembering elicited facts concerning his childhood. But he exhibited a gradient of retrograde memory impairment, such that memory of several years prior to the current time was almost completely lost or available in extremely limited fashion. It should be noted that the use of family collateral interviews was important in developing an episodic, retrograde memory test of facts and information specific to his life (Denney, 1996; Frederick, Carter, & Powel, 1995; Frederick & Denney, 1998). This type of procedure is designed to identify individuals who are feigning amnesia, but it may serve purposes of an actual assessment of memory as well. The ultimate issue opinion of the forensic examiner was that the defendant failed to meet CST criteria on the basis of his profound difficulty in assisting his attorney with the factual basis of the events surrounding the alleged robbery. In fact, he consistently confused the event in question with a previous charge of robbery for which he had already served 16 months; he admitted committing the crime, or so he thought, but did not recall having successfully completed his sentence. The court agreed, concluding that the defendant was incompetent to stand trial "at the present time," and he was remanded to a local psychiatric hospital for treatment and reassessment of his cognitive functions. The statute requires commitment to treatment until proven unrestorable. Thus, not only must the forensic examiner evaluate current functionality vis-à-vis competency but, if incompetence is found, he or she must also comment as to whether the defendant can be restored to competence, and if so, state the recommended treatment.

Competency to Stand Trial: "Amnesia" of Unknown Etiology

At the time of his arrest on charges of grand theft auto, JM, a 32-year-old male with an extensive criminal record, was HIV positive. The issue of CST arose in conjunction with the defendant's defense attorney, who indicated that JM had "amnesia for the alleged crime." JM was evaluated by a psychologist retained by defense counsel. JM asserted that he had no memory of the event in question. The defense expert's evaluation report concluded that JM had HIV-related dementia and was amnestic as a result and, therefore, incompetent to stand trial. JM's test results, as detailed by the defense psychologist's report, indicated profound cognitive impairment throughout all domains of cognitive functioning assessed. The Rey 15-Item Memory Test (FIT) was administered, and the results were interpreted as "normal," with 8 of 15 items correct. Memory scores on formal memory tests were universally below the first percentile. JM performed well below expectations on the CVLT Recognition subtest, raising suspicion. Many vague answers characterized the WAIS results. No sensorimotor testing was completed, nor were any tests of executive functioning, language, attention, or visual–spatial functions, beyond those on the Wechsler scales. Similarly, no tests of personality or psychopathology were administered (e.g., MMPI-2, Personality Assessment Inventory [PAI]). Despite these apparent limitations, the defense expert interpreted these findings as a "severe dementia syndrome ... likely associated with HIV or of other unknown etiology" [sic]. He opined that there was an underlying organic cerebral basis for JM's "obvious inability to recall the alleged offense"; therefore, JM was considered incompetent to stand trial.

The second author was contacted by the prosecutor in this case for a second opinion. He asked whether JM actually had AIDS or any history of opportunistic infections associated with the AIDS-related dementia complex (ARDC). He was informed that JM had no medical record to speak of and that the HIV-positive diagnosis literally had just been made—while he was in jail. There was no medical history beyond that, though the defendant had an extensive history of marijuana abuse.

The examination began with administration of the TOMM. JM correctly identified 20 items on Trial 1 and 18 items on Trial 2. These scores are well below expectations and below chance values. His VSVT results were consistent with feigning as well, with correct identification of less than half of both "easy" and "difficult" items. On the CVLT-II, JM performed worse than he did on the defense expert's exam. His WAIS-III scores were also worse, despite the expectation of a practice effect. On the MMPI-2, JM had an invalid profile with an elevated Infrequency–psychopathology (Fp; $T = 110$) and a Fake-Bad Scale (FBS) of 30 (Lees-Haley, English, & Glenn, 1991).

Furthermore, JM tested positive for HIV but demonstrated no signs of AIDS or any serious infection, or other medical disorder on recent medical examination. Results were clearly consistent with feigned cognitive dysfunction and noncredible test performance. In addition, although JM denied any recollection of the auto theft, when asked "indirect retrospective" questions, specifically designed for this evaluation using police records, JM earned a score of nearly 100% (Frederick et al., 1995).[5] Taking all of the data, presentation of the examinee, and history into account, the diagnostic conclusion was one of malingered neurocognitive dysfunction (MND; Slick, Sherman, & Iverson, 1999), and in the absence of any documented cause of possible cognitive impairment, the trial judge ruled him competent to stand trial. JM was ultimately convicted of grand theft auto and is currently serving 18 years in New Jersey State Prison. Incidentally, he began to cooperate with his defense counsel shortly after the judge declared him competent. This is not an uncommon ending to such cases in our experience.

Traumatic Brain Injury

Moderate and severe traumatic brain injuries (TBIs) typically result in lasting cognitive deficits, with a range of magnitude from mild to extremely severe depending on a host of factors, most notably the severity of the injury and neurological sequelae (Roebuck-Spencer & Sherer, 2008). Mild TBI,

TBI's without significant loss of consciousness, and high Glasgow Coma Scale scores typically result in no lasting cognitive deficits. Postconcussion complaints generally resolve to baseline within weeks or months; this is the so-called "postconcussion syndrome" (Mittenberg & Roberts, 2008). Sequelae of TBI can affect CST depending on the severity of the injury and what cognitive functions are impaired. The court will want to know whether the defendant can be restored, and this depends on the severity of the injury. A very severe injury with a lengthy coma and persisting deficits could potentially result in an unrestorable defendant. However, a mild TBI would be very unlikely to affect CST.

Competency to Stand Trial: TBI and Psychosis

RS was incarcerated on capital murder charges and awaiting trial at the county jail. He was charged with strangling his girlfriend and dumping her body in an abandoned and dilapidated automobile lot owned by a large, local body shop. Her body was "wedged between two cars," according to the police report and had been wrapped in clear packing tape, "mummy style." RS had been appointed a public defender, who began preparing the case about 6 weeks prior to his phone call to the second author.

The public defender reported: " . . . the strangest thing, he was very cooperative with me at first, then after his fall [see below] he seemed crazy and I couldn't understand him. He says he sees things and hears things. I ask him important questions about the events surrounding the alleged incident and he makes no sense to me. I suppose it was his brain injury."

Medical records from the emergency room (ER) of a university hospital were received, along with other, related discovery material, including reports completed by the correction officers on duty who witnessed the incident. RS had been at the county jail, going up a flight of stairs, when he slipped and fell, landing on his head and upper back/shoulders. He reported that he "blacked out" for a moment but was able to stand up and walk to a nearby chair. He reported to correction officers on duty that his head hurt quite a bit and that he was dizzy and felt nauseated and anxious. The correction officers, concerned and following standard protocol, contacted their supervisor, who had the inmate evacuated to a nearby ER for evaluation.

ER records upon review indicated that upon arrival, RS had been awake, alert, relevant, coherent, and cooperative. X-ray and magnetic resonance imaging (MRI) scans of his head and neck revealed no abnormalities. Vital signs and neurological exam were normal. RS complained of headache and back pain and ER staff decided to keep him overnight for observation. Nursing notes from the following morning revealed that whereas RS had been spontaneously verbal and cooperative prior to sleep the night before, in the morning he was mute and did not speak. Neurological and psychiatric consultations were ordered, as was a new brain scan. Neurological examination and MRI were "completely within normal limits." With the exception that RS did not speak, neurological examination revealed no underlying abnormality to indicate a new onset of aphasia. The neurologist was awaiting a psychiatric consultation. The psychiatric consultation suggested that RS was "selectively mute." The neurologist decided to transfer him to the psychiatry service for further observation. Later that day, once on the psychiatry ward, RS began to communicate with staff and told a nurse that he was seeing and hearing things. He said he saw "little mice and little men carrying things," and that he heard the sound "of the sand making noise on the beach." Notes from the psychiatry resident stated that RS was most likely experiencing an acute psychosis, NOS (not otherwise specified) and antipsychotic medication was ordered (olanzapine).

RS remained in the psychiatric unit for 3 more days, was considered "stable," and was discharged back to the jail, where his medication was continued. Several days later, RS's attorney requested a competency evaluation when he found RS to be "unintelligible" and thought that perhaps RS had sustained a serious brain injury when he fell and was now "completely messed up."

On examination, RS had a telegraphic speech quality, halting in midsentence. He answered questions in an approximate way and reported no memory for basic, episodic personal facts, such as his date of birth, birthplace, age, marital status, name of his parents, education, and the like. He reported auditory and visual hallucinations, as mentioned earlier, and claimed to be experiencing them during the clinical interview. On neuropsychological testing, he drew a house with trees and a walkway for the Rey-Osterrieth Complex Figure test. He remembered two items by Trial 5 of the CVLT-II and made 11 intrusions. On the Boston Naming Test he made absurd answers, calling the bench a "bucket" and the house a "red barn." WAIS-III FSIQ was 42. He obtained 22 correct on Trial 1 of the TOMM and 11 correct on Trial 2 (33/100, z –3.3, p = .0002). His documented below-chance failure on symptom validity testing (SVT) can best be understood as a deliberate choice to answer incorrectly, thus branding all neurocognitive test scores as noncredible. His reported "psychotic" symptoms were not consistent with any known form of psychosis or any genuine mental disorder, and appeared to be the product of someone pretending to be a mental patient (i.e., an "unsophisticated malingerer"; Morgan, 2008).

The defendant was a blatant malingerer; his symptoms made no sense whatsoever. The attorney was informed that RS's symptoms and presentation made no logical sense from a neurological or psychiatric perspective, and that his SVT performance was unequivocally consistent with malingering of cognitive impairment. After RS was confronted by the examiner, his symptoms rapidly and miraculously improved. His fall had resulted in a feigned "psychosis of opportunity."

The reader should note some important lessons that emerge from this case. On the one hand, as obvious as it may seem to most neuropsychologists, many unsophisticated malingerers have a grossly incorrect notion of even basic neuropsychological and mental health principles that professionals take for granted. However, not all malingers are so obvious. The other important lesson is that even well-educated professionals, such as attorneys and judges, may have no knowledge whatsoever as to what constitutes a real mental or neurological disorder, and may have no clue that their defendant is malingering.

Mental Retardation

A diagnosis of mental retardation is based on three criteria: IQ below 70, evidence of intellectual impairment prior to age 18, and a history of difficulty with day-to-day adaptive functions and skills (American Psychiatric Association, 2000). The Supreme Court's ruling in *Atkins v. Virginia* (2002) mandated that individuals with mental retardation cannot receive the death penalty. Briefly, in *Atkins*, petitioner Atkins was convicted of a capital murder by a Virginia jury and sentenced to death. Affirming, the Supreme Court of the Commonwealth of Virginia relied on *Penry v. Lynaugh* (1989) in rejecting Atkins's contention that he could not be sentenced to death because he was mentally retarded. The U.S. Supreme Court reversed this decision.

Incompetent individuals cannot be executed in the United States. The rationale for this emanates from several lines of inquiry (Denney, 2005b). The U.S. Supreme Court noted that societal views had changed since it decided the *Penry* case, such that executing a person with mental retardation should be considered "cruel and unusual punishment." The Court also concluded that a mentally retarded individual's "deficiencies do not warrant an exemption from criminal sanctions, but they do diminish [his or her] personal culpability" (*Atkins v. Virginia*, 2002, p. 328). The Court was doubtful that the retribution and deterrence aspect of capital crimes would have much meaning for those with mental retardation. Finally, those with mental retardation likely face an inappropriately high risk of execution because of false confessions, less effective assistance by counsel, being poor witnesses, and often having a demeanor at court that fosters the wrongful assumption that they lack remorse.

Mental retardation is a crucial issue with regard to competency to proceed cases, in that all competency issues ultimately deal with cognitive functioning. Since mental retardation spans a range of severity, courts have ruled that the presence of mental retardation alone is insufficient to meet the standards of *Dusky*. In essence, persons with mild mental retardation may be presumed to be competent if they can assist counsel, and have a rational and factual understanding of the charges against them and the proceedings. As in all cases of competency, the severity of the mental impairment, in this case, mental retardation, in conjunction with the complexity of the case and the demands placed on the defendant to understand the crucial issues and to participate adequately, is more related to the adjudication of competency than the sheer presence of a mental disorder or mental retardation. Having said that, however, "mentally retarded persons are categorically less culpable than the average criminal ... since by definition, they have diminished capacities to understand and process information, communicate, abstract reason and learn from mistakes, anticipate consequences, engage in logical reasoning, [and] to control impulses and to understand the actions of others" (*Atkins v. Virginia*, 2002, p. 328). Neuropsychologists are in a unique position to evaluate those very concerns, but only if they have the prerequisite training and understanding in criminal forensic matters and specialized forensic assessment instruments.

Assessment Instruments for Competency to Stand Trial

There are several empirically validated specialized assessment instruments for competency evaluations. According to a recent survey (Archer, Buffington-Vollum, Stredny, & Handel, 2006), the most frequently used instruments for assessing competency are the MacCAT-CA (Poythress et al., 1999), the ECST-R (Rogers et al., 2004), and the Competence Assessment for Standing Trial for Defendants with Mental Retardation (CAST-MR; Everington & Luckasson, 1992). These measures are described below. For a more extensive review of CST measures, see Grisso (2003).

MacArthur Competency Assessment Tool— Criminal Adjudication

This measure, developed by MacArthur Research Network on Mental Health and Law, is a shorter measure, derived from the MacArthur Structured Assessment of Competencies of Criminal Defendants (MacSAC-CD). There are 22 items divided into three sections entitled Understanding, Reasoning and Appreciation. This measure covers the ability to plead guilty, to stand trial, and to appreciate the nature of crimes; competency to make decisions; and outcomes of plea negotiations based on answering question about a vignette rather than the defendant's specific situation. Good reliability and validity are reported in the literature (Zapf, Skeem, & Golding, 2005). The MacCAT-CA scales are most frequently suppressed due to psychosis, which reflects the fact that most incompetency to stand trial is due to psychosis. The MacCAT-CA does not include embedded scales to identify feigned incompetency, and Rogers, Sewell, Grandjean, and Vitacco (2002) documented the measure's susceptibility to feigned incompetence. The scale developers recommend use of free-standing measures of effort to address this potential concern.

Evaluation of Competency to Stand Trial—Revised

The ECST-R is a standardized, semistructured interview designed as a screening measure to assess dimensions of CST. The ECST-R has three competency scales corresponding to the *Dusky* standards (Consult with Counsel, Factual Understanding of Courtroom Proceedings, and Rational Understanding of Courtroom Proceedings). Unlike the MacCAT-CA, the ECST-R focuses on case-specific information relative to the defendant and his or her relationship with counsel. It is suitable for adults age 18 and older and can also be used with mildly retarded (IQ of 60–69) adults. Gender-specific norms, as well as norms for three ethnic groups (European American, African American, and Hispanic), are provided. A unique additional feature is that the ECST-R provides a screen for feigned incompetence called the Atypical Presentation Scale (ATP), with questions probing purported impairment and symptoms specific to competence issues. The ATP evaluates whether the defendant is feigning either psychotic or nonpsychotic symptoms.

Competence Assessment for Standing Trial for Defendants with Mental Retardation

The CAST-MR is a structured interview comprising 50 questions organized in three sections. The interview covers Basic Legal Concepts, Skills to Assist Defense, and Understanding Case Events. Questions in the first two sections are in a multiple-choice format, whereas the section on understanding comprises 10 brief, open-ended questions. The test was designed with simple syntax, grammar, and vocabulary and the reading level is grades 2–6. The test has good psychometric properties (for a review, see Grisso, 2003), but has been criticized for limited predictive ability and the fact that, in a real courtroom situation, questions are not posed to the defendant in a multiple-choice format with simple grammar and syntax. Nevertheless, it is a very useful tool for evaluating competence in defendants with mental retardation. As with the MacCAT-CA, the CAST-MR has no imbedded validity indices and appears to be an easy test on which to feign mental retardation.

Conclusions

Many neuropsychologists are not routinely involved in CST evaluations, but when the defendant claims amnesia, when there is a suspicion of dementia or a recent head injury, or other neurological illness that could impair the cognitive abilities underlying competence, neuropsychological assessment is a valuable addition. Neuropsychologists bring their specialized expertise to the competency examination, including their knowledge of mental disorders and psychopathology, of the science of brain–behavior relationships and the impact of cognitive impairment on functional abilities, and their expertise in the detection of noncredible self-presentations, as in cases of exaggeration of deficits, feigning/malingering, and poor effort. In questions of competency to proceed, the neuropsychological examination may be a very valuable addition to the assessments provided by other professionals in assisting the trier of fact in criminal forensic settings.

Notes

Opinions expressed in this chapter are those of the authors and do not necessarily represent the position of the Federal Bureau of Prisons or the U.S. Department of Justice.

1. The prosecution, defense, or the court may raise the issue of competency at any time during the process (Melton et al., 2007), though it is most often raised prior to trial.
2. This fact demonstrates that governments may provide additional protections for the individual than what is required under the U.S. Constitution, but not less.
3. There may in fact be multiple mental health evaluations from mental health experts chosen by the defense, prosecution, and even the court.
4. For example, 18 U.S.C. § 4241(d) spells out the requirement that incompetent federal criminal defendants be committed to the U.S. Attorney General for inpatient mental health treatment to restore competency to proceed.
5. This retrospective test comprised questions such as "Well, I know you don't remember, but if you had stolen the car, what color would it be?" (Answer: "blue"—correct); "What street would the car have been parked on, Jackson or Myrtle?" (Answer: "Myrtle"—correct). Although customarily used to identify feigned amnesia, in this case, it actually demonstrated memory, because JM provided more correct answers than would have occurred by chance.

References

American Psychiatric Association. (2000). *Diagnostic and statistical manual of mental disorders* (4th ed., text rev.). Washington, DC: Author.

Archer, R. P., Buffington-Vollum, J. K., Stredny, R. V., & Handel, R. W. (2006). A survey of psychological test use patterns among forensic psychologists. *Journal of Personality Assessment, 87*(1), 84–94.

Ardolf, B. R., Denney, R. L., & Houston, C. M. (2006). Base rates of negative response bias and malingered neurocognitive dysfunction among criminal defendants referred for neuropsychological evaluation. *Clinical Neuropsychologist, 21,* 899–916.

Atkins v. Virginia, 536 U.S. 304 (2002) 260 Va. 375, 534 S.E.2d, 312, reversed and remanded.

Bonnie, R. (1992). The competence of criminal defendants: A theoretical reformulation. *Behavioral Sciences and the Law, 10,* 291–316.

Bonnie, R. (1993). The competence of criminal defendants: Beyond *Dusky* and *Drope*. *University of Miami Law Review, 47,* 539–601.

Boone, K. B. (2007). A reconsideration of the Slick et al. (1999) criteria for malingered neurocognitive dysfunction. In K. B. Boone (Ed.), *Assessment of feigned cognitive impairment: A neuropsychological perspective* (pp. 29–49). New York: Guilford Press.

Cima, M., Nijman, H., Merckelbach, H., Kremer, K., & Hollnack, S. (2004). Claims of crime-related amnesia in forensic patients. *International Journal of Law and Psychiatry, 27,* 215–221.

Cochrane, R., Grisso, T., & Frederick, R. I. (2001). The relationship between criminal charges, diagnoses, and psycholegal opinions among federal defendants. *Behavioral Sciences and the Law, 19,* 565–582.

Cooper v. Oklahoma, 517 U.S. 348 (1996).

Cornell, D., & Hawk, G. (1989). Clinical presentation of malingerers diagnosed by experienced forensic examiners. *Law and Human Behavior, 13,* 375–383.

Denney, R. L. (1996). Symptom validity testing of remote memory in a criminal forensic setting. *Archives of Clinical Neuropsychology, 11,* 589–603.

Denney, R. L. (2005a). Criminal forensic neuropsychology and assessment of competency. In G. J. Larrabee (Ed.), *Forensic neuropsychology: A scientific approach* (pp. 378–424). New York: Oxford University Press.

Denney, R. L. (2005b). Criminal responsibility and other criminal forensic issues. In G. J. Larrabee (Ed.), *Forensic neuropsychology: A scientific approach* (pp. 425–465). New York: Oxford University Press.

Denney, R. L. (2007). Assessment of malingering in criminal forensic neuropsychological settings. In K. B. Boone (Ed.), *Assessment of feigned cognitive impairment: A neuropsychological perspective* (pp. 428–452). New York: Guilford Press.

Denney, R. L., & Wynkoop, T. F. (2000). Clinical neuropsychology in the criminal forensic setting. *Journal of Head Trauma Rehabilitation, 15,* 804–828.

Drope v. Missouri, 420 U.S. 162 (1975).

Dusky v. United States, 362 U.S. 402 (1960).

Everington, C., & Luckasson, R. (1992). *Competence Assessment for Standing Trial for Defendants with Mental Retardation: Test manual.* Worthington, OH: IDS Publishing Corporation.

Favole, R. J. (1983). Mental disability in the American criminal process: A four-issue survey. In J. Monahan & H. Steadman (Eds.), *Mentally disordered offenders: Perspectives from law and social science.* New York: Plenum Press.

Ford v. Wainwright, 477 U.S. 399 (1986).

Frederick, R. I., Carter, M., & Powel, J. (1995). Adapting symptom validity testing to evaluate suspicious complaints of amnesia in medicolegal evaluations. *Bulletin of the American Academy of Psychiatry and the Law, 23,* 231–237.

Frederick, R. I., & Denney, R. L. (1998). Minding your "p's and q's" when using forced choice recognition tests. *Clinical Neuropsychologist, 12,* 231–237.

Godinez v. Moran, 509 U.S. 389 (1993).

Green v. United States, 365 U.S. 301 (1961).

Grisso, T. (1988). *Competency to Stand Trial Evaluations: A manual for practice.* Sarasota, FL: Professional Resource Exchange.

Grisso, T. (2003). *Evaluating competencies: Forensic assessments and instruments* (2nd ed.). New York: Springer.

Gudjonsson, G. H., Petursson, H., Skulason, S., & Sigurdardottir, H. (1989). Psychiatric evidence: A study of the psychological issues. *Acta Psychiatrica Scandinavica, 80,* 165–169.

Heck, A. L., & Herrick, S. M. (2007). Geriatric considerations in restoration of competence to stand trial: Two cases of impaired cognition. *Journal of Forensic Psychology Practice, 7,* 73–82.

Hubbard, K. L., Zapf, P. A., & Ronan, K. A. (2003). Competency restoration: An examination of the differences between defendants predicted restorable and not restorable to competency. *Law and Human Behavior, 27,* 127–139.

Jackson v. Indiana, 406 U.S. 715 (1972).

Larrabee, G. J. (2005). A scientific approach to forensic neuropsychology. In G. J. Larrabee (Ed.), *Forensic neuropsychology: A scientific approach* (pp. 3–28). New York: Oxford University Press.

Larrabee, G. J. (2007). Introduction: Malingering, research designs, and base rates. In G. J. Larrabee (Ed.), *Assessment of malingered neuropsychological deficits* (pp. 3–13). New York: Oxford University Press.

Lees-Haley, P. R., English, L. T., & Glenn, W. J. (1991). A fake bad scale on the MMPI-2 for personal injury claimants. *Psychological Reports, 68,* 203–210.

Medina v. California, 505 U.S. 437 (1992).

Melton, G. B., Petrila, J., Poythress, N. G., & Slobogin, C., with Lyons, P. M., & Otto, R. K. (2007). *Psychological evaluation for the courts: A handbook for mental health professionals and lawyers* (3rd ed.). New York: Guilford Press.

Mittenberg, W., & Roberts, D. M. (2008). Mild traumatic brain injury and post concussion syndrome. In J. E. Morgan & J. H. Ricker (Eds.), *Textbook of clinical neuropsychology* (pp. 430–436). New York: Taylor & Francis.

Morgan, J. E. (2008). Noncredible competence: How to handle "newbees," "wannabes," and forensic "experts" who know better or should know better. In R. L.

Heilbronner (Ed.), *Neuropsychology in the courtroom* (pp. 53–65). New York: Guilford Press.

Nicholson, R. A., & Kugler, K. E. (1991). Competent and incompetent criminal defendants: A quantitative review of comparative research. *Psychological Bulletin, 109,* 355–370.

Pate v. Robinson, 383 U.S. 375 (1966).

Penry v. Lynaugh, 492 U.S. 302 (1989).

Poythress, N., Nicholson, R., Otto, R., Edens, J., Bonnie, R., Monahan, J., et al. (1999). *The MacArthur Competence Assessment Tool—Criminal Adjudication: Professional manual.* Odessa, FL: Psychological Assessment Resources.

Poythress, N. G., & Feld, D. B. (2002). Competence restored—what forensic hospital reports should (and should not) say when returning defendants to court. *Journal of Forensic Psychology Practice, 2,* 51–57.

Reisner, R., & Slobogin, C. (1990). *Law and the mental health system* (2nd ed.). St. Paul, MN: West.

Roebuck-Spencer, T., & Sherer, M. (2008). Moderate and severe traumatic brain injury. In J. E. Morgan & J. H. Ricker (Eds.), *Textbook of clinical neuropsychology* (pp. 411–429). New York: Taylor & Francis.

Rogers, R., Salekin, R. T., Sewell, K. W., Goldstein, A., & Leonard, K. (1998). A comparison of forensic and nonforensic malingerers: A prototypical analysis of explanatory models. *Law and Human Behavior, 22,* 353–367.

Rogers, R., Sewell, K. W., & Goldstein, A. (1994). Explanatory models of malingering: A prototypical analysis. *Law and Human Behavior, 18,* 543–552.

Rogers, R., Sewell, K. W., Grandjean, N. R., & Vitacco, M. (2002). The detection of feigned mental disorders on specific competency measures. *Psychological Assessment, 14,* 177–183.

Rogers, R., Tillbrook, C. E., & Sewell, K. W. (2004). *Evaluation of Competency to Stand Trial—Revised professional manual.* Lutz, FL: Psychological Assessment Resources.

Schacter, D. L. (1986). Amnesia and crime: How much do we really know? *American Psychologist, 41,* 286–295.

Sell v. United States, 539 U.S. 166 (2003).

Slick, D. J., Sherman, E. M. S., & Iverson, G. L. (1999). Diagnostic criteria for malingered neurocognitive dysfunction: Proposed standards for clinical practice and research. *Clinical Neuropsychologist, 13,* 545–561.

State v. Lambert, 275 N.J. Super. 125 (1994).

State v. Otero, 238 N.J. Super. 649 (1989).

United States v. Liberatore, 546 F. Supp. 569 (N.D. Ohio 1994).

United States v. Liberatore, 62 F.3d 1418 U.S. App. (1995). Retrieved August 29, 2007, from *www.ipsn.org/court_cases/libertore_appeal.htm*

United States v. Wilson, 391 F.2d 460 (1968).

Vitacco, M. J., Rogers, R., Gabel, J., & Munizza, J. (2007). An evaluation of malingering screens with competency to stand trial patients: A known-groups comparison. *Law and Human Behavior, 31,* 249–260.

Warren, J., Fitch, L., Dietz, P., & Rosenfeld, B. (1991). Criminal offense, psychiatric diagnosis, and psychological opinion: An analysis of 894 pretrial referrals. *Bulletin of the American Academy of Psychiatry and the Law, 19,* 63–69.

Washington v. Harper, 494 U.S. 210 (1990).

Wieter v. Settle, 193 F. Supp. 318 (W.D. Mo. 1961).

Wilson v. United States, 391 F.2d 460 (D.C. Cir. 1968).

Wynkoop, T. F., & Denney, R. L. (1999). Exaggeration of neuropsychological deficit in competency to stand trial. *Journal of Forensic Neuropsychology, 1,* 29–53.

Youtsey v. United States, 97 F. 937, 940 (6th Cir. 1899).

Zapf, P., Skeem, J., & Golding, S. (2005). Empirical analysis of the factor structure of the MacArthur Competence Assessment Tool—Criminal Adjudication. *Psychological Assessment, 17,* 433–445.

Chapter 7

Neuropsychology in the Assessment of Mental State at the Time of the Offense

KATHY F. YATES
ROBERT L. DENNEY

Forensic neuropsychology, as it is applied in the criminal area, is the application of neuropsychological knowledge and technical expertise to assist the criminal justice system. As far as sanity is concerned, the question a forensic neuropsychologist investigates is whether some form of neuropathology caused an altered mental status, such that a criminal defendant would meet the legal standard for lacking criminal responsibility for past criminal activity (*insanity*). In other words, brain pathology to some degree or other may have contributed to the acts constituting the offense. In some instances, the behavior may have been completely due to such pathology. More often, it may not have eliminated the person's responsibility for the crime, but rather, lessened the defendant's responsibility (called *diminished capacity*). Even if the defendant is guilty to the fullest extent of the law, neuropsychologists can provide beneficial information to assist the courts in understanding whether or not there were special circumstances that may demonstrate reason for lessening the severity of sentencing, termed diminished responsibility or mitigating issues (addressed in much greater extent in Heilbronner & Waller, Chapter 9, this volume). Sanity evaluations are also called *Criminal Responsibility* (CR) or *Mental State at the Time of the Offense* (MSO) evaluations. Assessing whether a defendant was sane at the time of an offense is one of the most controversial questions forensic examiners are asked to address given that the purpose of such an exam is to identify individuals who should not be held morally responsible for their acts.

An insanity plea is pursued in about 9 out of 1,000 cases, and it is successful approximately 25% of the time (Wrightsman, Greene, Nietzel, & Fortune, 2002). Despite the apparent rarity of brain-injury-related insanity acquittals (Denney, 2005b, p. 435), neuropsychologists increasingly are being asked to assess whether brain pathology may contribute to criminal behavior. Brain injury can take many forms and result from various external trauma or any acquired brain change by vascular, encephalopathic, or disease process. In addition, impoverished cognitive functions resulting from disorders diagnosed in infancy, childhood, or adolescence, such as retardation, learning disorders, and pervasive developmental disorders, may contribute to criminal behavior. Neuropsychologists are uniquely positioned to address these important issues if they also have the prerequisite knowledge. To assist properly in such endeavors, the neuropsychologist needs to understand the legal standards related to criminal responsibility (Denney & Wynkoop, 2000).

Our primary goal in this chapter is to help the neuropsychologist better understand CR standards commonly used in federal and state jurisdictions, and the difference between diminished capacity, diminished responsibility, and related sentencing issues in regard to neuropathology-related mental disability at the time of the crime. In the process of covering the above issues, we will present the difference between *actus reus* and *mens rea* defenses, attempt to translate legal standards into psychologically meaningful concepts, and explore how specific pathologies may correspond to them.

Legal Conceptualizations for Criminal Responsibility

Six categories of circumstances exist under which a defendant may be excused for his or her crimes: insanity, diminished capacity, intoxication, infancy, entrapment, and duress or coercion (*Congressional Quarterly Supreme Court Collection*, 2005). The law recognizes that these circumstances may mitigate or eliminate criminal responsibility for a crime. Different legal standards (also known as *tests*) exist to establish whether a defendant was insane at the time of the crime. States vary widely in their adoption of insanity standards and in additional provisions regarding the trial process, verdict, and issue of treatment after verdict. Additionally, consider the following examples.

1. A defense of *diminished capacity* for a crime requiring specific intent is available in some jurisdictions (i.e., mental retardation).
2. Generally, a defense of *intoxication* is accepted only if the intoxication was involuntary. However, voluntary intoxication may be a defense when the crime requires specific intent.
3. *Infancy* pertains to the age of the defendant at the time of the criminal act. It is traditionally understood that children under the age of 14 are presumed to be incapable of forming intent necessary to commit a crime.
4. If it can be proven that the defendant was unfairly induced by the government to commit the crime, the defendant may be excused by the defense of *entrapment*.
5. Finally, the defense of *duress* or *coercion* may be applied when a crime was committed as a result of the use of force or threat of death or serious bodily injury by another person.

Entrapment is not a mental health–related issue, because it pertains to behavior of law enforcement personnel. Infancy is relevant for forensic mental health evaluators, because maturation not only may have played a part in the offense but it is also relevant to whether or not a youth is capable of participating competently in the legal process in general. The issue of maturation is addressed in chapter 10 of this volume. Coercion is generally not a mental health issue; however, criminal defendants who are mentally ill can occasionally believe they are being coerced, when in reality they are not. Such a mental illness–induced misperception would likely be evaluated under insanity or diminished capacity standards. We address issues that fall under the concepts of insanity, diminished capacity, and intoxication after we address issues of intent.

Mens Rea and Related Concepts

Four conditions must be met for criminal responsibility: (1) The defendant must have committed the act (legally called the *actus reus*); (2) the defendant's action must have caused the prohibited result (the crime); (3) the defendant must have committed the crime with the guilty "state of mind" (legally called the *mens rea*); and (4) there must be no circumstance constituting a legal defense for the charged crime (e.g., self-defense). In short, there must be the criminal act and the criminal intent. Thus, *mens rea* distinguishes a criminal offense from the same act committed either for some noncriminal purpose, such as self-defense or an act committed accidentally. According to Gifis (1991, p. 296), "Criminal offenses are usually defined with reference to one of four recognized criminal states of mind that accompanies the actor's conduct: (1) intentionally; (2) knowingly; (3) recklessly; and (4) grossly [criminally] negligent." *Recklessness* is defined as the conscious awareness that the defendant is creating a substantial and unjustifiable risk of criminal conduct, whereas *negligence* is defined as creating a substantial and unjustifiable risk of criminal conduct without conscious awareness, but under conditions in which a reasonable person should be consciously aware that the risk is being created (*Model Penal Code*, sec. 2.02(2), 1962).

All *mens rea* terms have ordinary language meanings, and it can be argued that non–Model Penal Code *mens rea* terms are equivalent to or are variants of the Code's terms (Morse, 1999). For example, to intend to do something is simply to do it on purpose. With the possible exception of premeditation, capacity for moral reflection, moral evaluation, and developed critical faculties is not required (Morse). However, Carson and Felthous (2003) have argued that the concept of *mens rea* is inadequately or improperly understood as a "state of mind" given these different categories of *mens rea* from a legal perspective. It is important for the forensic neuropsychologist to be aware of the statutes and case law in his or her jurisdiction in this regard. In our experience, judges tend to define intent in a much more basic manner (e.g., the "defendant intended to enter the bank and take money not belonging to him"). Jury instructions may prove to be the best source of defining or operationalizing this concept in any specific jurisdiction.

Intent refers to the mental state that must be present when a crime was committed (i.e., a guilty mind or *mens rea*); therefore, its meaning is also altered by the nature of the criminal offense. Common law has divided crimes into one of two categories of intent: specific or general, for the purpose of determining culpability. In *general intent crimes*, the prosecution simply must show that the defendant desired to commit the act that was the basis for the crime (intended to perform the proscribed act or closely related act). Knowledge that the act was unlawful is not completely necessary; only a vague, general level of awareness that he or she was likely committing a crime is needed. Rape, battery, felon in possession of a weapon, illegal reentry after deportation, and involuntary manslaughter are examples of general intent crimes. *Specific intent crimes*, such as premeditated murder, solicitation, assault, larceny, forgery, and embezzlement, require purpose plus deliberation. In other words, the defendant must possess an additional level of knowledge (or intent).

Malle and Nelson (2003) have suggested that a range of degrees of intention exists that corresponds with different mentally disordered states. In their view, skill and awareness need be present for an action to be performed intentionally. The awareness component specifies the state of mind at the time of the action, which implies knowing what one is doing, whereas the skill component refers to one's ability to perform the intended action (Malle & Knobe, 1997). As far as we are aware, courts have not adopted this conceptual framework. In this regard, there is a difference between mental health and law scholars debating such fine differences and the pragmatic application of the law by the courts. Forensic neuropsychologists are well served to be aware of the academic debates on such issues but not to forget the actual manner in which those who seek our services apply the law.

Although they are unique concepts, voluntariness and consciousness are linked, because both are psychological qualities of intent and legal *mens rea*. Both require conscious awareness and ability to perform the act, and anticipate consequences from the action (Barratt & Felthous, 2003; Carson & Felthous, 2003). Denno (pp. 601–618, as cited in Carson & Felthous, 2003, p. 562) points out that consciousness varies in degree akin to the volume of a radio, rather than "off or on" like a lightbulb. She posits that the varying degrees of consciousness and voluntary control result in gradations of criminal intent. Concurrently, Barratt and Felthous (2003) ask to what extent aggressive criminal acts are impulsive or reactive rather than planful, intentional, or proactive, and how these distinctions might impact forensic considerations for *mens rea*. They distinguish impulsive from premeditated acts, a distinction that they suggest is critical for determining whether a specific criminal act was voluntary. They explored to what extent aggressive acts were unconscious, that is, committed without thinking (impulsive or reactive) versus premeditated (planned, intention, proactive). Again, although important issues for research, these concepts may have little application in actual courts of law.

Insanity Standards

Lack of criminal responsibility, or insanity, is not a medical condition; it is a legal standard or finding. Thus, the definition of insanity changes secondary to the ideas of lawmakers, mental health and law scholars, and decisions of appellate courts. In addition to fluidity over time, the legal definition of insanity and the practice of the insanity defense varies between jurisdictions. In *Powell v. Texas* (1968), the U.S. Supreme Court revealed its appreciation for how insanity standards change over time, and the High Court has never established any particular insanity standard nor established the insanity defense as a U.S. Constitutional right.

The insanity defense is based on the supposition that it is not just to hold individuals accountable for their actions if mental disability deprived them of the ability to make rational or voluntary choices. In addition, it is generally held that such persons need special treatment rather than incarceration, because punishment is not likely to deter future antisocial conduct of these individuals. However, the mental disease must be related to the criminal behavior, such that the perpetrator is not morally culpable, and the mental disease must meet the threshold of the legal standard. A number of legal standards are used to determine whether a defendant was legally insane at the time of the crime, and they vary depending on jurisdiction. Current standards in the United States include the Insanity Defense Reform Act (IDRA), the American Law Institute's *Model Penal Code* (ALI Standard), and the Product Test. Prior to addressing each of these standards, we need to review an old, yet very important insanity standard.

The most well-known and influential, insanity test is the M'Naghten "right–wrong" standard of 1843. This is the substantive portion of that decision:

> To establish a defence on the ground of insanity it must be clearly proved that, at the time of committing of the act, the party accused was labouring under such a defect of reason, from disease of the mind, as not to know the nature and quality of the act he was doing, or, if he did know it, that he did not know he was doing what was wrong. (p. 210)

The M'Naghten's purely cognitive standard was initially adopted in the United States, and its influence has varied over the years. Subsequent insanity standards were developed in large part because of the strict limitations imposed by a pure right–wrong cognitive test. One such standard was the Irresistible Impulse Test (*Parsons v. State*, 1887), a broad, volitionally based standard, but it has fallen out of favor as a stand-alone insanity test. We now turn to those standards still in use within the United States.

Product Test (*Durham* Rule)

In contrast to the M'Naghten's narrow right–wrong standard, New Hampshire developed what was termed the "Product Test" (*State v. Jones*, 1871). The core aspect of this standard was adopted by the federal jurisdiction in Washington, D.C. (*Durham v. United States*, 1954). It was extremely broad and ill-defined, such that insanity could be any action that was a product of mental disease or defect. Difficulties with this standard became apparent over the following 20 years, when many individuals with untreatable personality disorders (even antisocial) were found insane. Attempts were made to tighten the legal definition of mental disease (*McDonald v. United States*, 1962) and to limit the extent of expert testimony (*Washington v. United States*, 1967). Although the federal standard was ultimately replaced in 1972, New Hampshire continues to use its form of the Product Test.

American Law Institute Standard

The American Law Institute (ALI), a legal think tank, drafted a *Model Penal Code* in 1955. This Code was formally adopted in 1962 and provided a definition of insanity that became known as the ALI Standard. It is occasionally referred to as the *Brawner* standard (*United States v. Brawner*, 1972). The standard is essentially a two-prong test that combined the M'Naghten (cognitive prong) and Irresistible Impulse standards (volitional or inability to conform one's behavior to the requirements of the law prong). In modifying the cognitive aspects of the M'Naghten standard, the ALI lessened the rigidity of an absolute knowledge of right or wrong to a "substantial incapacity" to "appreciate" (rather than to know) the difference between right and wrong. This shift recognized degrees of incapacity. The ALI broadened the insanity test so that individuals could be found insane on either the cognitive or volitional prong; substantial incapacity on both prongs was not required. In summary, the ALI placed a focus on both the defendant's understanding of his or her conduct and ability to control his or her actions.

Table 7.1 presents the key elements of the two-prong ALI standard. Please note the key terms in this standard: *mental disease or defect, substantial incapacity, appreciate, criminality* (or, optionally, *wrongfulness*), and *conform conduct*. The ALI (1955) also included a "caveat" paragraph proposing that repeated criminal behavior should not constitute a mental disease. The ALI test became the standard in the federal system by 1972 and remained so for many years. It is currently used by many states. It is also used to identify mitigating issues in some states during sentencing, but not during the guilt–innocence phase.

In Arkansas for example, Ark. Code Ann. § 5-2-312(a) (Repl. 1997) provides that "[i]t is an affirmative defense to a prosecution that at the time the defendant engaged in the conduct charged, he lacked capacity, as a result of mental disease or defect, to conform his conduct to the requirement of law or to appreciate the criminality of his conduct." Furthermore, Ark. Code Ann. § 5-1-111(d) (Repl. 1997) provides that a defendant must prove an

TABLE 7.1. Relevant Elements of the American Law Institute's Model Penal Code Standard for Insanity

The ALI standard contained this two-prong test, cognition and volition:

The defendant lacks substantial capacity as a result of mental disease or defect to:
1. Appreciate criminality (optionally, wrongfulness), or
2. Conform conduct to the requirements of the law.

Note. Adapted from American Law Institute (1955).

affirmative defense by a preponderance of the evidence. *Mask v. State* (1993) makes Arkansas law clear that once the prosecution meets its burden of proving the elements of the offense beyond a reasonable doubt, the burden shifts to the defendant to prove the affirmative defense of insanity by a preponderance of the evidence.

Insanity Defense Reform Act of 1984

The IDRA, Title 18, U.S.C. Section 17, defines the current federal test of insanity. The IDRA was developed in response to the public backlash resulting from the acquittal of John Hinckley, Jr., who was found not guilty by reason of insanity in the 1981 shooting of President Ronald Reagan, Press Secretary James Brady, and two law enforcement officers. The ALI had been the federal standard in place at the time.

There are significant differences between the IDRA and ALI standards. Most obviously, the IDRA eliminated the volitional prong, while retaining the cognitive component. It added the words *nature* and *quality* and retained *wrongfulness*. It maintained the use of "appreciate" regarding the defendant's understanding, and *mental disease or defect* had to be "severe." The federal statute made insanity an affirmative defense, where the defense must prove insanity by clear and convincing evidence (see Table 7.2). In Arizona the defense also carries the burden by clear and convincing evidence, but most states only require a preponderance of evidence to prove insanity.

The IDRA, as part of the overarching Crime Control Act, also limited expert opinion in paragraph (b) of Federal Rule of Evidence (FRE) 704. This paragraph restricted mental health professionals from providing an opinion in front of a jury on the ultimate issue of sanity and also, specifically, on the defendant's ability to appreciate the nature, quality, or wrongfulness of his or her behavior. This added limitation was based on the argument that mental health experts might have too much influence on the jury, because it was the

TABLE 7.2. Insanity Defense Reform Act Definition of Insanity (Current Federal Standard, Title 18, U.S.C. § 17)

A. *Affirmative defense.* It is an affirmative defense to a prosecution under any federal statute that, at the time of the commission of the acts constituting the offense, the defendant, as a result of a severe mental disease or defect, was unable to appreciate the nature and quality or the wrongfulness of his acts. Mental disease or defect does not otherwise constitute a defense.

B. *Burden of proof.* The defendant has the burden of proving the defense of insanity by clear and convincing evidence.

jury's role to determine the ultimate issue. Experts are still allowed to testify to the mental status of the defendant at the time of the alleged offense, however (*United States v. Dubray*, 1988). Although experts are not allowed to testify directly to the ultimate issue, they are directed to provide the ultimate issue opinion in their written reports [Title 18, U.S.C. § 4247(c)(4)(B)]. Finally, the IDRA established that, once found insane, the defendant is to be committed to the custody of the U.S. Attorney General for secure hospitalization and treatment. The acquittee is considered dangerous due to mental illness until proven otherwise and can be held until no longer dangerous due to mental illness (Title 18, U.S.C. § 4243).

Current Status of the Insanity Defense

A state-by-state chart identifying legal standards for insanity and other relevant provisions can be found in State Court Organization Table 38 in the U.S. Department of Justice, Bureau of Justice Statistics (1998). In summary, the following 26 states have adopted the federal IDRA standard, or some version of it: Alabama, Alaska, Arizona, California, Colorado, Florida, Georgia, Iowa, Kansas, Louisiana, Minnesota, Mississippi, Missouri, Nebraska, New Jersey, New Mexico, New York, North Carolina, Ohio, Oklahoma, Pennsylvania, South Carolina, South Dakota, Texas, Virginia, and Washington. The ALI (in part or in its entirety) is recognized by the following jurisdictions: Arkansas, Connecticut, Delaware, District of Columbia, Hawaii, Illinois, Indiana, Kentucky, Maine, Maryland, Massachusetts, Michigan, North Dakota, Oregon, Puerto Rico, Rhode Island, Tennessee, Vermont, West Virginia, Wisconsin, and Wyoming. New Hampshire continues to use a form of Product Test. Idaho, Montana, and Utah have abolished the insanity defense, but evidence of mental defect may negate an offense element, and mental health experts can testify on *mens rea* (Melton et al., 2007).

With regard to other provisions, 12 states have a bifurcated trial: California, District of Columbia, Florida, Maine, Maryland, Minnesota, Mississippi, New Hampshire, North Dakota, Oklahoma, Pennsylvania, and Wisconsin. This means that these states first try a defendant on the facts of the case to see whether the defendant was indeed the perpetrator. The court then holds a trial to ascertain whether the defendant was insane at the time of the acts. States are split on the issue of treatment after verdict. It is discretionary in 36 states and mandatory in 18 states. Inpatient treatment in a secure setting is mandatory in the federal jurisdiction. In Texas, treatment is discretionary for nonviolent crime and mandatory for violent crime. In all but three states, the release authority is the court or the chief administrative judge. In Massachusetts, Oregon, and Vermont, the hospital or some division of mental health services determines retention versus release.

Because of the substantial differences between insanity standards currently in use, it is imperative that neuropsychologists performing sanity evaluations learn the standard in effect for the jurisdiction in which the evaluation is to be conducted. We have seen many instances where the supposed forensic mental health expert used the wrong legal standard in formulating a forensic opinion. To better understand the mental health–related statutes, appreciation of various legal definitions is necessary.

Operational Definitions of Standard Key Terms

Here we address operational definitions of the key terms in the ALI and IDRA standards. Most ALI jurisdictions have followed the definition of *mental disease or defect* outlined in *McDonald v. United States* (1962), which defined this criterion as "any abnormal condition of the mind which substantially affects mental or emotional processes and subsequently impairs behavioral controls" (p. 851). Some debate remains as to what diagnosis constitutes disease or defect (Rogers & Shuman, 2000.) One viewpoint is that with the possible exception of antisocial personality disorder, any diagnosis in the fourth edition, text revision of the *Diagnostic and Statistical Manual of Mental Disorders* (DSM-IV-TR; American Psychiatric Association, 2000) would be sufficient. A contrasting viewpoint is that personality disorders should be excluded from consideration. This view is consistent with *United States v. Sullivan* (1976), which narrowed the scope of definition for mental illness, and *United States v. Salava* (1992), which excluded personality disorders as significant mental disease or defect.

Lack of substantial capacity suggests severe but not necessarily complete impairment in at least one of the twin prongs of cognition (wrongfulness) and volitional abilities (conformity of conduct) at the time of the offense (Huckabee, 1980). Rogers and Shuman (2000) suggest that substantial incapacity of the defendant's psychological functioning may result from a mental disorder causing interruption, disorganization, or gross distortion. *Interruption* is described as variable in nature and possibly difficult to assess given a typical absence of such behavior once a defendant is stabilized in an institutional setting (i.e., discrete manic episodes seen in severe bipolar disorder that may severely disrupt cognitive and volitional ability for brief periods). *Disorganization*, as seen in grossly psychotic individuals, may negatively affect the ability to perceive accurately and interpret the environment and interactions with others. Because of this, the individual may not appreciate the immediate situation and control subsequent conduct. *Gross distortion*, such as that seen during a paranoid delusion, can lead to a misinterpretation of interactions in the face of intact intellectual functions and a general ability to behave logically outside of the circumscribed delusion.

The term *appreciate* was incorporated into the ALI Standard from M'Naghten and retained in the IDRA standard. Rogers and Shuman (2000) suggest that in evaluating *appreciation*, the forensic expert assess the defendant's ability to understand and recognize the significance of his or her conduct. Specifically, in assessing the cognitive component of appreciation, the expert should ascertain the defendant's recognition/understanding of such actions, the expected outcome/consequences of the actions, and awareness of the significance of the actions. Such an assessment likely entails evaluating an awareness of what happened and what was expected to happen to both the defendant and the victim(s). Assessment of the emotional component of appreciation may be gleaned through query regarding the defendant's perception of the importance of his or her behavior and any emotional experience attached to such behavior (i.e., how "bad" the defendant's behavior was—from a criminal point of view). Rogers and Shuman offer several hypothetical situations as templates to access such information, which include the expert encouraging the defendant to consider his or her reaction if the defendant or a loved one was the victim of the crime; verbalizing the victim's emotional response to the crime; and assessing the defendant's reaction to such emotional expressions on the part of the victim.

Conform one's conduct represents the volitional prong of the ALI Standard and pertains to a conscious ability to choose or to hold back behavior leading up to and including the criminal act. Although a loss of behavioral control may be associated with a loss of cognitive control, it may also occur in individuals who do have awareness or insight into their compulsive behavior but are unable to control such behavior (i.e., obsessive–compulsive disorder). Rogers and Shuman (2000) suggest the assessment of several dimensions of this criterion, including capacity to conform, ability to conform, and "choicefulness." They suggest that *capacity to conform* relates to choice and whether or not the defendant exercised such capacity (as opposed to reckless or impulsive behavior that reflects on choice rather than capability to conform his or her behavior). *Ability* pertains only to the requirements of law for criminal behavior (i.e., deficits in behavioral control unrelated to criminal behavior do not qualify). Finally consistent with recommendations made by Halleck (1992), "choicefulness" of criminal behavior involves assessment of the defendant's perceived options and decision-making abilities, the deliberateness of actions, the choices available to the defendant at the time, and at what point the criminal action became inevitable.

Nature, Quality, and Wrongfulness

The IDRA incorporates the following three terms when addressing cognitive appreciation or the defendant's understanding of his or her behavior: *nature, quality,* and *wrongfulness*. Debate exists regarding the exact meanings of these terms in both judicial and forensic settings. For example, Rogers, Turner, Helfield, and Dickens (1988) found that 88% of the surveyed forensic psychologists and psychiatrists had erroneous beliefs regarding the three basic concepts of the Canadian insanity standard, including "disease of the mind," "appreciate the nature and quality," and "wrongfulness." They noted that "misconceptions abound among forensic mental health professionals in their understanding of 'appreciating nature and quality' " (p. 692). In Canada, this criterion has been defined legally as an understanding of one's physical actions and the likely outcome of such actions without necessarily including an emotional component either in understanding or expression (*Kjeldsen v. The Queen,* 1981). In the Rogers and colleagues study, the majority of forensic mental health professionals erroneously believed that an affective component of the defendant's presentation, as well as awareness of his or her actions on the community, should be considered as elements of "appreciate the nature and quality."

Unfortunately, no similar study has been conducted in the United States, and review of the legal definitions reveals that there has been no judicial clarification for "quality and nature." The First Circuit in the Committee Commentary to Instruction 5.07 Insanity [18 U.S.C. § 17] makes this point:

> The phrase "nature and quality [of defendant's conduct]" can be troublesome. It is not apparent what difference, if any, there is between the words "nature" and "quality." But given the lineage of the phrase to at least M'*Naghten's* case ... the safer course would be not to truncate the phrase. (First Circuit Committee on Pattern Jury Instructions Criminal, 1998, p. 126)

It is further noted that if both the insanity defense and a *mens rea* defense are offered based on an abnormal mental condition, when evidence shows the defendant failed to understand "nature and quality" of conduct, that evidence will tend both to help prove the insanity defense and to raise reasonable doubt about the requisite culpable state of mind. The Committee stated that this "overlap" problem can either be solved by adequate instructions or be avoided by omitting the "nature and quality" phrase from the insanity instruction, unless so desired by the defense. In this instruction, the two terms appear as one unit rather than two. Concurrently, in the explanation offered by the Virginia Supreme Court, as explained in *Price v. Commonwealth*

(1984), a two-criterion standard is presented in which nature and quality comprise one unit and wrongfulness the other:

> The first portion of M'Naghten relates to an accused who is psychotic to an extreme degree. It assumes an accused who, because of mental disease, did not know the nature and quality of his act; he simply did not know what he was doing. For example, in crushing the skull of a human being with an iron bar, he believed that he was smashing a glass jar. The later portion of M'Naghten relates to an accused who knew what he was doing; he knew that he was crushing the skull of a human being with an iron bar. However, because of mental disease, he did not know that what he was doing was wrong. He believed, for example, that he was carrying out a command from God. (pp. 106, 108–109)

Disagreement has also been noted among mental health experts as to whether *quality* and *nature* should be considered as independent or coexisting terms. Initially, Shapiro (1984, 1991, 1999) described the view that *nature* and *quality* had differences. This view is also embraced by the definitions of *nature* and *quality of conduct* as required in the M'Naghten standard offered by Rogers and Shuman (2000). *Nature of the act* addresses the very basic aspects of the act. It relates, for example, to the defendant's comprehension of the physical characteristics of the act and under what circumstances (e.g., did the defendant know the object was a gun out of which dangerous projectiles shoot?), and to an awareness of properties of some object (e.g., recognizing that an iron is an object that is hard and perhaps knowing its function—that it will become hot if it is turned on). *Quality of the act*, however, was generally thought to have a broader meaning than the purely physical component. It pertained to the consequences of the act, such that the harmfulness of the conduct, or its potential or actual consequences could be known (e.g., did the defendant understand the consequences of hitting the victim—that the dangerous projectile shooting out of a gun could cause an injury, or that hitting someone over the head with an iron could cause an injury?) A view of the two terms as related but independent is consistent with Canadian standards.

Shapiro and colleagues (Goldstein, Morse, & Shapiro, 2003) later modified this view to one consistent with the concepts of nature and quality as one basic concept. Concurrently, Melton and colleagues (2007) proposed a two-prong standard: (1) nature and quality and (2) wrongfulness. They suggested that most defendants who do not have the reasoning capacity to understand the nature and quality of the act in question would not appreciate the wrongfulness either. Research suggests that nature and quality are often ignored altogether as juries focus solely on the issue of wrongfulness (Goldstein, 1967, cited in Melton et al., 2007). This finding reflects the likely truth that most case facts regarding sanity under this standard focus on the defendant's understanding of wrongfulness; thus, for the forensic expert, knowing the relevant standard is so critical.

Wrongfulness has been defined in a manner that goes beyond simple criminality (acknowledging that an act is wrong or forbidden by law) when it includes a morally infused appreciation of one's acts. However, courts are split on this distinction. A literal or strict cognitive context of wrongfulness (criminality) leaves little room for application to most mentally ill individuals given the fact that most would state in the abstract that certain acts, such as murder, are wrong. The ALI Standard proposed that jurisdictions could adopt the term *wrongfulness* rather than criminality (Table 7.1). The distinction reflects the possibility that a criminal defendant may have appreciated that his or her act was criminal, but because of mental illness, believed the act was, nonetheless, morally justified.

Judge Cordozo in the 1915 New York Court of Appeals case, *People v. Schmidt*, analyzed this concept in great detail. Judge Cordozo reviewed the significant legal precedents of Britain and the United States regarding the definition of *insanity* with specific emphasis on whether or not *wrongfulness* meant simply awareness of criminality or whether it also included the moral awareness of wrongfulness. He noted that there was no instance in the many precedents reviewed in which the term *wrong* was statutorily limited to a legal rather than moral understanding. He provided this hypothetical illustration:

> A mother kills her infant child to whom she has been devotedly attached. She knows the nature and quality of the act; she knows that the law condemns it; but she is inspired by an insane delusion that God has appeared to her and ordained the sacrifice. It seems a mockery to say that, within the meaning of the statute, she knows that the act is wrong. If the definition propounded by the trial judge were right, it would be the duty of a jury to hold her responsible for the crime. We find nothing either in the history of the rule, or in its reason and purpose, or in judicial exposition of its meaning, to justify a conclusion so abhorrent. (p. 339)

The appeals decision concluded that the consensus of the United States at the time, as well as reason, dictated that the concept of wrongfulness should not be limited only to a legal understanding but to a moral one as well.

Federal jurisdictions followed this same line of reasoning. In 1970, the U.S. Court of Appeals for the 9th Circuit adopted *wrongfulness* in the definition of insanity and gave the example of a delusion leading to a belief in moral justification (*Wade v. United States*, 1970). In a similar case, the 9th

Circuit reiterated the limitation that whereas a defendant does not necessarily need to have a delusion to be considered insane, the moral justification must be a result of mental disease (*United States v. Sullivan*, 1976). The moral justification cannot be based simply on the fact that individuals with personality disorders often have difficulty accepting responsibility for their behavior. The 9th Circuit Court went further in 1977, declaring that juries should be instructed that wrongfulness can be interpreted as moral rather than criminal *only* if there are facts in the case that raise this unique distinction (*United States v. Segna*, 1977). *Wade*, *Sullivan*, and *Segna* are noteworthy for raising the issue of moral wrongfulness and outlining its use in the federal jurisdiction as it is applied to the ALI Standard in use in that jurisdiction at the time.

In 1988, the U.S. Court of Appeals for the 8th Circuit applied the same *Segna* clarification and procedure to the post-Hinckley IDRA insanity standard by providing the following conclusion (*United States v. Dubray*, 1988):

> Nothing in the trial record provides a basis on which the jury could believe that Dubray's understanding of moral wrongfulness somehow diverged from his understanding of the legal significance of rape. Because the moral/legal distinction was unnecessary to the jury's consideration of Dubray's defense, the trial court properly refused the defense's proposed instruction. (pp. 1101–1102)

Dubray also clarifies the FRE 704(b) limitation of testimony on the ultimate issue of sanity by allowing testimony on motivation, mental state, and diagnosis at the time of the offense. *Dubray* only governs federal jurisdictions in the 8th Circuit, but it appears that most other jurisdictions throughout the country have adopted this definition and application of *wrongfulness* as well.

Clinical Example of How Nature of the Standard Makes a Difference

In 1993, a man disassembled a smoke detector in an airliner after departing Phoenix, Arizona. Although this appears to be a rather benign event, it is a federal offense. His situation helps to clarify how insanity is demonstrated under the ALI Standard but not IDRA. This man, a high school wrestling coach displaying signs of manic behavior, started to believe he would make it on the U.S.A. Olympic wrestling team even though he had not wrestled competitively in years. He knew he needed to get to Philadelphia for the national tryouts. He loaded his car to the roof with personal possessions and food, and started driving out of Phoenix. As he left the city, he changed his mind and decided to fly to Philadelphia. He then turned the car around and started driving back to Phoenix. Once inside the city, he changed his mind again and started driving back to Philadelphia. He changed his mind (and driving direction) three times before he finally made it to the international airport in Phoenix. He left his car full of food curbside and carried his possessions to the ticket counter. He purchased his ticket with a credit card but was late for the departing flight. He ran to the gate and realized that he had left his video camera on the ticket counter. He ran back to the counter, retrieved his camera, and ran back to the gate just in time to board the plane. Once at cruising altitude, he decided he needed a cigarette. He went to the bathroom, took out a screwdriver, and disassembled the detector. With the detector hanging from the ceiling by wires, he realized that he needed coffee with this cigarette. Consequently, he returned to his seat and waited for the flight attendant to bring coffee. By this time the flight crew realized his behavior was erratic, because he was loud and disrupting their work. They found the altered smoke detector and locked the bathroom. The man began demanding to see the pilot. His behavior forced the captain to land the plan in New Mexico, where Federal Bureau of Investigation (FBI) agents were waiting to board the plane. The agents came on board and approached the defendant. The defendant realized that with his expert wrestling skill, he could easily take down the nearest agent. He slipped his leg around the agent in an attempted take down, and was quickly subdued, dragged to the back of the plane, and handcuffed.

The defendant spent a month in a county jail before he made it to the forensic hospital for mental health evaluation. By this time, his manic episode had predominantly been resolved by antipsychotic and mood stabilizing medications. He was friendly, pleasant, and very much in control of himself. He had excellent recollection of events during his manic episode. He realized that he actually had no realistic chance of getting on the Olympic team. He recounted his speed of thinking and poor judgment regarding his indecision over whether to drive or fly to Philadelphia. He recounted his thinking while in the airplane. He said he understood that tampering with a smoke detector was a criminal offense, and noted that he remembered being told such by the flight attendant before the plane took off. He said that he disassembled it thinking that he could smoke a quick cigarette and then reassemble the detector without being caught. However, he became distracted by his desire for a cup of coffee and returned to his seat. He said it then took too long for the attendants to bring the coffee to him. Investigative material substantiated not only his account of events but also the disorganized behavior.

All available information supported the fact this man had developed his second manic episode. It was apparent that at the time of the offense, he appreciated the nature and quality of tampering with a smoke detector. He also understood the wrongfulness of the behavior. He believed he could do it without getting caught simply because of his grandiose and disorganized thought process. Manic episodes can often demonstrate the difference between cognitive and volitional prongs of insanity standards. This man retained the cognitive appreciation for the nature, quality, and wrongfulness of his acts, but he was not able to control his behavior well enough to refrain from the criminal act due to mania. Because this case occurred in the federal jurisdiction after 1987, the IDRA applied. This standard has no volitional prong, and the man was considered sane based solely on his cognitive appreciation. It was explained in the report that he did not meet the current 18 U.S.C. Section 17 definition of insanity, but he would likely have met the insanity definition under the previous ALI Standard's volitional prong. This conclusion was placed in the report to let the judge know that the defendant was considered sane based strictly on the current standard, but he had been mentally ill enough to warrant an insanity finding under another widely used standard. The judge appreciated this fact and was able to provide a significant reduction in length of sentencing after the defense stipulated to the facts and pleaded guilty.

Intoxication and Insanity

Voluntary intoxication traditionally has not been allowed to form the basis of an insanity defense, regardless of the insanity test used by the jurisdiction. Currently, about one-half of U.S. jurisdictions explicitly bar evidence of voluntary intoxication to support an insanity defense, and 9 jurisdictions have not resolved the issue. However, 17 states allow an insanity defense to be predicated upon substance abuse when chronic abuse that has led to "settled insanity" can be demonstrated (Marlowe, Lambert, & Thompson, 1999; see, e.g., *People v. Free*, 1983). As with the traditional position, acute intoxication by itself cannot form the basis for the insanity. Rather, an independent syndrome must be diagnosed, such as substance-induced hallucinations or delusional disorder or substance-induced dementia. In this instance, the presence of psychosis meets the definition for *mental disease* or *defect*. Moreover, the syndrome must both predate and postdate the crime. If for example, the syndrome is present only during the period of acute intoxication, the syndrome is an insufficient defense; the condition must last for a reasonable period of time. Although substance-induced insanity traditionally required the mental defect to be "permanent," some recent cases have held that as long as the condition was present before and after the current instance of intoxication, it was sufficient to establish the condition as "fixed" for purposes of the defense, even it ultimately resolved (see *Porreca v. State*, 1981). Finally, the defendant's state of mind must meet the jurisdiction's legal test for insanity. Expert testimony is required in all such cases for an offer of proof of the presence of the independent and diagnosable mental disease or defect.

Conversely, it is easier to establish an insanity defense when the basis of the mental disease or defect is either involuntary or "pathological intoxication." *Involuntary intoxication* is a condition that is induced without the individual's consent either through fraud, duress, force, or contrivance by another; or when the individual has no reason to know the substance would cause the intoxication (i.e., side effects from prescription drugs). *Pathological intoxication* is defined by the grossly excessive degree of intoxication given the amount of the intoxicant ingested. As with involuntary intoxication, the individual has no reason to know that he or she is unusually susceptible to the substance. Specifically, the individual must lack actual knowledge about the potential effect(s) of the substance on his or her behavior, or about unusual effects or intoxicating qualities of a particular substance. A pathological- or involuntary-intoxication-based insanity defense is not an option if the defendant knew or had reason to know about his or her hypersensitivity to the substance. For example, if the individual had experienced an unusual reaction to the substance in the past, he or she could not use a defense of involuntary or pathological intoxication. Legal standards for an involuntary intoxication insanity defense vary significantly by jurisdiction (for further discussion of this variation, see Marlowe et al., 1999). Insanity defense based on involuntary or pathological intoxication is significantly different from the defense of automatism.

Automatism and Insanity

Although a fair amount has been written over the years about automatism, it is not a recognized diagnosis per se in the *International Classification of Diseases* (ICD-10; World Health Organization, 2003) or DSM-IV-TR (American Psychiatric Association, 2000) and this has led to the lack of a universally accepted definition of the term. Kalant (1996) provided the following composite definition of behavior-related automatism:

> Automatism is a behavior of which the person is unaware and over which that person has no conscious control. It is usually inappropriate to the circumstances, and may be out of character for the individual. It can be complex, coordinated and apparently purposeful and directed, though lacking in judgment. There is usually full or partial amnesia afterwards, for the period in which this behavior occurred. (p. 634)

In a medicolegal context, *automatism* refers exclusively to behavior and has been called "automatic behavior" (Blair, 1977). In medical terms, automatism refers to a syndrome of symptoms that occurs in a variety of conditions involving a disturbance of consciousness. Normal consciousness includes intact functioning of attention, concentration, interest, and apperception, as well as cognitive, affective, and conative traits. Cognitive traits include intelligence, memory, reasoning and judgment, whereas affect traits refer to emotions, sentiments and mood. Infections and toxic conditions can lead to a range of impaired consciousness, from dulling or clouding to delirium and coma. Prodromal symptoms may precede changes in consciousness when the individual is abnormally irritable, restless, intolerant (i.e., of noise), short-tempered and querulous, or generally ill at ease. Automatisms may be categorized as either organic or psychogenic depending on etiology.

Organic automatisms may result during acute or chronic intoxication (alcohol or drugs) and be associated with epilepsy, brain injury (cerebral contusion), anoxia, or metabolic diseases. For example, automatic behavior may occur with hypoglycemic conditions, especially those related to a diabetic condition. John Hughlings Jackson perhaps first used the term *automatism* in conjunction with bizarre behavior associated with temporal lobe epilepsy. However, this behavior comprises repetition of whatever the person had been doing just before the epileptic seizure or a new behavior that commenced with the attack but was inappropriate for the surrounding circumstances. Furthermore, the behavior was generally rather simple. Attacks of rage and violence, although rare, have also been noted during such seizures (Fenwick, 1986). However, the aggressive acts documented during epileptic automatism have generally been described as simple, stereotyped, unsustained, and never supported by a consecutive series of purposeful, or truly goal-directed, movements.

Blair (1977) noted that, from a legal point of view, automatism occurring in any organic condition typically is associated with minor offenses and perhaps antisocial or irresponsible behavior. Similar to the literature on aggressive acts during seizures, behaviors during various organic bases of automatism tend to be mostly routine, repetitive behaviors of low complexity, not associated with serious crimes, such as burglary, sexual assault, arson or homicide, unless the personality of the individual is a significant contributing factor. Although Kalant (1996) reported that there is no scientific evidence that automatism is directly caused by alcohol intoxication alone, regardless of the level of severity of intoxication, others have noted that automatism can take place during a number of alcohol-induced conditions, including delirium tremens, acute alcoholic hallucinosis, Korsakoff's syndrome, and alcoholic dementia (Leonard, 1972). In addition, a small number of drugs, called *dissociative anesthetics*, can produce automatism as a direct consequence of their pharmacological action in the brain (Jaffe, 1985). This group includes ketamine, phencyclidine (PCP) and related substances, often used as veterinary anesthetics. Concurrently, Blair (1977) acknowledged that large doses or strong preparations of psychedelic drugs, particularly in individuals who are particularly sensitive to the drug concerned, can result in extreme mental derangement, which can lead to any sort of crime, including ruthless assaults and murders. He attributed such action to the ability of these drugs to arouse illusory, delusory, and hallucinatory transcendental experiences—in which individuals are not consciously aware of or able to control their actions. An automatism defense is not an option if the defendant knew or had reason to know about his or her hypersensitivity to the substance. Although this defense rarely occurs, the mental state is not the issue. Rather, the defense negates the conduct itself, because the individual may be viewed as not having engaged in the requisite act of the offense (*actus reus*; e.g., see *Fulcher v. State*, 1981).

Psychogenic automatisms may result from hypnotic suggestion, prolonged stress, or psychopathological dissociations, or they may be feigned. Criminal acts are not likely to be the result of hypnotic suggestion. It is widely accepted that no one can be hypnotized to perform acts that he or she does not wish to perform or that are fundamentally contrary to moral or ethical principles. Automatism associated with prolonged strain typically is associated with unacceptable guilt, frustration or fear, or results from the immediate strain of acute mental trauma. Psychopathological dissociations include somnambulism, fugue states, multiple personalities, and feigned automatism. A diagnosis of somnambulism requires repeated incidents of sleepwalking. It is rare, if not unknown, for somnambulists to injure themselves; concurrently, they rarely indulge in serious crimes, though they may behave oddly or sometimes illegally. However, violent crime during somnambulism has been reported (Morce, 1968; Podlosky, 1960).

Automatism in hypnosis or dissociative states may be more purposeful and complex in character than behavior seen in other forms of automatism, but all forms of the behavior are characterized by the absence of normal consciousness and judgment. Also all true automatisms are characterized by amnesia following the attack (Kalant, 1996). See Blair (1977) for a comprehensive overview of the medicolegal aspects of automatism.

Although many individuals who claim to have been involved in some dissociative state during criminal activity pursue an insanity defense (Melton et al., 2007), an automatism defense differs from an insanity defense in important ways. An individual pursuing an insanity defense, who alleges that she or he is insane, must have a mental disease or defect, which is not a requirement for automatism. In addition, an individual who is considered insane typically was conscious of his or her actions at the time of the crime.

Although acts may be intentional and purposeful during automatism, they are outside of the conscious awareness of the individual.

Brain Injury and Insanity

Brain injury can take many forms. For our purposes in this chapter, *brain injury* is defined as any acquired brain change, whether traumatic, vascular, neurological, or encephalopathic. In the most cases, it appears that crimes carried out by individuals with extreme forms of neurological compromise are quite minor. These situations are dealt with at the time in what has been called *pretrial diversion* (Melton et al., 2007). Most commonly, individuals are returned to a hospital or to their residential setting and the issue is resolved informally. As a result, most forensic neuropsychological evaluations concern milder forms of pathology—pathology that does not rule out a person's ability to behave in ways that could be considered criminal.

Although the language for each insanity standard offers the potential for mental defect as the result of some neurologically based injury, research suggests the majority of individuals who pursue an insanity defense, or who are acquitted using this defense, have a major mental illness such as schizophrenia, another psychosis, or a major affective disorder (Nestor & Haycock, 1997; Steadman et al., 1993) Based on their review of six studies, Melton and colleagues (2007) reported that the presence of psychosis was usually required for a successful insanity defense. Rogers and Shuman (2000) reported that in a database on insanity acquittees, only 103 of the 5,573 not guilty by reason of insanity (NGRI) patients were diagnosed with organic mental disorders. They further reported that only 4.3% of the insane and 1.4% of the sane defendants had definite organic damage, and that organicity grossly impaired intentionality and behavior control in only one insanity defendant. Moreover, review of 456 consecutive sanity evaluation referrals to the U.S. Medical Center during the early 1990s indicated that only 17 defendants were diagnosed with an organic mental illness and none were considered insane (Denney & Wynkoop, 2000). Cochrane, Grisso, and Frederick (2001) reviewed 1,170 additional cases from this same database, spanning a longer period of time, and found little support for insanity opinions based on organic disorders.

It has been proposed that whereas an insanity defense with the IDRA standard would be difficult to support for individuals with mild or less obvious organic mental disease without psychosis (Denney & Wynkoop, 2000), such a defense might have a greater chance of success under the ALI Standard (Melton et al., 2007).

Diminished Capacity

Diminished capacity is a *mens rea* defense based on the premise that a decreased level of intent (of the mental state at time of offense) that does not rise to the level of insanity should lead to a decreased level of culpability. Additional considerations include nature of the defendant's intent (i.e., general vs. specific intent) as well as the differentiation between intent and motive. For example, it generally can be assumed that it is illegal to carry a weapon; thus, by carrying one, an individual's prerequisite intent typically is demonstrated (a general intent crime). This general intent is contrasted by a specific illegal action such as armed robbery, which requires specific intent. Concurrently, the law recognizes that the state of mind with which the act is carried out (intent) is different from the motive that prompts the act. In *United States v. Kimes* (2001), the 6th Circuit Court of Appeals made this observation:

> It is important . . . to distinguish between two different types of mental defect defense. The first, sometimes called the "diminished responsibility" defense, applies where the defendant's mental condition "completely absolves him of criminal responsibility regardless of whether or not guilt can be proven." [citing *United States v. Fazzini*, 871 F.2d 635, 641 (7th Cir. 1989)]. The second, often referred to as the "diminished capacity" defense, applies "where the defendant claims only that his mental condition is such that he or she cannot attain the culpable state of mind required by the definition of the crime." (citing *Fazzini*, 871 F.2d 641, pp. 805–806)

In *United States v. Gonyea* (1998), the court described the difference between the insanity defense and diminished capacity:

> The insanity defense . . . "is not concerned with the *mens rea* element of the crime; rather, it operates to completely excuse the defendant whether or not guilt can be proven" [quoting *United States v. Twine*, 853 F.2d 676, 678 (9th Cir. 1988)]. Therefore, "insanity is a defense to all crimes, regardless of whether they require general or specific intent. By contrast, the diminished capacity defense . . . is not an excuse. Rather, it 'is directly concerned with whether the defendant possessed the ability to attain the culpable state of mind which defines the crime.'" (citation omitted) [Thus] diminished capacity is a defense only to specific intent crimes. (p. 651)

The *Gonyea* Court concluded that the defendant's right to pursue a diminished capacity approach survived enactment of the IDRA [*United States v. Gonyea*, supra at 650 n.3, citing *United States v. Newman*, 889 F.2d 88, 91 (6th Cir. 1989)].

According to Marlowe and colleagues (1999) the most common basis for diminished capacity is intoxication. Intoxication at the time of a murder, for example, may preclude the level of required intent for first-degree, resulting in a jury finding of a lesser offense, such as second-degree murder or manslaughter. However, even severe clinical effects of intoxication generally do not interfere with capacity to form general intent. The greatest effects of acute intoxication are on impulse control, executive functions such as planning and sequencing, and motor coordination. When intoxicated, some individuals may be prone to aggressive behavior in response to some perceived or real insult. In such instances, then, the behavior may be intended but impulsive and poorly carried out. Without dissociation, delirium, or a psychotic reaction, intoxication evidence likely could only be useful to negate specific intent, but not general intent. Keiter (1997) provides an excellent overview of the history of the intoxication defense and the current position of each state on the use of this defense.

Diminished Capacity and Substance Abuse/Dependence

The *Egelhoff* opinion (*Montana v. Egelhoff*, 1996) examined the constitutionality of excluding intoxication evidence under federal law and found that the accused does *not* have a fundamental right to present evidence of voluntary intoxication in his or her criminal defense. State courts, however, have the right to admit such evidence, and approximately four-fifths of jurisdictions allow intoxication evidence in certain circumstances. See Marlowe and colleagues (1999) for a comprehensive review of the law related to voluntary intoxication and criminal responsibility in the 50 United States, District of Columbia, the U.S. Virgin Islands, and Puerto Rico. Forensic experts should be aware of the ways in which voluntary intoxication evidence can potentially be utilized given the statutes of the jurisdiction(s) in which they practice. Although jurors often have negative opinions about substance abuse and the abuser, failure to consider such information may constitute ineffective assistance of counsel under some circumstances. Moreover, substance abuse is the most common comorbid behavioral syndrome in criminal activity, including cases involving violence, abuse, and neglect (National Institute on Drug Abuse, 1993), and among psychiatric patients it is the strongest predictor of future violence (Steadman et al., 1998).

U.S. jurisdictions take one of four approaches to the use of evidence of voluntary intoxication to negate *mens rea*: (1) Twelve states bar the use of such evidence in *all* criminal cases to negate *any* element of the offense; (2) 20 states provide statutory language to permit such evidence where relevant to negate "an element of the offense" generally interpreted as applying to the *mens rea* component of "general intent" crimes (recklessness is specifically excluded in the majority of these jurisdictions); (3) 21 states permit evidence of voluntary intoxication to negate "specific intent" crimes; and (4) some states limit the admission of such evidence only to first-degree murder cases (used to negate the requisite element of premeditation or deliberation, thus reducing criminal culpability to second- or third-degree murder, depending on the state).

In some instances voluntary intoxication may reduce homicide liability to voluntary manslaughter, involuntary manslaughter, or criminally negligent homicide. On occasion, when a reasonable belief in self-defense may exist, it is a *complete* defense to any liability. For example, the victim points a toy gun at the defendant, who misperceives a threat. In this case, the defendant may not be liable, even if the danger was misinterpreted.

Finally, another type of homicide relates to the *felony murder doctrine*, which pertains to being charged with murder for an unintended killing during the course of a specific felony. If the unintended felony is a general intent crime (i.e., a store robbery) and the killing occurs during commission of the robbery, even if unintended and unplanned, the "intent" to kill is "transferred" from the intent to commit the robbery. If the crime is committed in a specific intent jurisdiction, voluntary intoxication may *not* be an available defense to felony murder (e.g., see *Daniels v. State*, 1998). However, if the underlying felony is a specific intent crime (e.g., burglary), then voluntary intoxication might be admissible to negate felony murder (e.g., see *Commonwealth v. Halbert*, 1991).

Certain classes of substances can produce profound effects on judgment and understanding, and cause serious misperceptions of reality, although consciousness is present. These drugs include amphetamines, cocaine, and even cannabis. In high doses, these substances may result in the user reacting with violence against real or imagined danger. Moreover, from a neurobiological perspective, a significant correlation has been found between abuse of various psychoactive substances and crime or violence. In addition, some of these drugs are known to have agitating effects on the central nervous system and have been shown to induce aggression in controlled settings, including alcohol (Fagan, 1993; Whitfield, 1990), stimulants, PCP, and cocaine (Marlowe et al., 1997). Weiss (2004) suggests that persistent use of PCP can result in a psychosis that is different from intoxication and produces behavioral effects that closely resemble schizophrenia symptoms. He argues that chronic PCP abuse/addiction might be used in the service of an insanity defense. However, the concept of insanity presumes an involuntary condition of mental disease or defect, a standard not consistent with intoxication or an artificial voluntarily induced insanity.

Diminished Capacity and Head Injury

Similar diminished capacity arguments can be made for the effects of neurological compromise. The persistent cognitive difficulties often associated with traumatic brain injury (TBI), such as a closed head injury, may be associated with criminal court concerns (i.e., impulse control, motivation, problem solving and judgment; Richardson, 1990). Although some aspects of brain pathology–induced impulsivity, lack of judgment, or dementia can rise to the level needed for a finding of insanity in some jurisdictions (more likely in ALI Standard jurisdictions), effects of such damage more likely have relevance for diminished capacity and a decrease in level intent. Even more commonly, however, these effects are successfully addressed at the time of sentencing under the diminished responsibility (mitigation) doctrine. Effects of neuropathology on criminality are addressed much more thoroughly by Barr in Chapter 8, this volume.

Diminished Capacity and Extreme Emotional Disturbance

New York State also has an affirmative defense termed *extreme emotional disturbance* [EED; Penal Law 25.00(2)], which acts as a form of diminished capacity. The standard is unique and has this statutory definition:

> The defendant acted under the influence of extreme emotional disturbance for which there was a reasonable explanation or excuse, the reasonableness of which is to be determined from the view point of a person in the defendant's situation under the circumstances as the defendant believed them to be. [L 125.25(1)(a)]

This defense is similar to a "heat of passion" defense, but broader in scope. If the jury finds the defendant committed the crime under an EED, the defendant may be found guilty of a lesser intent crime, such as manslaughter or any other appropriate crime rather than second-degree murder [PL 125.25(1)(a), 125.20 (2)]. EED is not available, however, for depraved indifference second-degree murder (*People v. Fardan*, 1993). Elements of an EED defense include the following:

1. At the time of the killing or attempted murder, the defendant suffered from EED.
2. The defendant acted under the influence of the EED (i.e., the killing or attempted murder was the product of the EED).
3. There is a reasonable explanation for the EED.

There are both subjective and objective components of an EED defense. The subjective element focuses on the defendant's state of mind at the time of the crime. This element requires evidence that the defendant's conduct was actually influenced by an EED (loss of self-control). This aspect is the element to be assessed by a forensic examiner. In many ways, this defense is similar to the Product Test for insanity, although it does not constitute a mental health–related acquittal. The evaluation of EED incorporates the same forensic evaluation process as an insanity defense.

Diminished Responsibility and Mitigation

A related term, *diminished responsibility*, refers to mitigating circumstances of the crime, factors most frequently considered during sentencing that warrant a lesser punishment. For example, individuals with frontal lobe damage often have impulse-control problems that may contribute to criminal acts. Concurrently, neurological compromise may lead to deficits in emotional and behavioral controls, as well as to impaired executive functioning, which may be relevant to a defense against criminal charges. However, it is likely that neither of these situations would have eliminated the defendant's ability to appreciate the nature, quality, or wrongfulness under IDRA. It is possible that such mental defects could have caused a substantial lack of capacity to conform conduct to the requirements of the law under the ALI Standard, but in most instances it is likely that the issues would have most success at the sentencing phase under diminished responsibility doctrine. In other words, the findings would have significant mitigating effects on the sentencing. This issue is addressed more thoroughly by Heilbronner and Waller, in Chapter 9, this volume.

Assessment of Criminal Responsibility

Unlike competence to stand trial examinations, which are like a snapshot of the defendant's current condition,[1] criminal responsibility exams are more like a movie, capturing a longitudinal view of the examinee, with a focus on the areas of mental functioning at the time frame immediately surrounding the alleged offense (Applebaum & Gutheil, 2007). Responsibility evaluations always have a past focus of attention. Once it is clear that a defendant is capable of understanding the limits to confidentiality, a careful and detailed interview should be conducted regarding the behavior, mental state, and any issues that could affect mental state around the time of the alleged crime. The examiner should pay particular attention to and assess for conditions that could impair the defendant's ability to control behavior, as well as impair understanding of the nature and/or wrongfulness of actions at the time of the alleged crime. Criminal responsibility evaluations should include a longitudinal view of the defendant, including a comprehensive clinical history (personal, social, educational, medical, psychiatric, and legal) as well as a mental status examination. A special focus is necessary for the period immediately before and after the alleged crime. Detailed descriptions from collateral sources of information also are critical (victims, witnesses, arresting officers, emergency medical professionals, as well as individuals well known to the defendant, e.g., family members, friends, coworkers or supervisors). Such information is crucial for external corroboration of the defendant's self-report and helps to minimize the problems associated with conducting an assessment of mental state retrospectively. When possible, it is recommended that the examiner obtain such collateral information prior to examining the defendant (Appelbaum & Gutheil, 2007).

A multiple data source model of criminal forensic assessment adapted from Mrad (1996) was applied to the practice of criminal forensic neuropsychology (Denney, 2005a; Denney & Wynkoop, 2000). This model is particularly relevant to the assessment of past mental states, such as that done in criminal responsibility evaluations. Use of the model, presented in Figure 7.1, helps to ensure that the evaluator incorporates relevant and important information in the criminal responsibility assessment rather than relying simply on the defendant's self-report and presentation when interviewed and tested. The first two columns represent necessary sources of information (from defendant self-report and corroborative sources). Each row represents a different period in time. Each of the boxes in a particular column should make some logical sense as far as consistency with each other, just as each row should have some logical progression from left to right. Self-report historical information should be reasonably consistent across information sources and provide reliable picture of the defendant's past mental states. The present row should provide a consistent and reliable picture of the defendant's presentation mental state. Lastly the middle row represents a specific period in time (typically mental state at the time of the offense [MSO], but can be past competency) and should make clinical sense in regard to the upper and lower row. Only after information from each of these general areas is obtained can an examiner provide a competent opinion regarding the ultimate issue (e.g., sanity). While framed in a specific manner in Figure 7.1, this model is consistent with other conceptual-

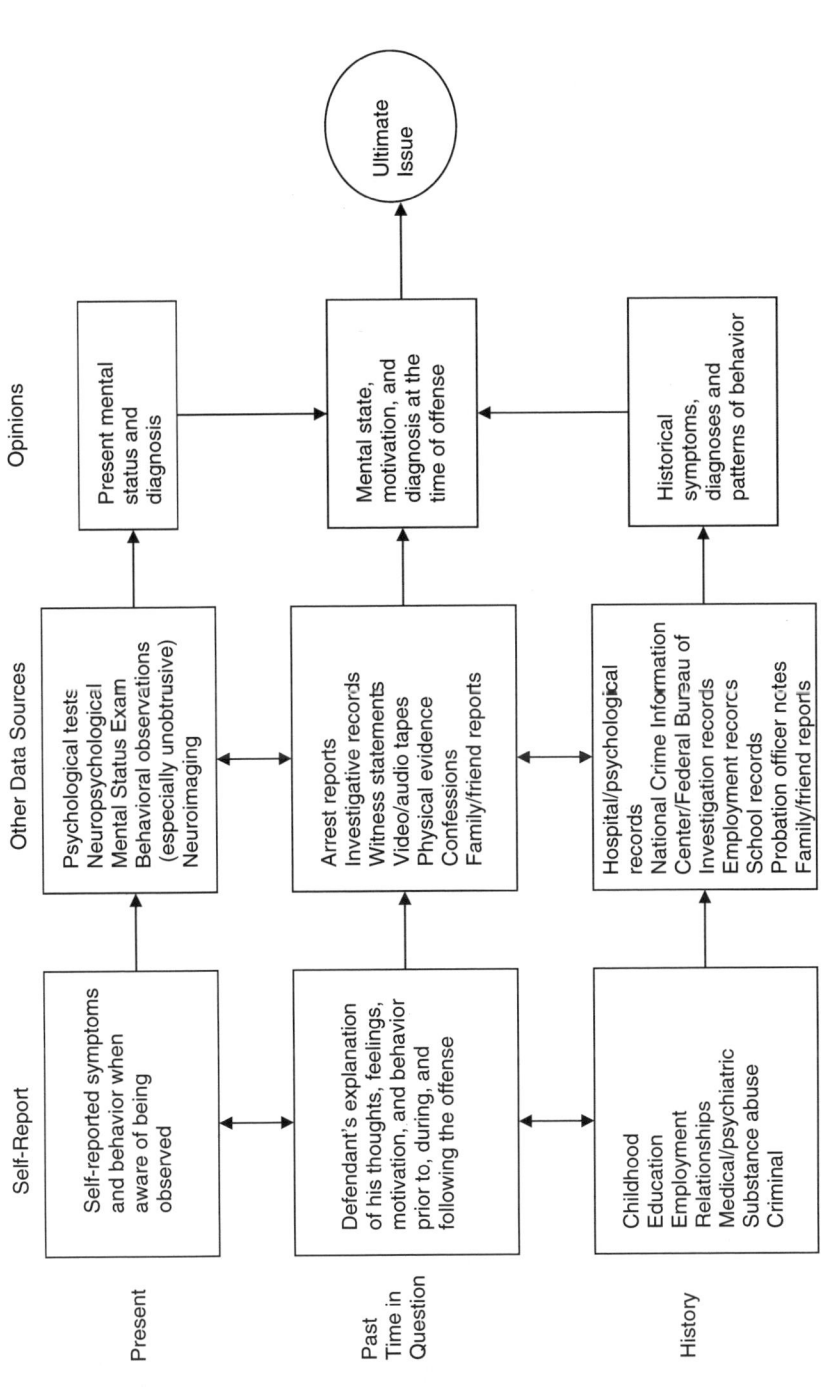

FIGURE 7.1. Multiple Data Source Model for the Assessment of Past Mental States. The left-hand column indicates period of time in question. Connecting lines represent avenues of expected consistency, with arrows leading toward opinions. Ultimate issue signifies the expert's opinion on sanity (it could also represent an opinion on retrospective competency). From Mrad (1996). Adapted with permission of the author.

izations of effective forensic assessment (e.g., Goldstein, Morse, & Shapiro, 2003).

Criminal Responsibility Assessment Instruments

Two free-standing instruments for insanity determinations include the Mental State at the Time of Offense Examination (MSE; Slobogin et al., 1984) and the Rogers Criminal Responsibility Assessment Scales (R-CRAS; Rogers, 1984).

The MSE was designed to "enable outpatient evaluators to 'screen out,' in the course of a brief interview, those defendants whose alleged criminal conduct clearly was not caused by 'significant mental abnormality'" (Slobogin et al., 1984, p. 305). Thus, the MSE is a *screening* measure for a range of potential legal defenses, including insanity, diminished capacity, automatism, and unconscious defense. The MSE consists of three parts: history of mental disorder, impairment at the time of the offense, and a current mental status examination. For the first two parts, a provided outline is used to structure a clinical interview approximately 1 hour in length. There appears to be no recent literature evaluating the effectiveness of the MSE, and it appears for the most part to have fallen out of use.

The R-CRAS (Rogers, 1984) was developed as a systematic model for the assessment of criminal responsibility. It is a reliable measure for retrospectively quantifying key symptomatology and applying standardized decision models associated with evaluations of criminal responsibility. The R-CRAS comprises 30 variables that are typically rated on 5- or 6-point scales, representing their increased relevance to psycholegal issues of insanity. The R-CRAS allows the examiner to quantify the impairment at the time of the crime, to relate the impairment to the appropriate legal standard, and to render an expert opinion with respect to that legal standard. Part I establishes the degree of impairment on psychological variables significant to the determination of insanity. Part II aids in rendering an accurate opinion on criminal responsibility with the ALI Standard. However, data are also available for the M'*Naghten* and "guilty but mentally ill" (GBMI; Rogers, Seman, & Clark, 1986) standards. For example, four additional assessment criteria were developed to examine specific components of the GBMI standard: impairment of judgment, behavior, reality testing, and capacity for self-care. *Impaired judgment* is defined as a lack of capacity to weigh alternatives, assess benefits–risks, and make decisions; it is distinguished from poor judgment and judgment not based on accepted social norms. *Impaired behavior* is defined as behavioral disturbances or symptoms that affect the individual's capacity to function and occur with a significant loss of volition. *Impaired reality testing* is defined as distortion and/or disorganization of (1) perceptual processes (i.e., ability to attend to, receive, and recognize external stimuli), (2) perception of external stimuli that are not present, and/or (3) cognitive processes (i.e., ability to integrate percepts and conceptualize external events in a consensually validated manner). *Capacity for self-care* is defined as the ability to take care of one's physical needs, maintain a minimally adequate home environment, and organize and carry out tasks necessary to sustain such an environment.

Validation studies indicate a high level of accuracy for classifying sane and insane subjects. Rogers and Ewing (1992) indicated that whereas the R-CRAS has psychometric properties consistent with traditional psychological tests, the measure was constructed to standardize and organize insanity evaluations. They warn against misuse of this measure and, according to manual instructions, the clinician should not render an ultimate opinion when incomplete or conflicting data exist. Overall, the measure has been useful in assisting in sanity classification (Rogers & Sewell, 1999), and has the most validity and reliability for guiding insanity determinations (Nicholson, 1999). It appears most appropriate for use with ALI and IDRA standards. Although the R-CRAS has its weaknesses (see Golding, Skeem, Roesch, & Zapf, 1999), it incorporates a multimodal assessment strategy that includes relevant legal criteria in a manner that is helpful to neuropsychologists learning how to perform sanity evaluations.

In Closing

Neuropsychologists have a great deal to offer the criminal judicial system. Neuropsychologists have expertise in assessment of neurobehavioral conditions that bear directly on issues before the courts. This assistance benefits not only the courts but also criminal defendants and society in general. There are conditions that relate directly to *mens rea*, such that neuropsychologists have an opportunity provide meaningful service. This service is only meaningful if provided in a competent manner. Neuropsychologists can only become competent to provide such services, particularly in areas of assessing past mental states, when they learn the legal standards and definitions, understand how neuropathology can affect mentation related to those standards, and appropriately incorporate a multiple data source model.

Notes

Opinions expressed in this chapter are those of the authors and do not necessarily represent the position of the Federal Bureau of Prisons or the U.S. Department of Justice.

1. It is important to note, however, that competence to proceed evaluations are occasionally requested retrospectively, termed *retrospective competency examinations*. In other words, the question is whether the defendant was actually competent when he or she went through a past legal proceeding (e.g., trial, pleading, waiving of *Miranda* rights).

References

American Law Institute. (1955). *Model Penal Code*. Philadelphia: Author.
American Psychiatric Association. (2000). *Diagnostic and statistical manual of mental disorders* (4th ed., text rev.). Washington, DC: Author.
Appelbaum, P. S., & Gutheil, T. G. (2007). *Clinical handbook of psychiatry and the law* (4th ed.). Philadelphia: Lippicott, Williams & Wilkins.
Barratt, E. S., & Felthous, A. R. (2003). Impulsive versus premeditated aggression: Implications for *mens rea* decisions. *Behavioral Sciences and the Law, 21*, 619–630.
Blair, D. (1977). The medicolegal aspects of automatism. *Medicine, Science and the Law, 17*, 167–182.
Carson, D. C., & Felthous, A. R. (2003). Introduction to this issue: Mens rea. *Behavioral Sciences and the Law, 21*, 559–562.
Cochrane, R. E., Grisso, T., & Frederick, R. I. (2001). The relationship between criminal charges, diagnoses, and psycholegal opinions among federal pretrial defendants. *Behavior Sciences and the Law, 19*, 565–582.
Commonwealth v. Halbert, 410 Mass. 534, 573 N.E.2d 975 (1991).
Congressional Quarterly Supreme Court Collection, electronic library. Retrieved October 11, 2005, from www.cqpress.com
Daniels v. State, 956 P.2d 111 (Nev. 1998).
Denney, R. L. (2005a). Criminal forensic psychology and assessment of competency. In G. Larrabee (Ed.), *Forensic neuropsychology: A scientific approach* (pp. 378–424). New York: Oxford University Press.
Denney, R. L. (2005b). Criminal responsibility and other criminal forensic issues. In G. Larrabee (Ed.), *Forensic neuropsychology: A scientific approach* (pp. 425–465). New York: Oxford University Press.
Denney, R. L., & Wynkoop, T. F. (2000). Clinical neuropsychology in the criminal forensic setting. *Journal of Head Trauma Rehabilitation, 15*, 804–828.
Durham v. United States, 214 F.2d 862 (D.C. Cir. 1954).
Fagan, J. (1993, Winter). Interactions among drugs, alcohol and violence. *Health Affairs*, pp. 65–79.
Fenwick, P. (1986). Aggression and epilepsy. In M. R. Trimble & T. G. Bolwig (Eds.), *Aspects of epilepsy and psychiatry*. Chichester, UK: Wiley Medical.
First Circuit Committee on Pattern Criminal Jury. (1998). *First Circuit Pattern Jury Instructions—Criminal*. St. Paul, MN: West.
Fulcher v. State, 633 P.2d 142 (Wyo. 1981).
Gifis, S. H. (1991). *Law dictionary* (3rd ed.) New York: Barron's.

Golding, S. L., Skeem, J. L., Roesch, R., & Zapf, P. A. (1999). The assessment of criminal responsibility: Current controversies. In A. K. Hess & I. B. Weiner (Eds.), *The handbook of forensic psychology* (2nd ed., pp. 379–408). New York: Wiley.

Goldstein, A. M., Morse, S. J., & Shapiro, D. L. (2003). Evaluation of criminal responsibility. In I. B. Weiner (Series Ed.) & A. A. Goldstein (Vol. Ed.), *Handbook of forensic psychology: Vol. 11. Forensic psychology* (pp. 381–406). New York: Wiley.

Halleck, S. L. (1992). Clinical assessment of the voluntariness of behavior. *Bulletin of the American Academy of Psychiatry and Law, 20,* 221–223.

Huckabee, H. M. (1980). *Lawyers, psychiatrists, and criminal law: Cooperation or chaos?* Springfield, IL: Thomas.

Jaffe, J. H. (1985). Phencyclidine and related compounds. In A. G. Goodman, L. S. Goodman, T. W. Rall, & F. Murad (Eds.), *Goodman and Gilman's the pharmacological basis of therapeutics* (7th ed., pp. 565–567). New York: Macmillan.

Kalant, H. (1996). Intoxicated automatism: Legal concept vs. scientific evidence. *Contemporary Drug Problems, 23*(4), 631–648.

Keiter, M. (1997). Just say no excuse: The rise and fall of the intoxication defense. *Journal of Criminal Law and Criminology, 87*(2), 482–520.

Kjeldsen v. The Queen, 2 S.C.R. 617 (1981).

Leonard, J. (1972). Drinks, drugs, and automatism. *Medical Legal Journal, 40,* 53–58.

Malle, B. F., & Knobe, J. (1997). The folk concept of intentionality. *Journal of Experimental Social Psychology, 33,* 101–121.

Malle, B. F., & Nelson, S. E. (2003). Judging mens rea: The tension between folk concepts and legal concepts of intentionality. *Behavioral Sciences and the Law, 21,* 563–580.

Marlowe, D. B., Kirby, K. C., Festinger, D. S., Husband, S. D., & Platt, J. J. (1997). Impact of comorbid personality disorders and personality disorder symptoms on outcomes of behavioral treatment for cocaine dependence. *Journal of Nervous and Mental Disease, 185,* 483–490.

Marlowe, D. B., Lambert, J. B., & Thompson, R. G. (1999). Voluntary intoxication and criminal responsibility. *Behavioral Sciences and the Law, 17,* 195–217.

Mask v. State, 314 Ark. 25, 869 S.W.2d 1 (1993).

McDonald v. United States, 312 F.2d 847 (D.C. Cir. 1962).

Melton, G. B., Petrila, J., Poythress, N. G., & Slobogin, C., with Lyons, P. M., & Otto, R. K. (2007). *Psychological evaluations for the courts: A handbook for mental health professionals and lawyers* (3rd ed.). New York: Guilford Press.

M'Naghten's Case, 10 Clark & Finnelly 200 (1843).

Montana v. Egelhoff, 518 U.S. 37 (1996).

Morce, H. N. (1968). Aberrations in legal psychiatry. *Journal of Forensic Sciences, 13,* 1–32.

Morse, S. J. (1999). Craziness and criminal responsibility. *Behavioral Sciences and the Law, 17,* 147–164.

Mrad, D. (1996, September). *Criminal responsibility evaluations.* Paper presented at

Issues in Forensic Assessment Symposium, Federal Bureau of Prisons, Atlanta, GA.

National Institute on Drug Abuse. (1993). Numerous factors implicated in drug-related violence. *NIDA Notes, 8*.

Nestor, P. G., & Haycock, J. (1997). Not guilty by reason of insanity of murder: Clinical and neuropsychological characteristics. *Journal of the American Academy of Psychiatry and Law, 25*, 161–171.

Nicholson, R. (1999). Forensic assessment. In R. Roesch, S. Hart, & J. Ogloff (Eds.), *Psychology and law: The state of the discipline* (pp. 122–173). New York: Kluwer Academic/Plenum Press.

Parsons v. State, 81 Ala. 577, 2 So. 854 (1887).

People v. Fardan, 82 N.Y.2d 638 (1993).

People v. Free, 447 N.E.2d 218 (1983), cert. denied 104 S. Ct. 200, 464; rehearing denied 104 S. Ct. 514; habeas corpus denied in part, 778 F. Supp. 431; on remand 818 F. Supp. 1098 (Oct. 29, 1992); habeas corpus granted in part 806 F. Supp. 705; vacated, opinion clarified, order held to be of no effect, affirmed in part, reversed in part 12 F.3d 700; rehearing and rehearing en banc denied 19 F.3d 389; cert. denied 115 S. Ct. 433.

People v. Schmidt, 216 N.Y. 324 (1915).

Podlosky, E. (1960). Somnambulistic homicide. *Medical Science and Law, 1*, 260–265.

Porreca v. State, 49 Md. App. 522, 433 A.2d 1204 (1981).

Powell v. Texas, 392 U.S. 514; L.Ed. 2d 1254 (1968).

Price v. Commonwealth, 228 Va. 452, 323 S.E.2d 106, 108-09 (1984).

Richardson, J. T. E. (1990). *Clinical and neuropsychological aspects of closed head injury*. New York: Taylor & Francis.

Rogers, R. (1984). *Rogers Criminal Responsibility Assessment Scales (RCRAS) and test manual*. Odessa, FL: Psychological Assessment Resources. Retrieved February 22, 2007, from *faculty.ncwc.edu/TOConnor/psy/psylect14.htm*

Rogers, R., & Ewing, C. P. (1992). The measurement of insanity: Debating the merits of the R-CRAS and its alternatives. *International Journal of Law and Psychiatry, 15*, 113–123.

Rogers, R., Seman, W., & Clark, C. C. (1986). Assessment of criminal responsibility: Initial validation of the R-CRAS with the M'Naghten and GBMI standards. *International Journal of Law and Psychiatry, 9*, 67–75.

Rogers, R., & Sewell, K. W. (1999). The R-CRAS and insanity evaluations: A reexamination of construct validity. *Behavioral Sciences and the Law, 17*, 181–194.

Rogers, R., & Shuman, D. (2000). *Conducting insanity evaluations* (2nd ed.). New York: Guilford Press.

Rogers, R., Turner, R. E., Helfield, R., & Dickens, S. (1988). Forensic psychiatrists' and psychologists' understanding of insanity: Misguided expertise? *Canadian Journal of Psychiatry, 33*, 691–695.

Shapiro, D. L. (1984). *Psychological evaluation and expert testimony*. New York: Van Nostrand Reinhold.

Shapiro, D. L. (1991). *Forensic psychological assessment*. Boston: Allyn & Bacon.

Shapiro, D. L. (1999). *Criminal responsibility evaluations: A manual for practice*. Sarasota, FL: Professional Resource Press.

Slobogin, C., Melton, G., & Showalter, S. (1984). The feasibility of a brief evaluation of mental state at the time of the offense. *Law and Human Behavior, 8*(3–4), 305–321.

State v. Jones, 50 N.J. 369 (1871).

Steadman, H., Mulvey, E., Monahan, J., Robbins, P., Applebaum, P., Grisso, T., et al. (1998). Violence by people discharged from acute psychiatric inpatient facilities and by others in the same neighborhoods. *Archives of General Psychiatry, 55*, 1–9.

Steadman, H. J., McGreevy, M. A., Morrissey, J. P., Callahan, L. A., Robbins, P. C., & Cirincione, C. (1993). *Before and after Hinckley: Evaluating insanity defense reform*. New York: Guilford Press.

United States Department of Justice, Bureau of Justice Statistics. (1998). *State court organization 1998* (Table 38: The defense of insanity: Standards and procedures (pp. 257–259). Retrieved May 5, 2007, from *www.ojp.usdoj.gov/bjs/pub/pdf/sco9805.pdf*

United States v. Brawner, US Court of Appeals, D.C. Cir., 471 F.2d 969 (1972).

United States v. Dubray, 854 F.2d 1099 (8th Cir. 1988).

United States v. Gonyea, 140 F.3d 649 (6th Cir. 1998).

United States v. Kimes, 246 F.3d 800 at 805-06 (6th Cir. 2001).

United States v. Salava, 978 F.2d 320 (7th Cir. 1992).

United States v. Segna, 555 F.2d 226 (9th Cir. 1977).

United States v. Sullivan, 544 F.2d 1052 (9th Cir. 1976).

Wade v. United States, 426 F.2d (9th Cir. 1970).

Washington v. United States, 390 F.2d 444 (D.C. Cir. 1967).

Weiss, K. J. (2004). "Wet" and wild: PCP and criminal responsibility. *Journal of Psychiatry and Law, 32*, 361–384.

Whitfield, C. L. (1990). Alcoholism, other drug misuse, and violence: An overview. In L. J. Hertzberb, G. F. Ostrum, & J. R. Roberts (Eds.), *Violent behavior: Assessment and intervention* (pp. 201–225). Great Neck, NY: PMA.

World Health Organization. (2003). *International statistical classification of diseases and related health problems* (10th rev.). Geneva: Author. Retrieved January 5, 2006, from *www3.who.int/icd/vol1htm2003/fr-icd.htm?navi.htm*

Wrightsman, L. S., Greene, E., Nietzel, M. T., & Fortune, W. H. (2002). *Psychology and the legal system* (5th ed.). Belmont, CA: Wadsworth, Thompson Learning.

Chapter 8

Neuropsychological Approaches to Criminality and Violence

WILLIAM B. BARR

Neuropsychologists applying their clinical skills in the criminal forensic setting face a set of unique challenges. One must not only be familiar with the legal basis of topics such as criminal responsibility and comprehension of legal rights but also have a critical understanding of neurobiological factors that have the potential to influence a given defendant at the time of the alleged offense or at trial. Over the past 25 years, technological advances, such as the development of neuroimaging and computer analysis, have led to an unprecedented growth in our knowledge about the brain and its influences on behavior. By virtue of training and experience, neuropsychologists are placed in a unique role allowing them to combine the results of this continually expanding literature with their own empirically based methods of analysis to inform the court about brain–behavior relationships relevant to the case at hand. The goal of this chapter is to provide the reader with a brief review of the neurobiological approaches to criminality and violence and to introduce what I call a "syndrome-based" approach to conceptualizing neuropathological influences on criminal behavior.

Before beginning, it is important to state the context in which information from a neuropsychological assessment of a criminal defendant can be put to greatest use. Until recently, the most commonplace standard was to have the court's behavioral expert inform the court whether the defendant was experiencing any form of psychiatric or neurological pathology that could potentially have influenced his or her behavior as a "mental disease or defect" at the time of the alleged crime (Dietz, 1985). Now, the growing trend is to include behavioral data within the context of a detailed analysis of available crime data and information from other relevant sources. One must be careful not to conclude simply that a defendant necessarily exhibited a lack of criminal responsibility by virtue of having a medical diagnosis. To avoid this, it is important to apply relevant legal standards to the facts of the case when providing an opinion on the influence of the defendant's mental state. The alleged offense is never a result of the defendant's brain in isolation, but rather the behavior of a living person acting within a set of environmental circumstances.

This chapter provides information that helps the reader to distinguish between a defendant with a predisposition for aggression or violence and one who has committed a violent act as a result of mental disease or defect. I use the term *aggression* to refer to attitudes or behavior that cause harm or pain to another. *Violence*, in turn, reflects a situation in which the aggression has been directed at another person. An act of violence, in most cases, results in the commission of a crime. Although this chapter emphasizes neurobiological influences on violence, one must realize that neurobiology is likely to have much less of an effect on criminal behavior than societal ills such as poverty or racism.

This chapter reviews scientific literature supporting the view that a number of neurobiological factors have the potential to influence violent behavior. Some of these factors are present in individuals at risk for committing violence, such as persons with certain forms of personality disorder, or those identified by having already committed a violent act, such as convicted felons. In each case, I espouse the view that neurobiology is rarely the sole cause of the violence. Each case must be viewed in a context based on not only the characteristics of the defendant but also a thorough analysis of the crime. Although these individuals are often referred to in the scientific literature as exhibiting features of psychopathy, I focus on the term *antisocial personality disorder* (APD) from the most recent edition of the *Diagnostic and Statistical Manual of Mental Disorders* (DSM-IV-TR; American Psychiatric Association, 2000). First, I review some of the neurobiological influences known to affect aggression and violence in animals and humans, and a method to differentiate these from the effects of developmental or acquired disease.

A Psychobiological Taxonomy of Aggression

Animal investigators have long known that aggressive behavior is varied and depends on the context in which it is observed. Different forms of aggression are associated with food seeking, fear, sexual behavior, and maternal protection, depending on the species and environmental factors. Initial insights into the neuroanatomical basis of aggressive behaviors were provided by a series of brain stimulation studies in the mid-1900s. Investigations in Switzerland by Hess and Brugger (1943) demonstrated that electrical stimulation in or near the hypothalamus caused some cats to exhibit the teeth baring, hissing, and piloerection characteristics now termed *rage reactions*. The investigators also found that cats stimulated in adjacent brain regions were prone to make direct attacks on other animals or objects placed in their immediate environment. The second form of behavior appeared to be more characteristic of that observed when an animal is stalking its prey.

Subsequent work by Flynn (1967) led to identification of the neuroanatomical basis of these behaviors. Rage reactions were found to occur in animals undergoing stimulation of the medial hypothalamus. Stimulation of the lateral hypothalamus, in turn, resulted in the more predatory form of behavior. In the latter case, high-intensity stimulation of the lateral hypothalamus caused the cat to make a quick, directed attack on a rat placed within the cage. During the attack the cat would focus on biting at the head and neck of the rat, while displaying little of the emotional arousal seen in the rage attack. At lower intensities of stimulation, the cat would circle the cage, ignoring the rat or making a small gesture at it in passing before commencing with the deadly attack.

Based on the results of those studies and subsequent work, researchers now commonly speak of two major classes of aggressive behavior (Meloy, 2006). *Affective aggression* is the form of behavior commonly seen in an animal's response to threat or frustration. It is characterized by what appears to be a total loss of inhibition. The aggression, as seen in many animals, is commonly accompanied by a high level of physiological arousal and often includes some form of vocalization. The resulting attack appears to be impulsive in nature and is often poorly organized. In contrast, *predatory aggression* appears to be a more purposeful and goal-directed form of behavior. The animal carries out the attack in a less emotional state and appears to be governed more by high levels of concentration and cognitive control. Some characterize this second form of behavior as more "cold-blooded" in nature.

There have been a number of attempts to use the distinction between affective and predatory aggression to understand criminal behaviors in humans (Blair, 2001; Eichelman, 1983; Meloy, 2006). An example of such an attempt is provided in Table 8.1. Taken in its most simplistic form, impulsive forms of violence such as "road rage" attacks, and mass murders in public places such as post offices or fast-food restaurants are examples of affective aggression. In such cases, the act may include violence toward random individuals and results in a disorganized crime scene. In contrast, the classic

TABLE 8.1. Application of the Affective/Predatory Dimensions to Humans

Model	Affective aggression	Predatory aggression
Psychological source	Emotional	Cognitive
Perceived threat	External or internal	None
Degree of planning	None: Reactive or immediate	Planned and purposeful
Human examples	Road rage attacks Mass killings	Serial murders Sexual predators

"serial murderer" provides a human example of predatory aggression. In this case, greater levels of organization and planning enable the perpetrator to exert control over the act and the victim, as reflected in an organized crime scene and the ability to evade capture, at least for a limited period of time.

Many have realized that most criminal behaviors are more complex phenomena than what can be explained by a simple dichotomy. For example, by adding the concept of compulsion, one can provide additional characterization of more "mixed" types of crime, such as compulsive fire setting or predatory sex crimes. As a result, a suggestion has been made to define the concepts of affective and predatory aggression as dimensional rather than categorical in nature (Meloy, 2006). Nonetheless, the use of dimensions that are known to occur in nature provide important information for persons who study criminology, who treat violent offenders, and who perform neuropsychological evaluations of criminal defendants. An example of the dimensional use of these concepts is provided in a coding scale for violent incidents developed by Cornell and colleagues (1996). Taking a neurobiological view in analyzing the crime is as important as analyzing the criminal.

Neurobiological Studies of Violent Offenders

The search for a physical cause of criminal behavior dates back to the 19th-century work of Cesare Lombroso (1876), who, influenced by Darwinism and the science of phrenology, specified a set of physical characteristics that he considered common to criminals. Research in this area took a negative turn in the mid-20th century as a result of the atrocities taking place in Europe during World War II (Volavka, 2002). The approaches used today began in the 1970s with the application of neurological models and newly developed imaging techniques to identify neurological abnormalities in offender populations (Lewis, Shanok, Pincus, & Glaser, 1979; Pincus &

Tucker, 1978). Our current understanding of the neurobiological underpinnings of violence is based on continuing advances in neuroscience that combine the results of both animal and human studies.

Sampling becomes an extremely important issue when discussing the relationship between violence and the brain. The following section reviews the literature examining the topic of neurobiological abnormalities in subjects exhibiting aggressive behavior. Some of the studies' subjects were selected from prison populations, with a demonstrated history of violent behavior, whereas others selected subjects from psychiatric samples at risk for violence, including those with APD. Results from both types of studies point to a likely interaction between biological susceptibility and environmental factors in the etiology of APD and violent behavior.

Influence of Neurotransmitters, Genetics, and Hormones

Our discussion begins with a review of the most basic neurobiological mechanisms known to have an influence on violent behavior. Knowledge of neuropharmacological influences provides us with a means of understanding potential causes of aggressive behavior and a foundation for developing pharmacological treatments. Results from animal studies indicate that serotonin plays a significant role in control of aggressive behavior (Krakowski, 2003). Lower levels of this transmitter are associated with higher rates of aggression. There is evidence that gamma-aminobutyric acid (GABA) has a similar inhibitory influence. Dopamine and norepinephrine are both known to potentiate aggressive behavior. Some researchers feel that natural control of aggression is influenced by maintenance of a balance between serotonin and other neurotransmitters (Volavka, 2002).

Results from human studies have revealed that decreases in central serotonergic function, as measured by cerebrospinal fluid (CSF) 5-hydroxyindoleacetic acid (5-HIAA), plasma tryptophan, platelet serotonin uptake, and neuroendocrine challenge are all associated with impulsive violence, though this may be limited to certain populations (Krakowski, 2003; Volavka, 2002). It has been shown that irritability or overreactivity to the environment is influenced through noradrenergic mechanisms, including monoamine oxidase (MAO) and catechol-O-methyl transferase (COMT) activity, providing a possible explanatory model that involves interactions with serotonergic activity. The use of alcohol is thought to interact with both of these mechanisms in a manner that leads to disinhibiting behavior (Raine, 1993).

No specific class of drugs has been shown to be effective for treating aggressive behavior in violent offenders. Aggression in psychiatric patients is commonly treated with antipsychotic medication or mood stabilizers (Volavka, 2002). Of these agents, clozapine and valproate are generally considered most effective. Other agents, such as beta-adrenergic blockers and benzodiazepines have also shown some efficacy for short-term control of aggression. There has been some controversy about the use of selective serotonin reuptake inhibitors (SSRIs) in spite of the observed relationship between serotonin and aggression (Walsh & Dinan, 2001). Although there is evidence that treatment with SSRIs may result in decreased aggression, some researchers have claimed that these drugs increase the expression of both suicidal and violent behaviors.

Beyond gender, results from studies on the demographics of violence indicate that age provides the most robust of all of the risk factors that have been studied. Most violent acts are perpetrated by males ages 15–25 (Krug, 2002). Results from twin and adoption studies provide strong evidence for genetic effects on criminal behavior, although it is difficult to separate these from other congenital influences, such as birth complications. Most of the evidence indicates a complex interaction between congenital factors and factors related to prenatal and perinatal care. Childrearing practices and social-environmental factors are also known to play a role in development of aggressive behaviors. For example, it has been shown that children raised in homes without siblings and/or those who undergo excessive bullying may be more prone to exhibiting aggressive behavior as adolescents and adults. Early abuse is also a significant factor in later development of impulsive aggression (Goodman, New, & Siever, 2004). Although studies show elevated rates of violent crime among African Americans, there is no evidence to indicate that ethnicity provides an effect independent of larger social and economic factors.

In consideration of the higher rates of aggression among males, one must consider hormonal in addition to societal factors, including higher rates of substance abuse in men. Research findings indicate activational effects of androgens on aggressive behavior in animals (Volavka, 2002). Human studies indicate that those with a history of violent behavior have slight elevations in testosterone levels, although the overall effect is somewhat small. Although there is evidence that administration of anabolic steroids leads to increased aggression in athletes and others, empirical support for this claim is not very strong. Evidence for the long-held assumption that violence is associated with chromosomal defects involving the extra Y chromosome (47, XYY) or extra X chromosome (e.g., Klinefelter syndrome, XXY) is also rather weak as a result of subject selection factors and the low base rates for this and other sex-linked chromosomal disorders.

Studies of female offenders indicate that those already prone to violence may experience an escalation in aggressive behavior during the late luteal phase of their menstrual cycles. However, women prone to experiencing premenstrual syndrome do not appear to be more prone to violence than others. Research on other hormonal factors, such as those involving insulin, has found a preliminary link between hypoglycemia, violence, and impulsivity, although it is not likely to be strong enough to support any future use of the "Twinkie defense," as in the widely publicized case of the accused murderer of San Francisco politicians George Moscone and Harvey Milk (*State v. White*, 1981).

Neuroimaging and Electrophysiological Findings

Our understanding of the neuroanatomical basis of aggression has advanced significantly in the past 40 years, since the reported stimulation studies involving the hypothalamus. Parallel work at that time with both animals and humans revealed the importance of the role of medial temporal lobe regions, particularly the amygdala, in modulating drives and aggressive behavior (Mark & Ervin, 1970; Papez, 1995). Technological advances in neuroimaging have now enabled us to turn our focus to the study of humans and the higher cortical regions responsible for inhibition and more complex forms of impulse control. What has resulted is the development of a neuroanatomical model of a complex circuit involving both cortical and subcortical brain regions. The circuit begins with input from subcortical and limbic regions, including the hypothalamus, thalamus, amygdala, and hippocampus. Intricate connections exist between these regions and cortical regions, including the insula, anterior cingulate, and prefrontal cortex. Lesion studies on animals and humans have suggested that a disruption of several key areas along this circuit leads to an increase in aggressive behavior (Volavka, 2002).

The study of aggression and violence has been advanced through results of both structural and functional imaging. The increased resolution afforded by magnetic resonance imaging (MRI) has enabled investigators to identify brain abnormalities among groups of individuals that had not been possible in studies using previous radiological techniques or postmortem specimens. Volumetric techniques combined with MRI have enabled investigators to also identify subtle abnormalities that are not always identified through standard radiological inspection in psychiatric samples. Even more knowledge has been gained through the use of functional imaging techniques, including positron emission tomography (PET), single-photon emission computed tomography (SPECT), and functional MRI (fMRI), which have enabled researchers and clinicians to identify areas of dysfunction in brain regions that are not necessarily marked by any obvious form of abnormality on structural imaging.

One of the first studies to use neuroimaging techniques in violence-prone individuals was performed by Raine, Buchsbaum, and LaCasse (1997).

This group used PET in association with an attentional challenge test in 41 individuals who were pleading not guilty by reason of insanity (NGRI) to charges of murder compared to 41 age- and sex-matched controls recruited from a university setting. The defendant group exhibited general reductions of glucose metabolism in a number of areas, including the prefrontal cortex and more posterior brain regions. Lower levels of left-hemisphere metabolism were observed in the amygdala, thalamus, and other aspects of the medial temporal lobe. Results of subsequent analysis of a subset of predatory ($N = 15$) and affective ($N = 9$) murderers revealed a greater degree of prefrontal dysfunction in the affective group, consistent with a hypothesis suggesting reduced impulse control in that group (Raine et al., 1998).

At least 15 additional neuroimaging studies of brain abnormalities in criminal offenders have been conducted over the past 20 years. The conclusion based on a number of recent reviews is that dysfunction in prefrontal regions is observed most consistently in studies using PET or SPECT (Brower & Price, 2001; Bufkin & Luttrell, 2005; Hoptman, 2003). Locations of the abnormalities were dispersed among various prefrontal regions, with no consistent evidence of any specific involvement of the oribitofrontal cortex. Results from studies to determine structural abnormalities in this region have been even more inconsistent.

Attention has recently shifted back to the study of temporal–limbic regions. A number of studies using PET and SPECT have demonstrated abnormalities in this region. These findings, unlike those associated with frontal lobe dysfunction, have been accompanied by structural abnormalities in the form of volume reductions in a number of limbic structures, including the amygdala and hippocampus. There has also been some indication that structural abnormalities in temporal–limbic regions are more prominently in the left hemisphere than in the right (Raine et al., 2004).

While the evidence may clearly support the existence of frontal and temporal–limbic abnormalities in criminal offenders, there is no evidence to indicate that any specific pattern of abnormality can cause the commission of a violent act. Research has shown that similar patterns of brain abnormality exist in a range of other conditions, including substance abuse and attention-deficit/hyperactivity disorder (ADHD), which are known to occur comorbidly in a significant number of criminals (Bush, Valera, & Seidman, 2005; Mena, Cuellar, Vargas, & Riascos, 2005). Additionally, there is ample evidence that the same abnormalities may also be seen in individuals with APD, with or without a history of violent behavior (McCloskey, Phan, & Coccaro, 2005; Schmahl & Bremner, 2006). Therefore, results of neuroimaging studies of violence are interesting from an academic standpoint but of questionable use in a forensic context, as a result of the lack of specificity of the findings.

Studies using electrophysiological methods have found additional evidence of neurological abnormality in violent offenders. Results from early electroencephalographic (EEG) investigations were limited to nonspecific findings, such as increases in slow wave activity (Gatzke-Kopp, Raine, Buchsbaum, & LaCasse, 2001; Raine, 1993; Volavka, 2002). However, results from studies using more refined techniques have found consistent evidence of dysfunction in frontal and temporal regions (Gatzke-Kopp et al., 2001; Hoptman, 2003). Some have posited a relationship between epileptiform abnormalities and violence (e.g., Pincus, 1981). Those using quantitative EEG have found abnormalities in more than 50% of violent offenders, although no findings have demonstrated specificity of these abnormalities in that group in relation to other, known clinical or offender samples (Raine, 1993). The findings from evoked potential studies have indicated a reduction in evoked potential (P300) amplitude in subject groups prone to violent behavior. Studies using a variety of psychophysiological techniques, including EEG, skin conductance, and heart rate, have shown that those prone to crime have a basic level of underarousal that may lead to violent activity in the form of sensation-seeking behavior (Raine, Venables, & Williams, 1990). Overall, the electrophysiological results are interesting, but suffer from the same specificity issues as the imaging studies.

Neuropsychological Findings

Neuropsychology has contributed significantly to our knowledge of the neuroanatomical basis of violent behavior. The findings have, thus far supported results obtained from neuroimaging and neurophysiological studies, while providing a more coherent link to the explanation of the behavior itself. Results from studies using psychological tests have demonstrated consistently lower levels of intelligence in samples of criminal offenders compared to the general population (Raine, 1993; Volavka, 2002). There has also been some indication of a more distinct relationship between low intelligence and violent crime. Results from large-scale factor-analytic studies indicate that intelligence is a predictor of APD and violence that is independent of many of the most common demographic predictors (Vitacco, Neumann, & Jackson, 2005).

Findings from studies using intelligence tests have been consistent with reports that individuals with learning disabilities and mild mental retardation are overrepresented in criminal and death-row populations (Lewis, Pincus, Feldman, Jackson, & Bard, 1986). There is evidence that the link between crime and low intelligence is not simply the result of studying lower functioning groups of criminals who fail to evade capture. One must consider that low intelligence is also linked to poor academic performance and restricted occupational opportunities, indicating that social, as well as biological, factors might explain the relationship between intelligence and crime.

Studies from the 1970s using large-scale neuropsychological test batteries demonstrated a pattern of left-hemisphere dysfunction in a wide range of samples, including violent males, criminal psychopaths, sex offenders, conduct disordered adolescents, sexual offenders, and schoolchildren with behavioral problems (Raine, 1993; Yeudall & Fromm-Auch, 1979). Those results were considered supportive of a theory proposed by Flor-Henry (1973), suggesting that criminal behavior is based on lateralized dysfunction in the left frontotemporal region. The results have been supported more recently by findings demonstrating verbal deficits in individuals prone to violence (Cohen et al., 2003). Taken together, these findings indicate that underlying weaknesses in verbal skills and expressivity might predispose some individuals (particularly men) to communicate aggressive impulses through violent behavior.

The field of neuropsychology has provided valuable findings on the relationship between criminality and frontal lobe dysfunction. Forensic investigators with a background in brain science have long recognized that aggressive individuals exhibit a number of the tendencies seen in patients with well-defined forms of frontal lobe dysfunction. Although results from numerous studies have provided evidence that individuals classified by psychopathic or criminal behavior exhibit lower scores on neuropsychological tests of frontal lobe functions, the findings are by no means consistent (Morgan & Lilienfeld, 2000; Raine, 1993). It has been suggested that much of the variability in findings can be attributed to variations in the definition of frontal lobe functions and the tests used, in addition to variations in the populations that have been studied (Morgan & Lilienfeld, 2000). Other criticisms have focused on whether the evidence of frontal lobe dysfunction in these samples is linked directly to APD or to the indirect effects of comorbid conditions such as substance abuse, brain injury, or ADHD. Thus, it appears that specificity is also an important issue when viewing the neuropsychological test findings.

It is clear that a more advanced application of neuropsychological theory is required to articulate fully the relationship between violence and frontal lobe dysfunction. Neuropsychologists have long realized that the frontal lobes are large, complicated structures that comprise a number of independent networks of neural activity (Cummings, 1995). From a clinical perspective, neuropsychologists have identified different patterns of cognitive and behavioral dysfunction, depending on the location of pathology within the frontal lobes (Stuss & Benson, 1984). Individuals with a disruption of the dorsolateral prefrontal cortex (DLPFC) or medial frontal cortex (MFC) are traditionally known to exhibit behavioral features of apathy, with an associated pattern of cognitive deficits affecting organization, initiation, and set shifting. In marked contrast, patients with pathology in the orbitofrontal cortex (OFC) exhibit a more "pseudopsychopathic" profile of behavior, characterized by personality changes and difficulties with emotional lability and impulse control. It is this latter group that has attracted the attention of those studying criminal behavior. Forensic neuropsychologists benefit from learning as much as they can about the range of behavioral changes in association with frontal lobe pathology.

Neuropsychological studies have revealed that individuals with APD perform comparably to controls on standard measures of executive functions, including the Wisconsin Card Sorting Test (WCST; Heaton, 1981), the Category Test (Heaton, 1981), and the Controlled Word Association Test (Benton, 1968), which are the measures traditionally associated with a disruption of the DLPFC or MFC (Blair et al., 2006; Morgan & Lilienfeld, 2000). In contrast, subjects with APD typically perform at lower levels than controls on measures requiring response inhibition or response modulation, including the Maze Test (Porteus, 1942), Trail Making B test (Reitan & Wolfson, 1985), Stroop Test (Golden, 1978), and go–no-go tasks (Luria, 1966), which are generally considered to be more sensitive to OFC dysfunction (Zald, 2006). The implication of these findings is that individuals with APD exhibit a specific set of cognitive deficits, including impulsivity, distractibility, and other features that might make them prone to antisocial behavior and violence.

More recently attention has turned to the study of the ventromedial cortex (VC) and its role in causing what investigators have called "acquired sociopathy" (Blair, 2001). Patients with lesions in this region are known to incur financial losses and to suffer social losses that appear to be the result of impaired decision making. This is thought by many to form the basis of the poor levels of judgment known to occur in some criminal offenders. Research on behavioral changes in patients following disturbance of the VC has demonstrated that in spite of relatively normal intelligence and language, this group performs poorly on measures of decision making (Bechara, Damasio, & Damasio, 2000). Studies using a measure known as the Gambling Task (GT) have demonstrated that this group is prone to make choices based on emotion or the possibility of immediate gain, as opposed to what might be in their best interest in the long term. It has been suggested that a disruption of the VC might interfere with the ability to suppress limbic input during decision making, rendering one susceptible to making impulsive decisions. While the GT has not yet gained wide acceptance as a neuropsychological test measure, preliminary findings indicate particularly low scores on this measure in a sample of death row inmates (Lewis, Yeager, Blake, Bard, & Strenziok, 2004).

A Syndrome-Based Approach to Assessment of Criminal Behavior

Information in the preceding section indicates that there is now sufficient scientific evidence to argue for the existence of number of neurobiological factors predisposing a given individual to violence. The findings raise a number of interesting questions for society and our legal system regarding the definition of what might be termed *pathological* behavior. To adopt an extremely liberal view that all violent behavior is pathological at some level would require a complete overhaul of our legal and correctional systems, to accommodate an increasing number of individuals identified as "not criminally responsible." In contrast, to ignore these neurobiological effects completely would lead to unjust levels of punishment in situations where individuals, under the influence of known neurobiological factors, commit acts that are the result of diminished control secondary to a mental disease or defect.

A neuropsychological evaluation to assess competency to proceed often differs from one designed to assess criminal responsibility. In the latter case, it is no longer enough simply to establish that a criminal defendant exhibits deficits on neuropsychological tests. One must now establish that the deficits, if any, fit a pattern that would render the defendant susceptible to committing the crime for which he or she is accused. One must also be in a position to establish that the observed deficit differs in severity or nature from what one would expect to see in someone with APD, alcoholism, or some other condition known to occur frequently in individuals that, by definition, are "naturally" predisposed to violence. Demonstrating a defendant's neuropsychological vulnerability to impulsivity also provides an important point for arguing diminished capacity and mitigation in cases of violent crime.

A Venn diagram depicting the forensic neuropsychologist's role in conducting evaluations of criminal responsibility is provided in Figure 8.1. If one assumes that both APD and criminality are associated with a certain level of frontal lobe impairment, the forensic neuropsychologist's position is that he or she must establish whether a defendant under examination exhibits a profile of impairment that by severity or nature is different than what one would expect solely from the defendant's status as a criminal. The ideal situation might involve a case in which someone accused of committing an impulsive–aggressive act is observed to have specific deficits on neuropsychological measures of response inhibition, such as the Stroop Test or a go–

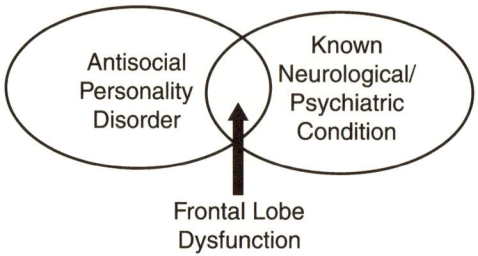

FIGURE 8.1. Venn diagram of the neuropsychologist's role in establishing criminal responsibility.

no-go procedure, with findings also supported by neuroimaging results demonstrating a well-defined lesion in the area of the OFC. Although such cases are rare, they are known to occur. Upon encountering such as case, a well-prepared neuropsychologist would be in a position to demonstrate these findings to the court with a clear and convincing argument.

The list of neurological and psychiatric disorders with the potential to affect criminal responsibility is not without limit. A sample list of these disorders and a method for classifying them on a neuropsychological basis is provided in Table 8.2. Category 1 includes a variety of conditions, including psychosis, dementia, and mental retardation, that would conceivably render a defendant, albeit for different reasons, unable to comprehend the nature of his or her actions as a result of generalized dysfunction. In Category 2, a set of conditions that affect the frontal lobes might potentially cause a defendant to act more impulsively or in a more extreme manner than one would predict for a criminal bound by the effects of APD or an associated form of

TABLE 8.2. Categories of Neuropsychological Syndromes with a Potential to Influence Criminal Behavior

1. Generalized deficit syndromes
    a. Schizophrenia
    b. Dementia
    c. Mental retardation
2. Frontal lobe syndromes
    a. Brain tumors
    b. Intracerebral hemorrhage
    c. Traumatic brain injury
3. Temporal lobe syndromes
    a. Complex partial seizures
    b. Intermittent explosive disorder
    c. Amnesia or fugue states

personality disorder. In Category 3, a set of conditions affecting the temporo-limbic system might lead a defendant to exhibit criminal behaviors while under a state of altered consciousness or amnesia. Further description of each of these conditions is provided below.

General Deficit Syndromes

Forensic neuropsychologists are often called on to assist in determining whether a criminal defendant understood the nature and consequences of his or her actions at the time of the offense and knew the actions were wrong. Three major classes of conditions might affect criminal responsibility, as defined earlier, for general reasons. First, the defendant may have been suffering from the effects of a psychiatric condition that caused a general impairment in reality testing. In other words, the defendant may have been experiencing symptoms of any one of a number of psychotic symptoms known to be associated with schizophrenia, bipolar disorder, or some type of psychosis attributed to a medical condition at the time of the crime for which he or she is charged. Second, the defendant may have demonstrated intact intellectual functioning at some point in his or her life but at the time of the criminal action was found to be under the influence of some form of neurological disease causing a general decline in cognitive functioning and judgment. In the third scenario, a defendant charged with a violent crime might have a lifelong condition affecting cognitive and social development, commonly labeled as mental retardation. In this situation, it would be argued that the defendant committed the crime unwittingly, as a result of mental impairment. In each of these cases, the neuropsychologist's task is to help the court determine whether the defendant meets criteria for the condition in question at the time of the forensic evaluation, whether there is evidence in the records that the defendant experienced symptoms of this condition in the past, and whether there is a probable link between the symptoms resulting from the condition and behavior exhibited by the defendant at the time of the alleged crime. Examples of these conditions are provided below.

Schizophrenia

The American public has an apparent fascination with the topic of violence and insanity, and it contributes significantly to continued stigma associated with severe mental illness. This discussion focuses on schizophrenia, although it is known that similar issues may arise when studying patients in the midst of the manic states of bipolar disorder and other conditions leading to thought disorder. While higher rates of violence are observed in patients with schizophrenia compared to the general population, it is also known that the vast majority of individuals with schizophrenia never commit a violent crime. Some attribute the higher rates to social factors, such as the deinstitutionalization movement over the past 50 years (Angermeyer, Cooper, & Link, 1998; Pearlson, 2000). However, looking at the numbers, the risk of violence in men with schizophrenia is only 1 in 3,000, whereas the risk observed in women is 1 in 33,000 (Walsh, Buchanan, & Fahy, 2002). It turns out that the majority of persons with schizophrenia who are considered prone to violence exhibit the same risk factors for violence as the general population. A history of previous violence, substance abuse, and noncompliance with medication are all considered significant predictors of future violence in patients with schizophrenia (Torrey, 1994). Those patients living alone appear less at risk for violence than those living in close proximity to their family members.

When evaluating a defendant with a possible diagnosis of schizophrenia, it is important to examine carefully the characteristics of his or her behavior before, during, and after the alleged crime. It is a serious mistake to assume that the defendant exhibited diminished responsibility simply because of his or her diagnosis of schizophrenia. It is important to understand the nature and severity of the individual's psychotic symptoms and how they relate specifically to the crime. Studies have shown that *positive symptoms*, including suspiciousness and persecutory delusions, are associated with higher rates of violence, whereas *negative symptoms*, such as social withdrawal, provide a negative predictor (Swanson et al., 2006).

Structured interview methods such as the Structured Clinical Interview for DSM-IV (SCID; First, Spitzer, Gibbon, & Williams, 1997) provide the "gold standard" for documenting symptoms of schizophrenia in clinical and research settings, but this instrument is used much more rarely in the forensic setting. When using any structured interview format, such the SCID, it is advisable to add other instruments, such as the Structured Interview of Reported Symptoms (SIRS; Rogers, Bagby, & Dickens, 1992) and the Minnesota Multiphasic Personality Inventory–2 (MMPI-2; Butcher, Dahlstrom, Graham, Tellegen, & Kaemmer, 1990), to assess the possibility of a response bias, such as an exaggeration of symptom severity.

The days of distinguishing between "organic" and "functional" psychoses are over. The origins of schizophrenia are now considered to be neurodevelopmental in nature, with symptoms developing with a relatively predictable pattern and time course (Pearlson, 2000). Neuroimaging studies have revealed a range of consistent brain abnormalities, including ventricular enlargement, sulcal prominence, reversal of "normal" anatomical asymmetries, and reduced volumes of temporolimbic structures. Many of the abnormalities have been found to exist more prominently in the left hemisphere (Flashman & Green, 2004). Neuropsychological studies have shown some level of impairment in nearly all areas of cognition, although a subgroup of individuals with schizophrenia and minimal impairment is known to exist. Some investigators have argued for specific impairment in executive functions (Berman, Illowsky, & Weinberger, 1988). However, more recent findings indicate particular weaknesses in episodic memory and vigilance. Research has shown that psychosis does not result in increased false positives on effort tests such as the Test of Memory Malingering (TOMM; Duncan, 2005; Tombaugh, 1996). However, decreased levels of effort have been identified using the Word Memory Test (WMT—Gorrison, Sanz, & Schmand, 2005; Green & Astner, 1995).

As an example, a 38-year-old man with a reported history of schizophrenia was arrested in New York City and charged with assault in the second degree for allegedly attacking a woman on the street. The man had been arrested in the past for similar episodes but, in each case, charges were reduced as a result of his reported mental state. A close examination of the medical record revealed a single admission for assessment of psychotic symptoms when the defendant was 19 years old. He had not received any psychiatric treatment since the age of 21, and he had been living on his own for the past 10 years. He gave a very vague description of his symptoms during the clinical interview, stating that "voices" told him to hit the woman. He was unable to provide any account of an accompanying delusion. There was no evidence of any obvious negative symptoms. Low levels of performance were obtained on neuropsychological testing, including measures of effort and motivation. He reported an inordinately high level of symptoms on standardized self-report instruments. The conclusion was that whereas there was documentation of a psychotic episode in the past, the defendant's more recent history and behavior did not coincide with what is typically seen in an individual with schizophrenia. The defendant was considered fit to proceed in the face of charges for assault in the second degree.

Dementia

I use the term *dementia* in this context to refer to an acquired condition resulting in cognitive decline that affects an individual's functional activities. Although the term is appropriate for description of decline across the lifespan, it is restricted in this discussion to conditions observed in the elderly. Violence is known to occur at much lower rates in this age group. Less than 2% of institutionalized felons are 65 years of age or older. However, elderly prisoners are known to have inordinately high rates of mental illness. Most crimes committed by the elderly are mild in nature, with driving offenses and shoplifting identified as the most common offenses. Homicides are extremely rare, with the majority found to be the result of driving mishaps. Thus, one should be cautious when considering a diagnosis of dementia in a trial involving a premeditated form of murder.

Dementia itself has been shown to be associated with violent behavior, although it is typically seen more as a confused form of acting out rather than an action associated with an underlying plan. For example, one might see a resident in a nursing home striking another for no apparent reason, but rarely would one find a person with dementia carrying out an elaborate plan for vengeance. Dementia is rarely the cause of violent crime. Those prone to violence may exhibit symptoms of an underlying depression or paranoid psychosis. One study on violence associated with Alzheimer's disease (AD) found aggressive acts in 52% of the patients with advanced forms of the disease (Eastley & Wilcock, 1997). The aggression was seen more often in males. Verbal outbursts were twice as frequent as any form of assaultive behavior. Agitation, screaming, and lack of cooperation with caregivers are also known to occur frequently in this population.

The causes of dementia in the elderly are varied. Frontotemporal dementias (FTDs) are characterized more often by extreme personality change and loss of judgment than are vascular dementia (VD) or AD. Formal criteria for establishing diagnoses of these conditions are readily available. A number of rating scales have also been developed to evaluate neurobehavioral changes in these samples. Studies show that patients with FTD are at more risk for agitation in the early stages of illness. The rates of agitation observed in FTD, AD, and VD become more equivalent as these illnesses progress (Srikanth, Nagaraja, & Ratnavalli, 2005).

Agitation in AD has been associated with frontal lobe deficit (Senanarong et al., 2004). The diagnosis of progressive dementia is typically associated with MRI findings that show generalized or regional cortical atrophy. Isolated lesions on MRI are seen most often in VD. Functional imaging in AD, using PET or SPECT, generally shows bilateral hypoperfusion in parietal regions, whereas in FTD patients exhibit regional reductions in frontotemporal regions. Neuropsychological test profiles in AD are characterized by a general decline in cognitive functions, with deficits in episodic memory and retrieval from semantic memory appearing most prominent. Research has shown that tests of effort can be used effectively with this population for assessment of malingering, although the rates of misclassification are slightly higher than those observed in the general population (Teichner & Wagner, 2004).

A 69-year-old business owner had a longstanding dispute with one of his employees. One day he allegedly shot and killed her after she had reportedly approached him angrily with a set of cutting shears. The defense attorney argued that his client had acted recklessly as a result of incipient dementia and could not have formed the intent to commit murder. A report from a neuropsychologist, retained by the defense, found evidence of impairment on memory testing, consistent with early AD. Repeat testing, performed by the prosecution's expert, found a number of reduced test scores, although low levels of performance were also seen on effort testing. A review of the medical record indicated no history of memory complaints or observations of reduced mental functioning. Doctors had never commented on the need for any type of neurological workup. Interviews with other employees revealed no obvious changes in the business owner's behavior in the year prior to the shooting, and the consensus was that the owner had "despised" the deceased employee. The defendant accepted a plea of murder in the second degree, after the prosecution argued that there was no evidence that the defendant was experiencing any identifiable form of dementia.

Mental Retardation

The topic of violence and developmental disability has been of interest, particularly with concerns about the presence of mental retardation in death-row inmates. Studies show that aggressive behaviors are common in institutionalized individuals with developmental disability, but this behavior is rarely seen in those living in the community. The vast majority of people with mental retardation do not break the law. However, other studies show that these individuals are overrepresented in prison populations. There are suggestions that this is because individuals with mild mental retardation are more likely to be apprehended, more likely to confess to a crime and be convicted, and less likely to be paroled than other prisoners.

As with other general deficit conditions, one cannot simply assume that a person is mentally incompetent by virtue of having a diagnosis of mental retardation. One must carefully examine the nature and consequences of the defendant's intentions and the resulting behaviors, as in any other context. One must not confuse the diagnosis of mental retardation with that of *learning disability*, a term commonly used to refer to a less severe or more specific disturbance of academic functioning. The diagnosis of mental retardation must be carefully established, both clinically and by history. It is a common mistake to focus solely on scores from IQ tests, which, typically, must be below a score of 70 to establish the diagnosis. All standard diagnostic classifications of mental retardation also include a requirement for accompanying impairments in adaptive functions, including communication, independent living skills, and ability to use community resources. It is necessary for the disability to have originated before the age of 18 years. To establish these criteria, it is often best to consult relevant medical, psychiatric, and educational records, as well as to interview collateral sources that can provide details about the defendant's early history and upbringing.

Neuropsychologists evaluating defendants with a possible diagnosis of mental retardation benefit from consulting diagnostic guidelines provided by DSM-IV-TR (American Psychiatric Association, 2000) and the American Association of Mental Retardation (AAMR; 2002). The latter definition pays special attention to limitations in functioning within the context of the individual's community according to local age and cultural standards. A comprehensive assessment of intellectual functioning often includes a large-scale measure, such as the Wechsler Adult Intelligence Scale–III (Wechsler, 1997), combined with an assessment of adaptive functioning such as the Vineland Adaptive Behavior Scales–II (Sparrow, Cicchetti, & Balla, 2005) or the Adaptive Behavior Assessment Scale (Harrison & Oakland, 2003). The causes of mental retardation are varied and include a combination of vaguely defined entities, such as perinatal stroke, as well as a number of specific disorders (e.g., Down syndrome, fragile X syndrome, and fetal alcohol syndrome). Findings on neuroimaging vary according to the particular etiology. Although aggressive behavior in these patients may be related to frontal lobe dysfunction, it is often difficult to establish a specific pattern of disorder in that region as a result of the generally diffuse nature of the pathology. Neuropsychological studies show common deficits in attention, short-term memory, and sequential processing, whereas language and visual–spatial abilities present in more varied fashion (Pulsifer, 1996). Low scores in restricted ranges make it difficult for neuropsychologists to establish specific deficits on measures of executive functioning. Data on standard tests of symptom validity are conflicting with regard to whether persons with mental retardation are prone to misclassification as "malingerers" (Michael, 2007; Victor & Boone, 2007).

Frontal Lobe Syndromes

Neuropsychological research has contributed significantly to the classification of various frontal lobe syndromes. As mentioned earlier, OFC and VC studies have advanced our knowledge of the neuroanatomical basis of impulsive aggression and acquired sociopathy (Blair, 2001). According to the most current theories, an individual with an OFC or VC lesion would be prone to exhibit impulsive forms of aggression in conditions of external provocation. The resulting violence would be the result of a failure to inhibit an aggressive impulse properly or to weigh the long-term consequences of one's behavior. A neuropsychologist examining a defendant accused of such a crime should thoroughly review his or her history and medical records to determine the presence or absence of a neurological condition that would render him or her susceptible to aggressive outbursts, and be able to document a plausible profile of impairment through neuropsychological testing.

As it turns out, focal lesions to the OFC and VC occur only rarely in nature, because placement of natural brain lesions often does not respect the boundaries of segmentation are typically seen in functional brain imaging studies. Brain tumors provide one of the most common etiologies. Experience has shown that astrocytomas, oligodendrogliomas, and meningiomas all have a predilection for the frontal lobes and may extend in some cases to more inferior regions. However, lesions of this area of the brain are rarely the result of an occlusive stroke, because cerebral infarcts are rarely limited to the distributions of either the medial or lateral orbitofrontal arteries, although ischemic changes of these vessels are known to result, on occasion, from iatrogenic effects of neurosurgical procedures performed in the region of the inferior frontal lobe. Focal disruption of the OFC is seen more commonly as a result of hemorrhagic process resulting from ruptures of anterior communicating artery aneurysms. Frontal lesions attributed to acute cerebrovascular events would be expected to develop rather rapidly, whereas symptoms from brain tumors would necessarily develop more slowly. In each case, the pathology should be quite easily viewed once the individual is examined through appropriate neuroimaging.

Determination of cognitive impairment secondary to frontal lobe pathology requires the clinician to document performances on tests of executive functioning that are lower than would be predicted from demographic factors and the examinee's measured level of intelligence. The challenge lies in the fact that the tests used for this purpose fit poorly with current conceptions of executive functioning. As mentioned earlier, standard measures of "frontal lobe" functions, such as the WCST and the Category Test, have been found to be relatively insensitive to pathology in the OFC and to behavioral measures of aggression (Morgan & Lilienfeld, 2000). Although research studies have demonstrated the sensitivity of response inhibition measures, including the Porteus Mazes and go–no-go procedures, such measures lack standardization and are not commonly used by clinicians in general practice. The development of newer batteries of executive functions, such as the Delis–Kaplan executive functioning system (D-KEFS; Delis, Kaplan, & Kramer, 2001) have the advantage of including multiple test indices that are normed together, although there is yet little information regarding the utility of this battery for documenting deficits associated with impulsive aggression. Similarly, little information is available for other frontal lobe batteries, such as the Behavioral Assessment of the Dysexecutive Syndrome (BADS; Wilson, Alderman, Burgess, Emslie, & Evans, 1996) or the Executive Control Battery (Goldberg, Podell, & Bilder, 2000), for identifying patterns of impairment associated with aggression. Neuropsychological assessment is clearly lagging behind advances made in cognitive neuroscientific studies on aggression and violence.

Focal frontal lobe pathology is seen more commonly in head trauma, particularly in cases where severe levels of traumatic brain injury (TBI) have led to focal hemorrhages or contusions that can be visualized on neuroimaging. In a well-known study of 279 Vietnam War veterans with penetrating head injuries, those with lesions in the VC were found to have an increased risk for aggressive and violent behavior (Grafman et al., 1996). Studies of severe TBI groups in rehabilitation settings using structured measures such as the Neurobehavioral Rating Scale (Levin, High, & Goethe, 1987) or the Overt Aggression Scale (Yudofsky, Silver, & Jackson, 1986) have documented aggressive behavior in over 70% of those receiving inpatient care. The violent behavior seen in this group is typically disorganized and develops outside the context of any obvious provocation. Aggression is seen in approximately 33% of those receiving outpatient treatment, with depression and early age at the time of the injury considered to be the most significant predictors (Baguley, Cooper, & Felmingham, 2006). Much of the aggressive behavior observed in outpatients is expressed in terms of domestic violence and failed interpersonal relationships. As in other studies, aggression is seen most often in males, subjects with low IQ, and in those experiencing socioeconomic difficulty. Concomitant substance abuse also plays a role in risk for violence in this population. TBI victims with a propensity for violence have been shown to exhibit lower scores on measures of executive functioning (Wood & Liossi, 2006).

It should be emphasized that the relationship between head injury and violence has been limited to studies of patients with severe forms of TBI. There is no research evidence of violent behavior in association with mild traumatic brain injury (MTBI). Although some studies of prison populations have reported MTBI incidence rates exceeding 80%, there was no means of controlling for bias in the reporting of head injury (Schofield et al., 2006; Slaughter, Fann, & Ehde, 2003). There are now reasons to doubt previously held assumptions about the persistence of symptoms resulting from MTBI. Results from large prospective studies of athletes indicate that symptoms of MTBI rarely persist more than 7–10 days (McCrea et al., 2003). However, risks for repeat injury and more persistent symptoms is seen in those with a history of three or more MTBIs (Guskiewicz et al., 2003). There is now reason to believe that multiple head injuries might place one at risk for developing dementia at a later age (Guskiewicz et al., 2005). At this point, there appears to be a relationship to early cognitive deficit, with no evidence that repeated MTBI makes one particularly prone to violence.

A 27-year-old man was charged with assault in the first degree after he allegedly attacked security guards from a nightclub with pieces of broken furniture he had found in the street. One of the guards had suffered severe facial injuries and loss of consciousness that extended nearly 72 hours. The defendant had argued that the guards insulted him, whereas the guards had in turn insisted that he had not understood their indications that he would not be granted admittance to the club. An examination of the defendant's medical history indicated that he had been involved in a serious motor vehicle accident at age 20 and had been in a state of coma for nearly 2 months. He had completed long-term hospitalization, followed by course of rehabilitation for TBI. Neuropsychological test results indicated an average level of functioning, with specific deficits observed on measures of working memory and executive functions, compatible with a profile of frontal lobe dysfunction. The findings were compatible with MRI results demonstrating the presence of prior pathology in the right frontal lobe. Hypometabolism in that region was observed on a PET scan. All of the findings were consistent with pathology that was observed during the course of the acute hospitalization. Charges were reduced in response to the defense attorney's argument that his client was functioning under a state of diminished capacity linked to the prior effects of TBI.

Temporal Lobe Syndromes

The final set of syndromes discussed in this chapter includes conditions that might affect one's awareness or memory of his or her actions or surroundings at the time of the offense. The most common scenario associated with these conditions is that an individual allegedly commits a violent act while in the midst of an epileptic seizure or in some type of amnestic state. Some may argue that unexpected changes in behavior resulting from seizures might explain the behavior of individuals who "just snap," resulting in commitment of an impulsive and violent act. What is common to all of these arguments is the potential for a disruption of temporal lobe systems responsible for memory, consciousness, and impulse control.

The general belief that people with epilepsy are more prone to violence than other individuals contributes to the stigma associated with this condition. Studies have demonstrated increased rates of aggressive behavior in patients with epilepsy (Hermann & Whitman, 1984). Similarly, there have been studies showing increased rates of epilepsy in offender populations (Bach-y-Rita, Lion, Climent, & Ervin, 1971). There is evidence that the aggression observed in patients with epilepsy occurs within the context of an accompanying psychosis, or while the individual is in the midst of a confusional state. Others claim that aggression is observed most frequently in patients with underlying personality disorders, or in those with histories of substance abuse. Although increased rates of violence might occur, it is not clear whether this is a direct effect of the epilepsy or a result of associated factors.

The claim in many cases has been that a defendant with alleged epilepsy committed the crime for which he or she is charged while in the midst of a seizure. To substantiate this type of claim, one must be certain that the individual actually has a history of epilepsy and that he or she has experienced complex partial seizures (CPSs), the type of seizures known to cause unusual forms of behavior. It would be extremely unusual for an individual to commit a violent act as a result of his or her first lifetime seizure. Documentation of abnormal EEGs should be present in the medical records. There should also be proof that the defendant had been under some form of active treatment with antiepileptic medication prior to the incident. It is also important to establish whether the individual experiences CPSs characterized by an alteration in consciousness, and whether he or she has a tendency to experience complex behavioral automatisms. Although the nature of automatisms across individuals is variable, they are typically characterized more by movements of the face and upper extremities than by any form of sequential behavior directed toward others.

Patients with CPSs often have stereotyped events, which means that they likely have experienced events identical to the behavior in question at some time in the past. A CPS typically lasts less than 2 minutes. It may be preceded by an aura and, in some cases, progress into a more dramatic generalized tonic–clonic (GTC) seizure. When determining the relationship between a seizure and an alleged offense, it is important to determine the estimated duration of the behavioral change(s) and whether the change(s) in question were likely to have occurred in the midst of the seizure or in the postictal period, which is in some cases characterized by an extended period of confusion. Seizures with these types of features are known to occur following focal dysfunction of the temporal lobe, and in many cases result from abnormalities of limbic structures, including the hippocampus and amygdala, which are known to be involved in mediation of emotions and drive states. Thus, this finding has made temporal lobe epilepsy (TLE) an entity of interest to clinicians and researchers who study violent behavior.

Increased scientific attention to the issue of aggression and epilepsy was prompted in the 1970s and 1980s by a number of high-profile murder cases in which the defendants were acquitted as a result of using an "epilepsy defense." This state of affairs prompted a large-scale study by many leaders in the field, who found little evidence to support the contention that anyone could have committed a violent act while in the midst of a well-defined epileptic automatism (Delgado-Escueta et al., 1981). The view continues to be that there have been no adequately documented cases of ictal aggression, in which an organized and directed attack on another individual has been found to occur as a manifestation of an epileptic seizure (Treiman, 1999). However, there is some support for the existence of brief, resistive violence at the completion of seizures in some patients, while they are in a state of postictal confusion.

Epilepsy is a clinical diagnosis that requires a history of well-defined seizures, supported by abnormal EEG results and, in some cases, positive findings on neuroimaging studies. As mentioned, documentation of the abnormal EEG is critical in the forensic setting. The "gold standard" for diagnosis of TLE is to observe videotaped episodes of seizure activity while the patient is undergoing simultaneous EEG recording, a procedure known as video EEG (VEEG). Individuals with TLE often exhibit characteristic abnormalities on structural neuroimaging, such as atrophy in the hippocampus or its surrounding region (Kuzniecky & Knowlton, 2002). Regional hypometabolism or reduced blood flow might also be seen in the temporal lobe when using functional imaging procedures such as PET or SPECT. Deficits in attention, memory, and executive functions are commonly observed on neuropsychological testing (Elger, Helmstaedter, & Kurthen, 2004). Individuals with epilepsy typically exhibit low rates of failure on measures associated with effort and malingering (Grote et al., 2000). TLE is also accompanied frequently by psychiatric disturbance. While there has been much emphasis on the study of psychosis and associated personality disorders in this population, the rates of these disorders pale in comparison to the rates of depression and anxiety observed in TLE (Devinsky et al., 2005).

A member of a street gang was charged as an accomplice in the robbery and assault of a middle-aged man in Greenwich Village, but he claimed that he could not recall any details of what had happened. The defendant had a history of epilepsy and had presented to a hospital emergency room the day before the incident, after experiencing a seizure. A court-appointed defense attorney argued that charges against his client should be dropped, because at the time of the alleged offense he was in a state of diminished capacity secondary to the effects of the seizure. A neuropsychologist was hired by the district attorney's office to help investigate the validity of that claim. Test results provided no evidence of impairment. All test scores were consistent with an average level of functioning, using demographically based norms. An examination of hospital records revealed that the defendant had indeed appeared for treatment after experiencing a GTC on the day in question, consistent with a documented history of primary generalized epilepsy. However, the records provided no evidence that the defendant was prone to experiencing any prolonged states of postictal confusion following a typical seizure. He was noted to report in at least one instance that he was usually able to resume activities at full capacity within an hour after his seizures. The defense attorney's attempt to have the charges dropped was rejected by the judge after she heard the prosecution's argument that the history was not consistent with the type of epilepsy that would cause a reduced state of awareness 24 hours after experiencing a seizure.

There has been particular interest in another subset of patients known to exhibit rapidly occurring aggressive outbursts. The behavior is typically not goal-directed and is known to occur at a level well out of proportion to the circumstances. This condition was initially given names such as "limbic rage," "episodic dyscontrol syndrome," or "limbic psychotic trigger reaction," because it was considered to be a "seizure-like" disorder emanating from the limbic system, characterized by extreme and unpredictable rage (Elliott, 1984; Pontius, 1981). In some cases, the condition was described as being preceded by a "fleeting psychosis" that comprised olfactory or visual hallucinations. Although the disorder was thought to relate in some way to TLE, there was no consistent EEG evidence of any abnormality in affected individuals. They were considered by some to represent a distinct diagnostic entity with limbic abnormalities that caused an imbalance in frontal control mechanisms (Pontius, 1981). The condition was also thought to occur in a large number of criminal offenders, some of whom had never exhibited prior evidence of epilepsy or any other form of neurological disorder.

The rapidly occurring rage attacks described earlier have obtained the more recent label *intermittent explosive disorder* (IED; Coccaro, 2000). IED is thought to occur in 6–8% of all psychiatric inpatients, is exhibited more frequently in males (3:1 ratio), and typically develops in midadolescence. The risk for its occurrence is doubled in persons diagnosed with APD or borderline personality disorder (BPD). As mentioned earlier, it is characterized by aggressive outbursts with a short onset and typically lasts less than 30 minutes. Behaviors include verbal outbursts, assault, and/or destruction of property. Results from a recent study of affected individuals demonstrated bilateral EEG and MRI abnormalities (van Elst, Woermann, Lemieux, Thompson, & Trimble, 2000). Other imaging studies have shown abnormalities in the region of the hypothalamus and in the amygdala. Some researchers have implicated abnormal functioning of the OFC in this population. There is little information regarding performance on neuropsychological testing in patients with IED. Efforts are currently underway both to formalize the criteria used to diagnose this condition and to find appropriate treatments.

The temporal lobes are known to play an important role in memory processing. Much has been written about the role that memory and its failures play in the testimony of witnesses in trials. One must also consider issues related to memory when evaluating information obtained from criminal defendants. Results from one small study indicated that 60% of defendants reported some form of disruption in recall of details of their crimes (Bradford & Smith, 1979). The majority involved "patchy" recall of the events. Over 20% reported periods of amnesia lasting more than 6 hours. Alcohol or intoxication with other substances was thought to be involved in 50% of the cases. Loss of memory due to "emotional" reasons was reported in 30% of cases. Other studies have suggested that many criminals have a tendency to feign memory loss to limit the amount of information that can be used against them in prosecution (Schacter, 1986; Victor & Boone, 2007).

The forensic neuropsychologist will benefit from having a possible etiology in mind when evaluating a defendant's claim of amnesia for the events surrounding his or her crime. One must first determine whether the defendant is reporting persistent memory loss for events occurring at the time of the evaluation, in addition to that at the time of the crime. In that case, the task is to document an acquired form of memory impairment that would possibly be related to the onset of dementia or, in younger subjects, a variety of causes, including head injury, substance abuse, or other forms of neurological dysfunction. In these situations, neuropsychologists are encouraged to use standard measures of memory, such as the Wechsler Memory Scale–III (WMS-III; Wechsler, 1997), the California Verbal Learning Test–II (CVLT-II; Delis, Kramer, Kaplan, & Ober, 2000), or the Rey Auditory Verbal Learning Test (RAVLT; Schmidt, 1996) to document the presence of memory impairment. If the defendant is reporting transient memory loss, then one must consider a range of other possible conditions, many of which require associated findings on the physical and/or neurological examination. It is important to ascertain whether the time of the crime was the first reported episode of the condition or whether the individual had undergone similar episodes in the past.

Transient global amnesia (TGA) and transient epileptic amnesia (TEA) are the two most common forms of transient memory disturbances related to neurological causes (Zeman & Hodges, 2000). TGA is characterized by a temporary form of anterograde amnesia that occurs for less than 24 hours. There is typically no associated loss of consciousness or personal identity. Memory is the only function that is affected. The cause of TGA remains poorly understood. Some consider it to be the result of cerebrovascular factors. TEA has very similar characteristics to TGA, but the etiology is more clearly defined, because it is typically seen in individuals with a documented history of epilepsy. Migraine, head injury, and intoxication are other conditions that might cause temporary memory loss.

One must also consider the possible effects of a dissociative disorder, particularly when the crime involved some form of emotional trauma. Memory loss secondary to dissociation often includes amnesia for personal events, in addition to details regarding the trauma (Coons, 1998). It differs from TGA or TEA, because it is known to reverse through hypnosis or administration of amobarbital. It is difficult to obtain documentation of memory impairment while a subject is in the midst of a transient memory disturbance. Thus, the neuropsychologist's task is to document whether any memory disturbance exists when the individual is not in episode and to examine medical records for evidence to support the existence of an associated medical condition. Additional measures of personality, including the MMPI-2 and scales developed for assessment of dissociation symptoms, such as the Dissociative Experiences Scale (DES; Bernstein & Putnam, 1986), should also be included. One must also give strong consideration to the possibility of malingering, as demonstrated by a number of studies of individuals showing unusual forms of amnesia (Denney, 1996; Frederick, Carter, & Powell, 1995).

Summary

Considerable evidence now indicates that neurobiological factors play a major role in manifestations of aggression and violence. Studies examining criminal offenders or persons identified as having APD indicate a variety of abnormalities, extending from abnormal neurotransmitter levels to a disruption of neuroanatomical networks. At the neurotransmitter level, an association between aggression and serotonin levels has been established, although it has not yet resulted in any form of effective treatment. A number of genetic and hormonal influences have also been recognized, with evidence that these may interact with environmental factors to result in a predisposition to violence.

In the past 20 years a number of valuable insights have been gained from neuroimaging, indicating frontal network disturbances in a number of groups that are prone to violent behavior. Findings from neuropsychological studies have indicated that these groups exhibit particular deficits on tests of response inhibition and decision making, providing a link to an underlying tendency toward impulsive behavior. Whereas the findings from these studies, taken separately, provide a rather compelling argument for a disruption of frontal networks responsible for impulse control in violent offenders, more research is needed to integrate findings from these separate lines of research and to identify indicators that separate individuals who are prone to violence from those with comorbid conditions, such as substance abuse and/or ADHD.

This chapter's discussion of the role of the forensic neuropsychologist has focused primarily on assessment of criminal responsibility and diminished capacity. Given what is now known about the neurobiology of criminality, the major goal of the neuropsychologist in this context is to demonstrate whether the defendant exhibits some form of neurological or psychiatric illness that would affect his or her mental capacity in a manner over and above what would be expected solely on the basis of having APD or an associated condition, such as ADHD or substance abuse. This chapter has provided a sample set of conditions that have the potential to affect a defendant's behavior in this type of manner. In each case, by examining details of the crime, as well as the available records, the neuropsychologist should be in a position to make a case that the defendant's behavior was or was not affected by mental disease or defect at the time of the offense. One should always conduct a thorough evaluation of the context of the behavior and never attempt to make an argument that the defendant lacks criminal responsibility solely on the basis of having a particular neurological or psychiatric diagnosis.

This chapter has provided evidence of a link between dysfunction in specific areas of the frontal lobe and a tendency toward impulsive forms of aggression. It is recommended that neuropsychologists working in criminal settings begin to include more measures associated with response inhibition and control in their test batteries. Neuropsychologists are also encouraged to develop new tests designed for this purpose, followed by collection of appropriate norms. Significant advances have been made in the neuroscientific study of aggression and violence over the past 25 years. Those using neuropsychological methods in a criminal forensic setting are encouraged to follow these advances closely to provide the court with information that is current, that addresses the needs of the court, and is scientifically sound.

References

American Association on Mental Retardation. (2002). *The AAMR definition of mental retardation*. Washington, DC: Author.

American Psychiatric Association. (2000). *Diagnostic and statistical manual of mental disorders* (4th ed., text rev.). Washington, DC: Author.

Angermeyer, M. C., Cooper, B., & Link, B. G. (1998). Mental disorder and violence: Results of epidemiological studies in the era of de-institutionalization. *Social Psychiatry and Psychiatric Epidemiology, 33*(13), S1–S6.

Bach-y-Rita, G., Lion, J. R., Climent, C. E., & Ervin, F. R. (1971). Episodic dyscontrol: A study of 130 violent patients. *American Journal of Psychiatry, 127*(11), 1473–1478.

Baguley, I. J., Cooper, J., & Felmingham, K. (2006). Aggressive behavior following traumatic brain injury: How common is common? *Journal of Head Trauma Rehabilitation, 21*(1), 45–56.

Bechara, A., Damasio, H., & Damasio, A. R. (2000). Emotion, decision-making, and the orbitofrontal cortex. *Cerebral Cortex, 10,* 295–307.

Benton, A. L. (1968). Differential behavioral effects on frontal lobe disease. *Neuropsychologia, 6,* 53–60.

Berman, K. F., Illowsky, B. P., & Weinberger, D. R. (1988). Physiological dysfunction of dorsolateral prefrontal cortex in schizophrenia: IV. Further evidence for regional and behavioral specificity. *Archives General of Psychiatry, 45*(7), 616–622.

Bernstein, E. M., & Putnam, P. W. (1986). Development, reliability, and validity of a dissociation scale. *Journal of Nervous and Mental Disease, 174,* 727–735.

Blair, K. S., Mitchell, D. G., Leonard, A., Newman, C., Richell, R., & Morton, J. (2006). Differentiating among prefrontal substrates in psychopathy: Neuropsychological test findings. *Neuropsychology, 20*(2), 153–165.

Blair, R. J. R. (2001). Neurocognitive models of aggression, the antisocial, personality disorders, and psychopathy. *Journal of Neurology, Neurosurgery, and Psychiatry, 71,* 727–731.

Bradford, J. M., & Smith, S. M. (1979). Amnesia and homicide: The Padola case and a study of thirty cases. *Bulletin of the American Academy of Psychiatry and the Law, 7*(3), 219–231.

Brower, M. C., & Price, B. H. (2001). Neuropsychiatry of frontal lobe dysfunction in violent and criminal behaviour: A critical review. *Journal of Neurology, Neurosurgery, and Psychiatry, 71*(6), 720–726.

Bufkin, J. L., & Luttrell, V. R. (2005). Neuroimaging studies of aggressive and violent behavior: Current findings and implications for criminology and criminal justice. *Trauma, Violence and Abuse, 6*(2), 176–191.

Bush, G., Valera, E. M., & Seidman, L. J. (2005). Functional neuroimaging of attention-deficit/hyperactivity disorder: A review and suggested future directions. *Biological Psychiatry, 57*(11), 1273–1284.

Butcher, J. N., Dahlstrom, W. G., Graham, J. R., Tellegen, A. M., & Kaemmer, B. (1990). *MMPI-2: Minnesota Multiphasic Personality Inventory–2: Manual for administration and scoring.* Minneapolis: University of Minnesota Press.

Coccaro, E. F. (2000). Intermittent explosive disorder. *Current Psychiatry Reports, 2*(1), 67–71.

Cohen, R. A., Brumm, V., Zawacki, T. M., Paul, R., Sweet, L., & Rosenbaum, A. (2003). Impulsivity and verbal deficits associated with domestic violence. *Journal of the International Neuropsychological Society, 9*(5), 760–770.

Coons, P. M. (1998). The dissociative disorders. Rarely considered and underdiagnosed. *Psychiatric Clinics of North America, 21*(3), 637–648.

Cornell, D. G., Warren, J., Hawk, G., Stafford, E., Oram, G., & Pine, D. (1996). Psychopathy in instrumental and reactive violent offenders. *Journal of Consulting and Clinical Psychology, 64*(4), 783–790.

Cummings, J. L. (1995). Anatomic and behavioral aspects of frontal–subcortical circuits. *Annals of the New York Academy of Sciences, 769,* 1–13.

Delgado-Escueta, A. V., Mattson, R. H., King, L., Goldensohn, E. S., Spiegel, H., Madsen, J., et al. (1981). Special report: The nature of aggression during epileptic seizures. *New England Journal of Medicine, 305*(12), 711–716.

Delis, D., Kramer, J. H., Kaplan, E., & Ober, B. A. (2000). *California Verbal Learning Test* (2nd ed.). San Antonio, TX: Psychological Corporation.

Delis, D. C., Kaplan, E., & Kramer, J. (2001). *Delis–Kaplan Executive Function Scale.* San Antonio, TX: Psychological Corporation.

Denney, R. L. (1996). Symptom validity testing of remote memory in a criminal forensic setting. *Archives of Clinical Neuropsychology, 11,* 589–603.

Devinsky, O., Barr, W. B., Vickrey, B. G., Berg, A. T., Bazil, C. W., Pacia, S. V., et al. (2005). Changes in depression and anxiety after resective surgery for epilepsy. *Neurology, 65*(11), 1744–1749.

Dietz, P. E. (1985). Why the experts disagree: Variations in the psychiatric evaluation of criminal insanity. *Annals of the American Academy and Political and Social Science, 477,* 84–95.

Duncan, A. (2005). The impact of cognitive and psychiatric impairment of psychotic disorders on the Test of Memory Malingering (TOMM). *Assessment, 12*(2), 123–129.

Eastley, R., & Wilcock, G. K. (1997). Prevalence and correlates of aggressive behaviours occurring in patients with Alzheimer's disease. *International Journal of Geriatric Psychiatry, 12*(4), 484–487.

Eichelman, B. (1983). The limbic system and aggression in humans. *Neuroscience and Biobehavioral Reviews, 7*(3), 391–394.

Elger, C. E., Helmstaedter, C., & Kurthen, M. (2004). Chronic epilepsy and cognition. *Lancet: Neurology, 3*(11), 663–672.

Elliott, F. A. (1984). The episodic dyscontrol syndrome and aggression. *Neurologic Clinics, 2*(1), 113–125.

First, M. B., Spitzer, R. L., Gibbon, M., & Williams, J. B. W. (1997). *Structured Clinical Interview for DSM-IV Axis I Disorders (SCID-I), Clinician Version.* Washington, DC: American Psychiatric Press.

Flashman, L. A., & Green, M. F. (2004). Review of cognition and brain structure in schizophrenia: Profiles, longitudinal course, and effects of treatment. *Psychiatric Clinics of North America, 27*(1), 1–18, vii.

Flor-Henry, P. (1973). Psychiatric syndromes considered as manifestations of lateralized temporal–limbic dysfunction. In L. Latiner & K. Livingston (Eds.), *Surgical approaches in psychiatry.* Lancaster, UK: Medical and Technical Publishing.

Flynn, J. P. (1967). The neural basis of aggression in cats. In D. C. Glass (Ed.), *Neurophysiology and emotion.* New York: Rockefeller University Press.

Frederick, R. I., Carter, J. E., & Powell, J. (1995). Adapting symptom validity testing to evaluate suspicious complaints of amnesia in medicolegal evaluation. *Bulletin of the American Academy of Psychiatry and the Law, 23,* 231–237.

Gatzke-Kopp, L. M., Raine, A., Buchsbaum, M., & LaCasse, L. (2001). Temporal lobe deficits in murderers: EEG findings undetected by PET. *Journal of Neuropsychiatry and Clinical Neurosciences, 13,* 486–491.

Goldberg, E., Podell, K., & Bilder, R. M. (2000). *The Executive Control Battery*. Sydney: Psych Press.

Golden, C. J. (1978). *Stroop Color and Word Test: A manual for clinical and experimental uses*. Los Angeles: Western Psychological Services.

Goodman, M., New, A., & Siever, L. (2004). Trauma, genes, and the neurobiology of personality disorders. *Annals of the New York Academy of Sciences, 1032*(1), 104–116.

Gorrison, M., Sanz, J. C., & Schmand, B. (2005). Effort and cognition in schizophrenia patients. *Schizophrenia Research, 78*, 199–208.

Grafman, J., Schwab, K., Warden, D., Pridgen, A., Brown, H. R., & Salazar, A. M. (1996). Frontal lobe injuries, violence, and aggression: A report of the Vietnam Head Injury Study. *Neurology, 46*(5), 1231–1238.

Green, P., & Astner, K. (1995). *The Word Memory Test*. Edmonton, Alberta, Canada: Neurobehavioural Associates.

Grote, C. L., Kooker, E. K., Garron, D. C., Nyenhuis, D. L., Smith, C. A., & Mattingly, M. L. (2000). Performance of compensation seeking and non-compensation seeking samples on the Victoria Symptom Validity Test: Cross-validation and extension of a standardization study. *Journal of Clinical and Experimental Neuropsychology, 22*(6), 709–719.

Guskiewicz, K. M., Marshall, S. W., Bailes, J., McCrea, M., Cantu, R. C., Randolph, C., et al. (2005). Association between recurrent concussion and late-life cognitive impairment in retired professional football players. *Neurosurgery, 57*(4), 719–726.

Guskiewicz, K. M., McCrea, M., Marshall, S. W., Cantu, R. C., Randolph, C., Barr, W., et al. (2003). Cumulative effects associated with recurrent concussion in collegiate football players: The NCAA Concussion Study. *Journal of the American Medical Association, 290*(19), 2549–2555.

Harrison, P., & Oakland, T. (2003). *Adaptive Behavior Assessment System–II (ABAS-II)*. San Antonio, TX: Harcourt Assessment.

Heaton, R. K. (1981). *Wisconsin Card Sorting Test Manual*. Odessa, FL: Psychological Assessment Resources

Hermann, B. P., & Whitman, S. (1984). Behavioral and personality correlates of epilepsy: A review, methodological critique, and conceptual model. *Psychological Bulletin, 95*(3), 451–497.

Hess, W. R., & Brugger, M. (1943). Das subkortikale zentrum der affektiven abwehrreaktion [The subcortical center of the affective defensive reaction]. *Helvetica Physiologica Acta, 1*, 33–52.

Hoptman, M. J. (2003). Neuroimaging studies of violence and antisocial behavior. *Journal of Psychiatric Practice, 9*(4), 265–278.

Krakowski, M. (2003). Violence and serotonin: Influence of impulse control, affect regulation, and social functioning. *Journal of Neuropsychiatry and Clinical Neurosciences, 15*(3), 294–305.

Krug, E. G. (2002). *World report on violence and health*. Geneva: World Health Organization.

Kuzniecky, R. I., & Knowlton, R. C. (2002). Neuroimaging of epilepsy. *Seminars in Neurology, 22*(3), 279–288.

Levin, H. S., High, W. M., Jr., & Goethe, K. E. (1987). The Neurobehavioral Rating Scale: Assessment of the behavioral sequelae of head injury. *Journal of Neurology, Neurosurgery, and Psychiatry, 50*, 183–193.

Lewis, D. O., Pincus, J. H., Feldman, M., Jackson, L., & Bard, B. (1986). Psychiatric, neurological, and psychoeducational characteristics of 15 death row inmates in the United States. *American Journal of Psychiatry, 143*, 838–845.

Lewis, D. O., Shanok, S. S., Pincus, J. H., & Glaser, G. H. (1979). Violent juvenile delinquents: Psychiatric, neurological, psychological, and abuse factors. *Journal of the American Academy of Child Psychiatry, 18*(2), 307–319.

Lewis, D. O., Yeager, C., Blake, P. Y., Bard, B., & Strenziok, M. (2004). Ethics questions raised by the neuropsychiatric, neuropsychological, educational, developmental, and family characteristics of 18 juveniles awaiting execution in Texas. *Journal of the American Academy of Psychiatry and the Law, 32*, 408–429.

Lombroso, C. (1876). *L'Uomo Delinquete* [Criminal man]. Milan: Hoepli.

Luria, A. R. (1966). *Higher cortical functions in man.* New York: Basic Books.

Mark, V. H., & Ervin, F. (1970). *Violence and the brain.* New York: Harper & Row.

McCloskey, M. S., Phan, K. L., & Coccaro, E. F. (2005). Neuroimaging and personality disorders. *Current Psychiatry Reports, 7*(1), 65–72.

McCrea, M., Guskiewicz, K. M., Marshall, S. W., Barr, W., Randolph, C., Cantu, R. C., et al. (2003). Acute effects and recovery time following concussion in collegiate football players: The NCAA Concussion Study. *Journal of the American Medical Association, 290*(19), 2556–2563.

Meloy, J. R. (2006). Empirical basis and forensic application of affective and predatory violence. *Australian and New Zealand Journal of Psychiatry, 40*(6–7), 539–547.

Mena, J. C., Cuellar, H., Vargas, D., & Riascos, R. (2005). PET and SPECT in drug and substance abuse. *Topics in Magnetic Resonance Imaging, 16*(3), 253–256.

Michael, J. S. (2007). Performance of mentally retarded forensic patients on the test of memory malingering. *Journal of Clinical Psychology, 63*(4), 339–344.

Morgan, A. B., & Lilienfeld, S. O. (2000). A meta-analytic review of the relation between antisocial behavior and neuropsychological measures of executive function. *Clinical Psychology Review, 20*(1), 113–136.

Papez, J. W. (1995). A proposed mechanism of emotion. *Journal of Neuropsychiatry and Clinical Neurosciences, 7*(1), 103–112.

Pearlson, G. D. (2000). Neurobiology of schizophrenia. *Annals of Neurology, 48*, 556–566.

Pincus, J. H. (1981). Violence and epilepsy. *New England Journal of Medicine, 305*(12), 696–698.

Pincus, J. H., & Tucker, G. J. (1978). Violence in children and adults: A neurological view. *Journal of the American Academy of Child Psychiatry, 17*(2), 277–288.

Pontius, A. A. (1981). Stimuli triggering violence in psychoses. *Journal of Forensic Sciences, 26*(1), 123–128.

Porteus, S. D. (1942). *Qualitative performance in the Maze Test*. Vineland, NJ: Smith.

Pulsifer, M. B. (1996). The neuropsychology of mental retardation. *Journal of the International Neuropsychological Society, 2*(2), 159–176.

Raine, A. (1993). *The psychopathology of crime: Criminal behavior as a clinical disorder*. San Diego, CA: Academic Press.

Raine, A., Buchsbaum, M., & LaCasse, L. (1997). Brain abnormalities in murderers indicated by positron emission tomography. *Biological Psychiatry, 42*(6), 495–508.

Raine, A., Ishikawa, S. S., Arce, E., Lencz, T., Knuth, K. H., Birhle, S., et al. (2004). Hippocampal structural asymmetry in unsuccessful psychopaths. *Biological Psychiatry, 55*, 185–191.

Raine, A., Meloy, J. R., Bihrle, S., Stoddard, J., LaCasse, L., & Buchsbaum, M. S. (1998). Reduced prefrontal and increased subcortical brain functioning assessed using positron emission tomography in predatory and affective murderers. *Behavioral Sciences and the Law, 16*(3), 319–332.

Raine, A., Venables, P. H., & Williams, M. (1990). Measures of arousal at age 15 years and criminality at age 24 years. *Archives of General Psychiatry, 47*, 1003–1007.

Reitan, R. M., & Wolfson, D. (1985). *The Halstead–Reitan Neuropsychological Test Battery: Theory and clinical interpretation*. New York: Hemisphere.

Rogers, R., Bagby, R. M., & Dickens, S. E. (1992). *Structured Interview of Reported Symptoms*. Odessa, FL: Psychological Assessment Resources.

Schacter, D. L. (1986). Amnesia and crime: How much do we really know? *American Psychologist, 41*(3), 286–295.

Schmahl, C., & Bremner, J. D. (2006). Neuroimaging in borderline personality disorder. *Journal of Psychiatric Research, 40*, 419–427.

Schmidt, M. (1996). *Rey Auditory Verbal Learning Test: A handbook (RAVLT)*. Odessa, FL: Psychological Assessment Resources.

Schofield, P. W., Butler, T. G., Hollis, S. J., Smith, N. E., Lee, S. J., & Kelso, W. M. (2006). Traumatic brain injury among Australian prisoners: Rates, recurrence and sequelae. *Brain Injury, 20*(5), 499–506.

Senanarong, V., Cummings, J. L., Fairbanks, L., Mega, M., Masterman, D. M., O'Connor, S. M., et al. (2004). Agitation in Alzheimer's disease is a manifestation of frontal lobe dysfunction. *Dementia and Geriatric Cognitive Disorders, 17*(1–2), 14–20.

Slaughter, B., Fann, J. R., & Ehde, D. (2003). Traumatic brain injury in a county jail population: Prevalence, neuropsychological functioning and psychiatric disorders. *Brain Injury, 17*(9), 731–741.

Sparrow, S. S., Cicchetti, D. V., & Balla, D. A. (2005). *Vineland Adaptive Behavior Scales, Second Edition (Vineland–II)*. Circle Pines, MN: American Guidance Services.

Srikanth, S., Nagaraja, A. V., & Ratnavalli, E. (2005). Neuropsychiatric symptoms in dementia—frequency, relationship to dementia severity and comparison in Alzheimer's disease, vascular dementia and frontotemporal dementia. *Journal of the Neurological Sciences, 236*(1–2), 43–48.

State v. White, 612 (117 Cal. App. 3d 270, 1981).

Stuss, D. T., & Benson, D. F. (1984). Neuropsychological studies of the frontal lobes. *Psychological Bulletin, 95*, 3–28.

Swanson, J. W., Swartz, M. S., Van Dorn, R. A., Elbogen, E. B., Wagner, H. R., Rosenheck, R. A., et al. (2006). A national study of violent behavior in persons with schizophrenia. *Archives of General Psychiatry, 63*(5), 490–499.

Teichner, G., & Wagner, M. T. (2004). The Test of Memory Malingering (TOMM): Normative data from cognitively intact, cognitively impaired, and elderly patients with dementia. *Archives of Clinical Neuropsychology, 19*(3), 455–464.

Tombaugh, T. N. (1996). *Test of Memory Malingering*. Toronto: Multi-Health Systems.

Torrey, E. F. (1994). Violent behavior by individuals with serious mental illness. *Hospital and Community Psychiatry, 45*(7), 653–662.

Treiman, D. M. (1999). Violence and the epilepsy defense. *Neurologic Clinics, 17*(2), 245–255.

van Elst, L. T., Woermann, F. G., Lemieux, L., Thompson, P. J., & Trimble, M. R. (2000). Affective aggression in patients with temporal lobe epilepsy: A quantitative MRI study of the amygdala. *Brain, 123*(2), 234–243.

Victor, T. L., & Boone, K. B. (2007). Identification of feigned mental retardation. In K. B. Boone (Ed.), *Assessment of feigned cognitive impairment: A neuropsychological perspective* (pp. 310–345). New York: Guilford Press.

Vitacco, M. J., Neumann, C. S., & Jackson, R. L. (2005). Testing a four-factor model of psychopathy and its association with ethnicity, gender, intelligence, and violence. *Journal of Consulting and Clinical Psychology, 73*(3), 466–476.

Volavka, J. (2002). *Neurobiology of violence* (2nd ed.). Washington, DC: American Psychiatric Press.

Walsh, E., Buchanan, A., & Fahy, T. (2002). Violence and schizophrenia: Examining the evidence. *British Journal of Psychiatry, 180*(6), 490–495.

Walsh, M.-T., & Dinan, T. G. (2001). Selective serotonin reuptake inhibitors and violence: A review of the available evidence. *Acta Psychiatrica Scandinavica, 104*(2), 84–91.

Wechsler, D. (1997). *Wechsler Adult Intelligence Scale–III*. San Antonio, TX: Psychological Corporation.

Wilson, B. A., Alderman, N., Burgess, P. W., Emslie, H., & Evans, J. J. (1996). *Behavioural Assessment of the Dysexecutive Syndrome (BADS)*. Oxford, UK: Thames Valley Test Company.

Wood, R. L., & Liossi, C. (2006). Neuropsychological and neurobehavioral correlates of aggression following traumatic brain injury. *Journal of Neuropsychiatry and Clinical Neurosciences, 18*(3), 333–341.

Yeudall, L. T., & Fromm-Auch, D. (1979). Neuropsychological impairments in various psychopathological populations. In J. Gruzelier & P. Flor-Henry (Eds.), *Hemisphere asymmetries of function in psychopathology*. Amsterdam: Elsevier North-Holland.

Yudofsky, S., Silver, J. M., & Jackson, E. K. (1986). The Overt Aggression Scale for the objective rating of verbal and physical aggression. *American Journal of Psychiatry, 143,* 35–39.

Zald, D. H. (2006). Neuropsychological assessment of orbitofrontal dysfunction. In D. H. Zald & S. L. Rauch (Eds.), *The orbitofrontal cortex.* Oxford, UK: Oxford University Press.

Zeman, A., & Hodges, J. R. (2000). Transient global amnesia and transient epileptic amnesia. In G. E. Berrios & J. R. Hodges (Eds.), *Memory disorders in psychiatric practice.* Cambridge, UK: Cambridge University Press.

Chapter 9

Neuropsychological Consultation in the Sentencing Phase of Capital Cases

ROBERT L. HEILBRONNER
DANIELLE WALLER

> Death is different
> —ANONYMOUS PUBLIC DEFENDER

The death penalty is different. It is an ultimate and irrevocable sanction. For that reason alone it warrants a greater degree of reliability (*Lockett v. Ohio*, 1978) in its application. All involved parties (e.g., judge, lawyers, experts, etc.) must operate at the highest level of ethics and professionalism, as mandated by their particular fields of expertise. Like other areas of forensic psychology consultations, neuropsychological consultations in capital cases involve the same four components: (1) clear recognition of the relevant psycholegal issues, including the implications of the evaluation methods and findings; (2) unwavering adherence to ethical standards, including informed consent, objectivity, and advocating for the data; (3) assessment methods that are both relevant to the issue in question and comprehensive in application; and (4) familiarity and reliance on the best empirical data and research perspectives (Cunningham & Goldstein, 2003). Becoming involved in a capital case is something that requires a personal assessment of one's morals; personal values; and views on the constitutionality of the death penalty, the role of government, and other important theoretical and philosophical issues. It is not for the faint of heart, which perhaps is one reason that very few neuropsychologists perform mitigation assessments as part of their practices and so little has been written on this topic.

A death penalty case is not a unitary phenomenon. It comprises two separate and very distinct phases: a trial phase and a sentencing phase. In a noncapital felony case, attorneys may put 99% of their time and planning into the trial portion of the case, with 1% reserved for a sentencing hearing. However, the sentencing phase of a capital case cannot be conceptualized as an afterthought. Indeed, the attorney and his or her team must give at least as much planning and attention to this phase as they do to the guilt–innocence phase. In fact, some capital cases are all about the sentencing portion of the case. In the sentencing phase of a capital case, experts frequently testify regarding the presence of mitigating and/or aggravating factors to provide information about the defendant's background or about circumstances of the crime that may influence the sentence the defendant is to receive (Cunningham & Goldstein, 2003). This is especially true in cases in which the guilt of the defendant is very clear and the defense focuses largely on efforts to convince the trier of fact (in capital cases, it is the jury; see *Ring v. Arizona*, 2002) *not* to impose a death sentence. In those cases, a life sentence without parole may be considered a victory by the defense team and the defendant.

Because of the emphasis on the sentencing portion of the case, it is incumbent on a defense attorney in a capital case to assemble a multidisciplinary team for each phase. This means finding and hiring an experienced mitigation specialist (otherwise referred to as a *forensic social historian*). The 2003 American Bar Association's guidelines for the appointment and performance of defense counsel in death penalty cases requires that a mitigation specialist be a member of the defense team. The decision to bring on certain experts, such as a neuropsychologist, to assist in the sentencing phase of the trial, is often in response to the recommendation of the forensic historian. In fact, the forensic social historian is one of the best sources of referrals for neuropsychologists in capital cases.

A capital case begins with the guilt–innocence phase of the trial. The verdict (guilty, innocent, not guilty by reason of insanity) determines whether the case continues to the sentencing phase. Once a jury finds the defendant guilty, then it must decide whether the defendant is eligible for death based on the facts of the crime. In Illinois, 21 eligibility factors allow someone to face the possible punishment of death. One such factor is the killing of a police officer. However, although the commission of this crime makes someone *eligible* for death, it does not automatically result in a sentence of death.

If a defendant has pled guilty or is found guilty of a capital offense, then a sentencing proceeding takes place. The information presented at sentencing is to be considered by, and to assist, the trier of fact in determining the appropriate punishment for the defendant. In many instances, the two options for sentencing are death or life in prison without the possibility of parole. The sentencing phase of a capital case comprises aggravation and mitigation. *Aggravation* is a presentation of the reasons the State is asserting that death is the appropriate sentence. Some examples of aggravating factors include the assassination of a government official or killing someone during the course of a felony (e.g., armed robbery). *Mitigation* is a presentation of the reasons the defense is asserting that death is not the appropriate sentence. A mitigating factor is one reason why a defendant should be sentenced to something less than death (Cunningham & Goldstein, 2003).

The U.S. Supreme Court has maintained that individual sentencing is a constitutional requirement when death is being considered as a punishment. This notion was eloquently stated by the U.S. Supreme Court in *Woodson v. North Carolina* (1976):

> A process that accords no significance to relevant facets of the character and record of the individual offender or the circumstances of the particular offense excludes from consideration in fixing the ultimate punishment of death the possibility of compassionate or mitigation factors stemming from the diverse frailties of humankind. It treats all persons convicted of a designated offense not as uniquely individual human beings, but as members of a faceless, undifferentiated mass to be subjected to the blind infliction of the death penalty. (pp. 303–304)

Each jurisdiction has its own set of specific circumstances (defined by legislators in each state and by Congress on the federal level) that, if found by the trier of fact to be present, might result in a verdict other than death. These factors are referred to as *statutory mitigating factors*. Some examples include the following: The defendant was mentally ill at the time of the crime; the defendant's use of drugs at the time of the crime impaired his or her judgment and impulse control; and the defendant has no prior record of violence and does not present a risk of future dangerousness. *Nonstatutory mitigating factors* include *any* evidence related to the defendant's background and circumstances of the offense that may be considered as mitigation in reaching a verdict (*Lockett v. Ohio*, 1978). Examples include the defendant's history of mental illness; his or her history of physical and sexual abuse as a child; his or her discontinuation of prescribed psychotropic medications in the weeks preceding the crime; and others. It is important for the jury to consider both the statutory and nonstatutory factors in sentencing. In *Hitchcock v. Dugger* (1986) a death sentence was ruled unconstitutional, because the jury was instructed to consider only the mitigating factors set out in state statute and the sentencing judge refused to consider nonstatutory mitigating factors.

Throughout the years, court rulings have identified specific topics or events considered constitutionally appropriate for presentation during mitigation. A number of cases cite the following factors as mitigating:

- ❖ Poor social background
- ❖ Physically abused as child
- ❖ Watched physical abuse of mother
- ❖ Emotional abuse/neglect as child
- ❖ Parent/stepparent alcoholic/drug user
- ❖ History of suicide attempts
- ❖ History of psychological problems/psychiatric hospitalizations
- ❖ Defendant is a follower, not a leader

Eisenberg (1999) identified a number of other factors that he felt should be considered as mitigating factors in the sentencing phase of a capital case (Table 9.1). Those (and some others not included) that appear to be particularly relevant from a neuropsychological perspective include organic brain syndromes, traumatic brain injury (TBI), epilepsy/seizure disorders, brain tumors, strokes, learning disabilities, attention-deficit/hyperactivity disorder (ADHD), drug and alcohol abuse/dependence, exposure to toxins, dementia, mental retardation, borderline intelligence, fetal alcohol syndrome, and developmental disorders.

Most challenges to the constitutionality of the death penalty have focused on issues related to the Eighth Amendment to the U.S. Constitution, specifically, the "Cruel and Unusual Punishment" clause. Interestingly, this clause, adopted from the English Bill of Rights in 1689, was developed

TABLE 9.1. Psychological/Neuropsychological Factors to Explore in Mitigation

❖ Abuse	❖ Memory disorders
❖ Alcoholic parents	❖ Mental retardation
❖ Absent parents	❖ Military service
❖ Attachment disorders	❖ Mood swings
❖ Attention-deficit/hyperactivity disorder	❖ Neglect
❖ Birth defects	❖ Poverty
❖ Borderline IQ	❖ Prison culture
❖ Criminal parents	❖ Remorse
❖ Cultural issues	❖ Runaway
❖ Death of a parent	❖ Sexual history
❖ Exposure to violence	❖ Sleep disorder
❖ Fetal alcohol syndrome	❖ Spousal abuse
❖ Gang affiliation/exposure	❖ Substance abuse/dependence
❖ Institutionalization	❖ Transcience/homelessness
❖ Juvenile history	❖ Traumatic brain injury
❖ Learning disabilities	❖ Toxins
❖ Organic brain syndromes	❖ Victimization
❖ Personality disorders	❖ Welfare effects on the family
❖ Malnutrition	❖ Youth of the defendant

Note. Adapted with permission of the author from Eisenberg (1999).

in response to torture, cruelty, and brutality directed against rebels revolting against King James II. In the United States, there have been a number of challenges to the constitutionality of the death penalty, too many to list in this chapter. However, the reader should be acquainted with the following cases for at least a preliminary understanding of the law and the death penalty, and the relevance of mitigating factors in the sentencing phase (see Appendix 9.1 for a more extended discussion of these cases).

- In *Lockett v. Ohio* (1978), the Court concluded that the sentencer "not be precluded from considering, as a mitigation factor, *any* aspect of a defendant's character or record and any of the circumstances of the offense that the defendant proffers as a basis for a sentence less then death" (p. 604, emphasis added).
- In *Eddings v. Oklahoma* (1978), the Court opined that although a sentencer can decide how much weight to give a mitigating factor, if any, a judge cannot exclude a mitigating factor from consideration. This case permitted the introduction of any evidence regarding a capital defendant's family history and background as mitigation.
- In *Skipper v. South Carolina* (1986), the Supreme Court concluded that mitigation evidence may include postoffense behavior. "Good adjustment" in jail while awaiting trial "might serve as a basis for a sentence less than death" (pp. 4–5).
- In *Atkins v. Virginia* (2002), the Court determined that defendants who meet the criteria for mental retardation were to be spared from the possibility of receiving the death penalty. Those who did not meet the criteria for mental retardation, but were still disabled, had their limited intellectual functioning deemed mitigating.
- In *Roper v. Simmons* (2005), the Court ruled that juveniles were to be exempt from the ultimate punishment. It ruled that the Eighth and Fourteenth Amendments forbid execution of persons who were under age 18 at the commission of the crime.

The Social History Investigation

The sentencing phase of a capital case is extremely complex, and many variables have to be considered on both sides. More often than not, defendants have an unusually high number of risk factors (see Table 9.2) that have hampered their development, adaptive functioning, and ability to make good choices in their lives. They have often been surrounded by crime, violence, and poverty, beginning in early childhood and continuing through adulthood. Many are products of a dysfunctional family; they suffer from psychological disorders and chronic substance abuse. In fact, clinical evaluations of

TABLE 9.2. U.S. Department of Justice Model: Predictors of Youth Violence

Individual psychological factors
- Hyperactivity, concentration problems, restlessness, and risk taking
- Aggressiveness
- Early initiation of violent behavior
- Involvement in other forms of antisocial behavior
- Beliefs and attitudes favorable to deviant or antisocial behavior

Family factors
- Parental criminality
- Child maltreatment
- Poor family management practices
- Low levels of parental involvement
- Poor family bonding and family conflict
- Parental attitudes favorable to substance abuse and violence
- Parent–child separation

School factors
- Academic failure
- Low bonding to school
- Truancy and dropping out of school
- Frequent school transitions

Peer-related factors
- Delinquent siblings
- Delinquent peers
- Gang membership

Community and neighborhood factors
- Poverty
- Community disorganization
- Availability of drugs and firearms
- Neighborhood adults involved in crimes
- Exposure to violence and racial prejudice

Note. From Hawkins et al. (2000).

death-row inmate samples have revealed a significant incidence of intellectual limitations, poor academic achievement, psychological disorders, neurological insult and neuropsychological impairment, family-of-origin histories of child maltreatment and abuse, parental substance dependence, and preincarceration substance dependence (Hawkins et al., 2000). Unfortunately, most capital defendants have very few "protective factors" (e.g., high level of education, good family background) to serve as buffers. All of this information must be investigated, compiled, and documented in the social history investigation.

Failure to perform a comprehensive social history investigation has been the cause of many reversals in capital cases. Indeed, attorneys may be deemed "ineffective counsel" due to a failure to investigate any and all mitigating factors. In two of the most recent cases, *Wiggins v. Smith* (2003) and *Rompilla v. Beard* (2005), the defense attorneys did not uncover and present relevant mitigating evidence that might have spared their clients' lives. As Justice Sandra Day O'Conner stated in *Wiggins*, "Had the jury been able to place petitioner's excruciating life history in the mitigation side of the scale, there is a reasonable probability that at least one juror would have struck a different balance" (p. 25).

The social history investigation strives to understand who the defendant is and how adverse risk factors impacted his life trajectory. Information is primarily gathered in one of two ways: through third-party interviews and extensive record collections. A simple rule is followed when deciding who should be interviewed and what documents should be collected: *everyone and everything!* Each fact in the history and each person in the past or present cannot be considered separately. Indeed, the cumulative effect of various risk and protective factors can only be understood by examining the material in a full, comprehensive manner. Often, it may not be possible to understand fully the importance and relevance of certain material and events until they have been gathered and reviewed in their entirety, and by all members of the legal team.

An example of this occurred with a case involving a death-eligible defendant. His many bouts of the flu, with high fever, ear infections, and seizures throughout his childhood, were well documented in the medical records. It would have been easy to disregard the relevance of the medical files if they had been considered as individual and separate events. However, when documented in a comprehensive, chronological fashion, the pattern of high fever and ear infections, with their possible mitigation implications (neglect in the home, neurologic disorder, etc.) became obvious and had a major impact on a number of jurors, leading them to spare the life of the defendant.

On some occasions the forensic social history investigator does not believe a particular record is significant, yet is informed of its value later on by one of the experts. For these reasons, *every* record is potentially important and should be passed on to the consulting experts, even if the social history investigator feels that they may not be all that significant in the final formulation of the experts' opinions. The basic data that should be gathered in every case include medical, mental health, social service agencies, academic, employment, military, and legal records. Indeed, any records that include information about any factors that might adversely affect the biopsychosocial and moral development of the defendant should be sought after, requested, and reviewed.

Significance of the Social History Investigation for the Expert

Reviewing previous medical records is obviously a necessary function of the expert, especially a neuropsychological expert. If the social history investigator has not provided them, it is very important that they are at least requested by the expert, and that this request is documented in the file in anticipation of rigorous cross-examination by a prosecuting attorney. A number of records are of particular interest to neuropsychological experts, especially those related to the medical, academic, and vocational histories of the defendant. These records have memorialized events as they occurred and are unencumbered by the defendant's real or alleged problems with faulty memory. Labor records of the biological mother, along with the birth records of the defendant, may contain invaluable information pertaining to any suspected trauma experienced by the defendant at birth. Often the Apgar score is easily obtained and may serve as credible evidence of possible central nervous system (CNS) injury. It is imperative that the expert review medical records from the defendant's hospitalizations secondary to motor vehicle accidents as a child, adolescent, or adult, including available records of statements from emergency medical technicians (EMTs), ambulance personnel, and witnesses; these kinds of records often require a separate request.

A large percentage of defendants in the criminal justice system have received various mental health services throughout their lives. It is important to remember that many of them have comorbid diagnoses, most often substance abuse/dependence and other *Diagnostic and Statistical Manual of Mental Disorders* (DSM-IV-TR; American Psychiatric Association, 2000) Axis I or II disorders. Once a defendant has been incarcerated following a murder, psychiatric diagnoses are often rendered as a result of a superficial, brief intake by a social worker or some other mental health professional, based solely on a defendant's self-report. Mental health records may be separate from the primary medical record in some prison systems and may require an FOI (Freedom of Information) release. Reviewing past mental health records is not only essential but it should also be done with a skeptic's eye. Often, the more inpatient psychiatric hospitalizations a defendant has had, the more inconsistent or unreliable the diagnoses. In a death penalty sentencing hearing, the goal is not to present a DSM-IV-TR diagnosis per se. Rather, the focus is on helping the jury understand how risk factors or an identified (neurological or psychiatric) impairment affected every aspect of the defendant's life and the subsequent choices he or she made throughout life.

Educational records provide details of a defendant's intellectual and academic functioning, originating early in life. These records are required by law to be kept for various numbers of years, depending on the state. In Illinois, the permanent file is kept for 60 years (usually in microfilm or, more recently, on CD-ROM). However, the temporary file, which contains the special education material, is required to be kept for only 7 years and will certainly not be available if the defendant has been out of school for a while. Whereas available records may provide documentation and evidence of disturbances mitigating to the defendant, collateral interviews with third parties are also extremely important. Along with anecdotes about temperament, intelligence, and behavioral patterns, family, friends, teachers, and employers can also provide insight into the possible changes that may have occurred in the defendant's personality over time (after an accident, following the loss of a parent, etc.).

For example, a defendant had been in an automobile accident 6 years before the offense. He was a passenger in a car that rolled over at least five times. He was rendered unconscious, and the initial Glasgow Coma Scale (GCS) score at the scene was 7 (*severe*). Acute magnetic resonance imaging (MRI) of the brain showed no evidence of intracranial lesion(s), but the defendant continued to have severe headaches and reported problems with his memory for many years afterward. Witnesses were able to provide details of significant changes in his personality and temperament. Indeed, it was quite clear that the defendant's life began a "downward spiral" shortly after the accident. Within 5 years of the crash, he had been charged with first-degree murder and was facing the death penalty. Before the accident, he had no criminal history whatsoever. This is the type of case in which a neuropsychological consultant can be particularly helpful. Indeed, a history of real or alleged TBI represents the most common scenario in which a neuropsychologist is consulted, followed by substance abuse/dependence, learning disabilities, and ADHD. Again, defendants' histories frequently include multiple events, disorders, and conditions to be examined alone and in combination: The social history investigator (more than the attorney) is usually the person responsible for understanding the totality of a defendant's life.

Bringing the Expert on Board

Timing

Although not always possible, the majority of a defendant's life history should already be assembled when a neuropsychological expert is retained to work on the case. However, that does not mean it is acceptable to retain an expert on the heels of opening statements. Optimal timing is when the multigenerational social history investigation is near completion and well before the trial is to begin. Indeed, an expert's ability to perform his or her job may be adversely affected if the team has not completed these tasks beforehand. One such essential task is gaining the defendant's trust. If the defendant does not trust the defense team (including the attorney), it is unlikely that he or she will trust the expert. The results can be drastic, varying from a noncooperative defendant to one that provides misleading, inaccurate information and severely compromises the team's efforts to obtain a more positive outcome (usually a life sentence vs. death).

Role

The defense team should understand each expert's role and have created specific referral questions to provide direction and focus. However, sometimes an expert is asked to go on a "fishing expedition," without much direction, to uncover things that may not be all that apparent to the other members of the team. The team may just be looking for anything to use in mitigation when it is fairly obvious that the client will undoubtedly be found guilty. Experts must understand that the evidence they uncover is not an excuse for the crime. Indeed, mitigation is conceptualized as an *explanation* for the path the defendant has traveled, a path that eventually led to the crime. It may also serve as a foundation for mercy and empathy.

The expert is retained *not* to provide a specific opinion but to provide the truth. Whether that truth helps or hurts the case is irrelevant. In numerous instances a neuropsychologist is retained only to discover that his or her test results indicate nothing abnormal or significant. Even more compelling are cases in which the defendant is determined to be malingering cognitive dysfunction or mental illness. In such cases, the expert may no longer be utilized, or the results may be configured into the mitigation theme in some other unexpected way. Regardless, the expert should not accede to pressure to provide a specific finding just to satisfy the theory of the defense team. Indeed, neutrality and honesty are essential elements of the expert's credibility on the stand in the present and future cases.

Mitigation assessments, including those that emphasize psychological and neuropsychological issues, should take into consideration a wide range of biopsychosocial factors. For this reason, they are usually broader and more comprehensive than other types of forensic assessments (Cunningham & Reidy, 2001; Liebert & Foster, 1994). Any and all factors that might negatively affect the physical, cognitive, psychological, neuropsychological, interpersonal, social, academic, vocational, civic, and moral development of the defendant should be considered (Cunningham & Goldstein, 2003). Rather than a focus on interviewing the defendant about the circumstances surrounding the crime, the emphasis is on obtaining a highly detailed, anecdotal, "multigenerational biopsychosocial" history. Most of this has been done by the forensic social history investigator or the forensic psychologist. Thus, the neuropsychologist is freed up to interview the defendant about historical events of particular relevance to his or her neuropsychological status and how it relates to the legal issue at hand (for a more extended discussion on the different roles of the neuropsychologist and forensic psychologist in criminal cases, see Heilbronner & Frumkin, 2003).

The history provided by the defendant should be confirmed by collateral examination or validated via available records, usually by the forensic social history investigator. Often, defendants do not remember their childhood medical histories, how many times they were admitted to the hospital, whether they lost consciousness when they were assaulted as an adolescent, and so forth. They may also be defensive or reluctant to admit to past events or shortcomings. This places some limitations on the quality and quantity of information that can be obtained. Although such information is potentially helpful to their case, defendants often do not want to admit to a history of learning difficulties, possible mental retardation, and other seemingly pejorative types of conditions.

Qualifications

The expert should be credible and able to speak clearly to the jury. Unfortunately, an expert begins testifying at a disadvantage. By and large, jurors are skeptical of expert testimony, particularly in capital cases. Many of them adhere to the misconception that experts are "hired guns," willing to render conclusions that have been "bought" by the prosecution or defense. To correct jurors' misperceptions, experts must first be aware that these misperceptions may exist. It is important for the attorney to spend some time during direct testimony to reveal the expert's experience and credentials. Explaining the significance of each credential (e.g., board certification, relevant publications, experience in criminal cases) helps the jury understand that the neuropsychologist is indeed an expert (i.e., possesses knowledge, skill, or experience beyond that of the average juror or layperson). It also provides a framework for the jurors in comprehending the high costs associated with the expert's work and testimony.

There have been occasions (often popularized by the local press) when an expert's credibility is completely destroyed because of misrepresentations during testimony or sometimes even an innocent oversight on a curriculum vitae. One such expert taught as a part-time, adjunct professor at a local college for a number of years. When he left that position, he did not place it in the chronological order in his curriculum vitae. Although it may have been a simple oversight on his part, his credibility was destroyed on cross-examination, when the prosecuting attorney made it appear that he was lying; the jury had a difficult time trusting him or believing his opinions.

An expert's credibility is bolstered when the jury appreciates that he or she has performed an exhaustive review of all the documentation. The review must be comprehensive and the time spent examining the defendant must be lengthy. It is not good practice to administer an abbreviated test (e.g., IQ test) when the defendant is facing death. The use of short forms of tests is also strongly discouraged. Typically, a comprehensive psychological or neuropsychological evaluation lasts many hours, sometimes days. Obtaining a comprehensive, detailed history usually requires 8–20 hours of interview with the defendant, exclusive of any testing (Cunningham & Goldstein, 2003). Often, this is done by the mitigation specialist, or by a forensic psychologist, if one has been retained (Heilbronner & Frumkin, 2003). Because neuropsychologists most often focus exclusively on neuropsychological issues, they typically do not spend as many hours interviewing the defendant. Instead, their time is devoted to an objective and comprehensive assessment of multiple neurocognitive domains and structured personality inventories (if there is no other mental health expert on the team). Jurors dismiss information they do not understand. For this reason, an expert must be clear, both in style and message. The expert must teach the jurors, explaining the issues as if to a junior high school classroom, but without being condescending. If jurors do not understand the jargon, they will miss the point. If they do not like the expert, they will not consider the message. In many ways, it is like theater: The expert performs for the jury in a way that looks effortless and genuine, yet at the same time convincing.

Foundation for Neuropsychological Consultation

Research and clinical evidence suggest a high incidence of neurological disorders among murderers and violent offenders (Blake, Pincus, & Buckner, 1995; Martell, 1992) and death row samples (Cunningham & Vigen, 2002; Lewis et al., 1988; Lewis, Pincus, Feldman, Jackson, & Bard, 1986). For this reason, neurological and neuropsychological consultations are indicated in most capital cases. In fact, their inclusion should probably be automatic in all capital cases. According to Cunningham and Goldstein (2003), this conclusion is based on two primary rationales. First, should neuropsychological deficits or a neurological disorder be identified, the brain dysfunction and its potential association with violent acts may be a significant mitigating factor in a jury's deliberation. Second, a growing body of research identifies brain dysfunction (especially in the frontal and temporal lobes) as a risk factor for serious violence. Medical conditions that affect brain function and are often associated with violence include fetal maldevelopment; elevated testosterone, serotonin, and cortisol levels; premenstrual syndrome; and others (Raine, 1993; see Barr, Chapter 8, this volume).

An often asked question is, "Does a neuropsychological evaluation used for mitigation purposes differ from that used in other circumstances?" In theory, there really should not be a strong difference between an evaluation used for an ordinary purpose versus one used for forensic matters, except for the particular psycholegal issue at hand. It may, of course, differ in a number of ways from an evaluation used for clinical purposes, especially the inclusion of multiple measures of symptom validity/effort (Denney & Wynkoop, 2000; National Academy of Neuropsychology, 2005). Beyond that, the evaluation should be comprehensive and assess multiple neurocognitive domains with reliable and valid neuropsychological measures. Particular emphasis should be directed toward areas of the brain (e.g., frontal and temporal) that have a demonstrated relationship to violence, impulsivity, poor judgment, and so forth. Outside of the Wisconsin Card Sorting Test (WCST; Berg, 1948), the Category Test (Reitan & Wolfson, 1985), the Trail Making Test (Reitan & Wolfson, 1985), and tests of verbal fluency, not many standardized measures have proven to be sensitive to frontal lobe pathology, especially in criminal defendants. Furthermore, the specificity and sensitivity of these instruments as measures of frontal lobe dysfunction are not excellent (Alvarez & Emory, 2006). The Delis–Kaplan Executive Function System (D-KEFS; Delis, Kaplan, & Kramer, 2001) is being used by many neuropsychologists who are involved in mitigation assessments; however, many of the resultant scores (including the primary and optional scores) appear to have questionable reliability and validity.

Beyond standardized neuropsychological testing, frontal and temporal lobe dysfunction may sometimes be inferred from a history of behavioral alterations, previous episodes of violence, poor judgment, and so forth. Of course, such events do not inherently mean that the defendant has sustained frontal or temporal lobe damage. Indeed, most individuals with documented damage in these parts of the brain do not engage in violence, murder, and so forth.

Another question that the neuropsychologist must consider is, "Should personality testing be included as part of a neuropsychological evaluation for mitigation purposes?" There is no hard-and-fast rule. A forensic psychologist's comprehensive assessment typically includes standardized (and less often, projective) personality instruments. In this situation, the neuropsychologist likely focuses exclusively on the neurocognitive and effort domains and not on personality testing (Heilbronner & Frumkin, 2003). If a forensic psychologist is not included as part of the team, then the neuropsychologist must decide, in consultation with the attorney, the pros and cons of doing a thorough personality assessment. On the one hand, the incidence of psychological disorders among murder defendants (Blake et al., 1995), as well as death-row inmates (Cunningham & Vigen, 2002), suggests that careful screening for major psychological disorders could be important to mitigation considerations. Does that mean including the Minnesota Multiphasic Personality Inventory–2 (MMPI-2; Butcher, Dahlstrom, Graham, Tellegen, & Kaemmer, 1989) or Personality Assessment Inventory (PAI; Morey, 1991)? No doubt, the answer requires familiarity with the reliability and validity of these instruments in general, and with a correctional population more specifically.

Defense attorneys often do not want the MMPI-2 administered in criminal assessments generally and in mitigation assessments more specifically, because it often reveals a 4-9 (antisocial personality disorder [ASPD]) type of profile. They fear that it will fuel the prosecution's position that the defendant has ASPD—something that would be looked upon negatively by the jury. However, it is important to point out that other types of conditions or response styles, besides ASPD, may result in a 4-9 type of profile. In fact, the DSM-IV-TR includes for consideration adult antisocial behavior under "Additional Considerations That May be a Focus of Clinical Attention." This category can be used when the focus of clinical attention is on adult antisocial behavior that is not due to a mental disorder (e.g., conduct disorder, ASPD, or impulse control disorder). There are a number of hypothesized causes of adult antisocial behavior, many of which are similar to the risk factors identified in Table 9.2, including sociological causes (e.g., peer pressure, use/abuse of alcohol and drugs, availability of handguns); family characteristics (absence of mothering, lack of parenting skills, alcohol and drugs in the parents); physical abuse (as a model for behavior, a source of injury to the child's CNS or impaired ability to control impulses and function in society); constitutional factors (history of accidents, CNS injuries, mental retardation, ADHD, etc.); and clinical signs and symptom (abnormal EEGs, soft neurological signs, neuropsychological deficits, etc.). Indeed, as Lewis (1989) has suggested:

> ... anything that affects the CNS in such a way as to diminish a person's appreciation of reality, capacity to think logically, and control of their impulses and emotions will compromise social functioning. Clearly, there is no single cause of recurrent, aggressive, anti-social behavior. Most neurologically impaired, physically abused, socioeconomically disadvantaged, psychiatrically disturbed, and intellectually retarded people are neither criminal nor aggressive. But, as evidence accumulates, it is clear that much recurrent anti-social behavior is the final common pathway of the interaction of these kinds of biopsychosocial vulnerabilities. (p. 1403)

To ascertain whether a neuropsychological evaluation is warranted in any particular case, it is important to consider the value derived from retaining such an expert. Neuropsychological evidence has clearly been shown to be of value in the forensic arena in general and in criminal cases more specifically (Heilbronner & Pliskin, 2003). If a defense attorney is going to argue that the defendant's brain dysfunction is a mitigating factor for the judge or jury to consider in sentencing, then it must be shown *by reliable and valid evidence*. The causal link between the documented brain damage and subsequent alterations in behavior that led to the alleged criminal behavior should be developed to the fullest extent. It may help the judge or jury to understand that brain damage is one of many risk factors that underlies the violent behavior of the defendant, and that the murder was not wholly the product of a willful choice, but was shaped, influenced, and compromised by a host of biopsychosocial factors. In essence, it may serve to reduce the "moral culpability" of the defendant (*Woodson v. North Carolina*, 1976).

One of the values of a neuropsychological assessment in sentencing is that it can provide the trier of fact with a normative description of the defendant's neurobehavioral strengths and weaknesses. It brings to the forefront quantified data on brain–behavior relationships that may be much more compelling than opinions based on mental status exams or clinical interviews. As an example, stating that the defendant scored at the 2nd percentile on the WCST may not mean all that much to a jury. But stating that "the defendant's score on a task requiring higher level, conceptual reasoning skills was so low that 98% of the population scored higher than he did" puts things in a clearer perspective. Relating his score on this test to his behavior in the real world is even more important. Indeed, in preparing a neuropsychological report or testifying before a judge or jury in a capital case, it is vitally important that the expert go beyond simply listing the test scores, percentiles, and so forth. For example, consider the following statement:

> It is abundantly clear, based upon a review of the defendant's history, my review of the records, interview of the defendant, and in consideration of the impairments he demonstrated on neuropsychological testing, that the moderate to severe deficits he demonstrates on tasks requiring higher-level reasoning skills is a problem that he has been plagued by ever since he was a young child. They appear to be a product of the multiple head traumas he sustained as a result of repeated episodes of abuse as a young boy. Indeed, he clearly showed these types of thinking difficulties in grade school, during his previous incarcerations at the juvenile facilities he was placed in, and in all aspects of his life. He does not appear to possess the capacity to reason and problem-solve at an age-appropriate level, and his impaired judgment and decision-making skills are one—and certainly a vital one of many—risk factors that contributed to delinquency throughout his life.

These kinds of statements are not an excuse for the crime, but they provide an important perspective as to how other forces have shaped the defendant's behavior over time.

In closing, a neuropsychologist, skilled in translating the results of neuropsychological testing to the real world, can provide useful information to a jury in the context of a host of other events from the life story of the defendant that may prove to be critical in the final determination of life or death. There are very few comparable situations in which neuropsychology plays such a vital and irrevocable role.

References

Alvarez, J. A., & Emory, E. (2006). Executive function and the frontal lobes: A meta-analytic review. *Neuropsychology Review, 16*, 17–42.

American Bar Association. (2003). *Guidelines for the appointment and performance of defense counsel in death penalty cases: Revised edition.* Chicago: Author.

American Psychiatric Association. (2000). *Diagnostic and statistical manual of mental disorders* (4th ed., text rev.). Washington, DC: Author.

Atkins v. Virginia, 536 US 304 (2002).

Berg, E. A. (1948). A simple objective technique for measuring flexibility in thinking. *Journal of General Psychology, 39*, 15–22.

Blake, P., Pincus, J., & Buckner, C. (1995). Neurologic abnormalities in murderers. *Neurology, 45*, 1641–1647.

Butcher, J. N., Dahlstrom, W. G., Graham, J. R., Tellegan, A., & Kaemmer, B. (1989). *Manual for administration and scoring of the MMPI-2.* Minneapolis: University of Minnesota Press.

Cunningham, M. D., & Goldstein, A. M. (2003). Sentencing determinations in death penalty cases. In A. Goldstein (Ed.), *Handbook of psychology: Vol. 11. Forensic psychology.* Hoboken, NJ: Wiley.

Cunningham, M. D., & Reidy, T. J. (2001). A matter of life or death: Special considerations and heightened practice standards in capital sentencing evaluations. *Behavioral Sciences and the Law, 19*, 473–490.

Cunningham, M. D., & Vigen, M. P. (2002). Death row inmate characteristics, adjustment, and confinement: A critical review of the literature. *Behavioral Sciences and the Law, 20*, 191–210.

Delis, D. G., Kaplan, E., & Kramer, J. H. (2001). *Delis–Kaplan Executive Function System.* San Antonio, TX: Psychological Corporation.

Denney, R. L., & Wynkoop, T. F. (2000). Clinical neuropsychology in the criminal forensic setting. *Journal of Head Trauma Rehabilitation, 15*(2), 804–828.

Eddings v. Oklahoma, 436 U.S. 921 (1978).

Eisenberg, J. R. (1999, November). *The role of the forensic psychologist in death penalty mitigation.* Workshop presented for the American Academy of Forensic Psychology, Chicago.

Hawkins, J. D., Herrenkohl, T. I., Farrington, D. P., Brewer, D., Catalano, R. F., Harachi, T. W., et al. (2000, April). *Predictors of youth violence.* Washington, DC: U.S. Department of Justice.

Heilbronner, R. L., & Frumkin, I. B. (2003). Neuropsychology and forensic psychology: Working collaboratively in criminal cases. *Journal of Forensic Neuropsychology, 3*(3), 5–12.

Heilbronner, R. L., & Pliskin, N. H. (2003). Clinical neuropsychology in the forensic arena. In G. P. Prigatano & N. H. Pliskin (Eds.), *Clinical neuropsychology and cost outcome research: A beginning.* Brighton, UK: Psychology Press.

Hitchcock v. Dugger, 481 U.S. 393 (1986).

Illinois General Assembly. Statute defining Power/Duties of the Office of the State Appellate Defender, 725 ILCS 105/10(c)(5).

Lewis, D., Pincus, J. H., Bard, B., Richardson, E., Prichep, L. S., Feldman, M., et al. (1988). Neuropsychiatric, psychoeducational, and family characteristics of 14 juveniles condemned to death in the United States. *American Journal of Psychiatry, 145,* 584–589.

Lewis, D., Pincus, J. H., Feldman, M., Jackson, L., & Bard, B. (1986). Psychiatric, neurological, and psychoeducational characteristics of 15 death row inmates in the United States. *American Journal of Psychiatry, 143,* 838–845.

Lewis, D. O. (1989). Adult antisocial behavior and criminality. In H. I. Kaplan & B. A. Sadock (Eds.) *Comprehensive textbook of psychiatry* (5th ed., Vol. 2, pp. 1400–1403). Baltimore: Williams & Wilkins.

Liebert, D. S., & Foster, M. D. (1994). The mental health evaluation in capital cases: Standards of practice. *American Journal of Forensic Psychiatry, 15,* 43–64.

Lockett v. Ohio, 438 U.S. 586 (1978).

Martell, D. (1992). Estimating the prevalence of organic brain dysfunction in maximum-security forensic psychiatric patients. *Journal of Forensic Sciences, 37,* 878–893.

Morey, L. C. (1991). *The Personality Assessment Inventory: Professional manual.* Lutz, FL: Psychological Assessment Resources.

National Academy of Neuropsychology. (2005). Symptom validity assessment: Practice issues and medical necessity. *Archives of Clinical Neuropsychology, 20,* 419–426.

Raine, A. (1993). *The psychopathology of crime: Criminal behavior as a clinical disorder.* San Diego, CA: Academic Press.

Reitan, R. M., & Wolfson, D. (1985). *The Halstead–Reitan Neuropsychological Test Battery: Theory and clinical interpretation.* Tucson, AZ: Neuropsychology Press.

Ring v. Arizona (No. 01-488), 536 U.S. 584 (2002).

Rompilla v. Beard, 545 U.S. 355 F.3d 233 (2005).

Roper v. Simmons, 543 U.S. 551 (2005).

Skipper v. South Carolina, 512 U.S. 154 (1994).

Wiggins v. Smith, 539 U.S. 510 (2003).

Woodson v. North Carolina, 428 U.S. 280 (1976).

APPENDIX 9.1. Case Summaries

Ohio v. Lockett

❖ **Date of decision by the U.S. Supreme Court**: July 3, 1978
❖ **Nature of the case**: Individualized mitigation
❖ **Facts of the case**: Sandra Lockett was found guilty of murder in Ohio. She had encouraged and driven the getaway car for a robbery that resulted in the murder of a pawnshop owner. After being found guilty she was sentenced to death.

An Ohio law required that individuals found guilty of aggravated murder be given the death penalty. The death penalty was mandatory unless (1) the victim had induced the offense, (2) the offense was committed under duress or coercion, or (3) the offense was a product of mental deficiencies.

The statute prohibited the Judge from considering mitigating factors at sentencing.

❖ **Issue**: Did the Ohio law violate Lockett's Constitutional rights by limiting the consideration of mitigating factors?

❖ **Holding and rationale**: Yes. The Supreme Court held that the Eighth and Fourteenth Amendments required, in all but the rarest capital cases, that the triers of fact be allowed to consider a number of mitigating factors before imposing the death penalty. These factors included any aspect of a defendant's character or record and any circumstances of the offense proffered as a reason for a sentence less than death. The Supreme Court held that the Ohio statute did not permit the type of individualized consideration of mitigating factors required by the Constitution.

Eddings v. Oklahoma

❖ **Date of decision by the U.S. Supreme Court**: January 19, 1982
❖ **Nature of the case**: Individualized mitigation and chronological age as a mitigating factor
❖ **Facts of the case**: On April 4, 1977, Monty Lee Eddings, a 16-year-old youth, and several younger friends ran away from their homes in Missouri. They drove Eddings's brother's car until they reached the Oklahoma Turnpike. Eddings had several rifles and a shotgun that he had taken from his father. Due to a traffic infraction, he was signaled to pull over by Officer Crabtree of the Oklahoma Highway Patrol. Eddings did so, and when the officer approached the car, Eddings stuck a loaded shotgun out of the window and fired, killing the officer.

Monty Lee Eddings was convicted in an Oklahoma trial court of first-degree murder for killing a police officer and sentenced to death. At the time of the offense the petitioner was 16 years old, but he was tried as an adult. The Oklahoma death penalty statute provides that in a sentencing proceeding, evidence may be presented as to "any mitigating circumstances" or as to any of certain enumerated aggravating circumstances. At the sentencing hearing, the State alleged certain of the enumerated aggravating circumstances, and Eddings, in mitigation, presented substantial evidence of a turbulent family history, of beatings by a harsh father, and of serious emotional disturbance.

The trial judge imposed a sentence of death and found that the State had proved each of the alleged aggravating circumstances. But he refused, as a matter of law, to consider in mitigation the circumstances of the petitioner's unhappy upbringing and emotional disturbance, and found that the only mitigating circumstance was the petitioner's youth, which circumstance was held to be insufficient to outweigh the aggravating circumstances.

* **Issue**: Did the trial judge err in not considering mitigation regarding Edding's history put forth by Eddings's attorneys in the sentencing phase?

* **Holding and rationale**: Yes. Monty Lee Eddings was convicted of first-degree murder and sentenced to death. Because this sentence was imposed without "the type of individualized consideration of mitigating factors . . . required by the Eighth and Fourteenth Amendments in capital cases, *Lockett v. Ohio*, we reverse."

Skipper v. South Carolina

* **Date of decision by the U.S. Supreme Court**: April 29, 1986
* **Nature of the case**: Mitigation evidence to be allowed for consideration; individualized mitigation
* **Facts of the case**: Ronald Skipper was convicted in a South Carolina trial court of capital murder and rape. The State sought the death penalty, and a separate sentencing hearing was held before the trial jury. Skipper's attorneys presented as mitigating evidence the defendant's own testimony and that of his former wife, his mother, his sister, and his grandmother. He then sought to introduce testimony of two jailers and a "regular visitor" to the effect that Skipper had "made a good adjustment" during the 7½ months he had spent in jail between his arrest and trial. The trial court ruled such evidence irrelevant and inadmissible, and the petitioner was sentenced to death.
* **Issue**: Did the court commit a constitutional error by not allowing the testimony regarding Skipper's conduct in jail to be presented and considered during sentencing?
* **Holding and rationale**: Yes. The trial court's exclusion of testimony denied his rights to present all relevant evidence in mitigation. The right to do so was established in *Ohio v. Lockett* and *Eddings v. Oklahoma*.

Atkins v. Virginia

* **Date of decision by the U.S. Supreme Court**: June 20, 2002
* **Nature of the case**: Execution of the mentally retarded
* **Facts of the case**: Daryl Renard Atkins was convicted of abduction, armed robbery, and capital murder. In the penalty phase of Atkins's trial, the defense relied on one witness and a forensic psychologist. The psychologist testified that Atkins was mildly mentally retarded. The jury sentenced Atkins to death.

The Virginia Supreme Court ordered a second sentencing hearing, because the trial court had used a misleading verdict form. During resentencing, the same forensic psychologist testified, but this time the State rebutted Atkins's intelligence. The jury again sentenced Atkins to death. The Virginia Supreme Court rejected Atkins's contention that he could not be sentenced to death because he was mentally retarded.

❖ **Issue:** Is the execution of mentally retarded persons "cruel and unusual punishment" prohibited by the Eighth Amendment?

❖ **Holding and rationale:** Yes. The Supreme Court held that executions of mentally retarded criminals are "cruel and unusual punishments," prohibited by the Eighth Amendment. Since it last confronted the issue, the Court reasoned that a significant number of States have concluded that death is not a suitable punishment for a mentally retarded criminal. Moreover, the Court concluded that there was serious concern whether either justification underpinning the death penalty—retribution and deterrence of capital crimes—applies to mentally retarded offenders, due to their lessened culpability.

"Construing and applying the Eighth Amendment in the light of our evolving standards of decency, we therefore conclude that such punishment is excessive and that the Constitution places a substantive restriction on the State's power to take the life of a mentally retarded offender," wrote Justice Stevens.

Roper v. Simmons

❖ **Date of decision by the U.S. Supreme Court:** March 1, 2005

❖ **Nature of the case:** Execution of juvenile offenders

❖ **Facts of the case:** Christopher Simmons was sentenced to death in 1993, when he was only 17 years old, in Missouri. A series of appeals to state and federal courts lasted until 2002, but each appeal was rejected. Then, in 2002, the Missouri Supreme Court stayed Simmons's execution while the U.S. Supreme Court decided *Atkins v. Virginia.*

Using the reasoning from the Atkins case, the Missouri court decided, 6 to 3, that the U.S. Supreme Court's 1989 decision in *Stanford v. Kentucky,* which held that executing minors was not unconstitutional, was no longer valid.

The opinion in *Stanford v. Kentucky* had relied on a finding that a majority of Americans did not consider the execution of minors to be cruel and unusual. The Missouri court, citing numerous laws passed since 1989 that limited the scope of the death penalty, held that national opinion had changed. Finding that a majority of Americans were now opposed to the execution of minors, the court held that such executions were now unconstitutional.

❖ **Issue:** Does the execution of minors violate the prohibition of "cruel and unusual punishment" found in the Eighth Amendment?

❖ **Holding and rationale:** Yes. The Court ruled that standards of decency have evolved so that executing minors is "cruel and unusual punishment" prohibited by the Eighth Amendment. The majority cited a consensus against the juvenile death penalty among state legislatures, and its own determination that the death penalty is a disproportionate punishment for minors. Finally the Court pointed to "overwhelming" international opinion against the juvenile death penalty.

Wiggins v. Smith

❖ **Date of decision by the U.S. Supreme Court**: March 24, 2003
❖ **Nature of the case**: Ineffective assistance of counsel for failure to investigate mitigation
❖ **Facts of the case**: Kevin Wiggins was convicted and sentenced to death for a 1988 murder in Maryland. He appealed, claiming that his attorneys' decision not to tell jurors about Wiggins's troubled childhood amounted to ineffective counsel, because it resulted in a harsher sentence. Prosecutors countered that the attorneys' decision had been carefully considered, and that a different decision would not necessarily have resulted in a different outcome. Therefore, they said, it was not ineffective counsel.
❖ **Issue**: Does a criminal defendant's attorneys' failure to investigate his background and present mitigating evidence of his unfortunate life history at his capital sentencing proceedings constitute ineffective assistance of counsel?
❖ **Holding and rationale**: Yes. The Supreme Court held that the performance of Wiggins's attorneys at sentencing violated his Sixth Amendment right to effective assistance of counsel. The Court reasoned that Wiggins's counsel did not conduct a reasonable investigation because, among other things, standard practice in Maryland in 1989 included the preparation of a social history report, which his attorneys did not commission even though the necessary funds were available. The Court concluded that Wiggins's counsels' failures prejudiced his defense.

"Had the jury been able to place [Wiggins's] excruciating life history on the mitigating side of the scale, there is a reasonable probability that at least one juror would have struck a different balance," wrote Justice O'Connor.

Rompilla v. Beard

❖ **Date of decision by the U.S. Supreme Court**: June 20, 2005
❖ **Nature of the case**: Ineffective assistance of counsel for failing to investigate
❖ **Facts of the case**: A Pennsylvania court convicted Ronald Rompilla of murder. During the sentencing phase, the prosecution presented to the jury Rompilla's previous rape and assault conviction, as an aggravating factor to justify the death sentence. They gave notice to Rompilla's attorneys of their intent to do so during aggravation. The jury sentenced Rompilla to death and the State Supreme Court affirmed.

Rompilla's new lawyers filed an additional appeal, arguing that Rompilla's trial counsel had been ineffective for failing to present mitigating evidence about his various personal problems. The state courts found that Rompilla's counsel had sufficiently investigated mitigation possibilities. After Rompilla filed a federal *habeas cor-*

pus petition, a district court reversed the sentence and ruled that the State Supreme Court had unreasonably applied the U.S. Supreme Court's 1984 decision in *Strickland v. Washington*. Had the state court followed that case, the district court ruled, the court would have found Rompilla's trial counsel ineffective for failing to investigate obvious signs of Rompilla's troubled childhood, mental illness, and alcoholism. The 3rd Circuit reversed.

❖ **Issue**: Did the Sixth Amendment right to effective counsel require Rompilla's counsel to try to obtain material that counsel knew the prosecution would probably use at the trial's sentencing phase?

❖ **Holding and rationale**: Yes. The Supreme Court held that Rompilla's trial counsel was ineffective for failing to make reasonable efforts to examine the file on Rompilla's prior conviction for rape and assault. Moreover, counsel had known the prosecution would probably present the prior conviction to the jury during sentencing. In that file, counsel would have found mitigating evidence about Rompilla's troubled childhood and mental health.

Chapter 10

Neuropsychology in the Juvenile Justice System

TIMOTHY F. WYNKOOP

As Tom Grisso (1998a) aptly states, "Few clinicians begin their careers intending to become experts in performing evaluations for the juvenile justice system" (p. iii). I agree with this anecdotal, yet well-informed, observation and believe that it includes neuropsychologists who serve the juvenile justice system as well. Regardless of the how the neuropsychologist comes to serve the juvenile justice system, he or she needs to acquire the requisite competence prior to independently serving any of the 1.5 million cases processed by juvenile courts annually. Most readers are probably aware of the dearth of literature on the application of neuropsychology to juvenile justice.

My aim in this chapter is to help interested neuropsychologists begin the process of acquiring competence in the application of neuropsychology to the juvenile justice system (i.e., juvenile forensic neuropsychology). The task is broad and daunting, because juvenile justice (which serves children, adolescents, and adults) is more complex than its criminal justice counterpart (which serves adults and juveniles tried as adults). For example, whereas the legal designation *juvenile* generally means anyone under the age of 18 not being transferred to criminal court, juvenile court jurisdiction can reach into adulthood. Three common examples of juvenile court jurisdiction over adults are when a juvenile offender receives a disposition that extends beyond the age of 18 (which in some states can extend into the mid-20s); when juvenile or family courts order evaluation and/or intervention for parents of a juvenile in some form of distress (e.g., delinquency, neglect, abuse); or when an adult contributes to the delinquency of a minor. Larger jurisdictions in metropolitan areas sometimes relegate the latter two examples to a family court division, whereas smaller, typically rural, jurisdictions may have only one court to serve all of these matters.

Furthermore, in the context of a serious youthful offender and potential blended sentence, and/or potential transfer to adult court, determining juvenile adjudicative competence can be far more cumbersome and complex than determining competence to stand trial in adult court (e.g., Barnum, 2000; see also Wynkoop, 2003). There is also great diversity in the practices of juvenile courts across and within jurisdictions, more so than in criminal courts, sometimes making generalizations difficult.

The assumption that most readers of this book have basic knowledge of the application of neuropsychology to criminal justice constitutes the basis for my approach to the application of neuropsychology to juvenile justice in this chapter. Consequently, I emphasize delinquency (i.e., the juvenile analogue to crime), as opposed to status offenses, custody issues, and so forth, and use criminal justice as a reference point whenever it is expedient to do so. I discuss juvenile justice in the United States (i.e., origin, philosophical issues, relevant case law, procedure), points of neuropsychological service to juvenile justice, relevant developmental issues (e.g., general maturation, adolescent general psychopathology, neuropsychology of delinquency), types of neuropsychological assessments in juvenile justice (including malingered cognitive deficit), and ethics (i.e., professional competence, personal professional development, informed consent, court-ordered evaluations). I then conclude with a call for neuropsychological input into juvenile justice policy decisions.

This chapter is intended to be a primer to provide a conceptual framework within which to apply one's knowledge of child development, pediatric neuropsychological assessment, and basic criminal procedure in service to the juvenile justice system. By the end of this chapter readers should be able to appreciate the complexity of service to the juvenile justice system, and the complexity and breadth of clinical and forensic skills needed to serve children in the justice system. Ultimately, I hope to help readers increase their level of competence and standard of practice in juvenile justice.

Juvenile Justice in the United States
Differences between Criminal and Juvenile Justice

Major differences between the criminal and juvenile justice systems are created by adversarial versus parental (*parens patriae* or "state as parent") processes, or punishment versus rehabilitation (or habilitation) for adults and juveniles, respectively. The distinction between punishment and rehabilitation for juveniles has not always existed in our law, and has seemingly failed over the past 20 years, causing statutory revisions that blur the lines of distinction between the two systems in some respects. A brief history of juvenile justice in the United States should foster further appreciation of its complexity.

Evolution of Juvenile Justice in the United States

The history of juvenile justice in the United States fits neatly into three broad epochs (Green, Heilbrun, Fortune, & Nietzel, 2006; Grisso, 1998a). The first epoch was pre-20th century, when our courts treated older children as adults, punitively. The common law from England, as it evolved in Colonial America, treated children under the age of 7 in the same manner as it treated insane persons, as not culpable for their own actions. Children between ages 7 and 14 were afforded some protection, in that the prosecution needed to prove that the child knew what he or she was doing at the time of the commission of the offense and that his or her behavior was wrong (i.e., analogous to M'Naghten). Children age 14 and older were treated as adults (Lou, 1927).

In 1899, the first juvenile court in the United States was established in Chicago by the Illinois legislature, with the mandate to correct, rather than to punish, wayward children (Greene et al., 2006; see Mack, 1909, for a more contemporaneous perspective). This began the second epoch, and coincided with the establishment of child labor laws and compulsory education for children, part of a broader societal context of child-related reforms (Bakan, 1972). In little better than the first half of the 1900s, all states except three had established juvenile courts. New rules and terminology were adopted that avoided the pejorative connotations of the criminal justice system. For example, there were status offenses (i.e., based on one's status as a juvenile; e.g., running away from home), and delinquency (i.e., acts that would be considered criminal for adults). Reform schools replaced prisons for the most incorrigible children.

The emphasis on rehabilitation instead of punishment permitted the juvenile courts to dispose of cases rather informally (e.g., with guidance from an officer of the court, remanding the child to the care of parents, requiring mental health intervention). However, this informality did not serve to protect children's procedural due process when more punitive measures were employed by the court. This led the U.S. Supreme Court to affirm (some may say *establish*) due process protections for juveniles (e.g., *Kent v. United States* [1966], *In re Gault* [1967], and *In re Winship* [1970] described below), which also had the untoward effect of promoting adversariness in many juvenile hearings (particularly *Gault* and *Winship*; see Feld, 1997).

The third epoch of juvenile justice history came about as the result of a wave of violent juvenile crime that occurred in the mid-1980s and led to legislative actions stiffening the penalties for delinquency, with the intention to increase community protection from violent youth (see Grisso, 1996, 1998a; Woolard, 2002). These legislative changes occurred in the wake of the adversarial consequences of *Kent*, *Gault*, and *Winship*, and also in the perceived failure of the juvenile justice system to live up to its promise of rehabilitation (see Green et al., 2006; Grisso, 1996). Examples of these changes include (1) stiffer, more punitive sentences for juveniles (Melton, Petrila, Poythress, & Slobogin, 1997), and (2) increased frequency of statutory and judicial transfers to criminal courts for children (typically, age 13 and older, although some jurisdictions allow transfer of children as young as 10 to adult court, while others do not specify a minimum age [Sickmund, 1996]) for an increasingly broader array of offenses. (*Note*. Aside from the death penalty [*Roper v. Simmons*, 2005], children transferred to criminal court are generally subject to the same penalties as adults [Wrightsman, Green, Fortune, & Nietzel, 2002], including life without parole [cf. *State v. Massey*, 1990]). In Ohio, for example, juveniles can be subject to Serious Youthful Offender and Dual Sentencing statutes, in which jurisdiction can be retained by the juvenile court through age 25, and can include harsh punishment if the juvenile does not participate well in rehabilitative efforts (a sword of Damocles approach; Wynkoop, 2003).

It appeared that the legislative pendulum had begun to swing back toward rehabilitation as the youth violent crime rate receded in the 1990s. However, with the more recent resurgence of violent juvenile crimes, this is doubtful. In the final analysis, a fair amount of tension exists between judges and legislators because of "get tough" statutory changes. For example, as I was writing this chapter, a juvenile judge told me that the state legislature did not trust juvenile judges to make good decisions, particularly as they relate to the best interest of the child.

Nonetheless, juvenile judges still exercise a fair amount of discretion. As Grisso (1998a) perceptively noted, despite the increase in punitive legislation, many juvenile judges still act in ways that they believe to be in the best interest of the child. For neuropsychologists serving the juvenile justice system, this legislative–judicial tension and the ability of juvenile judges to exercise wide discretion can create confusion (e.g., the rules and, hence, the neuropsychological needs may seem to change from courtroom to courtroom).

Philosophical Legal Issues in Juvenile Justice

Our society grapples with the existence and form of a separate juvenile justice system. Proposals range from elimination to reform. The latter seems to be the order of the day, for now anyway. However, even reform has its limits if the juvenile justice system is to maintain its integrity. This logic is reflected in the U.S. Supreme Court's decision in McKeiver v. Pennsylvania (1971): "If the formalities of the criminal adjudicative process are to be superimposed upon the juvenile court system, there is little need for its separate existence" (p. 1989).

The recent tension between parental and punitive roles of the juvenile courts is perhaps best epitomized in Justice Rehnquist's majority opinion in Schall v. Martin (1984):

> There is no doubt that the Due Process Clause is applicable in juvenile proceedings. "The problem," we have stressed, "is to ascertain the precise impact of the due process requirement upon such proceedings" (internal quotes from In re Gault, 1967, pp. 1436–1437). We have held that certain basic constitutional protections enjoyed by adults accused of crimes also apply to juveniles. . . . But the Constitution does not mandate elimination of all differences in the treatment of juveniles. . . . The state has a *"parens patriae* interest in preserving and promoting the welfare of the child" (Santosky v. Kramer, 1982, p. 766), which makes the juvenile proceeding fundamentally different from an adult criminal trial. We have tried, therefore, to strike a balance—to respect the "informality" and "flexibility" that characterize juvenile proceedings . . . and yet to ensure that such proceedings comport with the "fundamental fairness" demanded by the Due Process Clause. (p. 2409)

Problems with application of the full range of constitutional rights to juveniles include the contention that juvenile proceedings are civil (as opposed to criminal; cf. G.J.I. v. State, 1989), the lack of systems consequent to particular rulings (e.g., forensic hospitals for juveniles determined not competent to proceed), and legislation that creates specific classes of juvenile offenders (e.g., serious youthful offenders) and dual sentencing (Wynkoop, 2003).

Case Law in Juvenile Justice

There is growing case law relevant to juvenile justice at state and federal levels. Two U.S. Supreme Court decisions have particular import for juvenile justice in the United States, and neuropsychologists should be familiar with them. In the first, Kent v. United States (1966), the Court provided the basis for due process in juvenile legal proceedings by affirming juveniles' rights to legal representation, to avoid self-incrimination, and to confront and to cross-examine witnesses in transfer hearings (cf. Grisso, 1998a). In arriving at its decision, the Court stated, "There may be grounds for concern that the child gets the worst of both worlds: That he gets neither the protections accorded to adults nor the solicitous care and regenerative treatment postulated for children" (Kent v. United States, p. 1054).

In what is generally considered to be the most important juvenile due process rights case, *In re Gault* (1967), the Court held that juveniles have the right to a notice of charges against them, to legal counsel, to confront and to cross-examine witnesses against them, and to avoid self-incrimination (see also Green et al., 2006). In its decision, the Court alluded to juvenile proceedings as a "kangaroo court, characterized by arbitrariness, ineffectiveness, and the appearance of injustice" (Melton et al., 1997, p. 419). Furthermore, the Court in *Gault* concluded that the doctrine of *parens patriae* "proved to be a great help to those who sought to rationalize the exclusion of juveniles from the constitutional scheme" (pp. 1437–1438), and that *parens patriae* had been perverted de facto by the juvenile justice system (i.e., had become quasi-criminal, changed from its original meaning of the state's duty to protect dependent persons and their property—not necessarily to discipline or to rehabilitate them; cf. Melton et al., 1997). There were juvenile due process cases that preceded *Kent* and *Gault* (e.g., *Haley v. Ohio* [1948], *Gallegos v. Colorado* [1962]); however, the complete evolution of juvenile due process case law is beyond the scope of this chapter.

Other U.S. Supreme Court cases of interest in delinquency adjudication include *In re Winship* (1970), which requires that the beyond reasonable doubt standard be applied in delinquency hearings; *McKeiver v. Pennsylvania* (1971), which affirmed that juveniles do *not* have a right to trial by jury as a constitutional matter; *Breed v. Jones* (1975), which prohibits double jeopardy for juveniles; *Fare v. Michael* (1979), which established the *totality of circumstances* approach as the standard when deciding whether the juvenile has properly waived Miranda rights during interrogation; *Schall v. Martin* (1984), which reaffirmed due process in juvenile proceedings; and *Roper v. Simmons* (2005), which banned execution for those who commit murder prior to their 18th birthday (which is a transfer-related issue).

State court cases of interest include *In re Causey* (1978), in which the Louisiana Court of Appeals concluded that immaturity in and of itself could form the basis for adjudicative noncompetence for juveniles; *In the interest of S.H.* (1996), in which the Georgia Court of Appeals reversed and granted the right of competence to proceed to juveniles; *G.J.I. v. State* (1989), in which the Oklahoma Appellate Court ruled that juveniles were *not* accorded the constitutional right of competence to proceed (because juvenile hearings are rehabilitative or civil not criminal; Oklahoma is the only jurisdiction in the United States that has ruled in this manner); *State v. Massey* (1990), in which the Washington State Court of Appeals upheld a life without parole sentence for a judicially transferred 13-year-old defendant who committed aggravated murder; and *In re Williams* (1997), which allows Ohio juvenile courts to consider juvenile norms when deciding adjudicative competence (given that Ohio juvenile courts have to apply the adult standard for competence to stand trial to juvenile adjudicative competence for lack of a specific juvenile standard; see *In re Johnson*, 1983).

Returning briefly to philosophical legal issues, the trilogy of *Kent*, *Gault*, and *Winship* fostered adversarial conditions in the juvenile courts (Feld, 1997), thus limiting the Court's ability to act as parent in certain instances (i.e., benevolently dictating in the best interest of the child). However, there is legal theory that suggests these "rights" accorded juvenile defendants, particularly as relates to *Gault*, were formed out of the due process clause of the U.S. Constitution, not necessarily born out of the same need for adversarial process accorded to adult criminal defendants under the Constitution (Fondacaro, Slobogin, & Cross, 2006). Fondacaro and colleagues (2006) contend that the heart of the issue for juvenile justice is fundamental fairness, not necessarily that juvenile courts should mimic the adult criminal process. In other words, the amount of due process protection should be matched to the seriousness of the potential outcome.

This is by no means an exhaustive review of the relevant case law. Rather, it is meant to provide some insight into relevant case law for neuropsychologists who wish to serve the juvenile justice system, and to demonstrate that juvenile justice case law continues to evolve.

Juvenile Court Procedure

In many respects, delinquency proceedings mimic adult criminal procedure (Melton et al., 1997). For example, apprehension (i.e., arrest), can be followed by a detention hearing (an analogue to an adult bail hearing). After this, an intake hearing is conducted (analogous to a preliminary hearing), sometimes by a probation officer or magistrate, to determine whether there is probable cause to believe that an offense has been committed. At this point, however, the official still has the ability to divert the youth away from court proceedings, toward some form of intervention (e.g., parental control or mental health care).

If court proceedings are deemed necessary, then a petition is filed (analogous to indictment or charges), and the youth proceeds on to an adjudication hearing (i.e., trial—which can be quite adversarial). At the adjudication hearing, the state is represented by prosecution and the youth by counsel (either retained or provided). Plea bargaining can be conducted at any time in the process, similar to criminal court. However, the tendency is to bargain over disposition as opposed to the allegations in the petition, because the disposition can remain the same regardless of the allegations against the youth. A judge or magistrate presides over the adjudication hearing as trier of fact (recall that the right to trial by jury is not accorded to juveniles; see *McKeiver v. Pennsylvania*, 1971). If the petition is found to be true (analogous to a finding of guilt), then a disposition hearing is held (analogous to a sentencing hearing), for which the probation department prepares a social study report (analogous to a presentence report). The youth can be placed on probation or in a facility (analogous to community vs. institutional corrections). Placement can be in a detention center for a limited amount of time (analogous to county jail) or reform school (analogous to prison).

A notable difference between the juvenile and criminal justice systems includes legislative or judicial transfer from juvenile to criminal court (at issue is whether the juvenile system is the proper venue for the youth; see Melton et al., 1997). If the juvenile is transferred to criminal court, then he or she is treated as an adult (exceptions being application of the death penalty and pretrial detainment in which Joint Commission jail medical standards require separate facilities for anyone under age 18). Regarding disposition, juvenile court judges typically have more options open to them than do criminal court judges. Options typically include rehabilitation, punishment, mental health referral, or some combination of these (e.g., dual sentencing; Wynkoop, 2003). If the juvenile is considered to be a serious youthful offender (an option that exists in many states), he or she can be monitored by the juvenile court (either in or out of facilities) well into his or her 20s. Another option of juvenile court judges is to continue the disposition for a lengthy period of time (analogous to an abeyance), during which time the juvenile needs to maintain proper behavior or else face the wrath of the court as it makes its disposition decision (for a more thorough discussion of the processing of delinquency cases, see Grisso, 1998a). Appeals are generally handled via the criminal justice Appellate and Supreme Court systems.

Other differences between adult and juvenile justice systems arise in their respective administrative structures. For example, the lead juvenile court judge in the county is typically administratively responsible for the entire juvenile justice system in that county (often with State Supreme Court oversight). This includes hiring and administration of court staff, court officers (i.e., juvenile probation officers in most jurisdictions), detention personnel, diversion program personnel, and even evaluative and treatment staff (e.g., social workers, psychologists). The criminal court judge typically plays a less administrative role outside of his or her own court.

Additionally, juvenile court judges often allow officers of the court (e.g., juvenile probation officers) essentially to triage cases as to seriousness and to make recommendations as to the formality (or informality) with which cases should be disposed. For example, a case can be handled almost completely, and informally, by the officer, with the judge endorsing the officer's report. Juvenile courts tend to make use of magistrates as extenders of judicial authority. The more serious the alleged crime, however, the more the juvenile justice situation should resemble the adult situation, at least in theory (Fondacaro et al., 2006).

Points of Neuropsychological Service to the Juvenile Justice System

Although not written for specifically neuropsychologists, Grisso (1998a) describes several types of evaluations that psychologists may provide to the juvenile justice system. These include emergency evaluations (for juveniles recently arrested and detained, to rule out intent to commit suicide, or to rule out psychosis), ability to waive *Miranda* rights, transfer to criminal court, adjudicative competence (or competence to stand trial, if transferred to criminal court), insanity (more likely if transferred to criminal court), dispositional decisions (including rehabilitation or treatment needs, placement needs), treatment and/or treatment progress, and extension of the juvenile court's authority over an adolescent about to turn 18. To this list of evaluations, I add general consultation to the juvenile judges and staff; and providing training in cognitive, emotional, and behavioral development, developmental psychopathology, neurodevelopmental delay, and so on, some of which is recounted in the next section.

Neuropsychology Specific to Juvenile Justice

Neurodevelopment

The majority of children on whom neuropsychologists are consulted in the juvenile justice system are likely adolescent. However, there are also instances in which neuropsychologists are asked to evaluate younger children. My own observation has been that the younger the child, the more complex the case. For example, one of the first children on whom I was asked to consult was a 10-year-old boy with an IQ in the mildly defective range and profound academic learning disorders, who allegedly had caused the death of another child. Readily apparent in this example is that knowledge of human development, normal and abnormal, is a prerequisite for neuropsychological service to the juvenile justice system.

It is not my intent in this chapter, however, to review general neurodevelopment or child and adolescent neuropsychological assessment. Several outstanding available texts describe normal and abnormal neurodevelopment in depth (e.g., Anderson, Northam, Hendy, & Wrennall, 2001; Spreen, Risser, & Edgell, 1995; Yeates, Ris, & Taylor, 2000), and primers are available elsewhere (e.g., for social and neurocognitive sequelae to traumatic brain injury (TBI) that, although written more for civil litigation, also are relevant to juvenile justice, see Kolb & Fantie, 1997; Wynkoop, 2003; see also Donders, 2005a). Additionally, readers can consult Baron (2000) for a primer on neuropsychological assessment of children and adolescents, and Baron (2004) for a comprehensive text. What follows are some of the developmental issues relevant to juvenile justice.

As neuropsychologists are aware, development begins at conception (see Wynkoop, 2003). In fact, it is often informative to factor in weeks lost during gestation for children born prematurely when arriving at neurocognitive age expectations for younger children, and to explore complications of premature birth (i.e., it has been my experience that many parents neglect to mention natal and perinatal complications, unless specifically asked about them). For example, there is a local (Toledo, Ohio) base rate of 5% for intraventricular hemorrhage in 2- to 7-day-old neonates born at less than 33 weeks' gestation (the cognitive sequelae of which remain a matter of investigation). Additional gestational developmental questions are important to the forensic child neuropsychologist, such as maternal use of tobacco, alcohol, drugs, and medical services. Childhood maladies, premorbid functioning (in the event of central nervous system [CNS] insult), and social context are also important (Donders, 2005a).

General Maturational Issues

Developmentally, children tend to develop at different rates, and their development is confounded by "spurts, delays, or temporary regressions," and a lack of generalizability of skills learned in one context to other contexts (Grisso, 1998a, p. 28). Adolescents tend to "enact a persona to try it out," generally temporarily, but sometimes retaining some part of the persona, which becomes more fixed with time (p. 28). Adolescents also lack the life experience to behave in stable ways under stress (Grisso, 1998a).

Additionally, adolescents often harbor feelings of invincibility, a belief that they know most of what there is to know about life, and a tendency to focus on immediate or short-term gains at the expense of delayed outcomes. These attributes cut across intellectual and academic lines. Furthermore, the "know it all" attitude of some juveniles can lead to a false impression of an understanding of the court and its procedures (relevant to competence to proceed). Problematically, adolescents and children are more easily misled than adults. They are suggestible and lack judgment.

My experience with adolescents in nonclinical settings leads me to conclude that it is not uncommon to observe even in bright, generally well-behaved children a disconnection between acquired information and judgment. Take, for example, the academically bright, college-bound adolescent in his or her senior year of high school who neglects National Honor Society duties, risking expulsion from the society, without seeming regard for the potential ramifications of this behavior on college admissions. Furthermore, when the ramifications are explained, the student still does not seem to "get it." Then, consider that most of the youth that one serves in juvenile justice do not even posses the intellectual and academic advantages of this student.

Specific to forensic work, and the tendency to focus on immediate gains at the expense of long-range planning, consider false confessions by children. In many instances, youth tend to confess falsely to violent crimes at substantial rates, as high as 33% in one study, because they think they will be able to go home after confessing (Drizen & Leo, 2004). The point is even more salient when the rate of false confessions of juveniles (42%) is compared to that of adults (13%) among DNA-exonerated defendants (Gross, Jacoby, Matheson, Montgomery, & Paul, 2005). In one analogue study in which children and young adults were pressured into confessing that they had pressed a computer button that caused the computer to break down, there was a modest age effect with 12- to 13-year-olds confessing 78% of the time, 15- to 16-year-olds confessing 72% of the time, and young adults confessing 59% of the time (Redlich & Goodman, 2003). Such research serves to confirm the common sense notions held by the U.S. Supreme Court in the interrogation-related cases of *Haley v. Ohio* (1948) and *Gallegos v. Colorado* (1962), in which, respectively, a 15-year-old was considered "no match for the law" (p. 601) and a 14-year-old was "not equal to the police" (p. 54).

Adolescent General Psychopathology in Juvenile Justice

Grisso (1998a) recounts an unpublished epidemiological review by Otto, Greenstein, Johnson, and Friedman (1992), in which the prevalence of all forms of psychiatric disturbance among adolescents ranges from about 14 to 22%. Among delinquents, however, conduct disorder is seen in 50–60% (compared to about 1–10% in the general population; American Psychiatric Association, 2000); substance abuse/dependence in about 25–50% (compared to 5% for cannabis in the general population, with most other prevalence rates for substance abuse/dependence unknown; American Psychiatric Association, 2000); attention-deficit/hyperactivity disorder (ADHD) in greater than 20% (3–7% among school-age children in the general population; American Psychiatric Association, 2000); affective disorders in 30–75% (compared to 0.4–1.6% for bipolar disorders, 6% for dysthymia, and 5–12% for men and 10–25% for women with major depression, lifetime prevalence in the general population; American Psychiatric Association, 2000); posttraumatic stress disorder (PTSD) in 10–40% (8% lifetime prevalence in the general population; American Psychiatric Association, 2000); and psychosis in 1–6% (compared to roughly 1.5% or less in the general population across the lifespan; American Psychiatric Association, 2000). Comorbidity is fairly common among delinquent youth, particularly conduct disorder with another disorder. In short, delinquents seem to be plagued by more than their fair share of psychopathology.

Some caveats are in order. First, is the relatively high prevalence of PTSD among delinquents, suggesting that a neuropsychologist who assesses a juvenile offender may also be assessing a victim (i.e., one and the same person), and issues of prior and/or concurrent victimization need to be considered in developing a complete picture of the youth. Second, as Grisso (1998a) states, clinicians should avoid the temptation to end the diagnostic process once they observe symptoms of conduct disorder. Third, the diagnosis of conduct disorder should not be applied if the behavior is "simply a reaction to the immediate social context" (American Psychiatric Association, 2000, p. 96). Fourth, although conduct disorder is a prelude to antisocial personality disorder in adulthood, most children who meet diagnostic criteria for conduct disorder do not continue to offend in adulthood (American Psychiatric Association, 2000), thus limiting its predictive utility (which is pertinent to judicial transfer decisions).

Neuropsychology of Delinquency

Aside from some of the more obvious juvenile justice neuropsychology referrals, such as TBI, cerebrovascular accident (CVA), mental retardation (MR), and/or learning disabilities (LDs), there is growing neurobehavioral theory relevant to delinquency, particularly to violence. Researchers have studied social (e.g., family, environment) influences on criminal behavior and delinquency for decades. Emphases have traditionally been placed on psychological and sociological explanations, with cogent biological theories building momentum in recent years (Green et al., 2006). Although it seems fashionable to integrate the various theories into one biopsychosocial model, for our purposes I concentrate on CNS functions. A caveat before proceeding: The nature of neurodevelopment precludes simple downward extension of adult findings and theories to children. In fact, many pediatric neuropsychologists recognize simple downward extension of adult neuropsychological principles to children to be anathema, and rightly so. For example, there seem in some instances to be continuity of cognitive findings related to asocial behavior between adults and children (e.g., IQ), but not in general, nor in some very important ways (e.g., prefrontal frontal volume ratios; Kruesi & Casanova, 2006).

According to Raine (2002), "There is no doubt that genetic processes play an etiological role in childhood antisocial and aggressive behavior," and that "environmental processes produce physiological changes in both CNS and ANS [autonomic nervous system] functioning in a way that can predispose to antisocial and aggressive behavior" (p. 417). Implicated in this process have been increased levels of testosterone (controversial) and insulin, with low levels of serotonin (Coccaro, Kavoussi, & Lesser, 1992; DiLalla & Gottesman, 1991; cf. Toot, Dunphy, Turner, & Ely [2004] for animal analogue studies). Criminal populations are known to have higher base rates of head trauma than the general population (Barnfield & Leathem, 1998; Slaughter, Fann, & Ehde, 2003; Templer, Kasiral, & Trent, 1992). Positron emission tomography (PET) imaging suggests that some murderers have overactive amygdala, hippocampus, thalamus, and midbrain regions in the context of reduced prefrontal activation (Raine, Meloy, & Buchshaum, 1998; see also Raine & Yang, 2006). How some of these findings apply to children, however, is a matter of debate. For example, although Yang and colleagues (2005) demonstrated prefrontal differences between pathological (22–26% increase in prefrontal white matter; 36–42% reduced prefrontal gray–white matter ratios) and nonpathological lying in normal and antisocial adult controls, Kruesi and Casanova (2006) did not find the same differences in children (although this could have been an artifactual result of their small sample size).

IQ has long been of interest to criminologists. Criminal population IQs are known to be about 8–10 points lower on average than IQs in the general population (a possible artifact of studying only criminals who have been caught; Lynam, Moffitt, & Stouthamer-Loeber, 1993). In children, and continuing into adulthood, lower IQ early on (i.e., ages 8–10) has been associated with more convictions for violent crimes through age 32 (Farrington, 1995), an association that remains even when researchers controlled for race, social class, and motivation to perform on testing (Lynam et al., 1993).

Gestationally, malnutrition in the first and second trimester has been linked with antisocial personality in adults (Neugebauer, Hock, & Susser, 1999). Compared to controls, children malnourished early on demonstrated more hyperactive and/or aggressive behaviors at age 8, more externalizing behaviors at age 11, and greater conduct difficulties and more motor activity at age 17 (Liu, Raine, Venables, & Mednick, 2004). The relationship between degree of malnourishment and abnormal behavior has been dose-dependent.

There is also a strong interaction effect between gestational and/or birth complications and early maternal rejection (i.e., attempted abortion, placement in an orphanage-type setting during the first year) in the prediction of aggression and violence among children and adults (reassessed in their mid-30s; Raine, Brennan, & Mednick, 1994). In one large sample, persons with both of these factors in their background committed 70% of all the violent acts committed by members of that sample (Raine, Brennan, Mednick, & Mednick, 1996).

Researchers controlling for potential social and medical confounds found that maternal alcohol use (Fast, Conry, & Loock, 1999; Olsen et al., 1997; Streissguth, Barr, Bookstein, Sampson, & Olsen, 1999) and smoking (Brennan, Grekin, & Mednick, 1999; Rantakallio, Laara, Isohanni, & Moilanen, 1992) have also been linked in conduct disorder and/or violent behavior in children, with up to a fourfold increase (Weissman, Warner, Wickramaratne, & Kandel, 1999). When birth complications are paired with maternal smoking during gestation, the behavioral problems have lasted into adulthood (Brennan et al., 1999). Maternal smoking during gestation is known to reduce noradrenergic functioning, to disrupt cerebellar development, and to damage the basal ganglia, the first of which is hypothesized to inhibit sympathetic activity, including heart rate (Raine, 2002).

Minor physical anomalies (e.g., furrowed tongue, low-seated ears, adherent ear lobes; Raine, 2002) suggesting genetic abnormality or CNS insult (e.g., anoxia, infection, bleeding; see Guy, Majorski, Wallace, & Guy, 1983) near the end of the first trimester have been associated with aggression against peers as early as age 3 (Waldrop, Bell, McLaughlin, & Halverson, 1978). These anomalies have also been associated with violent behavior at age 17, independent of family problems (Arseneault, Tremblay, Boulerice, Seguin, & Saucier, 2000). Minor physical anomalies likely do not cause antisocial behavior, specifically violence, but they may provide a marker for an underlying cause(s) that influences cerebral functions leading to violence.

Slow resting heart rate in childhood is "the best-replicated biological correlate of antisocial and aggressive behavior in children" (Raine, 2002, p. 417), and "predicts antisocial and criminal behavior in adulthood" (p. 421). The reason(s) for this link remains unclear, but likely represents a third factor(s) that may be directly related to behavioral problems (e.g., reduced noradrenergic function, norepinephrine and/or dopamine dysfunction, low sympathetic nervous system arousal). Prediction of antisocial behavior via heart rate in adults has not held very well (possibly due to study design problems and/or the confound of physical development).

Spatial difficulties (when assessed at age 3) were found developmentally to precede verbal weaknesses (when reassessed at age 11) in children with a later history of antisocial behavior compared to normals (Raine, Yaralian, Reynolds, Venables, & Mednick, 2002). Adolescents age 16–17 with childhood persistent antisocial behaviors demonstrated impairment in spatial and memory functions relative to controls and to those with a limited time span of antisocial behaviors (Raine et al., 2005). Early-onset conduct disorder has been associated with reduced right temporal lobe and right temporal gray matter volumes on magnetic resonance imaging (MRI), more striking than slightly reduced prefrontal volumes when compared to age-, sex-, and handedness-matched controls (Kruesi, Casanova, Mannheim, & Johnson-Bilder, 2004).

In summary, our understanding of the biological basis of disordered conduct, particularly violent behavior, in children and adolescents is evolving. The most consistent findings have been related to violence (as opposed to property damage or victimless crimes). However, our understanding remains incomplete, is based mostly on correlational data, and is fraught with potential confounds and sometimes inconsistent findings, and with the obvious difficulty of applying group data to individual children. Consequently, it is not yet prudent to predict a tendency toward chronic behavioral disturbance or violence via neurocognitive or physical assessment of a child.

Types of Neuropsychological Evaluations in Juvenile Justice

Interestingly, although stating that there are few instances in which they "believe psychological testing to be an efficient means of gathering data to answer a forensic question" (p. 436) in juvenile justice, Melton and colleagues (1997) suggest that when a formulation is required to construct an educational plan for a child in need of services (e.g., an Individual Education Plan under the Individuals with Disabilities Education Act), intelligence, achievement, learning style, vocational interest, and personality should be assessed. This suggested evaluation format resembles a neurocognitive evaluation in many respects (particularly if one interprets *learning style* to include directing attention, multitasking, and decision making, and verbal versus visual–spatial strengths in a variety of areas, including learning and recall). They also suggest that the family and community context be assessed in preparation for multisystem interventions (which are demonstrably the most efficacious interventions at present; Melton et al., 1997). Again, considerations of family and community contexts are not foreign concepts to neuropsychologists.

Opinions about the need for psychological and/or neuropsychological assessment in juvenile justice aside, the practice of neuropsychology in the juvenile justice system is plagued by two demons. The first is that there is little need for full neuropsychological assessment in the vast majority of cases. The second is that juvenile justice systems nationwide are notoriously underfunded, and this limits the ability to fund lengthy and expensive test batteries (unlike civil litigation). Nonetheless, neuropsychology still has much to offer the juvenile justice system.

The juvenile forensic neuropsychologist needs to develop a sense for selecting tools that help to answer the referral question (e.g., competency to proceed, diversion) and when to apply them. Whenever neuropsychological assessment is helpful, the typical forensic evaluation caveats apply (e.g., use of collateral information, more documentation, assessment of symptom validity).

The most likely use of neuropsychological assessment in juvenile justice is determining competence (e.g., waive *Miranda* rights [Grisso, 1998b], confess, procedural, adjudicative [Grisso, 2005a, 2005b]), insanity [albeit rare in juvenile justice], and dispositional and/or treatment progress evaluations, in which there is a need to determine whether neurocognitive deficit causes or contributes to a juvenile's poor progress in treatment).

Oddly, cognitive maturity is not at issue in judicial transfer hearings. Rather, the determination to be made by the court is whether the juvenile system remains the proper venue for the youth, predicated on his or her predicted amenability to intervention. In other words, has the youth demonstrated that he or she can no longer benefit from rehabilitative efforts? Consequently, most juvenile courts faced with a transfer decision may not consider ordering a developmental neurocognitive evaluation. This is unfortunate, and may rob the court of useful information.

Although most of us in criminal forensic neuropsychology adhere to the adage that the best predictor of future behavior is past behavior (suggesting that past intervention failure is predictive of future intervention failure), the issue is not quite as straightforward with children and adolescents (see Grisso, 1998a). Two factors are relevant. First is whether the intervention has a proven track record of success. Obviously, not all interventions are effective, and it would be erroneous to conclude that because the youth did not respond to an ineffective intervention, he or she is not amenable to rehabilitation. Second is whether the intervention was suited to the child's developmental level (e.g., social, cognitive). Obviously, it would be erroneous to conclude that because the youth did not respond to an intervention not suited to his or her developmental level, he or she is not amenable to rehabilitation. These are failures of the system, not of the child. In summary, the intervention must be demonstrably effective at the youth's neurodevelopmental level at the time to conclude that there was really failure attributable to the youth (and that multiple intervention failures suggest that the youth is not amenable to intervention and should be transferred to criminal court). My experience has been that most psychologists and psychiatrists who conduct transfer evaluations are not as developmentally savvy as they should be. In this sense, developmental neuropsychology may have much to offer judicial transfer evaluations, even if the courts have yet to realize this.

In the final analysis, although not every evaluation in juvenile justice need be, or should be, a full neuropsychological battery, the neuropsychologist's knowledge of human cognitive and emotional development can be quite valuable in most any evaluation conducted for the juvenile court.

Malingered Cognitive Deficit in Children

Whereas malingered cognitive deficit by children is receiving more attention in the literature, empirical research lags behind (see Rohling, 2004; see also Wynkoop & Denney, 2008). There is, however, evidence that children lie and mislead, and that they do so in ways that meet DSM criteria for malingering. For example, young children have been found to prevaricate at rates approaching 20% compared with parental report (Stouthamer-Loeber, 1986). Additionally, a body of literature, primarily case reports, demonstrate that young children feign and/or exaggerate symptoms (i.e., 15 case studies since 1981 involving at least 44 children found in Medline and PsycInfo searches), and a National Institutes of Health (NIH) study found 11 cases of feigned illness among inpatient children from the early 1960s through the late 1970s (Aduan, Fauci, Dale, Herzberg, & Wolff, 1979). The children in these combined studies ranged in age from 8 to 17 years (Wynkoop & Denney, 2008).

The age at which children are capable of deception is becoming clearer. Some research suggests that toddlers can act deceptively and that non-caregivers have difficulty distinguishing when they are doing so (Lewis, 1993). By age 6, such skills are ingrained, although lacking in sophistication and planning (see Oldershaw & Bagby, 1997), and by about age 9 (or by fourth grade) children can successfully deceive their peers and parents (Quinn, 1988). Regardless, by the time that children reach the age at which they are likely to be seen by the neuropsychologist in the juvenile justice system, they have the capacity to deceive, and to do so convincingly and stealthily with strangers (e.g., evaluators).

Neuropsychologists lack information on base rates of malingered cognitive deficit in children in general (stratified by specific developmental level) and whether the typical adult detection methods will work with children (and with what children), and whether imbedded detection measures for instruments originally designed for adults and adolescents (e.g., Denney, 1999; Mittenberg, Theroux-Fichera, Zielinski, & Heilbronner, 1995; Spreen & Strauss, 1998) should be used with older adolescents (ages 16 and 17). About all that can be concluded with any degree of certainty is that neuropsychologists (including board-certified neuropsychologists) are not very good at detecting malingered cognitive deficit in adolescents using only conventional test batteries (see Faust, Hart, & Guilmette, 1988; Faust, Hart, Guilmette, & Arkes, 1988; to be fair, both studies generated some furor and disagreement; e.g., Bigler, 1990; Faust & Guilmette, 1990).

Models of Malingered Cognitive Deficit in Children

Whether adult models explaining deception and malingering can be accurately applied to children is an empirical question that is as yet unanswered (see Rogers, 1997; see also Frederick, Crosby, & Wynkoop, 2000, regarding motivation and effort). Presently, it seems reasonable to conclude that older children (i.e., adolescents) may be motivated to feign or to exaggerate symptoms using incentives similar to those of adults (e.g., financial gain, avoid punishment), but younger children may not be motivated by the same tangible rewards as adults (Oldershaw & Bagby, 1997). As Constantinou and McCaffrey (2003, p. 82) state, "Young children probably do not intentionally deceive for the same 'grown-up' incentives as adults and may not be able to appreciate the full consequences of their deception." For example, instead of money, younger children may deceive in an effort to gain attention. Regarding effort in children, Barkley (1997) discusses developmental issues relevant to effort on testing, such as attention and self-regulation, which again may differ from adults.

Detection Strategies for Children

Several methods for detecting malingered cognitive deficit have been promulgated, including symptom validity testing (SVT; i.e., a forced-choice paradigm), consistency of performance on items of similar difficulty, performance curve analysis, floor effect, magnitude of error, deficits in memory that are not consistent with known principles, and increased response latency to test items, examination of patterns of test performances, comparison of laboratory observations (e.g., symptoms or test results) with known neuropathological processes (i.e., typical performance), and comparison of test results with both collateral and surveillance information (Rogers, 1997; Wynkoop & Denney, 1999). Of these, it seems reasonable to conclude that the forced-choice paradigm and comparison of laboratory observations (e.g., symptoms or test results) with known neuropathological processes, collateral information, and surveillance information are useful with children. The other strategies would require either development of instruments (e.g., performance curve analysis) and/or research incorporating multiple developmental levels (e.g., typical performance, pattern of test performances, floor effect, response latency).

To date, only three peer-reviewed articles specifically validate detection of fabricated cognitive deficit in children under the age of 16. In the first study, 61 Greek Cypriot and 67 American children ages 5–12 years were able to perform adequately on the Test of Memory Malingering (TOMM), whereas only children 10 years and older were able to perform adequately on the Rey 15-Item Memory Test (Constantinou & McCaffrey, 2003). A second TOMM study (Donders, 2005b) suggested that as the age of children decreases from 16 to 6 years ($N = 100$), so too does their efficiency on the TOMM. However, greater than 90% of the children ages 6–8 still performed at the TOMM criterion level originally set for adults. What remains unclear is what constructs these tests are actually measuring in young children.

McKinzey, Prieler, and Raven (2003) extended the research using Raven's Standard Progressive Matrices (SPM) in the detection of malingered neurocognitive deficit in adults (Gudjonsson & Shackelton, 1986) to children (McKinzey, Podd, Krehbiel, & Raven, 1999). They asked 44 Viennese children ages 7–17 to take the SPM under two conditions: the first compliant, and the second after being told to "do as badly as you can." They found that the formula developed and cross-validated with adults was not as effective with children (64% false-negative rate), but that a 95% hit rate, with only 5% false negatives, was possible simply by considering children to be malingering if they missed any of the three easiest items on the test. Problematically, however, a child who is savvy enough, or who is taught to present more subtle impairment, may not be detected using this strategy.

Although we may not know much about the extent of child malingering, about 10–12% of children (ages unknown) fail the Word Memory Test (WMT), and 7.5% fail the Medical Symptom Validity Test (MSVT) (Green, 2003, presented but unpublished in Flaro, 2006; see also Green & Flaro, 2003), without identifiable external incentives to do so, and with clear decrement in performance for children less than 8 years of age (Courtney, 2006). In other words, in the context of age confounds, a large percentage of children do not appear to put forth maximum effort on testing (in the absence of external incentives to perform poorly), and there is a trend for younger children to have more difficulty on instruments designed to measure effort. Again, this is an application of an adult paradigm to children, for whom the construct of effort may be qualitatively different from that of adults (see Barkley, 1997).

In summary, it appears that at least some clinicians who evaluate children are applying specific measures to detect malingered cognitive deficit in their clinical batteries. Problematically, research in the area is scant and relies on projection of adult tests downward to children. As the field matures, we should expect to see more sophisticated research designs using simulated and/or real malingerers, exploring tests or procedures developed specifically for children based on developmental levels. Until more research is conducted on validity indicators in children, we are left to our own devices, which the current research demonstrates to be fairly weak.

Ethical Practice of Neuropsychology in Juvenile Justice

Professional Competence

According to Grisso (1998a), "Clinicians who perform evaluations in delinquency cases must have specialized knowledge and experience regarding children and adolescents," including development, aggression, delinquency, psychopathology, and assessment (p. 27). Federal Rules of Evidence (Rule 702) state that expert witnesses need to have "knowledge, skill, experience, training, or education," and many states have adopted similar statutory language. To this, Melton and colleagues (1997) add that the psychologist should have broad knowledge of available community services (i.e., mental health and otherwise) to make cogent recommendations to the juvenile court in their evaluations. In short, the requisite training and experience needed to provide competent services in juvenile justice mirror the complexity of the juvenile justice system itself.

Arguably, clinicians need a broad range of education and training in areas of general adult neuropsychology (to serve older adolescents and young adults), child neuropsychology (to serve younger children), and criminal forensic neuropsychology (i.e., the application of neuropsychology in the legal system), and guidance in the application of this knowledge to juvenile justice. There is no regulatory authority, nor sanctioned specialty training, in the application of neuropsychology to juvenile justice per se. However, the American Psychological Association (APA, 2002) and the American Psychology-Law Society/APA Division 41 Committee on Ethical Guidelines for Forensic Psychologists (1991; and Revision Draft 2.0 dated February 13, 2005) ethical guidelines stress competent practice in whatever professional endeavors are undertaken. Both neuropsychology and forensic psychology have educational and training standards to which the juvenile justice neuropsychologist should aspire, and the American Psychological Association ethical guidelines suggest means of gaining proper postdoctorate experience to practice competently.

A fine judge of competent neuropsychological practice in juvenile justice is the juvenile justice system itself. Unlike other areas of practice in which the psychologist gains experience and then plies a trade with little supervision or feedback, the provision of neuropsychological services in criminal and juvenile justice is scrutinized by a host of interested parties. For example, the expert is subject to scrutiny under oath, including adversarial cross-examination with attorneys who may be prepared by other neuropsychologists. Thus, we have a paradox of sorts. Although there are no specialty guidelines specific to the practice of neuropsychology in juvenile justice, the practice of neuropsychology in juvenile justice has the potential to be heavily scrutinized.

Personal Professional Development

Information regarding professional development from a personal perspective is grossly lacking in the literature on criminal forensic neuropsychology. Practice in juvenile or criminal justice poses some unique intra- and interpersonal issues, even for the most well-seasoned evaluator, issues that can potentially impinge on ethical practice. Being an expert implies objectivity, truth, and fairness. However, we are often asked to consult on persons who have committed horrendous crimes, and/or who often hail from social backgrounds and lifestyles that are foreign to us (Wynkoop, 1996). This interpersonal contact can cause the neuropsychologist to confront his or her own mortality or the mortality of loved ones (e.g., children), perhaps arousing his or her disdain for the child or youth subject of the consultation, or, conversely, identification and/or overempathization with the child (e.g., having unresolved issues of one's own physical or sexual abuse as a child, having children of the same age as the perpetrator). In other words, the emotional consequences of practicing in juvenile justice can be taxing, sometimes prompting an emotional shift from objective expert to advocate or to foe. To this end, Wynkoop and Kiselika (1994) proposed the Professional Identity Development (PID) model, which is applicable to those who practice in juvenile justice.

In brief, the PID is a heuristic meant to promote reflection on the part of those who plan to work in juvenile justice, rather than wandering into the field naively (which has been the case for many of us). Our model proposes that those interested in juvenile justice traverse several stages that, we hope, lead to sound professional development. The crux of the model is the internal conflict promoted by contact with delinquents (and/or criminals). The stages are as follows:

1. Precontact
2. Preparation
3. Contact/conflict

4. Boundary issues
   a. Rescuer
   b. Punisher
   c. Professional
5. Resolution/adjustment
6. Integration

In the first stage, *precontact*, the professional has yet to have substantive contact with juvenile justice clientele, but he or she has a stereotype based on any number of vicarious experiences (e.g., media, his or her own victimization). Then, he or she enters the second stage, *preparation* (e.g., course work, continuing education, collegial consultation), which can cause conflict with well-meaning family and friends expressing their fear for the professional's safety and/or disdain for delinquent youth (e.g., "How could anyone work with a sex offender?!").

Contact with delinquent youth (the third stage) tends to create internal conflict. The former preconceived notions of what delinquents should be like are challenged by the stark reality of human victimization, either by or of the delinquent youth, any of which can trigger personal fears and even denial (which can lead to pathological boundary problems with delinquents or criminals). This internal conflict leads to interpersonal *boundary issues* (the fourth stage; e.g., transference, countertransference), causing the professional to experience the ambivalence of being drawn toward the role of *rescuer* (e.g., overextending oneself to get the perpetrator out of trouble, going beyond the legal question at hand) or *punisher* (e.g., making disparaging comments about the alleged perpetrator). The ideal *resolution* (the fifth stage) is the establishment of *professional* interpersonal boundaries, and *integration* (final stage) of juvenile justice practice into one's own life experience and persona.

This is but a brief introduction to the PID model. Interested readers may consult Wynkoop and Kiselika (1994) and/or Wynkoop (1996). Of course, one can also consult a colleague and/or engage in therapy to help resolve such intra- and interpersonal issues.

Informed Consent and Court-Ordered Evaluations

One of the most sensitive issues in forensic neuropsychology is that of informed consent. The matter is even more complicated when dealing with children. Although I field questions of informed consent from my nonforensic colleagues occasionally, the conflicts are typically easily resolved with requisite knowledge of the American Psychological Association's (2002) *Ethical Principles of Psychologists and Code of Conduct* and a working knowledge of privilege (which, for this discussion, subsumes confidentiality). Consent and privilege are legal, not clinical, concepts.

Neuropsychologists are responsible for obtaining informed consent for an assessment whenever possible. Exceptions are when testing is legally mandated, when informed consent is implied (e.g., to obtain a job), or when decisional capacity is at issue (American Psychological Association, 2002). Additionally, when informed consent cannot be obtained from the person being assessed, the code of conduct requires that the person be informed of the "nature and purpose . . . using language that is reasonably understandable to the person being tested" (p. 1071), and it is wise to attempt to gain assent when consent cannot be provided.

Under routine clinical conditions, an adult provides consent for evaluation and/or treatment and controls the flow of the resulting clinical information. Children, on the other hand, unless emancipated (a *not* universally accepted construct from the common law), cannot provide consent to evaluation or treatment, nor do they exercise control over their clinical information (including their own access), so a legally responsible adult provides consent in proxy for the child. Essentially, the same rules apply when either an adult or a child is referred for forensic evaluation by defense counsel. However, when court-ordered into evaluation, neither the child nor the adult can provide consent, nor can either of them exercise privilege over the resulting evaluation information (including access to the evaluation results unless granted by the court or by law). If court-ordered, the holder of the privilege is the court, which greatly simplifies things. It is incumbent on the neuropsychologist to clarify who holds the privilege, who is providing consent for the assessment, and who receives the information and how that information is to be conveyed (e.g., defense counsel may not want a written report), prior to agreeing to provide the service.

Under ideal circumstances, the court orders the evaluation and holds the privilege, and this is explained in proper language to the child and his or her parent or guardian for the purpose of soliciting their assent. As privilege subsumes confidentiality and access to records, the only additional topic that needs to be covered to be in compliance with the American Psychological Association (2002) Code of Conduct is to mention who else may see the information under the circumstances (tempering this with the knowledge that the neuropsychologist actually has no control over whom the holder of the privilege chooses to share the information). If the evaluation is court-ordered, then the judge determines who has access to the evaluation data and report (with the caveat that there are often statutory requirements that dictate who else may have access to the report and/or evaluation data). Providing this information preveniently to the child and his or her parent or guardian is required under the Code of Conduct, and attempting to gain the assent of these parties is good practice. However, gaining assent from either the parent/guardian and/or the child is not necessary when the evaluation is ordered by the court. Remember, under these circumstances, one's relationship and duty is to the ordering judge, and he or she has provided the requisite consent via his or her order for evaluation.

Court Orders

Obtaining a court order for assessment serves a variety of functions. First, it allows neutrality. While providing fair assessment and opinion should be the goal of every neuropsychologist under all circumstances, attorneys are adept at massaging opinions. Even though the neuropsychologist is compensated for his or her time, and not for his or her particular conclusions or opinion in a case, when hired by one side or the other there is a natural tendency to please one's employer. Working directly for the court limits such problems. It has been my experience, that when working for one side or the other, it is wise to obtain a retainer prior to engaging the case, to limit the impact or even the appearance of bias.

Second, obtaining a court order clarifies the privilege, which subsumes confidentiality. It provides permission for the evaluation, even if parents and children are reluctant. Third, a court order helps to ensure payment for services rendered. Finally, a court order provides protection against malpractice claims.

Other Roles for Neuropsychologists in Juvenile Justice

This chapter has been heavily consultation-focused. This makes sense, given that this is the typical service of neuropsychology to juvenile justice, and that neuropsychologists are uniquely qualified to consult with probation officers or with intervention staff (or even to provide intervention themselves) on behalf of delinquents who suffer developmental delay or acquired neurological insult. However, consultation is not the only service that neuropsychologists provide to juvenile justice. In many respects, our service to juvenile justice is limited by our own creativity.

For example, there is much to be accomplished in terms of forming juvenile justice policy. Jurisdictions continue to grapple with significant issues, such as juvenile adjudicative competency (Grisso, 1998a; Wynkoop, 2003), and advisement of rights (Grisso, 1998b). Additionally, only Florida and Virginia have juvenile competency statutes, with mental health systems for juveniles considered not competent to proceed. In Ohio, we are asked to apply the "adult" competency to stand trial statute to children (the fact is, the statute was written for all defendants in Ohio courts, not necessarily with juveniles in mind). In the event that a child is adjudicated not competent to proceed, there is no comprehensive system in place for restoration, leading to dismissal of charges in many of these cases (Lipps, 2006).

It is easy to see that there is much to be accomplished in juvenile justice from a public policy perspective. Neuropsychologists with specific forensic experience can play constructive roles in helping to shape juvenile justice public policy via advice to local juvenile courts, state legislators, ad hoc committees, and State Supreme Courts (who often have judicial oversight; Wrightsman & Fulero, 2005). It has been my experience that the interested and informed neuropsychologist is typically welcomed warmly by juvenile justice policymakers.

Conclusion

From the outset, my goal in this chapter was to help interested neuropsychologists begin the process of acquiring competence in the application of neuropsychology to the juvenile justice system. Despite the daunting nature of the task, I believe that it has been accomplished. Unfortunately, the dearth of literature on the application of neuropsychology to juvenile justice speaks to the infancy of juvenile forensic neuropsychology. My belief, and my hope, is that the development of specialty practice in juvenile forensic neuropsychology will improve the nature of psychological services to the juvenile courts and to the children that the courts serve.

References

Aduan, R. P., Fauci, A. S., Dale, D. C., Herzberg, J. H., & Wolff, S. M. (1979). Factitious fever and self-induces infection: A report of 32 cases and review of the literature. *Annals of Internal Medicine, 90*, 230–242.

American Psychiatric Association. (2000). *Diagnostic and statistical manual of mental disorders* (4th ed., text rev.). Washington, DC: Author.

American Psychological Association. (2002). Ethical principles of psychologists and code of conduct. *American Psychologist, 57*, 1060–1073.

Anderson, V., Northam, E., Hendy, J., & Wrennall, J. (2001). *Developmental neuropsychology: A clinical approach*. Philadelphia: Psychology Press.

Arseneault, L., Tremblay, R. E., Boulerice, J. R., Seguin, J. R., & Saucier, J. F. (2000). Minor physical anomalies and family adversity as risk factors for violent delinquency in adolescence. *American Journal of Psychiatry, 157*, 917–923.

Bakan, D. (1972). Adolescence in America from idea to social fact. In J. Kagan & R. Coles (Eds.), *Twelve to sixteen: Early adolescence* (pp. 73–89). New York: Norton.

Barkley, R. A. (1997). *ADHD and the nature of self-control.* New York: Guilford Press.

Barnfield, T. V., & Leathem, J. M. (1998). Incidence and outcomes of traumatic brain injury and substance abuse in a New Zealand prison population. *Brain Injury, 12,* 455–466.

Barnum, R. (2000). Clinical and forensic evaluation of competence to stand trial in juvenile defendants. In T. Grisso & R. G. Schwartz (Eds.), *Youth on trial: A developmental perspective on juvenile justice* (pp. 193–224). Chicago: University of Chicago Press.

Baron, I. S. (2000). Clinical implications and practical applications of child neuropsychological evaluations. In K. O. Yeates, M. D. Ris, & H. G. Taylor (Eds.), *Pediatric neuropsychology: Theory, research, and practice* (pp. 439–456). New York: Guilford Press.

Baron, I. S. (2004). *Neuropsychological evaluation of the child.* New York: Oxford University Press.

Bigler, E. D. (1990). Neuropsychology and malingering: Comment on Faust, Hart, and Guilmette. *Journal of Consulting and Clinical Psychology, 58,* 244–247.

Breed v. Jones, 421 U.S. 519 (1975).

Brennan, P. A., Grekin, E. R., & Mednick, S. A. (1999). Maternal smoking during pregnancy and adult male criminal outcomes. *Archives of General Psychiatry, 56,* 215–219.

Coccaro, E., Kavoussi, R., & Lesser, J. (1992). Self and other-directed human aggression: The role of the central serotonergic system. *International Clinical Pharmacology, 6,* 70–83.

Committee on Ethical Guidelines for Forensic Psychologists. (1991). Specialty guidelines for forensic psychologists. *Law and Human Behavior, 15,* 655–665.

Constantinou, M., & McCaffrey, R. J. (2003). Using the TOMM for evaluating children's effort to perform optimally on neuropsychological measures. *Child Neuropsychology, 9,* 81–90.

Courtney, J. C. (2006, October). *Assessing child effort: A clinical sample from the U.S. and a non-clinical sample from Brazil.* Presented at the National Academy of Neuropsychology annual convention, Tampa, FL.

Denney, R. L. (1999). A brief symptom validity testing procedure for logical memory of the Wechsler Memory Scale—Revised, which can demonstrate verbal memory in the face of claimed disability. *Journal of Forensic Neuropsychology, 1,* 5–26.

DiLalla, L. F., & Gottesman, I. (1991). Biological and genetic contributors to violence: Widom's untold tale. *Psychological Bulletin, 109,* 125–129.

Donders, J. (2005a). Forensic aspects of pediatric traumatic brain injury. In G. Larrabee (Ed.), *Forensic neuropsychology: A scientific approach* (pp. 182–208). New York: Oxford University Press.

Donders, J. (2005b). Performance on the Test of Memory Malingering in a mixed pediatric sample. *Child Neuropsychology, 11,* 221–227.

Drizen, S. A., & Leo, R. A. (2004). The problem of false confessions in the post-DNA world. *North Carolina Law Review, 82,* 891–1007.

Fare v. Michael C., 442 U.S. 707 (1979).

Farrington, D. P. (1995). The development of offending and antisocial behavior from childhood: Key findings from the Cambridge Study in Delinquent Development. *Journal of Child Psychology and Psychiatry, 360,* 929–964.

Fast, D. K., Conry, J., & Loock, C. A. (1999). Fetal alcohol syndrome among youth in the criminal justice system. *Journal of Developmental and Behavioral Pediatrics, 20,* 370–372.

Faust, D., & Guilmette, T. J. (1990). To say it's not so doesn't prove that it isn't: Research on the detection of malingering: Reply to Bigler. *Journal of Consulting and Clinical Psychology, 58,* 248–250.

Faust, D., Hart, K., & Guilmette, T. J. (1988). Pediatric malingering: The capacity of children to fake believable deficits on neuropsychological testing. *Journal of Consulting and Clinical Psychology, 56,* 578–582.

Faust, D., Hart, K., Guilmette, T. J., & Arkes, H. R. (1988). Neuropsychologists' capacity to detect adolescent malingerers. *Professional Psychology: Research and Practice, 19,* 508–515.

Federal Rules of Evidence, *Rule 702,* Jan. 2, 1975, Pub. L. 93-595, § 1, 88 Stat. 1937; amended 2000.

Feld, B. (1997). Abolish the juvenile court: Youthfulness, criminal responsibility and sentencing policy. *Journal of Criminal Law and Criminology, 88,* 68–136.

Flaro, L. (2006, October). *Effort testing in the assessment of children.* Presented at the 25th Annual Conference of the National Academy of Neuropsychology, Tampa, FL.

Fondacaro, M. R., Slobogin, C., & Cross, T. (2006). Reconceptualizing due process in juvenile justice: Contributions from law and science. *Hastings Law Journal, 57,* 955–989.

Frederick, R. I., Crosby, R. D., & Wynkoop, T. F. (2000). Performance curve classification of invalid responding on the Validity Indicator Profile. *Archives of Clinical Neuropsychology, 15,* 281–300.

G.J.I. v. State, 778 P.2d 485 (Okla. Crim. 1989).

Gallegos v. Colorado, 370 U.S. 49. 52 (1962).

Green, E., Heilbrun, K., Fortune, W. H., & Nietzel, M. T. (2006). *Wrightman's psychology and the legal system* (6th ed.). Belmont, CA: Thomson-Wadsworth.

Green, P. (2003). *MSVT for Windows.* Edmonton, Alberta, Canada: Green's Publishing.

Green, P., & Flaro, L. (2003). Word Memory Test performance in children. *Child Neuropsychology, 9,* 189–207.

Grisso, T. (1996). Society's retributive response to juvenile violence: A developmental perspective. *Law and Human Behavior, 20,* 229–247.

Grisso, T. (1998a). *Forensic evaluation of juveniles.* Sarasota, FL: Professional Resource Press.

Grisso, T. (1998b). *Instruments for assessing appreciation of* Miranda *rights.* Sarasota, FL: Professional Resource Press.

Grisso, T. (2005a). *Clinical evaluations for juveniles' competence to stand trial*. Sarasota, FL: Professional Resource Press.

Grisso, T. (2005b). *Evaluating juveniles' adjudicative competence: A guide for clinical practice*. Sarasota, FL: Professional Resource Press.

Gross, S., Jacoby, K., Matheson, D., Montgomery, N., & Paul, S. (2005). Exonerations in the United States 1989 through 2003. *Journal of Criminal Law and Criminology, 95*, 523–560.

Gudjonsson, G., & Shackelton, H. (1986). The pattern of scores on Raven's Matrices during "faking bad" and "non-faking" performance. *British Journal of Clinical Psychology, 25*, 35–41.

Guy, J. D., Majorski, L. V., Wallace, C. J., & Guy, M. P. (1983). The incidence of minor physical anomalies in adult male schizophrenics. *Schizophrenia Bulletin, 9*, 571–582.

Haley v. Ohio, 332 U.S. 596, 601 (1948).

In re Causey, 363 So.2nd 472 La. (1978).

In re Gault, 387 U.S. 1 (1967).

In re Johnson, Ohio App. (1983).

In re Williams, 116 Ohio App. 3d 237, 687 N.E. 2d 507 (1997).

In re Winship, 397 U.S. 358 (1970).

In the Interest of S.H., 469 S.E.2d 810 (Ga. Ct. App. 1996).

Kent v. United States, 383 U.S. 541 (1966).

Kolb, B., & Fantie, B. (1997). Development of the child's brain and behavior. In C. Reynolds & E. Fletcher-Janzen (Eds.), *Handbook of clinical child neuropsychology* (2nd ed.). New York: Plenum Press.

Kruesi, M. J. P., & Casanova, M. F. (2006). White matter in liars. *British Journal of Psychiatry, 188*, 293–294.

Kruesi, M. J. P., Casanova, M. F., Mannheim, G., & Johnson-Bilder, A. (2004). Reduced temporal volume in early onset conduct disorder. *Psychiatry Research: Neuroimaging, 132*, 1–11.

Lewis, M. (1993). The development of deception. In M. Lewis & C. Saarni (Eds.), *Lying and deception in everyday life* (pp. 90–105). New York: Guilford Press.

Lipps, T. R. (2006, June). *Competency in juvenile court*. Paper presented at the Ohio Juvenile Judges Association Seminar, Oregon, OH.

Liu, J., Raine, A., Venables, P. H., & Mednick, S. A. (2004). Malnutrition at age 3 years and externalizing behavior problems at ages 8, 11, and 17 years. *American Journal of Psychiatry, 161*, 2005–2013.

Lou, H. (1927). *Juvenile courts in the United States*. Chapel Hill: University of North Carolina Press.

Lynam, D., Moffitt, T., & Stouthamer-Loeber, M. (1993). Explaining the relation between IQ and delinquency: Class, race, test motivation, school failure, and self-control. *Journal of Abnormal Psychology, 102*, 187–196.

Mack, J. (1909). The juvenile court. *Harvard Law Review, 23*, 104–122.

McCann, J. (1998). *Malingering and deception in adolescents: Assessing credibility in clinical and forensic settings*. Washington, DC: American Psychological Association.

McKeiver v. Pennsylvania, 403 U.S. 528 (1971).

McKinzey, R. K., Podd, M. H., Krehbiel, M. A., & Raven, J. (1999). Detection of malingering on the Raven Progressive Matrices: A cross-validation. *British Journal of Clinical Psychology, 38*, 435–439.

McKinzey, R. K., Prieler, J., & Raven, J. (2003). Detection of children's malingering on Raven's Standard Progressive Matrices. *British Journal of Clinical Psychology, 42*, 95–99.

Melton, G. B., Petrila, J., Poythress, N. G., & Slobogin, C. (1997). *Psychological evaluations for the courts: A handbook for mental health professionals and lawyers* (2nd ed.). New York: Guilford Press.

Mittenberg, W., Theroux-Fichera, S., Zielinski, R. E., & Heilbronner, R. L. (1995). Identification of malingered head injury on the Wechsler Adult Intelligence Scale—Revised. *Professional Psychology: Research and Practice, 26*, 491–498.

Neugebauer, R., Hock, H. W., & Susser, E. (1999). Prenatal exposure to wartime famine and development of antisocial personality disorder in early adulthood. *Journal of the American Medical Association, 4*, 479–481.

Oldershaw, L., & Bagby, R. M. (1997). Children and deception. In R. Rogers (Ed.), *Clinical assessment of malingering and deception* (2nd ed., pp. 153–166). New York: Guilford Press.

Olsen, H. C., Streissguth, A. P., Sampson, P. D., Barr, H. M., Bookstein, F. L., & Thiede, K. (1997). Association of prenatal alcohol exposure with behavioral and learning problems in early adolescence. *Journal of the American Academy of Child and Adolescent Psychiatry, 36*, 1187–1194.

Otto, R., Greenstein, J., Johnson, M., & Friedman, R. (1992). Prevalence of mental disorders among youth in the juvenile justice system. In J. Cocozza (Ed.), *Responding to the mental health needs of youth in the juvenile justice system* (pp. 7–48). Seattle, WA: National Coalition for the Mentally Ill in the Criminal Justice System.

Quinn, K. M. (1988). Children and deception. In R. Rogers (Ed.), *Clinical assessment of malingering and deception* (pp. 104–119). New York: Guilford Press.

Raine, A. (2002). Annotation: The role of prefrontal deficits, low autonomic arousal, and early health factors in the development of antisocial and aggressive behavior in children. *Journal of Child Psychology and Psychiatry, 43*, 417–434.

Raine, A., Brennan, P., & Mednick, S. A. (1994). Birth complications combined with early maternal rejection at age 1 year predispose to violent crime at age 18 years. *Archives of General Psychiatry, 51*, 984–988.

Raine, A., Brennan, P., Mednick, B., & Mednick, S. A. (1996). High rates of violence, crime, academic problems and behavioral deficits and unstable family environments. *Archives of General Psychiatry, 53*, 544–549.

Raine, A., Meloy, J., & Buchsbaum, M. (1998). Reduced prefrontal and increased subcortical brain function using positron emission tomography in predatory and affective murderers. *Behavioral Sciences and the Law, 16*, 319–332.

Raine, A., Moffitt, T. E., Caspi, A., Loeber, R., Stouthamer-Loeber, M., & Lynam, D. (2005). Neurocognitive impairments in boys on the life-course persistent antisocial path. *Journal of Abnormal Psychology, 114*, 38–49.

Raine, A., & Yang, Y. (2006). The neuroanatomical bases of psychopathy: A review of brain imaging findings. In C. J. Patrick (Ed.), *Handbook of psychopathy* (pp. 278–295). New York: Guilford Press.

Raine, A., Yaralian, P. S., Reynolds, C., Venables, P. H., & Mednick, S. A. (2002). Spatial but not verbal cognitive deficits at age 3 years in persistently antisocial individuals. *Development and Psychopathology, 14,* 25–44.

Rantakallio, P., Laara, E., Isohanni, M., & Moilanen, I. (1992). Maternal smoking during pregnancy and delinquency of the offspring. *International Journal of Epidemiology, 21,* 1106–1113.

Redlich, A. D., & Goodman, G. S. (2003). Taking responsibility for an act not committed: The influence of age and suggestibility. *Law and Human Behavior, 27,* 141–156.

Rogers, R. (1997). Introduction. In R. Rogers (Ed.), *Clinical assessment of malingering and deception* (2nd ed., pp. 1–19). New York: Guilford Press.

Rohling, M. L. (2004). Who do they think they're kidding: A review of the use of symptom validity tests with children. *APA Division 40 Newsletter, 22,* 1, 21–26.

Roper v. Simmons, Supreme Court Case No. 03-633, 543 U.S. 551 (2005).

Santosky v. Kramer, 455 U.S. 745 (1982).

Schall v. Martin, 467 U.S. 253 (1984).

Sickmund, M. (1996). *How juveniles get to criminal court* (U.S. Department of Justice, OJJDP Update on Statistics). Washington, DC: Office of Juvenile Justice and Delinquency Prevention.

Slaughter, B., Fann, J. R., & Ehde, D. (2003). Traumatic brain injury in a county jail population: Prevalence, neuropsychological functioning, and psychiatric disorders. *Brain Injury, 9,* 731–741.

Spreen, O., Risser, A. H., & Edgell, D. (1995). *Developmental neuropsychology.* New York: Oxford University Press.

Spreen, O., & Strauss, E. (1998). *A compendium of neuropsychological tests* (2nd ed.). New York: Oxford University Press.

State v. Massey, 803 P.2d 340 (Wash. 1990).

Stouthamer-Loeber, M. (1986). Lying as a problems behavior in children: A critical review. *Clinical Psychology Review, 6,* 267–289.

Streissguth, A. P., Barr, H. M., Bookstein, F. L., Sampson, P. D., & Olsen, H. C. (1999). The long term neurocognitive consequences of prenatal alcohol exposure: A 14-year study. *Psychological Science, 10,* 186–190.

Templer, D. I., Kasiral, J., & Trent, N. H. (1992). Exploration of head injury without medical attention. *Perceptual and Motor Skills, 75,* 195–202.

Toot, J., Dunphy, G., Turner, M., & Ely, D. (2004). The SHR Y-chromosome increases testosterone and aggression, but decreases serotonin as compared to the WKY Y-chromosome in the rat model. *Behavioral Genetics, 24,* 515–524.

Waldrop, M. F., Bell, R. Q., McLaughlin, B., & Halverson, C. F. (1978). Newborn minor physical anomalies predict short attention span, peer aggression, and impulsivity at age 3. *Science, 199,* 563–564.

Weissman, M. M., Warner, V., Wickramaratne, P. J., & Kandel, D. B. (1999). Maternal smoking during pregnancy and psychopathology in offspring followed to

adulthood. *Journal of the American Academy of Child and Adolescent Psychiatry, 38,* 892–899.
Woolard, J. (2002). Capacity, competence and the juvenile defendant: Implications for research and policy. In B. Bottoms, M. Kovera, & B. McAuliff (Eds.), *Children, social science, and the law* (pp. 270–289). Cambridge, UK: Cambridge University Press.
Wrightsman, L. S., & Fulero, S. M. (2005). *Forensic psychology* (2nd ed.). Belmont, CA: Thomson-Wadsworth.
Wrightsman, L. S., Green, E., Fortune, W. H., & Nietzel, M. T. (2002). *Psychology and the legal system* (5th ed.). Belmont, CA: Thomson-Wadsworth.
Wynkoop, T. F. (1996). Stress and burnout in crisis intervention. In J. Hendricks & B. Byers (Eds.), *Crisis intervention in criminal justice and social service* (pp. 320–360). Springfield, IL: Thomas.
Wynkoop, T. F. (2003). Neuropsychology of juvenile adjudicative competence. *Journal of Forensic Neuropsychology, 3,* 45–65.
Wynkoop, T. F., & Denney, R. L. (1999). Exaggeration of neuropsychological deficit in competency to stand trial. *Journal of Forensic Neuropsychology, 1,* 29–53.
Wynkoop, T. F., & Denney, R. L. (2008, January). *Detecting malingered cognitive deficit in children: Underpinnings and state of the current research.* Paper presented at Child Forensic Psychiatry Symposia, University of Toledo Medical Campus, Toledo, OH.
Wynkoop, T. F., & Kiselika, M. S. (1994). Multicultural issues and perspectives. In J. Hendricks & B. Byers (Eds.), *Multicultural perspectives in criminal justice and criminology* (pp. 3–39). Springfield, IL: Thomas.
Yang, Y., Raine, A., Lencz, T., Bihrle, S., Lacasse, L., & Colleti, P. (2005). Prefrontal white matter in pathological liars. *British Journal of Psychiatry, 187,* 320–325.
Yeates, K. O., Ris, M. D., & Taylor, H. G. (2000). *Pediatric neuropsychology: Research, theory, and practice.* New York: Guilford Press.

Chapter 11

Conducting Criminal Forensic Neuropsychological Assessments
PRAGMATIC CONSIDERATIONS

STEPHEN HONOR
JAMES P. SULLIVAN

Knowing how to arrange for and conduct neuropsychological examinations in the correctional setting with incarcerated defendants is essential to allow us to provide our services. In this chapter we discuss dealing with the referring/retaining attorney(s), the nature of such referrals, the necessary "paperwork," arranging for transportation, the logistics of correctional facility examinations, and the approach for conducting such privately retained examinations. This section is written from the point of view of appropriately qualified and independently practicing forensic neuropsychologists. Although many criminal forensic neuropsychological assessments involve charges of murder, clearly there are other types of lesser criminal charges that necessitate a neuropsychologist's involvement and neuropsychological assessment as well. In our experience, all cases involving murder have required conducting the formal examination in the jail. Criminal cases in which the defendant is out on bail are not discussed in this chapter.

Initial Contacts for Criminal Referrals

Referrals most often come from defense attorneys. Forensic neuropsychologists may also receive referrals from the prosecution or directly from the court. We present the defense referral first and in most detail. At the conclusion of the chapter a section addressing the unique aspects of court and state referrals is provided.

The defense referral typically comes about in one of two ways: a telephone inquiry from the defense attorney to discuss retaining the services of the neuropsychologist, or blindly receiving records/data in the mail regarding the case (usually medical and or legal records), with an accompanying letter requesting the neuropsychologist to review the material and to contact the attorney(s).

The neuropsychologist may be initially contacted by a private practice defense attorney or by an attorney representing a Capital Defense Unit, which exists in many states with capital punishment.

The initial contacts must include and deal with the following issues:

- Discussion of the nature of the case.
- What the attorney would like from the neuropsychologist (e.g., formal examination, review of records only, work product consultation, etc.).
- Time parameters.
- The fee structure and the manner in which fees are paid.
- Logistical/location factors (being retained in murder cases can involve travel to locations distant from the neuropsychologist's office, including other states).
- Availability of information that the forensic neuropsychologist will require to evaluate the particular case comprehensively and competently.
- Whether the attorney will also be utilizing the services of other professionals in the evaluation of the case (e.g., whether a clinical psychologist, psychiatrist, or neuropsychiatrist also will conduct independent examinations of the defendant; see Sullivan & Denney, Chapter 13, this volume).

During the first contact the neuropsychologist needs enough information to determine whether he or she has the necessary qualifications, experience, motivation, and availability to accept the case. Most commonly the first contact occurs on the telephone, and the neuropsychologist often needs to obtain at least a portion of the records before making such a judgment (e.g., information pertaining to the facts of the case, the charges, and any initial medical or legal information that will ultimately be a part of more comprehensively reviewed information). Let us assume that that determination has been made, and the neuropsychologist is ready to accept the case. It is important next to discuss with the attorney why he or she specifically wants a neuropsychologist's services and the legal issues involved (brain injury/dysfunction, competency, insanity, etc.); it is presumed that the selection of a forensic neuropsychologist has been made purposely because the attorney, or some other person involved with the case, believes there may be some question as to possible brain–behavior involvement that either needs to be explored or is already a basis of the attorney's defense strategy.

At this juncture not only does the neuropsychologist need to understand "where the attorney is coming from," but also the attorney needs to understand what the neuropsychologist can do, how it will be done, and the logistic and time considerations/constraints. This includes a frank discussion of the limitations of the neuropsychological examination and assessment. It is essential that the neuropsychologist understand the full role of a forensic neuropsychologist; it is not sufficient to be clinically competent in medical cases. The neuropsychologist must be able to appreciate the relevant factors in conducting forensic evaluations (e.g., questions of malingering/exaggerating; legal proceedings, such as review of videotaped confessions, interrogations, and depositions; the role of collateral data, including interviews of other parties, as well as review of interviews of such parties by other people; and anything else that potentially bears on an understanding of the defendant's behavior with respect to the commission of the crime). Here the forensic neuropsychologist may also have to deal with the fact that he or she is part of a "team" (i.e., if other professionals are involved, such as clinical or forensic psychologists/psychiatrists). In such situations we may have to collaborate with these others professionals, then understand how our contribution fits into the overall picture (Heilbronner & Frumkin, 2003). We must always maintain our independence and objectivity, and understand the "team" concept in that context.

Setting Fees

Having arrived at a basic understanding of the case and how we fit in, a discussion of fees is necessary and appropriate. This ranges from a *pro bono* commitment to payment of one's full fees for services. For our purpose in this section of the chapter, any discussion of fees assumes that the neuropsychologist is not working *pro bono*. Although there may in some cases be a "negotiation" of fees (more likely when the bill is to be paid by a state-supported agency [e.g., a Capital Litigation Unit of a state public defender system]), there is no reason the neuropsychologist should not be paid his or her usual and customary fee for such forensic work. Of course, depending on the circumstances of the case, the neuropsychologist may accept a lesser fee, for whatever reason (e.g., because the defendant is not able financially to afford a full fee).

Keep in mind that a full forensic evaluation in a criminal case requires a substantial amount of work and time, well beyond that invested in a clinical or medical examination: the time to review extensive records, the time involved in transporting oneself and one's equipment to and from a jail or prison (which, as previously stated, may involve travel to other locations [i.e., states] on at least some occasions), the time to interview the defendant extensively, the time involved in consultations with the attorney and other professionals (if also involved in the case), the time to *very carefully* score and interpret the tests and other data, the time to interview collateral sources, the time to write a comprehensive report, the time to prepare for testimony (including one's personal organization and review of all data before testifying), the time to meet with the attorney prior to testimony, and the time involved in actually testifying (which may take several hours or several days). Involvement in such criminal cases can be inconvenient (although in our experience attorneys and the courts do their best to minimize inconvenience, court systems have a life of their own and certain delays or inconveniences are not uncommon) and disruptive to one's office schedule, unless the forensic neuropsychologist is involved only in forensic cases and does not also conduct a clinical practice.

The fee arrangement needs to be clear, and it is always best written to avoid any misunderstandings as the case unfolds. The arrangement should include not only the fee but also the manner of payment (e.g., retainers and how they will be paid). When the forensic neuropsychologist has been retained by a private attorney, it is important to be paid the retainer in advance. In this context it is important to be clear as to who is the "client." Because it is not possible at the outset to know how much time will be required in a particular criminal case, it is important that the retaining attorney understand that, in addition to the initial retainer fee, additional fees will most likely be necessary. It is essential that the attorney understand that work on the case cannot begin until such advance fees are paid in consideration of two factors: (1) to make sure that the neuropsychologist is paid for his or her work, and (2) to avoid having the neuropsychologist give the impression that his or her work may be biased toward the referral source in order to receive payment eventually (thus possibly contaminating his or her objectivity and impartiality). It is also essential to include in such a document what would happen if whoever paid the fees were unable to continue funding the assessment. Unless the neuropsychologist completes the total evaluation, he or she is not in a position to write a final report or render testimony which means, in essence, that all prior fees are lost and the project cannot be completed (see Appendix 11.1 for a sample letter of financial agreement).

In the case where fees are paid by a state or state agency, the "up front" payment model may be different. In such cases, fees are typically paid after portions of the work are completed. A request for a partial retainer is not inappropriate, but in some cases it is necessary to provide services prior to receiving payment. In such situations bills may be forwarded for the review of records after is completed; bills for interviewing collateral sources may be forwarded when that component is completed; bills for the formal examination may be paid once the examination is completed, and so forth. When the evaluation requires travel, there are also expense fees (plane fare, tolls, meals, lodging, etc.). Whereas this is not as "ideal" as being paid "up front," given the structure of these entities, it may be the way "business" must be done.

It is imperative to keep accurate, documented records of all work, particularly in terms of the amount of time spent on case-specific activities. Because the neuropsychologist will be submitting a bill for his or her work, this document is essential to keep an accurate record of time to substantiate that bill. In forensic cases neuropsychologists conduct a fair amount of work on their own (e.g., reviewing records and collateral contacts, scoring and interpreting tests). One needs to keep scrupulous track of the time spent. This may include use of a "forensic worksheet" for such documentary purposes, submitted perhaps on more than one occasion, depending on the billing agreement (e.g., when retainer fees entail more than one payment). See Appendix 11.2 for a sample forensic worksheet.

Logistics of the Examination

We come now to conducting the evaluation, and dealing with the logistics of jails, court orders, and so forth. As stated earlier, when retained on criminal matters that necessitate conducting the formal part of the evaluation in the jail, travel logistics are quite relevant, whether traveling to another state or at least transporting oneself and one's equipment to another location. It is not necessary to remind readers that the materials can be "bulky." Even when conducting an examination in a location that does not require extensive travel, one still needs to get oneself and one's equipment from here (one's office) to there (the jail). It is therefore not uncommon to transport suitcases/valises filled with testing equipment and sundry items.

When conducting the examination in another state, one option is to contact a colleague who practices in that state and attempt to arrange the "loan" of some of the testing equipment. Not too long ago, Dr. Stephen Honor, from New York, was retained to conduct an evaluation in Missouri. He contacted a neuropsychologist colleague in Missouri, who was able and willing to lend him some of the bulkier testing equipment, obviating the need to bring that material to Missouri. Nevertheless, it was still necessary for Dr. Honor to bring some of his "favorite" tests from New York.

When working out of one's own state, it is necessary to determine beforehand whether it is necessary to obtain permission from the state to conduct an examination without having a license in that particular state. We must be knowledgeable and respectful of any such state requirements, because some states consider it a criminal misdemeanor or even a felony to perform neuropsychological evaluations without a state-specific psychology license. In our experience in several states, the attorney was able to obtain permission for an out-of-state neuropsychologist to conduct the examination without undue difficulty. See Tucillo, DeFilippis, Denney, and Dsurney (2002), Shuman, Cunningham, Connell, and Reid (2003), and Yantz, Bauer, and McCaffrey (2006) for a thorough discussion on this issue. Readers may also find state-specific requirements and contact information online at *www.asppb.org*.

Considering the matter of attire, it is suggested that one dress casually but professionally. Unless you are most comfortable dressing in a jacket and tie (or the equivalent for a female neuropsychologist) this is not necessary. The actual physical working environment is not really conducive to more "formal" attire. We want and need to maintain our professional "persona," but there is no reason to spend many hours in a less than comfortable room (e.g., small and not necessarily air conditioned) dressed as we normally would in other professional situations. Indeed, days spent at the jail are likely to be long and tiring.

Prior to departing for the correctional facility, the neuropsychologist double-checks to make sure he or she has what is needed in terms of testing equipment, test protocols, stopwatch, paper, pencils, and so forth. One is not in a position to run into another room to get what he or she may have forgotten. Not having what one needs can lead to frustration and delay of conducting certain tests.

At the jail one must first present identification and authorization to perform the evaluation. To be sure, it is essential that, prior to traveling to the jail, the neuropsychologist has made the appropriate arrangements. We have found that different jails in different states (and different jail locations even within the same state) operate differently. But in any case, one must not only have the right documents to present at the jail before gaining entrance to that facility but also be prepared to present those papers perhaps multiple times (which means that it is helpful to have a few copies of those papers lest one of the jail personnel abscond with the first set and delay the evaluation even further). Necessary documents include written authorization from the defense attorney to meet with the client, as well as required court orders. All of the materials that one brings inside are scrutinized, possibly more than once. For the most part, jail personnel are not familiar with neuropsychologists. Whereas on other occasions they may have admitted psychiatrists, clinical psychologists, and neurologists (specialists who mostly bring paper and pencil [a neurologist, possibly a medical bag]), the neuropsychologist may have to explain to a "nonenthusiastic" audience why he or she is lugging a suitcase, as if about to move in for a month.

In addition to bringing all relevant papers (one's name [and some formal means of identification such as a driver's license], the name of the inmate to be examined, a judge's order, dates of admission to the facility, the amount of time one will need), it is wise to make sure that the attorney has also ensured that such papers have already been filed with the facility. Show up without the proper papers and one is looking at a long delay even before being admitted to the jail (and this does not include the time required to locate and transfer the inmate).

Once one is inside the prison, personnel arrange to have the defendant brought to wherever the examination is to be conducted. That "someplace" is highly varied. More often than not there will be a table and two chairs, usually in a room with a partial glass door, so that jail personnel can "supervise" and look in as necessary. One is likely to have plenty of time for setup, which is not necessarily an easy task: "unloading" tests, arranging them in some kind of logical order, locating one's stopwatch, pads, pencils, pens, and so forth. If one does not do this properly, he or she will spend time hunting for what is needed. Find out where the bathroom is, either by asking or doing a little exploration while waiting for the inmate to show up, and the procedure to follow when going to the bathroom (often jail personnel will want an officer to "stand guard" outside of the door or actually remove the prisoner). The actual amount of time before one meets with the inmate is quite varied, depending on the nature and expansiveness of the facility. It is not unheard of to wait an hour or more (while the inmate is located and sometimes transferred from one building to another, or waiting until he or she finishes eating or recreation).

As an aside, be courteous and patient, because jail personnel can be a big help or a big hindrance. For the most part jail personnel are hardworking and cooperative, even if they do not have the vaguest idea what a neuropsychologist is or does. One's title and status (together with one's papers) usually lead to respectful behavior on the part of the jail personnel.

The defendant arrives with an "escort," probably in handcuffs and leg restraints (depending on the attitudes of staff in the given facility, as well as the past behavior of the defendant). One should remember, never having met the inmate before, be cautious, especially if one wants the jailer to remove those restraints. Correctional facility staff interact with this individual on a daily basis; they know how the person has been behaving during the past 24 hours. In this regard, it is not unheard of for the individual to have been extremely disruptive, disrespectful, and even aggressive toward facility staff. Additionally, correctional facilities generally have a classification process that dictates how much security and restraint is needed to interact safely with this individual. This process has been developed over years of interacting with violent offenders and should not be "tossed off" lightly. Ideally, the defendant's attorney will have prepared the prisoner for the neuropsychologist's arrival; of course, the neuropsychologist has no idea what the prisoner has been told about him or her. It is necessary, before doing anything "official," that the neuropsychologist discuss his or her role, how the examination will be conducted, and what will happen afterward. One option is to have the defendant's attorney present during the consent procedure; this procedure can actually circumvent delays, because defendants often have additional questions about the purpose of the evaluation and may need reassurance from counsel. If the attorney is not present at this introduction, it is doubly imperative that he or she verify having contacted the client and gained his or her consent before the neuropsychologist's arrival for the evaluation.

Informed Consent

An informed consent is essential and needs to include all of the relevant information: what one will be doing, how one will be doing it, who will have access to the information (attorney work product vs. general availability of information), and especially the fact that one is not guaranteeing the inmate that one's work will benefit his or her legal case. The informed consent must be in writing. Informed consents are not "one size fits all." Because neuropsychologists work in different situations, the informed consent must reflect the specific circumstances of the case. We have provided five informed consent forms in Appendices 11.1 and 11.3–11.6 at the conclusion of the chapter. They essentially represent forensic neuropsychological evaluation from a private practice standpoint. In that context, the participation of the criminal charged is voluntary. By the same token, it is important to recognize that there are court-ordered evaluations that the incarcerated individual does not legally have the right to refuse. In this instance, it is always best (but not dependent on one's ability to complete the evaluation) to obtain assent, but true consent is not genuinely possible.

Before discussing the consent forms, it is important to understand that a forensic neuropsychologist may be providing services and conducting evaluations in a variety of jurisdictions. We have both conducted such examinations in states other than our own. Therefore, it is necessary to be sure that the informed consent we use does not in any way conflict with the laws of that state or jurisdiction. In this regard, discussing the issue of informed consent and documenting it with the referring attorney may be beneficial.

We hope that a brief explanation of each informed consent form will help the reader understand the purpose of each form. Note that an important aspect of each form is the client's understanding of the nature of the services to be provided, and the fact that information gathered through interviews, review of records, and neuropsychological examination will not necessarily support the position of the client (whether the attorney, the individual charged with the crime, and/or the family of the individual charged with the crime).

Appendix 11.1 is an informed consent in a situation where the attorney(s) is (are) directly retaining the forensic neuropsychologist to evaluate his or her client. Although in the majority of cases fees are paid by the individual being charged with a crime (or his or her family), there are circumstances in which the attorney(s) is (are) the retaining entity.

Appendix 11.3 is the informed consent for the circumstance in which the individual charged with the crime is incarcerated and his or her family is retaining the forensic neuropsychologist on behalf of their family member. For example, one of the authors (S. H.) was recently retained to conduct a forensic neuropsychological evaluation of a young man in his 20s, arrested and incarcerated on a charge of causing "shaken baby syndrome." Although the family was referred by the young man's attorney, the initial consultation was held with the parents on behalf of their son. Prior to traveling to the jail to evaluate this young man, additional meetings with the parents were held to obtain information necessary to understand the complex variables in the case. This form was used in that instance.

Appendix 11.4 is that form used when the forensic neuropsychologist is dealing directly with an incarcerated individual after having been retained by the attorney. Although in such cases fees are not directly provided by the inmate, he or she is the individual with whom the neuropsychologist is dealing.

Appendix 11.5 is a notification of purpose for when the evaluation is court-ordered. Here, assent is sought but not absolutely necessary. Psychology ethics and the Specialty Guidelines for Forensic Psychologists (Committee on Ethical Guidelines for Forensic Psychologists, 1991; see Tyson & Sullivan, Chapter 2, this volume) require proper notification of purpose even in instances when the defendant or inmate does not have a choice in the examination. Providing proper notification of purpose can avoid potential violations of a criminal defendant's Fifth Amendment rights to be free from self-incrimination (Bush, Connell, & Denney, 2006; Denney, 2005b; Sullivan & Denney, 2003).

Appendix 11.6 is an informed consent form designed to be presented directly to the individual charged with the crime. Like Appendix 11.5, it focuses on the evaluee's awareness regarding the purposes of the evaluation and the manner in which that information may be used, but it can be used even in instances when the evaluation is requested by the defense. There is a small acknowledgment line after each paragraph, which the defendant should initial to demonstrate that the information has been read (or read to him or her), that an opportunity for questions and clarification has taken place, and that those answers have been provided.

Factors Relevant to the Examination

How the examination is conducted is, of course, entirely within the discretion of the neuropsychologist. Obviously, it entails extensive interviewing, along with extensive neuropsychological testing. In our experience, this part of forensic involvement often requires at least 2 full days. Because getting in and out of the jail and the logistics of transporting the inmate often consume a certain amount of time, it is wise to have work to do in those interim periods.

In our evaluations of criminal cases we, as forensic neuropsychologists, are likely to have been retained because of our expertise in brain–behavior relationships and in situations where there are concerns/suspicions or knowledge of a defendant's head or brain injury, or developmental disability (or any other reason that the attorney or the court suspects "brain involvement" relevant to the crime). We are less likely to be retained when the primary concern is psychological/psychiatric disorder or questions of insanity, or the general legal concept of mental disease or defect. Notwithstanding the records that we read in preparation for evaluating the inmate, and the extensive history provided by the inmate as a part of the examination, a thorough evaluation includes other, collateral data (interviewing of any individuals who have knowledge of the inmate). If we are "working the case" alone (i.e., no psychologist or psychiatrist has also been retained) it becomes more important to obtain this additional data that will not be obtained by anyone else in the case. In such cases, mental status at the time of the commission of the crime, including *mens rea* and *actus reus*, may also be an issue, and gathering extensive data beyond the formal neuropsychological examination is essential to understand and interpret the neuropsychological data properly (see Denney, 2005a). In this context we have found the retaining attorney or organization to be quite helpful. They may have conducted interviews of significant others and/or collateral sources; however, if this is part of the background information provided to us, we must determine whether the information they have already obtained is sufficient from a forensic neuropsychological perspective. If the information we need is not available from others' interviews, we may need to reinterview those individuals. This can include prison personnel who have observed that inmate over time. For example, if our data suggest frontal lobe–type syndromes, we would expect "jailhouse" behavior to be consistent with such a hypothesis.

In spite of the fact that the defendant is incarcerated, our examination and assessment may lead us to want additional medical information to understand further and/or confirm our findings. An example of such a situation in S. H.'s experience was a gentleman arrested for a particularly gruesome murder. The neuropsychological and collateral data suggested significant brain impairment. S. H. suggested additional neuroimaging data that might be useful. Because such a test could not be conducted "on premises," it was necessary for the attorney to arrange with the court to have the defendant transferred to a medical facility for the test. Such a suggestion leads to certain additional hurdles. Although the attorney is the one to deal with the legal issues, the neuropsychologist must be prepared to explain clearly, most often in writing, the basis of the request and why it is important to his or her ability to assess the case comprehensively. Should there be a medical consultant (e.g., psychiatrist or neuropsychiatrist), the neuropsychologist can work with that individual to justify such testing.

Evaluating defendants is, at the least, inconvenient because of the logistical and time requirement factors. Nonetheless, we must be quite sure that we are very thorough and extremely comprehensive (with objectivity taken as a given) in dealing with not only the neuropsychological data but also the legal personnel with whom we interact. In criminal cases such as those described herein (as opposed to personal injury cases) there is a good possibility we will wind up testifying in court. Suffice it to say that such court appearances can be arduous, time consuming (to be on the witness stand for 8 or more hours is not rare) and very adversarial. We need to be thoroughly prepared, both in terms of the work we have done (i.e., formal examination and collection of essential collateral data) and with respect to our interactions with the legal and/or medical and psychological personnel with whom we have interfaced during the course of our evaluation.

Attorney Contacts

Contacts with the attorney during the course of an evaluation are largely perfunctory, because until we complete our evaluations we do not have much to offer. There may be status "checks," since the evaluations often take several months at least and include reviewing the records, making arrangements when travel is required, the actual examination, scoring and interpreting the tests, consulting with the attorneys and/or any other "primary" players in the case, collecting collateral information, and writing a report, if one is requested (which depends on the overall strategy of the attorney—sometimes our testimony is offered without a report having been written, although our records will have been provided to the "other side"). Once the examination is completed, we can expect to put in time meeting or discussing the case with the attorney or other personnel involved in the case. This may be face-to-face and/or telephone communication (e-mail and the Internet should not be used to transmit information or discuss the case). In these postevaluation contacts it is the job of the forensic neuropsychologist to help the attorney understand the significance of the information obtained during the course of the evaluation, findings and what they represent, and how the work may or may not fit into the attorney's defense strategy. After putting in the great amount of work required to evaluate a criminal case, our findings may or may not support the expectations of the attorney. After receiving this information the attorney decides whether he or she wants a written report. We always need to remember that regardless of the hopes or expectations of the attorneys with whom we work, ultimately we can only advocate for our findings, which do not always fit with the attorney's attempts to defend his or her client.

Reports

Attorneys come in all sizes, shapes, and predilections. Our dealings with criminal attorneys are guided by what they want of us and the initial contacts, in which we discuss what they want in relation to what we can do. Report writing is a combination of our style in how we write our reports and the kind of a report the attorney would like—if he or she wants one at all. Clinically, it would be unusual not to write a report after completing a neuropsychological examination. It is not the same in forensic neuropsychology. Aside from our own styles in writing reports (extensive/detailed v. "bare bones"), the attorney determines the extensiveness of the report he or she may want. Certainly, to be clear, whatever goes into our reports must be both accurate and objective/unbiased (as much as we can control our own inherent biases); however, how much information goes into the report depends on communications with the attorney, since the nature of the report must fit into his or her plan to defend the client. To be very clear, again, we neither tailor nor omit information essential to our findings and conclusions to suit the attorney; this would be obviously and blatantly unethical. However, it is, in our opinion, perfectly ethical to provide a "summary" report, if that is requested by the attorney. Of course, all of the information that may not be in the report is a part of our file and in our records and, if we are to testify, is discoverable via our records or testimony.

Court-Ordered Evaluations

Court-ordered and state-requested evaluations are similar. For each, the neuropsychologist should be authorized, by signed court order, to conduct the assessment. The neuropsychologist's possession of a court order to do the evaluation means that the defendant has no legal right to refuse participation. From a pragmatic perspective, inmates and defendants may not cooperate with interviewing and testing even under a court-ordered evaluation, but the neuropsychologist will definitely provide some type of report to the court. Additionally, with some exceptions, information from court-ordered evaluations is generally not protected by attorney–client privilege. Conversely, depending on jurisdiction, information from defense-retained evaluations is often protected by attorney–client privilege (Melton et al., 2007). Consequently, the defendant should be advised that all information resulting from the court-ordered evaluation will be made available to the court and probably to the state as well.

Clearly, it would be misleading for the examiner performing a court-ordered evaluation to obtain an informed consent similar to that obtained in a defense-retained evaluation, because informed consent implies that the defendant has a legal right to refuse consent and/or discontinue participation at any time. Informed consent forms also, in criminal forensic evaluations, often state that obtained data are protected by attorney–client privilege, which is clearly not the case with court-ordered evaluations.

Nonetheless, it is necessary for the neuropsychologist conducting court-ordered assessments to explain his or her role and the purpose of the evaluation clearly to the defendant. This explanation should culminate in the defendant signing a "Notification of Purpose" form (e.g., Appendix 11.5), which summarizes these limits and qualifications, and is presented to the defendant, along with a copy of the court order, at the beginning of the assessment (Melton et al., 2007).

With these notable exceptions, the court-ordered or state-retained assessment is no different than an assessment requested by the defense. Nor should it be. As noted by the Committee on Ethical Guidelines for Forensic Psychologists (1991), for any expert working in the area of forensic neuropsychology the best, and the only ethically sound, position is one of advocating for the obtained data, regardless of the retaining agency. After all is said or done, working with incarcerated criminal defendants can be extremely interesting and rewarding, albeit time-consuming and logistically challenging.

References

Bush, S. S., Connell, M. A., & Denney, R. L. (2006). *Ethical issues in forensic psychology: Key concepts and resources*. Washington, DC: American Psychological Association.

Committee on Ethical Guidelines for Forensic Psychologists. (1991). Specialty guidelines for forensic psychologists. *Law and Human Behavior, 15*(6), 655–665.

Denney, R. L. (2005a). Criminal forensic neuropsychology and assessment of competency. In G. J. Larrabee (Ed.), *Forensic neuropsychology: A scientific approach* (pp. 378–424). New York: Oxford University Press.

Denney, R. L. (2005b). Section 2: Ethical challenges in forensic neuropsychology. In S. S. Bush (Ed.), *A casebook of ethical challenges in neuropsychology* (pp. 15–22). Philadelphia: Psychology Press/Taylor & Francis.

Heilbronner, R. L., & Frumkin, I. B. (2003). Neuropsychology and forensic psychology: Working collaboratively in criminal cases. *Journal of Forensic Neuropsychology, 3*, 5–12.

Melton, G. B., Petrila, J., Poythress, N. G., & Slobogin, C. with Lyons, P. M., Jr., & Otto, R. K. (2007). *Psychological evaluations for the courts: A handbook for mental health professionals and lawyers* (3rd ed.). New York: Guilford Press.

Shuman, D. W., Cunningham, M. D., Connell, M. A., & Reid, W. H. (2003). Interstate forensic psychology consultations: A call for reform and proposal of a model rule. *Professional Psychology: Research and Practice, 34*, 233–239.

Sullivan, J. P., & Denney, R. L. (2003). Constitutional and judicial foundations in criminal forensic neuropsychology. *Journal of Forensic Neuropsychology, 3*(4), 13–44.

Tucillo, J. A., DeFilippis, N. A., Denney, R. L., & Dsurney, J. (2002). Licensure requirements for interjurisdictional forensic evaluations. *Professional Psychology: Research and Practice, 33*, 377–383.

Yantz, C. L., Bauer, L., & McCaffrey, R. J. (2006). Regulations governing the out-of-state practice of psychology: Implications for forensic neuropsychologists. *Applied Neuropsychology, 13*, 19–27.

APPENDIX 11.1. Retainer Agreement for Criminal Cases

This is a retainer agreement between Stephen Honor, PhD, PC, and the law firm of:

_____, Attorneys-at-Law
Old Country Road
Carle Place, NY 11514

The above specified attorney/legal firm has retained Dr. Honor to conduct a defense neuropsychological evaluation in a criminal litigation case. The attorney/firm agrees to Dr. Honor's hourly fee of $____ per hour for all work required in the evaluation of the case, including:

- Evaluation of *all* records (legal, medical, educational, occupational, etc.)
- Interviews and neuropsychological testing
- Obtaining collateral data
- Attorney conferences/consultations (telephone or in person)
- Out of office conferences/consultations (portal-to-portal)
- Late cancellations (i.e., less than 24-hour notice) and "no-shows"
- Report writing
- Research regarding the case (when and if necessary)
- Any other time spent in the preparation of the case
- Hourly fees for travel, if it is necessary to evaluate an incarcerated client

Should court testimony be required, current court fees are $____ for the day. Fees for pretrial preparation (i.e., review of all material prior to court appearance) and pretrial attorney consultation will be based on the hourly fee specified above. Deposition fees are based on a full or three-quarter day. Prior to any testimony, a preparation meeting must be held with the attorney(s). Following deposition, a copy of the deposition transcript will be provided for review; such review is billed at the hourly fee.

Regarding report writing, the findings will be discussed with the attorney(s) prior to the writing of any report, the nature of which will be discussed beforehand. As an objective, unbiased examiner, it is not possible to change a completed report, because of ethical considerations that strictly prohibit such changes.

All fees are payable in advance. Court and/or deposition fees are fully refundable up to 48 hours prior to court/deposition appearance.

Dr. Honor agrees to conduct a thorough, comprehensive, and unbiased evaluation; conclusions will consider all data obtained and will be consistent with the findings of the evaluation and may not necessarily support the attorney's defense strategy. While time commitments will be respected and honored, Dr. Honor will require sufficient time to conduct the evaluation as specified above. Requests from the law firm must be *timely*, allowing for sufficient time to conduct the evaluation in a professional and competent manner.

The required retainer fee at this time is $____. Additional fees will be requested as necessary.

Name of Case: _____

Name of Law Firm Representative: _____

Signature of Law Firm Representative: _____

Date: _____

APPENDIX 11.2. Sample Forensic Worksheet

YOUR PROFESSIONAL LETTERHEAD

FORENSIC WORK SHEET

Name: _____

Law Firm/Attorney: _____

Case # (if any): _____

Date	Service	Time Spent	Fee	Comments

APPENDIX 11.3. Independent Forensic Neuropsychological Examination Consent Form—Criminal Cases

You or a family member have/has been referred for an independent forensic neuropsychological examination by:

- ❖ Defense attorney _____
- ❖ Prosecuting attorney _____
- ❖ Court/judge _____
- ❖ Doctor _____
- ❖ Police _____
- ❖ Other referral source _____

This referral is based on arrest and criminal charges that have been filed against you or your family member. You or your family member will be undergoing a comprehensive neuropsychological examination in regard to the criminal charges; the examination may be conducted on one or several separate days and will require a number of hours.

The examination consists of interview, including information pertaining to the alleged crime and premorbid (i.e., before the arrest) functioning; review of relevant medical, educational, occupational and/or legal records; information from collateral sources (i.e., "significant others"); and formal neuropsychological testing (testing of intellect, memory, concentration, mental organization, etc.). The purpose of the interviews and neuropsychological examination is to assess the cognitive and behavioral functions that may be relevant to the commission of the alleged crime, and to understand those factors relevant to your/your family member's behavior and mental state. The formal examination will be conducted either in my office or, in the case of incarceration, in the jail.

Although my services have been recommended by an attorney/law firm or the court, I am not an employee of any such entity, and the examination you undergo will be independent, objective and impartial. Although you will be responsible for all fees, paid in advance on a retainer basis, there is no guarantee that the findings will be helpful to your legal case.

You are to understand that I am not your treating doctor. Therefore, I have no treatment responsibilities to you. I am responsible to conduct a competent and unbiased examination.

Should this evaluation not be completed for *any* reason on the part of the individual to be evaluated or the retaining entity, no conclusions can be provided, and any money spent up to the time of termination cannot be refunded. Any unused portion of the retainer fee will be refunded to you if the examination is not completed. Since you are responsible for fee payment, you need to consider carefully your financial resources before agreeing to undergo the evaluation to be sure you are in a position to complete it.

Fees are based on an hourly rate, as specified to you, and include interviewing, testing, report writing, consultations with the attorney(s) and/or the court, as well as time spent in traveling. A Forensic Work Sheet specifying all billed hours is kept and is available to you at any time. _____

Given these procedures, your signature below indicates your voluntary agreement to participate in this forensic process and your acknowledgment that the forensic examination process has been explained to you and that you fully understand that explanation.

NAME_____ DATE _____

SIGNATURE_____ or

NAME OF FAMILY MEMBER _____

SIGNATURE OF FAMILY MEMBER _____

WITNESS NAME (IF ANY) _____

WITNESS SIGNATURE _____

APPENDIX 11.4. Independent Forensic Neuropsychological Examination Consent Form—Criminal Cases

Your defense attorney has retained me to conduct an independent forensic neuropsychological examination based on your arrest and incarceration on criminal charges. The examination may be conducted on one or several separate days and will require a number of hours.

The examination consists of interview, including information pertaining to the alleged crime and premorbid (i.e., before the arrest) functioning; review of relevant medical, educational, occupational and/or legal records; information from collateral sources (i.e., "significant others"); and formal neuropsychological testing (testing of intellect, memory, concentration, mental organization, etc.). The purpose of the interviews and neuropsychological examination is to assess the cognitive and behavioral functions that may be relevant to the commission of the alleged crime and to understand those factors relevant to your behavior and mental state at that time. Since you are incarcerated, the formal examination will be conducted in the jail.

Although my services have been retained by your attorney/law firm or the court, I am not an employee of any such entity, and the examination you will undergo will be independent, objective, and impartial. You are to understand that I am not your treating doctor; therefore, I have no treatment responsibilities to you. The "client" is the attorney/law firm or the court that retained my services. I am responsible only to conduct a competent and unbiased examination, the results of which will be provided to your attorney/law firm or the court.

Should this evaluation not be completed for *any* reason, no conclusions can be provided.

Given the above, your signature below indicates your agreement to participate in this forensic examination process and your acknowledgment that the forensic examination process has been explained to you and that you fully understand that explanation.

NAME_____ DATE _____

SIGNATURE _____

NAME OF WITNESS (if any) _____

WITNESS SIGNATURE _____

APPENDIX 11.5. Notification of Purpose—Forensic Psychological Examination

Purpose

You have been referred by _____ for an evaluation of your neuropsychological function and mental health status.

Procedures

You may be asked about the circumstances surrounding the alleged crime(s), your understanding of the case against you, how legal proceedings work, and your past and current psychological and neuropsychological functioning. You will be given tests and asked to complete forms that will help me to learn more about you. It may be necessary for me to talk with other professionals or family members and to review prior records to obtain additional background information that will be useful.

Reporting

Information collected during the evaluation will prepared for _____ in the form of a report. Therefore, any information that you provide to me may be used in the court proceeding against you. I may be subpoenaed to Court and required to testify. You and/or your attorney will have no control over my report or my testimony.

Role Clarification

I am functioning in the role of a court-ordered examiner. As such, I am not your personal doctor; nor will I give you any therapeutic or other advice regarding your situation.

Refusal to Participate

Since this is a court-ordered evaluation you have no legal basis to refuse participation. There may be legal consequences if you should choose to limit or cease your participation. You are strongly urged to discuss this with your attorney before making any decision not to participate. A report will be provided to the Court regardless of your participation.

My signature below indicates that I have read this statement (or have had it read to me). I have had an opportunity to ask questions about the evaluation and to have issues explained in terms that I understand.

Signature: _____

Print Name: _____

Date: _____

APPENDIX 11.6. Forensic Informed Consent Contract

This Forensic Psychological Evaluation is being conducted at the request of:

_____

and is therefore somewhat different than other psychological services. It is important for you to understand how a forensic evaluation differs from more traditional psychological evaluations. To indicate that you have read and understand this document I will be asking you to initial each section.

(Initial acknowledgment of above) _____

While the results of this evaluation may or may not be helpful to you personally, the goal of this evaluation is to provide information about how you are functioning psychologically to the individual or agency requesting the evaluation. In most cases, this evaluation is intended for use in some type of a legal proceeding. As such, the confidentiality of the evaluation and the results is determined by the rules of the legal system. If your attorney has requested this evaluation, he or she will receive a copy of my report and will control how it is to be used and who has access to the report.

(Initial acknowledgment of above) _____

Normally, the results of this evaluation are protected by the attorney–client privilege. Exceptions to this might include a determination on my part that you are dangerous to yourself or another person or if you reveal information regarding child or incapacitated adult abuse or neglect. I will also have to release the results of this evaluation if a court orders me to do so. There may be other examples where the laws require me to release the information obtained during this evaluation. We will discuss these situations on a case-by-case basis.

(Initial acknowledgment of above) _____

Should a decision be made by your attorney to use the report in a legal proceeding, the report and any information pertaining to it will probably be admissible into evidence, as well as any other information you have provided. If you have any concerns about the use or distribution of my report, you should discuss these issues carefully with your attorney. If someone other than your attorney requested the evaluation, that individual is my client and he or she has complete authority over the results, including whether any information will be released to you or anyone else. in addition, because the evaluation was requested by another party, and is not for the purpose of treatment or counseling, the confidentiality may have fewer legal protections. I will not release the information unless instructed to do so by the person or entity who hired me or when I am legally required to do so.

Your participation in this evaluation is entirely voluntary. If you feel anyone is causing you to participate against your will, please tell me now. I will not conduct this evaluation without your signature on this document. You also have the right to stop the evaluation at any time. There may be legal consequences if you stop the evaluation; therefore, it may be in your best interest to consult with an attorney before doing so. In addition, if appointments are not kept or are not canceled within 48 hours of the appointment time, the person requesting the evaluation may incur charges for the time that has been reserved for this evaluation.

(Initial acknowledgment of above) _____

The evaluation itself consists of two parts, an oral interview and testing (psychological and neuropsychological). In addition, it may be necessary for me to review other related materials such as court records, depositions, transcripts, medical records, educational records, and so forth. If at any time you have a question about any aspect of the evaluation or these procedures, please feel free to ask me. In addition, if at any time you need a break from the evaluation, please let me know and we will stop as soon as possible. Once the evaluation is complete, and with the permission of the requesting party, I may be able to have a meeting with you to explain the results and answer any questions you might have. Finally, your signature below releases me, James P. Sullivan, PhD, ABPP, from any liability associated with administering psychological and other tests to you or with evaluating or reporting on the results of such tests.

(Initial acknowledgment of above) _____

I have read and understand the above. If necessary I have requested additional explanation. I agree to the above:

Signature: _____

(Print Name): _____

Date: _____

Chapter 12

Presenting Neuropsychological Findings, Opinions, and Testimony to the Criminal Court

JERID M. FISHER

Offering expert neuropsychological findings, opinions, and testimony in matters of criminal litigation is fraught with numerous challenges and pitfalls that are far removed from nonforensic clinical practice. Denney (2005b) observed, "Neuropsychologists entering the arena of forensic practice need to prepare adequately for the heightened scrutiny that comes with the court of law" (p. 456). "Heightened scrutiny" understates this experience. In all likelihood, with the stakes so high, the neuropsychological expert can and should expect that his or her work and opinions will be subjected to microscopic and obsessive analysis by experts and attorneys representing the opposing side. The goal: to expose flaws in the expert's reasoning, as well as biases and other weaknesses, through vigorous cross-examination.

The demand for forensic neuropsychological expert testimony has become increasingly prevalent in criminal litigation settings. Denney (2005a) stated, "This trend is understandable given the apparent higher rates of brain injury among criminal populations. . . . Neuropsychology has something to contribute to criminal forensic matters" (p. 378). Criminal proceedings require a clear understanding of the defendant's cognitive functioning when there is a concern that it may be compromised. Impaired cognitive functioning has potential relevance to a range of legal issues confronting the criminal defendant, including (but not limited to) competency to stand trial (including claims of complete amnesia for the criminal act), waiver and understanding of *Miranda* warnings, mental state at the time of a criminal offense (hence, potentially setting the stage for a partial or complete defense [plea of insanity] to mitigate criminal behavior), as well as issues of mitigation or competency for the death penalty.

The expert neuropsychologist should bear in mind that he or she is merely a visitor to the legal domain. The courtroom is the attorneys' turf. The criminal legal system has unique paradigms and rules, far removed from clinical neuropsychological practice. Even neuropsychologists who possess civil litigation savvy will confront unfamiliar challenges engendered by criminal courts, procedures, and laws. Legal issues define the conduct of expert work in the criminal forensic setting.

This chapter provides practical information that should prepare the neuropsychologist to function more effectively as an expert in criminal matters, as well as ensure quality forensic work, report preparation, and trial testimony. Criminal forensic work is not for thin-skinned or weak-willed individuals. Hanson (2003) observed, "Despite our level of education, training and clinical expertise, our credentials are attacked, as is the very basis of the practice of Neuropsychology. We are forced to defend our profession and our professional reputation at every step of the process, which can be simultaneously intellectually stimulating and personally frustrating" (p. 4). Forewarned is forearmed; when participating in criminal forensics, the expert is not in Kansas anymore! Absent careful and meticulous pretrial work, the expert's ability to make a meaningful contribution to the trier of fact will be greatly diminished, if not neutralized. The forensic neuropsychologist may be subjected to withering cross-examination targeted at exposing weaknesses, flaws, and biases in his or her work. Should an expert have a long day of bruising and battering on the witness stand (as a consequence of poor practice techniques), one hopes it will be limited to a "one-trial learning experience."

Expert versus Advocate: The Issue of Dual Roles— What It Is and Why It Must Be Avoided

What is a dual role? In the forensic setting, a *dual role* most typically involves acting simultaneously as a treating neuropsychologist and a forensic expert with the same individual. An extreme example of such role conflict is described by Ewing (2003) in the matter of *Baskerville v. Culligan*. In this

1994 case, the expert witness in a sex discrimination case was not only the plaintiff's treating psychologist but also her sister! Although extreme, the challenges to impartiality are more than obvious from this case. It is not necessary, however, to be one's client's relative to contaminate the forensic role of impartiality with the treating role of advocate.

Why should neuropsychologists avoid the pitfalls created by assuming a dual role as both "treater" (advocate) and forensic (nonadvocate) expert? The answer is simple. The requirements of the forensic (impartial) role depart significantly from those more traditionally associated with a treating doctor (advocate) role. This topic has been discussed in detail elsewhere (Denney, 2005a; Fisher, Johnson-Greene, & Barth, 2002) and is addressed by an array of sources, including the American Psychological Association (2002) code of ethical conduct (Section 3.05a, Multiple Relationships), the *Specialty Guidelines for Forensic Psychologists* (Committee on Ethical Guidelines for Forensic Psychologists, 2006 draft; 6.03.01 Therapeutic–Forensic Role Conflicts), and Melton and colleagues (2007). Denney (2005a) provides a useful comparison table setting forth important differences between treating and forensic roles for mental health professionals. As Fisher and colleagues (2002) asserted in reference to the expert role, "Credibility is rooted in a freedom from bias. To achieve the necessary level of objectivity that is required to truly assist the trier of fact, the neuropsychologist must resist pressures to serve as a biased advocate while striving to offer impartial data driven opinions" (p. 8). Denney (2005b) observed, "Part of the unique knowledge base in criminal forensics is the realization that forensic evaluators do not share the same goals as general clinical providers. The client is typically not the patient, and the evaluator's alliance is with the truth as opposed to the patient or referral source" (pp. 425–426).

Assuming a dual role should be vigorously resisted by the forensic neuropsychologist, not only to preserve his or her credibility at the time of testimony but to ensure that information provided to the trier of fact is objective and free of subjective bias, which is permissible in a treating (advocate) role. Denney (2005a) admonished, "A neuropsychologist who is uncomfortable with the task of being an unbiased seeker of truth should avoid forensic practice." Similarly Dietz (1996) encouraged forensic psychiatrists to adopt the role of forensic scientist, with the goal of presenting findings and opinions with "scrupulous fairness." Trimble (2004) reported recent English legal decisions precluding a treating doctor from acting as an expert. One British trial judge opined, "Where it is demonstrated that there exists a relationship between the proposed expert and the party calling him, which a reasonable observer might think was capable of affecting the views of the expert so as to make them unduly favorable to that party, his evidence should not be admitted however unbiased the conclusions of the expert might be." Trimble concludes, "No treating physician can be in a position to be an SJE [single joint expert]!" (p. 180).

This is not to say that a treating neuropsychologist is precluded from testifying in court. The treating neuropsychologist should, however, act solely as a fact witness (testifying exclusively to direct observation) and avoid offering opinions or testimony about psycholegal issues. The *Specialty Guidelines for Forensic Psychologists* (2006 draft; 6.03.02 Expert Testimony by Practitioners Providing Therapeutic Services) asserts,

> For example, providing testimony on matters such as a patient's reported history or other statements, mental status, diagnosis and treatment provided, as well as expert opinion regarding the patient's response to treatment, prognosis, and likelihood of relapse or remission would not ordinarily be considered forensic practice even when the testimony is related to a psycholegal issue before the decision maker.

The treating neuropsychologist should be ever vigilant, however, to the efforts of an attorney (who is a vigorous advocate) to persuade him or her to offer forensic opinions about psycholegal issues. As Melton and colleagues (2007) noted, "Mental health professionals should be alert to situations that threaten to involve them in such dual relationships and, *when possible*, should decline the forensic evaluator role" (p. 92, original emphasis). Neuropsychologists who desire to cultivate reputations as credible forensic experts will avoid a dual role.

Admissibility and Laws Governing Expert Testimony

Expert testimony, in theory (when conducted properly), should assist the trier of fact to understand the evidence or an issue that may be in dispute. As Judge Learned Hand (1902) observed at the beginning of the 20th century, "Expert evidence must be reliable in order to have some possible weight on an issue.... Absent reliability, the evidence would not be relevant to the inquiry." Expert witnesses are permitted to testify not only to facts and perceptions but also to opinions and conclusions.

Contemporary rules surrounding the admissibility of expert testimony have been set forth in a series of decisions by the U.S. Supreme Court, as well as the U.S. Congress. The forensic expert should be familiar with these rulings. As set forth in the *Specialty Guidelines for Forensic Psychologists* (2006 draft), "Forensic practitioners are responsible for a fundamental and reasonable level of knowledge and understanding of legal and professional standards, laws, rules, and precedents that govern their participation in legal proceedings" (4.04 Knowledge of the Legal System and the Legal Rights of Individuals).

In 1975, Congress enacted the Federal Rules of Evidence to govern the admissibility of expert witnesses and testimony in federal courts. Rule 702, Testimony of Experts provided:

> [I]f scientific, technical, or other specialized knowledge will assist the trier-of-fact to understand the evidence or to determine a fact and issue, a witness qualified as an expert by knowledge, skills, experience, training, or education may testify thereto in the form of an opinion or otherwise.

Prior to 1975, many Courts looked to the *Frye* test (*Frye v. United States*, 1923) regarding issues of admitting expert testimony. The *Frye* test stipulated that an expert opinion was admissible if it was *generally accepted* within the expert's respective field. The Federal Rules of Evidence were passed by Congress to liberalize or broaden acceptable testimony.

The Federal Rules of Evidence did not specifically mention the *Frye* test and failed to address this general acceptance standard, which had been embraced by the courts for more than half a century. As a consequence, in the years after the Federal Rules were enacted, many courts were split on the issue of applying the *Frye* general acceptance test, or Rule 702, of the Federal Guidelines. In 1993, *Daubert v. Merrell Dow Pharmaceuticals* ended this debate when the Supreme Court empowered the trial judge to act as the courtroom "gatekeeper" in admitting or precluding scientific (expert) evidence. *Daubert* held that admissibility should be governed by reliability and relevance, and the likelihood that this evidence would assist the trier of fact.

Guidelines for conducting this gatekeeper function include the following evaluative questions:

1. Has the theory or technique been tested? What is the "testability" of the expert's theory or technique?
2. Has the theory or technique been subjected to peer review and publication?
3. What is the known or potential error rate in applying the particular scientific theory or technique?
4. To what extent has the theory or technique received general acceptance in the relevant scientific community (this is the old *Frye* test)?

Prior to testifying in jurisdictions governed by *Daubert*, it is critical that the forensic neuropsychologist work through these evaluative questions with the retaining attorney to ensure that his or her testimony will be admissible (pointing out how it can be presented so as to highlight the scientific basis of the evaluation and subsequent psycholegal opinions).

Subsequent to *Daubert*, the Supreme Court refined and expanded upon admissibility and expert testimony issues in several follow-up decisions (*Joiner v. General Electric Co.* [1997] and *Kumho Tire Co. v. Carmichael* [1999]) often referred to as the *Daubert* progeny. These decisions promoted an amendment to Federal Rule 702 in 2000. The revised Rule 702 provides clear direction as to the proper method of disclosing an expert's opinion to the opposing side. Rule 702, Testimony by Experts (Amended April 17, 2000, effective December 1, 2000) states:

> [I]f scientific, technical, or other specialized knowledge will assist the trier-of-fact to understand the evidence or to determine a fact and issue, a witness qualified as an expert by knowledge, skill, experience, training, or education may testify thereto in the form of an opinion or otherwise. If (1) the testimony is based upon sufficient facts or data, (2) the testimony is the product of reliable principles and methods, and (3) the witness has applied the principles and methods reliably to the facts of the case.

While federal jurisdictions embrace *Daubert* and the Federal Rules of Evidence, individual states may or may not. Thirty-three states use *Daubert* or a reasonable facsimile to guide admissibility; 11 states reject *Daubert*, and 5 states retain a non-*Daubert* standard without explicit rejection of *Daubert*. If doubts arise about the rules in the expert's state or locality, seek the advice of informed legal counsel.

Experts should also be familiar with two additional Federal Rules of Evidence (703 and 704) which have specific applicability to expert testimony. Rule 703, Bases of Opinion Testimony by Experts states:

> The facts or data in the particular case upon which an expert bases an opinion or inference may be those perceived by or made known to the expert at or before the hearing. If of a type reasonably relied upon by experts in the particular field in forming opinions or inferences upon the subject, the facts or data need not be admissible in evidence in order for the opinion or inference to be admitted. Facts or data that are otherwise inadmissible shall not be disclosed to the jury by the proponent of the opinion or inference unless the court determines that their probative value in assisting the jury to evaluate the expert's opinion substantially outweighs their prejudicial impact.

Rule 703, in theory, permits an expert to base an opinion not only on facts in evidence but also on facts not in evidence, and even on facts that might not be admissible if they were offered at trial, as long as the underlying facts dealt with the kind of information on which similar experts would rely in making non-litigation-oriented professional judgments. However, most courts will not allow an expert to testify to inadmissible facts unless as set forth in Rule 703: "The court determines that their probative value in assisting the jury to evaluate the expert's opinion substantially outweighs their prejudicial impact."

Rule 704, Opinion of Ultimate Issue, states:

(a) Except as provided in subdivision (b), testimony in the form of an opinion or inference otherwise admissible is not objectionable because it embraces an ultimate issue to be decided by the trier-of-fact.
(b) No expert witness testifying with respect to the mental state or condition of a defendant in a criminal case may state an opinion or inference as to whether the defendant did or did not have the mental state or condition constituting an element of the crime charged or of a defense thereto. Such ultimate issues are matters of the trier-of-fact alone.

Rule 704(b) was adopted in 1984 (following the Hinckley insanity verdict) to preclude qualified mental health experts and other expert witnesses from testifying as to whether a defendant's mental state or condition affected an element of the crime or an element of the defense (this is limited to the issue of insanity). In practice, however, application of this rule has been far more inconsistent and is the source of considerable controversy (Melton et al., 2007; Slovenko, 2006). Nicholson and Norwood (2000) observed,

> The question of whether mental health professionals should offer opinions concerning dispositive facts at issue before the court (i.e., Was the defendant insane at the time of the crime? Is the defendant incompetent to stand trial?) has been a point of continuing controversy and debate. Because ultimate decisions often involve questions of morality and justice that lie outside the mental health professional's domain of expertise, some scholars have argued that psychologists (as well as other experts) should not answer the ultimate legal questions; others, however, have challenged that view. (p. 12)

Slovenko (2006) asserted, "Rule 704 (b) is an unnecessary addition to the rules of evidence," [arguing] it " . . . makes expert witnesses less useful to fact finders because it promotes indirect and incomplete testimony" (p. 25). In practice, most jurisdictions not only allow but also encourage ultimate opinion testimony.

Melton and colleagues (2007) discourage mental health professionals from offering psycholegal opinions that address ultimate legal issues. These authors assert, "Conclusions on such ultimate legal questions [such as sanity, competence, dangerousness, etc.] are the responsibility of the judge and jury, and clinicians should resist drawing them" (p. 600). However, these authors describe research with judges, which revealed that expert opinions on ultimate legal issues were viewed as very important. Melton and colleagues observed, "Numerous pressures, some subtle and some not so subtle, push mental health professionals in the direction of ultimate-issue testimony" (p. 601). The interested reader should consult Melton and colleagues and Ciccone and Clements (1987) for further discussion of this issue. As a practical example of the inherent problems in ultimate opinion testimony, consider the question of future dangerousness. In death penalty cases, prosecutors routinely ask mental health experts to predict whether a convicted killer will be violent in the future. Edens and Petrila (2001) reviewed the use of the Hare Psychopathy Checklist—Revised (PCL-R) in death penalty cases, wherein scores from this test are used to support the position that a defendant will represent a "continuing threat" to society. After a careful literature review, the authors demonstrate the spurious empirical basis for use of the PCL-R for this purpose. Nevertheless, this evidence and expert testimony are often allowed. The American Psychiatric Association has maintained the official position that predictions of future dangerousness are unreliable (*Barefoot v. Estelle*, 1983). More recently, the Texas Defender Service (2004), in a study of 155 inmates, concluded that psychiatrists' predictions about future violence were wrong 95% of the time, notwithstanding the fact that Texas is one of only two states that allows "future dangerousness" to play a critical role in determining whether a defendant receives the death penalty.

Bias and Debiasing

Williams (1997) observed, "Expert witnesses must present themselves as scientists who compile data in the most objective way and sort through alternative hypotheses to explain data. They must also be aware of the types of bias to which they are prone" (p. 38). *The Specialty Guidelines for Forensic Psychologists* (2006, draft), Section 3-01.01 (Impartiality and Fairness) states, "Forensic practitioners treat all participants and weigh all data, opinions, and rival hypotheses impartially. . . . Forensic practitioners offer facts and opinions impartially and irrespectively of who retains, compensates, or calls them to present the evidence to the judicial process."

Williams (1997) outlines various subtypes of bias, which include confirmatory bias ("the tendency to seek and value supportive evidence at the expense of contrary evidence"), anchoring (a type of confirmatory bias in which the expert is exposed at the time of initial contact with the retaining lawyer [who is an advocate] to this individual's "spin" on the case and is subsequently influenced unduly by this formulation), and illusory correlation (which occurs when a relationship is perceived between events notwithstanding the fact that objective data fail to support this relationship). Williams illustrates illusory correlation by citing the example of an individual who was administered the Boston Naming Test (BNT), despite the fact that his first language was Greek. Assuming that this individual achieved a low score on the BNT (in English) and this finding is used to support a claim of brain injury, the expert's conclusion is wrong, because this low score is more likely the result of factors other than brain damage (the BNT standardization sample did not include people whose first language was Greek).

The issue of bias begs the question of how the expert witness can avoid conducting his or her work in a manner that may be perceived as biased? Although a cross-examining attorney is likely to assert that the expert is biased, it is incumbent that the expert's practice techniques continuously embrace the objective of excluding bias. At the end of the day, if an expert can confidently evaluate his or her work as unbiased and fair, he or she will be afforded a level of confidence that makes him or her relatively "bulletproof" to opposing counsel's accusations and attacks. One method to avoid the perception of bias is to adhere to the same procedures regardless of the retaining party, and to administer these procedures as set forth in their respective test manuals (i.e., avoid shortcuts or shortened forms [unless the individual being examined has some physical or mental limitation that precludes the usual method of administration]). As set forth in the *Standards for Educational and Psychological Testing* (American Educational Research Association, 1999), "Test users should follow carefully the standardized procedures for administration and scoring specified by the test developer, unless the situation or a test taker's disability dictates that an exception should be made" (p. 63). Lee, Reynolds, and Willson (2003), in a probing review of alterations in test administration, conclude that such deviations "can significantly change the psychometric properties of the tasks. Given the emphasis of *Daubert* and the 2000 amendment to Federal Rule of Evidence 702 on the reliability of the methods the expert uses in gathering data, changes in test administration that might affect the psychometric properties of a score take on a special significance in the forensic arena" (p. 72). These authors caution, "in forensic settings, especially given recent interpretations of the *Daubert, Joiner,* and *Kumho* Federal court rulings, examiners who use a non-standard administration format or materials will be vulnerable to challenges to the validity (bearing on the admissibility) and credibility (bearing on the weight) of any conclusions drawn upon their so-called scores" (p. 76).

Structured interviews are preferable to clinical "make it up as you go" interviews. The former allows for systemic data collection and invariant questioning of the same topic areas; the latter may not. Although a more controversial topic among neuropsychologists, a fixed battery of tests, as opposed to a flexible battery (in which test procedures are selected based on the referral questions), may ultimately be viewed as more reliable and valid in the forensic contest (see the "Assessment Issues" section of this chapter for relevant legal decisions). Of course, given the differing nature of referral questions in the criminal setting, it is not always appropriate to use an invariant battery of procedures. As an example, assessing brain damage entails different test procedures than evaluating competency to stand trial or competency to waive *Miranda* warnings. Regardless of procedures chosen, one should ensure that they are reliable and valid, and that the expert is trained to administer and interpret the results. If the expert does not know, rest assured that opposing counsel will likely confront the expert with this information during cross-examination.

The expert should query him- or herself, "If I had been retained by the other side, would my procedures, my analysis/interpretations, or my conclusions be different than those I have set forth?" If the answer is "yes," then the expert is sliding down the slippery slope of partisanship. Sweet and Moulthrop (1999, p. 77) set forth a series of self-examination questions intended to identify bias in neuropsycholegal peer review; however, these questions prompt identification of bias in the expert's own work as well:

- Do I receive referrals only from plaintiff attorneys or only defense attorneys?
- Do I almost reach conclusions favorable to the side that has retained me?
- Have I moved away from being an expert witness to being an advocate?
- Do I form opinions of plaintiff or defense populations prematurely, without having enough facts for a solid opinion?
- Have I taken a position, in very similar cases, when retained by an attorney from one side that I did not take when retained by the opposite side?
- Do I routinely apply the same decision–rules for establishing brain dysfunction no matter what side retains me?
- Have I been reaching the same diagnostic conclusion at a much higher base rate than my colleagues or at a higher rate than described in the literature?
- Has my initial written opinion been altered by the time of deposition or trial testimony?
- Does my emotional response to a case cloud or distort my objectivity?

Foundation

The criminal justice system abhors unreliable information that may mislead or unnecessarily confuse the trier of fact. Good forensic work draws upon multiple informational data sources to corroborate facts and conclusions. Although the prior assertion may seem like a blinding flash of the obvious, empirical research (Skeem, Golding, Cohen, & Berge, 1998, p. 542) reveals "poor rates of incorporation of third-party information" in forensic reports. As Skeem and colleagues (1998) noted, "examiners who fail to review and incorporate 'outside' evidence leave themselves vulnerable to adversarial attack. Attorneys can easily assail uninformed examiners on the witness stand with evidence that contradicts their reports or conclusions" (p. 542).

The forensic neuropsychologist should routinely insist on a wide range of archival record Discovery. Reviewing important and relevant archival records provides an objective understanding of the defendant's past and present behaviors across a broad range of functional domains. An effective forensic expert, in most circumstances, will need to review any and all records that could potentially shed light upon the functional and mental status of the individual. Fisher and colleagues (2002) recommended the following generic list of records for routine forensic Discovery (of note, the relevant records requested for review will vary as a function of the legal question under consideration; for example, prior criminal records would be more relevant to risk assessment than would questions of competency):

- Educational transcripts and standardized test results
- Cumulative school health records
- Employment and personnel records, including supervisory evaluations
- Medical records
- Ambulance and police accident records (if applicable)
- Military records
- Alcohol or other drug treatment records
- Mental health records
- Income tax returns
- Pharmacy records
- Neuropsychological reports and raw test data
- Legal documents

Nicholson and Norwood (2000) underscore the importance of collecting "third-party information" which includes records such as "medical, criminal justice, educational and employment," as well as "interviews with or review of statements by witnesses, relatives and victims" (p. 11). Nicholson and Norwood observed that this practice "is a central characteristic of forensic assessment that distinguishes it from traditional therapeutic assessment" (p. 11).

Melton and colleagues (2007), in referencing the forensic examiner's affirmative responsibility to seek archival data, assert,

> Such information is also important in terms of enhancing the examiner's credibility with the judge, jury, and attorneys. To the degree that these parties view the forensic examiner as the mouthpiece for the client's self-serving story, they will discount and potentially disregard the examiner's testimony or report. Efforts to corroborate statements provided by clients and to weigh it against information from other sources can significantly improve the weight assigned to the examiner's conclusions. (p. 53)

The forensic neuropsychologist should insist on a full review of relevant archival materials prior to rendering a forensic opinion. If these materials are not provided or are provided incompletely, then the expert should not feel pressured to offer a psycholegal opinion with any degree of certainty. It is preferable to refuse to offer an opinion than to set forth an opinion without adequate foundation.

Lees-Haley and Cohen (1999) have compiled a useful comparison table (Table 12.1) outlining 17 distinctions between scientific and pseudoscientific expert work in forensic neuropsychology. Among these comparisons, they assert that a scientific expert is an "advocate of objectivity, evidence, reason, logic" (p. 465).

Clearly, well-informed forensic opinions require a careful and meticulous review of important foundational data sources.

Assessment Issues

This section touches briefly on several important assessment issues (third-party observers, assessment of effort, flexible vs. fixed test battery, and use of experimental procedures), with special reference to the criminal forensic arena.

The chief goal of forensic assessment is impartiality. The expert should advocate for conclusions drawn from the data, but never for a specific side in a legal matter. To advocate effectively for the data, the expert must conduct his or her evaluation in manner that provides a high level of confidence in the conclusions drawn from the data. As Denncy (2005a) observed, "The evaluator must carry out the evaluation much like a detective would attempt to sleuth out the truth" (p. 383).

TABLE 12.1. **Distinction between Scientific and Pseudoscientific Experts in Forensic Neuropsychology**

Scientific expert	Pseudoscientific expert
1. Open-minded, but skeptical of all experts regardless of personal characteristics, such as credentials, years of experience, publications, number of degrees, sources of degrees, awards, titles, association memberships.	1. Insinuates validity of opinions based on personal characteristics such as credentials, source of degree, years of experience, organization memberships.
2. Views neuropsychology as a young research discipline with many issues yet to be resolved.	2. Views neuropsychology as sophisticated, with well-established ecological validity and high intradisciplinary agreement on standards and methods.
3. Describes procedures explicitly enough to permit replication and rebuttal, and encourages criticism and commentary from members of other disciplines.	3. Suppresses data, claims it is unethical to permit anyone besides members of the guild to evaluate and criticize neuropsychological tests or data, avoids disclosure of specific methodology, claims no one but insiders can understand data.
4. Openly explores alternative explanations for the data.	4. Presumes causation, minimizes investigation of other potential explanations, downgrades importance of alternative life stressors, claims only neuropsychological explanations apply to persons with possible brain injuries.
5. Advocate of objectivity, evidence, reason, logic.	5. Advocate of plaintiff or defense.
6. Relies on empirical data interpreted with reason or logic.	6. Relies on intuition, clinical experience, speculation, hunch, conjecture, imagination, what feels right.
7. Makes inferences from base rates, law of large numbers, descriptive data.	7. Generalized from small samples, anecdotal evidence, vivid illustrations, sensational data.
8. Welcomes reasoned criticism, questioning, cross-examination.	8. Resents and belittles cross-examination, overtly or covertly; treats criticism of neuropsychology as treason.

(continued)

TABLE 12.1. *(continued)*

Scientific expert	Pseudoscientific expert
9. Distinguishes between observation and inference, consensual/empirical data versus self-report data.	9. Blurs objective and subjective data, or denies the existence of any distinction between the two.
10. Reads and relies on empirical research literature, admits limitations of knowledge.	10. Relies on clinical experience in contradiction to well-researched findings.
11. Attacks methodology of opposing experts.	11. Attacks person of opposing expert, makes *ad hominem* arguments.
12. Seeks explicit definition of alleged patterns and support for such allegations in peer-reviewed empirical literature.	12. Claims to see patterns that are not apparent to opposing expert, claims existence of signature profiles that prove causation, but cannot recall citations of independently replicated empirical demonstrations of their existence.
13. Draws attention to overall predictive; power, consideration of all cells in table (true and false; positive and negative), points out that most sensitive test is sheer unfounded allegation.	13. Emphasizes sensitivity of tests, claims extreme accuracy.
14. Expects temporal logic, dose–response logic, reasonable consistency of data.	14. Overlooks or makes excuses for unusual temporal relations, contradictory chronologies, and vague or implausible dose–response allegations.
15. Responds to request for production of files by making materials available to the extent permitted by applicable laws and professional guidelines.	15. Responds to request for production of files and materials by seeking excuses to avoid disclosure and then by interpreting information requests as narrowly as possible to restrict access.
16. Treats attorney inquiries objectively by focusing on substantive matters addressed and avoiding invitation to respond to matters personally or emotionally.	16. Tends to be defensive in responding to attorney challenges to work and conclusions.
17. Accepts outcome as product of a specific form of dispute resolution.	17. Views outcome as endorsement or rejection of science depending on whether it agrees or disagrees with the expert's position.

The issue of third-party observers has been extensively researched and discussed in the literature (Constantinou, Ashendorf, McCaffrey, 2005; Duff & Fisher, 2005; Lynch, 2005), as well as in official position papers issued by the National Academy of Neuropsychology (Axelrod et al., 2000) and the American Academy of Clinical Neuropsychology (2001). The interested reader is referred to these sources for arguments to preclude a third-party observer from the forensic neuropsychological examination. In essence, this prohibition is based on legitimate concerns that a third-party observer represents a significant departure from the original test standardization, as well as a threat to neuropsychological test security. Third-party observation of forensic examinations should be resisted on multiple grounds.

One of the earliest articles (Binder & Johnson-Greene, 1995) describing the adverse effect of a third-party observer (the patient's mother) concerned Portland Digit Recognition Test (PDRT) performance. Employing an A-B-A-B design, each time the patient's mother was present, PDRT test performance declined significantly. This issue is of particular concern with respect to criminal forensic work. For example, a neuropsychologist who routinely works as a prosecution witness on death penalty cases allows a third-party observer during his examinations. If this neuropsychologist subsequently finds evidence of suboptimal performance on symptom validity testing (SVT), is he justified in concluding that the defendant was intentionally exaggerating/magnifying his test performance, or are SVT findings contaminated by the presence of a third-party observer? Obviously, testimony regarding possible malingering carries potentially grave consequences for the accused and can be quite prejudicial.

The subject of SVT is addressed in a position paper published by the National Academy of Neuropsychology (Bush et al., 2005). Issues such as the purpose and methods of SVT assessment are discussed. This paper asserts, "The potential for symptom fabrication or exaggeration is higher in forensic contexts than in many clinical contexts. As a result of the increased incentive to mislead the examiner, neuropsychologists have a responsibility to conduct more extensive assessment of symptom validity" (p. 423). Similarly, Bauer, O'Bryant, Lynch, McCaffrey, and Fisher (2007) assert, "Without the support of passing SVT scores, lowered scores on other cognitive measures remain suspect due to insufficient effort making valid conclusions difficult, if not impossible, to glean" (p. 216). The weight of the literature and prevailing thinking is sufficient to require SVT as an integral part of any forensic test battery. These procedures are no longer optional; omitting SVT from a forensic neuropsychological evaluation not only weakens the credibility of the expert's assessment but also acts as a neon sign for cross-examination regarding a very significant omission error.

There is the interesting story of Vincent Gigante, Mafia boss of the Genovese family, sometimes called the "oddfather," who for many years successfully malingered organic and psychiatric symptoms to avoid standing trial (Mossman, 2003). The forensic neuropsychologist in this matter opined that Mr. Gigante "currently has moderate to severe dementia which reflects significant underlying central nervous system dysfunction" (notwithstanding the fact that PDRT hard item performance fell at a chance level). Mr. Gigante subsequently pleaded guilty in 2003 to racketeering charges, admitting he had faked mental illness and dementia to teams (he outwitted 34 mental health examiners) of forensic psychiatrists and a neuropsychologist in an effort to avoid competency hearings from 1990 to 1997.

It is also not unusual for defendants to claim a crime-specific amnesia (Cercy, Schretlen, & Brandt, 1997; Clark, 1997; Trimble, 2004). Kopelman (1995) reported that 25–45% of criminals found guilty of homicide claimed amnesia for the event

Cima, Merckelbach, Nijman, Knauer, and Hollnack (2001) reported, "As a rule of thumb, 20 to 30% of offenders of violent crimes claim amnesia for their crime. Various reasons may be set forth for the amnesia, from head injury to dissociative states" (p. 32). As one of my former elder colleagues was fond of saying, "Amnesia is the perjurer's sanctuary." There are both legitimate (e.g., epilepsy or head trauma) and not so legitimate (e.g., avoiding responsibility) reasons to claim amnesia after committing a crime. Defendants alleging a crime-specific amnesia deserve to have their claims evaluated carefully, as long as we bear in mind the high base rate for malingering in this population (Jelicic, Merckelbach, & van Bergen, 2004). Cima and colleagues describe one famous example of feigned, crime-specific amnesia. Rudolph Hess, at the start of the Nuremberg trials for atrocities committed by the Third Reich, claimed he was amnesiac for the entire period of the Third Reich. Prominent psychiatrists examined Hess, concluding that his amnesia was legitimate. When it later became clear to Hess that his claimed amnesia prevented him from responding to allegations, he apparently announced that he had fooled his examiners and was feigning amnesia. Both Cima and colleagues and Jelicic and colleagues (2004) underscore the importance of using forced-choice procedures when evaluating claims of crime-specific amnesia (i.e., arguing that interview assessment is insufficient). Denney (1996) provides several case examples of crime-tailored SVT in detecting feigning in criminal defendants. He concludes, "SVT appears to be helpful in correctly identifying feigned remote memory loss within the criminal forensic arena" (p. 598). In more recent writings, Denney (2005a) provides practical details for tailoring an SVT to a specific claim of remote memory loss by the criminal defendant.

What makes scientific sense is not always compatible with the lawyer's role as advocate. I recently served as a consultant to a District Attorney (DA) after a particularly brutal multiple homicide. A middle-aged man with no previous criminal record stabbed his wife to death, then killed one daughter and seriously wounded another daughter. His lawyer, based on a defense psychiatrist's evaluation, claimed that his client had been in a dissociative state at the time of the instant offense and had a specific and dense amnesia for this horrific crime. This expert, serving in a consultative capacity to the DA, proposed assessment with a crime-specific SVT. However, the DA ultimately declined this suggestion, indicating that from a trial-strategy perspective, if the test results failed to detect suboptimal responding, it would bolster the defendant's amnesiac claim and his defense. For additional detail in the area of malingering, see Denney, Chapter 4, this volume.

The issue of what constitutes a necessary and sufficient forensic neuropsychological test battery has been the subject of debate and controversy (Heilbronner, 2004). Of relevance are several court decisions addressing the issue of a fixed versus flexible battery. Perhaps the best known (and misunderstood) case is *Chapple v. Ganger* (1994). This opinion has often been cited (erroneously) as supporting the use of a fixed versus flexible test battery in a forensic setting (Reed, 1996). In this case, a brain-injured child underwent neuropsychological evaluation (flexible test battery) with Dr. Catherine Mateer (at the request of plaintiff's counsel), who testified that her evaluation revealed evidence of permanent brain damage to the infant plaintiff. In rebuttal, the defense called Dr. Ralph Reitan (fixed test battery), who opined that the infant plaintiff, based on objective test results, had made a good recovery from his brain injury. In addition, they called Dr. Lynch, a consultant in neurosurgery and neurology, who opined that the plaintiff had made a full, uncomplicated recovery. The plaintiffs issued a *Daubert* challenge to the opinions of Dr. Lynch, but contrary to lore, they did not make the same challenge to Dr. Reitan, although the plaintiff argued "that Dr. Reitan's methodology is viewed by some experts as outdated" (p. 497). The trial court ultimately ruled in favor of the defense experts' opinions, noting the lack of medical and scientific evidence offered by the plaintiff ("As to the areas which show below normal scores, there is not sufficient scientific evidence to support the conclusion that these scores are indicative of permanent organic brain damage in children" [p. 1498]). However, the district judge did not discuss the clinical validity or clinical relevance of the two types of neuropsychological batteries in her decision. In his 1996 article addressing this decision, Reed noted, "Perhaps the brightest result of the *Chapple* decision, at least for clinical neuropsychologists, is that the federal courts under the *Daubert* standard will admit neuropsychological test results as scientific evidence and treat the clinical neuropsychologist as a medical, scientific expert witness" (p. 320). Reed further opined,

> Within clinical neuropsychology, professionals who use the validated or fixed neuropsychological test batteries to obtain reliable and valid objective test results will generally find the *Daubert* standard an easy threshold to pass; however, professionals who use only flexible neuropsychological test batteries to obtain valid and reliable objective test results will find the *Daubert* standard more imposing, if not impossible to pass. (p. 321)

McKinzey and Ziegler (1999) described their unsuccessful *Frye* challenge to a flexible battery approach. In this matter, Mr. Charles Sebastianelli was struck on the head by a milk carton crate on March 7, 1997, without alteration in consciousness. Later that month (March 27, 1997) he solicited the murder of a business partner and the partner's wife and son (of note, he had been soliciting the services of this would-be hit man for the 6 months prior to being struck on the head). Mr. Sebastianelli was arrested and charged with solicitation of murder. During police interrogation, he denied these allegations and invoked his *Miranda* rights. Mr. Sebastianelli was subsequently referred for neuropsychological evaluation and administered a flexible battery of tests. The consulting neuropsychologist, Dr. Norton, concluded that there were "some significant [albeit mild] abnormalities in both cognitive and emotional functioning" (p. 544), which she attributed to his March 7, 1997, concussion. As a result, "defense counsel offered Dr. Norton's report and proposed testimony as part of the defense theory that Mr. Sebastianelli's concussion prevented him from attaining the required level of intent" (p. 546). The prosecution retained the authors of this article, McKinzey and Ziegler, to challenge the admissibility of Dr. Norton's proposed testimony under *Frye*, arguing that her opinions were not reliable or scientific, and were "likely to sway the lay jury with the mantle of 'expert' " (p. 547). At the hearing, Dr. Norton argued in support of her methods, further testifying that whereas there were some need to control for malingering, "she did not use any test designed for that purpose since she found the literature unsettled" (p. 547). Additional and very significant limitations in the doctor's techniques and interpretations of findings were set forth during the course of this hearing: "Given the glaring deficiencies, we [McKinzey and Ziegler] argued, the doctor's testing was not done properly, according to the profession's generally accepted scientific principles. Her opinions, which relied upon her testing, were therefore equally unreliable, and should not be allowed" (p. 549). Notwithstanding these arguments, the judge refused to agree, stating that the jury could consider "the weight of the evidence" (p. 550). The authors concluded,

There is good news and bad news in this case example. The judge's decision to allow the flexible battery in, despite the criticisms, mean psychologists will rarely have any conventional testimony excluded.... If this case is any guide to the future, judges will not use *Frye* or *Daubert* to keep juries from hearing testimony, even when the psychological procedures are clearly flawed. (p. 550)

More recently, a New Hampshire Superior court, in a *Daubert* motion, in the matter of *Baxter v. Temple* (2005), precluded the findings/testimony of plaintiff's neuropsychologist (who determined that brain damage was present in a pediatric lead poisoning case after she used a flexible battery of tests referred to as the "Boston Process Approach"). The court ruled against a flexible battery approach in a forensic setting. The defendants argued that the plaintiff's expert's methodology was "not accepted in the appropriate scientific literature as a 'forensic' approach to assessing children with lead poisoning" (p. 6). Dr. Faust, the defense consultant, opined, "The goal of a clinical neuropsychologist ... is to advance the interest of the patient.... On the other hand, the role of the forensic neuropsychologist is to render an objective analysis even though such analysis may not advance the individual interest of the patient" (p. 13). Further argument was presented that the plaintiff's expert deviated from standardized administration by allowing the plaintiff extra time to complete specific tests, while omitting portions of other test procedures. Based on defense arguments, the court precluded testimony and evidence from the plaintiff's expert. The court opined that although the Boston Process Approach was "generally accepted in the scientific literature as a sound scientific approach to evaluating individuals for brain injury, the evidence failed to show that it is generally accepted in the appropriate scientific literature as a forensic approach to evaluating individuals for brain injury" (p. 17).

A final assessment issue concerns the use of experimental procedures in the criminal forensic arena. The *Specialty Guidelines for Forensic Psychologists* (2006, draft) observes (12.02, Appropriate Use of Assessment Procedures): "Forensic practitioners ordinarily use assessment instruments whose validity and reliability have been established for use with members of the population tested or other representative populations." To illustrate, several years ago, I was retained as an expert by the prosecution in a competency matter involving a defendant accused of attempting to murder his neighbor. Although more than enough physical evidence (including the firearm used in the crime, with the defendant's fingerprints, and an eyewitness to the shooting) linked the defendant to the crime, he steadfastly maintained that he did not commit the crime. Competency was raised by the defense because of the defendant's rigid insistence that someone else was the perpetrator; the defense neuropsychologist theorized that the defendant had a frontal lobe dementia. To support his frontal dementia theory, the neuropsychologist used an experimental test, the Bechara Gambling Task (Bechara, Damasio, Tranel, & Anderson, 1998), which he indicated (in his final report) was "a research task on which patients with lesions to the ventromedial frontal lobe show a pattern of performance that is distinctly different from the pattern of normals, schizophrenic patients and patients with diffuse brain damage. Patients with a mild variant of frontotemporal dementia show the same pattern of performance on a very similar research task." The neuropsychologist subsequently used these test results to support his testimony that the defendant had a frontal lobe dementia. Needless to say, the prosecutor focused like a laser beam on the use of an experimental test to form conclusions in a murder competency hearing. Following a very lengthy cross-examination of this neuropsychological expert witness, the defense stipulated to the defendant's competency and the guilt–innocence phase of the trial proceeded.

Of note, the National Academy of Neuropsychology issued a position paper (Bush, 2005) entitled "Independent and Court-Ordered Forensic Neuropsychological Examinations" that addresses many of these important assessment issues.

Forensic Reports

A forensic report, when well written, provides an easy-to-follow blueprint of the expert's evaluation and reasoning, and should incorporate the practice techniques discussed in this chapter. A good report allows the reader (typically a nonpsychologist) to understand the psycholegal questions addressed, the methods employed by the examiner, and the reasoning processes relied upon by the expert to draw the conclusions set forth with the appropriate degree of certainty required for the legal issue under consideration. Paradoxically, the most important rule of report writing is always, without exception, to refrain from knee-jerk preparation of a written report after an evaluation is completed. To wit, while preparing this chapter, I received a call from a local criminal defense attorney requesting a neuropsychological evaluation of an individual accused of committing multiple homicides. After an initial discussion about the facts of the case, as well as logistics regarding the conduct of an examination, the defense attorney admonished, "Please don't prepare a report when you have completed your examination. Call me to discuss your findings first." These instructions echo Melton and colleagues (2007, p. 522): "When the assessment is for an attorney, the examiner should generally offer an oral summary and let the attorney decide whether a written report is needed." Babitsky and Mangraviti (2002, p. 2) refer to this as "the Golden Rule of Expert Report Writing," noting that "experts should never, under any circumstances, create any written reports unless specifically instructed to do so by retaining counsel." When conducting an evaluation for the defense, the decision regarding report preparation falls on the shoulders of the referring attorney, not the expert.

Under no circumstances should an expert agree to provide a draft report to an attorney. Although providing a draft report to the retaining attorney may sound preposterous, an attorney may successfully pressure an expert for a draft report. This practice allows the attorney to exert a potential influence on the expert's opinion (and, at the very least, leads to the impression of undue influence) and completely contaminates the expert's impartiality. Babitsky and Mangraviti (2002) observed, "If opposing counsel can show that retaining counsel improperly influenced the expert's report, the expert will lose credibility and the report will be discredited.... Draft reports are discoverable. It is, therefore, the best practice for the expert to avoid producing any draft written reports and to refuse to let counsel influence the fundamental substance of the expert's findings, conclusions, and reasoning" (p. 3, original emphasis). Consistent with this position, the *Specialty Guidelines for Forensic Psychology* (2006 draft) asserts (14.01, Accuracy, Fairness, and Avoidance of Deception), "Forensic practitioners do not, by either commission or omission, participate in misrepresentation of their evidence, nor do they participate in partisan attempts to avoid, deny, or subvert the presentation of evidence contrary to their one position or opinion."

Nicholson and Norwood (2000), in a probing analysis of forensic psychological report writing, concluded, "Nevertheless, the available evidence reveals significant deficiencies in the reports of forensic evaluations submitted to the courts" (p. 40). They cite one study regarding attorneys' and judges' level of satisfaction with pretrial competency reports:

> In general, the attorneys and judges who responded did not appear to be satisfied with the degree of specificity contained in the mental health professionals' answers to the statutory questions regarding competence. The respondents complained that little attempt was made to individualize cases, and that reports should provide more extensive descriptions of defendant's background and history, psycholegal abilities (especially with regard to assisting an attorney), and psychiatric condition, as well as specific reasons for the expert's opinions. (p. 29)

In an earlier article, Skeem and Golding (1998) emphasized the forensic examiner's principal role—to describe the examinee's capabilities and deficits relevant to the legal issue at hand, along with the examiner's inferences and reasoning regarding the causes of the observed deficits. Skeem and Golding further observed, in light of the fact that court decisions are often based on reports submitted by mental health experts rather than courtroom testimony, that the omission of the aforementioned data and reasoning in a report should be viewed as a fundamental flaw.

Volumes have been devoted to the art and science of forensic report writing. The expert should bear in mind that a forensic report fulfills multiple functions. The expert report becomes an official record of the evaluation with details such as the number of contacts with the defendant and other third-party informants, records reviewed, procedures administered, results of these procedures, and summary and opinions.

The report should be written in an easy-to-read (nonjargon), nonpartisan format. Neutral topic headings should organize the report's contents. Topic headings not only improve the report's readability but are extraordinarily useful to the expert at the time of trial. When testifying, topic headings allow the expert to locate relevant information quickly. The ability to locate relevant information efficiently when testifying conveys to the jury that the expert is well organized (this impression will inure to the expert's benefit as a credible and careful practitioner). At the other extreme, the disorganized expert, forced to fumble for information, especially during cross-examination, may be viewed as sloppy, hence less credible. Credibility ultimately determines the weight the jury assigns to the expert's findings and opinions.

The initial portion of the forensic report should succinctly summarize information regarding the referral source and the purpose for the evaluation (e.g., competency to stand trial). Information about each and every interview and testing contact with the defendant should be provided, including the dates and times of these contacts, location of the evaluation, and individuals present. If third-party observers were an issue, it should be explicitly stated, along with any potential limitations created by this threat to the examination's validity. Details of the informed consent waiver provided to the defendant should also be explicitly set forth (Fisher et al., 2002).

The report should itemize data sources (in addition to interviews with the defendant), including all records–pictures–legal documents reviewed and third-party informants interviewed. As Babitsky and Mangraviti (2002) observed, "The more thorough the expert's investigation, the more credible the expert's conclusions will be. The thoroughness of the expert's investigation is directly related to the documents the expert reviewed" (p. 55).

The *Specialty Guidelines for Forensic Psychologists* (2006 draft; 14.03, Disclosing Sources of Information and Bases of Opinions) state, "Forensic practitioners affirmatively disclose all sources of information obtained in the course of their professional services. Forensic practitioners affirmatively disclose which information from which source was considered and relied upon for formulating a particular conclusion, evidence, opinion, or other professional product."

The expert's report should include relevant findings from structured interviewing with the defendant and third-party collateral informants, as well as archival data sources. These findings should be disclosed in well-organized subsections. Archival facts should be clearly tied to their data source (this facilitates source attribution during both direct- and cross-examination testimony). As an example, if the expert opines that the defendant has a brain injury as a consequence of a severe head injury sustained a child, this should be based not on hearsay but be directly (and easily) linked to a reliable archival source. A word to the wise: If information recorded in interview notes (or other forms of note taking from archival records) is subsequently excluded from the forensic report, the expert should be prepared for cross-examination regarding the motivation(s) underlying this omission, particularly if this omitted information contradicts the expert's opinions. Even relatively benign omissions, in the hands of a skilled cross-examiner, may result in a series of cross-examination questions about how the expert determines what is important versus unimportant information to include or exclude from his or her report. If a biased motivation can be demonstrated for excluding information from the expert's report (that is contained in the expert's notes), then the expert may be cast as a partisan advocate.

A separate section on behavioral observations should be included in the report. The expert should limit this to a detailed description of the defendant's interview and testing behaviors, absent judgments or inferences about these behaviors. The expert should also address comorbid variables that may potentially have an adverse (but extraneous) impact on contemporary test performance. Important comorbid variables to consider include prescription and illicit substance use/abuse, alcohol consumption, hours of sleep, and so forth. Absent direct discussion and consideration of comorbid variables in the expert's report, cross-examination may find fertile argument in the suggestion that extraneous comorbid variables could account for poor test performance (e.g., the defendant's lack of sleep interfered with new learning) rather than the etiology that is argued in the expert's psycholegal opinion(s).

The report should document a detailed and reliable test methodology that cannot be successfully challenged under *Daubert*. Test data from the expert's formal assessment(s) that address the psycholegal question(s) under consideration should be set forth in a separate report section.

The final section of the forensic report contains the expert's psycholegal formulation. This section integrates all the data into a coherent series of conclusions relevant to the legal question under consideration. Stick to the facts. Maintain a scientific and conservative tone of voice. Avoid offering eccentric opinions that are not supported by the mainstream peer-reviewed literature (e.g., opining that a severe brain injury does not result in enduring sequelae). Be mindful of the cautions set forth in the *Specialty Guidelines for Forensic Psychologists* (2006 draft; 14.02, Differentiating Observations, Inferences, and Conclusions): "In their communications, forensic practitioners are careful to differentiate among their observations, inferences, and conclusions. Forensic practitioners are prepared to explain the relationship between their expert reports or testimony and the legal issues and facts of an instant case."

Several additional caveats relevant to report preparation should be mentioned. Babitsky and Mangraviti (2002) provide a detailed primer of prohibited and discouraged language. As an example, they admonish the expert to avoid "friendly language directed at counsel," such as "It was nice having lunch with you yesterday," "Have a nice holiday," or "I trust this information will be of help." The narrative text and tone of the expert's report should embrace neutrality. Keep it impersonal. If not, rest assured that cross-examination will become very personal. Other traps to avoid include making statements such as "The research shows." . . . This assertion will assuredly open the door to a challenge to cite the specific research. Similarly, it is potentially dangerous to cite a specific "pro" research study in the expert's report. There will likely be statements contained in the specific reference that, given the nature of the adversarial beast, may be taken out of context (a favorite cross-examination tactic) to contradict the expert's opinion.

The expert's report should be proofread several times. Simple typographical errors, errors in dates, or misquoting a record can all be used to impeach the expert as careless. The argument is quite simple: If he or she made errors here, it will be suggested to the jury, then it is also likely that errors occur in other aspects of the expert's examination. Sloppiness is not tolerated in a forensic setting.

The expert's report should avoid disrespectful judgments or *ad hominem* attacks on opposing experts. A well-known and respected plaintiff's attorney in Rochester, New York (who retained me to assess his brain-injured client) recently forwarded a copy of the defense expert's neuropsychological report in this civil matter. The case involved a young woman pedestrian struck by a large, out-of-control delivery van. Her brain injury was quite severe, encompassing intracerebral bleeding and several weeks of unconsciousness. The defense expert's report acknowledged that the plaintiff had been injured but asserted with respect to my finding of a serious brain injury, "a brain injury was, thank heavens, not one of those injuries." In commenting on my review of the plaintiff's medical course as documented in the archival hospital file, the defense neuropsychologist opined, "In desperation, he [referring to me] mentions the Mini-Mental Status Exam. . . . She had a score of 18 out of 30." He later characterized my review of the neurobehavioral consequences of anterior brain injuries "as a wild attempt" to establish behavioral deficits in this plaintiff. Needless to say, *ad hominem* attacks diminish the credibility of the accusing party and should be avoided. In furthering this opinion, the *Specialty Guidelines for Forensic Psychologists* (2006 draft) section 14.05 (Commenting upon Other Professionals and Participants) states, "When evaluating or commenting upon the work product or qualifications of other professionals involved in a legal proceeding, or otherwise when acting as a rebuttal expert, forensic practitioners represent their disagreements in a professional and respectful tone, and base them on a fair examination of the data, theories, standards, and opinions of the other party or expert."

Sweet and Moulthrop (1999) offer a series of self-examination questions for the expert to ask when preparing a forensic report. These eight questions encompass many of the important issues discussed in this chapter:

1. Would a panel of peers, composed of experts of known standing, arrive at a consensus with me regarding each and every statement in my test findings and conclusions sections?
2. Have I included statements that are at odds with the mainstream literature on this subject?
3. How will I defend each statement in the report, if pressed to do so?
4. Have I omitted facts or evidence or neglected to address known facts or evidence that will contradict or detract from the position I have taken?
5. Have I varied in some meaningful way in the adversarial case from the clinical decision-making tasks that I routinely carry out for nonadversarial cases?
6. Have I placed only the amount of confidence in collateral information that it deserves?
7. Have I placed only the amount of confidence in my interpretive statements that is warranted by each test's psychometric characteristics?
8. Have I used exaggerated or dramatic descriptors? (p. 82)

An important closing thought concerns the weighty nature of the work performed by forensic neuropsychologists in the criminal arena, and the careful thought and preparation that is routinely devoted to forensic report preparation. This is a high-stakes venue; unlike the civil arena, there is much more at risk than money. The expert may be asked to offer opinions that affect the potential for a defendant to be put to death (*Atkins v. United States*, 2002), to be found guilty of a heinous crime, or to avoid responsibility for the same crime. Each expert should examine his or her own mental strengths and weaknesses before taking on these assignments. I have a close and highly respected forensic psychiatric colleague who, for personal reasons, does not perform death penalty work. I remember my own visceral response to a death penalty case (Barry, 2003; Fisher & Samson, 2003) involving a 40-year-old murder defendant who had eluded the diagnosis of mental retardation (MR), notwithstanding abysmal school performance and lifelong functional living problems. With the Attorney General of the United States insisting on the death penalty, the issue of MR became critical to whether the attorney general could pursue this penalty in the event of a guilty verdict. I was retained by the defendant's attorney with the specific question of whether his client would be excluded from the death penalty under *Atkins*. The point of this story is not to relate the facts of the case but to recall the pressures brought to bear to produce a report before the necessary leg work had been completed (e.g., conducting multiple third-party interviews with school officials and family members to ascertain why an MR diagnosis had never been made). I called the defense attorney and in a firm but friendly manner acknowledged the "hurry up and wait" nature of forensic work, while insisting on additional time to perform the necessary research either to support or reject the opinion that his client had MR, and hence was eligible–ineligible for the death penalty. This extra time was granted. In the end, I crafted a careful and well-documented forensic report, and the federal prosecutor's neuropsychologist essentially stipulated to my findings. The defendant was excluded from the death penalty (under *Atkins*). That my report had the potential weight to open or close the door to the death penalty was a responsibility unlike any other I have confronted in my 25-year career.

Practical Suggestions for More Effective Direct and Cross-Examination Testimony

Psychological expert testimony was granted the same weight as psychiatry in the matter of *Jenkins v. United States* (1962). This landmark decision addressed the issue of whether clinical psychologists could provide expert testimony to support a criminal defendant's insanity defense. In the original criminal trial, the court instructed the jury to disregard the testimony of three qualified psychologists on the grounds that they were not physicians. On appeal, the District of Columbia Circuit Court of Appeals held that psychologists were qualified as expert witnesses on the question of mental disease. This decision, while relevant to the issue of forensic psychological testimony and criminal responsibility, was precedent setting and presaged the use of psychological experts on a much larger range of issues. In the 21st century, testimony by forensic neuropsychologists is now commonplace in the courtrooms of America.

Discussing the theory of expert testimony versus actually testifying are two very different experiences. There is no substitute for the real thing. The focus here is on the practical. As testifying witnesses know, anxiety and fear are common emotional accompaniments to expert testimony. There is nothing aberrant about these pregame jitters, which are rational responses to what can be a challenging and difficult venue for even the most seasoned professional. The courtroom operates on an adversarial principle. Two sides face off as vigorous advocates for their respective clients; the overriding goal is to win. Unlike scientific settings, in which facts trump speculation, this paradigm does not always prevail in the judicial setting (notwithstanding *Daubert* and other Federal Rules of Evidence reviewed earlier). There are numerous "how to" [testify effectively] texts published by the American Psychological Association, as well as others (e.g., SEAK, Inc.) dispensing sage wisdom and advice for the testifying expert. Professional organizations that focus on perfecting expert testimony regularly host conferences to address these issues. The recently published book *How to Become a Dangerous Expert Witness* (Babitsky & Mangraviti, 2005) underscores the highly adversarial nature of the court room, with promises to teach the expert "how to bulletproof yourself and your opinions . . . how to defeat opposing counsel's deposition and cross-examination tactics . . . [and] how and when to take the offensive and turn the tables on opposing counsel." The analogies to aggressive armed conflict are obvious. For the seasoned trial expert these metaphors are easily appreciated; for the novice, words inadequately convey the gravity of sitting on the witness stand ("hot seat") for hours, undergoing a grueling cross-examination. In a classroom or a conference venue, the neuropsychologist–teacher is permitted the latitude and freedom to describe and discuss the nuances of information. In stark contrast, vigorous and skillful cross-examination may endeavor to limit the expert's testimony to one-word "yes" or "no" answers ("Dr., just answer the question, yes or no") or require the expert to read information that has intentionally been taken out of context (e.g., if the expert has a computer-generated Minnesota Multiphasic Personality Inventory–2 (MMPI-2) report narrative, a variety of hypotheses are set forth; the expert may be asked to read a single sentence from such a narrative that contradicts his or her formulation/opinions). Remember, the lawyer's central paradigm is to act as a zealous advocate for his or her client at almost any expense, even if this requires distorting the truth.

Robert Bennett (2000), in a speech to the Jacob Burns Ethics Center, observed that lawyers "have an obligation to adhere to the highest standards of ethical and moral conduct," yet "the zealous advocate often speaks and acts in ways that to many are morally questionable, less than candid, and do not promote respect for the law in the eyes of the public." Bennett asserted, "Sometimes, in our legal system, the truth must be sacrificed for more important principles," adding "at times we use our training and skills to discredit truth-telling witnesses hoping to make them appear as fools or liars." In the *United States v. Wade* (1967), Associate Supreme Court Justice White opined,

> Defense counsel has no comparable obligation to ascertain or present the truth. If he can confuse a witness, even a truthful one, or make him appear at a disadvantage, unsure or indecisive, that will be his normal course. More often than not, defense counsel will cross-examine a prosecution witness, and impeach him if he can, even if he thinks the witness is telling the truth, just as he will attempt to destroy a witness who he thinks is lying. As part of the duty imposed on the most honorable defense counsel, we countenance or require conduct which in many instances has little, if any, relation to the search for the truth. (p. 256)

Ultimately, the judicial system entrusts the jury to sort out the differing views offered by each side of a criminal case, in its search for the truth.

Although "how-to books," primers, and courses for expert witnesses are obviously useful, perhaps the most important aspirational rule for forensic neuropsychologists is consistently to conduct scientific and careful assessments. Strive to build a professional reputation as a truth seeker and unbiased expert, whose most important pursuit is to uncover the truth, regardless of whether it hurts or helps the retaining party. The expert who cultivates a "straight shooter" reputation garners respect in the legal arena and among professional colleagues. This does not mean the expert will be given a free pass on the witness stand. Even under the best circumstances, opposing counsel, if doing his or her job well, will seek to attack the expert's methodology, conclusions, and ultimately, the expert him- or herself. A wise old saying circulates in the legal community that goes like this: "If you have the facts, argue the facts. If you have the law, argue the law. If you have neither, just argue." This adage should be kept in the forefront of the expert's mind during a tough cross-examination, in which the expert may be accused of being a hired gun, a whore, or some other lower form of protoplasm. If the primary focus of the cross-examination is on the expert (and if the challenges are underserved), this may actually be a good prognostic sign. When neither the facts nor the law can be argued, the lawyer may just be arguing. When being grilled about money matters, such as how much one makes per hour, per day, or per annum, remember to answer in a nondefensive manner while mentally musing on the oxymoron (one hopes this bemusement is also shared by the jury) that a lawyer, of all professions, is accosting someone about earning too much money.

Lees-Haley and Cohen (1999) set forth three cardinal guidelines for neuropsychological testimony:

1. Practice scientific and ethical neuropsychology.
2. Direct your testimony toward the goal of using your specialized knowledge to help the jury understand the evidence or determine the facts in issue.
3. Speak in reasonable language, avoiding technical terminology not likely to be understood by the lay audience with which you are communicating.

Fourth, fifth, and sixth cardinal guidelines should include always tell the truth, always have a well-organized "at the ready" file at the time of trial testimony, and well before entering the courtroom, have a good understanding of the arguments set forth by method skeptics about neuropsychology.

The fourth guideline, always to tell the truth, seems straightforward, although in a culture where lying is accepted at virtually every tier of society, it is worth restating the obvious. Always tell the truth. Even if the truth "hurts" the expert's opinion in a particular matter, no amount of ego satisfaction or financial gain should persuade an expert to violate the sacred oath "to tell the truth, the whole truth, and nothing but the truth." Honest Abraham Lincoln is credited with saying "Always tell the truth, you'll have less to remember." Good advice.

The fifth cardinal guideline, to have a well-organized file, is critical to persuasive courtroom testimony. Organizing file materials in clearly labeled manila file folders, then placing these folders in one or more large expandable folders (which can be carried to the witness stand) forces the expert to tidy up the file (discard duplicates, etc.) and facilitates easy access to materials while testifying. If the expert, especially during cross-examination, is challenged about a factual point made in his or her report, it is critical that locating the archival "backup" be easy and effortless. Not only does this reduce the expert's autonomic arousal (i.e., imagine being challenged on the witness stand about a particular fact and, in response, fumbling through hundreds of pages of materials in search of a particular record as the jury, judge, and attorneys watch impatiently) but it also demonstrates to the jury that the expert has a clear knowledge of the facts and abhors disorganization. Whether the perception is fair or not, a disorganized expert's credibility will likely suffer in the eyes of the jury.

The sixth cardinal guideline concerns knowing what the critics of forensic neuropsychology are telling lawyers. A simple Google search of the phrase, "cross-examining the forensic neuropsychologist" yields pages of materials. One document (Gleason & Harp, 2001) titled "Cross-Examining the Prosecution's Mental Health Expert" directs the attorney to conduct a "background investigation" of the mental health expert, which includes obtaining the following documents: driving record, indications of alcohol- and drug-related offenses, credit history, criminal court records, insurance reporting history, and so forth. Very up-close and personal. This same document directs the cross-examining attorney to "define the goals of cross-examination" with the notation, "Destroy the expert. This is rather ambitious but the situation may lend itself to a scorched earth approach." Although it may be painful to read these documents, there is no substitute for knowledge. The expert witness should, at a minimum, own a copy of the two sets of volumes by Faust and Ziskin (1988) and Faust, Ziskin, and Hiers (1991), written for attorneys to challenge psychologists and neuropsychologists. As Faust and colleagues assert in the Preface to Volume I, *Brain Damage Claims: Coping with Neuropsychological Evidence*, "The great bulk of this material [scientific and professional literature] casts doubt upon, or negates, the expertise of neuropsychologists" (p. xv). These volumes, however, were written more than 15 years ago; fortunately, science marches on.

Being aware of information that is disseminated to attorneys about experts may yield significant dividends. In the North African desert, after Patton defeated Rommel, the Nazi tank commander known as the Desert Fox, Patton is rumored to have shouted in glee, "Rommel, you magnificent bastard, I read your book." Patton was referring, of course, to Rommel's book on tank warfare strategies, which Patton read before engaging and defeating the Desert Fox in this strategic tank battle. Patton possessed the ultimate advantage because he knew his opponent's strategies and tactics before the battle began. Four hundred years before Patton and Rommel, Miguel de Cervantes (1547–1616), participated in the sea battle at Lepanto (1571), echoing this sentiment. He admonished, "Forewarned is forearmed." Thus, if the testifying expert can learn anything from these warriors of the past, it is to be prepared and knowledgeable about the tactics employed by potential adversaries. Monitoring the websites of organizations such as the American Bar Association (ABA) and SEAK, Inc. may provide leads on workshops, books, and articles that are distributed to attorneys who cross-examine forensic neuropsychologists (e.g., the ABA markets a 2005 course book by Archer & Bigler, focused on various issues, including "challenging psychological test results and testimony [and] common errors made by neuropsychologists").

Staying with the theme of cross-examination as warfare, it may benefit the forensic expert to read Sun Tzu's *The Art of War* (1963/1988). Although more than 2,500 years old, Sun Tzu offers intriguing observations about warfare. He observes insightfully, "If your opponent is of choleric temper, seek to irritate him. Pretend to be weak, that he may grow arrogant." While Sun Tzu did not intend this commentary as a "how to" in handling a hot-headed, blustering attorney, regardless of the attorney's choleric temper, if the testifying witness remains calm, tells the truth, thoroughly knows the matter under litigation, adheres to the six cardinal guidelines set forth herein, as well as practicing the other "commonsense" suggestions set forth in this chapter, he or she will be well on the way to providing effective expert testimony that can neutralize and even trump a variety of cross-examination techniques. Brodsky (2004) notes, "Attorneys may chastise or corner witnesses during cross-examinations. Good witnesses stay effective and in control through simple, reflective, or method-oriented answers that come out as purposeful knowledge of attorney techniques" (p. 117).

The expert should endeavor to accept cases from both "sides" in the legal arena—defense and prosecution. Not only does this broaden the depth and breadth of the expert's experiential base but it also helps to immunize him or her against cross-examination inquiry, which may attempt to paint the expert as a partisan. Of course, practicality may limit this suggestion; that is, one side may simply not consult with the expert. The only remedy for this situation is to earn a reputation for excellent and unbiased work. In time, this reputation may prompt calls by the defense and the prosecution as one's good work is shared among legal colleagues.

Before testifying in court, the expert should meet face-to-face with the retaining attorney to discuss the flow and content of direct testimony. Blau (1984) provides an excellent outline for this pretrial conference (pp. 217–218). Each attorney has his or her unique method for conducting the direct examination; this should be appreciated prior to offering testimony. As an example, I have worked with one defense attorney who abhors structure in his direct *voir dire*. He poses questions in an open-ended manner, such as "Doctor, please tell the jury about your credentials" (followed by a pregnant silence as he anticipates a minisynopsis of this expert's curriculum vitae). This contrasts methods of other attorneys, who ask a series of leading questions, essentially line by line, about the author's curriculum vitae. Knowing the attorney's questioning style in advance will help the expert to prepare mentally for trial testimony. It provides the expert an opportunity to inform the questioning attorney about preferences or pet peeves. Perhaps, most importantly, the critical content goals of testimony can be highlighted. The expert should inform the questioning attorney about the best way to discuss the dry subject of neuropsychological testing and test results without losing the jury's attention. A face-to-face meeting permits the expert to underscore specific limitations in testimony. For example, the expert should not wait until he or she is at the end of direct testimony during a trial to inform the questioning attorney that, absent specific foundational records (which were not provided), he or she cannot offer an opinion with a reasonable degree of neuropsychological certainty.

Expert testimony should be easy to follow and understand. It is simple, straightforward, and terse. Good testimony avoids psychobabble, pomposity, or arrogance. Brodsky (2004) cautions, "Avoid being a smug witness by acknowledging you do not know everything [and] have not done everything" (p. 71). An effective expert witness should connect with jury members and have as his or her goal the mission of educating and informing them about relevant issues. The expert should make technical material understandable. When speaking from the witness box, one important issue to consider is where does one look? Most lawyers instruct the witness to make eye contact with the jury. This is probably good advice as long as the eye contact is not too intense or contrived. Much like a good public speaker, shifting gaze to various individuals while speaking can create a sense of inclusiveness. During cross-examination, the questioning attorney may intentionally position his or her lectern, such that it draws the expert's gaze away from the jury. This is a cross-examination tactic. Combat this ploy by looking at the attorney while the question is being posed, then while answering, make direct eye contact with jurors.

Direct testimony typically begins with the expert's qualifications and credentials (*voir dire*). Although it is important to inform the jury about important educational and professional accomplishments, avoid vanity or pomposity. The goal of *voir dire* is to provide evidence of the neuropsychologist's qualifications to offer expert testimony. Be aware that a well-qualified and respected expert may occasionally prompt opposing counsel to "stipulate to" the expert's qualifications (hence permitting exclusion of this portion of direct testimony). There may be more than one motive for such a stipulation. It may be a legitimate proposal to save time, based on opposing counsel's respect for the expert. However, it may also be a ploy to keep the jury from hearing about the breadth and depth of the expert's work. It is the retaining lawyer's decision (not the expert's) to accept or reject a motion for credential stipulation.

A word to the wise about credentials. Over the last decade there has been a proliferation of credentialing organizations, many with a forensic spin. I have reviewed forensic reports by other experts with 10 or more lines of "credentials" listed beneath their names. More often than not these "credentials" are of questionable credibility. Heilbronner (2004) reviewed the problem with "vanity boards" and observed, "It is not certain that judges, attorneys, and juries (let alone the general public) can distinguish between legitimate and vanity boards" (p. 318). The forensic expert is well advised to avoid presenting "cracker jack" credentials as proof of expert competency; the forensic expert has an affirmative responsibility to represent his or her credentials accurately. The *Specialty Guidelines for Forensic Psychologists* (2006 draft) echoes this sentiment (4.03, Representation of Competencies) asserting, "Forensic practitioners do not, by either commission or omission, participate in misrepresentation of their abilities, training, credentials, or qualifications or the manner in which they were obtained" (see also 5.01 (b), *Avoidance of False or Deceptive Statements*—2002 American Psychological Association Ethics Code). Parry (1998) provides instructions for judges listening to psychiatric and psychological evidence and testimony, admonishing, "Judges must also be wary of witnesses claiming certification by various 'mail order' boards, that do not require an oral examination or other indicia of a rigorous qualifying process." Be aware, that misrepresentation of credentials may be exposed on cross-examination in the hands of a well-informed attorney. A trial witness in Rochester was recently confronted during cross-examination about having bestowed Board Certification (he was the Chairman of the American Psychotherapy Association Executive Advisory Board, which is affiliated with the American College of Forensic Examiners) on a cat named Zoe D. Katz (Eichel, 2002; Hansen, 2002). During this expert's cross, a large image of this four-legged feline, Dr. Katz, was projected onto a screen while the cross-examination proceeded. Not a pretty picture. This cross-examination is now part of the public record, available to attorneys who question this practitioner in the future. It will likely hound (no pun intended) him forever.

Once *voir dire* accomplishes the expert's credential review, direct testimony typically proceeds to archival records reviewed and relevant findings (14.03, Disclosing Sources of Information and Bases of Opinions). This testimony should be fair and balanced. Archival data findings must be discussed without bias or spin. As *Specialty Guidelines for Forensic Psychologists* (2006 draft) directs (14.01, Accuracy, Fairness, and Avoidance of Deception), "Forensic practitioners do not distort or withhold relevant evidence of opinion in reports or testimony because this is potentially misleading, and is incompatible with their role as experts to the court or other tribunals." The *Guidelines* add, "This principle does not preclude forceful representation of the data and reasoning upon which a conclusion or professional product is based. It does, however, preclude an attempt, whether active or passive, to engage in partisan distortion or misrepresentation." Blau (1984) observed, "The expert witness is not required and should not attempt to advocate for one side or the other, shade the data in favor of one adversary or the other, omit pertinent facts or expand upon inconsequential elements of a presentation" (p. 225).

The expert is usually asked to describe the procedures administered (including interviews and formal tests) to address the question(s) under consideration (e.g., competency; capacity to understand and waive *Miranda* warning; presence of brain damage with neurobehavioral consequences that might be a mitigating factor in determining, if at the time of the crime, the defendant had the capacity to act with free will). It is important to give the jury a full appreciation of the scope of the assessment performed, without going into mind-numbing detail. Melton and colleagues (2007) remarked, "If tests ... were used, the clinician should be prepared to discuss their validity and to describe the method of test development" (p. 531). As I discussed in the assessment section of this chapter, refrain from using experimental procedures when conducting forensic assessments. Although these tests may be useful in clinical practice, by their very designation as experimental, they have no place in the courtroom. Notwithstanding this caution, if the examiner feels compelled to use experimental procedures, then at the very least he or she should heed the *Specialty Guidelines for Forensic Psychologists* (2006 draft) admonition, "When such validity or reliability has not been adequately established in the forensic context or with this population, forensic practitioners describe the strengths and limitations of any test results and interpretation and explain the extrapolation of this data to the forensic context" (12.02, Appropriate Use of Assessment Procedures).

Direct testimony concludes with a series of questions to prompt the expert's opinion. For the novice, there is a concrete quality to this portion of the direct. The attorney will first inquire whether the expert has an opinion about the issue at hand (e.g., "Do you have an opinion, Doctor, about whether Mr. Smith sustained a severe brain injury?"); the expected answer is either "yes" or "no." If the expert replies in the affirmative, then the attorney will ask, "And, Doctor, what is that opinion?" The expert should reply succinctly. In his or her answer, the basis for the opinion can be briefly highlighted ("Based on the results of my review of the archival records, interviews, and formal test results)", followed by the opinion ("The weight of the evidence supports my opinion that Mr. Smith sustained a severe brain injury with permanent cognitive and personality deficits"). Some attorneys will actually break this opinion into two sets of questions; that is, after the expert opines that the defendant sustained a severe brain injury, the follow-up question would ask whether this injury has resulted in permanent cognitive and personality deficits. Remember that the expert's role is to help the judge or jury understand an issue well enough to make a reasoned decision.

Cross-examination follows the direct examination. This is the time when questioning most often changes from pleasant to unpleasant. As discussed earlier, some attorneys view this as war. Melton and colleagues (2007) note,

Gone is the friendly, understanding expression of the attorney who has led direct testimony; in its place is the scowl or piercing stare of the opposing attorney, whose tone of voice and looks of astonishment convey to the jury the 'unbelievable' nature of the clinician's testimony. A variety of verbal and nonverbal ploys are tried in an effort to confuse or discredit the witness, the testimony or the witness's profession. (p. 592)

Cross-examination, as highlighted earlier, is the opposing counsel's opportunity to neutralize or even destroy the expert's direct testimony and opinions. Some attorneys accomplish this with a full frontal assault, others are more subtle. Brodsky (2004) describes the expert's perception of cross, as the time in the trial "that symbolizes whether they are powerful, competent, and masterful—or whether they are weak, incompetent, and ineffectual" (p. 69).

The brief space allocated herein cannot provide the reader with all the necessary tools for coping or responding to cross-examination. As referenced earlier in this chapter, Brodsky (1991, 2003, 2004), Blau (1984), and others have published texts on effective courtroom testimony that the novice, as well as the seasoned expert, should read. Although this chapter does not substitute for a more detailed review of these texts, some broad strokes on this metaphorical canvas have been offered here in an effort to reassure the competent and thoughtful expert that cross-examination can be weathered with the full weight of his or her opinions intact (as set forth during direct testimony).

Excellent work and a cool head are two keys for prevailing, or at the very least maintaining the status quo, during a difficult cross-examination. Although it is important to understand the various semantic ploys and traps used by cross-examining attorneys (examples listed by Melton and colleagues include "The infallibility complex and God only knows gambits"; "The unreliable examination gambit"; "The loaded question and lawyer as expert ploys" [2007, pp. 592–593]) to fool and confuse the expert, if the expert's work is inadequate, no amount of bobbing, weaving, or semantic gimmicks will rescue him or her from the jaws of cross. Assuming the expert's work is as good as it gets, what can the expert do to minimize the battering that cross-examination endeavors to visit upon the expert? There are several key mantras the expert should keep centrally in the back of his or her head. First, no matter how heated and confrontational the questioning becomes, the expert must remain calm and professional. If the cross-examining attorney raises his or her voice and applies verbal pressure, the witness does not escalate in kind. Always pause before answering. There is no rule that requires an immediate answer to a question. Take time to think. Reply to questions in a calm manner, no matter how tempting it may be to get angry or defensive. Avoid excessive displays of emotion.

Succumbing to this impulse will, unfortunately, enlighten the combative expert about the old adage, "In a mud wrestling contest with a pig, the pig loves it and you get dirty."

If a question is convoluted or not fully understandable, request that it be repeated or read back. Pay close attention to the wording of the question; remember, it was a lawyer who testified under oath about the meaning of the word *is*. Never guess or speculate. Always tell the truth. The expert witness should never go beyond his or her expertise. Consistently advocate for the data, not for the side paying the expert's bill. It is not necessary to have an answer for every question. The expert should admit when he or she cannot fully know or appreciate the defendant's internal schema. The defendant is the only person who can provide this answer. Thus, the expert can reply, "While it is true that Mr. Smith's performance on tests sensitive to effort was variable, his scores on two out of four of these measures fell in the noncredible range of performance. This is sufficient to raise serious concerns about Mr. Smith's effort during my evaluation of him."

The competent expert must also remember that years of education and training provide a wealth of knowledge about neuropsychology, far exceeding that of the typical cross-examining attorney. Knowledge is power as long as the expert does not become caught up in the tumult engendered by a difficult cross. Brodsky (2004) asserts, "Remember, you usually know more than they do. A lot more" (p. 10).

A list of often asked questions during cross-examination would occupy many pages and are discussed at length by Brodsky (2004). Heilbronner's (2005) "Ask the Expert" section queries Drs. Sweet, Greiffenstein, and Lees-Haley as to how they would answer cross-examination questions, such as "Doctor, do you regard neuropsychology as an exact science?" "Doctor do you consider [insert any text here] to be 'an authoritative text' in clinical neuropsychology?" The answers of these well-respected forensic experts are worth the read.

Here are some of my favorite (and most frequently confronted) cross-examination questions:

- *You are not a medical doctor are you, Mr. Fisher?* The best advice for this ploy is to answer in a nondefensive manner that you have a PhD in clinical psychology, with specialized training in neuropsychology.
- *How much are you being paid for your opinion (or testimony) today?* Issues of fees and attempts to undermine the expert's impartiality by implying that his or her opinions are for sale are common. Deal with the issue directly and nondefensively. Respond directly that you are paid X dollars per hour *for your time*. Be cautious of this sophomoric question, which is a semantic booby trap. You are being paid for your time. Your opinions are not for sale.

❖ *Dr. Fisher, do you have your curriculum vitae with you?* Be conscious, to whatever degree feasible, of what you have written or said over the years. Lawyers like to have it both ways; that is, if you have never published or have published rarely, you will be attacked for failing to make a contribution to the scholarly literature. On the other hand, if you have published, you can most certainly count on being cross-examined with these materials, regardless of the publication date. This author is frequently crossed with a paper he wrote more than 20 years ago, about the neurobehavioral consequences of various degrees of brain injury; that the science of mild head injury and forensic neuropsychology has made giant leaps since the 1980s is of no concern to the cross-examining lawyer. One lawyer actually had tables from this author's old paper blown up to jury-size exhibits. During a cross-examination, an attempt was made to degrade my credibility by showing that my current (2005) position regarding mild head injury did not agree with my position in the early 1980s, notwithstanding more than 20 years of innovation and discovery. I responded in a nondefensive manner that science, like the law, is in flux. Important findings regarding the neurobehavioral consequence of brain injuries have been made through careful scientific discovery and well-controlled research in the intervening two plus decades.

The expert should make it a practice to "Google" him- or herself from time to time. It makes for interesting reading. Ignorance is not bliss. Be cautious about having a professional website or advertising in lawyer directories as an expert witness. Anything is fair game for cross. I am amazed at what some professionals say about their credentials and work in a public forum.

The experienced expert understands that following cross-examination, the retaining attorney may conduct "redirect" questioning. In fact, The Federal Rules of Evidence 611 (b) dictate that "cross-examination should be limited to the subject matter of the direct examination and matters affecting the credibility of the witness." Following cross-examination, there is an opportunity for the attorney who called the expert to engage in redirect, which is limited to the scope of cross-examination. Again, after redirect, there may be additional recross, more redirect, and so forth. In contentious cases, the expert should expect several redirects and recrosses before being dismissed from the witness stand:

> The role of cross-examination, to be effective, is to destroy or diminish the persuasive effect of the expert's direct examination in the eyes and ears of the jury. This may effectively be accomplished without a substantive attack when the expert fails to practice her profession with the highest degree of diligence and adherence to the scientific method. "Preparation, knowledge, and methodical diligence are important keys to persuasive courtroom testimony." (Rehkopf & Fisher, 1997, p. 150)

Melton and colleagues (2007) have described anecdotal research that investigated juror perceptions and decision making regarding criminal court experts. Of note, factors that led jurors to discount an expert's testimony (regardless of whether an expert for the defense or prosecution) included not spending sufficient time investigating the case, seeing the defendant only shortly before trial, destroying records or notes, and appearing to be pompous and self-centered.

At the end of a long day on the witness stand, the neuropsychologist expert should be satisfied that he or she embraced the highest possible level of science and professional practice. Although it is unlikely that even the most competent expert will get out of the courtroom without a few bumps and bruises, one hopes that Monday morning quarterbacking will fail to uncover substantial lapses in forensic practice techniques or judgment (as set forth in this chapter). Where shortcomings are identified, the expert should take immediate steps to ensure their elimination from future work.

Common sense is an essential ingredient to good forensic work. Yet, as Mark Twain is credited as saying (I am paraphrasing), "If it is so common . . . why is it so rare?" Giuliano, Barth, Hawk, and Ryan (1997) observed, "Neuropsychology as a science is well inside the courtroom door. Reliance on empirical methods and peer review of research common to the field ensures that courts will be able to discern the scientific substance of Neuropsychology in general" (p. 27). These authors cautioned, however, that "the level of individual practice will continue to be the basis of our real reputation in court" (p. 27).

When acting in a forensic capacity, the neuropsychologist has an affirmative responsibility to embrace the best possible practice techniques. Doing less will ultimately diminish both public and judicial respect for the field of forensic neuropsychology.

References

American Academy of Clinical Neuropsychology. (2001). Policy statement on the presence of third-party observers in neuropsychological assessment. *Clinical Neuropsychologist, 15,* 433–439.

American Educational Research Association, American Psychological Association, & National Council on Measurement in Education. (1999). *Standards for educational and psychological testing.* Washington, DC: American Educational Research Association.

American Psychological Association. (2002). Ethical Principles of psychologists and code of conduct. *American Psychologist, 57*(12), 1060–1073.

Archer, R., & Bigler, E. (2005). *Presenting psychological and neuropsychological evidence*

in personal injury and medical malpractice cases. Chicago: American Bar Association.
Atkins v. United States, 536 U.S. 304 (2002).
Axelrod, B., Barth, J., Faust, D., Fisher, J., Heilbronner, R., Larrabee, G., et al. (2000). Presence of third-party observers during neuropsychological testing. *Archives of Clinical Neuropsychology, 15*, 379–380.
Babitsky, S., & Mangraviti, J. (2002). *Writing and defending your expert report*. Falmouth, MA: SEAK, Inc.
Babitsky, S., & Mangraviti, J. (2005). *How to become a dangerous expert witness*. Falmouth, MA: SEAK, Inc.
Barefoot v. Estelle, American Psychiatric Association Brief Amicus Curiae, No. 82-6080, 1982.
Barry, D. (2003, May 18). A capital case, and a defendant who may be retarded. *New York Times*, p. B1.
Baskerville v. Culligan International Company, 1994 U.S. Dist. LEXIS 5296 (1994).
Bauer, L., O'Bryant, S., Lynch, J., McCaffrey, R., & Fisher, J. (2007). Examining the Test of Memory Malingering Trial I and Word Memory Test Immediate Recognition as screening tools for insufficient effort. *Assessment, 14*(3), 215–222.
Baxter v. Temple, No. 01-C-0567 New Hampshire (2005).
Bechara, A., Damasio, H., Tranel, D., & Anderson, S. (1998). Dissociation of working memory from decision making within the human prefrontal cortex. *Journal of Neuroscience, 18*(1), 428–437.
Bennett, R. (2000, February 8). *Ethics, advocacy, and the criminal defense attorney*. Lecture presented at the Jacob Burns Ethics Center, New York.
Binder, L., & Johnson-Greene, D. (1995). Observer effects on neuropsychological performance: A case report. *Clinical Neuropsychologist, 9*, 74–78.
Blau, T. (1984). *The psychologist as expert witness*. New York: Wiley.
Brodsky, S. (1991). *Testifying in court: Guidelines and maxims for the expert witness*. Washington, DC: American Psychological Association.
Brodsky, S. (2003). *The expert expert witness*. Washington, DC: American Psychological Association.
Brodsky, S. (2004). *Coping with cross-examination and other pathways to effective testimony*. Washington, DC: American Psychological Association.
Bush, S. (2005). Independent and court-ordered forensic neuropsychological examinations: Official statement of the National Academy of Neuropsychology. *Archives of Clinical Neuropsychology, 20*, 997–1007.
Bush, S., Ruff, R., Troster, A., Barth, J., Koffler, S., Pliskin, N., et al. (2005). Symptom validity assessment: Practice issues and medical necessity. *Archives of Clinical Neuropsychology, 20*, 419–426.
Cercy, S., Schretlen, D., & Brandt, J. (1997). Simulated amnesia and the pseudomemory phenomena. In R. Rogers (Ed.), *Clinical assessment of malingering and deception* (pp. 85–107). New York: Guilford Press.
Chapple v. Ganger, 851 F. Supp. 1481 (E.D. Wa. 1994).
Ciccone, R., & Clements, C. (1987). The insanity defense: Asking and answering

the ultimate question. *Bulletin of the American Academy of Psychiatry and the Law, 15*(4), 329–338.

Cima, M., Merckelbach, H., Nijman, H., Knauer, E., & Hollnack, S. (2001). I can't remember your Honor: Offenders who claim amnesia. *German Journal of Psychiatry, 5*, 25–34.

Clark, C. (1997). Sociopathy, malingering, and defensiveness. In R. Rogers (Ed.), *Clinical assessment of malingering and deception* (pp. 68–84). New York: Guilford Press.

Committee on Ethical Guidelines for Forensic Psychologists. (2006, January 11). *Specialty guidelines for forensic psychologists* [2nd official draft]. Retrieved from http://www.ap-ls.org/links/SGFP%20January%202006.pdf

Constantinou, M., Ashendrof, L., & McCaffrey, R. J. (2005). Effects of a third party observer during neuropsychological assessment when the observers a video camera. *Journal of Forensic Neuropsychological, 4*(2), 39–48.

Daubert v. Merrell Dow Pharmaceuticals, 509 U.S. 579 (1993).

Denney, R. L. (1996). Symptom validity testing of remote memory in a criminal forensic setting. *Archives of Clinical Neuropsychology, 11*, 589–603.

Denney, R. L. (2005a). Criminal forensic neuropsychology and assessment of competency. In G. Larrabee (Ed.), *Forensic neuropsychology: A scientific approach* (pp. 378–424). New York: Oxford University Press.

Denney, R. L. (2005b). Criminal responsibility and other criminal forensic issues. In G. Larrabee (Ed.), *Forensic neuropsychology: A scientific approach* (pp. 425–465). New York: Oxford University Press.

Dietz, P. E. (1996). The quest for excellence in forensic psychiatry. *Bulletin of the American Academy of Psychiatry and the Law, 24*, 153–163.

Duff, K., & Fisher, J. (2005). Ethical dilemmas with third party observers. *Journal of Forensic Neuropsychology, 4*(2), 65–82.

Edens, J., & Petrila, J. (2001). Psychopathy and the death penalty: Can the Psychopathy Checklist—Revised identify offenders who represent "a continuing threat to society?" *Journal of Psychiatry and the Law, 29*, 433–481.

Eichel, S. K. D. (2002). Credentialing: It may not be the cat's meow. Retrieved August 31, 2007, from *www.dreichel.com/articles/dr_zoe.htm*

Ewing, C. (2003). Expert testimony: Law and practice. In I. B. Weiner (Series Ed.) & A. M. Goldstein (Vol. Ed.), *Handbook of psychology: Vol. 11. Forensic psychology* (pp. 55–68). Hoboken, NJ: Wiley.

Faust, D., Ziskin, J., & Hiers, J. (1991). *Brain damage claims: Coping with neuropsychological evidence* (2 vols.). Los Angeles: Law and Psychology Press.

Fisher, J., Johnson-Greene, D., & Barth, J. (2002). Evaluation, diagnosis, and interventions in clinical neuropsychology in general and with special populations: An overview. In S. Bush & M. Drexler (Eds.), *Ethical issues in clinical neuropsychology* (pp. 3–22). Lisse, The Netherlands: Swets & Zeitlinger.

Fisher, J., & Samson, L. (2003). Mental retardation and capital offenses: Case history. *APA Division 40 Newsletter, 21*(2), 3–5.

Frye v. United States, 293 F. 1013 (D.C. Cir. 1923).

Giuliano, A., Barth, J., Hawk, G., & Ryan, T. (1997). The forensic neuropsychologist: Precedents, roles, and problems. In R. McCaffrey, A. Williams, J. Fisher, &

L. Laing (Eds.), *The practice of forensic neuropsychology* (pp. 1–36). New York: Plenum Press.

Gleason, K., & Harp, R. (2001). *Cross-examining the prosecution's mental health expert.* Unpublished chapter, Kentucky Department of Public Advocacy.

Hand, L. (1902). Historical and practical considerations regarding expert testimony. *Harvard Law Review, 40*, 56.

Hansen, M. (2002, October 25). See the cat? See the credentials?: Psychologist's scam gets his pet "board certified." *ABA Journal eReport 1*(41). Retrieved August 31, 2007, from www.dreichel.com/articles/dr_zoe.htm#Zoe_aba

Hanson, E. (2003). The role of the neuropsychologist as an expert witness. *National Academy of Neuropsychology Bulletin, 18*(2).

Heilbronner, R. (2004). A status report on the practice of forensic neuropsychology. *Clinical Neuropsychologist, 18*(2), 312–326.

Heilbronner, R. (2005). *Forensic neuropsychology casebook.* New York: Guilford Press.

Jelicic, M., Merckelbach, H., & van Bergen, S. (2004). Symptom validity testing of feigned crime-related amnesia: A simulation study. *Journal of Credibility Assessment and Witness Psychology, 5*(1), 1–8.

Jenkins v. United States, 307 F.2d 637 (D.C. Cir. 1962).

Joiner v. General Electric Co., 522 U.S. 136 (1997).

Kopelman, M. D. (1995). The assessment of psychogenic amnesia. In A. D. Baddeley, B. A. Wilson, & F. N. Watts (Eds.), *Handbook of memory disorders* (pp. 427–448). New York: Wiley.

Kumho Tire Co. v. Carmichael, 526 U.S. 137 (1999).

Lee, D., Reynolds, C., & Willson, V. (2003). Standardized test administration: Why bother? *Journal of Forensic Neuropsychology, 3*(3), 55–81.

Lees-Haley, P., & Cohen, L. (1999). The neuropsychologist as expert witness: Toward credible science in the courtroom. In J. Sweet (Ed.), *Forensic neuropsychology fundamentals and practice* (pp. 443–468). Lisse, The Netherlands: Swets & Zeitlinger.

Lynch, J. (2005). Effect of third party observer on neuropsychological test performance following closed head injury. *Journal of Forensic Neuropsychology, 4*(2), 17–26.

McKinzey, R., & Ziegler, T. (1999). Challenging a flexible neuropsychological battery under Kelly/Frye: A case study. *Behavioral Sciences and the Law, 17*(4), 543–551.

Melton, G. B., Petrila, J., Poythress, N. G., & Slobogin, C., with Lyons, P. M., Jr., & Otto, R. K. (2007). *Psychological evaluation for the courts: A handbook for mental health professionals and lawyers* (3rd ed.). New York: Guilford Press.

Mossman, D. (2003). Daubert, cognitive malingering, and test accuracy. *Law and Human Behavior, 27*(3), 229–249.

Nicholson, R., & Norwood, S. (2000). The quality of forensic psychological assessments, reports, and testimony: Acknowledging the gap between promise and practice. *Law and Human Behavior, 24*(1), 9–44.

Parry, J. (1998). Courtroom admissibility of psychiatric and psychological evidence. In *National Benchbook on psychiatric and psychological evidence and testimony.* Washington, DC: American Bar Association.

Reed, J. (1996). Fixed vs. flexible neuropsychological test batteries under the Daubert standard. *Behavioral Sciences and the Law, 14*(3), 315–322.

Rehkopf, D., & Fisher, J. (1997). Neuropsychology in criminal proceedings. In R. McCaffrey, A. Williams, J. Fisher, & L. Laing (Eds.), *The practice of forensic neuropsychology* (pp. 135–151). New York: Plenum Press.

Skeem, J., & Golding, S. (1998). Community examiners' evaluations of competence to stand trial: Common problems and suggestions for improvement. *Professional Psychology: Research and Practice, 29*, 357–367.

Skeem, J., Golding, S., Cohen, N., & Berge, G. (1998). Logic and reliability of evaluations of competence to stand trial. *Law and Human Behavior, 22*(5), 519–548.

Slovenko, R. (2006). Commentary: Deceptions to the rule on ultimate issue testimony. *Journal of the American Academy of Psychiatry and the Law, 34*(1), 22–25.

Sun Tzu. (1988). *The art of war* (S. B. Griffith, Trans.). Norwalk, CT: Easton Press. (Original work published 1963)

Sweet, J., & Moulthrop, M. (1999). Self-examination questions as a means of identifying bias in adversarial assessments. *Journal of Forensic Neuropsychology, 1*, 73–88.

Texas Defender Service. (2004). *Deadly speculation: Misleading Texas capital juries with false predictions of future dangerousness*. Houston: Author.

Trimble, M. (2004). *Somatoform disorders: A medicolegal guide*. Cambridge, UK: Cambridge University Press.

United States v. Wade, 388 U.S. 218 (1967).

Williams, A. (1997). The forensic evaluation of adult traumatic brain injury. In R. McCaffrey, A. Williams, J. Fisher, & L. Laing (Eds.), *The practice of forensic neuropsychology* (pp. 37–56). New York: Plenum Press.

Ziskin, J., & Faust, D. (1988). *Coping with psychiatric and psychological testimony* (4th ed.). Marina Del Rey, CA: Law and Psychology Press.

Chapter 13

A Final Word on Authentic Professional Competence in Criminal Forensic Neuropsychology

JAMES P. SULLIVAN
ROBERT L. DENNEY

In the preface we expressed our hope that this text would serve to assist interested and motivated neuropsychologists working in the criminal forensic area to pursue, develop, and maintain authentic professional competence rather than a "mere pretense of expertise." Which procedures and resources can we employ to attest to attainment of authentic professional competence? In concluding this text we offer a brief review of relevant state guidelines, the three tiered model of the "Villanova Conference" recommendation, and a summary of the American Board of Forensic Psychology (ABFP) position on the development and evaluation of competencies in forensic psychology. Finally, we discuss the collaborative model presented by Heilbronner and Frumkin (2003) as an alternative to full competence in criminal forensic matters. In presenting that model, we assume that readers are already generally familiar with the Houston Conference (Hannay et al., 1998) and the American Board of Clinical Neuropsychology (ABCN) positions on the development and evaluation of competencies in clinical neuropsychology. Although we may strive for genuine competence in criminal forensic work, we can never forget the solid neuropsychological principles in which we were trained.

Representative State Guidelines

During recent years, states have started to spell out basic eligibility requirements for experts to be appointed by courts in criminal proceedings. Farkas, DeLeon, and Newman (1997) discussed the results of a survey of 55 U.S. States and Territories regarding policies about psychologists' standing as qualified forensic examiners in criminal matters. They found considerable variability. Although 90.4% of the 52 responding jurisdictions allowed psychologists to testify as experts, only 19.2% required forensic professionals to be certified as forensic examiners by additional training, examination, or both. Just over 17% required specialized training, 11.5% required examinations, and 3.8% required a specified amount of experience in performing criminal forensic evaluations. Since that publication, several states have modified regulations. Most recently, Texas passed Senate Bill 1057, which outlines qualifications for appointment as a forensic examiner in criminal competence matters (Article 46B):

(a) To qualify for appointment under this subchapter as an expert, a psychiatrist or psychologist must:
   (1) as appropriate, be a physician licensed in this state or be a psychologist licensed in this state who has a doctoral degree in psychology; and
   (2) have the following certification or experience or training:
      (A) as appropriate, certification by: (i) the American Board of Psychiatry and Neurology with added or special qualifications in forensic psychiatry; or (ii) the American Board of Professional Psychology in forensic psychology; or
      (B) experience or training consisting of: (i) at least 24 hours of specialized forensic training relating to incompetency or insanity evaluations; (ii) for an appointment made before January 1, 2005, at least 5 years of experience before January 1, 2004, in performing criminal forensic evaluations for courts; or (iii) for an appointment made on or after January 1, 2005, at least 5 years of experience before January 1, 2004, in performing criminal forensic evaluations for courts and 8 or more hours of continuing education relating to forensic evaluations, completed in the 12 months preceding the appointment and documented with the court.
(b) In addition to meeting qualifications required by Subsection (a), to be appointed as an expert a psychiatrist or psychologist must have completed six hours of required continuing education in courses in forensic psychiatry or psychology, as appropriate, in either of the reporting periods in the 24 months preceding the appointment.
(c) A court may appoint as an expert a psychiatrist or psychologist who does not meet the requirements of Subsections (a) and (b) only if exigent circumstances require the court to base the appointment on professional

training or experience of the expert that directly provides the expert with a specialized expertise to examine the defendant that would not ordinarily be possessed by a psychiatrist or psychologist who meets the requirements of Subsections (a) and (b).

Senate Bill 1057 does not spell out the exact nature of the training or course work required, but it notes the training should be in the area of relevant forensic examination. The Farkas and colleagues (1997) survey reveals that 26.9% of the jurisdictions required completion of government-sponsored classroom training programs that ranged from 2 hours' to 7 days' duration. Those neuropsychologists in mandated jurisdictions need to obtain the government-sponsored training to practice in criminal forensics. For others wishing to obtain additional didactic training on forensic issues, the American Academy of Forensic Psychology offers workshops at various places in the country throughout the year. Training is also available at the American Psychological Association's Division 41 (American Psychology–Law Society) program at the annual convention, as well as Division's yearly winter meeting. Finally, the National Academy of Neuropsychology and the American Academy of Clinical Neuropsychology routinely offer workshops in criminal forensic issues as well.

Villanova Conference

In 1995, a conference of practicing forensic psychologists, academicians, and attorneys was convened by the Education Directorate of the American Psychological Association at the National Invitation Conference on Education and Training in Law and Psychology. This conference produced recommendations regarding training in psychology and the law that incorporated three levels: *Entry*, *Proficiency*, and *Specialty* (Bersoff et al., 1997).

Entry Level—The Legally Informed Clinician

"All professional psychologists would receive basic education in law as it applies to professional practice, including information about confidentiality and privileged communications, and appropriate procedures for responding to subpoenas for clinical records and personal notes" (Bersoff et al., 1997, p. 1305). It was proposed that this level of competence should be met by all professional psychologists, and the core knowledge required for this level could be obtained within the graduate program. In essence this level of legal-related competence should be held by all practicing psychologists, not just those seeking forensic practice.

Proficiency Level

"Psychologists attaining this midlevel expertise may be trained through general professional programs, with an emphasis on forensics; training programs offering a 'concentration' in forensic psychology; or, for already trained clinicians, through extensive continuing education or postdoctoral programs" (Bersoff et al., 1997, p. 1306). The authors envisioned graduate programs offering coursework, practica experience, and research opportunities related to forensic psychology that students could take as an elective concentration while proceeding through the program. The proficiency level of training was suggested as the most common form of training in forensic psychology.

Specialty Level

"Beyond intensive and in-depth understanding of case law and extensive training in forensic skills, the forensic specialist would work with a variety of populations" (Bersoff et al., 1997, p. 1306). The authors envisioned forensic specific programs that trained forensic psychologists, oftentimes with joint JD and PhD graduate training, specialty internships, and/or forensic postdoctoral fellowships. The most definitive indication of such specialty level of training and experience is demonstrated by attainment of the Diplomate in Forensic Psychology from the American Board of Professional Psychology. We recommend this level of achievement for those neuropsychologists who seek truly to become experts in criminal forensic matters. In that light, we would caution the reader against seeking "specialty" certification via vanity boards or "added qualifications" that are not established as demonstrative of true expertise in forensic matters from organizations that are not uniquely forensic in nature (e.g., neuropsychology board with "added qualification" in forensics). Such "credentials" do not rise to the level of specialty training in forensic psychology and may in actuality not exceed that of the expertise of the entry-level clinician.

ABFP and Professional Competence

As suggested in the Texas Bill and the Villanova Conference, legitimate board certification in forensic psychology is the clearest indication of competence to practice in the area of criminal forensics, even for neuropsychologists. We recognize, however, that not all neuropsychologists practicing in the criminal forensic arena will seek board certification. Nevertheless, there is a core area of knowledge needed to practice competently in the criminal forensic arena. In the section titled *Competence*, the Ethical Principles of Psychologists and Code of Conduct (EPPCC; American Psychological Association, 2002) maintains that "(f) when assuming forensic roles, psychologists are or become reasonably familiar with the judicial or administrative rules governing their roles" (p. 5). The American Board of Forensic Psychology (ABFP; 2003) has developed a document outlining the fundamentals of forensic psychology. Although written as a guide to the core knowledge requirements for individuals applying for ABFP certification, we suggest that this document can be a helpful guide for neuropsychologists seeking additional criminal forensic training.

Under "Fundamentals of Law" the document includes the following relevant statements relevant for criminal matters:

> Candidates should know basic legal concepts and terminology. These include . . . : Burdens of proof and standards of persuasion; evidentiary rules; fundamentals of . . . criminal procedure; . . . criminal competencies; . . . legal citation methods; elements of an offense; criminal intent; and mental status defenses to criminal charges.
>
> Candidates should be able to describe the workings of the adversary system and the structure of the legal system, including different kinds of courts and jurisdictions and their relationship to parties and to each other. They should be aware of the roles and responsibilities of the judge, jury, attorneys for the prosecution and defense in criminal matters. . . . They should understand the position of the psychologist as a consultant and expert witness, the legal basis for these roles and the controversies surrounding such activities. They should know the difference between a fact witness and an expert witness, and what is required, allowed, and objectionable in the presentation of expert testimony. They should understand the limits of expert testimony and its effective presentation . . .
>
> Candidates should be knowledgeable about the Constitution and its relationship to forensic psychological issues. They should be aware of the First Amendment rights guaranteeing freedom of speech and religion, and their relation to "right to refuse treatment" cases. They should also be knowledgeable regarding Fourth Amendment protections against unreasonable search and seizure; Fifth Amendment rights to avoid self-incrimination and their relationship to criminal competency examinations, and to issues of guilt and responsibility; Sixth Amendment rights to legal counsel and trial by jury; and Eighth Amendment rights forbidding cruel and unusual punishment and their implications for prison and hospital policies. Candidates should be aware of the due process and equal protection clauses of the Fourteenth Amendment, and their implications for . . . mental health law. (p. 2)

Under "Fundamentals of Criminal Mental Health Law and Systems," the document outlines the following requirements:

Candidates who conduct criminal examinations as part of their practice should be able to describe the process which guides a defendant through the legal system in the state in which they practice. They should demonstrate knowledge of what constitutes a criminal offense in the area in which they practice and be able to discuss the legal process that culminates in a legal decision, from arrest to adjudication and sentencing.

Candidates should be familiar with the historical antecedents and standards that are relevant to criminal competencies. Knowledge of criminal competencies should include, but is not limited to, the case law that describes those capacities that are usually associated with a defendant's competency to stand trial, competency to plead guilty, competency to waive Constitutional rights, and competency to be executed (. . . if the state in which the candidate practices has the death penalty). Similarly, candidates who practice within the area of criminal forensic psychology should demonstrate knowledge of the philosophical and historical bases that have contributed to state and federal case law and statutes related to criminal responsibility. They should know who bears the burden of proof and the standard of proof in these types of proceedings. Candidates should be aware of the issues related to providing ethical expert testimony in criminal proceedings, including statements regarding a defendant's risk for future violent behavior.

Candidates should also be able to discuss the various dispositional outcomes of those individuals determined by the court to be incompetent to stand trial, found guilty but mentally ill, or acquitted by reason of insanity [depending on their state's particular procedure]. Candidates who provide treatment to this forensic population should be familiar with competency restoration, and the debate involving treatment designed to restore incompetent defendants to competency. They should be able to explain the process that can culminate in involuntary commitment, the types of treatment these patients will receive, and factors that a forensic psychologist may wish to consider prior to either returning a defendant to court or releasing the defendant with mental illness to the community. For candidates who live in states that have a conditional release program, they should be prepared to discuss the state regulations relevant to this practice. (p. 4)

Whereas knowledge of these issues is suggested for competent practice, it is likely not wholly sufficient. Supervised experience in applying this knowledge is likely also needed. The EPPCC (American Psychological Association, 2002) maintains, in the subsection titled "Boundaries of Competence," that "(a) psychologists provide services, teach, and conduct research with populations and in areas only within the boundaries of their competence, based on their education, training, supervised experience, consultation, study, or professional experience" (p. 4). Furthermore, " psychologists planning to provide services, teach, or conduct research involving populations, areas, techniques, or technologies new to them undertake relevant education, training, supervised experience, consultation, or study" (p. 5). The Farkas and colleagues (1997) survey revealed that some states require supervised experience to serve as court appointed experts in criminal matters (Michigan requires 6 months of supervision, with an examination process that comprises supervisor evaluations over the course of supervision). Given the American Psychological Association ethical code and recent proliferation of state requirements, some supervised experience in applying psychological principles to criminal forensic matters is clearly warranted for competent practice of criminal forensic neuropsychology. As of this writing the length and nature of this supervision has not been identified.

Covering each of the areas outlined by the ABFP document is well beyond the scope and purpose of this text. For an outstanding and thorough review of each of these areas, the reader is referred to Melton and colleagues (2007).

A Collaborative Model of Practice

An alternative model of practice is for the clinical neuropsychologist to work collaboratively with forensic experts. Indeed, there is a legal strategy whereby the neuropsychologist evaluates solely the neuropathological and neurocognitive condition of the defendant, while a forensic mental health expert addresses the forensic question in light of the neurocognitive findings. In this regard, Heilbronner and Frumkin (2003) propose a two-tier model of practice that incorporates both a neuropsychologist and a forensic psychologist.

In the first option, "the clinical neuropsychologist works as a consultant, providing the neuropsychological data to a forensic psychologist, who then ties in the neuropsychological data to the legally-relevant criteria, based upon his or her knowledge of the case law and professional standards in the area" (Heilbronner & Frumkin, 2003, p. 9). In this option, the neuropsychologist is working for the forensic mental health expert (the client, in this case). Here the forensic expert will incorporate the neuropsychology conclusions in formulating his or her opinion and will likely be the primary expert witness on the case, if testimony is needed. One of us (Denney) has often provided expertise as neuropsychologist in this manner for forensic experts (both psychologists and psychiatrists) within the forensic assessment unit of the U.S. Medical Center for Federal Prisoners. Commonly the forensic expert attaches the neuropsychology consultation report to his or her report as an addendum. On other occasions, he or she would simply refer to the neuropsychology consultation report as an additional source of information, just as he or she would the medical history and physical examination and other sources of data obtained during an inpatient mental health evaluation. In some instances both of us are requested to provide testimony; in other instances, testimony is only required from the clinician providing the ultimate issue opinion. The neuropsychology expert testimony is limited to issues relevant to the clinical, neuropathological, and neurocognitive findings, whereas the forensic expert testimony is focused on issues specific to the ultimate issue before the trier of fact.

Heilbronner and Frumkin (2003) provide an additional option in their model, in which the referring attorney hires both a forensic expert and a neuropsychological expert to evaluate different but related concerns. They note that these two experts could be hired concurrently to address their respective areas of expertise at the outset. They also note the possibility that one expert (typically the forensic expert) is hired initially but subsequently recommends the input of a neuropsychological expert. The neuropsychologist could possibly also enter the case initially to address mitigating issues, for example, only to find the facts of the case suggest the need to evaluate retrospective competence, or some other specific forensic question (sanity, coercion/false confessions, competence to waive the right to trial, etc.). Here, the forensic expert would then enter the picture, because the neuropsychologist recognizes that he or she is not competent to perform such a specifically focused forensic evaluation. The authors provide the following summary regarding the collaborative model:

> But, in criminal cases, offering opinions in relative isolation, with the exception of examining the notes or evaluations of others, should be the exception rather than the rule. Indeed, the forensic psychologist and clinical neuropsychologist are most effective when both are working on a case, serving as a consultant to each other. It is good planning, forethought, and money well spent when an attorney recognizes the importance of, and the need for, both kinds of evaluations. (p. 11)

We recognize that not all neuropsychologists want to become experts in criminal forensic matters to the *specialist*, or even *proficiency* level. It is for these individuals that the collaborative model of criminal forensic neuropsychology works well. It is incumbent that neuropsychologists, and forensic mental health experts, realize where their respective expertise ends and remain willing to make this limit known to referral sources. We hope, however, that more neuropsychologists will see the benefit of striving for the specialty level of expertise in criminal matters.

Conclusion

The chapters in this text are properly viewed as points of departure for continued investigation and development of professional competence in each of the particular areas examined. As mentioned in the opening chapter, as recently as 1999, clinical neuropsychologists conducted criminal forensic assessments only very occasionally (Sweet, 1999). It is our firm conviction that times have changed; that clinical neuropsychology has most definitely arrived in the criminal forensic venue and is here to stay. Furthermore, it is our sincere hope that this text will encourage readers to raise the collective quality of neuropsychological involvement in the criminal forensic area through renewed individual commitment to ethical rigor, professional excellence, and, ultimately, authentic professional competence.

Note

Opinions expressed in this chapter are those of the authors and do not necessarily represent the position of the Federal Bureau of Prisons or the U.S. Department of Justice.

References

American Board of Forensic Psychology. (2003). *Fundamentals of forensic psychology: Description of forensic specialty areas: Revised 2003*. Retrieved from December 10, 2003, from *abfp.com/pdfs/fundamentals_of_forensic_psychology.pdf*

American Psychological Association. (2002). Ethical Principles of Psychologists and Code of Conduct. *American Psychologist, 57*, 1060–1073.

Bersoff, D. N., Goodman-Delahunty, J., Grisso, J. T., Hans, V. P., Poythress, N. G., & Roesch, R. G. (1997). Training in law and psychology: Models from the Villanova Conference. *American Psychologist, 52*, 1301–1310.

Farkas, G. M., DeLeon, P. H., & Newman, R. (1997). Sanity examiner certification: An evolving national agenda. *Professional Psychology: Research and Practice, 28*, 73–76.

Hannay, H. J., Bieliauskas, L. A., Crosson, B. A., Hammeke, T. A., Hamsher, K. deS., & Koffler, S. P. (1998). Proceedings: The Houston Conference on Specialty Education and Training in Clinical Neuropsychology. *Archives of Clinical Neuropsychology, 13*(2). Retrieved December 9, 2007, from *www.theaacn.org/position_papers/Houston_Conference.pdf*

Heilbronner, R. L., & Frumkin, I. B. (2003). Neuropsychology and forensic psychology: Working collaboratively in criminal cases. *Journal of Forensic Neuropsychology, 3*, 5–12.

Melton, G. B., Petrila, J., Poythress, N. G., & Slobogin, C., with Lyons, P. M., Jr., & Otto, R. K. (2007). *Psychological evaluations for the courts: A handbook for mental health professionals and lawyers* (3rd ed.). New York: Guilford Press.

Sweet, J. J. (1999). Introduction. In L. A. Bieliauskas (Series Ed.) & J. J. Sweet (Vol. Ed.), *Series on neuropsychology, development, and cognition: Vol. 2. Forensic neuropsychology: Fundamentals and practice* (pp. xvii–xix). Lisse, The Netherlands: Swets & Zeitlinger.

Index

Page numbers followed by *f* indicate figure, *t* indicate table

Acquired sociopathy, 248–249
Actus reus, 205, 336
　defined, 206
Ad hominem attacks, avoiding, 372–373
Adamson v. Chiovaro, 1998, 61
Addington v. Texas, 441 U.S. 418,430 (1979), 31
Admissibility issues, 38, 55–90
　applied in criminal cases, 71–75
　case vignettes, 56–58
　Daubert impact, 76–81
　for Grisso measures, 161–166
　for GSS, 161–162, 166–170
　history of, 58–62
　and Insanity Defense Reform Act, 65–68
　and presentation of findings to court, 352–356
　and qualification of experts, 68–71
　and rules governing competency and insanity defense, 62–65
　and wrongful disclosure, 81–84
　See also United States v. José Santos-Bueno, 1997
Adolescents
　developmental assessment in, 303–304
　general psychopathology in, 305–306
　malingered cognitive deficit in, 311–314
　maturational issues in, 304–305
　See also Juveniles
Advocacy
　avoiding, 381–382
　versus providing expert testimony, 350–352
Affective disorders, in adolescents, 305
Aggravating factors, 275
Aggression
　affective versus predatory, 240, 241*t*
　focal frontal lobe pathology and, 258

　neuroanatomical basis of, 244–246
　psychobiological taxonomy of, 239–241
　serotonergic/noradrenergic function and, 242
　social-environmental factors in, 243
　treatment of, 242–243
Ake v. Oklahoma, 470 U.S. 68 (1985), 15, 25–26
Alcohol abuse/dependence
　maternal, aggressive behavior in children and, 308
　as mitigating factor, 276
　serotonergic/noradrenergic function and, 242
Alternative Suggestibility Scales, 169
Alzheimer's disease, aggression associated with, 254
Amendments, constitutional, 14–17
American Board of Clinical Neuropsychology, position on professional competence, 391
American Board of Forensic Psychology, 46
American Board of Forensic Psychology and American Psychology—Law Society, 4–5
American Law Institute, insanity standard of, 209, 210–211, 210*t*
　versus IDRA standards, 211–212, 218–220
　jurisdictions recognizing, 212
　operational definitions in, 213–218
American Psychological Association
　ethical guidelines on competent delivery of services, 39–40
　Ethical Principles of Psychologists and Code of Conduct, 32, 395–397
　guidelines for informed consent, 33–34
　and mixing of professional roles, 50–51
　release of test data and, 46–48
　standards of, 46

401

Amnesia
    and competency to stand trial, 189–193
    crime-specific, 364
    feigned, 189–190
    forms of, 190
    retrograde, 118–122
    transient epileptic, 263
    transient global, 263
    of unknown etiology, competency to stand trial and, 192–194
Anchoring, 356–357
Anesthetics, dissociative, automatism and, 222–223
Antipsychotic medications, for aggressive behavior, 242–243
Antisocial personality disorder, 239, 247
    intermittent explosive disorder and, 262
    intrauterine malnutrition and, 307
    neuropsychological studies of, 248
Anxiety, exaggeration of, 94
APD. *See* Antisocial personality disorder
Appellate courts, 6
    deference to district courts, 70
Archival records
    presenting, 381
    retrieving, 359–360
Arkansas, insanity standard in, 210–211
Art of War, The, 378–379
Atkins v. United States, 2002, 373, 374
Atkins v. Virginia, 2002, 16, 23–24, 65, 124, 196–197
    and mitigating factors in sentencing phase, 277
Attention-deficit/hyperactivity disorder, 245, 247
    in adolescents, 305
    as mitigating factor, 276
Attorney
    contacts with, 337
    strategies of, 375–376, 382–383
Automatism
    definitions of, 221–222
    epileptic, 260–261
    insanity defense and, 221–224, 223–224
    psychogenic, 223

Bail, excessive, 16
Barefoot v. Estelle, 1982, 356
Barefoot v. Estelle, 1983, 26
Baskerville v. Cullgan, 1994, 350–351
Bates v. State, 56
Baxter v. Temple, 2005, 78–80
Bechara Gambling Task, 368
Behavior
    impaired, defined, 232
    pathological, 249
    See also Criminal/violent behavior
Bell v. Thompson, 2005, 57

Beneficence, 39
Bergson v. Ray, 61
Berman v. Kuckarski, 2006, 82
Beta-adrenergic blockers, for aggressive behavior, 243
Bias, 356–358
    avoiding, 357–358
    subtypes of, 356–357
Billiot v. State, 1995, 65
Bonner v. ISP Technologies, Inc., 2001, 61
Borderline personality disorder, intermittent explosive disorder and, 262
Boston Process Approach, 78–79, 367
Boulder Conference, 58
"Brain Damage Claims: Coping with Neuropsychological Evidence," 378
Brain dysfunction
    cases involving, 56–62
    medical conditions causing, 284–285
Brain injury
    assessment of, 205
    defined, 224
    insanity defense and, 224
    penetrating, competency to stand trial and, 190–192
    See also Traumatic brain injury
Brain overclaim syndrome, 67
Brain regions, aggression-related, 244–247
Brain tumors
    criminal/violent behavior and, 257
    as mitigating factor, 276
Brain–behavior science, skepticism about, 61–62
Brawner standard, 210
Breed v. Jones, 1975, 300
Brown v. Mississippi, 1936, 18, 149
Broyles v. Reilly, 1997, 82
Buckler v. Sinclair Refining Co., 1966, 60

California v. Burnett, 1987, 163
Calloway v. State, 1995, 63
Cameron, diminished capacity and, 66
Capacity for self-care, defined, 233
Capital Defense Unit, 327, 329
Capital murder cases, 10
    and consequences of forensic opinions, 9–10
    insanity defense and, 65
    sentencing phase of. *See* Sentencing phase
Capital punishment. *See* Death penalty; Execution
Carpenter v. Yamaha Motor Corp., 2006, 83
Carter v. State, 1997, 163
Case citations, guide to, 17
Case law, 5
    and guidance for informed consent, 37–38
    in juvenile justice, 299–301
    psychologist competency and, 44
Case vignettes, evidence admissibility and, 56–58

Causey, 1978. See *In re Causey, 1978*
Chapple v. Gangar, 1994, 80–81, 365
Children
  informed consent and, 316–318
  malingered cognitive deficit in, 311–314
  See also Adolescents; Juveniles
Circuit Courts of Appeals, 6, 6t
Citizens, constitutional rights of, 14–17
Civil forensic settings, NRB in, 97–98
Clinical interviews, in evaluation for *Miranda* waiver, 142–143
Clinical neuropsychology, settings for, 1
Coercion, defense of, 206
Cognitive deficits, feigning, 2
Cognitive test results, poor effort and, 91–92
Collaborative model of practice, 397–398
Colorado v. Connelly, 1986, 139
Committee on Ethical Guidelines for Forensic Psychologists, 34, 35t–36t, 36
  guidelines on forensic psychologist competence, 40, 41t–43t
  and mixing of professional roles, 51–52
Commonwealth v. Halbert, 1991, 227
Commonwealth v. Soares, 2001, 167–168
Commonwealth v. Zamarripa, 1988, 122
Competence
  cases involving, 32
  versus diminished responsibility/capacity, 67–68
  entry of plea and, 64
  key factors in, 20–21
  professional. See Professional competence
  retrospective determinations of, 62
  rules governing, 62–65
  training and education and, 44–46
  and types of witnesses, case law, Federal Rule of Evidence 702, 44
  to waive *Miranda* rights, 137–140
  for waiving *Miranda* rights, evaluation of, 140–149
Competence Assessment for Standing Trial for Defendants with Mental Retardation, 198–199
Competence restoration, 22
  limits to, 184–185
Competence to be executed, 184
Competence to be sentenced, 182–183
Competence to plead guilty, cases involving, 19–20
Competence to proceed, 176–203
  assessment instruments for determining, 197–199
  case examples, 189–197
    amnesia, 189–193
    mental retardation, 196–197
    traumatic brain injury, 193–196
  and competency to be executed, 184
  and competency to be sentenced, 182–183

  and competency to waive rights to trial/counsel, 181–182
  defined, 176
  Dusky and, 177
  versus legal sanity, 176
  legal standard for, 177–181
  as legal versus psychological concept, 180
  and limits to competency restoration, 184–185
  model for evaluating, 185–187
  neuropsychological testing for, 176, 187–189
  New Jersey definition, 178
  versus questions of knowledge or willingness, 179–180
  threshold for initiating inquiry into, 181
  Wieter v. Settle and, 179, 179t
Competence to stand trial, 20–21
  assessment instruments for, 197–199
  and consequences of forensic opinions, 9–10
  Dusky and, 64
  mental retardation and, 65
  penetrating brain injury and, 190–192
Complex partial seizures, aggressive behavior and, 260
Comprehension of *Miranda* Rights, 145–148
Comprehension of *Miranda* Rights—Recognition, 145–148
Comprehension of *Miranda* Vocabulary, 145–148
Computerized Assessment of Response Bias, 108–110
Conduct disorder, 305–306
Confessions
  cases involving, 18–19
  challenges to, 135
  false, 135–136
    coerced–reactive, 153
    by juveniles, 305
    processes related to, 155–156
    psychological risk factors for, 154–155
    research on, 151–152
    voluntary versus coerced–compliant, 152–153
  false and involuntary, 149–154
  physically coerced, 18
  Reid technique for eliciting, 149–150
  reliability of, expert testimony and, 153–154
  See also *Miranda* waiver/confession cases
Confirmatory bias, 356
Conform one's conduct, definitions of, 214
Constitution. See U. S. Constitution
Constitutional law, U. S. versus state, 5–7
Constitutional rights, Fourteenth Amendment and, 16–17
Cooper v. Griffin, 1972, 139
Cooper v. Oklahoma, 1996, 179
Counsel, right to. See Right to counsel
Court orders, in juvenile settings, 318

Courts, parallel systems of, 6
Crane v. Kentucky, 1986, 153
Credentials, expert witness, 380–381
Crime Control Act, 211
Criminal adjudicative process, 7, 8f
Criminal courts, malingering and, 122–123
Criminal forensic issues, clinical neuropsychology applications, 2–4
Criminal forensic neuropsychology
  dichotomous classification system in, 31
  foundations of, 1–29
  as unique setting, 7, 9–14
Criminal forensic psychology
  defined, 4
  five I's and, 3, 32
Criminal forensic settings, NRB in, 98–99
Criminal justice system
  adversarial approach in, 31, 48–49
  competencies in, 178t
  versus juvenile justice system, 296–297, 302–303
  sequence in, 8f
Criminal legal system, 5–7
Criminal litigation, admissibility of expert testimony in, *Daubert* and, 76–78
Criminal offenses, defined, 206–207
Criminal referrals, initial contacts for, 327–328
Criminal responsibility
  assessment of, 229–233, 231f
    instruments for, 232–233
  conditions for, 206–207
  forensic neuropsychologist's role in establishing, 249–250, 250f
  legal conceptualizations for, 205–206
  See also Mental state at time of offense
Criminal/violent behavior, 238–272
  brain injury and, 281
  due to defendant predisposition versus mental disease/defect, 239
  frontal lobe syndromes and, 250–251, 250t, 256–259
  generalized deficit syndromes and, 250–256, 250t
    dementia, 250t, 253–255
    mental retardation, 250t, 255–256
    schizophrenia, 250t, 251–253
  genetic factors, 243
  in juveniles, 306–309
  neurological and psychiatric disorders with potential to influence, 250–251, 250t, 286
  neurological disorders and, 284–285
  risk factors for, 277–278, 278t
  syndrome-based approach to, 238, 249–251
  temporal lobe syndromes and, 250–251, 250t, 259–264
  See also Aggression; Violent offenders

Cross-examination
  attorney strategies in, 382–383
    minimizing effects of, 383–384
  enhancing effectiveness of, 374–386
  Federal Rules of Evidence and, 385
  frequently used questions in, 384–385
"Cross-Examining the Prosecution's Mental Health Expert," 377–378
Cruel and unusual punishments, 16, 276–277
  and competency to be executed, 184
Cunningham v. Montgomery, 1995, 61

Dangerousness
  cases involving, 26
  future, predicting, 356
Daniels v. State, 1998, 227
Daubert v. Merrell Dow Pharmaceuticals, 1993, 32, 44, 68–70, 375
  and admissibility of expert testimony in criminal litigation, 76–78
  avoiding challenges by, 371
  clarifications of, 70–71
  evidence admissibility and, 56, 73–78
  and fixed versus flexible test batteries, 365–366
  fMRI evidence and, 67
  on gatekeeper function of judge, 353–354
  Grisso tests and, 162, 163
  Gudjonsson Suggestibility Scales and, 166–167
  testing bias and, 357
Death penalty
  aggravating factor in, 275
  appropriateness of, 16
  cases challenging constitutionality of, 277
  cases involving, 22–24, 24–25
  challenges of consultations in, 273–274
  constitutionality of, 276–277
  as cruel and unusual punishment, 65
  eligibility factors in, in Illinois, 274
  expert's self-examination and, 373–374
  future dangerousness and, 356
  in Georgia, 22–23
  in Ohio, 23
  prohibition of
    for juveniles, 298
    for mentally regarded criminals, 124
  prohibitions of, mental retardation, 374
  trial phase, 274
  See also Capital murder cases; Execution
Death penalty appeals, basis for, 16
Deception
  child's capacity for, 311
  detection of, 104
  evaluating, 77
  on GSS and GCS, 161
Deception test, 68

Index

Defendant
   academic functioning of, 280–281
   in capital crimes, social history investigation of. *See* Social history investigation
   competent, 177. *See also* Competence
   constitutional rights of, 14–17
   indigent, 25–26
   innocent, confessions by, 135–136
   interactions with, at prison, 333
   mental health history of, 280
   rapport versus therapeutic alliance with, 10
   reading comprehension level of, 141
Delinquency
   emphasis on, 296
   neuropsychology of, 306–309
   versus status offenses, 297
Dementia
   causes of, 254
   criminal/violent behavior and, 253–255
   as mitigating factor, 276
Depression, exaggeration of, 94
Detroit Edison Co., v. NLRB, 1979, 82, 83
Developmental disorders, as mitigating factor, 276
Diagnostic and Statistical Manual of Mental Disorders, fourth edition, text revision
   attitudes toward definitions of, 213
   malingering defined by, 96–97
Dickerson v. United States, 2000, 19, 138
Diminished responsibility/capacity, 204
   versus competence and insanity, 67–68
   confusion about, 66
   defense of, 206
   extreme emotional disturbance and, 228–229
   head injury and, 228
   insanity defense and, 225–226
   mitigation and, 229
   substance abuse/dependence and, 226–228
Disorganization, 213
Dissociation, exaggeration of, 94
Dissociative anesthetics, automatism and, 222–223
Dissociative disorder, criminal/violent behavior and, 263–264
District courts, gatekeeping functions of, 70
District of Columbia Circuit Court of Appeals, 6, 6t
Dot Counting Test, 106–107
Downs v. Perstorp Components, Inc., 1999, 61
Drope v. Missouri, 1975, 21–22, 64
   competency to proceed and, 181
Dual role, definition and example, 350–351
Dual Sentencing statute, 298
Due Process Clause, 177, 182
Duress, defense of, 206
Durham rule, 209

Durham v. United States, 1954, Product Test and, 209
Dusky v. United States, 1960, 19, 20–21, 62, 139, 182
   and competency to be sentenced, 183
   and competency to proceed, 177
   and competency to stand trial, 64, 197

Eddings v. Oklahoma, 1978, and mitigating factors in sentencing phase, 277
Education, psychologist, 44–46
Educational plan, construction of, 309
Eighth Amendment
   cases involving, 23–24
   and constitutionality of death penalty, 276–277
   mental competency and, 65–66
   wording and significance, 16
Emotional disturbance, extreme, insanity defense and, 228–229
Entrapment, defense of, 206
Epilepsy defense, 260–261
Epilepsy/seizure disorders
   aggressive behavior and, 259–260
   as mitigating factor, 276
   temporal lobe, 260
Epileptic automatism, 260–261
Episodic dyscontrol syndrome, 262
Estelle v. Smith, 1981, 15, 24–25, 32
   informed consent and, 37
Ethical issues, 30–54
   competency and, 38–46
   conclusions and recommendations, 52–53
   court orders in juvenile system, 318
   informed consent, 33–38
      for children, 316–318
   in juvenile justice neuropsychology, 314–318
   versus moral values, 30
   and multiple relationships, 50–52
   and release of test data, 46–50
Ethical Principle B, 38
Ethical Principles of Psychologists and Code of Conduct, 32, 395–397
Evaluation of Competency to Stand Trial—Revised, 187, 198
Evidence
   rules of. *See* Federal Rules of Evidence
   See Neuropsychological evidence
Execution
   competence to undergo, 64–65, 184
   See also Death penalty
Executive Car & Truck Leasing, Inc. v. DeSerio, 1985, 60
Expert testimony. *See* Neuropsychologist expert testimony
Experts, qualifications of, 68–71
Extreme emotional disturbance, insanity defense and, 228–229

Fabianke v. Weaver ex rel. Weaver, 1988, 61
Factitious disorder, versus malingering, 96
Fare v. Michael, 1979, 300
Farretta v. California, 1975, 15
Federal Rules of Evidence (FRE), 15
  FRE 403, 77
  FRE 611, 385
  FRE 702, 77, 353–354
    and admissibility of expert testimony, 38
    amendment of, 71
    neuropsychologist testimony and, 73–74
    psychologist competency and, 44
    in *United States v. José Santos-Bueno*, 71
  FRE 703, 354–355
  FRE 704, 354–355
  FRE 704(b), 355
  enactment of, 353
  release of data and, 48
Fees, setting, 329–330
Felony murder doctrine, 227
Felony track, 7
Fetal alcohol syndrome, as mitigating factor, 276
Fidelity and Responsibility principle, 38
Fiduciary role, defined, 38
Fifth Amendment
  cases involving, 24–25
  Miranda v. Arizona and, 63
  violations of, 18–19
  wording and significance, 14–15
Findings, presenting. *See* Presenting neuropsychological findings
Fines, excessive, 16
Five I's, 3, 32
Florida Department of Transportation v. Piccolo, 2006, 82–83
Forced-choice digit recognition tests, 108–111
Ford v. Wainwright, 1986, 65, 184
Forensic evaluation
  methodology in, 10, 12
  Mrad's multiple data source model and, 12, 13f, 14
  nontherapeutic nature of, 10
  prevalence of, 32
  roles in, 11t
  See also Neuropsychological assessment
Forensic mental health assessment, 137–138
Forensic neuropsychologist
  attire of, 331
  avoiding dual roles, 350–352
  collaborative model of practice and, 397–398
  competency of, 38–46. *See also* Professional competence
  entry level, 393
  fiduciary role of, 38
  in juvenile settings. *See also* Juvenile justice system
    competency of, 314–315
    professional development of, 315–316

multiple relationships and, 50–52
obligations of, 39
proficiency level, 394
qualification requirements, 44
responsibilities of, 30–31
roles of, 9–10
specialty guidelines for, 41t–43t, 49t
specialty level, 394
See also Neuropsychologist expert testimony
Forensic neuropsychology. *See* Criminal forensic neuropsychology
Forensic psychology
  graduate and specialty training in, 394
  graduate programs in, 45
Forensic reports, 368–374
  avoiding attorney influence on, 369
  content, 370–372
  Golden Rule of, 368–369
  presentation to criminal court, 368–374
  prohibited and discouraged language in, 372–373
  self-examination questions for preparation of, 373
Forensic social historian, 274
Fourteenth Amendment
  cases involving, 23, 25–26
  Due Process Clause of, 182
  Dusky and, 177
  mental incompetence and, 62
  violations of, 18
  wording and significance, 16–17
Frederick's conceptual model of test performance, 95–96, 95f
Frendak v. United States, 1979, 64
Frontal lobe defense, 66–67
Frontal lobe syndromes, 66
  criminal/violent behavior and, 250–251, 250t, 256–259
Frontal lobes, dysfunction of
  criminal responsibility and, 249–250, 250f
  criminality and, 247–248
Frye standard, 44, 353
Frye v. United States, 1923, 32, 44, 68, 69, 353
  challenge to flexible battery approach and, 366
  Daubert and, 76–77
  general acceptance test and, 69
  Grisso tests and, 162, 163
  Gudjonsson Suggestibility Scales and, 166–167
  Rule 702 and, 73–74
Fulcher v. State, 1981, 223
Functional magnetic resonance imaging
  in aggression/violence studies, 244
  legal use of, 67
Furman v. Georgia, 1972, 16
Future dangerousness, predictions of, 356

Gallegos v. Colorado, 1962, 300, 305
Gault, 1967. See In re Gault, 1967
General acceptance test, 68–69
General Electric Co. v. Joiner, 1997, 70, 73. See also Joiner v. General Electric Co., 1997
General intellectual ability, measures of, 105–117
Generalized deficit syndromes, in criminal/violent behavior, 250–256, 250t
Generalized tonic–clonic seizures, 260
Genetic factors
  in childhood antisocial/aggressive behavior, 306–307
  in criminal/violent behavior, 242–244
G.I.W. Southern Value v. Smith, 1985, 61
G.J.I. v. State, 1989, 299, 300
Godinez v. Moran, 1993, 15, 19–20, 64, 181–182, 186
Graduate programs, 45
  in forensic psychology, 394
Green v. United States, 1961, 183
Gregg v. Georgia, 428 U.S. 153 (1976), 22–23
Grenitz v. Tomlian, 2003, 61
Grisso competency evaluation criteria, 186–187
Grisso tests, 145–149
  admissibility issues, 161–166
  critiques of, 163–166
Gross distortion, 213–214
Gudjonsson Compliance Scales, in assessment of voluntariness of Miranda waivers/confessions, 160–161
Gudjonsson Suggestibility Scales, 155, 157–159
  admissibility issues, 161–162, 166–170
  malingering and deception on, 161

Hagen v. Swenson, 1975, 61
Haley v. Ohio, 1948, 300, 305
Hand, Judge Learned, 352
Hare Psychopathy Checklist—Revised, 356
Head injury, diminished capacity and, 228
Head trauma, focal frontal lobe pathology and, 258
Health Insurance Portability and Accountability Act, test information requests and, 47
Hinckley, IDRA and, 65–66
Hitchcock v. Dugger, 1986, 275
Homicide
  amnesia and, 118–119
  criminally negligent, voluntary intoxication and, 227
  epilepsy defense and, 260–261
Hormones
  aggression and, 243
  criminal/violent behavior and, 242–244
Houston Conference, position on professional competence, 391

How to Become a Dangerous Expert Witness, 375
Howard v. State, 1985, 62
Huntoon v. TCI Cablevision, 1998, 61
Hutchinson v. American Family Mut. Ins., 1994, 61
Hypothalamus, aggression and, 244

Illusory correlation, 357
Impaired behavior, defined, 232
Impaired judgment, defined, 232
Impaired reality testing, 232–233
In re Causey, 1978, 300
In re Gault, 1967, 138, 297, 298, 300
In re Johnson, 1983, 301
In re Patrick W., 1978, 139
In re T.S.D. v. Florida, 1999, 163
In re Williams, 1997, 300
In re Winship, 1970, 297, 298, 300
In the interest of S.H., 1996, 300
Infancy, defined, 206
Information
  access to, 48–49, 49t
  pseudoscientific, 360, 361t–362t
  reliable, 359–360
  third-party, 359–360
Informed consent, 33–38
  APA guidelines, 33–34
  case law guidelines, 37–38
  for children, 316–318
  Committee on Ethical Guidelines for Forensic Psychologists, 34, 35t–36t, 36
  guidance for, 32
  pragmatic considerations, 333–335
Innocence Project, 153
Insanity
  versus diminished responsibility/capacity, 67–68
  legal, standard for, 65
Insanity defense
  automatism and, 221–224
  brain injury and, 224
  current status of, 212–213
  diminished capacity and, 225–226
  IDRA versus ALI standards of, clinical example, 218–220
  jurisdictions abolishing, 65
  prevalence of, 205
  rules governing, 62–65
  variations in standards for, 213
  voluntary intoxication and, 220–221
Insanity Defense Reform Act of 1984, 62, 65–68, 209, 211–212, 211t
  versus ALI standards, 211–212
  Hinckley and, 65–66
  jurisdictions adopting, 212
  nature, quality, and wrongfulness definitions in, 215–218

Insanity Defense Reform Act of 1984 (cont.)
    neuropsychologist testimony not precluded by, 72–73
    operational definitions in, 213–218
    standards of, versus ALI standards, 218–220
Insanity standards, 208–212
    changes in, 208
Intent, defined, 207–208
Intermittent explosive disorder, 262
Interrogation
    audio- or videotaped recordings of, 141–142
    versus interview, 151
    right to stop, 19
Interviews
    clinical, in evaluation for *Miranda* waiver, 142–143
    versus interrogation, 151
    structured, 357–358
Intoxication
    defense of, 206
    involuntary, 221
    pathological, 221
    voluntary
        insanity defense and, 220–221
        mens rea and, 226–227
IQ
    in criminal population, 307
    Miranda waiver and, 143–144
Irresistible Impulse Test, 209

Jackson v. Indiana, 1972, 22, 184, 185
Jail
    logistical considerations, 331–332
    neuropsychologist–defendant interaction in, 333
Jenkins v. United States, 1962, 58–60, 374
John v. Im, 2002, 61
Johnson, 1983. See *In re Johnson*, 1983
Joiner v. General Electric Co., 1997, 354
    testing bias and, 357
    See also *General Electric Co. v. Joiner*, 1997
Judgment, impaired, defined, 232
Jury
    misleading, expert testimony and, 75
    responses to expert testimony, 386
Juvenile crime, violent, in 1980s, 298
Juvenile justice system, 7, 295–325
    administrative structure of, 302
    case law in, 299–301
    court procedure, 301–303
    versus criminal justice system, 296–297, 302–303
    ethical neuropsychology practice and, 314–318
    evolution of, 297–298
    forensic psychologist competence in, 314–315
    and malingered cognitive deficit in children, 311–314
    neuropsychology-specific issues in, 303–309
        adolescent general psychopathology, 305–306
        general maturational issues, 304–305
        neurodevelopment, 303–304
        neuropsychology of delinquency, 306–309
    non-consultation-focused neuropsychologist roles in, 318–319
    parens patriae and, 296–297
    philosophical issues in, 298–299
    points of neuropsychological service to, 303
    policy development in, 318–319
    rehabilitation versus punishment in, 297
    types of evaluations in, 309–311
Juveniles
    defined, 295–296
    and exemption from death penalty, 277
    inadequate interventions for, 310
    Miranda protections and, 138
    pretrial diversion track and, 7
    punishment versus rehabilitation of, 297–298
    transfer to criminal court, 302
    See also Adolescents

Kent v. United States, 1966, 297, 298, 299
Kinsey v. King, 1982, 61
Kjeldsen v. The Queen, 1981, 215
Krevitz v. Savoy Heating and Air Conditioning Co., 1981, 61
Kumho Tire Co. v. Carmichael, 1999, 70, 73, 354
    testing bias and, 357

Landers v. Chrysler Corp., 1998, 61
Landmark cases, 17–26
Law
    Constitutional, 5–6, 6t
    legislative, 5–6, 6t
Learning disabilities
    aggressive/violent behavior and, 246–247
    GSS and, 168–169
    as mitigating factor, 276
Learning disability, versus dementia, 255
Legal constructs, core, 3
Legal issues, psycholegal opinions about, 355–356
Legal sanity
    versus competency, 176
    See also Insanity defense; Insanity Defense Reform Act of 1984
Legislative law, 5–6, 6t
Life sentence without possibility of parole, 274–275
Limbic psychotic trigger reaction, 262
Limbic rage, 262
Locket v. Ohio, 1978, and mitigating factors in sentencing phase, 277

Lockett v. Ohio, 1978, 23, 273
Lugo v. Citicorp Mortgage, 1994, 61

MacArthur Competence Assessment Tool—Criminal Adjudication, 187, 197–198
Madrid v. Univ. of Ca., 1987, 61
Magnetic resonance imaging, in aggression/violence studies, 244
Malingered cognitive deficit, in children, 311–314
   detection strategies for, 312–314
   models of, 312
Malingered neurocognitive dysfunction, 99, 193
   base rate of, 101
   Slick criteria for, 101–104, 102f
Malingering, 12, 91–134. *See also* Negative response bias
   adaptational model of, 97
   assessment of, 104–118
      with embedded indices of neurocognitive NRB, 117
      in evaluation for *Miranda* waiver, 145
      with free-standing measures of NRB, 105–117
      future directions in, 123–124
      with multiple NRB indices, 118
      with self-report measures of psychiatric disturbance, 118
   base rate of, 99–101
   classification of, 101–104
   and competence to stand trial, 188–189, 195–196
   components of, 93–97
   crime-specific amnesia and, 364
   criminal courts and, 122–123
   by criminal defendants, 98–99
   criminological model of, 96
   diagnostic accuracy of, 99–101
   explanatory models of, 96–97
   versus factitious disorder, 96
   on GSS and GCS, 161
   motivations for, 91
   versus negative response bias, 101, 103
   negative response bias and, 93–96
   pathological model of, 96–97
   peer-reviewed papers on, 91, 92f
   prevalence rates, 97–99
Malnutrition, abnormal behavior and, 307
Manslaughter, voluntary/involuntary, voluntary intoxication and, 227
Mask v. State, 1993, 211
Mass murder, 240, 241t
Maternal rejection, juvenile aggression and, 307–308
Maturational issues, assessment of, 304–305
McCarthy v. Atwood, 2005, 61

McDonald v. United States, 1962, 209
   mental disease/defect defined by, 213
McKeiver v. Pennsylvania, 1971, 299, 300, 301
Medical Symptom Validity Test, 114–116
   for children, 313
   medical, 116–117
Medina v. California, 1992, 179
Memory, short-term, measures of, 107–117
Memory impairment
   and competency to stand trial, 189–193
   feigned, symptom validity testing for, 119–122
   remote. *See* Remote memory loss
Memory processing, temporal lobes in, 262–263
Mens rea, 206–208, 336
   defined, 206–207
   diminished capacity and, 225
   evidence proving lack of, 65–66
   voluntary intoxication and, 226–227
Mens rea defense, 205
Mental disease/defect, in *McDonald v. United States*, 1962, 213
Mental examination, court-ordered, 63
Mental health case law, 3–4
Mental health evaluation, defense counsel's knowledge of, 24–25
Mental health professionals
   lack of legal knowledge, 3–4
   treatment versus forensic roles for, 11t
Mental illness
   cases involving, 61–62
   diagnostic criteria for, 65
   See also Insanity defense
Mental retardation
   aggressive/violent behavior and, 246–247
   cases involving, 24
   and competence to stand trial, 65, 196–197
      assessment of, 198–199
   criminal/violent behavior and, 255–256
   criteria for, 196
   and exemption from death penalty, 124, 277, 374
   feigned versus genuine, 124
   versus learning disability, 255
   as mitigating factor, 276
   VIP and, 106
Mental State at the time of Offense Examination, 232
Mental state at time of offense, 204–237
   automatism and, 221–224
   brain injury and, 224
   criminal responsibility and
      assessment of, 229–233
      legal concepts for, 205–206
   and current status of insanity defense, 212–213

Mental state at time of offense (cont.)
  diminished capacity and, 225–226
    from extreme emotional disturbance, 228–229
    from head injury, 228
    from substance abuse/dependence, 226–228
  diminished responsibility and mitigation and, 229
  extreme emotional disturbance and, 228–229
  head injury and, 228
  impact of standard, 218–220
  insanity standards and, 208–212
  intoxication and, 220–221
  and *mens rea*, 206–208
  and operational definitions of standard key terms, 213–218
  substance abuse/dependence and, 226–228
Miles v. Stainer, 1997, 64
Minner v. American Mortgage & Guaranty Co., 2000, 60
Minnesota Multiphasic Personality Inventory–2, 252
Miranda rights, 366
  competency to proceed and, 176
Miranda v. Arizona, 1966, 18–19, 63
  requirements of, 137–138
Miranda waiver/confession cases
  competency and, protocol for evaluating, 140–149
  defendant competency and, 137–140
  evaluation protocol
    clinical interview in, 142–143
    psychological testing in, 143–145
    record review in, 141–142
    specialized tests in, 145–149
  Grisso tests and, 164–166
  psychological evaluation in, 135–175
  psychotic defendant and, 149
  types of waiver and, 138–139
  voluntariness and, evaluation protocol for, 154–161
  See also Confessions
Miranda warnings, 18, 62, 63, 350, 358
Misdemeanor track, 7
Misskelley v. State, 1996, 167–168
Mitigating factors, 22, 23
  examples, 275–276, 276t
  nonstatutory, 275
  statutory, 275
Mitigation
  defined, 275
  diminished responsibility and, 229
Mitigation assessments, 282–283
Mitigation specialist, 274. *See also* Forensic social historian
M'Naghten "right–wrong" standard of 1843, 209, 210, 214, 215, 216, 232, 297

Model Penal Code, 210–211, 210t
  insanity standard of, 209
Montana v. Egelhoff, 1996, 226
Mood stabilizers, for aggressive behavior, 242–243
Moran v. Burbine, 1986, 20, 139
Morrison v. United States, 1990, 64
Mrad's multiple data source model, 12, 13f, 14
Multiple data source model, 12, 13f, 14
Murder
  mass, 240, 241t
  serial, 241, 241t

National Academy of Neuropsychology, test security and, 47
Nature, IDRA definition of, 215–217
Negative response bias, 12
  aspects of, 93–95
  in civil forensic settings, 97–98
  and competence to stand trial, 189
  in criminal forensic settings, 98–99
  free-standing measures of, 105–117
    Dot Counting Test, 106–107
    forced-choice digit recognition tests, 108–111
    for general intellectual ability, 105–107
    Medical Symptom Validity Test, 114–116
    Nonverbal Medical Symptom Validity Test, 116–117
    Rey 15-Item Memory Test, 107–108
    for short-term memory, 107–117
    Test of Memory Malingering, 111–112
    Validity Indicator Profile, 105–106
    Word Memory Test, 112–114
  versus malingering, 101, 103
  multiple indices of, 118
  neurocognitive, embedded indices of, 117
Negligence, defined, 207
Nelson v. Nelson, 58
Neurocognitive deficits, ruling out, 2
Neurocognitive testing, below-random performance on, 101, 103–104
Neurodevelopment, assessment of, in children, 303–304
Neuroimaging studies
  and evaluation of truthfulness, 77–78
  legal use of, 67
Neuropsychological assessment
  in capital cases
    expert qualifications in, 283–284
    versus noncapital cases, 285
    role, 282–284
    social history investigation and, 283–284
    timing, 281–282
  for competency to stand trial, 187–189
    instruments for, 197–199
    consent forms, 343–345
    court-ordered, 338–339

forms for, 334–335, 340–348
impartiality in, 360, 363–368
informed consent contract for, 347–348
in juvenile justice system, 303–311
   of adolescent general psychopathology, 305–306
   of delinquency, 306–309
   of general maturational issues, 304–305
   of malingered cognitive deficit, 311–314
   of neurodevelopment, 303–304
   types of, 309–311
for malingering. *See* Malingering, assessment of
Miranda waiver/confessions and, 170
notification of purpose form, 346
pragmatic considerations, 326–348
   attorney contacts, 337
   court-ordered evaluations, 338–339
   informed consent, 333–335
   initial contacts for criminal referrals, 327–328
   logistics, 330–333
   relevant factors, 335–336
   reports, 337–338
   setting fees, 328–330
prevalence of use, 1
retainer agreement for, 340–341
sample worksheet, 342
state-specific requirements for, 331
Neuropsychological consultation
   assumptions about, 9
   foundation for, 284–288
Neuropsychological evidence
   admissibility of. *See* Admissibility issues
   prevalence of application, 55
Neuropsychologist expert testimony
   admissibility and laws governing, 352–356
   versus advocacy, 350–352, 381–382
   bias in, 356–358
   credentials of, 380–381
   and *Daubert* and Rule 702 admissibility standards, 73–75
   direct and cross-examination in, increasing effectiveness of, 374–386
   exclusion of, *Daubert* and, 78–81
   guidance for, 375–378
   history of, 58–62
   and *Jenkins v. United States*, 1962, 374–375
   jury misled or confused by, 75
   language of, 380
   minimizing effects of cross-examination strategies, 383–384
   presentation to criminal court. *See* Presenting neuropsychological findings
   pretrial conferences and, 379–380
   prohibitions against, 61
   versus pseudoscientific testimony, 360, 361t–362t

   relevance of, 74
   reliability of, 73–74
   and wrongful disclosure of tests, 81–84
   See also Admissibility issues
Neuropsychology, relevance to judicial system, 1–2
Neurorehabilitation patients, rapport versus therapeutic alliance with, 10
Neurotransmitters, criminal/violent behavior and, 242–244
Nicholson v. American National Insurance, 1998, 122
Nonmalfeasance, 39
Nonverbal Medical Symptom Validity Test, 116–117
North Carolina v. Butler, 1979, 63

Organic brain syndromes, as mitigating factor, 276

Parens patriae, 296–297
Parsons v. State, 1887, 209
Pate v. Robinson, 1966, 21, 63, 181
Pathological behavior, 249
Patrick W., 1978. *See In re Patrick W.*, 1978
PCP abuse/addiction, 227–228
Penry v. Lynaugh, 1989, 24, 196
People v. Fardan, 1993, 228
People v. Free, 1983, 220
People v. Gettings, 1988, 64
People v. Hawthorne, 56
People v. R.R. & G.A., 2005, 61
People v. Schmidt, 1915, 217
Perceptions of Coercion in Holding and Interrogation Procedures, 166
Personality disorders
   intermittent explosive disorder and, 262
   malingering and, 96–97
   See also Antisocial personality disorder
Personality testing
   in assessment of voluntariness of *Miranda* waivers/confessions, 160
   in capital cases, 285–286
   in evaluation for *Miranda* waiver, 144–145
"Petition for the Recognition of a Specialty in Professional Psychology," 4–5
Plea entry, competency and, 64
Police coerciveness, *Miranda* waiver and, 139–140
Portland Digit Recognition Test, 108–110, 363–364
Positron emission tomography, in aggression/violence studies, 244–245
Posttraumatic stress disorder, in adolescents, 305–306
Powell v. Texas, 1968, 208
Pregnancy complications, juvenile aggression and, 307–308

Presenting neuropsychological findings, 349–390
  admissibility and relevant law, 352–356
  assessment issues in, 360–368
  bias and debiasing and, 356–358
  foundation for, 359–360
  suggestions for increased effectiveness, 374–386
Pretrial conferences, 379–380
Pretrial determinations, 76
Pretrial diversion, 7
  brain injury and, 224
Pretrial motions, 63
Price v. Commonwealth, 1984, 215–216
Prison
  logistical considerations, 331–332
  neuropsychologist–defendant interaction in, 333
Product Test, 209, 229
Professional competence, 38–46, 391–400
  American Board of Forensic Psychology and, 391, 394–397
  APA guidelines and, 39–40
  and collaborative model of practice, 397–398
  and Committee on Ethical Guidelines for Forensic Psychologists, 40, 41t–43t
  in juvenile justice settings, 314–315
  representative state guidelines for, 392–393
  Villanova Conference and, 393–394
Professional Identity Development model, 315–316
Psychiatric disturbance, self-report measures of, 118
Psychological testing
  avoiding bias in, 357–358
  in evaluation for *Miranda* waiver, 143–145
  experimental procedures in, 367–368
  fixed versus flexible test batteries in, 358, 365–368
  wrongful disclosure of results, 81–84
  See also Neuropsychological assessment
Psychosis
  in adolescents, 305–306
  exaggeration of, 94
  traumatic brain injury and, 194–196
Public policy, in juvenile justice setting, 318–319
Punishment
  competency and, 64–65
  cruel and unusual, 16

Quality, IDRA definition of, 215–217

Racial stereotyping, influence of, 225
Rage reactions, neuroanatomical basis of, 240
Raven's Standard Progressive Matrices, 313

Reading comprehension, defendant's level of, 141
Reality testing, impaired, 232–233
Recklessness, defined, 207
Record keeping, 330
Rector v. Clark, 1991, 65
Referrals, criminal, initial contacts for, 327–328
Reform schools, 297
Reid Technique, 149–150
Release of data, 49t
Remote memory loss
  complaints of, 118–122
  symptom validity testing for, 119–122
Reports
  assessment, 337–338
  See also Forensic reports
Rey 15-Item Memory Test, 107–108
Right to counsel
  competency to waive, 181–182
  waiving, 19
  See also Sixth Amendment
Right to trial, 15
  competency to waive, 181–182
Rights, waivers of, 135
Ring v. Arizona, 2002, 274
Road rage, 240, 241t
Rogers Criminal Responsibility Assessment Scales, 232–233
Rompilla v. Beard, 2005, 279
Roper v. Simmons, 2005, 65, 298, 300
  and mitigating factors in sentencing phase, 277
Ross v. State, 1980, 60
Rules of evidence. See Federal Rules of Evidence
Rush v. Megee, 1871, 58
Rustenhaven v. American Airlines, Inc., 2003, 61

Sanchez v. Derby, 1989, 61
Sanity, legal, versus competency, 176
Santosky v. Kramer, 1982, 299
Schall v. Martin, 1984, 299, 300
Schizophrenia
  criminal/violent behavior and, 251–253
  origins of, 252–253
Seiling v. Eyman, 1973, 20
Seizures
  complex partial, 260
  generalized tonic–clonic, 260
Selective serotonin reuptake inhibitors, aggression treatment and, 243
Self-care, capacity for, defined, 233
Self-incrimination
  privilege against, 14–15
  See also Fifth Amendment
Sell v. U.S., 2003, 185

Sentencing phase, 273–294
  basis for expert consultation in, 284–288
  social history investigation in, 277–279
  expert's participation and, 281–284
  significance for expert, 280–281
Serial murderers, 241, 241t
Serious Youthful Offender statute, 298
Serious youthful offenders, monitoring of, 302
Serotonin, aggressive behavior and, 242
SGFP. *See* Committee on Ethical Guidelines for Forensic Psychologists
Shaw v. Delo, 1992, 65
Short-term memory, measures of, 107–117
Simmons v. Mullins, 59–60
Single-photon emission computed tomography, in aggression/violence studies, 244–245
Sixth Amendment
  cases involving, 19, 24–26, 37
  Miranda warnings and, 63
  wording and significance, 15
Skipper v. South Carolina, 1986, and mitigating factors in sentencing phase, 277
Sleepwalking, diagnosis of, 223
Slick criteria, 101–104
Smoking, maternal, aggressive behavior in children and, 308
Social history investigation, 277–279
  failure to perform, verdict reversals and, 279
  purpose of, 279
  significance for neuropsychological expert, 280–281
Social Security Disability referrals, NRB rate for, 98, 99
Sociopathy, acquired, 248
Somnambulism, diagnosis of, 223
Specialty Guidelines for Forensic Psychologists, 25, 351, 352, 356, 369, 370, 372, 373, 381, 382
Specialty training, in forensic psychology, 394
Standard 9.04, 46–47
Standard progressive matrices, 313
Stare decisis, 19
State Senate Bill 1057, 392–393, 394
State v. Beam, 1985, and abolishment of insanity defense, 65
State v. Broom, 1995, 62
State v. Card, 1991, and abolishment of insanity defense, 65
State v. Cayward, 1989, 153
State v. Clemons, 1997, 63
State v. Griffin, 2003, 163
State v. Jones, 1871, 209
State v. Korell, 1984, and abolishment of insanity defense, 65
State v. Lambert, 1994, 179
State v. Lee, 1997, 63
State v. Massey, 1990, 298, 300
State v. Phillips, 1992, 163

State v. Rogers, 2000, 66
State v. Romero, 2003, 167–168
State v. Whitaker, 1990, 163
State v. White, 1981, 244
Status offenses, versus delinquency, 297
Stereotyping, infuence of, 225
Stroke, as mitigating factor, 276
Structured Clinical Interview for DSM-IV, 252
Structured Interview of Reported Symptoms, 166, 252
Substance abuse/dependence
  in adolescents, 305
  insanity defense and, 226–228
  as mitigating factor, 276
Substantial capacity, lack of, 213
Suggestibility
  Gudjonsson Scales of, 155, 157–159
  psychological variables related to, 159–160
  Shift type, 169
Supreme Court
  state, 7
  U. S. *See* U. S. Supreme Court
Symptom validity testing, 363–364
  for children, 312
  for remote memory loss, 119–122

Temporal lobe epilepsy, 260–261
Temporal lobe syndromes, 259–264
  in criminal/violent behavior, 250–251, 250t
Temporal lobes, in memory processing, 262–263
Test batteries
  fixed versus flexible, 358, 365–368
  See also Psychological testing
Test data
  inconsistencies in, 94
  prohibitions against release of, 47
  release of
    APA regulations, 46–48
    and Committee on Guidelines for Forensic Psychologists, 48–50
  versus test materials, 47
Test of Memory Malingering, 111–112, 313
Test performance, Frederick's conceptual model of, 95–96, 95f
Test security, 47
Testimony. *See* Neuropsychologist expert testimony
Testosterone, aggression and, 243
Texas State Senate Bill 1057, 392–393, 394
Therapeutic alliance, lack of, 10
Third-party observer/recording device, 82
Third-party observers, 359–360
  arguments for precluding, 363
Thompson v. Bell, 2006, 57
Training, psychologist, 44–46
Transient epileptic amnesia, 263
Transient global amnesia, 263

Traumatic brain injury
  and competency to stand trial, 193–196
  criminal/violent behavior and, 281
  focal frontal lobe pathology and, 258–259
  insanity defense and, 228
  mild, 258
  as mitigating factor, 276
Trial
  bifurcated, 22
    states using, 212–213
  speedy and public, right to, 15
Trial courts, 6
  adversarial atmosphere of, 375
Truthfulness, evaluating, 77
T.S.D. v. Florida, 1999. See In re T.S.D. v. Florida, 1999
Twinkie defense, 244

U. S. circuit courts of appeals, 6, 6t
U. S. Constitution
  federal powers defined by, 5
  key amendments to, 14–17
U. S. Supreme Court, 6
  landmark cases of, 17–26
United States v. Banks, 1991, 63
United States v. Brawner, 1972, 210
United States v. Cameron, 1990, 73
United States v. Crocker, 1975, 138
United States v. Dubray, 1988, 212, 218
United States v. Frisbee, 1985, 65
United States v. Gonyea, 1998, 225
United States v. Greer, 1998, 122–123
United States v. Johns, 1984, 62
United States v. José Santos-Bueno, 1997, 71–75, 78
United States v. Kimes, 2001, 225
United States v. Liberatore, 1994, 182–183
United States v. Major, 1996, 153–154
United States v. Marenghi, 1995, 63
United States v. Newman, 1989, 225
United States v. Pohlot, 1987, 65–66
United States v. Raposo, 1998, 167
United States v. Renfroe, 1987, 64
United States v. Riggleman, 59
United States v. Salava, 1992, 213
United States v. Schneider, 1997, 73
United States v. Segna, 1977, 218
United States v. Sullivan, 1976, 213, 218
United States v. Wade, 1967, 376

Validity Indicator Profile, 105–106
Valiulis v. Scheffeos, 1989, 61
Venn diagram
  of frontal lobe dysfunction in criminal responsibility, 249–250, 250f
  of frontal lobe role in criminal responsibility, 249–250, 250f
Ventromedial cortex, acquired sociopathy and, 248–249
Victoria Symptom Validity Test, 108–111
Videotapes, 82–83
Villanova Conference, 44–45, 391, 393–394
Violence. See Criminal/violent behavior
Violent offenders
  influence of neurotransmitters, genetics, and hormones, 242–244
  neurobiological studies of, 241–249
    neuroimaging and electrophysiological findings in, 244–246
    neuropsychological findings in, 246–249
Virginia Code, self-incrimination and, 15
Voir dire, 380–381

Wade v. United States, 1970, 217–218
Waivers
  intelligent, 138–139
  knowing, 138
  unintelligent, 139
  voluntary, 139–140
  See also Miranda waiver/confession cases
Washington v. Harper, 1990, 185
Washington v. United States, 1967, 209
Westbrook v. Arizona, 20
Whitaker v. Parker, 58
Wieter v. Settle, 1961, 179, 179t, 180
Wiggins v. Smith, 2003, 279
Williams, 1997. See In re Williams, 1997
Wilson v. United States, 1968, 119, 190
Winnans, 58
Winship, 1970. See In re Winship, 1970
Witnesses, types of, psychologist competency and, 44
Woodson v. North Carolina, 1976, 275, 287
Word Memory Test, 112–114
  for children, 313
  non-English versions of, 113–114
Wrongfulness, IDRA definition of, 215, 217–218

Youtsey v. United States, 1899, 62, 177

RA1147.5 .C55 2008
Clinical neuropsychology in
the criminal forensic
setting